Yigal Allon, Native Son

JEWISH CULTURE AND CONTEXTS

Published in association with the Center for Advanced Judaic Studies of the University of Pennsylvania

David B. Ruderman, Series Editor

Advisory Board
Richard I. Cohen
Moshe Idel
Alan Mintz
Deborah Dash Moore
Ada Rapoport-Albert
Michael D. Swartz

A complete list of books in the series is available from the publisher.

Yigal Allon, Native Son

A Biography

ANITA SHAPIRA

Translated by Evelyn Abel

PENN

University of Pennsylvania Press

Philadelphia

The publication of this volume was assisted by a grant from the Lucius N. Littauer Foundation.

Copyright © 2008 University of Pennsylvania Press

All rights reserved. Except for brief quotations used for purposes of review or scholarly citation, none of this book may be reproduced in any form by any means without written permission from the publisher.

Published by
University of Pennsylvania Press
Philadelphia, Pennsylvania 19104–4112

Printed in the United States of America on acid-free paper

10 9 8 7 6 5 4 3 2 1

A Cataloging-in-Publication record is available from the Library of Congress

ISBN-13: 978-0-8122-4028-3
ISBN-10: 0-8122-4028-6

Contents

List of Abbreviations   vii

Preface: Last Rites   ix

 1. Mes'ha: The Beginning   1
 2. Kadoorie Agricultural School   35
 3. Ginossar   53
 4. The Start of Security Work   79
 5. British-Jewish "Cooperation"   109
 6. The Palmah: Beginnings   126
 7. The Palmah, 1943–47   141
 8. Countdown to Statehood and the Onset of War   178
 9. The Ten-Day Campaigns   209
10. Commanding Officer of the Southern Front   238
11. Triumph and Tragedy   282

Epilogue: The End of Things   298

Notes   323

Bibliography   363

Index   369

Acknowledgments   385

Abbreviations

AHC	Arab Higher Committee
BGA	Ben-Gurion Archive
BGD	Ben-Gurion's Diaries
BGWD	Ben-Gurion's War Diary
BZI	Ben-Zvi Institute
CGS	Chief of General Staff
CZA	Central Zionist Archives
GAR	Ginossar Archives
GHA	Givat Haviva Archives
HA	Haganah Archive
HGS	Haganah General Staff; after 15 May 1948, Israel Defense Forces High General Staff
HNHO	Ha-Noar Ha-Oved
HSHT	Ha-Shomer Ha-Tza'ir
ICA	Jewish Colonization Association
IDF	Israel Defense Forces
IDFA	Israel Defense Forces Archive
IZL	Revisionist National Military Organization
JA	Jewish Agency
JA-PD	Jewish Agency's Political Department
JSP	Jewish Settlement Police
KA	Kadoorie Archive
KM	Kibbutz Me'uhad movement
KMA	Kibbutz Me'uhad Archive
KMC	Kibbutz Me'uhad Council
KMP	Kibbutz Me'uhad Publishing House
KTA	Kefar Tavor Archive
LA	Labor Archive
LAHA	Le-Ahdut Ha-Avodah
LA-HE	Labor Archive, Histadrut Executive
LA-LI	Labor Archive, Lavon Institute
LeHI	Lohamei Herut Israel (Israel Freedom Fighters) or the Stern Gang
LPA	Labor Party Archive

LPA-BB	Labor Party Archive, Bet Berl
PICA	Palestine Jewish Colonization Association
S.N.S	Special Night Squads (Wingate's)
SHAY	Haganah Intelligence Service
UNSCOP	United Nations Special Committee on Palestine
UNRRA	United Nations Relief and Rehabilitation Administration

Preface
Last Rites

Yigal Allon was the man and mark of a generation: the generation bred in Eretz Israel during the struggle for Jewish statehood. This book is dedicated to him and his era, when he and his peers in the elite Palmah fashioned the country's first youth culture, setting the tone for those who came after.

"Palmahniks" were neither highbrow nor cultivated but a young brigade of daring volunteers. Apart from a handful of writers and poets who sprang up from within, most had little use for the trappings of culture or social graces. And yet their defining experience, which was to stay with them throughout their lives, became *the* cultural inspiration of the young. The type of person spawned by the Palmah was not without fault. There was about them a callow rawness, an upstart's brashness, the shallowness of men of action, the intolerance of the self-absorbed. They judged both themselves and others mercilessly, knowing no compassion. Yet they were also capable of openness and high-flying idealism, extraordinary acts of friendship and comradeship, reticence and loftiness, humility and dedication. They had a measure of pride that in their youth took the form of arrogance and over the years was widely translated into independence and self-sufficiency, a personal autonomy, so to speak. Many of the Palmah veterans flowed with the times, changed their lifestyles, forgot the ideals of their youth. All, however, retained that core sense of belonging and fellowship formed on those heady, faraway nights of campfires, coffee, and song. Those who detached themselves from the past were spared the anguish of recent decades when the old kibbutz order collapsed, taking with it values that had been the bedrock of their lives.

Others, such as the Palmah's erstwhile intelligence officer, Zerubavel Arbel, never resigned themselves to the change. In an interview I had with him at Kibbutz Maoz Haim in order to write Yigal biography, he described, with wonder and wistfulness, the yawning gulf between himself and his father, whom he held in affection. The intellectual parent, a teacher at the historic Herzliya High School, and the son, who had built the IDF's field intelligence, were separated by an unbridgeable chasm of lost Jewish culture. The father was vastly more educated; the son was far handier in physical wisdom and the lore of action. Theirs, in microcosm, is the story of the generation gap between founding fathers and native sons in the land of Israel. It was the native sons and their devotees who shouldered the task of establishing the state of the Jews.

Arbel, like many Palmahniks, loved the land of Israel with his very fiber, knew its every wadi, its every groove. The Bible occupied a place of honor, and he read it like a guide book for its history and geography. He led me to a lookout over the Jordan Valley to point out the route taken by the Jabesh-gileads on their way to Beisan (Beit She'an). The biblical story is brief: the Philistines came upon the bodies of King Saul and his sons, slain in the battle on Mount Gilboa. They cut off Saul's head, stripped him, and hung him and his dead sons on the walls of Beisan. When the news reached the men of Gilead across the Jordan River, they walked all night long to Beisan, took down the bodies, buried them in their own land, and fasted for seven days. They had never forgotten the young Saul's goodwill when he saved them from Nahash the Ammonite. For Arbel, this final kindness, the last rites the Gileads performed for Saul, was a founding myth: again and again he would gaze at the route the Gileads took that night, cherishing their noble gesture to a defeated king fallen on the sword. For Allon, too, the story of Saul was a central motif. He loved the biblical character who had begun life like Cinderella and had ended it like the hero of a Greek tragedy. It was the tale of a lad towering head and shoulders above his people, worn down by political squabbles, by a savagery and chicanery he could not deal with. Was Arbel intimating that Allon's fate was a modern version of Saul's tragedy? Perhaps he was underlining the importance he himself attributed to a biography of Allon—the last rites for a dead commander who in his youth had delivered the people of Israel and won the hardest of Israel's wars.

I chose not to tell Allon's whole life story but only his story until the end of the War of Independence, the "War of Liberation" as that generation called it. The war was a watershed between Yishuv society and statehood. Whatever the continuity between them, the Yishuv and the state represented totally different human, social, and cultural entities. The main account thus stops in 1950 with the conclusion of Allon's military career. It was the end of an era both in his personal life and in Israeli realities. It was the end of one era, and the start of another.

Allon's story is not about the victors of a historical narrative but about those consigned to oblivion in Israel's public discourse. Those who perished on the upward climb without making it to the top also deserve a voice in collective memory. For without the story of the forgotten, history would be incomplete. This book stands as the last rites to them, the fallen of the first generation of native sons.

Chapter 1
Mes'ha: The Beginning

When Yigal Allon, born Paicovich, reached bar mitzvah age, he, like all the boys at Kefar Tavor/Mes'ha, was called up to the Torah. Yet the ritual merited no mention in his memoirs. Instead, he recorded the test of courage his father put him to that day. Yosef Reuven Paicovich—known by all as Reuven—summoned the boy to the silo and said, "By putting on phylacteries you still do not satisfy *all* the main commandments; today, you are a man and, from now on, you will have your own weapon."[1] With these words, he handed the boy a semi-automatic Browning.

Allon could not contain his excitement. But there was more. That night, Reuven sent him out to guard a remote field on the colony's northern edge. Known as *Balut* in Arabic, *Allon* in Hebrew, after its oaks, the field abutted the convoy route from Transjordan to the Mediterranean. To reach it, Allon had to walk some five kilometers. He arrived at about 8 P.M. with fear as his constant companion: it was his first stint of guard duty on his own. He took cover amid rocks and oak trees, starting at every sound and rustle in the fields. He fervently hoped that the robbers would rest from their labors this night, but it was not to be: just after midnight a passing convoy came within earshot. He saw three men get off their horses and start stuffing sacks with the sorghum that had been gathered. Reuven's instructions had been very clear: should thieves come, Allon was to let them go about their business at first; then, he was to call out warnings in Arabic and, then, shoot to miss in order to avoid escalation. He was permitted to shoot to hit only if they drew near. Allon recounted: "I followed all the instructions. I got over my fright. And Father's orders too made sure [that I would do] as I was told."[2] Far from being alarmed by Allon's calls, however, the bandits dug in and returned the battle cry. Allon shot into the air; he was answered by the cocking of guns. He had no instructions left, and his thoughts came hot on the heels of one another: Should he shoot to hit? Should he flee under darkness? What if he hit one of them? What if he himself were hurt? All at once, help materialized. His father came storming in from the side, spitting and spewing curses in heavily accented Arabic and firing above the robbers' heads. Just like in a western, the robbers jumped onto their horses and made off. Yigal Allon summed up: "My joy was double that night: not only did I meet the test, but Father *saw* me do it. I can't imagine how I would have looked him in the eye had I not acted as I did."[3]

It was a rite of passage in a frontier community where all adult men carried arms. Initiation into male society demanded proof of courage, symbolizing a value system imparted from father to son. Reuven Paicovich may have had a greater dose of courage and belligerence than his fellow villagers, but this does not diminish the transformation that had taken place in the value system of Jewish men who had settled the wilds of Galilee only twenty years earlier.

Yigal Allon was born in a small village at the foot of Mount Tabor and spent most of his first twenty years there. His early experience, as seen through the eyes of a boy, was described in *Bet Avi* (My father's house): it was a world of intimacy with the land, of the fragrance of baking bread, of the delights of the threshing floor on a summer night, of neighborly squabbles and brawls, of tests of courage and displays of physical prowess. The village depicted by the adult Allon was bathed in the magic that maturity lends to childhood. The farther he wandered from Mes'ha, the more his descriptions benefited from the distance of time and place, toning down imperfections and enhancing the charm of his salad days.

The Paicovich family saga began in Grodno, White Russia, at the crossroads between Vilna in the north and Bialystok in the south. Its Jewish community, one of the most important in Lithuania, dated back to the twelfth century and had produced scholars and sages.[4]

The saga opens with Yigal's grandfather, Yehoshua Zvi Paicovich, in the second half of the nineteenth century.[5] Earlier generations were apparently unremarkable, and certainly not scholarly. The Paicoviches were a family of means. Yehoshua was a builder; his wife, Rachel, managed the family hardware store.[6] Reuven entered the world in 1873, a year after Shmuel, the firstborn. As a child, he was drawn to "un-Jewish" pastimes: roaming the fields, dipping in the waters of the Niemen River, climbing a tree. He was especially fond of animals and secretly kept a dog and a cat in the attic despite the Jewish ban on pets for reasons of impurity. Often enough, his exploits earned him the feel of a fatherly thwacking.[7]

In 1890, Yehoshua decided to move to the land of Israel with the two older boys, Shmuel and Reuven; according to family tradition, he was a devout adherent of the Lovers of Zion movement. Additionally, his boys were now of conscription age in White Russia, and he had no intention of offering them to the czar's army. Some citizens of Grodno had immigrated to America, but Yehoshua set his sights on Palestine.[8]

It was a ten-hour train journey from Grodno to the Black Sea port of Odessa, where ships set sail for Palestine. Manning the gangplank was a towering gendarme possessed of the furry *kicme* headgear and a daunting sword. But he was no fool: spying Yehoshua and the two boys, aged sixteen and seventeen, he detected draft dodgers! With a stomp of the foot and thunder in his voice, he made it plain that they would not slip away. Thus spoke the figure of authority. Unruffled, the slight, unimposing Yehoshua stepped to the side and dabbed his perspiration with a handkerchief. He placidly withdrew a few rubles from his pocket and proffered them to the rampaging gendarme. It was Reuven's first lesson in dealing with the powers that be: the man underwent an instant metamorphosis. Patting the boys on the cheek, he murmured, "children, children," and bade them a pleasant journey to "their Palestine."[9]

A week later, the three disembarked into the hustle and bustle of the port of Jaffa, where the Arab porters impressed them as aggressive and untamed, and they could not understand their cries. They headed for the Jewish colonies, finding work in the vineyards of Rishon Lezion, Rehovot, and Nes Ziona. Mostly they turned over the earth and prepared it for planting with the help of a hoe. For a day's hard labor, they earned seven Turkish pennies, barely subsistence money. It is not clear how long they were so employed: one account indicates two years; another, only a few months.[10] In any case, they were soon known as hard workers, and Yehoshua Ossowetzky, a former agent of Baron Edmond de Rothschild in Nes Ziona who was now in charge of Jewish settlement in the Lower Galilee, invited them to the newly founded colony of Rosh Pinnah. Paicovich's building skills could be put to good use there, and they accepted with alacrity.

From that day on, the Galilee was Reuven's home. The hilly landscape spellbound him. Mount Canaan beckoned him. Within days he had scaled to the top, a curious act in the eyes of the residents of Rosh Pinnah, who felt little urge to commune with nature. He spent several years building Rosh Pinnah and dreaming of farming: of obtaining a tract of land from the baron or the Jewish Colonization Association (ICA).

The dream remained out of reach. Meanwhile, he made a name for himself as a valiant young man, and the matchmakers took notice. In his words, "a meeting was arranged, she liked me, I liked her and, in time, I was married to Chaya, daughter of Reb Alter Schwartz, of blessed memory, and set up home."[11] This depiction may have done for Reuven's time and society, but it was too prosaic for his sons. They wanted romance. And in their rendering of the parental encounter, Reuven spied a caravan of donkeys descending from Safed to Rosh Pinnah; mounted on one of them was a black-eyed maiden who immediately lit his fire.[12] This biblical portrayal is the version that became ensconced in the family saga. One way or another, in 1894 Reuven Paicovich and Chaya Ethel Schwartz were wed.

Chaya came from an old Safed family. Her mother was the granddaughter of the rabbi of Buczacz, a source of pride for Chaya. The family tradition holds that the family had lived in Safed since the Middle Ages; one branch had departed for Buczacz and service in the rabbinate, though following generations had returned.[13] Reb Alter Schwartz, Chaya's father, was one of seventeen young, married yeshiva students to join the pioneer Elazar Rokeach in the establishment of a new farming village. The group purchased land from the Arab village of Ja'uni for what became the Jewish Gei-Oni.

Gei-Oni was plagued by drought, and the colonists lost their assets. In 1882 a Lovers of Zion delegation from Romania toured the country to acquire land for settlement. Captivated by the vistas of Gei-Oni, they bought out the first settlers. Four of the original families refused to sell and joined the Romanian group,[14] which renamed the site Rosh Pinnah. One of the four was Reb Alter Schwartz. He, however, soon sold out to the baron, served a two-year rabbinical stint in Alexandria, and, upon his return, began to work for the baron as a supplier, a position he retained until his death. Chaya was his firstborn.[15]

Reuven and Chaya lived with Reb Alter for some five years, producing two sons during that time, Moshe and Mordekhai. In 1898, construction began on the new colony of Mahanayim, near Rosh Pinnah. Reuven was asked to lend his building skills and guide the newly arrived ultra-Orthodox immigrants from Galicia in the ways of the land. In return, he hoped to obtain a property at Mahanayim and finally settle down to farming. He gave three years of his life to Mahanayim, built a house, invested every penny he managed to save from working at the site, and brought his wife and children to live with him.

But the Lovers of Zion movement that backed the project suffered serious financial and social setbacks. In 1902–3, Mahanayim was abandoned and its lands were ultimately annexed to Rosh Pinnah.[16]

Reuven found himself back at square one: out of pocket, out of work, thirty years old with a wife and three children to support (a third son, Zvi, had meanwhile joined the family). The future looked bleaker than ever. In 1900 the baron handed over the administration of his colonies to the ICA. The First Aliyah wave of immigration to the land of Israel was in crisis, having lost faith in the enterprise. Farmers of the relatively sound, orchard-based Jewish colonies on the coastal plain upped and left the country by the dozens. Many in Palestine's new Jewish Yishuv lent an avid ear to the Uganda Plan (the idea of establishing a Jewish colony in East Africa under British protection), for who knew better than they how arduous it was to settle the land of Israel. Reuven decided to try his luck in America, the "*goldeneh medineh.*" His decision, in 1905, stemmed from a sense of impasse and despair. Should he get on his feet in the United States, he planned to bring his family across. Should he fail, he would return to Palestine. His conscience would at least be clear that he had not missed the opportunity of a lifetime.[17]

He shared his plans only with his wife, who was once again with child. He divided the little remaining money from Mahanayim into two: half for Chaya and the children, who stayed with her father; the other half for himself. Early one morning he rose, mounted a donkey laden with bags, and rode it to Beirut. From there, he sailed to Marseilles and then on to the United States. Three weeks later he disembarked in New York.

America did not smile on Reuven. He found life on the Lower East Side alien and longed for open, star-studded skies and green fields. He was a diligent laborer earning adequately for the times. But he made no real money. What he did manage to put aside, he referred to as *kishke gelt*—whatever his gut could spare. After two years, he returned to Palestine. America had turned out to be a false dream.[18]

Left with no alternative, he swallowed his pride and applied to the ICA for a leasehold at one of the Lower Galilee settlements under development. He explained his inclination for manual labor, his aspiration to live off farming, his yearning for the soil. The officials—as he told it—not only agreed to settle him but even allowed him to choose one of four sites. But when the time came to make good on the promise, Rosenheck, the ICA clerk, reneged on the offer and directed him to Mes'ha, that is, Kefar Tavor.[19] Whether fact or fiction, the incident marked Reuven with a life-long hostility toward ICA officials.

It was not a choice area for farming and settlement. The Eastern Lower Galilee gets little precipitation, and natural springs are few. The harsh conditions had driven most of the Arab villagers out in the nineteenth century,[20] and the region was overrun with marauding Bedouin. Force was the law of the land. Tribes arbitrarily fought one another, provoked the Ottoman government, and mercilessly attacked village after village. By the close of the nineteenth century, even the most optimistic estimates put the entire population there at only tem thousand.[21]

In the nineteenth century, destitute peasants were crushed by loans they were unable to repay. Lands slipped out of the hands of cultivators and into the hands of capitalists or the government. The southern part of the Eastern Galilee became state land and was purchased by Sultan Abed al-Hamid; the northern part was taken over mostly by wealthy effendis from Nazareth, Acre, Damascus, and other places. Here, then was an opportunity for Jewish settlement agents to acquire sizable tracts. The largest Jewish land-buyer was Baron de Rothschild. His agent, Yehoshua Ossowetzky, picked up 30,000 to 50,000 dunams (7,500 to

Figure 1. The Paicovich family: mother, Chaya; father, Reuven; and three sons: Moshe, Mordekhai, and Zvi. Photographer unknown. Courtesy of the Allon family.

12,500 acres; 3,000 to 5,000 ha) from an Arab living in Syria. These transactions took place in the 1880s and 1890s. Jewish settlement in the area began at the end of the nineteenth century and the beginning of the twentieth.[22]

Jewish settlement of the Eastern Lower Galilee was associated with the transfer in 1900 of Baron de Rothschild's villages and assets in Palestine to the ICA. Founded by Baron de Hirsch in 1891, the ICA aimed to ease the lot of Eastern European Jews by promoting their agricultural settlement around the world, particularly in Argentina. Unconnected to Zionism, it wished to see Jews emigrate and become "productive." On top of his holdings, Rothschild gave the ICA more than 15 million francs to help set Palestine's Jewish villages on a firmer footing. The ICA opened up a new department to deal with agricultural settlement in Palestine.[23]

Rothschild's move angered and alarmed the colonists. Mainly, he was motivated by the colonies' stagnation: after eighteen years of hard work and huge investments—estimated at £1.6 million—they were still not self-sufficient. The transfer of their administration to the ICA signaled a new approach. The ICA stopped subsidizing wine, which had artificially raised income; vineyards were uprooted for lack of demand and other crops were introduced. And settlers were allowed far more autonomy in the internal management of village affairs. In the space of a few years, the colonies were at long last self-sufficient and even enjoyed a measure of ease. They grew and prospered during the Second Aliyah immigration wave of 1904–14.

In the Lower Galilee, the ICA hoped to solve the problem of landless farm laborers and second-generation farmers by inaugurating a relatively cheap form of settlement. In the first decade of the twentieth century, it founded six villages: Sejera, Kefar Tavor (Mes'ha), Yavne'el (Yemah), Bet-Gan, Melahamiya (Menachemiya), and Mitzpeh. Rothschild, in the veteran settlements, had been guided by the model of a European village based on sophisticated agriculture and run by comfortable or wealthy farmers. The ICA envisioned a modest village where the farmers earned their bread by the sweat of their brows.

The crops chosen for the Lower Galilee were those better suited to dry farming. Because income was expected to be relatively low, each unit was enlarged to 250–300 dunams (62.5–75 acres; 25–30 ha). In the opinion of the ICA, a plot of this size could support a family even if it were farmed extensively.[24] The ICA provided the plot, undertook to build the homestead, and extended a loan for the purchase of animals and equipment: plows, wagons, seeds, oxen, and so forth. In return, the settler undertook to cultivate the entire unit with the help of his family, using hired labor only in high season. From his own pocket, he was to handle land amelioration, irrigation installations, and (road) infrastructure. He received the unit on lease and was to pay the ICA 25 percent of the harvest as did tenant farmers in Arab villages to their landlords. The loan was to be repaid gradually. The ICA transferred title only after years of trial and proof of aptitude for farming. The system of tenancy made it possible to settle people with no means of their own at quite a low cost; at the same time, the settlement company retained the leverage to make sure that a farmer honored his commitments and cultivated the land made available to him. Settlers not up to the task could be evicted and sometimes were.[25]

Reuven's allotment was at the foot of Mount Tabor, a domed peak towering over the region in splendid isolation and casting its shadow over the small village on its eastern flank. Graced by a dense oak woodland (later sacrificed for fuel by Arab villagers), it boasted two monasteries (one Catholic, the other Greek Orthodox), and appeared mysterious, even ominous. Kefar Tavor was on the ancient Via Maris from Egypt to the Fertile Crescent. Straddling the gateway from the Lower Galilee to the Jezreel Valley, it was in a strategic position.

The pristine scenery could not disguise Mes'ha's sorry location on a thirsty ridge of the Eastern Lower Galilee.[26] Children may have taken great pleasure in the dry wadis and ruins around the colony,[27] but the basic water shortage went unsolved. It was the chief cause of Mes'ha's troubles, misery, and sluggishness, and frequent drought only made the situation worse, damaging crops and drying up springs.

Reuven Paicovich and his family were not Mes'ha's first settlers. The colony was established in 1900 and its early founders—some twenty-two in number—had included two groups: first- and second-generation farmers from Metullah and Rosh Pinnah, tough Galilee rustics who made do with little and had already tasted frontier settlement; and the offspring of orchard colonists from Zikhron Ya'acov and Shfeya, who were considered more pampered by the farmers mentioned above. The guiding principle behind the ICA's choice of settlers was fitness for farming and prior experience. Many of the settlers already had families, although some were single. They did not know one another beforehand and antagonism soon developed between the groups from Galilee and Zikhron: everyone wanted the derelict huts at the site left over from the abandoned Arab village, and there was no end to quarrels and resentment. The same was true when it came to the allotment of fields. In short, Kefar Tavor's members were known as hotheads, a "title" they did everything in their power to defend.[28]

The village was laid out in the usual cross: a long street lined on both sides by a row of houses with red tile roofing from Marseilles. This street was bisected by a shorter street, perpendicular to the farmers' houses and containing the public buildings: the synagogue, the school, the teachers' houses, the doctor's house, and the council premises. Every home was fenced off and backed by outbuildings: a stable, a barn, a chicken coop, a tool shed, and a shack for the Arab hired hand and his family. A defensive stone wall ran along the rear of the farmyards to protect the homesteads from marauders.

It was not a welcoming community: "In this small, this tender body, so much strife, conflict, and carping," an item in *Hashkafa* described Mes'ha, "happy faces and laughter—no way."[29] On its third anniversary in 1903, Mes'ha was crowned with the Hebrew name of Kefar Tavor by the visiting Zionist leader Menachem Ussishkin.[30] The settlers persisted with the old name. It was partly one, partly the other: a failing village patterned after the old Arab format; a Jewish colony striving to belong to the new Hebrew Yishuv.

In those early years of real pioneering, stark hardship, and a gnashing determination to gain a grip on the Lower Galilee, one of Mes'ha's residents was Joseph Vitkin, a precursor to the Second Aliyah and the principal of Mes'ha's school for two years. His letters are filled with an unmistakable wretchedness, even if we discount personal circumstances, physical infirmity, and loneliness, severed as he was from any living being he could talk to. The letters reflect Mes'ha's young face: a poor, miserable village that drowns in mud and is cut off from the world with the first rain. "I detest these crude and alarmingly rotten surroundings, to an unbelievable extent," Vitkin wrote.[31] Vitkin's attempts to inject a mood of nationalism in his pupils and even in the farmers of the colonies by appealing to voluntarism and the general good were met with bitter derision: how easy it was for him, who could be sure of his meal, to preach idealism and making do to people who worked themselves to the bone and went hungry for bread.[32] The high-brow Vitkin found no common language with the farm workers whose children were his educational charges. He felt that he failed to leave a mark on the children: "The environment is stronger . . . and all that we sow within the school walls in the long term and with great emotional effort is uprooted in the short term."[33]

Mes'ha was synonymous with dereliction. When the teacher Asher Ehrlich and his wife, Dvora, arrived at Mes'ha in 1905 to replace the exhausted Vitkin, they found twenty-two abandoned houses, the tenants having returned their homesteads to the ICA. Some of the houses—recently built—were already cracked and dilapidated. In the entire village, there was not a spot of green—no grass, no flowers, no fruit trees. These were luxuries ruled out by the lack of water. But, in any case, the population did not have a feel for ornamentation or a need to introduce beauty into their lives. In this respect, Mes'ha resembled the Eastern

European *shtetl* where Jews did not hanker after aesthetics, especially in public areas; aesthetics were a trivial goyish pursuit of non-Jews.[34]

Vitkin, in one of his letters, bemoaned the hills of Mes'ha that closed in on it and robbed it of a horizon, of open space. But Mes'ha's residents were quite comfortable with the narrow vistas handed them by fate. In time, those who stayed on despite the privations very likely explained their endurance in Zionist terms. The romanticism of their twilight years lent an aura of idealism to the ordeals of youth and maturity. If truth be told, however, their *aliyah* to Eretz Israel had been a combination of love of Zion—the fruit of *midrash*, *aggadah*, and liturgy—and the hope of a better living in Palestine. The tidings that Baron de Rothschild was settling Jews on the land and that other agencies too were involved in the endeavor attracted Jewish immigrants to Palestine. Yet they were a mere trickle. The great current flowed toward American shores. There is no way to quantify or appraise the ratio between emotional nationalism and personal expediency in the hearts of those who turned to Zion. Often, those guided by expediency lost their hearts to the country and never were to be dislodged from it, not even by a dozen oxen, while those who came in search of King Saul's Hills of Gilboa or Gideon's Ein Harod broke on the rock of reality, abandoning the country of their dreams in disillusionment. Of Mes'ha's residents it may be said that their Zionism came after the fact and despite everything; they certainly paid a high price for their Eretz Israel.

To the extent that they ever had dreamed of the country and their lives in it, the dream had been as narrow as their village horizon: to dwell each under his vine and fig tree in the Promised Land. They had no problem with the traditional lifestyle of the *shtetl*. Religion played a central part, molding individual and public spheres. *Kashrut* was self-evident, and everyone attended synagogue on the Days of Awe. Only the doctor was allowed to absent himself since, as everyone knew, he was well-versed in external wisdom and therefore exempt from the rules governing ordinary Jewish mortals.[35] In principle, Mes'ha's inhabitants did not suffer from overeducation. As was typical of a Jewish *shtetl*, those with schooling consisted of the teacher, the doctor, and the pharmacist, although not in all cases.

Mes'ha was a mirror of the faults and virtues of a *shtetl*: arguments and intrigue were regular fare, and the infighting in some years caused the council to change its composition more than once. Yet, there was also a sense of mutual concern: when disaster struck—a householder's death, lengthy illness, and so forth—the council would strive to extend assistance while the women lent a hand with housework and everyday needs. Men, too, could rise to gestures of magnificence, plowing or sowing a neighbor's fields. In normal times, though, every farmer jealously guarded his own acreage and kept to himself.

The move of Mes'ha's residents from the *shtetlach* or villages of their births to Kefar Tavor did not entail modernization, a new self-image, or a new worldview. But when an Eastern European Jewish village is planted in the Wild West of the Palestine frontier something's got to give. The Lower Galilee sprouted a frontier culture complete with romance, symbols, and heroes, with its own lifestyle and code of conduct. The Paicoviches fit right in.

In November 1908, Reuven signed a contract with the ICA and became a tenant farmer on the lands of Um-J'abal—"the mother of mountains" in Arabic.[36] The best fields had already been taken. Newcomers were given remote plots, several kilometers to the north of the village, on the lower slopes of Mount Tabor (at the site of today's Kibbutz Bet Keshet). The virgin soil was so stony in parts that the earth could not be seen. It bordered the lands of a-Zbekh, the strongest, most dangerous Bedouin tribe in the area. The Zbekhs claimed ownership of some of Um-J'abal, while the ICA had plans to extend its holdings into a-Zbekh's territory. Thus, tension over land was already in place, even before anyone took a hoe to the ground.[37]

Paicovich's field neighbors too were recent arrivals. One was a Yemenite Jew named Zefira; the other, Mattveyov, was one of the Russian converts to Judaism who settled in the Galilee. Come the rainy season, the three planned to plow their fields together. But the route to their fields passed through a-Zbekh territory and the tribesmen blocked their way. The farmers thought they might outwit them: they tried their luck at dawn, they tried in the middle of the night, but it made no difference. Whenever they showed up, the Bedouin were out en masse to greet them, until one day Reuven's patience snapped. Booming with rage, he demanded the right of passage. Seeing that this made no impression, he drew his rifle and fired into the air. He had every intention of continuing to shoot when he noticed that one of the elders wished to approach. Reuven was too angry even to listen at first, though in the end he heard the Bedouin out—from a distance. The tribesman informed him that from now on the a-Zbekhs would accept them as neighbors and allow them through. Paicovich's reputation was sealed. From then on in a-Zbekh eyes, he was brave and indomitable. Sipping cups of coffee, they wondered who he was. A Jew? Certainly not: Jews were *walad el-mitta* (mortals), that is, cowards who did not defend themselves. A Muslim or a Christian? Evidently, no. Ultimately, they concluded that he was an Insari, a member of the north Syrian tribe of Ashuri known for their courage. Paicovich's sons adopted the appellation. At family affairs, he became "al-Insari" to them.[38]

Paicovich threw himself into farming with all the love and energy of a man who had at last realized his life's dream. With infinite toil, rudimentary tools, and no mechanization whatsoever he cleared his fields stone by stone and used the stones to mark off his land. He actually enlarged his holding to 350 dunams (87.5 acres; 35 ha), a takeover that won recognition from the ICA.[39]

His love for the soil was almost sensual. As if born to farming, he would pick up a clod of earth and relish its taste. Every stalk of grain fallen from the wagon he retrieved with a loving hand. He had his children or a laborer trail behind the wagon to collect whatever fell off—a practice that his neighbors variously interpreted as either mingy or thrifty.[40] Meticulous and orderly, he took great care of his tools and his harvests. The rows he sowed were painstakingly straight. The olive grove he cultivated had no match, and his vineyard earned high praise from visiting ICA officials who marveled at the talents of the novice farmer. He raised potatoes in his vegetable garden and, by his own account, every potato that he managed to grow was treated with the reverence Jews reserved for a perfect citron.[41]

Paicovich was known in Mes'ha as a smart farmer adeptly managing his holding. Industrious, persevering, and surrounded by a bevy of sons learned in the lore of the land from the cradle, he had the advantage over his neighbors. What's more, he was tall and strong, and took easily to physical work. A hard and stubborn man, he could hold his own in negotiations. As a result, the family was not counted among the colony's poor. Poverty and wealth, however, are relative concepts.[42]

Life revolved around work. Chaya rose in the wee hours to do her chores and to prepare food for the field hands. She would rouse the family and, at first light, Reuven would set out with the boys. They were not seen again until nightfall and, sometimes, especially during harvest, they continued working past dark. After the day's work, the boys would hitch a wagon and ride to the spring to fill barrels of water for drinking and household needs. The houses in Mes'ha had no running water until the 1930s and trips to the spring were a daily ritual. Alighting at the source, the boys would lower a can into the water, fill the barrels, and carefully cover them with sacks to protect the water from road dust. At home, again with great care, they would empty the barrels into vats kept in the farmyard. The route to the spring cut through fields with bumps and potholes, and on occasion the barrels arrived home half-empty. The spring could not supply the colony's demand and in drought years—which were frequent—it would be dry by summer's end. Its waters were turbid; as soon as several farmers had drawn their fill nothing remained for the rest. The water level was on everyone's lips as farmers passed one another to and from the spring.

Water was a source of friction with the Arab neighbors too: in periods of drastic shortage, Mes'ha's young would get into fights trying to pilfer water from guarded Arab wells. Water wars were an annual occurrence. Two Mes'ha boys were once caught red-handed yet continued to draw water rather than flee. Finding themselves surrounded, one of the boys shot into the air, mustering the entire colony to their rescue. Before matters could escalate, a soft-spoken teacher by the name of Entebi stepped in and rebuked the Arabs; he shamed them for their un-neighborly behavior, depriving the thirsty colony of drinking water.[43]

In these conditions bathing and laundry were obviously a luxury, particularly in summer. For decades, this was the situation at all settlements in the Lower Galilee. It is little wonder that one girl from Yavne'el carried a lifelong memory of an immaculate first-grade teacher with not a fly on her, while clusters of insects hovered over the children's faces.[44]

Life at Mes'ha followed the agricultural cycle and seasons: in the autumn, everyone looked out for the first rains. When they came, the land was prepared for sowing. Oxen were used for plowing until they were replaced by mules in the transition from the light Arab plow to the European kind.

In winter, the village was totally cut off and enveloped in heavy mud, inside and out; no one arrived, no one left. Roads were unpaved and a journey to Tiberias or Nazareth could not be made without a donkey. Later, under the British Mandate, the outside world was opened up by train service from Afulah. The rainy season was a time for repairs. Housewives used the long winter nights to sew clothes for the family or to sell and earn a little extra money. Families sat around tables lit by oil lamps. The oil was imported in tins and sold by the measure, and the filling and the lighting of the lamp was an art in and of itself: if a lamp died out, the children were generally charged with relighting it, taking care not to get burned by the hot glass.[45] On nights such as these, Reuven Paicovich would read to his children from Hebrew literature: Abraham Mapu, Peretz Smolenskin, Mikha Joseph Berdyczewski, I. L. Peretz.[46] Winter was also the season for studying since in the spring and the summer children twelve and older would accompany their fathers to the fields, making up school assignments in the evenings after a hard day's work.

Spring was heralded by the return of Mes'ha's cattle to the village. Spare in flesh and produce, the herd consisted of Arab cows unflatteringly known as "tails." In winter, when a thin mantle of green covered the hills, Arab cowhands would lead them to pasture north of the colony—"on vacation" according to the local jesters. Two months later, the cows came home, filling the air with mooing and lowing as each found its way to its master's yard and every farmer spotted his beast.[47]

Summer's sign was the threshing floor: the entire family with the exception of the farmwife would scramble to bring in the grain out of harm's way, be it from natural or human elements. To guard the harvest from thieves, everyone slept in the granary. Girls and young women brought along food and drink, someone would reach for a harmonica, and the sound of song would soon be heard. Couples seeking privacy clambered to the top of the piled-up sheaves, away from prying eyes.

Mes'ha may have been lean, but it did not suffer from hunger. Most of the food was home grown. The seeds from the harvest were ground at the Kafr Kama flourmill, which worked like a charm, unlike Mes'ha's contraption. For the children, the walk to Kafr Kama, a Circassian village, was like a holiday: in addition to the half day off from work, there was the anticipation of waiting in line for their turn at the mill, of buying sweets for a penny, of roaming through the narrow village lanes—all of it was a lingering adventure.[48]

For cooking and baking, the Arab outdoor *tabun* was used. The first settlers to arrive in the Lower Galilee had erected the usual barred range, but the lack of wood for fuel soon posed a problem, while rising smoke made housework grueling. Into the breach stepped the wife of the *harat*, the Arab laborer: kneading together grass and earth, straw and water, she marked off a *tabun* in the ground to present the women with a superior technical upgrade. It was fueled three times a week with the help of slow-burning, kneaded animal droppings, but since matches were not always handy, great care was taken to keep the embers alive. The *tabun* became hearth and home.[49]

The food was simple and natural: bread, milk, cheese, and butter. Eggs from the chicken coop were plenty and were often sold to a wholesaler in exchange for such luxuries as herring or *halva*. Cooked food was based on cereals and legumes: bulgur, *cholent*, and so forth. Meat was less common, although for the Sabbath and holidays a hen would be slaughtered. Fruit and vegetables were bought from Arabs hailing from the water-rich Bet-Netofah Valley who made the rounds of the villages. Mes'ha's vegetable patches yielded only herbs, onions, and sometimes a potato.[50]

In times of trouble, the hardships of living in an out-of-the-way village were all too palpable: if illness struck, the bumpy wagon ride to a hospital in Tiberias or Nazareth could well hasten a patient's end. In winter, the trip was out of the question altogether and the sick simply had to cope on their own. For childbirth, the *bobbeh* or midwife was called in—she was a Mes'ha institution in herself.

The village was too small to support good services. It had no store worthy of the name, medical treatment was poor, and the school left much to be desired. Rosh Pinnah, in contrast, was already a small town boasting various service providers from artisans to ICA officials, as well as farmers. The service providers were able to maintain a store and their presence lent the colony a sense of relative ease.[51] Mes'ha had none of these.

Predictably, Mesh'ha's relations with its Arab neighbors were complex from the first. Although the interaction was rather simple and unsophisticated, at the same time, it had many aspects: hostility was tempered by affection, dependency by self-sufficiency, aggression by friendship, and distance by closeness. Mes'ha's attitude stemmed neither from ideology nor politics; largely, it was an extension of the attitude *shtetl* Jews had toward the Russian or Ukranian *muzhik*s who brought Jews the produce of their fields and gardens, sold them their butter and eggs, and at their stores bought the provisions they required for their farms—rope, nails, tools. The *shtetl* Jews' singular attitude to the country *goyim* reflected both Jewish uniqueness and the Jewish anomaly: on the one hand, Jews were contemptuous of the *goyishe* dunderheads, who were the butt of their ridicule and deception; on the other hand, Jews had a gnawing fear of the *goyim*'s violent outbursts: come pogroms, all of Jacob's wisdom would prove useless against Esau's brawn. In Mes'ha on the whole, however, calm reigned as business dealings and interdependence spilled over onto the personal plane, sparking friendships and loyalties across national and religious divides. To a great extent, the relations between Mes'ha's residents and their Arab neighbors were patterned along these lines.

Built on the ruins of an Arab village abandoned in the latter half of the nineteenth century, Mes'ha did not face the sort of strife that had poisoned Metullah's early years (when the Druze claimed dispossession). It did come under attack from a-Zbekh Bedouin—though not more so than other villages, whether Arab or Jewish. Marauding was the Bedouin way of life and roving tribes had declared war on settled homesteaders. Added to this was the rivalry over water, with the wars of the herdsmen taking on biblical dimensions at times. But it was not a national conflict. Much like the Wild West where cattlemen were pitted against homesteaders, everyone did as he wished; to survive, a man—no matter how inherently nonviolent—had to learn to shoot, to fight, to ride a horse, and to defend his life, his honor, and his property.

Mes'ha's residents drew a sharp line between friendly and unfriendly neighbors. Kafr Kama, where they sent their children to grind flour, was very friendly. The Maghreb villages whose population stemmed from North Africa were not considered dangerous. From beyond the hills, fruit and vegetable sellers came to peddle their produce. And within the village itself, each and every farmyard had a shack for the *harat* and his family. A *harat* was usually a landless peasant who hired himself out in exchange for 20 percent of the harvest. He worked alongside the farmer in any job that needed doing, plowing and sowing, reaping and threshing. His wife would spend the day with the farmer's wife, helping with the housework, seeing to the *tabun* fire, washing the laundry, and doing the heavy work. Their children, too, would lend a hand and they played with the Jewish family's children, speaking a Yiddish mixed with Arabic and Hebrew. The farmer and the *harat* would take their meals together in the field, tasting one another's morsels. If a cow was stolen from the farmyard, the *harat* joined in the chase after the thief. During harvest, he too was recruited for guard duty. Nonetheless, the idyll was shattered at times: a *harat* might be suspected of pilfering from the farmer's harvest and his wife and children "accused of" impertinence and a lack of hygiene. Quarrels could degenerate, a *harat* and his family resorting to violence against the farmer.[52] But this show of muscle, as in Russia, was the exception to the rule; it made no real dent in the way of life. The lack of green, the smoke of the *tabun*, the argot of playing children, the dirt, and the neglect all lent Mes'ha the appearance of an Arab village, no different from its surroundings.

The ICA's contracts stipulated that hired hands could be used only in the high season, and Reuven Paicovich's contract stated explicitly that only Jews could be hired.[53] It was an impossible demand. Mes'ha's residents hailed from Rosh Pinnah, Metullah, and Zikhron Ya'acov. All of these communities, especially the last, had used Arab labor, and their former residents saw no reason to change in their new location. Besides, integrating into the surroundings meant also fostering Jewish-Arab relations. The guarding of Mes'ha was thus placed in the hands of one Hamadi, the most infamous local bandit, while *harat*s were accepted into Mes'ha's homes. They knew the local conditions forward and backward; they taught the farmers the secrets of the fields while their wives taught the farmers' wives the secrets of the *tabun*. But this situation caused Mes'ah to have a population that consisted of more Arabs than Jews. And a niggling fear lingered among the Jews that "the Arabs would rise up one day and make mincemeat of their Jewish exploiters."[54]

The mixture of intimacy and dependence often spawned true affection; some *harat*s became part of the family, remaining loyal even through the hard times of riots and bloodletting. Other relationships ended in lifelong enmity. Unlike the colonies that did not employ Arab labor, at Mes'ha, Arabs were not strangers, not an unknown quantity. Their persons, language, conduct, and customs were part of the village tapestry; they were not foreign, but flesh of the land, integral to the landscape. The ideology of "Jewish labor" that dictated against employing Arabs created a complete separation between Eretz Israel and Palestine—in consciousness if not in actuality. The former was entirely Jewish and not overly welcoming to Arabs; the latter was Arab, a foreign land that aroused anxiety and alienation in the Jews: to them, Palestine was mysterious, ominous, intangible.

At Mes'ha, Arabs may have been neighbors or friends or even thieves, but there was nothing mysterious about them. They were real. Of course, this had no bearing on the larger picture of Jewish-Arab relations in the land of Israel, questions that were still sealed in the future, especially for people with a horizon blocked by Mount Tabor. At Mes'ha, Jewish-Arab interdependence peeled away the mystery, which, potentially, could have formed a cultural, national shell.

In this land where everyone did as he wished, the regime intervened only in extreme instances. Amid the eternal conflict between Bedouin and peasantry, law and order was to spring from the society itself. The history of the Second Aliyah reserves a fondness and place of honor for the colonies of Galilee based on field crops: they were the crucible of the independent Jewish agricultural worker, who proved capable of organizing farm work without the need of supervisors. The beginnings of the so-called Labor settlement apparently lay in the attempts and initiatives of individuals to introduce into the Lower Galilee Jewish laborers in place of Arab *harat*s and Jewish guards in place of the Arab master thieves customarily employed. At Mes'ha, the appearance of Jewish farmhands was connected with a man who became a local legend, the teacher Asher Ehrlich.

After Joseph Vitkin despaired of himself and his pupils, he suggested to Asher Ehrlich, who lived in Rehovot, that he replace him as principal. The neglect and backwardness that so depressed Vitkin and the hills that so stifled him—these he described to Ehrlich in glowing colors, firing his idealism with a Zionist educational challenge. Ehrlich, who had been born in a Jewish farming village on the banks of the Volga, Nehar-Tov, and who had endured a four-year ordeal in the czar's army, was tall, strong in body and soul, brave, and proud. The "long teacher"—*al-muallem a-tawil*, as the Arabs called him—was a walking example to Mes'ha's youth of the need for "Jewish muscle."

Working on the premise of a healthy mind in a healthy body, he regaled pupils with tales of Maccabean heroism and led them on excursions around the Tabor, unveiling before them the delights of Eretz Israel—its plant and animal kingdoms, its trails and landmarks—and teaching them to have no fear of Arab villagers or casual wayfarers. A chance encounter of his with Bedouin went down in the settlement's annals: one night, while walking alone from Melahamiya to Mes'ha, he came upon two horsemen. One of them asked him for a light. Ehrlich pulled out his gun and offered him the barrel. To Ehrlich's everlasting glory, the Bedouin fled for their lives. He was able to impress his pupils because he manifested qualities necessary for the wilds of Galilee: communion with nature, physical prowess, courage, and a proud defense of life and property. In the Wild West, decency, determination, and physical strength can triumph over the forces of evil and anarchy. This was the role Ehrlich filled at Mes'ha.[55]

He won Mes'ha's hearts not only because of his personal endowments but also because he was ready to help the farmers beyond the call of duty. He lobbied for them before the ICA and initiated a loan fund to see the needy through to harvest. Building on these successes, he tried to institute his long-standing plan of introducing Jewish labor. He did not find Mes'ha to his taste, with its image as a mixed colony where children spoke a brew of Hebrew and mumbo jumbo, with its street that was not Jewish in either form or character, with the fact that its safety was guarded by an outlaw. To him, the import of Jewish labor was the Archimedean screw that could transform Mes'ha into Kefar Tavor. He traveled to Judea, where his infectious enthusiasm motivated others to return with him, marking the start of what was to become the Second Aliyah's push toward Galilee. All at once, a new spirit infused Mes'ha. Ehrlich made space in his house for a clubroom, and the singing of the hired hands soon dissolved the nighttime terrors and the loneliness that had swaddled the village at dark. Children suddenly had new role models: Jewish guards in *abaya*s and *keffiyeh*s cut dashing figures with their decked-out horses, their ammunition belts, and their weapons. Their imagination fired, Mes'ha's youth longed to be like Beraleh Schwiger or Yigael the guardsman—a son of Metulla, that is, of Galilee.[56]

Mes'ha, for one brief moment, was a social and public hub. Here the Second Aliyah founded Ha-Horesh, Galilee's first workers organization, as well as Ha-Shomer, a body of Jewish guardsmen (which was established on the seventh day of Passover, 1909). Jewish guards and Jewish labor were coming into their own. But the moment passed. Ehrlich became embroiled in a major squabble and was forced to leave the colony.[57] With his departure, the bubble burst. A year later the contract with Ha-Shomer for Jewish guards was terminated, the Jewish hired hands were gradually fired, and the *harat*s were restored to Mes'ha's farmyards.[58]

Like that of Mes'ha, Reuven Paicovich's attitude to the Arab milieu was ambivalent. His courage stood out from his first day in the country[59] and his memoirs include hair-raising exploits about near-death encounters with highwaymen and miraculous deliverances due to his unfailing heart. He gave at least as good as he got and he tried to teach his sons to fight for life and honor. It was not an abstract message, but something concrete translating immediately into physical engagement. It was the ABCs of Galilee—vital to survival. After the a-Zbekh incident, Paicovich's neighbors understood that it was best not to tangle with this strong-willed man who itched for a fight, and they chose other fields for their spoil. But if they needed reminding, all they had to do was stray onto his property.

His reputation preceding him, Reuven was welcomed into Bedouin tents to sit and sip coffee with a-Zbekh elders between one scuffle and another. It was a reputation in which al-Insari's sons too basked, and rightfully so: the boys were hardly fist-shy; as soon as they came of age, they showed themselves eminently capable of thwarting thieves and trespassers.

The frays were governed by ritual and were rarely life threatening. Both Arabs and Jews were careful to stop short of killing lest they stir up blood vengeance, known as *gom*, and all that it entailed. By an unwritten law of the Galilean wilds, deadly weapons were shunned unless there was absolutely no choice. Paicovich played by the rules of the game.

He observed the rules when it came to Jewish labor as well. National pride was one thing and hiring Jews another. He was already living at Mes'ha during the brief transition to Jewish labor when some fifteen farmers took Jewish workers into their employ. But not he: his name does not appear on any list of farmers using Jewish laborers. He saw no need. Arabs may have been rivals, robbers, constant opponents, but they were part of the landscape; there was no contradiction. Paicovich's *harat*s were part of his household and when the need arose the *harat*'s wife nursed his son.

He was not an observant Jew. According to Allon, Reuven was cured of religion after being thrashed by his father for playing with a puppy.[60] En route from Odessa to Jaffa, he bickered with ultra-Orthodox passengers who were making the voyage in order to die in the Holy Land. They took exception to his abstinence from prayer; he showed them lofty contempt, undiluted by a scrap of Jewish compassion.[61] His wife, Chaya, was highly devout and abided by all of the commandments, minor and major. She kept a kosher home, observed the Sabbath and the holidays with all of their traditional dishes, and lit the candles. It is safe to assume that Reuven did not make the blessing over wine. But he was the center of her universe, and she was careful not to force her ways on him. His feet knew the route to the synagogue but they took him there only on the High Holidays.[62] He had a Lithuanian skepticism for anything that did not stand up to proof of reason or perception. The boys all took after him, adding a further distinction to this Mes'ha family. Generally speaking, the fathers' generation was pious; it was only later that most of the sons turned their backs on religion—not so the Paicovichs. And yet, within a few short years, Paicovich became one of the colony's leading figures, in all likelihood because of his other virtues.[63] In 1912 he became a member of the council, a seat he retained intermittently until the onset of British rule.[64]

Hard, strict, pedantic, Reuven's penny pinching was famed: he cut every cigarette in two, smoking half at a time and saving the leftover tobacco in a small box to use later in his pipe.[65] Dearth can lead to minginess, and the residents of Mes'ha learned to hoard every sheaf of wheat and every matchstick. But Paicovich never featured among the colony's poor. His parsimony was ingrained in his life and character. The main thread of his life was the work ethos—man was born to toil. His extreme individualism set the tone in his home. He had no time for small talk, never invited his neighbors home, never visited them for a glass of tea with *tzuker*, as they called it. Nor did he participate in joint village projects. Proud, reserved, and suspicious, he chose to work on his own with his family and his *harat* rather than rely on others. To his sons, he strove to pass on his independence, meticulousness, love of work, and courage. Of them, he demanded that they tell the truth, take responsibility for their actions, and lovingly accept punishment for their misdeeds, large or small.[66] His integrity was ruthless, he did not know the meaning of mercy, and despite his diligence, conditions at Mes'ha never brought him the measure of ease he had hoped for. Eventually, he was forced to bury his pride and turn to the ICA for assistance.

Their first few years at Mes'ha were good to the Paicoviches. In 1909, their only daughter was born and named Deborah after the biblical prophetess with a connection to Mount Tabor. Eliav (born during Paicovich's trip to America) and Deborah were still toddlers, but Moshe, Mordekhai, and Zvi already composed an able work force helping their father run the farm. Chaya lent the home its warmth and softness. Kind and gentle in nature and appearance, she sought to round the "sharp corners" in her husband's personality. As the household's bookkeeper, she would sometimes secretly manage to return to a farmer requiring seeds before Passover change from the money her husband had charged him. Without advertising the fact, she lent money to the needy of the village. She shielded the boys from their father's wrath, Reuven's parenting being based on "spare the rod and spoil the child." In the cramped conditions of the small house—the dining room was at once the lounge, the kitchen, and the center of family life, while the bedroom served everyone (in summer, the children slept outdoors on mats)—she managed to cook, sew, and keep her home clean and tidy. Possessions were few and soon became worn in a house that had cried out for renovations from day one. Only rarely did she permit herself a luxury, such as visiting her father in Rosh Pinnah. The journey took a whole day and Paicovich was not given to visiting his father-in-law.

The disruptions wrought by the First World War did not bypass Palestine or Mes'ha. Men were conscripted into the army or forced to labor for the war effort. Livestock was requisitioned for military needs. In some sense, Mes'ha's lot improved: since the country was cut off from the rest of the world and there was famine in the towns, the price of wheat soared. Like all Galilean colonies raising cereals, Mes'ha was spared hunger and even succeeded in selling spare produce. Paicovich and his two older boys, Moshe and Mordekhai, had been called up. Moshe, never having had a yen for fieldwork, had attended the Herzliya High School and excelled in languages; the Turks soon made him an officer. Mordekhai and his father were ordinary soldiers. In 1917, when the Ottoman fate was sealed, Mordekhai and Reuven snuck home, eluding the search for deserters. Yigal was born about a year later. He later laid his birth at the door of his father's dramatic return from the dread of war.[67]

Yigal was an afterthought in a rather mature family. By the time he was born, his father was forty-five, his mother about forty-two. His sister, who was closest to him in age, was nine, his oldest brother, twenty-two. One story from Mes'ha about his birth said that his mother feared for his life because he was so small. The midwife consoled her: don't worry, she said, this little one will yet head the Mes'ha Council![68] After Yigal made a name for himself, becoming the colony's most illustrious son, the tale became part of the Mes'ha legend.

He was born in heady times of great expectations. Until then, Paicovich had given his children traditional Jewish names. He now outdid himself; he called the boy Yigal—a typical Eretz Israel name redolent of the exultation following the Balfour Declaration and the British conquest. No more dispirited Diaspora names, such as Moshe or Mordekhai or Zvi. "Eliav"—for the child born while the father was in American exile—expressed Jewish resignation to an inauspicious fate: may God be with both the tender newborn and the father. "Deborah," though prompted by the scenery outside the window, still belonged to the lexicon of common Jewish names. But "Yigal"—the redeemer—suggested new times, a different sort of life experience, high hopes, and a commensurate self-confidence. It was exceptional among Mes'ha's children. It bespoke great expectations and nationalist goals.

Allon's memoirs describe the early 1920s at Mes'ha. Presumably, the stories were told and retold so that he absorbed them as a babe on his mother's lap. One episode that took pride of place in the family saga concerned Mes'ha's cattle robbery.

One cloud-free Sabbath morning in the early summer of 1920, as most of Mes'ha's old-timers stood in the synagogue wrapped in prayer shawls, the serenity was shattered by a lad bursting in with the cry that the entire herd had been stolen. The residents of Mes'ha were shocked. Such a

Figure 2. Allon in the arms of the husband of his Arab wet nurse. Photographer unknown. Courtesy of the Allon family.

thing had never happened before—not even under the Turks. For it to happen now—in the British era—when the troublemakers seemed to have retired and stopped harassing the colony . . . They quickly pulled themselves together, quit their prayers and the synagogue, and, undeterred by the holy Sabbath, set out in hot pursuit. Paicovich was not at the synagogue, and the news of a robbery on this tranquil morning hit him like a bomb at home. Zvi hastily grabbed for his weapons in order to join the other young men in the chase. Reuven held him back momentarily, for fear of the *Gom*. But Zvi paid no attention. Paicovich, as the chairman of the council at the time (by his own report), went to see to the colony's defense against a possible raid by the Bedouin neighbors to the north: the robbery and chase could well whet their appetite for an attack on the disconcerted village. The robbers had come from Transjordan and scurried to get back across the Jordan under cover of Wadi Bira, driving the herd eastward. In their flight, they ran into an ambush laid by Mes'ha's "posse." One of the robbers was killed in the dust-up, and others appeared to be hurt. Mes'ha also suffered losses: Moshe Klimantovsky, the son of a widow who managed her farm alone, was slain. Two others were wounded: Nahman Karniel and Zvi Paicovich.

With Yigal in his mother's arms—so the story goes—his mother and father stood outside their home anxiously awaiting news. All at once a rider came into view. It was Zvi; he had left home on his feet only to return atop someone else's horse. "*S'iz gornisht, imi*" ("It's nothing, my mother"), he shouted, his shirt soaked in blood. Chaya fainted. Horse and rider continued on to the pharmacy, but before he could get there, Zvi also fainted. Vigilant neighbors rushed to dismount him and dress his wounds. Mes'ha's pharmacy served as a clinic and even an infirmary, and Zvi lay there for several weeks before being transferred to a hospital. It was a year before he returned to farm work.

The loss of the handsome, amiable Klimantovsky cast a pall over Mes'ha the next day. The two other casualties hovered between life and death and the air was heavy with the stillness of the grave. It was unexpectedly disturbed by noise on the northern road, not far from Paicovich's home. He took his rifle and went out to investigate. A horde of merry Bedouin were firing guns and riding toward the village. Thinking them a wild mob come to finish yesterday's piece of work, he planted his feet on the main road, cocked his rifle, and faced them, a man alone. He warned them not to try to enter the village. Nearly falling over themselves, the Arabs explained that they were on a wedding procession, a *fantasiyeh* in honor of the bride's coming to the groom, and no one had the right to block the main road that ran through Mes'ha. Paicovich would have none of it—the village was in mourning, he said, the wounded required quiet, and the bereaved families could not abide the rowdiness; the procession would *not* pass through Mes'ha! Having said this, he was not a man to back down from what might have been an unnecessary confrontation. Some of the merrymakers soon recognized him and spread the word that it was wiser not to lock horns with al-Insari. The procession turned toward a byroad.[69]

Reuven's intrepid stance and Zvi's injury nourished many a tale, magnified by the fact that a year later, Klimantovsky's sister married the second Paicovich son, Mordekhai. The episode contained all of the ingredients of the Wild West, including the sense that the authorities could not be relied on to ensure the safety of the settlers.

Its wider context, however, is virtually absent from descriptions by the residents of Mes'ha. In this period, the whole of the Galilee—Lower and Upper—was in turmoil. But the connection to Emir Faisal's deposition in Damascus by the French escaped Mes'ha's notice. To the settlers, the raid from Transjordan was a local clash; it was not related to the serious skirmish that had taken place at Tzemah a month before (on 23 May 1920) between the Indian army stationed there and Bedouin attempting to invade from the desert. The people of Mes'ha saw the raid as more of the same, as an extension of the constant battle over grazing land and water sources: a conflict between the lawless and the law-abiding folk. It rankled them that their Arab neighbors—far from coming to their aid—had actually helped the robbers. Nevertheless, the nationalist awakening washing over the colony in those days did not make them view their neighbors as having the same aspirations. The perceptions of Wild Galilee were still paramount.

In the thick tension following the incident, Jewish settlers in the Galilee and the Jordan Valley submitted a strong protest to the military governor in Tiberias for the lapse in peace and security. As a result, the Indian army was stationed at colonies in the Upper and the Lower Galilee, and, after a couple of weeks of uncertainty and fear of war, calm was gradually restored and life reverted to its normal course.[70]

This unsure interval highlighted Mes'ha's virtues and faults. The courageous stance on life and property, the unhesitant enlistment of the young in battle, reflected the great distance traveled by former denizens of Lithuanian *shtetlach* to Eastern Galilee's untamed frontier. Nearby colonies equally stood up to the test: Yavne'el, for instance, made immediate provisions to supply Mes'ha with a daily shipment of milk (preboiled, of course, so as not to spoil on the way). In contrast, when it was suggested that farming be organized communally, with everyone working together on a different field each day, the residents of Mes'ha could not get their act together: those with nearer fields balked; those with better work animals refused to help neighbors whose beasts were a cut below.[71]

Paicovich was among the main victims of the robbery, losing five cows and five bulls. Only one other farmer lost more, and only two others matched him[72]—meaning that his was one of the more prosperous farms in the village.

It was, in many respects, a peak period in Mes'ha's history and in the Paicovich annals. In the war years, as noted, grain fetched high prices and Mes'ha had plenty of grain. In 1917–18, the rain was generous, producing a bumper crop. Afterward, a constant decline set in, both in harvests and prices.[73] Successive drought brought on a plague of field mice that ate away at the meager yields for three consecutive years. Settlers had to borrow money from government sources and the ICA.[74] Attempts to diversify cereal farming with dry orchards failed. Only olives and almonds could be grown without irrigation. The vines had succumbed to disease during World War I, almonds were economically unviable, and even olives, so common in Arab villages, did not do well at Mes'ha.

In the Jewish Yishuv in those days, the Third Aliyah immigration wave enlarged the population and injected a boost of initiative, action, and building. Innovation and experimentation were the name of the game, whether in agriculture and industry or in new settlement forms, such as the cooperative *moshav*, the *kvutza* or large commune (the forerunner of the kibbutz), or the "labor battalion" (contract workers who lived in collective equality). The times were infused with a burst of youthful energy and the joy of creation. But not at Mes'ha. It seemed to have sunk into slumber, hardly touched by the changes sweeping over the Yishuv. And yet, for a short moment it too seemed to come alive, in the "war of the generations" in the colonies of the Lower Galilee. But victory went to the "old."[75]

The triumph of conservatism over renewal found expression in the old farming methods. Mature farmers had little interest in new inventions or mechanization. Uneducated and naturally suspicious, they had no use for the new-fangled notions banging at the doors of their small world. In particular, they were wary of anything that smacked of "bolshevism"; to them, it stood for everything that nipped individual independence and freedom of action.

The question of Jewish labor lay at the heart of the controversy between the "progressives" and the "conservatives." Everyone agreed that the colony was too small and the Jewish settlers so few as to threaten its existence. Mes'ha's street retained an essentially Arab character, as in the period of the Second Aliyah. The number of Arabs living there was certainly no less—and sometimes even more—than the number of Jews. The cattle robbery of 1920 gave the Jews of Mes'ha a moment of alarm that their Arab neighbors, including the friends and kinsmen of their *harats*, would join forces with the thieves. In 1921, thirty-two Jews were reportedly hired as annual workers at Mes'ha, apparently on the same conditions as *harats*. They soon organized evening Hebrew classes, and outside lecturers included them on their circuit.[76] All of a sudden Mes'ha was part of the Yishuv. Yet in less than a year, the number of Jewish workers dropped to nine, after having inspired a local counterculture: a Bnei Binyamin club, an organization of second-generation settlers, was founded in the colony, and most of Mes'ha's young joined it. Culturally, it did not amount to much. But it accented—and exacerbated—the rivalry between farmers, who considered themselves middle class, and Jewish laborers, who leaned toward the Zionist Left.[77]

By 1921 it was clear that the dry farming of cereals could not support hired labor, whether Jewish or Arab, and that a radical solution was needed for the colonies' woes—to reduce the size of the farm units and switch over to intensive farming.[78] Of course, no one had the energy to tackle the farmers, the ICA, or the objective conditions. The lack of internal cooperation and the unwillingness of the farmers to establish a representative organization with financial and electoral clout prevented the Galilee's settlers from constituting the political force that could have improved their lot.

In the eyes of the young Yigal, however, these were the best years. With the exception of his eldest brother, Moshe, who, after his release from British wartime imprisonment, left Mes'ha to work on the Haifa railway, the whole family was together. His mother, Chaya, showered the fair child of her "old age" with love and pampering, while Reuven, too, was not immune to his charms. On one heart-stopping occasion, Reuven, driving a mule-wagon laden with goods, spied Yigal alone in the fields. Unable to rein in the animals because of the weight of their load, he cried out from afar for the child to move out of the way, but to no avail. Yigal slid beneath the wheels. Only after he saw that the child had suffered minor cuts was Reuven able to breathe again. But the incident was apparently traumatic enough for him to recall it fifty years later.[79] Yigal's version of the same incident was different: Reuven, he said, commanded the doctor to save the child or he would have his head.[80]

Those happy years were dominated by the mother's quiet presence. The adult Allon described his parents' home—with its scents and dishes, with the serenity of a Sabbath eve descending on it, as the hub that it was for the colony's guards and guests—as a short season of motherly grace. It was soon taken from him: after finishing her housework one Friday, Chaya sat down to rest, keeled over, and lost consciousness. The doctors summoned to her bedside did not hold out any hope, while neighbors rallied round to succor an abruptly motherless family. She was gone within the week. The young child could not but feel the change, although nothing prepared him for his last encounter with his mother: "Suddenly, my father came, picked me up in his arms, and carried me to the room where she lay. . . . I didn't understand what was happening, but the silence of the family poised around her bed said it all. My father lowered me toward her and I kissed her forehead. If my memory does not betray me, she even turned her eyes on me, which suddenly lit up with the supreme effort of an impossible smile."[81] She was around forty-nine.

The loss was tremendous. Paicovich, only in his early fifties, refused to remarry, whether out of loyalty to her memory or the difficulty of adapting to someone new. The house began to empty out. Even before Chaya's death, Mordekhai had joined the Bnei Binyamin organization of farmers' sons to found the colony of Binyaminah. Deborah, fourteen, dropped out of school to assume responsibility for the home and to raise Yigal. Paicovich was never a social animal. After his wife's death, there were no more visitors to the home and his public prestige waned. Gloom increasingly nestled between the four walls.

Allon wrote of his father as the dominant figure in his and the family's life. He sketched a man strong and brave, honest and unimpeachable, a proud man standing up to ICA officials, unafraid to take on the authorities or to fight against wrong. In Allon's hands, Reuven was either the Gary Cooper of the Galilee or a member of the enlightened landed gentry. Contemporaries, however, painted a far different portrait, as did Paicovich's own memoirs. No one doubted his courage, toughness, or pride. But broad-mindedness or spunk against the "wicked" PICA? Yigal seems to have resorted to wishful thinking. (In the early 1920s, the ICA became the PICA—the Palestine Jewish Colonization Association.)

The relations between Mes'ha and the PICA shed light on the character of the colony and its settlers. Mes'ha was founded with the intention that the farmers would stand on their own two feet after receiving an initial loan from the ICA. Reality, however, got in the way. The farmers were not shy about asking for additional assistance, while the officials, by nature, risked being snared into providing support and fostering dependency, despite all good intentions to the contrary.

Affairs came to a head in the 1920s. The PICA was hard put to balance the books, whereas the farmers had grown accustomed to requesting handouts for all and sundry. Their applications centered on important issues, such as water supply, as well as on minor items. When it came to public institutions—the school, the synagogue, the ritual bath or the community center—the residents of Mes'ha took it for granted that the PICA was to erect them. And when the harvest failed, they thought it only right that the PICA pay the government the land taxes due on their behalf. The PICA was fed up: the more it helped the farmers, the less they helped themselves.[82]

Paicovich was no different. He too enjoyed being on the receiving end of the PICA's loans and benefits. Notwithstanding the image of a proud pauper that he liked to tout, he was neither all that poor nor all that proud.

His sense of the PICA's wrongdoing went back to the very beginning, when the ICA's Rosenheck had refused him the choice of a colony. But it only grew worse, and after the earthquake of 1927 and the ensuing argument over home repairs, his bitterness took firm root. As he told it, the PICA fixed the cracks in the houses of the other farmers, but not his; he ascribed it to the organization's dislike of him, his pride, and his independence. He dashed off at least four letters to the PICA administration asking that his house be repaired or exchanged for another. In one letter, he noted: "Permit me to mention here that I have already been a farmer at Mes'ha for twenty years and I never come to the officials with a demand for help."[83] He was not eager to turn to the PICA, he said, but it was now a matter of necessity. The administration remained unimpressed: "We cannot, to our regret, meet your request since we have no budget for same.—Besides, it is time that the farmer understood that the maintenance [and] repair of his house comes under his care—not ours."[84] Paicovich did not let up. In December 1934 he again pressed the PICA for repairs and again was told that the "repair of the buildings falls on the farmer, not on our company,"[85] as indeed the leasehold contract stated. It was a typical response from PICA officials weary of the endless demands made by Mes'ha's farmers; it was not a sign of discrimination. Paicovich made no repairs. He left the house in splendid dilapidation as eternal evidence of his being wronged by the PICA.

The PICA-Paicovich cup of bitters grew fuller with another affair, that of the Mikveh Israel Agricultural School. Paicovich submitted Yigal's application in 1931 and the boy passed the entrance exam. But Paicovich had no intention of paying school fees out of his own pocket. He hoped that they would come from the PICA: it provided six scholarships for which all of the children in its colonies could apply. There were thirty applicants; Yigal was not selected. A year later, Mes'ha's only successful candidate quit the school, Paicovich reapplied, and Yigal redid the exam. This time Paicovich stressed the fact that Yigal was a motherless boy and noted the importance of an agricultural education for the future of both boy and farm. Again, Yigal was not among the six winners.[86]

Paicovich may have been unable to afford the fees, although that is open to doubt: according to Allon, the farm owned a pricey, pedigree horse. And when the boy desired a mule, money materialized for this as well. But nothing when it came to education. Reuven did not think that it was up to him to pay for his son's education, especially since there was a chance that the PICA would. The matter of house repairs and the school episode may have had something in common: Paicovich was not prepared to lay out money for what others could obtain from the PICA free of charge.

The PICA's impatience with Paicovich reflected its annoyance with Mes'ha as a whole. In 1930, the residents of Mes'ha filled out a questionnaire presented to them by John Hope-Simpson, who was exploring the feasibility of colonization following the unfavorable report on Zionist settlement produced by the British Shaw Commission on the Palestinian Disturbances of 1929. Based on the questionnaire, the village had thirty farming families at the time and a total debt of Palestine £7,000. They employed forty *harat* families and another thirty-five temporary workers. None of the hired hands was Jewish.[87] At the time, the PICA leaned toward a rescue plan devised for the colonies by the Yavne'el "progressives": intensive farming, smaller units to boost productivity, mechanization (a tractor and a combine), the seed cycle, modern amelioration and fertilization, and improving livestock with superior strains. The entire plan meshed with the problem of Jewish labor. Smaller units and mechanization were meant to reduce manpower and give preference to skilled, trained labor. Yavne'el adopted the program with the PICA's support. Mes'ha rejected it. One of the voluble opponents to modernization was Paicovich. In Mes'ha's dispute with the management of the Galilee Farmers Federation, Paicovich charged: "You (the federation) and PICA must change your attitude toward us."[88] In other words, the fault lay not with Mes'ha's methods but with the attitude of official bodies.

The dispute grew sharper in the summer of 1931, with Mes'ha rejecting every suggestion to change its lifestyle and let the *harat*s go. The PICA imposed sanctions. Spurning a request from Mes'ha's farmers to help them obtain outside work, it explained: "Even if we had funds for employment at Kefar Tavor—we would not use them in view of the farmers' negative position on every suggestion to improve the situation and upgrade agriculture. They object to the seed cycle and to any change in working methods—things that already exist at most of their sister colonies in Lower Galilee." The conclusion was: "So long as the farmers do not change their views on these questions—they can expect no help from us."[89]

The colony's Z. Eshbol complained: "Because of Arab labor, Mes'ha has fallen from grace in the eyes of [PICA] officials and the federation." In the spirit of Paicovich's earlier demand, he called for understanding and caution in officialdom's attitude toward Mes'ha.[90] But while Mes'ha refused to "reform," the PICA refused to extend assistance.

In 1932, a sunken well at Yavne'el fortuitously yielded abundant water, changing the prospects of the Lower Galilee farm and carrying everyone along in a wave of optimism. The discovery seemed to justify the methods of the modernists after the fact. Craving water on their land too, the residents of Mes'ha did not bother to consult the PICA and dug a well at their own expense. The PICA deemed the unplanned excavation a waste of money. Still, there was no denying that it was a novel local initiative. What's more, with the PICA's help, a group of Mes'ha's farmers got together to purchase a jointly owned tractor.

Following sterile attempts and sterile investments by the PICA, finally, in 1932, Mes'ha's homes and farmyards were supplied with running water. An entire saga can be written about the water problem, informed by Mes'ha's bungling in making its demands and the PICA's in meeting them; the former suffered from articulation problems, the latter from technical incompetence. The efforts to install a functioning system went back to 1926 and were a resounding failure, which was virtually imitated in 1932. Given the day-to-day hardships endured by the settlers, one can sympathize with their bitterness and suspicion of the PICA, although this hardly excuses their passivity or inability to organize for the common good.[91]

The early 1930s were full of improvements at Mes'ha. In 1933, electricity came to the village. As usual, there were grumblers who refused to contribute to the required funding, but, in retrospect, all welcomed it.[92] In addition, the opening of the Kadouri Agricultural School in 1934 made it necessary to pave a road to Tiberias and Afula.

Following Yavne'el's success, Mes'ha seemed to accept the new farming arrangements. For its part, the PICA helped in the acquisition of a tractor and planned for a combine as well. Paicovich had no part in the tractor's purchase. He continued to toil alongside his *harat*.[93]

Paicovich's conservatism may have been one of the reasons that, one by one, his sons quit the farm. Zvi settled in Netanya and even Eliav, the only farmer among them, gave up agriculture and moved to the city. Allon's explanation was that they could not obtain holdings at Mes'ha. This is inconsistent with the fact that there were about a dozen abandoned farms at Mes'ha, and the colony was desperate to increase its dwindling population. Besides, Paicovich's holding alone was certainly large enough to support two families, albeit based on the new cultivation methods. The trouble was that he was set in his ways and refused to hear of change. In the stifling atmosphere of a gloomy home and backward farm, the brothers chose to seek their fortunes elsewhere.

Their departure was a blow to Paicovich. He had envisioned an entire neighborhood populated by an extended Paicovich clan. Now, here he was at the start of the 1930s, in a house with only his youngest son, Allon.[94]

The young Allon was left with a dour father who cast a giant shadow and was the fount of kindness and correction, love and frost, closeness and remoteness, a man for whom any show of affection was a sign of weakness. The mature Allon wrote little of this time, but, reading between the lines, one senses a wistfulness. When the boy hurt himself falling from a galloping horse, he received no embrace or sympathy; instead, he was told to get right back on (without the saddle that had torn) and take himself to the pharmacy. Allon tried to put off the ride to the next day. Reuven wouldn't have it. Remarked the adult Allon: "He loved me, I knew that, but in his reactions he was always reticent and Spartan."[95] The fact that Allon was the child of his old age took some of the edge off his relentlessness. Moreover, he grew increasingly conscious that Yigal alone, of all his sons, was still on the farm—his last hope. He blamed himself for the boys' departures, pinning it on his own restrictiveness. Yet he did not spare Yigal; the boy could be sure of a hiding if he neglected farm duties or schoolwork.[96] Allon's awe of his

Figure 3. Allon as a child in Me'sha. Photographer unknown. The Davar Collection. Courtesy of the Lavon Institute for the Study of the Labor Movement, Tel Aviv.

father was mixed with a constant desire to please him, to acquit himself with flying colors in the tests he set him.

Growing up in his father's shadow, Allon was filled with admiration for al-Insari's unflinching stance in the clashes with Arab neighbors that made up the rhythm of life. The brushes with robbers sparked no particular animosity. On the contrary: just as there were Arabs who stole, there were Arab *harat*s who shared the family farmyard. One account tells of Allon being nursed by a *harat*'s wife. In time, his natural playmates were the *harat*'s children. During summer vacation, he would spend two weeks with a family of Arab friends at Kafr Ein Mahl, near Nazareth, basking in all the pampering and attention he lacked at home.[97] Scaling the Tabor with his father, the two would sidetrack to a Bedouin tent and a warm welcome from neighbors with whom they had exchanged blows. The frontier code of conduct valued valor, daring, resolve.

Young Allon's world was circumscribed by Mes'ha's narrow horizon and anti-intellectual society. Education was not a consideration in the PICA's selection of settlers, and frontier society, by its very nature, values physical attributes over "spiritual" qualities. Allon painted Paicovich as a cultured frontiersman with a love of books and reading.[98] This portrait too seems to have been drawn by wishful thinking: Paicovich's letters to the PICA, like others from Mes'ha, were written in broken Hebrew, although there is no doubt that he respected education and made sure Allon was not remiss about his studies.

Allon was a conscientious pupil. An extant letter that he wrote when in second grade, to an ill teacher, is illustrated with a picture at the bottom showing Allon himself sick in bed.[99] In 1928, at the age of ten, he wrote a poem and a composition for the school newspaper. The composition is a specimen of the high-sounding language of the Hebrew Enlightenment (Haskalah) upheld at Mes'ha's school—one could not have too much of it.[100] He contributed also to the quiz section, suggesting riddles that required a fair mastery of the Bible. The raw material for the newspaper must have been vetted by a careful eye because a letter he wrote two years later to the teacher Ephra'im Derekh shows quite a few errors of style. The Haskalah's flowery phraseology features here as well: "Out of doors, the wind wails," Allon wrote, "and I am seated alongside whispering embers and writing you the letter." The letter sheds light on the curriculum: arithmetic class was not up to scratch. The pupils (the fifth grade, apparently) learned a series of topics, from grammar to crafts, together with the eighth. For Bible studies, it was common to memorize whole chapters. The children wrote a good many compositions. Allon's special writing talent was on "My Family Memories" and "My Favorite Animal." He comes across as a nice, obedient child, amiable to his teachers, scholastically ambitious, without any sense of rebellion.

Mes'ha in the 1920s did not attract enviable schoolmasters. Top teachers chose to live in the city or in the villages of Labor settlement. In 1933, the school won the high commissioner's prize for raising silkworms and gardening. The awards did not solve the problems of a leaking roof in winter or a plague of flies in summer. In the 1930s, an effort was made to improve the school's exterior and install an ornamental garden, which even won the Wauchope Prize. The children threw themselves into the task eagerly. Not so the parents, who considered gardening and ornamentation as a whole an unjustified waste of precious water.[101]

Even if the school did not really broaden the children's vistas, it apparently left its stamp in several areas of study: Bible studies, Hebrew litera-

Figure 4. Class of elementary school, Mes'ha. Allon sits in the middle line, first from the right. Photographer unknown. Courtesy of the Allon family.

ture, and Jewish history. It was in fact a "nationalist" curriculum, aimed at bonding the child to the people and the land, especially the latter. In general, Jewish history in Exile was depicted as one long chain of persecution. In Allon's imagination the Crusades were so tied to the Inquisition that when he traveled to Nazareth with his father he was careful not to bend down near a church lest it be understood as kneeling before the cross. He had no such misgivings about Islam, having learned in school that Muslims were tolerant of Jews, with the emphasis on Spain's Golden Age.[102] The Bible was the local history book: Saul and his sons; the prophetess Deborah; Barak, the son of Avinoam; Yael and Sisera; Gideon—all had waged their campaigns within an arrow's shot of Kefar Tavor. The Bible was the source of legitimacy for an instinctive sense of ownership felt by youth rooted in the country's soil.

The myth that had the greatest impact on young Allon was the story of Saul, to which he returned again and again: the lad who had been taken from behind the herd to become king of Israel. He and Mes'ha's other children were spellbound by Saul Tchernichowsky's ballad, "Be-Ein Dor," their hearts pounding at the poet's words when he visited their village. "Just imagine"—the mature Allon would quote the poet he had heard in the spring of his life—"how great King Saul was. The history was written by David's sycophants, and even they did not manage to dwarf him. And if that is how he emerged from their hands, one may easily imagine how great a man he really was."[103] Much like Kefar Tavor's own boys, Saul was the pure, innocent country lad, the sacrifice of both the "sullen and displaced" Samuel, who ignored political considerations and the ways of war, and of David, who though he may have been the "sweet Psalmist" yet was ready to join the Philistines in their war against his own people. In Mes'ha's childhood world, the preference for Saul—the handsome tragic figure of the Book of Samuel—over David, the devious victor who did not shrink from wrongdoing or bloodshed, was self-evident, especially since Saul's brave war was waged near the village and Ein Dor was visible from the window. The love of Saul, the noble victim, and the rejection of David, the reckless victor, was anointed with Reuven's blessing: the one and only kiss Allon ever received from his father was after Tchernichowsky's talk, when the excited child bared his heart to Reuven, objecting to David and identifying with Saul.[104]

A product of the Mes'ha of the 1920s and 1930s, Allon lived in a world that was imprinted with "earthiness." Love of nature, of landscape, of the surroundings were givens. Life was molded by work. The daily routine, the yearly cycle, prosperity, and dearth, all revolved around the farm. Allon was born into agriculture without agony or agonizing. It may have been hard, but it was a fact of life.[105]

The realities gave rise to a very simple value system: a concept of primary, almost biblical, justice—of "an eye for an eye"; relations of "give and take" with the Arab neighbors; courage and physical prowess; a farmer's love of the land; loyalty to the family, to the village, to the country, to the nation. The measure of a man was how he lived up to these values.

Daily life at Mes'ha no doubt posed a challenge to these values since the villagers hardly excelled in mutual help or cooperation. Extreme individualism occasionally degenerated into downright selfishness. Allon must have been aware of this, and it may explain his omission in *Bet Avi* of neighbors' names, including those of boyhood friends. Perhaps he consigned them to anonymity because the mention of any one person might have offended those not named. Or, perhaps if he had done otherwise, relating to Mes'ah as it was, he could not have painted its picture as he did: naïve, but pretty and wholesome. The myth of Wild Galilee with his father cast in the role of tough, stern, dauntless sheriff, a myth he constructed by carefully selecting certain fragments and ignoring others—was the foundation of his worldview and the source of his pride. When he was to come into contact with youth of the Zionist movement, including those steeped in Labor traditions and proudly brandishing Labor's banner, the only asset he could offer in return was his father's house, rooted in the land, a rock of its rocks, an oak of its oaks. Against slick and worldly city youth, he held out the authenticity and simplicity of a country boy, the aristocracy of the land.

Chapter 2
Kadoorie Agricultural School

Allon's first meaningful introduction to the world beyond the horizon was at the Kadoorie Agricultural School. He entered Kadoorie as a child of Mes'ha and emerged from it determined to leave his native village.

Once Reuven Paicovich realized that his youngest son was not to benefit from a Mikveh Israel education out of the PICA's pocket, he began to nurse a fresh hope: Yigal would attend the newly built school next door to Mes'ha, on lands adjoining the Paicovich holding at Um-J'abal—meaning Kadoorie. The public storm surrounding its founding was typical of the Jewish Yishuv at the time, when Zionist fervor imbued every deed, big or small, with value and significance beyond ordinary mortal measure. Only in this sort of atmosphere could a school's establishment turn into a national project, an open controversy, the focus of animosity and suspicion toward the British authorities, and a source of pride and sense of overall achievement for the Jews. Kadoorie—before it ever even rose—came to represent British injustice toward the proud Jewish Yishuv.

It all began with a misunderstanding: the last will and testament of one Ellis Kadoorie, an Iraqi-born Jewish millionaire who had lived in Hong Kong and bequeathed a third of his legacy, £1 million, to his majesty's government for the building of a school in his name in Palestine or Iraq.[1] The bequest, soon enough, was given the following complexion by the Zionist press: an upright Zionist Jew wished to leave money for a Jewish school in the land of Israel, when along comes "wicked Rome"—that is, the British—which helps itself to part of the gift for an Arab agricultural school in Tul Karm.[2] This Zionist interpretation was passed down as bald fact from one generation of Kadoorie pupils and graduates to another.

As it happens, the government of Palestine was interested in building a Jewish high school in Jerusalem. But the legendary teacher Asher Ehrlich threw a spanner in the works: he began to lobby for a Jewish agricultural school around the Jezreel Valley, and, in 1925, a whole series of institutions, colony councils, community bodies, and so forth signed and submitted a petition to High Commissioner Herbert Samuel to earmark the funds for an agricultural school in the Lower Galilee and the glory of local education. Mes'ha added its voice to "the people's will," as it stated in its application to the high commissioner.[3] The government of Palestine endorsed the idea of a Jewish agricultural school similar to the Arab school in Tul Karm, and the question of location came up for discussion. Several sites vied for the honor and the not inconsiderable benefits—a road, a well, and a boost to the consumer population. The felicitous choice ultimately fell to a hillock between Sejera and Mes'ha, bordering on a-Zbekh lands at the edge of the Tabor, and, following divine and human delays, construction began in 1931. The edifice designed by government engineers was expansive and tasteful: the barn alone was fairer than any of the buildings in all of the local colonies put together, as were the living quarters, classrooms, laboratories, and other enhancements.

The school belonged to the government of Palestine, coming under its Department of Agriculture. The department financed it, was to appoint the principal and teachers, and set the curriculum. At one of the early planning stages, Herbert Samuel suggested that it be an English school, only to provoke more furor: Jewish money was to go for a non-Hebrew school in the land of Israel?! The British backed down. They promised to build a Hebrew school with a Jewish principal and teachers, and a number of Yishuv representatives on the school board. Hereafter, government officials consulted with the Jewish Agency (JA) on all school matters. In Tul Karm, in contrast, the principal was indeed English and the school's character was British colonial.

At the suggestion of the JA, Shlomo Zemach was appointed principal.[4] This ideal candidate was an agronomist, a writer, and an educator, and the zealous champions of Hebrew could breathe easy.[5] The fact that he belonged to the Ha-Poel Ha-Tza'ir Party, as did Chaim Arlosoroff, the director of the JA-PD at the time, presumably did not harm his nomination. He was appointed in 1933 and began to prepare actively for the school's opening in 1934.

Allon acceptance at Kadoorie involved protracted negotiations between Paicovich, Zemach, and British officials about the boy's fees. Paicovich was of the opinion that the school's proximity to Mes'ha entitled his son to a full scholarship. In his address to Mes'ha, High Commissioner Arthur Wauchope had mentioned that one of the village children had been accepted at the new school. Paicovich understood that "the high commissioner meant that the lad study at the government's expense for the benefit of the village nearest the school."[6] The motif "the lad of the village nearest the school" was reiterated in Paicovich's letters as sufficient cause to relieve him of payment. The fees had been set at Palestine £24 per year, no mean sum at the time: an agricultural worker earned only 20 pennies (*grush*) a day, and a teacher about £5 a month. Given Mes'ha's financial straits, it is hard to imagine that Paicovich could come up with the full sum. Zemach wanted a local child at the school and was sympathetic to Paicovich's circumstances. To make it easier for him, he employed Allon for about a year in the school's construction prior to its opening, in the hope that the boy would save up for the fees.[7] Though the fate of Allon's wages is undocumented, they certainly did not go for fees. After Zemach finally digested the nature of Paicovich's objection to school fees, he referred him to the Department of Agriculture. Paicovich did in fact obtain an exemption—but only for the cost of a day pupil. Since boarding was compulsory, he had to make up the difference, Palestine £12 per year. He was thunderstruck: part of the sum had already been waived and he had imagined that boarding would be a pittance! He delivered an ultimatum to Zemach: either Zemach would allow Yigal to attend for £6 a year or Paicovich would remove the boy from the school.[8] Zemach ultimately agreed.[9] Paicovich's "thank you" letter, announcing the first remittance in December 1934, quite some time after school had started, was penned by Allon.[10] How the boy felt throughout the haggling, which smacked of wretchedness, both Paicovich's and the village's, is anybody's guess.

The school officially opened on 20 June 1934 at a state ceremony under the patronage of the high commissioner. Regular studies began that autumn, following a summer preparatory course, which Allon attended. The school was to teach agriculture to graduates of the tenth grade. The first twenty-four pupils were handpicked out of some two hundred candidates,[11] an elect group boasting a number of very bright stars indeed.

Yigal first met his classmates in the summer of 1934. The new pupils—strangers to the setting and the landscape, to farming and Arab neighbors—found themselves welcomed by a fair-haired, blue-eyed youth riding bareback. Most of them were around sixteen; he was about a year younger—no mean difference at that age. But he knew the place and its ways, while they were outsiders. Apart from Amos Brandsteter of Yavne'el, only Yigal hailed from the Lower Galilee. Moreover, he was familiar with Kadoorie, having worked there while it was being built.

The curriculum represented a compromise between applied and theoretical agriculture. Theory was on a high level. The teachers had been carefully drawn from top professionals in different fields: animal husbandry, chemistry, physics, economics, soil science, fertilization, and so forth. The British who designed the program were partial to the assumption that farmers needed to know nothing but their trade, and they limited the curriculum to scientific and technical subjects. Humanities did not feature in the formal syllabus.[12]

Figure 5. At Kadoorie Agricultural School. Allon is standing, third from the right. Photographer unknown. Courtesy of the Allon House Archives, Ginnosar.

The standard of education was far more demanding than Mes'ha's schooling, and, after studies began, Allon found himself among the weakest pupils. He found physics and chemistry particularly hard,[13] and his first half year at Kadoorie required supreme effort. Applying himself with determination and diligence, he managed not to fail. His teachers helped him, especially Zemach, whose eye he had caught. But more valuable still was the help he received from classmates. Those who had attended good schools, such as Amos Brandsteter, Arnan Azaryahu—nicknamed "Sini" (Chinese) because of his slanted eyes—and top student Joel Prozhinin, who had won the Wauchope Prize, helped the poorer students, such as those who came from Kefar Giladi and our lad from Mes'ha. The school atmosphere was not competitive. Rather, there was a sense of togetherness and companionship with the strong aiding the weak.

After his first half year Allon was able to sigh with relief, believing himself equal to the task he had undertaken. He remained an average student until the end of his career at Kadoorie, neither shining nor disgracing himself.

Allon's academic standing did not affect his social position. He made up for his lack of scholarship with traits and talents learned at Mes'ha: he could ride a horse, hitch a wagon, wield a two-mule plow. Who knew farm work as well as he? City boys found it hard to rise to barn work or fieldwork at the crack of dawn; Allon was used to it. After his training at home, the four hours of daily work demanded by Zemach were a piece of cake. The farmer in him, nature's child that he was, made him a model at Kadoorie. Sure, it was good to know chemistry, but other knowledge was just as important: how to clear the land of stones, how to plow, to plant, to sow, to reap. These skills soon propelled Allon into a strong social position, whatever his intellectual achievements may have lacked.

Kadoorie was not the Eton of Eretz Israel, though more than a few of the country's prominent sons were to attend it over the coming decade. It did not turn out gentlemen or prepare students for high society. It did not provide a broad education, but it strove to produce highly trained farmers for the colonies and the settlements of the Labor movement. It did, however, abide by some of the norms and behavior of English boarding schools. Attending boarding school meant being cut off from home, from family, and from familiar surroundings. Pupils were allowed home on holiday once every three months. Parent's day was held at the school twice a year. Pupils seem to have found ample compensation for the break with home in the fellowship of peers and the warm relations they developed with teachers.

It was a boys' school, as was common for boarding schools in Britain, though less so for those in Palestine, where secular society championed women's equality and mixed learning was customary. In fact, shortly before Kadoorie's inauguration, the Ben Shemen Youth Village had opened under Dr. Siegfried Lehmann as a joint boarding school for boys and girls. The absence of girls at Kadoorie certainly affected the school experience. The emphasis tended to be on male qualities, such as physical prowess, practical jokes, and a degree of uncouthness. To counter the lack of female company and cut their manly teeth, the boys would pay visits to Nahalal, where there was a girls' school, to Tel Yosef, where there was a youth village, and sometimes even to faraway Haifa.

Kadoorie also adopted from the education of an English gentleman the code of honor. Two stories exist as to its source: one ascribes it to Zemach, the other to the student body. Either way, there was a gentleman's agreement against copying during exams, with teachers showing their trust by staying out of the classrooms. As often happens when supervision devolves on a peer group, the boys were more zealous than their teachers about the honor system. If anyone faltered by glancing at a textbook, the student council soon informed Zemach of the breach (without, of course, supplying the malfeasant's name) and called for reexamination. The code held good for smoking as well. Because Zemach's wife, a doctor, deemed the practice most harmful, a decision was made—and kept—to ban smoking from the school grounds.

The school day was very full: in the summer, pupils would rise at five; in the winter, at six. Cowhands rose at three. Classroom work lasted six hours, and farm work, four. Formally, pupils finished their duties at 4 P.M. and were free for homework, preparing for exams, idle—and not so idle—conversation, games, or going out. The boys took their studies seriously, especially those such as Allon who found the going uphill. Lights-out was at 9 P.M., but studies often stretched late into the night with the help of a flashlight.

Sports featured strongly in student life and were encouraged by the school. Dares—such as scaling the Tabor in pouring rain—were run-of-the-mill. But the favorite pastime was soccer. The small Kadoorie student body turned out a winning team for the Galilee Cup, thus stretching its reputation well beyond the region. Soccer held the boys and filled hours of play and talk. In a friendly game between the two Kadoorie institutions, the triumph of the Jewish school over the Arab one was veritably a national honor.

Actually, the boys as well as Zemach were highly conscious that their every deed and prank reflected on the Jewish image in British eyes. The very fact of British supervision charged teachers and students with guarding Jewish honor before the powers-that-be. Every few months, they were treated to a visit by Mr. Dowe, the inspector of the Department of Agriculture of the government of Palestine,[14] the momentous occurrence occasioning a feast. The school kitchen would cook up a storm compared to the regular fare, preparing, among other things, roast chickens. Being especially fond of the dish, the students—according to one story—would break into the kitchen and generously partake of the luxury before Dowe even arrived. Or, according to another story, they would burst into the dining room as soon as Zemach, Dowe, and Dowe's entourage had left it and fall upon the leftovers with the gusto of adolescent boys. Once, Dowe forgot something in the dining hall and he returned with Zemach only to catch the boys red-handed. Zemach did not know where to hide: what *would* the British think of Jewish conduct now?![15] Dowe, the son of a modest farming family and a swineherd in his youth,[16] presumably did not regard the boys' actions as overly "disgraceful." But Zemach and his boys were mortified.

The consciousness of guarding the national honor also came to the fore in another incident: two of Kadoorie's boys were invited to dine with the high commissioner. One of the two, Sini, was seated next to a British official. All of the warnings he had been given about Jewish honor rang in his ears and whenever the waiter offered him tantalizing delicacies, he courteously asked for a mere mouthful—after all, everyone knew that in polite company one did not exhibit appetite. Sini thus walked away from the meal as ravenous as he had come to it. Amos Brandsteter, in contrast, had been seated next to a Jewish official and had indulged his appetite to his heart's delight.

School subjects, as described earlier, were aimed at enriching the mind but hardly the soul. Pupils coming from regular high schools arrived at Kadoorie with the intellectual and emotional baggage instilled by humanist-oriented curricula. History, literature, Bible were the foundation stones of education in the city. Allon had received none of this emphasis. Zemach, an author among agronomists and an agronomist among authors as he liked to refer to himself, was alert to the paucity of Kadoorie's syllabus. He would take the time to converse with students about literature and even ask the capable ones to write papers, which did not fall short of any produced at nontechnical schools.[17] For some of the pupils, including Allon, the talks with Zemach opened up new worlds.

But on the whole, their world was small and circumscribed, centering on peers and school matters. They were not bothered by "big questions." This was true also of top students from educated bourgeois homes. Life revolved around exams, teachers, pranks, soccer, work, and girls—they were ordinary adolescents, after all. The pecking order was determined by physical excellence.

Like the rest of Yishuv society, the boys were affiliated with either the Left or the Right, either Labor or Revisionists. The first twenty-four, as it happened, were equally divided between Ha-Noar Ha-Oved, the youth movement of the Labor Federation (Histadrut), and Maccabi Ha-Tza'ir, which was connected to the middle class. Everyone anxiously awaited the arrival of a twenty-fifth student: Israel Krasnianski, the tie breaker, tipped the scales in favor of Ha-Noar Ha-Oved,[18] resulting in the election of an all-"socialist" student council (consisting of Prozhinin, Brandsteter, and Sini). The elected members were a conscientious lot, but their sense of responsibility was no match for Sini's desire to get his hands on a steering wheel. One night, he and a few others "borrowed" the agricultural instructor's car and set off for Afula. They knew a heady sense of mastery—they could drive! True, they could not find the rear gear, but this did not make the occasion any less momentous. When it was time to turn around, they simply lifted the vehicle and faced it in the right direction. Back at Kadoorie, they learned that the Arab guard had spotted their exit and reported them to the principal. Zemach made it plain that recklessness was inconsistent with a seat on the student council. By consensus, which was common practice at Kadoorie, Sini was ejected, making room on the council for a member of Maccabi Ha-Tza'ir—Allon.[19]

Allon had been involved in Maccabi Ha-Tza'ir at Kefar Tavor, where he had actually initiated and established the Mes'ha branch, an act that was a clear reflection of the village public mood: on the right of the political spectrum, yet not too far right. Maccabi Ha-Tza'ir was a middle-class, quasi-youth movement. Apart from socializing, its dominant activity was sports. Most of all, for the youth of Mes'ha, it represented a contrast to the Left, the Left that maligned them and demanded that they employ Jewish labor. Given Mes'ha's conditions, the mere fact that local youth organized to found a branch of the league was in itself an achievement. Allon's role in the affair had placed him at the forefront of Mes'ha's youth. His membership in Ha-Maccabi Ha-Tza'ir showed that he toed the line, that he accepted his father's worldview. He may have belonged to a poor family in a poor village, he may have been highly conscious of his poverty, but he likened himself to members of the middle class whose rituals and traditions he shared. His friends at Kadoorie, in contrast, who were pampered lads from "established" homes, saw themselves brandishing the socialist flag and identifying in their mind's eye with the wretched of the earth.[20] In substance and the type of youth it attracted, Maccabi Ha-Tza'ir had a petit-bourgeois air. Its "respectable" role models wore cravats at a time when the rest of the fledgling country still sported frayed collars. It lacked the drama and protest of Betar (the Revisionist youth movement), the daring and dedication of Labor youth. In an era when the young thirsted for commitment, it defended no cause. It breathed flat air, free of either danger or great dreams.

Allon remained true to Ha-Maccabi Ha-Tza'ir even after coming to Kadoorie and being exposed to other ways and ideas. However, his co-option to the student council as its representative marked the start of a fast friendship with members of Ha-Noar Ha-Oved, especially Amos and Sini (who was pardoned some months later and restored to the council). The three were to remain on the council until the end of their studies.

His friendship with Ada Zemach scored him an important social point. The principal's daughter was the only flower in Kadoorie's female desert. Ada studied at Haifa's Re'ali School and thus did not live at Kadoorie, but she came home on weekends and vacations. Pretty, delicate, learned, she was unlike any of the girls Yigal had ever met. Though a couple of years younger than him, she was his intellectual superior. She loved literature, belonged to the Left's literary bohemia that sprouted up around the rebellious poet Alexander Penn, read avidly, and was open to the unconventional and the avant-garde. To Allon, she symbolized the whole new world he was introduced to at Kadoorie. To Ada, a city-slicker, the handsome Allon had the appeal and freshness of a farmer and boy of nature. She was impressed by his horsemanship and

Figure 6. Ada Zemach. Photographer unknown. Courtesy of the Allon House Archives, Ginossar.

attracted by his simple manners. What's more, the fact that he was older than she and more savvy about boy-girl relationships made up for her scholarly lead. She took pleasure in parading him before her high school friends when he visited her on weekends. At the same time, his involvement in Maccabi Ha-Tza'ir and his petty-bourgeois traits somewhat marred the image of the natural farm boy she had constructed. Still, the fine pair were not together often enough to play up the shortcomings, and their missing one another went a long way to stifle doubts that might have surfaced in a closer relationship.

Their friendship began when Allon worked at Kadoorie before school started. It lasted for four years, until Ada finished high school and Yigal decided to join the Ginossar kibbutz group. It was a young love, significant to both. In the best romantic tradition, they were mostly self-absorbed when they were together, hardly ever discussing either Kadoorie or the great big world. Ada's head was full of the Spanish Civil War. Allon, like most Kadoorie boys, took no notice of it. But he certainly had a thirst for literature—her chief interest. He was at home in her house and often met her father, which only whetted his appetite. The pupils at Kadoorie liked to believe that Zemach and his wife did not overly approve of the relationship between their daughter and the Mes'ha farm boy, but the truth is that they accepted him as part of the family. He continued to show Zemach respect until the end of his life.[21]

The idyll was shattered in Yigal's second year at Kadoorie. Beginning in the autumn of 1935, tensions rose in the country. The fallout from Mussolini's war in Abyssinia sowed war panic and the economy slumped. A shipment of Haganah arms, hidden in a crate of cement, was intercepted at the port of Jaffa and shook up the Arab street. Even at Kadoorie, events in the country suddenly jerked the boys to attention. Sini reviewed the situation in a letter to his parents, ending on a note that smacked of Zemach: "Hopefully, it will be possible for us to go on building and consolidating. And if it is decreed that the world revert to the pre-flood era, it will find us ready to resist."[22] This curious contradiction between the apocalyptic forecast and the firm confidence that the pupils of Kadoorie (or of the Yishuv) would prevail seems to have been a basic element of education in Eretz Israel: it inculcated a sense that there was nothing the people could not do, no test the people could not meet. The consciousness that catastrophe was sure to come, and that the people would be called to stand in the breach, was inbuilt in the ideology. The appearance of these components in Sini's letter of October 1935 hints at an emerging awareness among the young that they were growing up into a dangerous world with a direct bearing on them; it was as if, suddenly, the curtain blocking their field of vision had risen, and the horizon stretched into the distance.

Kadoorie's small world suffered also from a tension of its own. Zemach inspired admiration from the pupils, but he was less able to manage the teaching staff, and his relations with some of them soured.[23] In his view, he owed allegiance to the British authorities who had appointed him to head the school. Precisely because he had always been a Zionist and had been nominated by the JA-PD, he sought to show one and all, and particularly the British, that he comported himself correctly as warranted by a state school.[24]

His prudence in dealings with the British was not to the liking of teachers, employees, and even pupils. Wagging tongues began to accuse him of being overly solicitous about British money and British property, and they found willing ears among the students. Matters came to a head with Zemach's decision to dismiss the teacher Siegfried Hirsch. In his memoirs, Zemach attributed the decision to the latter's frequent, unjustified absences. Hirsch apparently managed to persuade the pupils that he was being fired for being involved in the Haganah and because Zemach, a British lackey, objected to the Haganah operating in the school framework.[25]

The reaction of the pupils came close to rebellion. They resolved to intercede to rescind Hirsch's dismissal. To do so obviously meant to badmouth Zemach before the British. Their national responsibility aroused, the staunch champions decided first to consult the man who would be most interested in hearing about the ousting of a *nationalist* teacher from Kadoorie—that is, David Ben-Gurion, chairman of the JA Executive. The natural candidates for the mission were two council members affiliated with Labor, Prozhinin and Sini. One fateful day, Sini telephoned Ben-Gurion's home, introduced himself as the son of a man known to Ben-Gurion, and said that he and a few others from Kadoorie's graduating class wished to discuss a serious issue with him. Sini explained that they could come only in the late afternoon or evening; Ben-Gurion replied that he would see them whenever they came. And so it was: the two lads snuck away from Kadoorie after the day's activities and hitchhiked to Tel Aviv, arriving around midnight. Ben-Gurion greeted them in his pyjamas and heard them out in silence. They then gave him the draft of the petition they meant to send to the authorities, and he promised to consider the matter.[26]

Memory can play false. According to our heroes, the episode ended with Ben-Gurion's apparently burying the document. As it turns out, however, the affair was serious. The student council took two extreme actions: first, it sent off a letter to the high commissioner asking that Hirsch's dismissal be revoked. Second, it sent off a formal petition to the JA-PD, declaring that "the students' faith in the [school] leadership had been thoroughly shaken" and demanding that the Yishuv leadership and those in charge of the school "look into the situation and reverse it." The letter was signed by the twenty-four pupils of Kadoorie's first graduating class.[27] For Zemach, it was a slap in the face.

The first signatory was Allon, and the petition even looks like it was written in his hand. He still belonged to Maccabi Ha-Tza'ir and was not chosen to approach Ben-Gurion. But—eagerly or not—he was a full partner to the student conspiracy against his benefactor. Throughout this difficult period for Zemach, Allon continued to come and go in his home as he pleased. In his talks with Ada, the subject never came up, not once. Zemach was truly upset: not only had Allon placed himself against him, on the side of the teacher and pupils, but he had done so in secret, without telling him about it. "*Yigal was a Mes'her bokhur*" (a Mes'ha sonny) Zemach noted, filling the epithet with all his scruples about behavior he considered treacherous, ungrateful, and cowardly.[28]

The last peace-time activity to take place at Kadoorie was the trip of the graduating class to Egypt. It was to cap the end of studies and inaugurate a tradition of graduate trips to a neighboring country also under British rule, except that reality intervened and the school trip in early 1936 was apparently the only one of its kind. Arab riots soon broke out, upturning everything. Zemach had meant to lead the trip, and the students were to be the guests of Egypt's Department of Agriculture. But after learning of the student rebellion, Zemach announced that he would not be accompanying them. Nevertheless, he made sure to tell the council that it was responsible for the students' behavior and it was to make sure that they not disgrace the Yishuv.[29]

In April 1936, the Arab Rebellion erupted. (It was known in the Yishuv as the 1936–39 Disturbances.) It set into motion a new era, eventful and fateful for the Jewish Yishuv, which had known demographic growth, economic boom, and steady reinforcement since 1932. All of these developments had been viewed by the Arabs with dismay. While they too enjoyed prosperity, it could not compensate for their apprehension that the land was slipping away from them, changing virtually overnight from an Arab to a European country. The Rebellion was aimed at halting the process, at preventing the Jews from becoming the dominant factor in Palestine.

Tension was thick. Life at Kadoorie went on, but the environs seethed. The pupils felt left out of the action: the school was protected by British police, and despite its relative isolation it was not in any danger. The boys were asked to keep to themselves and avoid unnecessary sparring with Arabs. This was the local translation of the Yishuv policy of restraint, adopted in the face of the Arab revolt and terror. Jews were to demand British protection rather than embark on vengeance or retaliation. In practical terms, this meant holing up within Jewish settlements, never straying beyond the fence. Fields and barns were torched, trees cut down, years of toil lost—with no reaction. There were reasons for this policy: the Yishuv leadership hoped that this time—unlike the course they had chosen in 1929—the British would be unable to portray the unrest as a clash of two peoples; it was eminently clear that the blame lay with the Arabs and their resort to violence. The British government would have to defend the Yishuv from attack and, perhaps, even issue it the necessary means of defense. The hope was that the Yishuv would be allowed to set up a legal, Jewish defensive force, supervised and financed by the British. None of these considerations of high policy made it any easier for the boys of Kadoorie. They itched to be let loose for daring, heroic, patriotic exploits.

At the start of May 1936, a few weeks into the riots, Kefar Tavor's water facility was set alight about 150 meters from Kadoorie's fence. The arson was committed at night when the pupils were dead to the world, hearing nothing. The two resident policemen did not allow the pupils to be woken in order to extinguish the fire, either because—as they said—they did not want the tracks of the perpetrators blurred or because the firefighters would make excellent targets in the light of the flames. In the morning, the boys rose to a sooty pump, a broken motor, and a burned-down building. Here was an exploit indeed right under their noses—and they had literally been caught napping. Great was their shame, which was made worse by the rejoicing of Arabs released from custody after the scouts failed to discover anything.[30]

One summer day, a-Zbekh shepherds were spotted leading their flocks up Kefar Tavor's fields next to Kadoorie. The fields were Paicovich's, at Um-Jabal. Allon and a few of the boys and laborers ran to grab hoes to chase off the trespassers. The shepherds started to retreat, then stopped, raising instead the Arab alarm, the *Faza'a*. Bedouin flocked to the scene and soon outnumbered the contigent from Kadoorie. But the boys stood their ground. They conducted an orderly battle of retreat and even managed to wound seriously two of the Arabs; they themselves incurred no injuries. Meanwhile, the action had been discerned at Kadoorie. Led by Zemach, the teachers took two of the rifles on the premises and set out as reinforcements. Allon described the fight as a battle he had headed, organized, and directed. This leadership role is not remembered by other participants. In any case, it seems that Yigal called out to the teachers to fire in the air to miss, for fear of escalation. He had absorbed Mes'ha's long-standing code: caution lest blood be spilled, yet resolve to give as good as one got.[31]

But this was not yet the end. A-Zbekh Arabs complained to the authorities of aggression and the police descended on Kadoorie to detain the pupils involved.[32] They, including Allon, were carted off to jail in Tiberias. The adventure did them no harm and certainly added to their peer prestige. Allon was proud to have carried on the family tradition: both his father and brothers had been "privileged" to imprisonment and captivity under the Turks.[33] The whole episode took only a few days. The boys were released on bail paid by their parents.

Like almost everything else in that period, the trial of Kadoorie's youngsters turned into a national brouhaha. The JA-PD engaged the Haganah's hotshot attorney, Aharon Hoter-Yishai, and paid his legal fees of Palestinian £8.[34] Hoter-Yishai listened to the youngsters and told them what to say in court. After talking with them for half an hour, he chose Allon to act as the key witness. This appears to be the earliest evidence about the sort of impression Allon made on strangers. Hoter-Yishai chose a lad he judged to be above the rest: handsome, credible, articulate, naturally shrewd, and with a good grasp of the situation. If the brawl did not distinguish Allon from the others, his court appearance crowned him spokesman and ringleader.[35] In the courtroom, Allon claimed self-defense against trespassers and physical assailants. This version, buttressed by the personality of Hoter-Yishai, who overawed the prosecutor, was accepted by the British judge and the boys got off scot-free.[36]

In the summer of 1936 Kadoorie was shut for security reasons and the students were sent home. The truth was that the boys were not eager to stay to defend the school when their parents' farms were in danger. Studies apparently resumed in December and on 24 March 1937, Kadoorie's first graduating class completed its studies. Allon was nineteen.

Many of the pupils had joined the defense forces during the school's closure. Sini served as a *ghaffir* (a temporary police guard) at the village of Kefar Javetz, under a British sergeant. Brandsteter and Allon were guards in the bloc of Tiberias and the Lower Galilee, under Nahum Shadmi (Kramer) of the colony of Melahamiya. The duties seemed to be the same at every location: guard duty by day and defense patrols by night. "Since we have arrived, there have not yet been any shots"—Sini grumbled in his letter to his parents—"let's hope this will change or I'll die of boredom."[37] By his lights, the situation did not improve even though the *ghaffir*s at Kefar Javetz served as "a mobile squad to danger spots," that is, they were the spearhead of the defense forces. "As for my spirits, one should not hope for any improvement before one decent attack because I am being consumed by idleness," Sini continued to carp two weeks later.[38]

Allon didn't complain. As ever, Mes'ha offered stirring pursuits of Arab marauders. The chase was the same as it had always been except that now Yigal proudly boasted a guard's headgear (the *kolpak*—a tall fur hat), his possession of live ammunition was legal, and killing was permitted. At night, he and his friends would head for Mes'ha's fields to douse fires, putting themselves at risk from sniper shots from Arab gangs.[39] On these escapades he did not appear exceptional.

At this stage in their young lives, the boys regarded the fights, chases, gunshots, and danger much as though they were aspects of a thrilling game. Their parents may have worried about them, but they themselves had not yet experienced loss, and the danger was intoxicating, a boost of alertness and a burst of adrenalin. Only youths untried in the pangs of war could write to his parents as Sini did.

The glory of defense service aside, agricultural settlement retained its rank as the crowning achievement of practical Zionism in Eretz Israel. Out of twenty-two graduates of Kadoorie's first graduating class, seventeen aimed to be farmers. The others chose either to study further—mainly agriculture, abroad—or to enter public service.[40] Many of them regarded higher studies as near treason.[41] In those few months between the resumption of studies and the end of the first graduating class, when the young men talked about plans for the future, one of the ideas touted was the establishment of a fifty-unit farm. As graduates of a government school, they hoped to be in line for assistance: to obtain a holding, preferably on state lands in the Beisan Valley frontier, where both water and danger were abundant. Their eyes lit up at the thought of promoting the national good while treading a common path. In January 1937, thirteen members of the first two graduating classes organized and applied to the Government of Palestine for a piece of land.[42] The signatories included Arnan Azaryahu (Sini), Joel Prozhinin, and Yigal Paicovich.

The application was denied. The government replied that it did not intend graduates of Kadoorie to found a settlement of their own; rather, they were to fan out across the country and use their knowledge to boost agriculture as a whole. Furthermore, any assistance given to Jewish Kadoorie graduates would have to be matched for Arab Kadoorie graduates, entailing an expenditure beyond its means. In general, there were little available land, and the government preferred to place what there was at the disposal of the JA to use as its discretion.[43]

Amos Brandsteter did not sign the application. He knew very well that he would be returning to his father's farm in Yavne'el. Not so Allon. His memoirs say that he entered into the plan half-heartedly.[44] Nevertheless, his signature was the first step in his break with Kefar Tavor.

Kefar Tavor may have been home, but certain aspects of it caused him distinct discomfort. He never invited any of his friends to his house. Not even Ada ever crossed the threshold. If a friend happened to accompany him on his way home, he made sure that he did not come inside but waited for him outdoors. He seems to have been ashamed of the poverty, which is strange since poverty was not looked down upon, especially not in his circles. Ada was puzzled by his behavior: true, her own family occupied a fine home at the time, and her father earned the enormous salary of Palestine £500 a year, but this was one period in a long life that had known hardship and struggle. For Ada, poverty carried no social stigma. This was not so for Allon: he regarded it as a blot, as something to be hidden.[45]

Perhaps, it was the shabbiness, not just the poverty, that accounted for his attitude. The house was run down, having gone without a woman's touch for years. Rickety walls stood unrepaired, no ornaments or luxuries of any kind graced the premises. Within these bare walls, there lived an old man and a boy. Allon's home was not like any of those of his friends, not even the poorest among them.

Since Kadoorie, he saw Mes'ha with different eyes. Compared with Ada, its plain, simple girls held no charm for him. Compared with the modern agriculture he learned at Kadoorie, Mes'ha's farming methods, including his father's, appeared terribly backward. Even the local school, which he remembered fondly and had built up before his new friends, had lost its luster.

Allon, in *Bet Avi*, attributes his leaving Mes'ha primarily to the ideological changes in him during his second year at Kadoorie: "The ideological consideration began to vie within me with natural sentiment,"[46] "the social-moral uniqueness of kibbutz life; the qualitative standard of living; equality and mutual responsibility" were values that drew him with magic strings to the concept of the kibbutz, he said. "From day to day, I became increasingly convinced of the justice of the kibbutz way for the Yishuv, the nation and human society, and from day to day my desire to belong to it grew."[47] Was this really the case? Ideology was not discussed at Kadoorie. Among themselves, the boys would prattle on about soccer, girls, security actions. The question of a kibbutz composed of Kadoorie graduates came up only in their last few months. But it was not an intellectual conviction, merely the way of life favored by the country's top youth. Few of Kadoorie's graduates had been exposed to the enriching food for the soul served up by youth movements. They lacked the values education absorbed by members of youth movements. In this sense, there was very little difference between the youth of Maccabi Ha-Tza'ir and the youth of Ha-Noar Ha-Oved at Kadoorie. The latter's onsite activities amounted to twice yearly visits by a movement coordinator. The socialist-Zionist bricks that built the ideological foundation and motivation for kibbutz life were not inherent in Kadoorie's cultural world.

Allon grappled with the decision in talks with Ada and even more so in his letters to her. He seemed to find it easier to express his reservations in writing. Unfortunately, the letters have been lost, but their substance was clear enough and confirmed by the accounts of his friends. Ideology played a marginal role. The decisive factor was his feeling that Mes'ha was a dead end; a curtain on the new horizons he had glimpsed since coming to Kadoorie. A return to Mes'ha was a life sentence of retrogression, of poverty without compensation or challenge, in a backwater marginal to the great drama unfurling in the country. Apart from his sense of guilt at abandoning his father—and shattering the old man's hopes that the child of his old age would carry on the family farm—Mes'ha did not beckon him.

The kibbutz, in contrast, symbolized the new world: the company of young people, a hazardous location, a tractor instead of a plow, creating something from scratch. More than an explicit worldview, it was a proclamation of belonging to a dynamic current, to the Yishuv's creative forces at the time.

There was also the question of his future relations with Ada. Ada had finished the Re'ali School and was also considering her next move, whether to go to a university and study literature or join Allon on a kibbutz. Two things were clear: she would not go to Mes'ha and he would not pursue further studies. But going to a kibbutz together was an option. In the end, Ada chose to study at the Hebrew University in Jerusalem. It was the termination of their four-year relationship.[48]

The decision to leave Mes'ha and the Paicovich farm was very difficult for Allon—comparable, perhaps, to the decision of Diaspora youngsters to quit home and country and make *aliyah* to the land of Israel. It spelled rupture with a wealth of loyalties: childhood landscapes, the land and the farm, the father who nursed hopes and had expectations of him. Like pioneering *aliyah*, it was a new start and complete break, clean, clear-cut, life defining. It molded his life, but also his father's—for there was no one left to shoulder the burden of the farm now, and Paicovich was seventy. The choice was between Allon's life and his father's. At that moment of hard—even cruel—truth, the nineteen-year-old Allon found the strength to opt for the future.

The meeting at which he announced his decision to his father must have been one of his greatest trials. According to Allon, Paicovich told him that he had the right to do as he saw fit—even if he had not consulted his elder. But by saying that he, Paicovich, would go on living at Mes'ha, the lonely old man saddled Allon with a heavy sense of responsibility for his father's fate.[49] Emotional blackmail comes in many forms and is not necessarily direct. Paicovich may have hoped that Allon's decision was not final, that he would think better of it and return to Kefar Tavor.

A chain of events now conspired to turn Allon's intent into fact. Paicovich took sick and Allon had to hospitalize him in Haifa, near the home of his daughter, Deborah, and her family. Allon meanwhile stayed on at Mes'ha, having promised his father that he would not go to a kibbutz until the summer farm work was done. After the reaping, threshing, and storing of grain, he was faced with a dilemma: his father was in a hospital in Haifa, where the family wanted him to stay, with or near his daughter or one of his sons. Allon was all alone on the farm and the farm was a yoke around his neck: a homestead with livestock and poultry could not be left for a single day. It was one thing to talk about leaving, another to actually do so when there was no one else to take over. That summer, lonely and in a ramshackle house, he was more conscious than ever of the noose his father had placed on him. He was suffocating. In this mood, he decided that if he wished to live, he had no choice but to dismantle the farm and sell off the inventory. Only a draconian measure could free him of his native village. Only thus could he be the master of his fate.

It was a daunting decision, likely fueled by desperation and the typical egoism of the young. His mind made up, he acted quickly, feverishly. Livestock, poultry, wheat—everything was sold off. Every cow he let go added to his sense of freedom. In the end he was left with a pair of mules, a year's feed of barley for them, and a wagon. He harnessed the mules to the wagon, loaded the feed, and set out, a man alone on the perilous roads of Eretz Israel in the summer of 1937.

He headed for Netanya and his brother, Zvi. He had done his calculations. He figured out that if Zvi were to hire out the wagon and mules for work in Pardes Hannah, the earnings would allow Reuven Paicovich to live comfortably. After spending the night at Kefar Hasidim, Allon and his wagon arrived in Haifa in the morning. He sped to the eastern train station where his brother Eliav worked, only to be reprimanded: how had he taken it in his head to make the dangerous trip from Kefar Tavor to Haifa?! But this was nothing compared with Eliav's fury when he heard what Allon had done. Beside himself, he ran to get Moshe, the eldest brother and his superior on the railway. Allon now felt the wrath of both brothers. How dared he, without consulting anyone, eradicate the toil of decades at a single stroke? Worse still, Reuven had to hear of it while hospitalized. Allon chose to let his brothers inform their father. He took the mule wagon and continued along the coastline from one brother to another, from Mordekhai in Binyamina to Zvi in Netanya, being met everywhere with shock and rage. The further he journeyed, the more the magnitude of what he had done sank in. He was terrified by the thought of the inevitable encounter with his father. But Paicovich's reaction was surprisingly mild. After hearing what Allon had done, he was silent for a moment. Then, he turned to his sons: "And you let him travel alone in these times?"[50] By the time Allon came to visit, Paicovich had no scolding or preaching for him. Whatever anger he may have felt succumbed to relief that the boy was unharmed, despite his rashness.[51]

Neither his brothers' fury nor fear of his father's reaction made him regret the deed: by selling the farm he had purchased his freedom, and nothing equaled his sense of liberation. He dispensed with self-reckoning; it had been a campaign for his own self opposite his father's great shadow. And, as in every campaign containing an Oedipal component, Allon emerged with a sense of victory mingled with guilt. In time, the guilt produced *Bet Avi*. The triumph produced Yigal Allon.

Chapter 3
Ginossar

Allon's posthumous papers contained a draft for the opening of an autobiography beginning with his move to Ginossar: "The heavy truck pulled up at a . . . junction, one of the roads leading to the settlement of Migdal. The genial driver from Kibbutz Kefar Giladi parted from me with a warmth underlined by wishes for full integration into the kibbutz. . . . I hefted my heavy knapsack onto my back and crossed the road on foot towards the young kibbutz. I crossed the Rubicon, and did not look back."[1]

Yigal's crossing of the Rubicon meant forsaking his father's world for that of his young friends. The generation gap deepens in times of revolution and rapid change. Even if parents belonged to Eretz Israel's founding generation of brave, hardy revolutionaries, so great were the differences between them and their children that communication became forced and superficial. Things were worse still in the case of most of the parents, who had only recently disembarked on Jaffa's shores. Their understanding of what was going on in the country was limited, their lives passing in a kind of partial fog of bewilderment and incomprehension.

It is little wonder, then, that the youth bred in Jewish Palestine regarded themselves as a tribe apart from their parents and adults in general. Their primary frame of reference was the peer group. It, in every sphere, determined the behavioral norms, from articles of fashion to styles of speech, from the approach toward school to the attitude toward parents. The power it exerted on its members—virtually tyrannical—was seen as an expression of their release from adult authority, of an exodus from bondage to freedom. The peer group, or *hevreh* as it was called, was a company of willing partners to a particular path, a specific lifestyle.

"Good" *hevreh* went to live on a kibbutz. Going to a kibbutz entailed identifying with a youth group. Such was the force of the perceived generational differentiation that it lent the sense of togetherness an emotional bond reserved in other societies for tribe or family: here, the *hevreh* were the tribe. Those who didn't "belong" felt like outsiders, out of place, ostracized.

The fact that Yigal went to a kibbutz was above all a mark of belonging to the *hevreh*. Graduates of the Kadoorie school had no doubt that joining a kibbutz was the right thing to do. Choosing Ginossar was accidental. Kadoorie had a visit from Yehoshua Rabinowitz (Baharav), a member of the Ha-Noar Ha-Oved (HNHO) *kevutzah* (group)[2] at Migdal. He spoke to the graduates about the hardships of life at Migdal in the Ginossar Valley, about the attempts to settle on the PICA lands along the Sea of Galilee at the mouth of Wadi Amud—an area that teemed with lawless gangs and where no Jewish plowman had ever set foot. He painted a picture fraught with tension and hazard: shortly before his visit, armed bands had fallen upon members working in Migdal's orchards and wounded one of them. Knowing his audience, he overstated the perils: night after night, there were gunshots, he said. Their imagination lit, Kadoorie's *hevreh* decided to go to Migdal.[3]

A young *kevutzah*, subsequently known as Kevutzat Ha-Noar Ha-Oved Migdal, had arrived at the colony of Migdal in 1934 to work and wait for a leasehold to a collective settlement of its own. The nucleus consisted of graduates of Tel Aviv's school for workers' children who had gone on to study agriculture at the Ben Shemen Youth Village.[4] Most of them had trained on *hakhshara* farms of Hever Ha-Kevutzot and preferred to keep a neutral profile in terms of affiliation with a kibbutz movement. In 1935, they were joined by a group from Kibbutz Ein Harod that sought a connection with the Histadrut's HNHO youth organization as a preliminary to tying up with the Kibbutz Me'uhad (KM) movement. For years, the veteran core at Migdal, associated with Hever Ha-Kevutzot, held sway: they too identified with HNHO, but they carefully guarded their independence of any kibbutz movement or stream.[5]

In the Plain of Ginossar, the PICA owned some five thousand dunams (1,125 acres; 500 ha) of land. Part of this was tilled by Arab villagers from Abu-Shusha, next to Migdal, and part was tilled directly by the PICA under its own manager with the help of Arab laborers. At the eruption of the Disturbances, the PICA realized that the solitary Jewish manager was in danger. It now agreed to a proposal from Abraham Hartzfeld of the Histadrut's Agricultural Center to lease lands to Kevutzat HNHO, Migdal, and the group was hired to turn over the soil and uproot the wild blackthorn north of the plowed area. During the work there was tension in the air. On one occasion, the guard was late in spotting a gang attacking from Wadi Amud, and one of the plowers was wounded.[6]

When Yigal arrived in July 1937, several months after his friends from Kadoorie, the course of the *kevutzah* had already been decided: in February 1937 Kevutzat HNHO, Migdal signed a contract with the PICA; the *kevutzah* was to buy the hay the PICA had sown at Ju'ar (Ginossar's Arabic name) for Palestine £250 and harvest it.[7] The entire plain north of Migdal had not a single Jewish settlement and served as a transit route for bands from Syria and Transjordan. This lawlessness aroused the *kevutzah*'s slim hope that it would be permitted to settle on these lands. The reason it gave was that it would guard the hay from arsonists; the goal, however, was to set down stakes in the plain, in the hope that the PICA would subsequently find it hard to dislodge the group. Abraham Hartzfeld was party to the calculations and encouraged the *ketvutzah*.

On the eve of Purim, March 1937, a convoy set out from Migdal to the cultivated area and, within days, the members of the *ketvutzah* had raised a tower-and-stockade settlement—one of the hallmarks of that frenzied period: some ten dunams of land were fenced off, and within this area a watchtower was thrown up, a gravel-filled fence was built, and one hut, then another, were knocked together, along with a few tents. The small camp, it was explained to the PICA official, was necessary to protect the site.[8] The PICA's Palestine director, who was based in Haifa, forthwith notified the members of the *kevutzah* that as soon as they had gathered the produce they were to dismantle the guard post and hut and get off the land.[9] The *kevutzah*—now called Kevutzat Ginossar for the first time—made no promise.[10] Meanwhile, Hartzfeld stepped up his pressure on the PICA to settle these young pioneers who had shown such dedication and readiness to defend the land in those hard times, for this was the most effective way to ensure Jewish ownership over the land and make good use of the water-rich fertile soil in the area.[11]

By the time Allon arrived, it was no secret that the PICA did not share Hartzfeld's viewpoint. He treated the PICA's holdings as national land; it regarded the Ginossar camp as trespassing. Yet the young men and women clearly had no intention of leaving, continuing to hope for some sort of accommodation. The PICA wasn't interested: it wanted the *kevutzah* off its land. The Agricultural Center tried to placate the PICA, taking care not to dent its prestige or mar relations with the Rothschilds, the company's owners. Ginossar's members were also prepared to placate the PICA—as far as lip service went.

The PICA had the law on its side, along with the financial power of a large settlement company and the force of political pressure: so long as the conflict with Ginossar remained unresolved, the national institutions, including the Jewish Agency (JA) and the Agricultural Center, could not assist the young settlement. The budgetary stranglehold caused Ginossar severe hardship in the early years and was a direct result of the PICA's pressure. Nevertheless, the PICA's public position was also the source of its weakness: it was no ordinary private company; rather, it was driven by Zionism and was not immune to the influence of settlement bodies and Jewish public opinion. There was thus little chance that it would use force to evict this *kevutzah* of fine young people, even if they were squatters. Nor was it reasonable that it would appeal to the law since turning to the British could provoke an outcry.¹² The Ginossarites bet on the PICA's feeble reaction, and relations settled into a regular pattern: an attempt was made to negotiate; the *kevutzah* acknowledged its wrongs and promised to behave better in the future if the PICA forgave it its sins and recognized the status quo; the PICA refused to relinquish its holdings, demanding the *kevutzah*'s removal; and negotiations collapsed. But every such failure led to further encroachment by the *kevutzah*, to another fact on the ground in blatant, audacious defiance and total disregard of the PICA's objections.

The determination of the young to stay at Ginossar no matter what was echoed in their battle cry of "Ginossar and only Ginossar." Apart from the site's beauty, which chained them with love, its farming potential was enormous. "Better that we sit here waiting for this land for a year, two, three, five, for even then we will draw more from this soil than from any other," said Israel Levy, then Ginossar's central figure.¹³ As time passed, the bond to the land only tightened. Time was in their favor, for each passing day there meant another patch tilled, another pipe laid, one more birth, one more burial.

When Allon came on the scene, the pattern of the dispute over Ginossar's illegal camp was already set, and he took an extreme position on the matter of placating the PICA. When it became clear that the clash would squeeze the group financially, Allon made a statement at one of the assemblies that became Ginossar's catchphrase: "We will sow two hundred dunams of wheat and ten dunams of onions and we'll eat bread and onion."¹⁴ This bravado—undoubtedly nourished too by his great love for the bulb that showed up in his every salad—summed up Ginossar's resolve.

Allon seems to have been eager for the confrontation with the PICA. He could not have been oblivious to the difference in Ginossar-PICA relations and those between Mes'ha's old-timers—his father included—and the PICA. Mes'ha's farmers had faced the PICA cap in hand. In contrast, Ginossar's young were the active element, pushing the PICA into a resigned, passive corner. The role reversal between initiator and submitter, between the party in control and the party forced to knuckle under, must have put a song in his heart.

A few months later, at the height of the Arab Rebellion in August 1938, Ginossar's land-grab aims took another step forward: one weekend, as the PICA official in charge indulged in his Sabbath rest, the *kevutzah* mobilized to install a small pumping station, pipes, and an irrigation line from the Sea of Galilee to a 20-dunam tract; the group also planted a vegetable garden. The PICA issued a strenuous protest: the group was to remove the pipes and uproot the tomato plants.[15] Two weeks later the PICA received an inordinately courteous letter requesting its permission to create a winter vegetable garden at Ginossar—an idea "that can shore up our stamina in these troubled times and further bolster our readiness to preserve the integrity of the PICA's lands at Ju'ar as we have done to date."[16] The letter ended with the disingenuous hope that when the PICA decided to settle these lands, it would look on the Ginossar *kevutzah* as a suitable candidate. In vain did the PICA protest and threaten legal action.[17] The *kevutzah* blithely went about its business, affably ignoring the company.

In the autumn of 1938 the Arab Rebellion peaked and the local security situation badly deteriorated. In one incident, an Arab gang fell upon a Jewish neighborhood in Tiberias and, meeting no opposition, killed, wounded, and plundered (see the next chapter). As far as security personnel were concerned, this only made the small settlement point on the Kinneret shore all the more important. Meir Rotberg, of the Haganah High Command, applied to the PICA not only to leave Ginossar in place but to enlarge it (11 October 1938).[18] He was seconded by the Haganah's district commander, Nahum Kramer (Shadmi), who wrote to the PICA to expand the settlement point and fortify it properly.[19] Hartzfeld too suggested that the PICA broaden the settlement for security reasons, undertaking to have the *kevutzah* removed should conditions change. The PICA mulled over the matter with long letters going back and forth between the Haifa executive and the Paris head office. Hartzfeld's innocent proposal aside, the PICA's people knew very well that if they officially recognized the *kevutzah* on the land, this would mark the start of their concession to settlement there. The PICA wavered.

Ginossar's members did not. On 4 November 1938, some weeks after negotiations started about extending the site, they began to move the entire outfit from Migdal down to Ginossar. For about a year and a half, part of the *kevutzah* had lived in two huts at the lower camp, working and guarding the lands on the plain, while mothers, children, pregnant women, and some of the men continued to live in the old camp at Migdal. Communication between the two parts was problematic if not downright dangerous, and the separation was not healthy for internal cohesion. Beyond the very real security and social worries, however, the *kevutzah* wished to exploit the situation to establish its home at Ginossar. "We have come out well with the PICA"—Sini wrote his parents on an optimistic note—"it seems that after the Tiberias incident they are more inclined to give in to every demand made in the name of security, and there is hope that we will succeed in going down to Ginossar this week in peace. It also looks as though the money question will be resolved with ease and we will settle on our land."[20] But the PICA, it transpired, did not swallow the bait and Ginossar's members were furious. The PICA dilly-dallied in its response to the Haganah, which was seen as a snub to security personnel, inconceivable insolence, and a quasi-license for independent action.[21]

The move down to Ginossar was organized as a military operation to the very last detail: it was scheduled for a weekend when the PICA officials in Tiberias could be expected to relax their supervision over the intrepid squatters. The huts were moved in toto by rolling them along pipes. Construction material had been prepared in advance to fortify the enlarged settlement point and secure the dining hall and children's quarters. Everything was well planned—and then the heavens intervened. Contrary to all forecasts for clement weather and moonlit nights for that Friday in early November, it started to pour without letup. The members got soaked to the bone, the truck got stuck in the mud and had to be extricated by a tractor, and the entire schedule was thrown off kilter. Mustering the heroic effort that became part of the Ginossar saga, the members managed to knock together two extra huts for shelter from the rain, but all hope of completing the move in two days was lost.[22]

The PICA, of course, was incensed: the impudence of these young people had exceeded all bounds. The Haganah High Command announced that it had no hand in the affair; it had not given the *kevutzah* permission to do what it had done. Hartzfeld and the Agricultural Center also fumed: they too had not been consulted and had certainly not given their consent. But once the dust settled—or the mud dried—the question again arose of what was to be done about this endearing company of squatters. Ultimately, the PICA limited its reaction to denying members of the *kevutzah* employment in its local public works. This strapped the group financially but did not endanger its existence.[23]

"Now, our main difficulty is our relations with the national institutions [namely, the JA and other central Jewish bodies]. The PICA is ostracizing us, Hartzfeld threw our delegate out of his office, Kofer Ha-Yishuv [a body that supported endangered settlements] canceled its promised assistance under pressure from the PICA, and every month we have about P£100 of bonds to pay"[24]—Sini described the repercussions of having seized the land. The Agricultural Center was truly annoyed. Yet, when the PICA withheld payment owed to the *kevutzah* for work done, Hartzfeld remonstrated. "It is unthinkable that the PICA executive employs such measures," he declared.[25]

The move to Ginossar launched a new chapter in the *kevutzah*'s life. Financially, the group still relied chiefly on outside jobs, though members tilled a vegetable patch, which was a kind of auxiliary farm, and began to raise animals, building a chicken coop, a cowshed, a sheep pen.

They also tried their hands at fishing in the Sea of Galilee. One of the quickest branches to develop was the children's house, lending members a sense of permanence, of home.

Life at Ginossar's small farmyard was far from easy. Every three months, Dr. P. Lander of the Histadrut's Health Fund made the rounds with an eye to preventive medicine. After the doctor inspected hygienic conditions and living quarters, he stated in his report for April 1939 that "the camp is in a terrible anti-sanitary state." The kitchen, dining room, and their surroundings were full of flies and garbage rolling about nearby. The shower was not yet finished and there was a lot of rubbish near it as well, and as to the toilets—the less said the better. He ended the report thus: "This sort of camp state could be a source of all types of infectious diseases and malaria."[26] The next report, in July 1939, reported a sharp improvement in hygiene, especially in the delicate respects mentioned above.

Yet the basic problem of overcrowding remained. Ginossar had sixty men and forty women at the time, including twenty-two families with twelve small children. All of these people lived in two huts of seven tiny rooms, three tents, and five lean-tos. Families did not have their own rooms or tents, and couples often had to share with a redundant "third"—the notorious "Primus" from the early 1930s when growing *aliyah* swelled the kibbutzim.

Collective welfare, as a rule, took precedence over individual life. A member had to be prepared to submit to group judgment in all affairs. One member wished to attend his sister's wedding. Since this entailed a loss of work days, the question was brought before the general assembly; because it did not sanction the trip, the member left the kibbutz.[27] The members agreed that every family was to have only one child at first. When a young mother fell pregnant for a second time, the general assembly discussed the option of abortion (which was voted down).[28] It did not occur to anyone to protest the public discussion of intimate affairs. In the case of a couple that separated, the woman demanded that the *kevutzah* oust her ex-partner;[29] the question discussed by the assembly was whether her pressure should force the man out. Nobody objected to the group's right to decide matters of personal status if they affected the character or vitality of the small society. The ambition of members to pursue a specific occupation or further studies was considered a luxury no young kibbutz could afford.[30] One of the typical reasons for asking for leave was "parental assistance," that is, the need to help aging parents who had no financial support apart from a child on a kibbutz. To counter the problem of absence, such members were asked to persuade their parents to come live at the kibbutz.[31] Considering the conditions at Ginossar—overcrowding, no minimal sanitary standards, polluted drinking water, endemic fevers[32]—it was an impossible demand. The person who made it was Allon: "True, parents would have to make an acknowledged effort to adapt to the *kevutzah*"—he said—"but if their situation is so hard, they can come to the *kevutzah* and find in it a solution for themselves and for the *kevutzah* on this question."[33]

Dearth was rife. Legumes were the staple diet: bean soup and more bean soup. Meat hardly ever featured on the dining hall table. The food was flat, prepared by a young woman never initiated in the art of cooking by her mother. But given the ordeal of cooking in the heat of the Jordan Valley and in Ginossar's primitive kitchen, the poor girl who slaved away could hardly be blamed.[34] Ginossar's newsletter from the end of October 1938 tells of a decision by the kibbutz assembly to send a member to help and encourage a sister *kevutzah* that had just settled at Hulata (to the north). This formal resolution was never put into practice because the warehouse could not supply the slated member with a pair of shoes.[35] Only in March 1940 did a radio arrive at Ginossar, and it, a big, shiny Philips, then common in kibbutzim, was allotted a place of honor in the dining hall. The Ginossar newsletter reported the event: "It must have a fixed, permanent place, on some cupboard or special crate in the corner of the dining hall, rather than continue to stand on the piano; this is inconvenient and, what's more, not good for the piano. It would also be a good idea to make some sort of cover for the radio, of cloth or wood, otherwise the flies in the dining hall—which are not few—will change its shiny color to speckle-bound."[36]

In these conditions, some strong cohesive force is needed to counter a temptation to leave. This role was filled by the PICA. Ginossar's collective character was consolidated in its wrangling with the PICA. The slogan "Ginossar and only Ginossar" evolved into lyrics for songs in *hora* circle dances, the speech of skits, and the battle cry of those hard times, protesting against the whole adult world. Constant tension and uncertainty about the future lent collective life the spice of danger that molds solidarity. Everyone felt responsible for the farm's survival. Anyone leaving Ginossar quit not only the kibbutz but also the battle, abandoning comrades to struggle along on their own. This had nothing to do with socialism but with the sense of siege felt by an endangered group. In many frontier communities, the security situation filled the role of social linchpin. At Ginossar, the PICA played a similar role.[37]

Allon's reputation preceded him to Ginossar. His friends from Kadoorie had sung his praises, and the *kevutzah* knew to expect a brave young hero, a born farmer who did not flinch from clashes with Arabs. Upon entering the yard at Migdal, he was immediately assigned to the small camp at the bottom of the plain, where the more daring members tilled the PICA's lands. And that first night, he was posted to the middle shift to guard from 12 to 2 A.M.[38] Allon did not manage to reach any great heights at Ginossar, for within months, Nahum Kramer (Shadmi) appropriated him for a sergeants' training course given by the Haganah. Allon left.

Nevertheless, his heart was already lost to Ginossar. In 1936 the *kevutzah* was enlarged by a group of German-Jewish youth educated at Tel Yosef. They had been on a kibbutz for two years now and found it all overwhelming: the Hebrew language, the collective life, the hard work. The period was rough: it was the start of the Arab Rebellion and the tenderfoots were called on for guard duty on top of their daily work load.[39] Ginossar's members began to grumble that the "match" with the group from Tel Yosef had been a mistake. Nor was the crowd from Kadoorie sympathetic to the heartbreak of the German girls who were asked to deposit in the common warehouse all of the fine clothing they had brought with them—their mementos from a faraway home. Some, however, were charmed by the foreign girls who were so different from those they were accustomed to. Sini and his friends told Allon that they were reserving the prettiest one—Ruth Episdorf—for him.[40]

Ruth Episdorf had immigrated to Palestine from Germany in 1934. Her family stemmed from Poland, although her father had served in the German army and the family had taken pains to integrate into German society. Her father was a sales agent, her mother a housewife. Hitler's rise to power was traumatic. At fifteen, Ruth, was expelled from school, putting an end to her formal studies. Her father died of a heart attack, and as the family sat *shiva* in mourning for him German soldiers burst in on them in search of him. The shock was too much. The family's vague Zionism gelled into practical action. Ruth joined the Habonim youth movement, which emphasized returning to the land of Israel and settling on a kibbutz. This became the ideal that illuminated the darkness of those days in her native country. The three Episdorf sisters immigrated to Palestine; Ruth arrived with the training group at Tel Yosef. Her mother deferred her own emigration, not wishing to be a burden on her daughters. Ultimately, she delayed too long and met her death in the Lodz Ghetto.

Ruth's sights were set on working in the cowshed. But city girl that she was, she did not take easily to physical toil and so did not meet the challenge at Tel Yosef. At Ginossar, she again tried her hand in the cowshed. Later, she was proud to be assigned to fieldwork. In the early years, she fell prey to various illnesses, including typhus and malaria. There were emotional difficulties too: she lacked the mentality and social traditions of Yishuv society, which was predominantly "Russian"; and moreover, there was the shame of hailing from the country of the Nazis. She felt inferior to the young native Jews around her—and they certainly did not go out of their way to make things any easier. She eagerly adopted the pinafore, the embroidered blouse, and the elastic-bottomed shorts, an outfit that was almost a status symbol of the new society. The desire to "assimilate" was strong, and even if there was little sensitivity to or understanding of the woes of an individual, a foreigner, an orphan, there was something spellbinding about Ginossar's young society: it had the air of a band of boys and girls on a desert island; a whole world that consisted only of themselves.[41]

All of the girls at Ginossar were attracted to Yigal: apart from his reputation as a farmer and warrior, he was handsome, nice, cheerful, and good-hearted.[42] It was only natural that his choice would be Ruth, the "star" of the German group, as his friends said.[43] He was everything an immigrant girl could wish for: his manly qualities aside, he was native born, a sabra personified, and well-ensconced in the society to which she aspired to belong. Their very different cultural backgrounds added mystery and charm to the relationship. But they had also undergone a similar experience—a severance of roots: Allon from Mes'ha and its world; Ruth from the land of her birth and parental home. For both, Ginossar held out the promise of a new start, hope for a future not lodged in the past.[44]

A mere few months separated Allon's break with Ada Zemach and his attachment to Ruth. Was this an indication that he had been hurt by Ada's refusal to join him on the kibbutz? Whatever the case, his relationship with Ruth was on an entirely different footing: With Ada, he had been older and more experienced in affairs of the heart, even as he was her inferior socially and culturally. With Ruth, he was the dominant partner from the start, having the social and cultural edge as well. Neither was broadly educated and, in this sense, they were equal. But he, of course, had the added advantage of a native over an immigrant.

They must have been the best-looking couple at Ginossar if not in the whole Jordan Valley. They soon moved into a family room, which meant half of a room in a hut along with another family and the infamous "third." Formal marriage, according to the laws of Moses and Israel, took place later, apparently around 1939, in a mundane atmosphere stripped of the romance surrounding their move to the family room. One day, after work, Allon and Ruth simply drove to a rabbi in Tiberias accompanied by two members of Ginossar who served as witnesses. The rabbi lent them a ring for the ceremony and that was that.[45] There were no relatives present, not his father or brothers, not her sisters.

Ruth soon understood that Allon would be away a lot, yet it never even entered her head to complain. Security came first and everyone was enlisted, in spirit if not in fact. Security work epitomized the apex of commitment and lent an aura to both the volunteers who performed

Figure 7. Yigal and Ruth Allon. Photographer unknown. Courtesy of the Allon family.

and those who were close to them. Allon was well liked by the members of the *kevutzah* even though in the difficult years of 1938–40, he spent little time at Ginossar.[46] And then something happened that suddenly brought him home.

Ginossar took advantage of the eruption of World War II on 1 September 1939 to further extend its vegetable tracts and planted fields. The pretext was that the emergency made it necessary to farm every bit of land lest wartime imports be stopped and/or the Arabs worked the lands and thereby gained rights to them.[47]

Up until that time, the Arabs of the Ju'ar village of abu-Shusha had used part of the waters of the Rabadiyeh spring and left the rest to flow into the Sea of Galilee. Like some of the village lands, the spring was the property of the PICA though the Arabs held it and Ginossar sought to obtain legal rights to it. The members of Ginnosar began by talking to the villagers and even reached an agreement: after the abu-Shusha lands were irrigated, the waters were to be channeled across Ginossar lands. But the Arabs broke the agreement and diverted the spring waters to the wadi on the approach to the village, from there to spill into the lake. The diversion was accomplished by placing a large rock in the channel to direct the flow. After the agreement was broken several times, the British stationed its Jewish Settlement Police (JSP) to guard the water.[48] On 27 October 1939 a mobile, three-man JSP patrol was attacked. One member was hurt and his firearm was stolen. The guards shot into the air to raise the alert and call for help. A squad was organized at Ginossar with Allon (who had been recalled from Tiberias, where he served at Haganah's headquarters) commanding the counterattack. At nightfall, the toll was three wounded Arabs and two dead, including abu-Shusha's *mukhtar* himself—Sheikh abu-Fais Hamis, a notable landowner.

After the battle, the JSP guards among Ginossar's members reported to the Tiberias police station to furnish an account of the incident. They said that an armed gang had assaulted the guards, that the others had rushed to their defense, and that the Arabs were hit in the course of the fighting, with one of the guards also wounded. Ten of Ginossar's members were recorded as having taken part. Allon, who was no longer attached to the JSP, was not included on the record: had he admitted to possessing nonlegal arms, he could have faced life imprisonment or even hanging.[49]

Times were tense and confrontations between the Jewish Yishuv and the British authorities were frequent. The British had crushed the Arab Rebellion with an iron hand. But, at the same time, they embarked on a policy aimed at winning Arab goodwill or at least ensuring quiet by stymieing the development of the Jewish National Home. The White Paper produced by Colonial Secretary Malcolm McDonald and promulgated in May 1939 severely restricted Jewish immigration and purchase of land and announced the intention of his majesty's government to establish an independent state in Palestine in another ten years, a state with an Arab majority. The transition from Jewish-British cooperation during the Arab Rebellion to Jewish-British confrontation entailed painful adaptation: it meant a change of tactics and going underground. The Ginossar affair slipped into these new relations. The routine report by and recording of the ten members at the police station now led to an official investigation, followed by detention and imprisonment in Acre jail to await court martial. Things looked grim: first, there was the fact of being tried in a military court rather than a regular one; and second, it soon turned out that not a single Arab suspect had been apprehended. Still, Ginossar's members were not overly perturbed about the outcome: after all, it had been a clear case of self-defense, an incident like dozens of others that had taken place during the Rebellion. Nor was the Jewish Agency's Political Department (JA-PD) especially worried, though it did engage the services of two top attorneys.

Allon was well-known to the villagers of abu-Shusha. Having lived his whole life among Arabs, he had been the natural candidate to negotiate with them on the spring water. In addition, he seems to have had friends in the village; according to one version of the battle, during the fighting, Mukhtar Hamis, who was later killed, saved Allon's life by preventing shots from being fired at him.[50] The villagers of Abu-Shusha swore that he had been among the assailants, but there was no corroborating evidence. At the trial, he served as an aide to the defense, especially on the military aspects: weapons, shooting, field movements, and so forth, details that were vital to the court proceedings but obscure to the lawyers.

In the end, the excellent defense of the able lawyers performed no magic and Ginossar's ten members were sentenced to long prison terms. The verdict came as a shock: no one had expected a conviction or, certainly, so draconian a sentence. It was a harsh blow to tiny Ginossar, which was stripped suddenly of ten of its prominent, active members, including a core of its founders, among them Israel Levy and Yehoshua Rabinowitz, the farm manager and *mukhtar* respectively. In October 1940, Ginossar's external secretary, Absalom Zoref, was also put out of commission. While walking in the fields near Acre in the hope of catching a glimpse of his jailed friends there, he came across three Arabs and was stabbed in the stomach. Zoref was laid up in the hospital for months before the wound healed.[51] Ginossar was a ship without a helm, and Allon had little choice but to come to its rescue. Thus began his intensive period at Ginossar.

Allon was the key figure on the kibbutz for about a year and a half. One indication of his vital presence was a letter of protest dashed off by Israel Levy from prison to Ginossar when he learned of Allon's recruitment for work with the Haganah (June 1940): "Ginossar's plight makes it necessary for Yigal to play a role at home, and he, too, morally and socially, must fight to be available to the *kevutzah* in its special circumstances, nor can the [national] institutions ignore this demand."[52] In this period, Allon left his mark on Ginossar. It was the only time in his life that he was actively involved in the kibbutz.

The goal he set for himself was for the *kevutzah* to gain control of all the PICA's lands not tilled by Arabs in the Jordan Valley. He began with a small step. One night, members of the *kevutzah* were recruited to plant 10 dunams (2.25 acres, 1 ha) of bananas, adding to the 200 or so sown dunams they had already cultivated. The PICA responded with a legal suit against Ginossar's officials, including Allon. Public opinion, however, was with Ginossar. It granted the act legitimacy, which was symbolized by the fact that Hartzfeld spent the seder night of Passover 1940 with Ginossar's prisoners in Acre, while the Labor leader and mentor Berl Katznelson chose to spend the holiday with the young *kevutzah*.[53]

As soon as the holiday was over, Hartzfeld wrote the PICA saying that,

66   Chapter 3

in view of the *kevutzah*'s courage and stamina, he could not accept its removal from the land; he suggested that the PICA resign itself to the situation, recognize Ginossar's right to settle there, and even lease to it 600 dunams of Ju'ar land for the war period so that it could farm it legally.[54] When France fell, and contact between the PICA's executive in Haifa and its head office in Paris was cut off, Hartzfeld stepped up the pressure.[55] The Haifa office refused to take responsibility without instructions from Paris, although it did agree to Ginossar's request to drop the banana suit.[56] Allon had just promised the PICA not to venture beyond the 200 dunams cultivated by Ginossar, yet he immediately presented the members of the *kevutzah* with an expansion plan.[57] The first stage called for constructing a concrete building, a sign of permanence, unlike the rickety shacks and tents that could be easily taken down. The pretext was security—a building to shelter children in times of emergency.[58] To Allon and his friends, this was merely and clearly a further stage in the battle with the PICA, a test of how far Ginossar could go. Meanwhile negotiations proceeded with the PICA on formally regulating relations between them.

The PICA's response was eventually forthcoming. Ginossarites spotted the PICA's tractors overturning the soil around them, and they feared a plot. Had a Jewish settlement with no less right to the land than Ginossar reached an agreement with the PICA, leasing from it the lands that Ginossar believed should come to it? The fear was real and the settlement in question was the colony Migdal.

The PICA had in fact leased 250 dunams (62.5 acres, 25 ha) to Migdal. Allon now showed his mettle. Young and unknown, he nevertheless displayed leadership and resolve, calling on his powers of persuasion to recruit tractors from kibbutzim in the Jordan Valley. The tractors moved into action at the close of the Sukkot holiday, plowing all that could be plowed in the whole PICA area. The outcry was not long in coming: Ginossar, this time, had acted not against the PICA—which was naturally suspect in the Yishuv's Zionist eyes—but against a small, poor colony. After much haggling, the two sides agreed to accept Berl Katznelson's arbitration and the land was divided in two: the part on the west side of the road went to Migdal; the part on the east to Ginossar. The agreement was sealed on 2 December 1940 with the signature of Yigal Paicovich. Berl Katznelson's handwritten endorsement in the margin gave it the weight of his authority.[59]

The affair highlighted some of Allon's valuable qualities. He was eager to do battle with the PICA, which he appraised to have no fighting spirit. He was prepared to resort to piracy and subsequently to stand behind it.[60] At the same time, he grasped the importance of public opinion and took pains to explain Ginossar's position in the press and before the Yishuv's institutions. He also showed an understanding of Migdal: in public he may have contended that it did not require the disputed lands; off the record, he acknowledged its real need. This, apparently, was one of the reasons that he agreed to compromise in contrast to his staunch and steady defiance of the PICA.[61]

The Migdal affair threw him into close contact with Berl Katznelson, one of the key Labor leaders. The determined *kevutzah* fighting for its right to till the land kindled Berl's interest. He had most probably had a soft spot for Ginossar even earlier, for its refusal to join any single kibbutz stream and fiercely maintain organizational independence. Katznelson, campaigning at the time to unify all the kibbutz streams into one movement, felt affection and kinship for these young people who were actually living his doctrine. When, to add to their woes, ten of their members were arrested, as mentioned earlier in this chapter, he spent the 1940 Passover seder with them. He also helped them obtain a loan of P£200 to extend the irrigation fittings.[62] His position reinforced Hartzfeld's favorable attitude to Ginossar. Katznelson sought to untangle the mess with the PICA and apparently was also involved in the resumed negotiations between the two. And, of course, he helped resolve the conflict with Migdal, which could have damaged Ginossar's public image.[63]

Katznelson's special attitude to Ginossar is also seen in the role he played in another important step taken by Allon in those years. Allon decided to acquire a tractor for the farm, which, until then, had relied on mules and horses. His expansion plan entailed uprooting jujube shrubs that covered extensive areas. This called for a tractor. In addition, the tractor was a status symbol, the last word in progressive farming as opposed to the backward agriculture of cereal-based colonies. He found a new D-2 tractor—a feast for the eyes—at Tel Aviv's Caterpillar agency, which was run by a man named Segal. But it cost P£200—a vast sum for Ginossar then. Allon, however, was not a man to be daunted. He secured a loan from an unknown benefactor: according to the same Segal, who ran the agency, it was he who lent the nice young man the sum.[64] Allon never disclosed the source. In any case, the tractor was both a technological revolution and a boost for the morale. Still, the loan had to be repaid. Allon tried to obtain a loan at the Anglo-Palestine Bank, a cautious financial institution not in the habit of issuing loans to parties lacking credit and securities. He thus turned to Katznelson who interceded with the bank and won its agreement. But the bank demanded that the Histadrut executive underwrite the loan. Taking himself to the Histadrut offices, Katznelson convinced the treasurer Zalman Aharonowitz (Aranne) to serve as the guarantor. The said sum was P£160 and the *kevutzah* deposited a promissory note. The Histadrut executive signed on the note as guarantor. Signing for Ginossar—was Yigal Paicovich.[65]

Apparently, someone materialized to pay off the loan, for Ginossar never honored the note. It was left to gather dust in the Histadrut Executive files. But the main thing is that Ginossar had a tractor, and Allon had proved his ability to act in the world of the Histadrut leadership, which was not at all simple.[66]

The events only confirmed Allon in his estimation that the more the *kevutzah* created facts on the ground, the more they sapped the PICA's opposition. In January 1941, a few months after the sizable land-grab and conflict with Migdal, Allon proposed to the kibbutz assembly that another 500 dunams of the PICA's land be plowed, land still covered by dense scrub and thus untilled. The plan was carried out only eight months later. But it was typical that Allon had already charted this aggressive course in January, winning the support of his fellow members for the policy.[67]

Allon's third important step at Ginossar was to set it on the road of affiliation with the KM movement. Ginossar, as stated, was established by youngsters trained at farms identified with Hever Ha-Kevutzot, the association of small *kevutzot*, such as Deganyah, which identified with the Mapai Party's right wing.[68] Yet members also had close ties with the secretariat of the HNHO youth movement, which pulled in the direction of the KM, Mapai's left wing. The question of affiliation with a specific kibbutz stream had already surfaced in the early days at Migdal. The *kevutzah* clearly had to absorb new members, and members were to be had only from a kibbutz movement. The tension between the desire and need to enlarge and the fear that the newcomers would predominate over the founders—as had happened at several collective farms—led to internal struggles. The choice on the table was between the two streams of the Mapai.[69] Israel Levy pushed for joining Hever Ha-Kevutzot lest HNHO trainees to Ginossar tip the balance in favor of KM. Most members were not yet ready for affiliation. They decided to keep their ties to the HNHO and through it to supplement their manpower on an as needed basis rather than attach themselves to any kibbutz stream at this stage.[70] The kibbutz "neutralism" of the HNHO *kevutzah* at Migdal conformed to Katznelson's banner of "uniting all the kibbutz movement" and was one of the reasons for the close relations between the veteran Labor leader and Ginossar's young.

The KM movement apparently hoped that Ginossar would ultimately hitch up with it, though for the moment, it refrained from taking any action. Its great advantage over Hever Ha-Kevutzot lay in its large reserves of manpower. In the interim, it was not afraid to cast its bread upon the waters; it allowed German-Jewish youth groups trained at Tel Yosef—one of its kibbutzim—to join Ginossar.

The question of movement affiliation was discussed at length at Ginossar on the Jewish New Year of 1940. The advocates of association with KM were headed by Absalom Zoref, who supplied both ideological and practical reasons. To keep alive the collective idea—he argued—it was necessary to band together with other kibbutzim who lived by the same lights. Affiliation also offered agricultural training and support, manpower supplements, loans, and assistance with education and culture.[71] In the ensuing show of hands, a large majority voted for affiliation; a small majority voted for affiliation with the KM. Since it had been agreed that a two-thirds majority was warranted to make a decision, the matter was deferred.

Allon had played a marginal role in the affiliation controversy until then. His friends thought that he did not really understand the language used by graduates of pioneering youth movements, that the fine differences between the various kibbutz movements eluded—and likely did not interest—him. Yet it was plain to him that the *kevutzah* was at a crossroads, in a transition from its days of genesis, with all of the hardships, uniqueness, and loneliness, to a spurt of growth. At this juncture, it was vital to obtain the patronage of a large kibbutz movement that could guide, advise, extend financial backing, and wield political clout in the institutions of the Histadrut.

Toward the end of 1940, Allon pressed Ginossar to come to a decision. The small *kevutzah*'s important members, led by Israel Levy, were in Acre prison as, in fact, were most of the founders still clinging to nonaffiliation. But the staunchest advocate of affiliation, founding member Absalom Zoref, was also neutralized and in the hospital. Allon took the bull by the horns and did what these members could not bring themselves to do: he made a decision.[72] He, too, had a "red line" he would not cross; he would not countenance a split in the *kevutzah*. Nevertheless, he was more decisive than his friends in the old guard. He brought the matter to a vote without allowing further debate, tabling a motion to this effect at the kibbutz assembly of 30 November 1940: he said that because the members who were either in prison or in the Labor Legion in Sodom were unable to take part in the discussion, it was only fair that the members at Ginossar forgo influencing the outcome with further discussion.[73] It sounded like the pinnacle of justice, but the fact was that the process of discussion had been exhausted and it was time to settle the issue. Of those present at the assembly, 80 percent voted to join the KM movement. The die was cast, and with a large enough majority to preclude resentment. This was no random majority foisting its will on a large minority. Ginossar was ripe for a decision, but it needed the resolute Allon to act as midwife.

As Ginossar's official, de facto leader at the time, it was Allon who submitted the affiliation request to the Kibbutz Me'uhad Council (KMC) convening at Kibbutz Givat Ha-Sheloshah (17–19 January 1941). This was his first public appearance of any kind and it took place at a forum—the kibbutz council convention—that made it almost a tribal initiation, an outsider's test of worthiness.

Allon chose to push through kibbutz affiliation at one of the most critical moments in the history of the Jewish Yishuv. On the war front, France had fallen and Britain stood alone fighting for its life, the same Britain that the Jews considered their ally, in whose army they wished to serve—and which treated them coolly. In December 1940, a few days before the convention of the KMC, the air was heavy with the drama of the *Patria*: the ship that was to convey to Mauritius in the Indian Ocean illegal immigrants—Jewish refugees who had made it to Palestine from Central Europe—was blown up. More than 250 immigrants were killed in the Haganah action that had been aimed at staying the deportation. The shock reverberated through a Yishuv divided between the action's supporters and its opponents. A few days later, Jewish refugees from another ship, the *Atlantic*, were expelled to Mauritius amid a demonstration of British ruthlessness and Yishuv helplessness. The other power with whom the Left longed to identify, the Soviet Union, had also proved a disappointment: the alliance between Soviet Russia and Nazi Germany (the Molotov-Ribbentrop Pact of August 1939) was a stubborn blot despite all attempts made to explain it. Nor did Russia's attack of Finland (December 1939) improve the image of socialism's motherland. The KMC convention was overshadowed by a sense of the Yishuv's isolation in Palestine and Jewish isolation around the world.

Most of the KMC convention was devoted to a report from members of He-Halutz, Poland's Zionist pioneering organization that educated its members along the lines of the KM. The group had fled from the area of German conquest early on in the war and built up a fair pioneering movement in Lithuania. After some time, the Soviets allowed some of the pioneers "stuck" in Vilna to leave for Palestine and they finally arrived in the country after an adventuresome journey. The newcomers reported on the efforts to guard Jewish national identity against the assimilation onslaught by the Communist regime, on the strivings of pioneers to reach Palestine, and on manifestations of anti-Semitism in the land of the Soviets.[74]

For Allon, the deliberations were an eye-opener, a whole other world: "Those people showed me many new things about He-Halutz [members] that I didn't know," he later reported to the Ginossar assembly, adding somewhat patronizingly, "their fluent Hebrew is especially remarkable."[75] He learned "that of all the countries from which Eretz Israel absorbed pioneers, Poland took the most important place,"[76] an admission indicating just how unfettered he was by knowledge of the

KM's social roots. Jewish experience beyond the boundaries of the Yishuv filtered down to him for the first time. True, he had been confronted with the question of immigrant Jews earlier: in March 1940 Ginossar had discussed absorbing a German youth group that was at Kibbutz Afikim, and he had defended the equality between immigrant and local youth against contrary opinions.[77] But his stance on that occasion can be explained by his relationship with Ruth, herself a German Jew. At the KMC, the native son had to reflect on problems completely beyond his ken, from the trials of the Jewish people to ideological questions, such as the attitude toward the Soviet Union.

Though a stranger to the KM crucible, his impressions touched the heart of the matter: "At these deliberations I saw the element of mutual help between people who had reached safe shores and comrades living in the Diaspora. How sincere and caring the concern for them, as if it were one big family." And he added: "I was especially moved by the promptness to discuss getting people out [of Europe] despite the perils."[78] He witnessed an inner solidarity diametrically opposed to Mes'ha's individualism; a sense of collective togetherness, a devotion to this same large family that takes responsibility for its members but also imposes duties and obligations; and, finally, the dynamism of the KM as well as its eruptive self-sacrifice and all embracing sense of responsibility—all of this Allon felt instinctively in the council atmosphere, in the memorials that so impressed him, in the words of He-Halutz representatives.

His intuitive grasp of the essence of the KM, absorbed from the atmosphere and his immersion in that specific social, human experience, found expression in his public address on the KMC's closing evening. He declared that Ginossar wished to join unreservedly, unquestioning of the movement's ways or leadership. The kibbutz audience must have found this joyful conformism heartwarming: they already had enough rebels of their own, they needed no more.

In describing Ginossar's settling on the land, Allon underscored aspects that could be expected to fall on eager ears. First, he emphasized the "redemption of the land" from Arab hands, reiterating this component and perhaps exaggerating its importance. With the exception of the incident of the "water war," Ginossar had not seized any land tilled or claimed by Arabs. It had always been careful to take over land that was indisputably owned by Jews. The land-grab from the PICA and bringing the PICA to resign itself to the act were presented as a daring maneuver by young people on a mission to redeem national land, which, strangely enough, encountered resistance from the landowners.[79] Second, the difficulties with the PICA, with the Agricultural Center, with the British authorities—Allon portrayed all of these as a character reference of excellence, making Ginossar fit for the KM.[80] When, in summing up, Allon said, "We bring with us the deed, the deed of the KM: the building of a [settlement] point unassisted,"[81] he displayed true understanding of the body to which he was seeking admittance.[82]

Ginossar's acceptance to the KM was unanimous. The handsome, curly-haired Allon achieved fame and glory that night. Though his address suffered from stylistic shortcomings and might have benefited from a little "refugee" Hebrew, his articulation and grasp exceeded all expectations, especially as he had not been bred on youth movement traditions. David Zakai of the Second Aliyah, a member of Mapai and one of *Davar*'s veteran journalists, was so impressed that he mentioned the speech in his column of "Briefs" (21 January 41). He described a "fairly tall and bright-eyed youth . . . speaking with understated warmth and able humor of the internal and external hardships that found his group of friends . . . and how they resolved not to abandon 'their Ginossar.' . . ." It was Allon's debut in the daily press.

Allons' account to the Ginossar assembly of the KMC proceedings and of the commitment undertaken by Ginossar upon joining the KM movement contained a measure of zealousness and a demand for utter loyalty. It was the passion of the newly converted who had just seen the light.

It was his first political commitment as an adult, freely made. His need to show loyalty to the movement that had taken him in was to remain a lifelong habit. Loyalty to the kibbutz was not merely political, but total, of the kind one reserves for tribe and family. In such cases, disagreement or disobedience or a decision to leave takes on added meaning beyond narrow politics, and is judged in value terms as deviation or betrayal. The atmosphere of the KM held sway on many people, its leadership consciously cultivating it. On Allon it had a powerful effect, especially as he had come to the kibbutz without prior bonds. The lad who sold his father's farm at Mes'ha and severed his childhood roots now found a new family ready to adopt him. It spawned in him a sense of commitment from which he would never break loose.

Several weeks after these events, Berl Katznelson invited Allon to take part in a month-long seminar he was giving in Rehovot. The wide-ranging symposium was to touch on history and Jewish philosophy, Hebrew literature, socialism, world politics, the history of Zionism, and the history of the Yishuv's Labor movement. Participation was by personal invitation to people chosen by Katznelson as he saw fit and was based on his impression of their talents, openness, and leadership qualities. The KM frowned on Katznelson's custom of circumventing its secretariat and approaching young members directly. The kibbutz lived by group decisions. It soon put pressure on the selected candidates to turn down the invitation, and quite a few did.[83]

Allon very much wanted to attend. The kibbutz assembly was asked to approve the absence of two members from Ginossar for the period of a month. Regarding one member, David Borochov, there was no problem. This was not so in the case for Allon: Allon was the secretary of the kibbutz and the farm's functioning might suffer from his absence. Two key members were enlisted to support his participation: Absalom Zoref, who had just returned from the hospital, and Sini Azaryahu. Zoref explained the significance of Allon's attendance: "He was among the last to be exposed to the movement's basics and it is important that he take part in the course."[84] Sini stressed the added value to the *kevutzah*'s cultural life. Those arguing against Allon's attendance made sure to note that though they were not envious, the good of the farm came first.[85] The vote split, with thirteen in favor and fifteen against.

The vote notwithstanding, Allon did attend. For Allon, the seminar seems to have been his first exposure to any systematic, humanist education. Lecturers such as the Kabbalah scholar Gershom Scholem; the historian Ben Zion Dinaburg (Dinur), a future minister of education; the writer Haim Hazaz; and the intellectual Zalman Rubashov (Shazar), a future state president, unfurled before him a universe of which he had been ignorant, cultural riches whose lack he had been unaware of. In addition, the lectures by prominent figures from the Histadrut and Zionist movements—Ben-Gurion, Golda Meir, the KM leader Yitzhak Tabenkin, the Haganah head Eliahu Golomb, and so forth—had a great impact on him: horizons broadened, the world picture changed, the dimensions of reality expanded immeasurably. The seminar was dominated by Katznelson's personality, Socratic charm, the founts of his knowledge, the idealism that oozed from his every pore, the inspiration that he was to his following. It is little wonder that the boy from Mes'ha, who only a few years back had still admired his village teachers, fell under a spell that had captivated men "mightier" than he.

Nor was Katznelson indifferent to Allon.[86] Ever on the lookout for excellent youth with human and movement potential, Katznelson saw in Allon the qualities that caught his eye. He was intelligent, open, curious, thirsty for knowledge, handsome, and engaging. On seminar Saturdays and sometimes Friday nights, participants would get together socially and relate a life experience. Allon told of his path from Mes'ha to the *kevutzah*, and then of Ginossar's wrangles with the PICA. He spoke simply, in plain language, to the point, both pleasingly and modestly. The fair youth, describing with resolve and self-confidence Ginossar's land-grab, left a lasting impression on listeners as one of the seminar's high points.[87] Kibbutz activists had first noticed Allon at the KMC; in Rehovot, he came to the attention of Mapai's leadership and young intellectual elite.

74   Chapter 3

Amid all of these exciting events, Allon continued to apply himself to Ginossar's affairs. One of the main tasks on the agenda was the speedy release of its imprisoned members. To begin, this meant reaching an accommodation with Ju'ar abu-Shusha by means of the traditional Arab *sulha*. A public *sulha* had been held in March 1940, a couple of months after the devastating sentence. The conditions were worked out, that is, gifts were awarded the families of the slain and other sheiks and notables involved, a black tent was put up at the site of the killing, and an offering was prepared with all of the trimmings—a festive meal of mutton cuts in bowls of rice. The ceremony was attended by envoys from both sides, by the regional governor, military and police officers, and ordinary dignitaries. When the guests assembled, the victim's relatives stood and shook hands with Ginossar's representatives, including with Allon, Ginossar's *mukhtar*. They then placed a knotted *kaffiyeh* into their hands to symbolize the peace sealed between the sides. The bereaved family did not appear gratified by the procedures and had no stomach for the fare. Not so, the governor. In a valiant display of civic duty and unhampered by the absence of cutlery, he reached for the food to the glee of the gathered guests, their appetite in no way dampened. It was the first peace treaty concluded between a Jewish settlement and its Arab neighbors since the Arab Rebellion.[88]

In January 1941, Allon initiated a joint appeal from abu-Shusha and Ginossar to the military authorities asking that the prisoners be pardoned since calm had been restored between the parties.[89] In May 1941, five of the prisoners were released, and in August 1941, the remaining five were released in a general pardon declared for prisoners of the Disturbances.[90]

On 9 February 1940, the Ginossar newsletter carried greetings from Absalom Zoref to Yigal and Ruth Allon on the birth of their daughter, Nurit. "Sorrow shared is sorrow halved," Zoref wrote, jokingly alluding to the infant's gender and attesting to the prevalent attitude to sexual equality. The child was lovely and her parents rejoiced. She was late to develop, but in a society of young, new parents, the warning signs went unnoticed. Only when she was two did the parents take her to a specialist, who diagnosed her as retarded. Their denial was typical of parents dealt so harsh a blow. She is so pretty! She sings so nicely, she says a few words! She repeats words over and over again, she repeats movements. The medical field at that time did not distinguish between the various forms of mental or emotional retardation and certainly had no solutions to offer. Nor could anyone tell the young parents whether the problem was genetic. For years, Ruth and Yigal Allon thus refrained from having any more children.

The severity of Nurit's problems gradually became clearer. In these years, Allon was away a lot on security work and steadily achieving success. But he did visit a great deal and his letters are filled with deep concern for the child, his love for her, and his sense of helplessness. "I am so jealous when I see a child that says 'Father,'" he confessed to one of the women at Ginossar.[91] Nurit's shadow stalked him through his most glorious triumphs, embittered his and Ruth's life, and agonized them both. In public, Allon was the young success with the open smile; he was good-tempered and calm. But this image hid his wretchedness, heartbreak, and sense of impotence in the face of fate. There were two Yigals: the Palmah commander radiating youth, good looks, success, and sabra mischievousness; and Nurit's father, hanging between despair and hope, between various treatments and different doctors, and finding no consolation. Allon's ability to don a mask, to dissemble, developed in the wake of Nurit's plight. His cheerful face did not mirror his heart, and it became his mask in times of both joy and sadness, so much so that it was difficult to get his real measure.

In this same period, 1941, Allon brought his father to live at Ginossar.[92] The kibbutz circumstances had changed much in the preceding year as a result of its physical expansion, the advent of the tractor, and Ginossar's admittance to the KM movement and concomitant financial aid. Helping parents now became feasible and Allon was among the first, if not *the* first, to bring his father to Ginossar.[93] The old Paicovich had returned to Mes'ha in an attempt to recoup the farm that Allon had so thoroughly dismantled. But age and loneliness were against him. When he fell ill, his daughter, Deborah, took him home to live with her in Haifa. He was not fond of city life, however. When Allon suggested that he come live with him at Ginossar, he was pleased, although he wanted to make sure that Allon considered Ginossar his home and would not leave it: his heart would not stand yet another rupture, as both Mahanayim and Mes'ha had been.[94] Yigal and Ruth Allon accorded Reuven half the shack at their disposal and they moved into a tent, an improvement as far as they were concerned over bi-family living quarters.[95]

As far as is known, Reuven did not complain about the living conditions at Ginossar. Nevertheless, it was a hard life: he was an old man living in a small hot shack without a toilet or other minimal conveniences and eating a diet that was sparse and inferior. Paicovich was not accepted as a regular member of the kibbutz but as a member's parent. No one was interested in his advice or opinions. Lonely and unneeded, he wandered about the yard, grumbling in anger at the neglect. Toward the end of his life, he who had been a patriarch and a farm owner was expendable, necessary to no one. Allon showed him respect and treated him sensitively, but he was gone most of the time and old Paicovich had to make his own way through the maze of kibbutz society, which was young, foreign, and impatient. And he lacked the talent for it. His relations with his daughter-in-law were hardly warm: only an angel could win Paicovich's heart, and Allon's wife, the purloiner of his son, would likely have failed even if she had been an angel. It was Ruth who bore most of the burden of caring for him and quite naturally most of the resentment.

There was a dripping water tap next to the small shack and Reuven planted a eucalyptus seedling near it. The tree flourished and, one holiday, the kindergarten teacher brought her small charges to pick twigs for wreaths. Catching sight of them through the window, Reuven was enraged. He picked up a stick and went after the teacher and her wards, flailing about in all directions. Absalom Zoref, who was friendly with Paicovich and was sometimes summoned from work in emergencies to calm the old man down, was now sent for. "Mr. Paicovich, what happened?" he asked when he arrived at the shack. Paicovich had meanwhile cooled off somewhat, and for an answer he gave the tragic story of his life: he had had a dream, he said, to build at Mes'ha a village of Paicoviches. And, look, all his sons had left it and wandered far away. In the end, he had hoped that Allon would come build the farm. But this dream too was dashed, for Allon went to a kibbutz. This eucalyptus, he said, is a monument to his life's dream, and monuments should be left alone.[96]

Whether or not Allon acknowledged the calamity he had brought down on his father and the misery he had sentenced him to is a moot question. To the extent that Paicovich could show warmth, their relations remained warm and close. With his other sons, he refused to keep in touch, barely agreeing to spend the Passover seder with them in the year that Allon was out of the country. The sons contributed to Paicovich's upkeep on the kibbutz, though this remained unknown to him lest he balk.[97]

In early 1942, there was a sense of relative prosperity at Ginossar. The jujubes were uprooted by a powerful tractor and the newly exposed 500 dunams of arable land were plowed. The work began on the day that the second batch of prisoners was released. Within a few months time, Ginossar's cultivated area doubled. Now, since the authorities encouraged intensive agriculture, Ginossar applied for a government loan to install irrigation. It received P£2,000 and in 1942 it erected a water plant.[98] The PICA was flummoxed. Every fact the members created on the ground increased Ginossar's holdings and challenged anyone to try to evict the residents from their homes. The living conditions did not improve: the farm's flourishing did not translate down to the individual level. Spot checks by the health fund doctor still resulted in alarming sanitation reports. The daily per capita budget stood at 37 mil. Dirt in the kitchen and dining hall made visitors cringe, as did the overcrowding. As for the levels of cleanliness and services in the laundry, the dairy, the showers, and the toilets—the less said the better.[99] Family living quarters were still unbearable. In vain did the doctor issue warnings about epidemics. Ginossar's members were preoccupied with other things.[100] The most important of these, with the exception perhaps of building a new children's house, was the farm's expansion. In 1943 a group of parents in Tel Aviv organized to help Ginossar by paving a road to the kibbutz—in members' eyes, a wasteful luxury. The plan was to raise some P£400 from parents "of means" with the contractor doing the work providing the remainder as a loan.[101] It is not clear if the plan was executed. The idea, however, expressed both parental anxiety at Ginossar's isolation and confidence in the permanence of the settlement site.

In October 1942, the PICA's director, a man named Gottlieb, arrived from France, and a new exchange of letters began with Ginossar.[102] This time, other personalities also entered the picture, such as Henrietta Szold, Norman Bentwich, and Hans Beit, the latter two being directors of Aliyat Ha-Noar (Youth Aliya), which brought refugee youth to Palestine. An attempt was made to enable the *kevutzah* to remain where it was while assuaging the PICA's injured pride. At the end of 1946, a formula materialized—Ginossar was to publish a public apology. Thereafter, the talks revolved around the sum of compensation due the PICA for ten years of Ginossar's unlawful use of the lands.[103] Eventually, the sum of P£6,000, was agreed on, to be paid out in installments. On 22 December 1947 the daily press carried Ginossar's apology for having settled land "intended for other settlers" without permission from and in disobedience to the PICA. "We hereby express our regret for our past actions and also ask for the PICA's pardon for [things] we publicized that later turned out to be inaccurate."[104] The PICA book was closed. It is not clear if Ginossar in fact made the payments. The compensation was presumably forgotten in the upheavals of the War of Independence. Ginossar's young were vindicated, their stubbornness and impertinence had held out against a bureaucratic, legalistic, and stodgy institution. Not only did they emerge with Ginossar in their possession; they even managed to mold Yishuv public opinion in their favor. The PICA came to be seen as a failing settlement agency, obtuse about the demands of the national good.

The epilogue was still to come. In 1952, Yigal and Ruth Allon, who were in England, were invited to the home of Baron James de Rothschild. Allon, basking in the glory of the War of Independence, took the opportunity to lay before the baron both Paicovich's and Ginossar's complaints about the PICA's officials. The Palestine officials, it emerges from the documentation, did not act independently; the baron had been well aware of what had been going on even if he had not been directly involved in the details. Nevertheless, both the host and his guests found it convenient to regard the officials as the root of all evil. Following the conversation, the PICA modified its attitude to Ginossar.[105]

In November 1941, the poetess and future paratrooper to occupied Hungary, Hannah Szenes, spent some time at Ginossar and wrote down her impressions:

> I see in the society a number of advanced people among whom I'm sure I could find interest and friendships; although the society as a whole is not spirited enough I still have the impression of a good society. More precisely: [it is] a society made up of many good individuals but devoid of a social voice. This lack is expressed in all common areas from the reading room to the general assembly . . . a considerable number of members are certainly missing a clear collective awareness, their ties to the kibbutz [are] love of place, a simple social bond. They feel good here, factors that can sometimes hold a person at a place better than any awareness, but they are not promoting or developing society life sufficiently or in the desired direction.[106]

Hannah Szenes seems to have hit the nail on the head. Her assessment was true not only of most of Ginossar's members, but perhaps of most of the youth who went to kibbutzim in those days. It was certainly true of Allon. Ginossar was the first stage in his education, assimilation, and internalization until the movement that adopted him became an integral part of his personality. It was a process that began in the years of his apprenticeship at Ginossar.

From the end of 1941 onward, Allon's work at Ginossar dwindled more and more. On 9 February 1942, Ginossar advised the district officer in Tiberias that Yigal Paicovich had ceased to serve as *mukhtar* due to an illness warranting a lengthy hospitalization.[107] Allon was having problems with his shoulder as a result of a run-in with a cow while riding a motorcycle on Haganah duty.[108] The unromantic encounter had occurred in May 1939, leaving his shoulder dislocated. The illness referred to in the letter, however, seems to have been of a conspiratorial nature, for only in June 1943 did he undergo the necessary surgery.[109] From February 1942 onward he was busy with ventures best kept under wraps at the time. From this stage onward Ginossar occupied an important place in his and his family's life but his absences outstripped his presence there. His vitality was given to security affairs.

Chapter 4
The Start of Security Work

In April 1936 a new era opened in the history of Palestine. Concurrent with modern Jewish settlement in the country, the dispute between Jews and Arabs over possession of the land became a life-and-death struggle. The brief chronology of Zionist settlement was interspersed with the eruption of riots that earned the lukewarm designation of "Disturbances." Until 1936, these could be explained away with a variety of reasons that veiled the root cause: a clash between two peoples over one piece of land. In the wake of the Disturbances of 1936 (as the Jews called them; the Arabs called them the Arab Rebellion), the conflict's national character could no longer be ignored. As in previous outbursts, this time too events began with rioting in Jaffa and the killing of Jewish passersby. But the political coloring soon became clear in the establishment of the Arab Higher Committee and a general Arab strike. The strike was aimed at forcing the government of Palestine to change its pro-Zionist policy, especially to halt the large immigration that, since 1932, had doubled the country's Jewish population. The strike lasted for half a year and, this time, the British did not back down. Ultimately, the rulers of Arab states had to step in to extricate their Palestinian brethren from the situation. They asked the strikers to end the strike and enable His Majesty's government to dispatch a royal commission to Palestine to investigate the problem thoroughly. The Peel Commission, named for its chairman, had wide-ranging powers and concluded that the Mandate had failed because its working assumption—that the two peoples could coexist—had proved false. It recommended that Palestine be partitioned into two new independent states—one Jewish, one Arab—to satisfy the national aspirations of the two peoples. The Jews accepted the solution amid mixed feelings, unleashing a controversy that was to last for years: supporters favored creating a Jewish state immediately, even if only *in part* of the country; opponents refused to yield an inch of the land, even if it meant risking the lot. The Arabs rejected the recommendations outright and resumed the rioting, which in 1938 took on the dimensions of a revolt. At the time, the Arabs inhabited the country's hilly spine and the British, like the Jews, were careful not to stray into areas under their control. Order was not restored until 1939 and then only by the British bearing down with ruthless military force.

The period of the Arab Rebellion, to a large extent, overlapped with the formative years of Allon's generation. Just as the dream of socialism had blazed in the founding generation and the (1905 or 1917) Russian Revolution had been that generation's defining, existential, and intellectual experience, the physical contest over the land filled the same role for the generation born and bred in Palestine's Yishuv. This generation did not dwell on politics, strategy, or long-term thinking. It faced an immediate challenge that required neither explanation nor justification: to defend the life, property, and honor of Jews in Palestine.

The Arab uprising took the Yishuv by surprise and wreaked havoc although, ostensibly, the writing had been on the wall. One indication of growing Arab extremism in the country had been Sheikh Iz a-Din al-Kassam's terrorist group operating in the Jezreel Valley and Galilee in the early 1930s; it finally fell in a battle termed by Ben-Gurion "the Arabs' Tel Hai"—a reference to the legendary, heroic stand of Jewish defenders against Arab attackers at the country's northern tip. In 1935 the Arab press rattled with news of an attempt by Haganah to smuggle in arms. Britain's Parliament thwarted efforts by High Commissioner Arthur Wauchope to set up a legislative council in Palestine. The Jews grew stronger and the Arab population more frustrated. Added to this were the political tensions in the Middle East due to the Italo-Ethiopian war in the autumn of 1935, which exposed the underbelly of the British lion. And yet, when the eruption came, the Yishuv was not prepared for it—not emotionally or organizationally or militarily.

The Yishuv was informed by the key ethos and concept of upbuilding: the Yishuv as a whole and the Labor movement in particular saw themselves as the builders of the country. The right to the land was won by working it; ultimately the land would belong to those who "redeemed" it from the wastes, who transformed a wilderness into a living home. In the Yishuv's self-image, its key mission was peace, bringing progress and prosperity to all of the inhabitants. This "defensive ethos" rested on the belief that the land could be acquired by peaceful means. It was closely related to the other two ethoses of upbuilding and making the desert bloom, and all that they entailed.

To go from this dream to the Arab Rebellion was a rude awakening. The Yishuv believed that its life was at stake. It had to learn how to fight, and at once. Hereafter, the emphasis shifted to developing means of resistance, a test and effort that drew the top talents. Emotionally, the changing priorities were more digestible to the generation that had just come of age and was less committed than the founding generation to the ethos of upbuilding. "You may wonder, Father, at the military spirit that has come over me"—wrote Israel Galili to his parent. "Not so. The wish to live, the instinct to do something and the love of freedom are what led me now to view Jewish enlistment in the Haganah as the immediate center of gravity."[1]

The first shortcoming exposed by the Arab Rebellion, then, was the Yishuv's lack of an ethos in support of fighting. The second shortcoming exposed by it concerned organization and management. The importance of the military arm of the national liberation movement—the limited, underground Haganah—and the need to place it at the disposal of the movement's political echelon, represented by the Jewish Agency (JA) and the Zionist Executive, was late to be recognized and hard to acknowledge. The Arab Rebellion upturned traditional thinking and acting, and yet consensus, though vital, remained elusive.[2] Formed in 1920, the Haganah was still not central to national consciousness or priorities. Internally, it was riven by political rivalry. Only in 1939 did the various political parties in the Yishuv finally agree to form a Haganah National Command to oversee the Haganah's activities. It was composed as a steering committee of civilians, equally representing the Left and the Right, and it lasted until statehood.

The third deficiency was military capability: military leaders had no answer to the challenge posed by the Arab onslaught. Security personnel clung to a military conception of passive resistance; in the event of Arab attack, settlements were to hold the assailants at bay until the British army arrived to disperse them. It was considered an achievement just to prevent the aggressors from entering a Jewish settlement. The Arab Rebellion, characterized by prolonged aggression, confounded the settlements and the security establishment. Daily life and functioning were disrupted by the need for nighttime guard duty and the frequent alarms raised against ambushes. In addition, transportation came under attack. For the first time, the Arabs tactically resorted to obstructing traffic routes. The roads became perilous and vehicles passing through Arab areas did so in organized convoys.

Mostly, the Arabs chose the cloak of night for their operations. As dark descended, dread set in: what would the night bring—shooting at windows, the burning of fields, the chopping down of trees, or an attack on the whole settlement? A single volley of shots was enough to banish sleep from an entire community, rousing everyone to their positions. Guards sped to high lookouts, a spotlight—if there was one—sliced through the darkness, and mothers tried to soothe children while hiding them beneath the beds. The settlement fence served as the defensive border. Beyond it stretched the black of night commandeered by the assailants. From their posts, defenders would see fields being torched and watch their sweat and toil go up in smoke. Common wisdom had it that it was better to incur damage to property rather than to the body. The assumption was that the Disturbances would soon die down. Until then, the Jews were to prepare for self-defense but take no undue risks.

This conception reflected a mixture of ideology and a lack of combat skills. The desire to avoid escalation in the Jewish-Arab national conflict, to refrain from bloodshed, and to have peace were ideological components. Soon, an additional consideration came into play: the Jewish political leadership had had its fill of riots and inquiry commissions that came to investigate the causes and left with conclusions placing aggressors and defenders on an equal footing. The leadership wished to highlight the one-sidedness of the Disturbances—Jews were being attacked without retaliating, and it was incumbent on the government, which was responsible for law and order, to come to their defense. Furthermore, following every wave of unrest, the British tended to make political concessions to the Arabs. By highlighting the guilty party, the leadership hoped to make it tricky for the government to reward the aggressors at the expense of the Zionists. Indeed, despite Arab demands to the contrary, Jewish immigration did continue this time as the government refused to bow to violence. Added to this was another political factor: the prospect of incorporating Jews into the defense network and creating a legal military force under British command. The longer the Disturbances lasted and the more severe they became, the political advantages of this policy of restraint, as it was known—taking no initiative for either assault or counterterrorism—overshadowed its conceptual roots.[3]

Still, there was the purely prosaic military incapability and lack of an operational response to the new Arab tactics. In Allon's view, "Initially, the consideration of restraint stemmed simply from the unavailability of a force [able] not to [show] restraint."[4] The truth is that even the "big wide world" did not know how to deal with guerilla warfare at the time. The British army, too, from whom the Jews learned the ins and outs of war, found itself hard put to cope with night raids by small units vanishing back into their villages. Response was slow to develop.

It remains a moot question of who actually imparted the new theory of war to the Yishuv's young. Opinion is divided over Yitzhak Sadeh and Elijah Cohen (Ben-Hur), on the one hand, and Orde Wingate, on the other. What is certain is that in the years 1937–39 the combat methods of Palestine's Jews were radically revamped, spelling a veritable revolution.

Heralding the turning point was the appearance in the Jerusalem Hills of the mobile squad, which moved from point to point as needed rather than being stationed at any one spot. The unit was soon issued a vehicle and, in stark contrast to the helplessness and inexperience of frontier settlers, it whisked people with military experience to trouble spots.⁵ This was the start of what became known as "going beyond the fence": no longer accepting passive resistance inside a settlement while abandoning fields and orchards, but defending the entire area right up to nearby Arab villages. Arabs were no longer the sole masters of the night and fields; these now became part of the Jewish arsenal as well. To this end, small units were created to be able to move quickly and quietly. The ammunition also changed since only short-range weapons could be used at night, employing brief but concentrated firepower. The submachine gun made its debut alongside the grenade, the preferred weapon of nocturnal combatants. Capping these developments was the art of the ambush, which utilized the night and fields to strike and fire at entrapped armed bands.

Yitzhak Sadeh, one of the fathers of the mobile squad, claimed that he had acquired his knowledge of sorties in the Russian army, both in a reconnaissance unit during the First World War and, more so, in the Red Army during the Civil War.⁶ Those training schools had taught him a number of basic principles—unconventional frameworks, improvisation, mobility, and optimization of manpower and weapons.⁷ The solution that took shape was elegant in its simplicity and, in retrospect, seems almost self-evident. Sadeh's greatness was that he arrived at it from within, in collaboration with colleagues and followers. He grasped the nature of the revolution and was able to infuse in those around him a sense of the importance of things.⁸ It was a theory of war supported by a young base, the generation then coming of age. On his dry runs with the mobile squad in the Jerusalem Hills, Sadeh found the young ready to try out his new methods, unflinching and itching for action.

Allon's case was typical of the way that Sadeh recruited his "soldiers": Allon began his formal career in security work in the summer of 1936. That August, he was inducted into the Jewish Settlement Police (JSP),⁹ an auxiliary force formed by the British to help furnish defense for Jewish settlements throughout the country. It was the common track for young Jews: here, draftees were trained in the use of arms and kept on the alert to come to the aid of beleaguered settlements, escort convoys, or provide cover for farmers working in the fields. The JSP served two masters: one, British and official; the other, the Haganah and underground. This hardly made their lives any easier. On the contrary, often it resulted in entanglements that demanded all of the diplomatic skills of Yehoshua Gordon, their commander and the liaison between the two chains of command.¹⁰ In any case, many of rural Palestine's young men, including Allon, received their initial training in the JSP's paramilitary framework.

Yigal's military activity was more or less a natural outgrowth of his childhood involvement in the ritualistic squabbles between the residents

84   Chapter 4

Figure 8. Allon as a sergeant of the Jewish Settlement Police, 1937. Photographer unknown. Courtesy of the Haganah Archives, Tel Aviv.

of Mes'ha, notably his father, and the a-Zbekh Arabs. For him, as for other residents of Mes'ha, the notion of holing up within Mes'ha's walls while Arabs destroyed fields and orchards was foreign and unreasonable. Mes'ha's villagers had always "gone beyond the fence" without any explicit policy. Allon carried with him the memories of the 1929 Disturbances, when his father went out to guard and left him, an eleven-year-old boy, all alone. He would scramble up to the attic, remove the ladder to keep the rampagers away, and wait with an axe in hand, a provision Reuven had made for his self-defense. The mere thought of having to use the "weapon" had made him queasy and given him nightmares.[11] But that had been years ago. The sense of helplessness of that experience was now replaced by robust action.

Allon, early in his career in the JSP, caught the eye of Nahum Kramer (Shadmi), the commander of the Tiberias bloc of the Haganah. In no time at all, Allon was appointed the commanding officer of the tender, an eight-man van outfitted with rifles, guns, and usually a Louis machine gun, along with—contrary to British orders—"illegal" grenades. In theory, the vans were financed by bloc settlers for their defense and placed at the disposal of the bloc's settlement police. In practice, the vehicles were purchased by the JA executive. The British had no objection to the JSP improving its mobility; they themselves would sometimes use the vehicles and manpower during the Arab Rebellion. But the pretense was kept up that the vehicles were a local initiative for settler needs in order to ward off possible accusations about the JSP's dual command. The vans were considered the height of operational advancement at the time, and their effects were certainly felt in the field. They were soon converted into armored cars impregnable to the light firearms used by Arab rebels. Every bloc had its own van and commanding officer, who was appointed by the bloc commander.

Allon already had the reputation of a shrewd, daring young man in the JSP when he met Yitzhak Sadeh. His description of the encounter approached the biblical: in the summer of 1937, as he was turning a threshing sledge—monotonous work ordinarily done by Arab laborers who, however, were staying away because of the Rebellion—a boy ran up and summoned him to his father's house. The boy was the son of Mes'ha's Haganah commander, and Allon, he said, was wanted because of the arrival of a high-ranking Haganah officer. Allon's first impression of Sadeh was disappointment: he was tall, portly, balding, and spectacled, and he had an oleaginous growth on his forehead; he looked sloppy in shorts, drooping knee socks, and frayed sandals, and, if this were not enough, he was missing several teeth. Not thus had Allon imagined the military hero.[12]

The Haganah had just decided to set up a new subdivision of field companies and Sadeh was recruiting promising candidates. He had managed to persuade the Haganah's senior cadre that the field companies should operate under their own command, drawing manpower from all over the country.[13] He was looking for recruits with a track record and he inducted members of the mobile squads and young men who had made a name for themselves in the JSP. This is how he came to Allon.

He suggested to Allon that he join the new national contingent and bring along his friends from Mes'ha. Yigal may have found Sadeh off-putting, but he agreed at once: he had been selected for an elite unit and any other response was inconceivable. Under Sadeh's instructions, he mustered his peers at dusk for a night exercise and the group set out through the dark fields. Sadeh, in front, hardly set a good example: his foot managed to find every stone, every twig, shattering the silence. And yet, the solid figure striding at the head of the column radiated confidence. The purpose of the exercise was to lay an ambush near the Maghrebi village some four kilometers from Mes'ha. The ambush was laid, the flanks secured and prayers offered for the sighting of an armed gang. The prayers went unanswered. Sadeh ordered "his troops" to fire several volleys in the air toward the village and return to Mes'ha. In Allon's yard, he sat them down around a small campfire to sum up: the goal, he said, was to harass the Arabs so as to end their mastery of the night. Surprise attacks in Arab areas would force them to assign manpower for village defense, hampering their offensive capability in Jewish areas. There was to be no personal terror against Arabs—he stressed—but attack was to be answered by attack, forcing the Arabs onto the defensive.[14]

For Allon and his friends it was an epiphany: "Fragmented thoughts that had long flashed through our minds suddenly came together in a full-blown doctrine. We were all impelled by a terrific feeling and we knew instinctively: he's the man."[15] Though this description may have been colored by subsequent encounters between the two men, there is no denying the strong impression Sadeh made on the boys champing at the bit. Here was an adult who spoke little and did a lot; who not only did not shrink from danger but was eager for battle; who proposed simple, obvious, bold, and effective operational strategies. And above all, he had the charisma to imbue confidence in his followers and shower them with love. The romance between Sadeh and the Yishuv's young began with the field companies and spawned a new generation of active warriors.

In the months following, Allon was busy dismantling his father's farm and moving to Ginossar. He continued his duties in the Tiberias bloc of the JSP under Nahum Kramer and was soon called up by the field companies for a five-day officers' training course at Kibbutz Ayelet Ha-Shahar.[16] It was the Haganah's first practical course in field weapons and fieldcraft. The focus was on battle drill. It included target practice with guns, and grenades, the use of machine guns, and an introduction to sabotage. Hours were spent on fieldcraft and night walking.[17] The cadets learned to devise a plan of action, allot and organize manpower and equipment, read maps, set up inter-unit communication, reconnoiter, and, above all, to lead men in battle.[18]

The course was aimed at producing squad commanders to train bloc personnel. At Ginossar, for example, Allon then gave a course on the friction grenade, which to detonate properly required a few seconds' delay between releasing the safety pin and hurling the grenade. Allon would stand next to the learner and have the latter count to ten before letting it fly, while the rest of the pupils took cover behind mounds of earth—just in case. In one of the drills, an apprentice left out the counting. He released the pin and made ready to throw the grenade. Everyone tensed. Allon clamped the man's arm and prevented the motion. The pupil struggled to get free. Allon coolly continued the count to ten and only then did he allow his charge to continue. None of those present ever forgot the incident.[19]

From December 1937 to January 1938 there was a six-week course for platoon commanders, the equivalent of today's officers' course. Some fifty young men took part, and the course went down in Haganah's history. All at once, there was an entire cadre of military commanders, an esprit de corps of personal and professional relationships that was to stay with the participants throughout their security responsibilities for years to come. The course dealt with corps management based on German and Russian army literature. The Haganah's commanders often pored over the material, especially the theory of organizing battalions and even larger formations. Drills, however, took place at the platoon level and peaked at the company level.

All the practical experience gained till then in field operations was funneled into the course. Participants included top field company commanders, who brought to it fresh military thinking, an impetus for action, and the shrewdness of war: apart from Allon, there was Moshe Dayan, Joseph Hamburger (Yossi Harel), Meir Davidson, Shlomo Rabinowicz (Shamir), Shimon Koch (Avidan)—to mention only a few of the figures who were later to become highly prominent. The revolution wrought by Yitzhak Sadeh and his compeers yielded its first human fruit here—a group of military leaders thinking and acting in commando terms but possessed also of the theoretical basics for operating larger military corps. The course was meant to train platoon commanders; in retrospect, it trained generals. For many of the participants, it was the highest-level army course they ever took. It certainly was for Allon.

Allon was one of the bright lights in the course, albeit not *the* bright light. The very fact that he stood out in this capable group said much for his abilities and potential. He was rough and unpolished, a rustic in refined company. His Hebrew, too, was different: he sprinkled his speech with Arabic and his accent was the accent of the Galilee. He was not garrulous and at social gatherings he did not have much of a presence. But there was an easiness about him that did impress at least one participant, Joseph Hamburger. Though of average height, Allon looked tall and lean, with an open face drawn up in fine Modigliani lines to a high forelock. He was light of step, quick to grasp, free with people—a natural military leader. His rural background was considered an advantage, the open fields were his home turf. He displayed intelligence, shrewdness, and boldness. Especially conspicuous was the ease with which he commanded, not needing to pull rank to win cooperation. He had that quality that made people want to follow him.[20]

The person who most impressed the group was another participant, Moshe Dayan, who was destined to become Allon's rival down the road. To the extent that one can speak of an aristocracy in the Yishuv's unassuming, classless, egalitarian society, the Dayans belonged to it: they were among the founders of Deganyah, the "mother of *kevutzot*": members of the most illustrious small-holders cooperative, Moshav Nahalal; and public figures. Moshe's mother, Deborah, also proved herself a gifted author. In addition, in 1935, the young Moshe married Ruth Schwartz, the daughter of Rachel and Zvi Schwartz, graduates of the famed Herzliya High School. Zvi Schwartz was one of the few young Jewish Palestinians to study in London in the 1920s, and, upon his return, he filled important positions in the Zionist institutions in Jerusalem.

Moshe's home was not wealthy. Poverty and daily struggle were common, perhaps no less so than at the Paicoviches' home in Mes'ha. But at the Paicoviches' the hardship was a disgrace, while at the Dayans' it was a matter of form. Paicovich's poverty did not stem from any sort of ideology; the family was poor because he failed to get rich. Not so the Dayans at Nahalal. They regarded their austerity as a voluntary, conscious sacrifice for the cause of building the country. Poverty was not a punishment for failure; it was the entry ticket into a just society. Moshe Dayan did not consider his home inadequate and it never occurred to him to be ashamed of it. Allon, in contrast, regarded his home as a blot to conceal. The "aristocracy" lent its poor meaning, a sense of belonging, and a concept of dearth by choice. Ordinary paupers viewed their status as something to shed.

The poverty of the Dayan household was strictly materialistic. Intellectually and culturally, the fare was rich. Moshe's mother was an inspiration with naturally refined taste despite the mud outside her door. Books, poetry, intelligent conversation were run-of-the-mill in the Dayan home, accessible with no exertion. In spirit, the world of the Russian intelligentsia irradiated the life of the country boy without him having to spare it a thought.[21]

Allon's village and home were radically different, their paucity beyond the materialistic. He had a long hard road to travel just to arrive at the starting line of the Yishuv's Labor aristocracy.

Moshe Dayan came across as a brilliant young man with a wonderful sense of humor, an amusing storyteller who had the group in stitches. However, within minutes, he could suddenly clam up. These moods came and went, and were seen by his peers as depressive. He was clever, highly intelligent, and there was no doubt about his leadership ability. Yet it was different from Allon's: Dayan lacked Allon's lightness. He was not liked. People followed him out of esteem. But he had to bring more pressure and authority to bear to achieve the results that came to Allon effortlessly.[22]

One lifelong difference between the two men, which was obvious even this early in their development, was that Dayan built his authority without paying attention to people, while Allon built his on close relationships with those around him. Whether because of personality or upbringing, the fact is that Dayan grew up enveloped in a mother's love, her firstborn on whom she pinned all of her hopes. From day one, he had a sense of being chosen and he needed no outside reinforcements to feel wanted or liked. Allon, from early childhood, had lacked maternal love: Reuven Paicovich could not fill the place of Yigal's dead mother. As a child, it had seemed to Allon that his father's love, when given, was a reward for living up to Reuven's stringent expectations. Allon sought constant reinforcement from the immediate human environment. He emitted caring, and his milieu responded with love. It was a source of both his strength and his weakness. At this stage, there was as yet no rivalry or evident tension between the two men, though there was no special friendship either.

The second important connection Yigal made at the course was Israel Galili. Although Galili was only seven years Allon's senior, he might have belonged to a different generation. Galili and his family had immigrated to the country on the eve of the First World War. His father had stopped in Russia and "got stuck" there for the duration. Meanwhile, the family went hungry and the young Galili peddled almonds and doughnuts at army bases around Tel Aviv and Jaffa. Getting a job in layout at the Ahdut Press, he was introduced to the Labor movement and the Laborites frequenting the premises. He initiated the founding of Ha-Noar Ha-Oved (HNHO), the Histadrut Labor Federation's movement for working youth against exploitation and want, and at the age of sixteen he became its secretary. Galili was a quasi-intermediate link between the founding generation and the native sons. In age and education, he belonged to the younger generation. But there was something about him, an early maturity, that gained him the company of Labor's fathers, primarily Berl Katznelson and Yitzhak Tabenkin. From these mentors, he learned the traits of teacher and counselor, seeking a way to his pupils' hearts in order to mold them.

In 1935, Galili, at the age of twenty-four, submitted to pressure from Shaul Meirov and became his right-hand man at the Haganah Command. It was a period of building new frameworks and a continuous need for promising talents. Katznelson and Tabenkin had taught Galili to spot youth movement types, but there were more functions to fill than talents to fill them. This made the job of "talent scout" vital.[23] Galili traveled up and down the land meeting with bloc commanders, listening, gaining impressions, and mentally filing information about one young person or another. When the time came for a commanders' course, he would pick the participants from his "filing system" and drop in at the course venue to meet the people in question, speaking with them individually. The conversations were ideological; military tactics were not among Galili's chief concerns.[24]

He had heard about Allon from Nahum Kramer. Kramer often praised his young subordinate and relied on his acumen.[25] Tabenkin, too, sang the praises of the boy from Mes'ha. Galili met with him at the Kefar Vitkin course and came away with a high opinion. As Galili was rushing to get back to Tel Aviv at the end of the day, due to curfew, his car failed him and he had to return to the base. He asked the guard where he might sleep and was told to choose one of the cadet beds. He chose Allon's, and the two found themselves sharing a bed for the night and filling hours with talk. This was the start of their personal friendship. Allon now had two "fans" among Haganah's top brass: Yitzhak Sadeh and Israel Galili. An unknown young man, recently of Mes'ha, could hardly have asked for a more auspicious beginning.

The course turned out a series of van commanders: Yigal—the Lower Galilee bloc; Dayan—the Nahalal bloc; Meir Davidson—Kefar Yeladim (Jezreel Valley); and Shlomo Rabinowicz (Shamir)—Ayelet Ha-Shahar (the Upper Galilee).[26] Their new status came to the fore in the major settlement-security act of the period—the founding of Kibbutz Hanita.

Hanita symbolized the breakthrough into settlement areas where Jews had not set foot before—the Western Upper Galilee—and was the Zionist response to the Arab Rebellion: we shall not be moved from here. The response was self-nurturing, reinforced by the Hanita myth itself: ultimately, the Arab Rebellion makes us stronger—to wit, the building of the port of Tel Aviv, tower and stockade settlements, Hanita, and so forth. This conception is not corroborated by historical analysis; the Arab Rebellion led to a slow-down in the building pace of the Jewish National Home and endangered its further development. But as a myth to boost morale in times of trial, it had considerable importance. Hanita stood also for open confrontation with armed Arab gangs: here was a Jewish settlement, straddling the gangs' route from Lebanon to Palestine. Hanita thereby epitomized two myths, defender and settler both.

In addition, Hanita illustrated the Yishuv's improved organization. Its establishment was conducted like a military operation. On hand for the action were Ya'akov Dori, the Haganah's senior commander (the post of chief of staff had not yet been created), Yitzhak Sadeh, commander of the field companies, and several other of the Haganah's top brass. Zvi Ben-Yaacov headed the operation. He had under him a few dozen JSP guards with legal ammunition, and three platoons of the field companies, that is, three vans, under Meir Davidson, Moshe Dayan, and Yigal Paicovich respectively. In addition, people had been recruited from surrounding settlements and placed for training under another graduate of the Kefar Vitkin course, Joseph Hamburger.[27]

Hanita's first night saw a daring attack by Arab gangs on the Jewish invaders. The attack succeeded, ending in the deaths of two of the Haganah's men. It succeeded mainly because the field companies recruits, contrary to everything they had just learned in the course, did not deploy on the hills around Hanita but stayed within the camp. On the second night, the platoons formed a circle around the camp. A few days later, in the afternoon, a convoy of vehicles with laborers building a road to Hanita was attacked. This time, two vans sortied on a counterattack, engaged in a brief battle, drove the armed gang from its fortified positions, and incurred no casualties.[28] For the participants, it was, so to speak, an exercise using live ammunition to assimilate the course material they had just learned.

Several days later, the vans of Allon and Dayan returned to their permanent stations, leaving Meir Davidson's van at the site. A famous photograph from the history of Hanita's founding shows Yitzhak Sadeh embracing two charming young men: Yigal Allon and Moshe Dayan (see Figure 9).[29] Thereafter, Davidson remarked that the world is divided into two: those who do, and those who pose for pictures.[30] But the fact is that at Hanita everyone gave of their best: the men were young, eager for battle, and devoted to the cause. Tensions and ironies still lay in the future.

Soon afterwards, the van commanders were promoted to ranks and positions recognized by the British: in April 1938 a sergeants' course was given at Sarafand by the 14th Royal Scotch Regiment under Moshe Zalizky (Carmel). It was attended by salient participants of the Kefar Vitkin course and left graduates with the sense that they were part of a regular army framework. More importantly, it awarded them JSP sergeant stripes and with them the right to command JSP companies, to carry arms, and, in part, emerge from the underground.

Figure 9. The establishment of Kibbutz Hanita, 1938. From left to right: Moshe Dayan, Yitzhak Sadeh, Yigal Allon. Photographer unknown. Courtesy of the IDF Archives.

As a result, Allon and his peers simultaneously belonged to two entities: they were field company commanders for and under the Haganah; and they were officers in the JSP, financed by and under the British. This ambiguous chain of command hardly improved the delicate relations between the British and the Zionist institutions. The British knew about the "dual command" and occasionally let drop something to show their slightly arrogant underlings that they were not babes in the woods. But they could not accept a direct blow to their authority. The situation demanded a tact and maturity not always found in the young commanders.

When it came to the Haganah's discipline, Allon was a zealot. Since he knew no English, he found it hard to converse with British officers. He claimed that he answered only to the Haganah Command and took his orders only from it, a rather unreasonable contention on the part of a JSP sergeant.[31] Some months after the sergeants course, he caused an incident that brought down the wrath of Yehoshua Gordon, the director of the JA department in charge of Settlement Police affairs. A British colonel had asked Allon to place his van at his disposal. The van had meanwhile been converted into an armored vehicle and the colonel wanted it for a British countermeasure in the Arab Rebellion (in early November 1938). Allon refused. He informed the colonel (presumably via a translator) that the van belonged to the Jewish Agency, that he was under the Agency's command and, that according to his orders, the van was not to leave Jewish areas.[32] The declaration speaks volumes for Allon's inexperience in dealing with the British authorities. The colonel was furious: these Jews! It was on their behalf that the British were in fact fighting, yet they withheld necessary equipment, making excuses that lent credence to the suspicion that there was a JSP underground command, subordinate to the JA.

Allon had the support of the local Haganah commander—after all, you can't punish a good lad for showing excessive loyalty—who mollified the colonel in a chat warmed by whiskey. But Gordon was beside himself: Allon was to steer clear of situations in which Jews refused to cooperate with the military authorities. The incident induced Gordon to issue a circular to sergeants: "Army orders are to be carried out forthwith without hesitation or doubt. Sergeants should make no excuses nor enter into any political negotiations or arguments with the authorities, who demand that their orders be carried out."[33] Allon hardly excelled in relations with British officers later, too. This may have stemmed from the lack of communication, or the arrogance of a young commander who found it hard to swallow what in British eyes was his relatively inferior status, or from his Yishuv education, which was pervaded by suspicion of the British even in the period that the British protected Jewish Palestine.

The policy of restraint got the backs of young activists up. In time, the practice of permitted reprisal was adopted, although not of personal terror. This policy was adopted in order to create a distinction between the Haganah and the Revisionist National Military Organization (IZL) founded in 1931 by breakaway Haganah members, whose support came from right-wing circles. Since 1938, the IZL had abandoned restraint and taken to committing personal terror against Arabs. The Haganah maintained that there should be some direct linkage between the reprisals and the acts that provoked them, a view not shared by the IZL. The Haganah repeatedly stressed the difference: innocent Arabs were not to be harmed; retaliation was aimed only at those guilty of hurting Jews.[34]

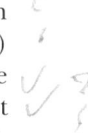

It was easier to set policy than to abide by it: the definition of "guilty Arabs" was open to interpretation. The Haganah Command tried to avoid harming women, children, and the elderly, but how could their safety be ensured in an attack on a house in an Arab village? Moreover, who could guarantee that the Arabs injured in an attack were the guilty party? For those at the fighting level, evidence that rioters hailed from a specific village seems to have sufficed for that village to be punished. The fighters accepted the idea of collective responsibility as imposed by Bedouin in blood vengeance on an entire village or tribe.

"There are people who say, and I second them, that in the conditions of the Orient, in the customs of the Orient, a blow—in response to any act—need not necessarily be against the assailant himself," Allon pronounced: "According to Arab tradition, it is enough to know the assailant's village to have grounds for settling accounts with that village. . . . If Jews are harmed, Jews killed, and it is impossible to strike at the assailant himself, one must strike at the tribe. . . . This is something they understand." Allon expressed this opinion some years later, but it applied also to the period of the field companies.[35]

Questions about what was and was not permissible continued to plague the field companies, which, for the first time, empowered relatively large, diverse social groups to employ force. For many, it was an initial, direct introduction to the open country and its Arab inhabitants. For others, it was an extension of their lives in Arab surroundings. The Disturbances had sown hatred of Arabs, which was a new element: the number of Jewish casualties, the brutality of the assailants, the lack of mercy for women and children all had an effect, engaging the passions of the young recruits. The field companies were stationed at vulnerable positions that had already suffered losses, and this knowledge, like the potential danger, heightened suspicion and hostility.[36]

Given these feelings, the gray area between what one should and shouldn't do was rather broad at times, whether on the personal level or in skirmishes. An anonymous member of the field companies, with an enthusiasm for Beethoven and Werfel, felt both embarrassed and compassionate when a dignified older Arab making his way home was detained in an ambush. The frightened man broke down only to receive a rifle butt in the face. The music lover noted: "Something moved within me. Can such a sight be witnessed with equanimity?"[37] The actions carried out with the British captain Orde Wingate, though in many respects invigorating, did not foster sensitivity toward Arab villagers. According to rumor, Wingate would line up all of the men of a suspect village and shoot every tenth one.[38] The anecdote itself may have been just rumor, part of Wingate's psychological warfare. But true or not, it reflected a ruthlessness previously unknown by the young men.[39]

Allon treated Arabs as he always had, with guarded familiarity and none of the inhibitions stemming from education or disposition. He was unemotional about war and killing, practical, cold, uninvolved. The reports of the Lower Galilee Mobile Guard, signed by no. 4—evidently Allon[40]—were matter-of-fact: they described clashes, ambush tactics, pursuit, fire, his or Arab subterfuges, and the lessons learned. Nothing in his words was indicative of attitude. He was noncommittal in describing the use of force; he might just as well have been speaking about plowing or sowing.[41] His opinion in favor of the principles of the Arab *gom* blood vengeance was supplemented by the observation: "We have to get over the moral difficulties we come up against in such actions."[42]

On the question of "purity of arms" (or clean hands), the High Command showed an ambivalence that filtered down through the ranks. Two incidents from this period—the actions in Tiberias and Lubya—show just how blurred the boundaries were.

The incident in Tiberias was traumatic for Allon, for Nahum Kramer, and for their men. Although Allon and Kramer were exonerated in the subsequent inquiry, Allon, it appears, did not totally absolve himself.[43] On the evening of 2 October 1938, an armed Arab band burst into Tiberias and massacred nineteen Jews, including eleven children. Earlier, Wingate's Special Night Squads (SNS) had been disinformed about an armed gang on the hill between Tiberias and Yavne'el and on Mount Kinneret. The SNS had set out to waylay the gang, requisitioning the Tiberias van. At 8:00 P.M., they heard shooting from Tiberias but were not overly concerned, because, as stated in the report (by Allon, evidently), the noise sounded like the "usual gunshots."[44] Manning the lookout with British army personnel, the recruits in the van never imagined what was happening in town: one Arab force had entered the lower city, torched the British Government House and police station, and tried to damage other government offices. The lone JSP policeman in town had fired at the attackers until he ran out of ammunition. At the same time, another force had clambered up the steep rise to the neighborhood of Kiryat Shmuel; the attack came from an unexpected and completely exposed flank. The neighborhood men were at defense posts. The women and children were at home. They were slaughtered without mercy. It was a repeat of the massacre in Hebron of 1929. The Arab gang went about its deadly business undisturbed, while in town no one knew what was going on.[45]

The gang's retreat and the ambush at Karnei Hittin gave rise to one of the better-known stories abut Allon: Allon, it was said, intercepted them and in a "classic maneuver" made short shrift of them, obliterating the disgrace of Tiberias. So *Davar* reported the incident and so contemporaries came to view it in time.[46] The truth was less glorious. As the shots increased from the direction of Tiberias, Allon asked the British officer in charge to set up ambushes on the lanes leading to Arab villages, to block the retreat of the gangs. This was routine procedure. The officer agreed and the squads proceeded to the points of ambush. En route, the scouts spotted a gang moving to the east. The officer gave an order to open fire, the Louis machine gun began to rattle, and Allon's men used their rifles. The officer then gave an order to charge. The squad charged. But when they reached the Arab casualties, some of the men ("about fifteen") chose to ransack the bodies rather than continue fighting. In the ensuing chaos, most of the Arabs managed to get away.[47] Allon's men learned of the massacre only when they returned to the colony of Mitzpe. Reporter no. 4 (Allon) attributed the attack's failure to "a developed lust for booty in (Jewish and English) army circles."[48]

It was Wingate's forces who carried out the retaliation for the Tiberias massacre. When Wingate learned what had happened, he impulsively ordered his men to mass on the village of Daburiyeh, where he had been wounded in a previous action. It was a simple case of vengeance: "We rode on a bad, bumpy road, each of us inwardly planning to kill and destroy and ease our hearts somewhat."[49] Some 15 Arabs were killed and many wounded and arrested. Had they taken part in the massacre in Tiberias? It is hard to know. In educational terms, the message conveyed by this unplanned action and its uncertainty about the identity of the guilty party was different from the Haganah's idea of "purity of arms." Since Wingate's troops were also field company troops, they no doubt absorbed both the message and its legitimacy.

The second incident, the action in Lubya, again underscored the ambiguity. Lubya was a very large village on the road from Haifa to Tiberias and the Jordan Valley. The action followed the murder near the village of a Jewish driver from Kibbutz Afikim. The commander of the operation was Shlomo Rabinowicz (Shamir), the commander of the Haganah field units in the area,[50] and the men taking part were subordinate to Kramer (Shadmi), the commander of Galilee. Allon brought some of his friends from the colonies while Joseph Hamburger was there with a force of his own. All of these were joined by David Shaltiel, who was newly returned from unnerving years in Dachau after being apprehended in 1935 for procuring arms. The superabundance of officers was not exactly a show of confidence in the rank and file.[51] Some of the participants were under the impression that the operation had been authorized by higher echelons. Nevertheless, it seems to have been a local initiative, approved by Nahum Kramer and no higher.[52]

The plan was to enter Lubya and hit a prominent house, though there was no information that this is where the driver's killers had come from. Nevertheless, the purpose was to strike at a house in the heart of the village "to make an example of it." The troops set out from Sejera at last light and progress was slow. They arrived at their destination around midnight, dogs barked but aroused no disquiet. The house was located.

Rabinowicz, Allon, and Hamburger led the approach, stopping in the shadow of the house to organize. At that very moment, the door opened and a man stepped outside. Coming into the dark, he did not immediately notice the men, although he seems to have brushed against one of them and sensed that something was amiss. Shlomo Rabinowicz drew his Toopie. He placed it at the man's head and pulled the trigger, but the gremlins got there first: the gun jammed. Allon leapt forward and drew his own gun. The same thing happened: his gun also jammed. The man started to scream, causing Hamburger to rush in with his submachine gun. This worked. As to what happened next—opinions are divided. One version has it that the action ended at this point and the men began to concentrate on retreat. A second version has it that Hamburger released several rounds into the house before retreating. Yet a third version says that amid the arrangements to retreat, Rabinowicz remarked, "We're not done yet!" The men returned to the house and threw a few grenades inside. They did not bother to evacuate anyone.[53]

Some years later, Allon described the sequence of events in incidents of blood vengeance in 1938: "We would come to a village, to the house pointed out by the dogs [of the guilty party], we would remove the people from the house, we would move them and the neighbors out of the way, we would create a human chain around the house so that no one could get near, and we would blow up the house."[54] This is not what they did at Lubya. Neither in planning nor in execution was any attention paid to "purity of arms." An editorial in *Davar* (22 June 1939) had harsh words for the "shots that murdered the elderly and women and spilt the blood of an infant and a dying man."[55] The editor seems to have believed that it was an IZL operation—reinforcing the hypothesis that the Haganah's High Command did not know about it. The IZL, in contrast, sent the personnel involved its congratulations.

Allon was not apt to mention the operation among those he took part in. Nevertheless, like the other participants, he did not seem to have been disturbed by the moral aspects. He had a long account to settle with Lubya and, according to what he knew of Arab norms, the idea that one should strike only at those who struck at you was not common practice.

There is no evidence that Nahum Kramer was reprimanded for the affair in Lubya. Allon might well have inferred that though "purity of arms" was the drift, the aspiration, it was not binding in the heat of an operation. At times, Allon and his friends also did things on duty without prior approval—for instance, in retaliation for the torching of the Yavne'el granary, the field company set fire to nineteen granaries in the area, although they had no orders to this effect.[56] Nahum Kramer probably knew about it, at least after the fact, but, again, who was going to discipline dedicated, good lads for overzealousness?

The year 1939 was fateful for the world as a whole, especially for Jews, and revolutionary change came also to the small world of Palestine. Overnight, the Yishuv's British allies turned into enemies, locking the country's gates, preventing Jewish immigration, restricting Jewish land purchase, and arresting the continued development of the Jewish National Home. As war loomed, Britain was interested in winning Arab support: it could count on Jewish support in this war against the Nazis. But to bring the Arabs on board, to ensure calm in the Middle East and safety on imperial roads, it had to curry Arab favor at the expense of the Zionist movement.

The White Paper of 1939, termed a "betrayal" by Ben-Gurion, was a clear signal to Allon and his peers that their suspicion of these foreigners had been justified. Their latent anti-Britishness now had legs to stand on. But apart from demonstrations, what could the small Yishuv do, surrounded as it was by foes and dependent on the British? For the young and gung-ho, raring to prove themselves, the dissonance between the Yishuv's impassioned rhetoric—which was Ben-Gurion's special forte— and its pathetic action stiffened their lack of trust in the founding fathers whose excessive rhetoric often came to mask inaction.

The drama of Palestine was a marginal precursor of the great European drama unfolding with the eruption of World War II in September 1939. Ben-Gurion immediately tested a new motto: "We will fight the Germans as if there were no White Paper and we will fight the White Paper as if there were no war against the Germans."[57] It had a nice ring to it. But the Yishuv was hard put to meet either challenge. The battle against the White Paper slowly dissipated; the British would obviously brook no disorder in wartime. Enlistment in the British army proceeded at a snail's pace. The British were far from enthusiastic about taking in Jewish volunteers, either because they believed that they would be training an army that would be fighting them one day or for fear of what the Arabs would say—the very reasons, if truth be told, that the Jews wished to enlist. On the personal level, volunteering for the British army was prompted by a desire to take part in the worldwide campaign against the forces of evil. Nonetheless, the political leaders wanted to capitalize on these aspirations and reap political fruit. They were most interested in forming Jewish battalions within the British army, under a Jewish flag and preferably a Jewish commander, much like those in World War I: for the generation of the current leaders (Ben-Gurion, Eliyahu Golomb, Ben-Zvi, and so forth), service in the Jewish Legion in World War I, in British uniforms, had been their formative military experience.

Jewish-British cooperation in the framework of the JSP increasingly waned. The van fell from grace. Men who only yesterday had fought under British patronage were now being harassed and searched for possession of illegal weapons. When the field companies were dismantled, Allon left the JSP (mid-1939) and joined the Haganah's permanent staff. He lost the van, his heart's delight and the first vehicle he had ever had at his disposal. In its stead, the Haganah issued him a motorbike and he would race up and down the roads to Tiberias and Ginnosar. This was the cause of his mortifying accident—a collision with a cow near Ginossar.

The outbreak of the war did not radically change the functioning of the Haganah. The second officers' course at Yavne'el was held as scheduled, as if all were right with the world. The course commander, Raphael Lev, had been an officer in the Austrian army and was invited by the Haganah to instruct it. Lev had been in the country only a few years and spoke a halting Hebrew, which made his deputy, Moshe Zalizky (Carmel), the key figure. Allon and Moshe Dayan were both among Zalizky's subordinates. On 2 October 1939, two British officers from Tiberias dropped in by surprise and, without overly taxing their perspicacity, grasped that this was no sports camp as they had been informed, but a military base with illegal arms. Both sides were nonplussed, hardly knowing what to do: the British officers were not eager to act against people with whom they had so recently cooperated; moreover, how were they supposed to arrest an entire base? For their part, the Haganah personnel wondered if they should arrest the officers or let them go. In the end, the common sense of the officers triumphed over the rash pugnacity of the cadets. The British were allowed to leave the base in one piece. But, the base obviously had to be dismantled, the course and all of the weapons and gear transferred to a training facility at Ju'ara (a wooded and secluded area near Mishmar Ha-Emek, where all future activity by the Palmah was to take place), and all evidence of illegal goings-on camouflaged. The gear was moved in a number of trucks. However, in view of army roadblocks and checks, it seemed too dangerous to move people this way. The men were thus to make their way to Ju'ara on foot. This would take two nights and they were to spend the day resting up at Kibbutz Ein Harod. About twenty of the men were sergeants or corporals in the JSP. Had their participation in the Haganah course come to light, they would have faced heavy penalties for a breach of military discipline. This group was thus to leave separately under Yigal Paicovich and rendezvous with the other group of forty-three late in the night near Moledet. The course officers were in charge of the operation, and one of the scouts was Moshe Dayan.[58]

Allon decided to take his people to Mes'ha at once. He was of course at home there and could conceal them until they set out for the night-

Figure 10. During the commanders' course in the Haganah, 1939. Allon stands first on the left. Photographer unknown. Courtesy of the Haganah Archives, Tel Aviv.

time trek. This decision freed him of the lengthy predeparture arrangements that delayed the other group for three hours and in the end spelled their downfall. In time, he took credit for having sized up the situation in advance.[59] Allon and his JSP men rested in his father's yard at Kefar Tavor until sundown. Two hours past midnight, they arrived at the appointed meeting place. But the second group did not show up. They settled down to wait behind a ridge, out of sight of the Transjordan Frontier Force patrolling the nearby pipeline of the Iraq Petroleum Company. An hour passed, then two—there was no sign of the second group. Finally, the spotter informed Allon that a group that looked like Jews had just been stopped by a unit of the Frontier Force. From his hiding place in the light of dawn, he saw the other group being apprehended a few hundred meters away. Not wasting a single minute, he and his men hotfooted it to Ein Harod and safety. There was no longer any thought of continuing the course at Ju'ara. Members of the JSP were told to report to their precincts at top speed to cover up their absence in the station logs as best they could.[60]

In time, the affair of the forty-three became a subtle bone of contention between Allon and Dayan. No reader of *Bet Avi* can ignore Allon's emphases, offsetting his own behavior with that of Dayan's, who—at the time of writing—was his rival. The care taken to leave early, the caution shown in the choice of a resting spot, and the route chosen for the trek to Ein Harod were meant to highlight opposite developments in the other group. Dayan was not the commander of the other group, merely its scout. But his position was dominant and Allon hinted at his responsibility for the fiasco. By the same token, Dayan's biographer took the trouble to stress that not Dayan but his commanders were to blame for the sorry outcome.[61]

The key issue was the failure to resist arrest. The unit detaining them was a service unit of the Frontier Force and numbered less than twenty people. The forty-three could certainly have gotten away. Instead, they allowed themselves to be captured complete with their weapons, showing no resistance, including Dayan. Allon stresses in *Bet Avi* that his group had been prepared for a run-in with the British and were determined not to be taken, even if it meant opening fire.[62] Forceful resistance during the confiscation of arms or arrest by the British was not something the Haganah condoned: the British conducted weapons searches resulting in trials for illegal possession. There was a good deal of anger over this in the Yishuv, but matters never went as far as forceful resistance. Allon, in *Bet Avi*, wrote as he did because his aim was to goad Dayan.

By coincidence, both Allon and Dayan interrupted their service in the Haganah for a year and a half: Dayan because of the detention of the forty-three men in the prison at Acre; Allon because of the "water war" that restored him to Ginossar. In any case, a process seems to have unfolded in that period that distanced Dayan from the Haganah's nerve center and drew Allon closer to it. But there were no external signs of this: in fact, in 1941, when the first two Palmah companies were created, Allon was put in charge of Company A and Dayan of Company B. But looking back, developments seem to have taken effect in 1940 that, to no small degree, determined the two men's future development.

Dayan's relations with the rest of the forty-three in prison were poor, leaving them with a bad taste in their mouths. This projected onto the attitude toward him of other figures as well. Dayan acted as his own man, refusing to bow to group opinion. His egocentrism and unbridled individualism stood out in prison conditions and put people off. Prison life was tough, yet he did not conceal his disdain for group members who were weaker and/or less intelligent than he, eliciting the disapproval and even disgust of other prisoners. On the one hand, he could be pleasant and friendly, winning people over easily with his story telling, a talent that ultimately saved him from ostracism. His own commander, Zalizky, had formed an unfavorable impression of him, and when Israel Galili stole into prison, disguised as a plumber (to dissuade the forty-three from attempting escape), he and Zalizky had a long talk. The two men were fellow travelers from their HNHO days and Kibbutz Naan, and Galili pumped him about their acquaintances among the prisoners. When he asked about Dayan, Zalizky said, "He holds nothing sacred." Galili was taken aback; he tried to persuade Zalizky that he must be mistaken. But Zalizky would not budge. He went on to cite conduct that showed up Dayan as having no values.[63] In a society that saw itself as resting on the loftiest human ideals, to go against convention was not to be a refreshing nonconformist; it was to defy the most basic value of preferring the general good over one's own. A self-proclaimed socialist society found it hard to digest Dayan's social unconcern. The Haganah's top brass knew of the bad feelings between Dayan and the other prisoners. Yitzhak Sadeh held him in esteem, though he showed no love for him as he did for Allon or Hamburger.[64]

In this same period, Allon more and more proved that he was made of the "right" fiber: he was an active member of a kibbutz; he was invited to Katznelson's month-long seminar in Rehovot, where he impressed a great many people; he had the ear of the Histadrut's bigwigs about Ginossar's affairs; and he was held in affection by Berl Katznelson. He was probably known to the Haganah leader Eliyahu Golomb as well, though there is no direct evidence of this. Nor is it known when Galili introduced him to Ben-Gurion; at any rate, it is reasonable to assume that it was in this period.[65] The fact that Ginossar had joined the Kibbutz Me'uhad movement (KM) and Allon's speech before its council consequent to this momentous event served as further proof that he was a lad "after our own hearts," flesh of our flesh: he understood how things were, accepted authority, and respected the right values.

In a society in which the leaders regarded the idealism of the youth movement as the desirable (though not always attainable) standard, Allon was seen as having internalized from Labor fathers the social norms and proper approach to the balance between the individual and society. He radiated the mixture of youthful innocence and idealism that they sought in their successors. Moreover, apart from being an "important lad," Allon was a "good lad." The same could not be said of Dayan.

The Haganah's political leadership was greatly concerned that these values be internalized by Yishuv youth ready and raring for action. People such as Eliyahu Golomb, Shaul Meirov (Avigur), Israel Galili, Berl Katznelson, and Yitzhak Tabenkin saw the realization of Zionism not only as the realization of the aims of a national movement, but as a moral virtue to right the wrongs of generations against an ancient, long-suffering people. Their passionate faith in the redemption of the Jewish people was bound up with lofty hope for the redemption of the world. This concept was instilled in the youth of Palestine's Labor Yishuv.

In the period of the field companies and early World War II, the Yishuv's young activists were not noted for a clear identification with these values. Though some of the field company commanders were graduates of the youth movements, the atmosphere at the training base was that of a military barracks, not that of the Labor Yishuv. It was a key period in molding the image of a generation totally immersed in the Haganah: "We"—said Shosh Spector (secretary of the Haganah and adjutant of Palmah)—"are the essence of the generation whose lifelong theme was security; who did not concern themselves with anything else—[who] concerned themselves with this!"[66] Their thinking was simple and single-minded: defense of Jewish life and honor. The rest didn't interest them.

They were not bookish. Most of them had little education and a narrow worldview. Zvi Spector was the intellectual of the group. Zvi was born in Jerusalem in 1915; his father had immigrated with the Second Aliyah; his mother came from a well-born Sephardic family, the Toledanos. The marriage failed, his mother committed suicide, and Zvi was raised by a maternal aunt in Jerusalem. For years he went by the name of Zvi Toledano. He attended the Rehavia Gymnasia, was a good student, and read English, French, and Arabic. He then went to university in England, but he returned to Palestine after two years. According to one version his return was due to lack of funds; according to another, it was due to the Disturbances.[67] Upon his return, he enlisted in the Haganah and was captivated by Yitzhak Sadeh. Spector's biography was unusual for the lads of Labor Palestine: who went to university rather than to kibbutz at that time? And if one did go, who went abroad, where one could be enticed away from loyalty to the country? Spector did not live by the dos and don'ts of the Labor movement. In 1940 he was so influenced by long talks with Shaul Meirov that he told Shosh, his wife, that he meant to join Mapai. But, at the same time, he was dismayed by their constant poverty and kept suggesting to her that they spend some time in Rhodesia, Kenya, or some other location in the British Empire, where they could raise rubber and grow rich.[68] The idea of leaving Jewish Palestine for a romantic, faraway adventure was not foreign to the youth of Jerusalem: Joseph Hamburger and his friends planned to join the Spanish Civil War. In the end, Hamburger was invited to join the Haganah's permanent staff and he ended up at Hanita instead of Barcelona. His friends went on to Spain never to be seen again.[69]

Spector was an army man through and through with no ideological ties, social conscience, or moral inhibitions. In this, he seemed to be characteristic of the entire group. They were soldiers who had either been recruited one by one or volunteered for duty without any movement backing and regardless of their movement affiliations. They were a band of individualists, many of them lone wolves eager for action, who fell under the dark spell of adventure, danger, and power.

The man to discern their spiritual emptiness was Yitzhak Sadeh. Sadeh won their admiration with his unconventional solutions and knack for providing a pithy outlet for their cravings. They liked to relate to him as "the old man" for he gave their actions and thinking legitimacy. They were somewhat embarrassed by the bohemian Sadeh who was fond of frequenting cafes and restaurants to indulge in wine and good food. But this too had an offbeat charm. From his experience in Russia's civil war, he understood the importance of cultural symbols and myths fostered by poetry, prose, and camaraderie to forge a combat unit's motivation. The Red Army adeptly conscripted writers and poets to compose stirring lyrics and epics that accompanied soldiers into battle, rousing their warrior souls and boosting their sense of justice. Sadeh's attempts to infuse the field companies with this substance did not succeed: when he tried to outfit his charges in spiritual accouterments, he could not penetrate their impervious cultural wall and basic lack of refinement.

The period of Europe's "phony war" and frozen front after Poland's fall (September 1939–March 1940) was followed by the great defeats of French and British forces in the spring of 1940. The war suddenly became a grave matter, and mighty Britain stood alone. In June 1940, Italy declared war on England and France and its bombers brought the war to Palestine's doorstep. The eastern part of the Mediterranean Basin turned into a battle arena. The fighting in the Balkans, the conquest of Greece and Crete by the Germans, and the capture in Crete of Palestinian Jews serving in the British army drove home just how close the war was. In 1940, British and Italian forces locked horns in the western desert in North Africa. After the Italian losses, a German expeditionary force was sent in and the war prospects changed: the British took a thrashing from the Germans under Rommel. In the spring of 1941, all anyone could talk about was the possibility that the British would be retreating from Egypt and Palestine. The Yishuv's serenity, it transpired, had been misguided. Suddenly, it was threatened with extinction.

The atmosphere in the Yishuv grew gloomier from day to day. A German invasion seemed imminent. "There is no strength to face tomorrow," Katznelson wrote in his diary.[70] No one knew what to expect of the Germans. It was thought that the Yishuv might reach some sort of modus vivendi with them: the Germans could wish to utilize the Yishuv's productivity, and people would be found willing to collaborate with them. One idea broached was to evacuate the entire Jewish population on the heels of the British, or at least the young so that they could continue their role in the war effort.[71] The sense of uncertainty was keen. When Yiftah Spector, the future commander of the Israeli Air Force flight school and a conscientious objector during the Second Intifada, was born in 1940, his father refused to have him circumcised: In this mad world, where no one knows what will be, why saddle the boy with Jewish heritage? Failing to convince him, Shosh Spector asked the doctor to perform the circumcision and just get it over with. Zvi Spector bandaged the baby at home—in utter silence.[72]

The air was such that ideas buzzed about organizing the Yishuv or at least its active elements for one glorious, last-ditch stand. The thinking of the security elites focused on organizing defense around Mount Carmel or the Hills of Ephraim.[73] At Kibbutz Afikim, instructions were given to repair the children's shoes so that they would be ready to set out on the long march to Mount Carmel.[74] The Spectors were in the throes of packing to move to Jerusalem (Zvi was to take up a new appointment and Shosh was to serve as the adjutant of the Jerusalem District), when Yitzhak Sadeh came to tell them of the plan to make a stand in a fortified area in the Carmel mountains and of the formation of a commando unit to take action behind enemy lines after the Germans occupied the country. Said Shosh, "Yiftah is so heavy—how am I to drag him on my back in the hills?"[75] But Zvi responded to Sadeh's call at once, even though he had only just recovered from a near-fatal car accident and was still limping.

This was the kernel of the Palmah: seeds of thought spawned, on the one hand, by the dark cloud stalking Britain's reversals in North Africa, and, on the other hand, by British readiness in the shadow of this catastrophe to cooperate with Palestine's Jews. On 14–15 May 1941, the Haganah's National Command made the decision to establish the Palmah (the Hebrew acronym for Peluggot Mahatz—crack commando units). In its structural outline, Zvi Spector was to fill a senior position—chief instructor, the core of a Palmah general staff—which as yet was a far-off dream.[76]

The first legend about the Palmah was born before the force itself. At dawn on 18 May 1941, the Sea Lion motorboat set sail from Haifa Port with twenty-four people aboard: twenty-three Haganah recruits and one British officer. Their mission was to blow up the oil refineries in Tripoli, Lebanon, which were now under Vichy control. It was one of the first joint operations between an arm of British intelligence and the Haganah. The man in charge of the operation was Yitzhak Sadeh and he enlisted his top people. It was important to Sadeh to show the British that the Jews were capable of carrying out a daring, dangerous commando operation. He thereby hoped to persuade them to make further use of his boys' talents.[77] The detachment contained most of the cadets of the Haganah's marine company, which had spent several months training at sea. It was to be the first measure independently planned and commanded by cadres from Jewish Palestine. The cadets were primed for action: months of training with no real mission had been demoralizing. Their superiors, however, had their doubts.

Beyond the operation's military logic—neutralizing the refineries on the eve of the British conquest when they themselves would need them—Sadeh was concerned about the execution and necessary manpower. For a start, he had demanded integrated land and marine forces; the danger of relying on the sea alone, without diversionary tactics on land, was too great. He also demanded a British warship, even if only a small one, since the Sea Lion was a non-armored, police coastal boat that could not provide cover for the disembarking troops. The British officers rebuffed his demands one by one, claiming they were unfeasible.[78] Faced with the option of calling off the operation altogether or carrying it out despite the danger, he chose to proceed.

The participants related to the action as an operational challenge: an exploit that signified promotion. Sadeh wanted to personally take command of the force, but Israel Galili forbade it. Galili, too, was worried about assembling so many capable officers in a boat the size of a nutshell and sending it out on a mission never before executed in the country, but he did not bring his weight to bear against the operation.[79] Two days before the operation, Sadeh asked Zvi Spector, one of his golden boys and the apple of his eye, to volunteer for the job. Spector was still limping and clearly would not be able to accompany the men onto land. Nevertheless, he was placed in charge of the operation, even though he was not a seaman and had only two days to absorb the material.

Despite his hesitations, deep down Sadeh did not seem to have been really worried. He was confident that the boys would return hale and hearty. The next day in Tel Aviv he bumped into Joseph Hamburger (Yossi Harel), a seaman serving abroad who happened to be home on leave. He told Yossi that he had missed the chance of a lifetime: too bad that he hadn't come home a few days earlier for then he could have taken command of the boat. The two traveled to Haifa together to watch the sea from the roof of a high building and wait for the return of the Sea Lion. After four days passed with no sight of the boat, fear clutched at Sadeh's heart.

Because of the secrecy of the operation, Sadeh, David Hacohen, Shaul Meirov, Haganah commanders, and members of the JA's political department could not say anything to the men's families. Relatives were left up in the air for months, dangling between hope and despair. They felt that everyone was avoiding them.[80] The British were supposed to officially inform the JA about the loss of the boat, and the Agency was to pass on the information to the families. The British dragged their feet. There was no official notification until October 1942, almost a year and a half after the boat's departure. The JA notified the families that their loved ones had gone missing without a trace while on a valiant mission.[81]

The Haganah was robbed of more capable talents than is reasonable to expect in a sole military operation. Sadeh's habit of singling out, befriending, and cultivating promising young men had played against him this time: he liked to work with the best and the ablest, and the manning of the boat reflected this preference.[82] Only by chance did Meir Davidson, Shlomo Rabinowicz, and Joseph Hamburger—all leading lights in the field companies—not number among the fallen.[83] At one stroke, Sadeh lost a hefty chunk of the Haganah's young elite leadership. The marine company was wiped out along with its instructors, who had been permitted by Sadeh to join the operation.

The loss continues to tease historians: What would the Palmah's command have looked like had these men lived? In fact, what happened was that one echelon of command vanished and another, different from it, sprouted up in its place. The story of the Sea Lion was less the prelude to the history of the Palmah than the closing episode of the period that preceded it.

The Sea Lion's casualties became the Palmah's first heroes before the Palmah actually even existed. The story had all the ingredients of a heroic romance: a daring mission crossing geographical and operational boundaries; crewmen known for their dashing exploits; a cloak of secrecy around the act and the actors; and finally, a veil of mystery that has never been lifted around their disappearance. The last component, more so than the others, seems to have placed the episode in the genre of a never-ending story, an enigma still waiting to be resolved. The speculations have never stopped. One hypothesis is that the boat ran into a submarine. Some accounts described a clash between crewmen and Vichy forces near to shore. Some claimed that the boat and crew had simply sunk. Others said that a few of the men had been captured by the French and carried off to parts unknown. In all of the searches for it, no more was ever dredged up than a pair of khaki shorts embroidered with a Hebrew name and a scouts' belt with three Hebrew letters.[84] The story of the boat was told around Palmah campfires—and could never be told enough. The force had not managed to carry out its mission, yet the myth remained undented. The commando operation was one of the most daring and one of the largest—if not *the* largest—wartime missions of the Jewish Yishuv; it is not surprising that it became legendary. The Palmah needed heroes, especially because of its forced inaction in its early years.

The connecting link between the sea commando and the Palmah was Yitzhak Sadeh. Through him, the crew could be converted into the Palmah's "very own," Yishuv lads who rose above themselves to acts of valor.

The Sea Lion was the first brave myth about the generation bred in Jewish Palestine. Despite the many differences between the boatmen and the Palmah, this was the crucial point. It was not the Maccabees or Bar-Kokhba of long ago, nor Trumpeldor at Tel Hai more recently, but the legendary sea commando with whom the Palmah could most easily identify: they spoke the same modern Hebrew, thought in the same Yishuv terms, breathed the same air. Unlike the myths that sprouted up about the Schutzbund or the Spanish Civil War, the sea commando did not aspire to change the world in far-off places but had volunteered for a mission here and now. It was a tale without pathos, pretension, or bombast, a tale of ordinary lads, except for that one exalted moment.

Chapter 5
British-Jewish "Cooperation"

The years 1941–43 were the most dramatic the Yishuv had ever known. Twice in that brief period the Yishuv faced the threat of destruction, which was averted only by the upheavals of war. The real fear that gripped those at the top, who saw themselves as responsible for the Yishuv's safety and security, trickled down to the broader public. Yet life went on, plying an everyday course as if Rommel's victories in the western desert did not pose an existential threat. Political squabbles continued as if the foe were not knocking on the door of Palestine.

Mapai, the pivotal party of the Yishuv and the Zionist movement, was riven by a twofold dispute. One was a power struggle between the pro-Soviet, leftist, Faction B minority led by Yitzhak Tabenkin—and encompassing about one-third of the party, including part of Kibbutz Me'uhad (KM) and part of the party branch in Tel Aviv—and the moderately socialist party majority, led by Ben-Gurion and Berl Katznelson. The other dispute was over policy, dividing "activists" from "moderates." The activists included the three leaders mentioned above and virtually the entire security establishment. The moderates were party leaders filling important positions in the Histadrut Labor Federation and in the Jewish Agency (JA). The disagreement revolved mainly around the White Paper: whether to keep up the struggle against the stringent British regulations during the war, or to shelve it for the duration

The activists were further split over the question of emphasis: Should the Yishuv urge its young to enlist in the British army against the common foe, or should it create an independent Jewish military force, an "army out of uniform," in Palestine? Some considered the former option supremely important in order to gain know-how and experience and, perhaps, somehow make contact with Jews in Europe; some thought the latter option was vital in order to prepare a fighting force that would one day have to meet the British and Arabs on the battlefield; others, such as Shaul Meirov and Eliyahu Golomb, saw no contradiction between the two. Both courses of action had solid backing. Members of Mapai enlisted in both (although the contingent of Mapai supporters in the KM tended to join the British army, while the left-wing Faction B supporters chose the "army out of uniform").

The young, on the whole, were activists, but they were in a quandary: there was precious little outlet for action. One way around the dilemma was found in "cooperation" with the British; all at once, the hammer and the anvil came together.

As early as 1940, Zionist leaders began to talk to anyone willing to listen in the British regime about the advantages of utilizing the Zionist movement in the fight against Hitler: the movement after all had branches all over Europe and thousands of young people at its disposal, members of He-Halutz who could be used for sabotage or intelligence in Axis-occupied countries. Upon Germany's conquest of western Europe, the British looked on the plan as attractive; they needed intelligence networks. Negotiations were conducted with Admiral John Henry Godfrey, the head of marine intelligence, but the matter was soon referred to Department D, whose function was to erect, foster, and encourage underground movements in the occupied countries. In the labyrinth of British intelligence, this department came under the War Office and Britain's Ministry of Economic Warfare.[1]

Several factors exerted an influence: the Yishuv's political interests, the hope of developing instruments of independent Jewish action, and vague plans to get through to Jews in conquered Europe. The JA leadership emphasized the first aim, while the Haganah Command emphasized the second. Both strove to clinch for the Zionist movement the status of a fighting party in the somewhat naïve hope that symbolic participation in the war might later yield political fruit. They therefore tried to make sure that Yishuv combatants would be under the command of representatives authorized by the JA; that the Haganah Command would have a say about its people taking part in any operation; and that its agents would not be salaried but merely reimbursed for expenses.[2]

The Zionist calf was more eager to suck than the British cow was to suckle: the initiative for cooperation may have emanated from London, but the government of Palestine did not know of it until a rather late stage, nor was it enthusiastic about it. The British in Palestine were convinced that the Zionists were building up a force to be used against them in the future and they were alarmed by any display of Jewish independence. One avenue found for cooperation was intelligence: cloak-and-dagger activities are easy to deny after the fact. The same cannot be said about a readily identifiable military unit. As a result, the Jewish Brigade was established only in 1944 after much shilly-shallying, although cooperation had actually begun four years earlier.

The first cooperative measures took place in the Balkans. In the spring of 1941, after Britain's resounding defeats in Greece and then

Crete, and the emergence of the North African threat, the idea was broached of cooperation in the Middle Eastern arena. In Syria, which was controlled by Vichy France, a network of agents was set up under the young Palestinian Jews Tuvia Arazi and Joseph Fein; it spread propaganda against Germany and for Free France. When a British invasion of Syria and Lebanon appeared imminent, a two-man Palestinian Jewish force was sent to sabotage the Aleppo airport and neutralize a German base that threatened the British from behind. And when the plan came up to take out the refineries in Tripoli, again young Palestinian Jews were sent on reconnaissance.[3]

It was as a part of the British-Yishuv cooperation that the Sea Lion with twenty-four people on board had embarked on its failed mission. The Haganah Command was rather annoyed when various reports about the boat inaccurately attributed the command to the British officer Anthony Palmer (who was there as an observer): the whole beauty of the operation was that it had been planned by Jews and was under Jewish command![4]

The tragedy of the Sea Lion coincided with the initial steps to form the Palmah. From the order that ushered it in, there was no way of knowing that this was the core of a permanently mobilized Yishuv force, directly subordinate to the Haganah High Command and, as things developed, not bound to any particular district. What was unique about the Palmah at this stage was that its company commanders (the first two being Yigal Paicovich and Moshe Dayan) were asked to recruit volunteers for the new force, picking the people that they judged suitable. For their part, the recruits always had to be at the ready, for any mission inside or outside the country, whether "with the British army or against the army."[5] This directive lent the new induction a spirit of dashing adventure. The idea was to create an elite force much like the commando units in the European war arena, whose fame had reached the shores of Palestine.

Based on the reports of the two recruitment officers, the men enlisted in each of the two companies were different. Dayan found it hard to muster veterans of the Arab Rebellion, volunteers who at the time had served in the field companies, or the Jewish Settlement Police (JSP). Some of them had enlisted in the British army, some were filling posts in the Haganah, and some had settled down to civilian life with no desire for additional security work. He thus had to induct novices who were untried in battle.[6] Allon seems to have had more success with veterans. He rounded up young men from the Galilee, the Beisan Valley and the Jezreel Valley, many of whom, he claimed, had served in the field companies.[7]

Amid their efforts to obtain top recruits, Allon and Dayan received an order to supply several dozen men to serve as trackers and scouts for the British army, which was poised to invade Syria.[8] The invasion of Syria went down in Zionist history in two lines of a song: "We'll yet remember under rain of lead/how in Syria marched the Palmah." Judging by the epic lines, the impression was of an entire brigade having been on the march, of having conquered Syria by its own efforts. The truth was less spectacular; had the events not occurred at a turning point in the Palmah's annals, they probably would not have earned more than a footnote in the history of Britain's conquest of Syria and Lebanon. The role of the Jewish scouts was minimal. They drew maps of the region: Allon's platoon reconnoitered the area of Marjayoun and then around the Beaufort Castle. Dayan's platoon reconnoitered the western zone, near the Iskandaron Bridge on Lebanon's coastal road. The entire operation was amateurish. The young Jewish lads from Palestine had never scouted in Lebanon before and had to rely on Arabs who knew the lay of the land and all its trails and wadis. These were smugglers, robbers, or ex-leaders of armed bands.[9]

The mission was two-pronged: first, the scouts acted in enemy territory for about a week, drawing maps, marking alternative routes and bridges, taking note of enemy manpower. Then came the invasion, which was spearheaded by Australian troops. Their directness and simple manners won over the young men of Jewish Palestine who were co-opted to their units. The Australians were to guard the bridges in their zone against French sabotage. Dayan was with the unit guarding the Iskandaron Bridge; Allon was with the unit at the Hardalah Bridge. Both missions turned out to be pointless: the French bombed the coastal road itself south of Iskandaron, thereby hampering the British advance along this axis. Iskandaron Bridge was not blown up, but it became irrelevant. The Hardalah Bridge, in contrast, was held for nearly twenty-four hours by the Australian soldiers and Palestinian recruits. In the end, they were compelled to retreat after the main British force failed to capture Marjayoun. The French blew up the bridge so that it too lost all strategic importance.

The operation won Dayan a hero's glory: when he learned that the French had turned their backs on the bridge he had been sent to guard, he scrounged about for action. On the advice of an Arab scout, he suggested to the Australian commander that the troops capture the nearby police station. The result was that the force got in over its limit. Instead of sleepy local policemen, they found French soldiers armed to the hilt and battling it out. Dayan displayed courage and resourcefulness. He lost an eye. And, ever after, the tale of his one-man assault on the building as he hurled a grenade inside was told around Palmah campfires. Though the British did not decorate him, the Hebrew press crowned him in laurels.[10] Allon did not earn the same distinction. His unit consisted of two Jews—himself and Yitzhak Henkin—and seven Australians. There was not much they could do when dozens of Frenchmen materialized before them with a machine gun. Though they withdrew under heavy fire, they acquitted themselves honorably; Henkin, wounded in the foot, clamped down on his pain on the walk back to the evacuation point at Kleyah. There was, however, no heroic tale here.[11]

Both Dayan and Allon were highly conscious of the operational limitations of the Jewish force in the British attack on Lebanon, which became known as the "invasion of Syria": "We were unprepared"—Allon recounted—"and our contribution even though important was small. Our action received no mention in any order of the day."[12] Both men regarded the necessity for Arab scouts as a Haganah failing.[13]

Neither had any doubt that they could have conducted the operation better than the British—nor were they embarrassed to say so. Dayan, upset that his unit could not carry out the mission and keep open the British advance along the coast, claimed that the failure lay with the orders he had received from the force to which he was attached: had the mission of securing the whole road (!) been in the hands of Palestine's Jews, failure would have been averted.[14]

Similarly, Allon contended that the British had waged the campaign on the Marjayoun front "according to the regular old methods as described in the literature of the First World War,"[15] and thus, even though the Australians had fought bravely, the frontal attack on Beaufort Castle had failed. Before setting out on the campaign, on 7 June 1941, Allon had suggested to the colonel in charge that most of the force come at Marjayoun from behind on the night of the attack and take it by surprise. The British officer had heard him out attentively and patiently, commenting, in typical British fashion, that his suggestions were very interesting indeed but that the campaign plan had already been decided and could not be changed; moving considerable forces to Marjayoun's rear was thus not an option.[16] Allon was convinced that his plan, had it been adopted, would have signaled a breakthrough in the British campaign in the Lebanon Valley, speeding the British army to the large Riaq airport in Syria, some 100 kilometers from the Palestinian border.[17] His military thinking was impressive: he was, after all, young and the sum total of his military experience was restricted to the van. The indirect approach he suggested was advanced and sophisticated, not only in terms of Haganah but also apropos Britain's standing army, as can be gleaned from the colonel's courteous reply.

The conspicuous disparagement of the British army in Dayan's and Allon's reports stemmed from a slew of factors, which, taken all together, boiled down to the prejudice of Eretz Israel. Anti-British education had begun not with the 1939 White Paper but at the onset of the British conquest. Their foreign language, modus operandi, and western-colonial style of rule all rendered the British incomprehensible to the Yishuv. Suspicion of the government, in general, and the West, in particular, coalesced. Moreover, many of the generation bred in Labor Eretz Israel dismissed Britain as an imperialist power—one could only guess at its evil intentions! To top it all off, the young people of the Yishuv had been raised to believe there was *nothing* they could *not* do. Their self-confidence, nurtured by a mixture of ignorance, arrogance, and the daring of youth convinced that they had been born for greatness, ultimately may have been the strongest weapon in the Palmah armory. At the same time, it proved quite a hurdle in the fragile cooperation with the British and a source of much misunderstanding.

In describing how he readied his men for action, Allon added the following: "When the order was given to prepare for action, the platoon assembled to hear words of general explanation from its commander about the anticipated danger to the country from a situation of having the Vichy army on the northern border, about the significance of the invasion, about the value of our participation, as well as general instructions that applied to the whole unit."[18] The importance of fostering motivation, of treating soldiers as equals in a military action, the appeal to their reason and emotions—here, for the first time, we see Allon's intuitive grasp of all of these issues. Young though he was, he was not content with issuing orders. He explained the action's rationale, national importance, and contribution to the course of the war. Like his suggestion to outflank the castle guard from the rear, so his approach to command seems to have come from an innate insight.

Germany's attack on Russia (22 June 1941) marked a new stage in the history of the war, though the repercussions of this stage were not yet felt in Palestine. Soviet defeats in the summers of 1941 and 1942 alarmed the British about a German pincer action with Rommel's troops in the south and German armies possibly breaking through from the Caucasus in the north. Britain's regional military heads were more worried about a German invasion of the Middle East via the Caucasus than an attack by Rommel, and they set policy accordingly.[19] British military circles, especially the intelligence units, were gearing up to evacuate Palestine and Syria willy-nilly and retreat to Iraq or even India.

Jewish-British wartime cooperation followed a regular rhythm, speeding up as the situation deteriorated, slowing down as things relaxed. It was so transparent that staff of the JA's Political Department found cause to regret an emergency's passing: if only the urgency had lasted a little longer, cooperation might have reached great heights.[20] It was no accident that Department D referred to JA-PD representatives, with whom the department was in contact, by the code name of "Friends" and it encompassed all the Zionist bodies: the high commissioner in Palestine and his entire government may have held a different opinion, but the military authorities had no doubt about the loyalty of the Jews in times of trouble. This was not true of the Arabs, many of whom volubly wished for an Axis victory.

Against this background, the British (with Jewish consent) decided to establish two operative programs in case the British actually did quit the region: the Palestine scheme and the Syrian scheme. The former at first was planned as a top-secret network made up of a select few and commanded by Moshe Dayan, who meanwhile had recovered from his wound. Formed at the end of 1941, the network was to set up wireless stations behind German lines to supply the British with intelligence. In 1942, in light of Rommel's advance, the British decided to expand the Palestine Scheme and create also a sabotage network to neutralize vital junctions after their withdrawal. This program, suggested by the Haganah to the British and devised by Yohanan Ratner and Yitzhak Sadeh, served as a flywheel for the Palmah's development.

A network of Palestinian Jews had been active in Syria in 1940 with the aim of spreading anti-German propaganda and disinformation. Its cover was blown by the capture of Tuvia Arazi. Now the British wished to establish an expanded network of saboteurs to move into action in Syria once the Germans conquered that country. It was to disrupt communication lines and strike at strategic transit hubs. An additional body was to act as a fifth column, spreading propaganda and assassinating pro-German local leaders and German agents. It was to be so deep underground as to conceal its actions from civil authorities in both Syria (the French) and Palestine. To this end, Department D required the help of the "Friends" and "their network."[21]

The JA-PD—headed by Reuven Zaslani (Shiloah)—was eager to meet every British request in order to demonstrate the effectiveness of Zionist assistance. But there was no correlation between eagerness and capability. This had already been evident during the invasion of Lebanon, when the Jews were asked to supply reconnaissance and had to resort to Arab scouts. The same thing now happened in Syria, causing problems and tension from the very start. The British wanted to form the Syrian network at once. The Jews had no experience in setting up an espionage network, let alone one outside the country. Thrown together in haste, it foundered initially: it was manned by young Jews who hailed from Syria and whose eastern appearance and knowledge of Arabic was their ticket into the country. It soon transpired, however, that they lacked the military experience and the daring and "chutzpah" of the youth of Eretz Israel. A new tack was called for. In their stead, Palestinian Jews were recruited and trained for action in Syria. The trouble was that training takes time and practice, commodities that the recruits did not have. Amateurism bordering on irresponsibility resulted in sending young men to Syria with hardly any knowledge of Arabic and, in some cases, not even an eastern accent.[22] There was no proper appraisal of the difficulties involved in planting such people in a foreign society with its different culture, lifestyle, religion, and customs. The first attempt to set up a network failed.

In August 1941, Allon reconnoitered in Syria and produced a memorandum to the Haganah Command. His working assumption was that the network had to be built around motivated people, to be chosen according to suitability rather than origin: it is easier to learn a language and get to know a place than to acquire the necessary qualities of a secret agent. He proposed a network equipped with wireless transmitters at four foci: Beirut, Damascus, Aleppo, and Tripoli. The agents would have to assume a local identity and find work while maintaining utter secrecy vis-à-vis the French authorities.[23] In terms of organization and operational methods, his program seems to have been executed.

The first commander of the Syrian scheme was Abdu (Israel Ben Yehuda), who was replaced by Aharon Lishavsky. Allon, the commander of the Palmah's Company A at the time, kept tabs on what was happening in Syria. In the summer of 1941, the faltering Syrian mission was the only serious operation undertaken in the framework of the British-Yishuv cooperation.[24] The JA-PD was thus in a hurry to implement a new Syrian scheme, under a new command. This is how Allon came to head it in January 1942.[25]

Yigal took over a unit suffering from growing pains. Lack of preparation, lack of knowledge, lack of precise instructions had all left their mark. The reports of unit members reflected the idleness of cafe denizens in Beirut and other cities but provided no truly important, strategic information.[26] There were fifteen recruits, five of them unsuitable. Allon sent them home and set about finding replacements and training the unit. There were two training courses for the Syrian platoon,[27] built around imparting general knowledge and drills about the destinations, modus operandi, wireless transmissions, sabotage, cover maintenance, conduct and contact in enemy territory, and so forth.

At the same time there was a growing recognition of the need to train undercover agents to live and operate among Arabs within an Arab environment. The intricacies of undercover work only became clearer after the first aborted experiences: the early agents were rather easy to spot as non-Arabs, or, if they were taken for Arabs, their covers did not match their speech or behavior. A good cover required learning the ins and outs of Islam: all of its factions; all of its different leaders, forms of worship, and liturgies; movements and maxims; eating habits; attitudes toward the elderly and toward women, toward the eminent and the lowly; as well as village speech patterns and customs as opposed to the mores of educated urbanites. In short, undercover work was not merely a matter of assuming a disguise and some typical gestures. It was the internalization of an entire way of life and culture, down to the last detail. It entailed lengthy, intensive study at the hands of professionals able to help the young men become invisible in a traditional, closed society and to guide them through the cultural maze and lurking pitfalls.

Once a trainee had become proficient in Syrian Arabic and acquired a reasonable knowledge of local customs, there was still a number of hurdles to overcome: first, the very penetration of Syria; second, the procurement of appropriate documentation; and third, the setting down of local roots—a steady source of income as an employee or businessman, and a permanent address. Nevertheless, the planting of an agent in Syria was relatively easier than going undercover in Palestinian society. Syrian society was made up of a mélange of peoples and tribes with different traditions, accents, beliefs, and leaders. The extensive construction of British army bases in the war years spurred on population movement in the Fertile Crescent; Iraqis mingled with Houranis, northerners migrated to the south. In this disorderly shake-up of existent frameworks, young men from Palestine were able to find camouflage.

The border was in fact open. Some entered on the strength of a Palestinian Arab passport, some by stealing across. This was neither hard nor particularly dangerous—if caught, the miscreants were simply escorted back to the Palestinian border. Others entered in Allon's car, disguised as British soldiers.[28] Allon himself did not go undercover. His fair locks and blue eyes did not fit the Oriental profile. He entered Syria as an employee of Solel Boneh, the large Histadrut construction company. Agents, too, worked for Solel Boneh, which was prepared to hire young "Houranis" without asking too many questions. The work furnished the young men with an opportunity to gain experience, make Arab friends, and don the credible cover of a laborer who had migrated for economic reasons. Solel Boneh also served as the conduit for the transfer of necessary operating funds to Syria: among the many payments remitted to the company by various British authorities, there was money for the Syrian platoon.[29]

As for documents, Allon chose not to accept forgeries from the British because he was worried about leaks, especially as the forgers were generally Arabs. He insisted that his men rely on their own guile to obtain "authentic" documents. It was a long, painstaking, and often risky process, and by November 1942, only twelve of them had managed to secure reliable papers.[30] Allon seems to have felt that he cared more about the men's personal safety than did the British, that their main concern was the mission's tactical success.

From the start, relations between the Jewish "Friends" and British officers were politically guarded even if on the personal level they were occasionally good. The British wanted help and they wanted it immediately, particularly after their disgraceful surrender to the Japanese in Singapore in February 1942. Sabotage and intelligence work behind enemy lines looked like an enticing way to make up for this military fiasco. To bother about safeguarding the lives of a number of Palestinian Jews when the blood of thousands of Englishmen was being spilled in the war did not strike them as a top priority. They pressed for the urgent implementation of the Syrian and Palestinian schemes; if training were warranted, it was to be operational—the use of wireless, sabotage, identifying enemy objectives, and so forth—strictly military functions. Questions of cover and safety were secondary.[31] The British did not plan on long-term cooperation; they wanted an immediate response to a potentially downhill situation. As far as they were concerned, the cooperation's plans were to be operational—if at all—by the summer of 1943.[32] As a result, they were always on their guard. They tried to maintain control over what was going on, they were worried by signs of independent Jewish action, and they wavered between cooperation and their basic suspicion of the Yishuv's Jews, none of which was unnatural for a party that had stopped being an ally yet had entered willy-nilly into a new sort of coupling. At the height of the cooperation honeymoon in the spring of 1942—with the adoption of Ratner's broad plan to mark sabotage and commando targets so as to thwart German forces in their conquest of the country and strike at strategic points after the conquest—P. T. Wilson, the general in charge of the entire operation and on the whole considered a friend by the Jews, wrote: "I was warned when I came to Palestine that if you gave the [Jewish] Agency an inch, they took an ell. It seems unfortunately to be true."[33]

Without a doubt, the British assumption that the Jews were trying to exploit the situation to their own advantage had a basis. Still, as an ally cooperating in times of trouble, the British overreacted to any departure from written instructions. Invited to Mishmar Ha-Emek to view the Palmah's first passing-out ceremony (at the end of basic training), Wilson, present for the lowering of the blue-and-white flag, saw it as no less than an expression of "fevered nationalism," against which Allied forces were fighting Germany. He thought it proper to condemn sharply the JA's inculcation of the young and warn that the Zionist project would meet a bitter end if it embarked on the road of conquest in the Levant.[34] Given the balance of forces at the time and the mood of the young, the assertion was highly exaggerated. Nor was it entirely comprehensible in view of his brief acquaintance with the realities of Palestine. He seems to have been fed information by Mandate officials and British officers hostile to the idea of a Jewish National Home.[35] Shertok, the head of the JA-PD, responded that it was true that "the poor are generally expected to be humble and swallow their pride, but why is it that the Union Jack is regarded as a perfectly healthy expression of patriotic feeling whereas our White and Blue is resented as a symbol of 'fevered nationalism'?"[36] Wilson, as was said earlier, was considered open-minded and favorably disposed to the Zionist enterprise. This was probably why he was removed from both his post and Palestine within a few months.[37]

Beyond the basic suspicion, however, there was the political problem. Whenever the British military authorities, especially the intelligence service, came up with a plan for cooperation, the British political authorities, local and at home, were quick to clip its wings. Even with the outcome of the war still uncertain, before the battle of el-Alamein, the initiators of the Palestine scheme were asked to curtail it. The JA-PD's attempts to break through the highly curbed frameworks led to a notice that to cross the line was to endanger cooperation as a whole. A benign officer explained to Reuven Zaslany: "When you realize that our preparations in Palestine are largely to meet an eventuality that will probably never materialize, you understand why major policy cannot be sacrificed for such preparations."[38]

To this pattern of relations Allon brought his own basic assumptions and soon found himself at loggerheads with the British. The British had earmarked sabotage and intelligence missions for the Syrian platoon, with the emphasis on the latter. Allon, in contrast, held that "the function that we set ourselves was first of all to hurt the enemy as much as possible."[39] Not only was this a different definition of the aims, but graver still, it was a sign of an attempt to independent action. Moreover, Allon seems to have viewed the problem of Syria through the prism of Palestine. Reports from agents in the Syrian scheme dealt with overheard cafe conversations about armed bands, the attitudes of locals to Zionism, and other topics that may have been interesting to the JA-PD but were of dubious use to the British.[40] Having a different goal and thinking in terms of the continuation of the network to the Yishuv's benefit even should the British decide to dissolve it, Allon sought to assure the platoon's independence. The issue of procuring documentation became, for him, an instrument to guarantee that his men would not have to rely on the British. For the same reason, apparently, he refused to supply the names of his undercover agents to the British officer with whom he worked.[41] Yet another sign of independence was the wireless course given to the platoon's members at Tel Aviv's Exhibition Grounds;

the British partners learned of it only when they were asked to see to the release of a wireless operator apprehended on a random police patrol.⁴²

So long as the Middle East campaign in the sands of el-Alamein remained undecided, the British were prepared to resign themselves to Allon's conduct. More importantly, they showed understanding and patience for the approach of the JA-PD, which claimed that it—not the British—had the command of Zionist forces.

Allon held that he was answerable to the Haganah or, at worst, to the JA-PD. This was not so for Moshe Dayan, the commander of the corresponding Palestine Scheme: Dayan believed that if and when Germany conquered the country, the network could be effective only if it was directly connected to the British and under British command. He took pains to obtain the rank of a British officer, which was totally unacceptable to Allon. The two had ripping arguments about the question of authority.⁴³ As far as Allon was concerned, cooperation with the British was an accidental stage in the development of an independent Jewish military force. Dayan invested less energy in guarding the independence of such a force, nor, it seems, did he see any special value in it.

As mentioned earlier, prior to the battle of el-Alamein, relations were highly correct. If the British had any reservations about Allon's functioning or the Syrian scheme they kept these to themselves. On 14 November 1942 (that is, a few days after the mop-up in the western desert) three British officers responsible for the Syrian scheme met with Shaul Meirov to exchange views and all pronounced the scheme good, necessary, and worthy of continuation. Their favorable attitude to Allon came across in the discussion. In fact, they were prepared to assign him a deputy.⁴⁴

Within a few months the entire picture changed. Allon described the unfolding of events two years later at a quasi-summing up of cooperation at the JA-PD. He pinned the blame for deteriorating relations on a British officer, Captain P. G. Francis, who had replaced the sympathetic Hammond. Francis, Yigal said, had made it his cause to smash the platoon's independence, provoking Allon in order to force him to accept British authority. Nor was the problem solved when Francis was replaced by another officer, Charles Hewer, who treated the Jews more kindly. Hewer may have been pleasant, but—according to Allon—the basic drift remained the same: gone were the days when the British were prepared to see the Jews as allies under a semi-autonomous command.⁴⁵

As the British partners saw it, Allon's comportment amounted to a severe breach of military discipline. Major J. M. Collard, the senior officer in charge of the Syrian scheme, complained that Allon acted contrary to his instructions, making no attempt to cooperate with British officers.⁴⁶ Collard was so frustrated that he demanded that Allon, who had been hospitalized then for surgery (to set his collarbone), not be returned to the platoon command. He was to be replaced by Abdu (March 1943).[47] The JA-PD agreed.

Precisely at that time, the British formally and courteously informed the JA-PD in writing of the dissolution of the Palestine scheme.[48] Cooperation with the Palmah was also terminated.[49] Only the Syrian scheme continued to function. Circumstances had changed and the British now wished to place the Syrian network on a different footing. Concomitant with the change in the command of the Scheme, it was to be reduced to a skeletal framework and assigned manpower supplements as needed.[50]

A few months later, following disagreements between Abdu and Hewer, things were made explicit. Major Gardner wrote to Shaul Meirov: "The man in operational charge of the party is Charles Hewer, and this must admitted." The status of every person in the Syrian platoon, he noted, was identical to that of a soldier on active service, and "any act of indiscipline or disobedience on his part—is misconduct by him, for which he can be dismissed without notice and without compensation."[51] This the Haganah refused to accept.

The dispute over authority was compounded by disagreement over the unit's management. The young people from Eretz Israel spent extended periods in foreign parts, cut off from home, family, and a supportive environment, and forced into protracted inaction—a predicament that caused no few complications. Allon was inclined to show understanding and, to relieve the pressure, allowed them home leave. The British, in contrast, were used to spending years in foreign service and regarded this as an indulgence: just as a British soldier did not sail home every few months, so a Palestinian soldier in Syria was not entitled to leave his post! In some cases, apparently, the recruits abused the privilege of leave: they delayed their return to Syria on one pretext or another, idling away their time at home.[52] The question of control was exacerbated once it became clear that the platoon was not to be included in active operations. Inaction affected morale and sometimes produced inappropriate behavior. Matters were made worse by arguments over money: the JA-PD was emphatic that the men serving in the framework of cooperation receive no wages[53] in order to highlight the uniqueness of the lads of Eretz Israel vis-à-vis other agents in British service. The fact is that although members of the Syrian scheme did not receive direct payment their families in Palestine did receive a monthly stipend. The British regarded this as a regular salary for all intents and purposes; it was normal practice for army people.[54] The British acquiesced in demands they considered reasonable, such as severance pay, but firmly rejected the idea of global payments for clothing or expenses. They insisted that the recruits find work or some sort of occupation as part of their cover and live at the standard of Syria's lower class.[55] The Palestinian recruits found it hard to comply with this demand.

Allon did treat his men indulgently. To them, he was somewhere in between a father figure and a priest hearing confession, a psychologist and a nanny. There was an element of dependency in their attitude to him, which they expressed in uninhibited admiration. The special relationship is illuminated by their farewell greeting to him in the platoon newsletter, which seems to have appeared only once and at Allon's initiative: "We are forced to part formally and dryly from the friend who guided us and took care of us, from the commander who raised us up from the rubbish pits to the pinnacle of recognition, from the pillar of light that walked before us for a whole year."[56] Yigal used the close personal relations he fostered to inspire Zionist motivation and a sense of national responsibility. These did not always stand up to the test. But without them, it is doubtful that the platoon could have endured. For many of the men, the encounter with Allon was *the* formative factor that changed their lives.[57] For some, the dependency and reliance lasted for years, with them paying visits to his home in Tel Aviv as if to a father.[58]

Allon's response to the dependency was an increased sense of responsibility. Like a compassionate father rather than a tough commander, he was alert to their problems and difficulties. He handled their personal problems as if they were part of a commander's functions. Similarly, he tended to shield them from criticism. At the JA-PD summing-up of cooperation in 1944, the Haganah liaison officer David Hacohen expressed himself in terms of implied criticism of the platoon's members. Fed up with inaction, some had left their Syrian posts and taken frequent leaves in Palestine, he said, adding that in consequence, the platoon had been terminated in the summer of 1943. To avert humiliation, the JA-PD had decided to cease its operations and had notified the British accordingly.[59] Reuven Zaslany, in his letter to his British counterpart, Major Gardner, had requested that the Syrian scheme be cancelled, noting, on the one hand, that there was slim chance of the platoon ever being used since the danger on the Middle Eastern front had passed. On the other hand, Zaslany described the blow to morale (a euphemism for extended leaves, card playing, and the squandering of funds) that would come once the men realized they would not see any real action.[60] Allon rushed to his men's defense, although he knew very well that the moderate criticism was based on fact. The only reason for the failure, he said, was the attitude of the British, who were determined to liquidate the scheme because of its independent spirit. On financial matters, he took the defensive, arguing that during his stint as unit commander he had tried to impress upon the men the importance of making do with little, "but since their conditions were easy at the start, it was difficult for them to get used to harder conditions later."[61]

The spat between Allon and Zaslany sheds light on the dissension between the Haganah's political and military controllers—the JA-PD and the operational cadre. The political level sought to cultivate relations with the British. The operational echelons sought to foster an image of treacherous Albion. Major Gardner complained that whenever he met with Shaul Meirov or David Hacohen they were soon in accord, but whenever he met with the military levels it felt like a contest of rivals.[62] "Let us remember"—Allon wrote in a piece on cooperation—"we are partners in this war against a common enemy. But this partner of ours is also sometimes our enemy, and we have to know when he is with us and when he is our foe."[63] In his eyes, the importance of the Syrian platoon was the training it offered in advent of the struggle to come in the foreseeable future.[64]

These variant positions affected the end result of cooperation. For example, the Palmah pilfered weapons from the British intelligence school on Mount Carmel. The JA-PD had no doubt that the rash act had been one of the factors in souring relations with the British partners and ending cooperation. The Haganah, however, regarded the deed as a valuable contribution to the defense forces. At the same time, the Haganah, especially Galili, who felt responsible for the men, resented the cavalier British attitude toward endangering the lives of recruits to the cooperation's "business." He had already voiced an objection at the end of 1942 and, in protest, had asked to be released from "the business of David," that is, of Hacohen and Moshe Dayan.[65]

Whether by chance or otherwise, the JA-PD faithfully represented the stance of Mapai's majority, especially that of Ben-Gurion. The JA-PD did not share Galili's opinion of the British or of cooperation, and the differences immediately donned political garb: just as the Palmah was the favorite child of the Kibbutz Me'uhad, so cooperation—like enlistment into the British army—came to symbolize identification with the Mapai majority.

The differences between the "Haganah Party" and the JA-PD did not reach open confrontation, although neither side was at ease: the former stressed the JA-PD's irresponsibility about its commitments; the latter stressed the undoing of cooperation because of short-sightedness.[66] In the course of time, particularly at the second level of the Haganah command, the differences became part of a larger discussion, the question of a uniformed versus a non-uniformed army. Was the military force meant to score political points or to win on the battlefield? This was the key issue. The young, such as Allon, took a simplistic view. There was none of the sophistication that marked Golomb's, or even Galili's, multifaceted approach. Allon regarded the military force as a means to decide the issue of Palestine. He foresaw an inevitable clash with the country's Arabs and wanted to prepare for it. This conception was a legacy of the Arab Rebellion, when Jewish-Arab confrontation became the dominant experience of his life. High politics and extramilitary considerations were foreign to his way of thinking. In this respect, he faithfully represented the Haganah's young cadre.

Allon commanded the Syrian platoon for little more than a year. He planned its deployment and its modus operandi, and to a large extent he was responsible for broadening the concept of undercover work and the training program. He also had an influential input on the rules of undercover work. It was he who determined that the network was not to get mixed up in Zionist activity or with local Jewry,[67] a rule that was broken in the 1950s with dire consequences (for example, Operation Susannah in Egypt, which led to the Lavon Affair). The Palmah's Arab platoon, which still had numerous exploits before it, was an outgrowth of the Syrian platoon, its accomplishments, and its lessons. Beyond all this, Allon proved himself a leader of men, even if their education and mentality differed from his—he was able to mold disparate individuals into a highly motivated, tightly knit group prepared to make the ultimate sacrifice.

In a sense, the Syrian scheme, like its sister Palestine scheme, was an aborted option. As a result, it could not test the virtues of the men and the organization, only their weaknesses. Allon did not return from Syria in glory. In fact, the British dismissed him. The Haganah Command does not seem to have attached any importance to the British opinion of him. As far as is known, no one considered his dismissal a black mark. Dayan, who wholeheartedly supported the cooperation, finished his assignment in the Palestine network with thanks from the British.[68] Allon received a sharp reprimand. Once more, Allon's strength in the affair came to the fore at the military level. Here, he showed himself adaptable and remarkably capable of learning and improvisation. But in the sensitive sphere of relations with partners-rivals such as the British, he again displayed none of the sophistication warranted by the situation. As in the battle with the PICA, as in the "water war" with Ginossar's Arab neighbors, he took a head-on tack, willing the outcome to be decided by force. His aggressive antagonism toward anyone beyond the ken of his social-political identification—an approach that had succeeded both against the PICA and his Arab neighbors—led to his relative failure in the Syrian episode. However, in a society that places utter, unalloyed allegiance at the top of its scale of values, Allon's shaky diplomacy was actually considered an advantage.

It was quite some time before he recovered from the surgery on his shoulder (at Hadassah Hospital on Mount Scopus in Jerusalem in February 1943). In June of that year, he was still in rehabilitation. Ginossar's secretariat took this opportunity to apply to the Histadrut's Central Appeals Committee on member recruitment and firmly demand the return of Ginossar's two members, Yigal and Sini (who had served in Dayan's network). The farm situation was desperate, so much so that the kibbutz had asked another, veteran kibbutz to allocate it a member for key jobs at Ginossar. A copy of the letter was sent to Israel Galili and the matter seems to have ended there,[69] for Allon did not return home. Instead, straight after his recuperation, he was assigned to the Palmah's headquarters.

Chapter 6
The Palmah: Beginnings

Allon was not reckoned among the Palmah's founders. According to Galili, the Palmah was the brainchild of several senior Haganah figures in the turbulent spring of 1940 after France fell to Germany. The swift surrender of the Low Countries and France was alarming: it looked as if nothing could stand in Germany's way. There was a real and present danger—and it was on the doorstop. The idea of recruiting a standing force had been bandied about by the Haganah and voiced by Golomb[1] since the period of the field companies. It now received new validity.

The faith in an independent Jewish force to meet the danger did not stem from military logic: if British troops were to withdraw from Palestine, how could a Jewish force withstand German might, and over time at that? But there is no arguing with faith, especially as it had proved an enduring fount of moral strength and prudent action. Its roots lay not in the military sphere, but in the basic stance and actions of the Yishuv's Labor movement from its inception: Palestine's Jews could not rely on British gentiles; they had to do everything themselves.

Because of political opposition, the Palmah was established only a year later, in the spring of 1941, coinciding with Germany's first offensive in the western desert. It was born in anxiety, over the approach of the war front to Palestine's still waters. The prospect of Britain withdrawing its army was ominous. What was to be done? The question was discussed in various frameworks from early on in 1942. At the Kibbutz Me'uhad Council (KMC) at Givat Brenner in April 1942, devoted largely to security,[2] Golomb spelled out the need to prepare for the country's defense against possible invasion. He added that the consolidation of a sizable Jewish force could be a key factor in Britain's decision not to evacuate Palestine.[3] This guarded optimism about the positive influence of a Jewish defense force soon petered out. From the end of May 1942 onward, the anxiety bordered on hysteria: the Germans launched an offensive and within weeks, Tubruk—the fortress between the sea and the desert, the symbol of staunch British resistance—fell to Rommel's troops (21 June 1942). On 29 June, the Germans took Marsa Matruh in Egypt and the road to Alexandria appeared clear. The British counteroffensive was thwarted, and they retreated to el-Almein.

July 1942 found the Yishuv in the grip of keen fear. Never before had the Jews so well understood their dependence on British defense, now that they were faced with the prospect of being abandoned by them. On 1 July, a top-level delegation comprising representatives of the Vaad Leumi (the National Committee, which was the title of the National Council of the Jews of Palestine), Moshe Shertok, the head of the JA-PD, and Eliyahu Golomb, the head of the Haganah, presented itself to High Commissioner Harold McMichael. They were resolute and dignified: they did not wail, they did not plead, they made concrete demands for bolstering the Yishuv's fighting capability. McMichael was extremely courteous, funereal almost, but he made no promises. When the delegation laid before him its fears of an Arab attack on the Yishuv in the event of a German invasion, he replied that not all Arabs were cut of the same cloth, that there were decent Arabs too; altogether, the Jews would do well to desist from incitement with talk of a Jewish army, a Jewish state, a Jewish commonwealth (a seeming allusion to the Biltmore Program approved in May 1942).[4] "I must admit that we did not sense much sympathy during the conversation," Golomb commented dryly afterward.[5] In the end, the British agreed to fortify the country's borders in the south, which they had not done earlier. But they were in no great hurry: "As of today, the border is still open," Galili warned some days later.[6]

The high commissioner also met with two members of the National Committee, Yitzhak Ben-Zvi and Avraham Katznelson, on their own. Though it is not known what went on, the meeting must have been dramatic. The Yishuv's leaders seem to have learned from informal chats between Haganah personnel, JA-PD figures, and British officers, who were possessed by undisguised panic, that the British meant to quit the region.[7] Apparently the question of a British evacuation was discussed at this meeting with the commissioner, and when the substance of the discussion was disclosed, it raised a furor. Totally unauthorized, the two respectable leaders proposed to the high commissioner that he declare Palestine a demilitarized zone in the advent of a British retreat, in the hope of ensuring the Yishuv's survival. One account has it that they sought to secure prisoner-of-war status under Red Cross protection for Palestine's Jews; the British were to announce that if the Germans harmed Palestine's Jews, the British would retaliate against German POWs. Underlying the request was the assumption that it would be worth the Germans' while to leave the Yishuv alone since it could prove useful to their war machine.[8] News of the meeting infuriated Mapai's activists. They saw it as a sign of panic, of an incipient readiness to collaborate with the Nazis in case of conquest, and of the Yishuv's humiliation before the British, as if the Jews were prepared not to fight the Germans so long as they could save their own skins.⁹

The episode exposed the prevalent mood of a considerable part of the Yishuv. When Jewish community leaders under Nazi conquest are judged and found wanting for having misunderstood Germany's intentions, for their futile attempts to conduct talks with the Germans, and for their pathetic, naïve belief that by proving useful to the German war machine they could at least save the community's young—one would do well to remember the positions of the Yishuv's leaders when they feared a similar fate.

The existential dangers hovering over the Yishuv also produced denial. At a Kibbutz Yagur assembly, members objected: "Why sow terror? One can no longer listen to this style of dread!"¹⁰ Many perceived the Germans as rational people one could talk to. Some were of the opinion that the German attitude differentiated between Diaspora Jews and Palestinian Jews: "There are those who say they hate only Diaspora Jews, but Jewish workers in Palestine—no way"!¹¹

Two additional suggestions reflected the desire to protect and preserve the core of the Yishuv for the postwar period. One stemmed from Haganah personnel and spoke of the Yishuv's youth retreating together with the British army. If those remaining in Palestine were doomed, it was better that the fighting force be saved for the ongoing struggle and the country's reconquest when the time came.¹² The other spoke of evacuating women and children from the country, to save at least the noncombatants.¹³

Ultimately, all of the proposals were abandoned. A sense that there was no alternative gradually sank in; it was conscious and pervasive. Given the previous instances of British retreat around the world, there was little hope that in the chaos of withdrawal and the evacuation of British personnel the army would spare logistic resources and organizational manpower for the local population. Besides, there was the basic question—evacuation to where? Where, in this colossal, worldwide shake-up, could be considered a safe haven?

The more immediate and concrete fear was that British withdrawal would unleash an attack by Palestine's Arabs on the Yishuv. The High Command believed that the Arabs were biding their time to settle accounts from the Arab Rebellion.¹⁴ The Nazis were considered a mythological enemy, virtually on the scale of natural elements; the very thought of a contest with them was grasped in mythological terms. In contrast, the Arabs were a familiar, known quantity; against them, conventional defense was feasible.¹⁵ Apprehensions about the domestic foe added impetus to the idea of creating the nucleus of an independent Jewish force.

The Yishuv's leadership and the Haganah Command were well aware that there was little chance of their succeeding, where the British had failed, against German forces. It was equally clear that the country's geography, lacking broad expanses or strategic depth, made it impossible to wage partisan warfare after the Soviet or Yugoslavian models.[16] The intention was "to create an actual line of defense and hope to hold it."[17] The Yishuv's forces were to concentrate in the region of Mount Carmel, a natural fortress. The British were to help with massive fortification and provide anti-aircraft capability, which had proved effective against Italy's bombing of Haifa. This area, it was hoped, with Allied help would be able to hold out for several months until the British retook Palestine. This is how Allon described the plan a few years later, adding: "It was a realistic plan, much more realistic than Tubruk and its sand dunes, which were exposed to enemy aircraft."[18]

The plan was delegated to Yitzhak Sadeh, Yohanan Ratner, and Von Friedman (Avisar),[19] and Galili spun a mythological image around it: it was to be "a 'Musa Dag,' a Masada."[20] Allon assessment aside, at the time its planners seem to have regarded it as a last stand, a bastion doomed to extinction, a flaming descent into hell, like the historic Masada. Thus, when news came of the Warsaw Ghetto uprising in the spring of 1943, Eliyahu Golomb saw fit to remark: "That's the sort of stand we thought about when there was talk of an imminent invasion of Palestine."[21]

Attesting to the plan's desperation and symbolism is the fact that when Germany did stand at the gates of Egypt, and contingency measures against invasion were vital, the line of retreat to the Carmel region was not put into motion. Instead, it was decided not to desert a single populated site, a single settlement point, nor to evacuate women and children; the Yishuv was to prepare for all-out defense, fighting for every inch of the land.[22]

In the end, the Yishuv was not put to the supreme test. There was no German invasion. But the discussions about it are indicative of the public mood, public reaction, and public leadership in that anxious period. The leaders were divided according to different readings of the situation. Only certain cadres, particularly those connected with the Haganah, dared gaze into the abyss and see possible annihilation. They wanted to make sure that the destruction be remembered as a lesson in valor, a testimony to the dauntless spirit of the "new Jew," falling in battle against impossible odds. That, in a nutshell, was the Carmel plan.

The summer of 1942 went down in the history of the Yishuv as a duel between the ridiculous and the sublime. The dispatch of the Palmah's Company A to Negba and Dorot to defend the Negev against Rommel's armored corps might have come from the theater of the absurd. The company was commanded by Zalman Mart, with subunits under Aharonchik Spector, Assaf Simhoni, and Nahum Sarig. That summer, the company marked the completion of two months of training with a trek in the Huleh Valley, capped by an inter-unit match for the volleyball championship. Ten minutes before the game's end, with Sarig's unit clearly in the lead, a car drove up to deposit Giora Shinan of Afikim. Shinan and Sarig conferred in hushed tones. Then, Sarig approached Sini Azaryahu, who was the captain of his team, to tell him that the game had to be stopped and the men had to fall into formation. Sini remonstrated: another ten minutes and the unit will have won! Sarig stood his ground. The game was stopped, the men fell in, and Shinan, introduced as a member of the Haganah High Command—a mysterious and awe-inspiring title—announced that Rommel had broken through Egyptian lines and the British were on the retreat. The High Command had therefore decided to send Company A to the Negev to stop the Germans. The men understood the urgency when they heard Shinan explain that they were to leave the next morning by vehicle: the Haganah did not spend money on transportation unless there was a good reason! The rest of the day was devoted to preparations. Toward evening, the peppy defenders decided to celebrate the dramatic turn of events and someone drove off to Metullah to fetch a few bottles of wine. Amid singing and merrymaking, one of the commanders got plastered and tottered about, shouting: "We're going to stop Rommel, we're going to stop Rommel!"[23] But there was disappointment in store: owing to the Haganah's logistic problems, the company did not receive rifle issues before setting out. It went down to the Negev without weapons or provisions. These caught up with the company ten days later. The men took this as a slight to the fighting unit and were resentful. They had answered the call, and they were repaid with cavalier treatment. No logistic reasons in the world could mollify them.[24] The incident, in time, served as one of many examples of the High Command's perceived hassling of the Palmah from the very start.[25]

The episode took its place in the Palmah's mythology via a line of the same song that converted the British action in Syria, which had been joined by a number of future Palmahniks, into a bona fide Palmah operation: "When a small company was sent to the Negev/With sticks instead of rifles." The focus was on the rifles. No one bothered to ask how it was that a company of 120 men, with or without rifles, had been sent to stop Rommel's tanks. The very idea that a Palmah company, no matter how well-trained (and Company A was not), could face off successfully against German troops was not only absurd but suicidal! The High Command apparently regarded it as a desperate attempt to stem a dam with a finger! But this was not how the young volunteers saw it: dispatched to the Negev, not one raised any doubts or wondered out loud about the sense or chances of the operation. They greeted the mission with enthusiasm, just as the twenty-three Jewish volunteers on the Sea Lion had welcomed their ill-fated mission.

The summer of 1942 was traumatic in all of the arenas of war. The swift German progress on the Russian front was no less astounding or alarming than Rommel's successes. At summer's end, however, the German offensive had reached its limit: at Stalingrad, near the Volga, Germany's troops were stopped; in the western desert, under General Montgomery's new command, the British retreat was halted. Temporary stability on the war fronts provided the Yishuv's security planners with a respite. They were now able to think in terms of a year or two rather than days or weeks.

The two major problems were recruitment and the Palmah's material maintenance. The Jewish Agency (JA) Executive and the National Committee had issued a first conscription order in May 1941, drafting all single people between the ages of twenty and thirty into the British army. Until then, some eight thousand Palestinian Jews had enlisted spontaneously. The volunteer spirit rose and fell with the tensions of war.

Enlistment in the British army dwindled owing to disillusionment as the young idealists wishing to serve their people realized they could expect no more than service job assignments. In addition, Britain's anti-Zionist policy was a deterrent. Especially rankling was its immigration policy, denying Jewish refugees from war-torn Europe the safe haven they sought in Palestine.

The end of 1940 had seen the shipping incidents involving the *Patria* and the *Atlantic*. In early 1944, these were compounded by the *Struma* affair, in which a refugee ship sank in the Black Sea, exposing Britain's callous, obtuse policy regarding Jewish refugees. Yet another expression of Britain's anti-Zionist policy was its refusal to form Jewish battalions under a Jewish flag, as the JA demanded. Taken all together, these factors took the shine out of enlistment.

But, as in everything else in the Yishuv then, politics also entered the equation. In the KM, stress was placed on the independent Jewish force, which was not to be abandoned in favor of British conscription. Soon enough, Mapai's Faction B, which was part of the Left, evinced reservations about signing up with the British army. Mapai's majority, however—especially the members of the KM (some 40 percent of which belonged to this majority)—came to regard British conscription as the hallmark of their unique activism.

The choice between the British army or the Palmah thus became a symbol of political identity. To complicate matters even more, many supporters of the KM leadership chose to fight the Nazis, while many loyal members of Mapai chose to enlist in the Palmah. The identity lines were crossed in both directions, according to the dictates of one's heart or the hand of chance.

The body to suffer most from dwindling ranks upon conscription was the Haganah. Its people were the most obvious candidates. As the volunteer downpour thinned to a drizzle, the Yishuv leadership found itself embarrassed: it had been in the habit of proclaiming the Yishuv's readiness to volunteer en masse. Voices now clamored for the Haganah's enlistment in the British army, rank and file. The Palmah too suffered from a drop in volunteers in this period.[26] Despite resentment of Britain and its policies, there was good reason to enlist in the British army, especially on moral grounds to help fight Hitler. For many of the young, who should have constituted the Palmah's natural reserve, this was enough.

Haganah's personnel and the advocates of British conscription thus found themselves at odds. The heads of the Haganah, especially Eliyahu Golomb, had no interest in a controversy over which army to join, whether "in uniform or out of uniform." He supported both. Both, to him, were complementary arms of a Jewish defense force. Nor did Tabenkin seek controversy; he considered it superfluous and damaging to the activist camp. But from the next level down, identification with one of the arms—the Haganah—had already spawned animosity toward the other—the volunteers for the British army. The bad feelings derived largely from the sense of weakness and the competition for a bite of the same "poor man's lamb."

The controversy engendered an "us" versus "them" mentality. Rather than solidarity against the majority who dodged service, the two recruitment arms experienced a conflict of interests over manpower. The weapons used against the persistent call to draft the entire force into the British army included a carefully fostered self-importance and sense of higher values, a touted superiority over British army conscripts, and an emphasis on "we, we"—which was exaggerated and often unjustified. These were also weapons against their own despair in view of the Yishuv's overall apathy to the war effort.

The conscription orders made a distinction based on age: conscripts in their twenties were meant to join the British army; those from seventeen to nineteen were to assume various national tasks in autonomous, Jewish local frameworks. Some of the Haganah's commanders wanted to keep the younger element in the country as its only remaining manpower pool for its own inducted force. They were to fill settlement functions and join the "non-uniformed" formations.

A struggle revolved around the nineteen-year-olds: which military body was to get them?[27] It was suggested, apparently by Golomb, that two hundred or even four hundred Palmahniks join the British army.[28] The tussle to keep nineteen-year-olds for the Palmah and to prevent manpower losses from the Palmah to the British army was at the root of the discussions on the Palmah's future in the summer and autumn of 1942.

The major concern about the Palmah's future regarded its financing after the period of cooperation with the British ended. To this end, a proposal was made to integrate the Palmah into the kibbutzim of Labor settlement. As far as is known, Yitzhak Tabenkin was the first to broach the idea. By May 1942, Galili had already spoken of the new arrangement as a fait accompli: "The Palmah will be enlarged to fifteen hundred people. The personnel will have to support themselves by working."[29]

No fanfare accompanied the Palmah's absorption into the KM kibbutzim. It was virtually imperceptible. At the height of anxiety about a German invasion, the KMC at Ein Harod (5 July 1942) adopted a vague decision, one of many relating to the Yishuv's defense: "The Kibbutz Council announces the readiness of Kibbutz Me'uhad Movement settlements to absorb the special security companies standing guard over the country."[30] The decision enabled Palmah companies to stay on the kibbutzim and formalize the status quo since, earlier too, its bases had been on kibbutzim or in bordering woodlands. The difference was that now Palmah members had to work as well: they were supposed to train for sixteen days a month and spend the rest of their time working for their living.

The KMC at Kibbutz Naan made the decision binding (21–23 September 1942) and the movement issued a loan to the Histadrut Labor Federation for the Palmah's upkeep. Financially, this placed a burden on each and every kibbutz. Tabenkin summed up the situation in a spirit appropriate to the occasion: "If we emerge from the war whole, we will get our money's worth from the Haganah one day, and if we do not emerge whole—it is not this money that we will necessarily be needing . . . *meanwhile the Palmah will exist!*"[31]

The decision, as said, merely sanctioned an existing situation. A temporary arrangement was codified, and an emergency measure became an integral part of kibbutz life.

The lodging of the Palmah units in kibbutzim was not greeted enthusiastically by the recruits. Conscription did not take off. All of the estimates about inducting thousands of volunteers into the Palmah within three months proved overly optimistic. At this moment, with the Palmah's "work and training camps" in crisis for lack of numbers, opposition reared from within: the veteran core of Palmah recruits showed signs of malcontent. They had enlisted to form an autonomous, well-trained Jewish force to serve at home and defend the Yishuv when necessary. They found themselves frustrated by inaction, sunk in kibbutz life, stripped of any sense of military achievement. Moreover, there was only a slim chance of their ever seeing any real action. They lost their sense of purpose, their self-esteem, just as news began filtering in about the extermination of European Jewry. The Yishuv's conscripts in the British army felt similarly. They had bitter, angry words about their inane tasks, the waste of time, and the lack of purpose. But those who had sworn allegiance to His Majesty could not leave; they were forced to resign themselves to the gray, depressing situation. In this respect, the members of Palmah were better off: they could vote with their feet. They could find a reason to return home or—more commonly—to enlist in the British army, where at least a soldier was a soldier rather than a farm laborer with military pretensions.

Galili was not surprised. He had foreseen the discontent when the idea of a "work and training camp" first came up. He thus began to look for a way to make a virtue of necessity, in the sacred tradition of the Labor movement. He put forth the idea that the "work and training camps" were more than an empirical solution to the prosaic problem of keeping manpower on hand; they had inherent value: "In my eyes, the idea of work and training is an exciting idea," he said, "[and] the hankerings I have about an ideal army—*it's an army of working and training.*"[32] Israel Idelson, at the KMC at Naan, offered an example of just such an army that combined work and training, namely the Red Army during the Russian Civil War, which even had a distinct name that most closely translated into a "working army."[33] The Soviet example was a cultural code to get the message across: not only did this form of organization have the advantage over various Western armies; it also had the creative intelligence characteristic of a new, revolutionary society. Regular armies lent themselves to corruption. But an army that devoted part of its time to work left no time for foolishness. Exposed to the blessed influence of physical labor, and agriculture at that, such an army would experience a purifying, educational value that required no explanation.[34]

This reasoning and its healthy dose of self-righteousness met with a good deal of resentment at the Palmah's bases: "They developed the idea of work as an ideal for the Palmah. People greeted it derisively. *We needed no moral preaching about love of labor.*"[35]

When the High Command sized up the bitterness and spreading malcontent, it resorted to the common youth movement approach in disputes between leaders and the rank and file: there was no compulsion from above, but rather a "friendly discussion among comrades." First, the youngsters were allowed to vent, then the older members rose to explain the gravity of the situation and why the decision had to be accepted. The system usually worked: the catharsis, achieved by letting the youngsters pour out their hearts against "the powers that be," mellowed them for the next stage of accepting discipline.

On 19 October 1942, the Palmah's Company B gathered in the chicken coop of Kibbutz Ramat Ha-Kovesh—under the command of Meir Davidson—for a "discussion" with Galili and David Nameri of the Haganah High Command. The young voiced their disappointment at the gulf between what they had believed they had been asked and wished to do and the soul-destroying reality; the kibbutzim were careful to uphold the labor quota—they complained—but nobody bothered about the training quota. Davidson, true to the High Command, preached in the vein of "the Command knows best." Even so, he too protested sharply: if there is no money, you don't build an army.[36] Given the frustration and anger, the financial straits inspired drastic remedies. The Yishuv was booming, everyone was benefiting financially from the war, and yet, in relative terms, the monetary contribution to the war effort of Palestine's Jews fell far below that of England's citizens. "Against such a Yishuv, all measures are acceptable, preaching is not enough. Just call on us—we'll get it done."[37] The allusion was to the LeHI (the breakaway Stern Gang from the IZL), which did not shrink at raising funds by robbing banks and extorting the Yishuv's wealthy. The Palmah's young men could identify with these actions. They were embittered, kicking and screaming—but they expected the rebellion to be led by their legitimate leadership, that is, the Haganah High Command.

The wise Galili chose to respond softly. Underscoring the historic importance of an independent Jewish defense force, he said: "I am not sure that all comrades grasp how much the fate of the country's Jews and the fate of the country's political future depend on these talks," flattering the men and stoking the rebellious unit's sense of self-importance.[38] His message was plain and familiar: you may be right, but the corollary of your being right will lead to the force's liquidation, whereas acceptance of the decision will ultimately lead to its strengthening. Most of the men present submitted. Davidson, however, left the Palmah and enlisted in the British army, which was a serious blow. A few dozen others followed suit. The majority, however, resigned themselves to the program of work and training even if it meant gritting their teeth. Despite the wave of drop-outs, the hard core remained loyal to the Palmah.[39]

The decision to enlarge the Palmah to thirty-five hundred conscripts out of the five thousand earmarked for internal security (taken at the 47th Histadrut Council) embodied the Palmah's changing image. It meant that the Palmah would be a popular force, open to all: there were not enough recruits to meet the earlier criteria of an elitist army. The idea did not sit well with some of the staff of the High Command.[40] Yitzhak Sadeh was far from enthusiastic. He preferred a tight, select force to mass conscription of people of dubious military caliber. Only in time, under the influence of Tabenkin and Galili as well as Allon, did he change his mind and formulate a new doctrine that the young and healthy could be whipped into a fighting force if they were trained properly.[41] Nor were all of the rank and file enthusiastic about the idea of quantity at the expense of quality.[42] They demanded that a highly skilled cadre of squad and platoon commanders be trained to constitute the skeletal command of an extended army when the time was ripe.[43] It is one of the ironies of fate that this is more or less what happened in the end. In any case, from that point on, the Palmah's recruits were no longer chosen on the basis of soldierly competence; any able-bodied person could join. While the masses did not exactly come running, the Palmah stopped being a military order and became a unit of enlisted civilians. And, like it or not, it had to adapt to the needs and wishes of those civilians.

The youth movements were the most natural, obvious pool of potential recruits for the Palmah. They, from the start of conscription in World War II, had been grappling with the dilemma of national priorities: Did pioneering settlement still top the scale? Were members to enlist in the British army or in an internal defense force? Or, were they to continue fostering their own social cohesion in advent of group training for agricultural settlement? No national leader of any stature had declared that the settlement mission now took second place to the military task. On the contrary; the leadership was just as conscious as the movements of the importance of maintaining reserves for settlement. The youth movement motto of "to farms and to arms," designated complementary—not contrary—aims.

And yet there was a problem: the scale of values may not have changed—or at least it was unclear that it had changed—yet the heart said otherwise. As war raged across the world and daily headlines screamed of poundings or pluck, as the Nazi foe chalked up more and more gains, it was hard for the young to remain uninvolved. How could they be content with the calm of kibbutz life—even if they had been taught all of their lives that there was no cause more noble than physical labor, no task more important than expanding Zionism's foothold in the land of Israel? The upshot was that many youth movement graduates enlisted in the British army. Others headed for the Palmah or the Jewish Settlement Police. Thus, instead of agricultural training, members opted for military service, stripping the youth movements of their manpower for settlement.

The agreement about work and training camps, signed between the kibbutz movements and the Palmah in the summer of 1942, for the first time made the defense force the business of Labor settlements. Suddenly, there was an immanent connection. Also that summer, the idea came up of inducting youth movement members not as individuals but as groups in order to preserve their tightly knit social units for future kibbutz life.

Youth movements functioned from the sixth grade upward. When they reached the age of eighteen, members were expected to organize in a *hakhshara* or training group, living as a commune and usually working in agriculture, whether on a kibbutz or as hired hands in farming colonies. After a number of years (depending on the availability of settlement points) they formed the nuclei of *kevutzot* or kibbutzim. The Palmah ultimately mobilized the training groups as a whole. This proved more advantageous to the youth movements as it kept the groups intact, stemming individual, would-be dropouts who had their sights on either the British army or the Palmah.

Between November 1942 and January 1943, the two youth movements affiliated with KM—Ha-Noar Ha-Oved (HNHO) and Ha-Mahanot Ha-Olim—mulled over sending their training groups to the Palmah. The step entailed a radical shift in outlook: overnight, priorities were to change.

Equally worrisome was the future of the social framework: youth movements were being asked to divest themselves of their mature echelons, their strength and manpower for movement drives and urban branch instructors, and hope for the best.

The first movement to conclude its agonizing and agree was HNHO. The general drift was favorable, whether for fear that further conscription of individual members might break up the groups or out of its typical sense of duty. On 30 December 1942, the decision was endorsed by the movement's highest forum.[44] The HNHO's long, hard journey to the Palmah was at an end. In 1943, five of its training groups enlisted in the Palmah.[45]

Ha-Mahanot Ha-Olim's path to the Palmah was more winding. It drew its numbers from middle-class, high-school students who had been raised to believe in "self-realization" on a kibbutz as the movement's crowning achievement. Establishing settlements and perpetuating the movement through these were considered essential. During the war, it established two kibbutzim, Bet Ha-Aravah and Hamadyah, and it had to man them. The manpower was to come from its agricultural training groups. The number of youth movement graduates was small to begin with, which only made every candidate vital and the decision about his or her future fateful (in November 1942, there were forty-seven continuing "graduates," that is, mature members heading for agricultural groups, and this was considered quite a large group).[46] For its part, the Palmah hoped that Ha-Mahanot Ha-Olim would serve as a trailblazer for other youth movements targeting high-school students. Those associated with Mapai (Gordoniya and the Tzofim [Scouts], in addition to HNHO and Ha-Mahanot Ha-Olim) awaited Ha-Mahanot Ha-Olim's decision as they tended to follow its lead. In addition, Ha-Mahanot Ha-Olim initiated and strongly influenced an organization of high-school graduates founded in 1942.[47] So that even though it was quite small, it carried considerable weight.

The discussion at Ha-Mahanot Ha-Olim regarding the enlistment of the training groups to the Palmah stretched for about half a year without any resolution. The council at Hamadyah (21–22 May 1943) decided that of its eighty members, scattered over six kibbutzim in agricultural training, forty would join the Palmah.[48] But there seems to have been pressure from below to enlist since the number of actual recruits exceeded the movement's allotment. In any case, only in 1944 was the conscription of agricultural trainees completed, after the agreement concluded between the youth movements and the Palmah.

Mapai was divided over conscripting youth movement graduates into the Palmah. These were the elite young men and women associated with Labor, the natural candidates for the most important missions: either settlement or security. At the same time, the internal struggle sharpened between the Palmah "party" and the British army "party." As it became clear how low the Palmah figures were, the recruitment propaganda became more and more vehement. Since there was little glory to speak of, the propaganda proclaimed the Palmah's supposed superiority over the British army. This attitude was prompted by several elements: the tendency of Palestine's Jewish youth toward high self-esteem, if not downright arrogance; the typical conceit of the KM that was apt to dismiss everyone outside of its own orbit; and the sense of crisis caused by the paltry enlistment into the Palmah. To stop the flow from the Palmah to the British army, Allon and even Galili considered the touted differentiation vital to the esprit de corps. Those who left the Palmah, even if for the army, were maligned as deserters quitting the battlefield. In vain did Tabenkin remonstrate: "Someone who leaves the Palmah and is to fall on the Tunisian front—are we to call him a deserter? This is a deserving judgment?"[49] The more the Palmahniks and especially their leaders came up against adversity—whether in relations with the kibbutzim, the disappointing enlistment, the constant lack of funds, or the public stigma clinging to young people out of uniform despite the exemption papers in their pockets—the more convinced they became that it was they who shouldered the Jewish people's future force, yet it was they who were being shortchanged, who suffered discrimination, who were the victims of misguided politics. From the other side, the more they differentiated between themselves and British army recruits—who were encouraged by Moshe Shertok and the Mapai majority—the more the Palmah became identified with the opposition in Mapai, Faction B.

The autumn and winter of 1942 were the Palmah's formative period. For better or for worse, this is when its basic guidelines, its composition, and, in retrospect, also its character and functioning, were shaped. It had been a professional, achievement-oriented military detachment; it became something that was not an army yet filled a military role. Its adoption by Labor settlement set it in the world of ideas. In its new form, the Palmah was actually the Labor movement's last, great, inspired invention, before Labor lost its creativity in the self-destructive process on which it then embarked. Like all of Labor's imaginative inventions, the Palmah was not preplanned; it was molded gradually and painfully through trial and error. Reality led the way and set all of the rules. Like Labor settlement, the Histadrut Labor Federation, Labor industry, the health fund, and so forth, the Palmah sprouted up in a social and political climate that made experimentation possible. The need of its begetters to repeatedly cite the example of the Russian past and Soviet present points to the specific intellectual world on which it fed and rested. But the idea of the Palmah, as devised in the autumn of 1942, was the original product of Jewish Palestine. It had no precedent.

The integration of Palmah camps into Labor settlements and the group induction of youth movement graduates into the conscripted force bequeathed to the Palmah the world of youth movement values with all of its childish postures and provincialism, but also its summits of idealism, passion, and disdain of routine; its conformism and coercion; and its humanism, based on moral absolutes. Rather than a barracks, the Palmah became a complete social universe with its joys and sorrows, its peaks of elevation and pits of despair.

There is a clear hierarchy on the scale of commitment to social groups. Some bodies entail very limited loyalty in terms of devotion, time, and emotional energy. Others elicit total dedication. The kibbutz, perhaps, heads the commitment scale: those who join abide by its social contract and way of life every minute of every day. This contract is not the external allegiance of a military barracks but the complete submission to a society of one's choice as the most significant reference group. Social dynamics reinforce the bond between the individual and society, which becomes the individual's home, family, and source of human contact. This sort of bond and the supreme commitment consequent to it were transferred from the kibbutz and youth movements to the Palmah bases. Little by little, amid contradictory impulses at times, an "alternative society" sprang up there.

The entire process, which determined the fate of the Palmah, proceeded without Allon's involvement. After the British removed him from the command of the Syrian unit, and after he recovered from the surgery to his shoulder, he was reassigned to Palmah's headquarters. It is not clear what position he filled in those days. But soon afterward, Yitzhak Sadeh's deputy, David Nameri, got fed up with the Palmah's inaction and followed his heart to the clandestine endeavors of "illegal immigration," bringing Jewish refugees to Palestine. Allon became the Palmah's second-in-command.

Chapter 7
The Palmah, 1943–47

In the five years between Allon's return to the Palmah's headquarters and the outbreak of the War of Independence, his leadership qualities solidified and earned recognition. He started out as one of several young, native military leaders who became prominent in the Haganah and field companies and then in the Palmah. He ended the period as the indisputable leader of the young born and bred in Eretz Israel.

Allon's fit with the "new" Palmah, after its boosting by youth movement *hakhsharot*, was far from self-evident. In fact, it was rather surprising. Allon had not grown up in a youth movement; its magic world was alien to him. The boys and girls who shared their adolescent crisis in "the movement" were molded by a worldview, a moral ethos; they had formed a profound solidarity and close friendships; they had forged a sense of togetherness. Youth movements took advantage of peer-group socialization at this critical age to instill commitment to two value systems: Zionism and socialism. Zionism was passionately bound up with patriotism; socialism, with the idea of equality. Both infused the idea of self-realization: to settle the land (that is, go to a kibbutz) was to be true to these two guiding principles. The *hakhsharot* brought to the Palmah's bases not only boys of little physical prowess but girls, who till then had been kept out of sight of the Haganah's and the Palmah's commanders; they brought also the lifestyle of idealistic groups that, were it not for the Palmah and the special conditions of the 1940s, would probably never even have thought of military pursuits. They brought an innocence that set the dominant norms, even if it was not shared by all. It was a source of emotional strength, a quasi-vaccine against oversophistication, cynicism, and realism. These qualities proved vital in the tests ahead.

Allon did not belong to this world of youthful romanticism, with its yearning for purity and justice and its belief in individual duty to live by one's principles. He had little to contribute to the group's everyday social culture—the campfire circle, the coffee *finjan*, the songs and dances. He did not tell tall tales, did not compose stories, could not sing and danced little. Yet, he was accepted without question as the leader of the Palmah. In time, he came to symbolize the native born and all their charm, audacity, and daring. He was the symbol of Eretz Israel youth, courageous, simple, and natural, who understood the call of the hour as against the old politicians—those who spoke in high-sounding terms that had outlived their time.

The Palmah to which Allon returned from Syria was not the same organization that he had left a year and a half earlier. The cooperation with the British had ended. The Palmah's headquarters, originally in Haifa and closely allied with British intelligence, now found itself under surveillance by the British Criminal Investigation Department (CID). As the conflict between the Yishuv and the British sharpened, the Palmah was forced to find cover in the secret Jewish republic, that is, in labor settlement areas. Most of the Palmah companies were put up on kibbutzim in the Galilee and in the valleys—Jordan, Beisan, and especially Jezreel. The Palmah's headquarters quite naturally sought shelter in the same area. At first, it moved to Kibbutz Alonim, and then, after money was raised to build a large shack at Kibbutz Mizra, an additional branch was set up there.[1]

The Jewish fighting organizations of the Mandate period are commonly—and erroneously—presented as belonging to four undergrounds: the Haganah, the Palmah, the IZL, and the LeHI. Understandably, former members of the latter two wish to create an equivalence between their organizations and the Haganah, as if all were of equal importance. In truth, the Haganah was the people's military organization answering to the Jewish Agency; it was partly a citizen militia, partly an underground army. The Palmah was the Haganah's regular detachment, the operative arm of the underground army rather than a self-standing body. The commander of the Palmah was Yitzhak Sadeh. The Haganah High Command included the following figures: Yaakov Dori, the Haganah's chief of general staff (CGS), a position formed only during World War II; Moshe Sneh, the chief of the Haganah's National Command, which was the civil authority over the Haganah (and which broke down thus: 50 percent Histadrut representatives [the Left] and 50 percent representatives of "civilian bodies" [the Right]); and Israel Galili, the aide to the head of the National Command and the individual responsible for appointments. Above all of these was Eliyahu Golomb, the head of the Haganah, who had no official, defined position. Shaul Meirov, the head of the Mossad for Aliyah Bet—the body organizing clandestine immigration of Jewish refugees—was also part of the same, semi-formal High Command. Another authoritative figure with no official position was Berl Katznelson, a confidant and consultant. Ben-Gurion, chairman of the Jewish Agency, was not involved in the everyday running of the Haganah until early 1947. But everyone, without exception, deferred to him; it never occurred to them to act contrary to his opinion.

It was a time of inaction and reduced tension; the war had moved away from the country's shores. The historic turn had come in early 1943 with the British victory at el-Alamein and the decisive Soviet offensive at Stalingrad. Economically, the Yishuv was flourishing, although this did not make the Yishuv's representatives any readier to allocate funds for the underground army. Acts of valor were taking place in the big wide world while the Palmah was sentenced to idleness.

Meanwhile, Allon became the Palmah's second-in-command. His appointment remains shrouded in mystery. No one remembers exactly when the personnel change took place, but the choice seems to have enjoyed consensus and was accepted as perfectly natural. Dayan, who might have been a contender, had not returned to the Palmah after being wounded in Syria. The only one to demur was Shimon Koch (Avidan), who had hoped for the appointment himself. Avidan had been a member of Germany's Communist Youth and the party's fighting unit. He had commanded a Palmah company and then the so-called German Platoon, which was designed to operate behind enemy lines. He was experienced and respected. But Sadeh chose Allon. No one claimed that it was a political choice, Allon being a member of KM and Avidan of its sister movement, Ha-Kibbutz Ha-Artzi Ha-Shomer Ha-Tza'ir. Allon's leadership was accepted without question, with the same ease that marked his personal relations.[2]

Sadeh never dealt with organization and administration. His seconds, Giora Shinan and then David Nameri, saw to the Palmah's functioning. Allon pursued the same course but elevated both the job and the organization. Apart from his leadership skills, he excelled in administration and management, while his persuasiveness was a byword in the Palmah.[3] In those years it was he who made sure the Palmah would continue to exist.

Despite the great age difference between them, there was a special bond between Sadeh and Allon. Zvika Dror cites Sadeh's daughter, Aza, who accompanied her father to buy a present for Allon's twenty-fifth birthday. Why Allon and not others, she asked. Sadeh answered: "You must know that Yigal is not like anyone else—he is your brother." Dror also quotes the poet Nathan Alterman, Sadeh's close friend: "He [Sadeh] loves him [Yigal] as one does a beloved."[4] Palmahniks knew that there was no point in complaining to Sadeh about Allon; Allon had his full backing. Some complained that Sadeh pampered him, that he was blind to his faults, for example, to his inclination to promote those he was fond of above others no less deserving.[5]

Sadeh's greatness lay in his leadership, originality, and uniqueness.

He found administrative work tedious. He allowed Allon to conduct staff meetings and when he grew impatient he began to rap his fingers on the table. Allon would conclude the meeting with a wink to the officers and then sit with them to wrap up details. In time, Sadeh took to perusing a newspaper at the meetings. He would seem to be paying no attention, but then he would interrupt to express an opinion, and his word was law.[6]

Allon treated Sadeh with love and solicitude, always protective of his honor. He would pick up the grain of an idea Sadeh had thrown out and work it into a concrete plan. The ability "to translate Yitzhak," as Shosh Spector put it, was no mean task. Often, he spoke in semi-riddles. Allon was able to intuit his intent and glean the elements suitable for the Palmah. Sadeh could function within the narrow framework of personal acquaintances, of people who respected him, were alert to his shortcomings, and able to shield him from himself. This was the secret of the symbiosis between the two.[7]

The other members of the Palmah's headquarters remembered no disagreements between the two. Yet they did not always see eye to eye: Allon was for conscripting girls into the Palmah—Sadeh against; Allon was for conscripting the youth movment *hakhsharot* into the Palmah—Sadeh against. Allon soon attained a position of independence: he began to appear alongside Sadeh at the regular meetings of the Palmah's headquarters with the CGS or the head of the National Command, and the High Command accepted it as fact.[8]

Sadeh's leadership radiated from him. Whatever he did, he did in his own inimitable way. He would attract attention merely by entering a room. Allon had no such presence. Sadeh might hug you, but it never occurred to anyone to hug Sadeh. Allon, yes—he was approachable. Sadeh never deluded either himself or anyone else with the idea that they were equals. Allon gave everyone that feeling, that they were the same as he, that he was in lieu of an older brother worth listening to.[9] Rather than a serious maturity, Sadeh emitted an "old man's" youthful naughtiness: he loved wine, pretty women, good food. He and Alterman, two of the generation's greats, often amazed the Palmahniks with the way they could hit the bottle. If Sadeh discerned a spark of literary talent in anyone, he would invite the lad to one of his favorite cafes, thereby cultivating a generation of authors and poets. The puritanical Palmahniks found quite a bit of charm in Sadeh's somewhat bohemian abandonment. He was their first exposure to unconventional behavior, to dash and daring, which only enhanced his aura: Sadeh was allowed to be different. He would strike a revolutionary pose, recounting his exploits in the Red Army during Russia's civil war (probably without mentioning his adventures in the White Army), and leave the youngsters open-mouthed. The Red Army, in World War II, fired the imagination.[10]

Sadeh had the fascination of the stranger and the extraordinary. Allon's prominent qualities were the exact opposite. He was always clean and tidy. He was able to do the impossible—to feast with his fingers in an Arab village and emerge neat as a pin. Sadeh's ostensibly revolutionary sloppiness was countered by Allon's Mes'ha conventionalism. Sadeh was impossible to imitate. Allon was not. He was accessible, yet able to create an atmosphere in which no one could refuse him. He never lost his temper, he was not remembered to have ever raised his voice.[11] He understood what motivated men and played on individual heartstrings. To some, this was contemptible: they called Allon a *siasnik*, a politician: if he pats you on the shoulder, watch out—he's out to get you. They would urge him to talk straight. But even the critics of his appeal to flattery and acknowledged political skills could not resist his charm when it was turned on them.[12]

In norms of conduct, Sadeh sent out mixed messages. On the one hand, he could treat irresponsibility lightly, especially on the part of those he liked. On the other hand, he drove home moral behavior. A Palmah unit, it is told, once gave a meal in his honor at Givat Brenner, with the boys supplying the food and even managing to "pinch" tinned meat for the occasion. When Sadeh he received his plate, he said thank you and commented that he did not eat stolen food. That was all it took. No one touched the tinned food that evening or, probably, even afterward. In one famous escapade, a group of youngsters traveling by train to Berl Katznelson's memorial hopped off at a station and began haggling with an elderly Arab vendor of watermelon. As the train started to pull out, the youngsters rushed to board without having paid, to the accompaniment of the vendor's wails. Alterman got wind of the affair and wrote it up in his newspaper column, "Ha-Tur ha-Shvi'i." Sadeh had the piece circulated among all of the Palmah's units.[13] The ambivalence about moral norms characterized both Sadeh and Allon; it was one of the factors in the Palmah's virtues as well as vices.

Allon dealt with all the nitty-gritty: budgets, vehicles, disagreements, contact with commanders and the High Command. He developed the Palmah's distinctive circles of decision making. The process of discussion and culture of consultation was borrowed from the youth movements, as was the idea that the lowliest soldier was entitled to express his opinion on organizational and operative measures.

The culture of consultation suited the character of the conscripted *hakhsharot* and the framework of "work-and-training camps." Rather than formal discipline, the onus was on the individual to show personal responsibility for and individual commitment to the general good. A Palmahnik did not obey his commanders because that is what it said to do in the rule book but because he accepted their authority; and after voicing his opinion he abided by the decision taken, even if he believed it wrong. As early as the Syrian campaign Allon had typically explained to his subordinates the purpose of the operation, its tactics, and the commanding officer's thinking. The practice suited his personality and satisfied his soldiers.

The Palmah was characterized by a dismissive attitude to army protocol, order, and discipline. Apart from an absence of badges of rank or lack of distance between officers and juniors, there was also sloppy dress, owing, to some extent, to dearth, but also to "the barefoot army's" disparagement of bourgeois manners.

Dori and Sadeh reflected opposing schools of thought. Dori had a knack for organization and had set up the Haganah's General Staff (HGS). He was responsible for the Haganah's structure until the formation of the Israel Defense Forces (IDF). Pedantic and meticulous, he took no unnecessary risks. Sadeh, in contrast, argued that the real world was not like textbooks. It was important to know how to take the enemy by surprise. This was an intuitive talent not acquired in army drills or procedure. The natural, daring adept, who was perhaps lax about formal discipline but excelled on the battlefield, was to be prized. Each, Sadeh and Dori, stressed his own strong point: the one, precise planning; the other, improvisation. Dori hardly shone in the latter, Sadeh paid little attention to the former. Allon knew this to be Sadeh's weakness, and he covered for him.

In the autumn of 1945, Dori went to the United States to procure arms, bruised and battered by the low priority accorded by the civilian National Command to the military arm, and the wont of Palmah commanders to circumvent his authority. Sadeh was made acting CGS and Allon was appointed to replace him in the Palmah.

In the two years from the summer of 1943, when Allon became Sadeh's second-in-command, until the autumn of 1945, a popular Palmahnik song went: "We will yet rise up, rise up comrades-in-arms/just let the old man [Sadeh] give the order."[14] But the order was never given. In that period, Allon and the rest of the Palmah's headquarters focused on devising alternatives to active duty, knowing that an idle underground was doomed. Enthusiasm was lost, the volunteering spirit wasted away. The fear was that the recruits would feel cheated and wish to leave, whether for home, the British army, or some other outlet for their frustration; they could easily join undergrounds not atrophying under self-imposed paralysis, such as the IZL (from the start of 1944) or the LeHI.

The Palmah kept itself busy with activities requiring virtually no weapons. It valued physical prowess—sports, endurance, face-to-face combat, jujitsu. The prestige of physical training was enhanced by the personal example of Sadeh, whose athletic and boxing skills amazed his young charges. Competition helped foster team spirit (how better to encourage group identification than by a tug of war?) and was part of the test of personal courage in Omega jumping. In addition, there was fieldcraft. Since the days of "going beyond the fence," fieldcraft, orienteering, and night walking had come to stand for pluck, much like the declaration of Jewish mastery over the land: no part of the country was closed to Jewish trackers. In fact, those years of disturbing inaction saw the development of scouts, both as a lesson of the disgraceful invasion of Syria, when Allon and Dayan had been forced to rely on Arabs, and because of the recognition of their importance. The Palmah's trackers assembled "files" on hundreds of Arab villages against future contingencies. These included maps with routes of approach and retreat, topography (another major topic), key buildings, water sources, and landmarks. Sabotage featured strongly; the Palmah had assimilated the art during the frantic days prior to the Battle of el-Alamein, when the Haganah and the British had prepared for a possible German invasion. There was little training in personal weapons and scant use of live fire. In contrast, the grenade, a product of the new military arms industry, was both common and useful.[15] Physical endurance and scouting were further drilled in the Palmah's treks to the Judean Desert, where various exercises in the use of arms could proceed without fear of unwelcome visits by the British police. The treks too forged team spirit. Water discipline (abstention due to dearth), the strong helping the weak up cliff sides, the tension over running into Bedouin, the evening campfires—all of these boosted the social dynamics that molded the profile of the native generation. It was the youth-movement heritage in military-security garb. The treks took place in areas of historic significance: Masada, Herodium, Bet Horon, Bet Zekharyah, and other battle arenas of Judah Maccabee. Twinning the romance of past and present raised morale and masked the pathetic lack of military means.

The constant search for occupation expanded the Palmah's spheres of activity. When hope arose of sending a volunteer unit disguised as Germans behind enemy lines, the Palmah quickly threw together the above-mentioned "German Platoon" whose members had a good command of the language and pored over the etiquette and procedures of the German army. The British did not use the platoon in the end. Instead, Avidan and other members took their special talents to postwar Germany on missions of vengeance. Another sphere revolved around the Marine Platoon: the clandestine immigration of Jewish refugees was expected to resume after the war, on a large scale. The Marine Platoon was set up to train seamen and captains to man immigrant ships. All of the members of the Palmah underwent extensive sea drills in the period of inaction.[16] Attempts were also made to create an air unit and train pilots to fly light aircraft under the façade of civilian activity. The pilots were to serve as back-up for trackers in uncovering armed bands if and when the need arose.[17]

In terms of integrating the *hakhsharot* into the Palmah and consolidating its character, 1945 was a critical year. Several processes took place simultaneously. First, the initial cohort of Palmah recruits completed two years of training. They could not be held indefinitely. World War II was drawing to a close and there was less justification for lengthy conscription. As a result, the principle of reserve duty was introduced: the soldiers were to remain connected to the Palmah after their discharge from "work-and-training camps" and their return to "civilian life." Relatively large numbers of young people could thus be trained despite the limited absorption capacity of the bases.

Second, to help foster commitment beyond ordinary military allegiance, the idea of Palmah frontier outposts came up: the *hakhsharot* finishing active training would settle frontier areas. It was another stage in the symbiosis between the role of the youth movement, to prepare reserves for agricultural settlement, and the role of the conscripted force, to prepare manpower for the defense of settlements. The Palmah's first frontier outpost was at Bet Keshet on land formerly owned by the Paicoviches.

Third, the Jewish Brigade was established as part of the British army and the Jewish Agency demanded that the *hakhsharot* help meet the manpower requirements. More than a third of the Palmah's members came from the *hakhsharot* at the time. Had the demand been met, the Palmah might have disintegrated. The youth movements preferred to keep the *hakhsharot* groups intact in the framework of the Palmah and refused to fill their quotas.[18]

In the Palmah's mythology, the idea took root that the Jewish Agency Executive under Ben-Gurion "had it in for them." The disagreement over recruitment quotas played a key role in this mythology. The notion that the Palmah was being shortchanged evolved into a myth that was to go from strength to strength.

In early 1944—after refraining from anti-British action and even cooperating with the British in the war years—the IZL under its new commander, Menachem Begin, declared a revolt against the British government of Palestine. The timing was related to considerations of the IZL on the Yishuv front, not necessarily to developments in the international arena: an Allied victory was assured, but Germany still controlled most of continental Europe and the invasion of Normandy was as yet far off. Begin announced that as long as Britain fought the Nazis, the IZL's fighters would not harm military installations, only administrative facilities of the government of Palestine. The distinction was unacceptable to both the British and the Yishuv's leadership. The IZL, for lack of funds, did not hesitate to intimidate Jewish businessmen, who purchased peace in hard currency. Hundreds of merchants and even institutions associated with the Histadrut paid protection money. Their intimidation and extortion, public announcements, measures against the British police and the CID—all of these made the IZL a strong presence on the Yishuv street.

In the summer of 1944 the Haganah was informed that the British government had decided to form a Jewish Brigade. Churchill intimated to Chaim Weizmann, the president of the Zionist Organization, that after the war a Jewish state would rise in Palestine. The Yishuv's leaders received the news as auguring a future shift in British policy toward Zionism. The IZL's provocative actions were seen as sabotaging the chances of any such development. Eliyahu Golomb and Moshe Sneh met with Begin. According to Sneh's report, Begin refused to rein in the IZL: the IZL's importance lay only in its fighting, he claimed. If it desisted, it would have no raison d'etre.[19] However, the LeHI, according to Golomb, did agree to unconditionally freeze its actions.[20] But three weeks later, on 6 November 1944, Lord Moyne, a member of the British war cabinet and its representative in the Middle East, was murdered in Cairo by two members of the LeHI. The shock was complete. It was a declaration of war on Britain during the war against Hitler. Apart from its being morally repulsive personal terrorism, there was profound apprehension about the British reaction: Would immigration be stopped? Would the British step up weapons searches and crack down on the local armed forces?

There had already been talk of obstructing the IZL and rendering it inactive in the summer of 1944. In the fall, the Jewish Agency, followed by the National Committee (23 October 1944) and then the Zionist Executive (24 October 1944), adopted the harsh decision to stop the IZL but still did not act on it. Moyne's murder was a watershed. In its wake, the JA Executive formally informed the British authorities that it was prepared to cooperate fully against the Jewish terrorist gangs. The Histadrut's Sixth Convention convened a special session (20 November 1944) aimed at mustering broad public support for the decision. Ben-Gurion spoke out sharply against the Yishuv's harboring terrorists and for cooperation with the authorities: in the absence of cooperation, they would not "succeed in stamping out this evil."[21] There was no such thing as independent Jewish action; the state-in-the-making had no state powers. There were no prisons, nowhere to conceal large numbers of people, no means to pay costs of such a recourse. Arrest and imprisonment were necessarily government functions.

At the end of October 1944, a KMC resolution stipulated that "the terrorist bands are a Jewish form of world fascism"; it called on the organized Yishuv to put an end to terrorism and disable the bands—on one condition: "The terror must be prevented by independent, autonomous Yishuv action."[22] The condition reflected Galili's approach; in August 1944 he had strongly opposed cooperating with the British, which he termed *She'at Nefesh*—"Revulsion." "I have been turning the matter over again and again since last night and it does not sit well with either my heart or my head," he had written to Sneh. "I think the move, if carried out, is fraught with disaster and will lead to the opposite effect."[23] But two weeks afterward, the picture changed because of Moyne's murder and the JA's announcement of cooperation with the British. As much as they hated cooperating with the CID, Galili and his colleagues could not bring themselves to go against the general public on so critical an issue.[24] Amid the sessions of the Histadrut Convention, the Le-Ahdut Ha-Avodah Party (LAHA, which had split from Mapai earlier that year and was based mainly on a faction from Kibbutz Meuhad) continued to fret. In the end, it decided to abstain in the vote without explanation; it did not wish to give the appearance of launching a public campaign against the "open season" (the *saison*), as the campaign was named by the Palmah. The escape clause for conscientious objectors was the freedom to choose whether or not to participate in the hunt.[25]

According to testimony by Galili, Allon and CGS Ya'akov Dori, the "open season" was organized within the Haganah and by its own bodies: the SHAY, its Secret Service, and the Palmah. A headquarters was set up for the purpose and Dori was put in charge of the whole operation. Allon was his deputy and Shimon Avidan was the operations officer. The operation was already under way when it transpired that the SHAY intended to hand over to the British the IZL members abducted by the Palmah. At this point, Allon resigned. Avidan replaced him. Allon was altogether opposed to the Palmah's members taking part in abductions even if the investigation and handover were in the hands of the SHAY. When matters came to a head with the High Command, Yitzhak Sadeh supported Allon, as did Israel Galili. According to Allon, to avoid making Palmah members act against their consciences, he suggested that the Haganah ask for volunteers for the operation.[26] In most cases, Galili said, the SHAY conducted all contact with the British so that the Palmah could keep its hands clean.[27] The idea of "volunteering" stemmed from the KM's resistance to cooperating with the British. This was also the reason for Allon's basic objections; he never stopped believing that the cooperation with the British in the *saison* had been a grave mistake. Galili, in contrast, at the end of his life did find room to defend Ben-Gurion's stand in the affair.[28] Like others in the KM, Allon was all in favor of thwarting and immobilizing the dissenters, but only if the Haganah did it. By his account, he suggested that the information the SHAY possessed be used to carry out extensive arrests of members of the IZL countrywide (about three hundred people), to detain the members in Labor settlement facilities, to interrogate them thoroughly, and then to release them under surveillance. This, he said, would put a stop to the IZL's actions without any need to cooperate with the British. The plan was not accepted by the SHAY or Dori. Instead, piecemeal arrests were carried out and in most cases the detainees were handed over to the British.[29] Whether or not Allon's plan was feasible, whether or not it was more than a mere idea thrown out in the discussion, remains a moot question. In any case, rumor circulated that Allon was planning a "Bartholomew's Night" massacre of the dissenters—very likely an exaggeration of the said plan.

While members of the Palmah were not compelled to take part in the *saison,* there was no real volunteering either: "You were told that you had to—and you went," said Dov Chesis, the *saison*'s coordinator in the Tel Aviv area. "I remember telling Yitzhak Sadeh that it was eating me up. He did not order me to stay, but [he] noted [that] one also does things that are uncomfortable when necessary."[30] Meir Pa'il, a Palmah commander who became a historian, explained that there was no call for volunteers; all that was said was that conscientious objectors did not need to participate. Most stayed.[31]

The campaign against the IZL was seen as a battle over the image of Israel's future society and government. Avidan, who replaced Allon as the *saison*'s operations officer, lived with the trauma of the Nazi takeover in Germany. He saw the *saison* as a crusade against dark forces.[32] Many people shared his view, notably members of Kibbutz Artzi, but also rank-and-file Palmahniks. Allon and Galili did not think otherwise. They regarded the *saison* as a power struggle to control the street, influence public opinion in the Yishuv, and allow the Haganah freedom of action. The IZL was the enemy because it was backed by public forces of the Revisionist Movement and even "civilian" [that is, center and right of center] parties. The LeHI may have attracted those Palmah members who were hungry for action, but it posed no political threat. This is the paradox: Lord Moyne's murder provided the rationale for the *saison.* But the *saison* was not against the organization of the perpetrators; it was against the IZL, which condemned the LeHI's practice of personal terrorism.

The ambivalence of the Palmah's commanders about the *saison* did not escape their juniors' eyes: Allon was all for taking on the IZL. He thought that if it could not be done without "revulsion" then at least it should be done properly. The message he sent out to Palmahniks was thus not total opposition; rather he "abstained." The abstention itself could be interpreted affirmatively, almost as a nod: therefore, the Palmah could both take part in the *saison* and emerge with clean hands.[33]

In the short term, it was considered an advantage to take part in the *saison*, but there were long-term risks (which were probably still unclear at the time). Having parted company after the Syrian period, Allon and Dayan now crossed paths again. Dayan, ambitious and politically savvy, was one of the SHAY's key figures in the *saison*. But he was reluctant to mention it later, according to his biographer.[34] Allon was doubly cautious. According to one account, he took pains not to be identified with the *saison* and let people know that he dissociated himself from it. Yet he was loathe to forfeit all that he had gained in the eyes of the High Command and even Ben-Gurion. He struck a balance: the Palmah contributed volunteers and Avidan carried out the work with messianic fervor.[35] Avidan resented Allon and other members of the KM for their fence-sitting: he regarded Allon's dissociation as a sign of political ambition, guiding him to skirt a dubious matter.

It is not unusual for one current of a national liberation movement to cooperate with the regime against another. The phenomenon is familiar from the histories of national and revolutionary movements, and the Jewish liberation movement was certainly not unique. It is, however, always a traumatic development. And the trauma spawns myths about just and unjust, loyalists and traitors. Galili's apprehension that the "revulsion" would turn public opinion in the Yishuv in favor of the dissenters and crown them as saintly freedom fighters was not borne out at the time. But as time passed and the dissenter narrative gained legitimacy in Israel's political upheavals it became increasingly difficult to explain the events of the autumn and winter of 1944–45. What had appeared reasonable—barely, agonizingly—in the charged atmosphere of 1944, disturbed the serenity of armchair viewers in the final quarter of the twentieth century. The handover of IZL members to the British became an important propaganda card of the Right in the battle over collective memory.

A mere nine months after the end of the *saison*, the erstwhile bitter rivals became allies in the Jewish Resistance Movement, fighting shoulder to shoulder against the British. This may be the most convincing evidence that the two sides walked a tightrope in their mutual relations, carefully avoiding actions that could have caused an irreparable rupture.

As the Zionist leadership saw it, the conclusion of World War II with an Allied victory should have tipped political accommodations in the Middle East in favor of the Jews for their support of the Allies; the Arabs, despite the White Paper, had evinced treachery and clear leanings toward the Axis. The Jews had no doubt that the whole world understood the enormity of their wartime catastrophe and shared their feeling that it was time to make amends, time for some sort of deed to balance that out—if only somewhat. This "deed" was supposed to be a Jewish state in Palestine.

The British government was in no hurry to make plain its intentions. British elections were scheduled for the end of July 1945, and during the campaign the Labor Party reiterated its firm support for annulling the White Paper and opening the gates of Palestine to Jewish refugees. It even reaffirmed its platform clause about encouraging Arab emigration from Palestine. By now, however, Ben-Gurion and his fellow leaders were well acquainted with the habit of British political parties to express support for the Zionist movement when in opposition and ignore their promises when in government. They were thus hardly surprised when the honeymoon ended once the Labor Party came to power and the new government showed no inclination to change its policy. At the end of August 1945, the British government informed Chaim Weizmann, the president of the Zionist Organization, that it would allow a monthly quota of fifteen hundred immigrants into the area. The Jews took the announcement as a slap in the face.

At the same time, Earl Harrison, President Truman's special envoy to the displaced persons' camps in the American-occupied zone of Germany, published a report exposing the humiliating, disheartening attitude in the camps toward Holocaust survivors. American-Jewish public opinion was shocked. Truman asked the British to immediately allow one hundred thousand Jewish refugees from Europe into Palestine, based on American estimates at the time of the numbers of Jews in the displaced persons' camps in Germany. The request was politely brushed off by the British prime minister, Clement Attlee. Nevertheless, in growing recognition of impoverished Britain's reliance on its wealthy allies across the sea, Attlee proposed setting up an Anglo-American Enquiry Commission to study the problem of Palestine and make recommendations. Time was on Britain's side: the longer the question of Palestine dragged on and faded from international public opinion the easier it would be for Britain to implement its anti-Zionist policy. Moreover, how long could Holocaust survivors, some of whom had been homeless for six years, continue to live out of suitcases in German displaced persons' camps without any prospect of rebuilding their lives? From the Zionist perspective, the problem of the one hundred thousand cited by Truman as the flagship of his humanitarian support for Jews was a two-edged sword: on the one hand, it vitalized and morally justified in world public opinion the Zionist struggle for opening the gates of Palestine to Jewish refugees. On the other hand, the problem of the displaced persons could possibly be solved in isolation from the question of a Jewish state in Palestine: the refugees might find shelter in other countries, such as the United States. Alternatively, the British foreign minister, Ernest Bevin, might allow a one-time provision for the immigration of one hundred thousand refugees and, with that, remove the issue from the international agenda. In the end, Bevin hardened his heart and refused to stray from British policy, whereas the United States allowed a limited number of Jewish refugees into the United States only after the State of Israel was founded. But in the summer of 1945, there was no way of knowing that this was what was going to happen, and the question of Palestine seemed more urgent and fateful than ever.

To dramatize the question of Palestine for world public opinion and drive home to the British government that it could not determine matters unilaterally, the Yishuv's leaders adopted a two-pronged course. One was to encourage the flow of Eastern European refugees to Germany, where they gathered in displaced persons' camps to await the next leg of their journey as "illegal" immigrants to Palestine. This was to keep up survivor morale and keep alive the hope of reaching safe shores in Palestine. It was also to be a daily reminder to the world and especially the American public that, as yet, a satisfactory solution to the refugee problem had not materialized. All sectors of the Yishuv approved of this course of action. The other avenue, however, was controversial from the start. It was formulated at the first large Jewish conclave to convene since the Zionist Congress of 1939—the London Conference of August 1945, at which, notably, Ben-Gurion and Sneh discussed using force against the British. In early October 1945, Ben-Gurion telegrammed instructions to Sneh (who had returned to Palestine) to embark on the anti-British struggle, including recourse to "Route S" (that is, sabotage). This change of policy led to the establishment of the Jewish Resistance Movement.[36]

The negotiations concerning the Resistance Movement were largely conducted by Sneh, the head of the Haganah National Command, under instructions from Ben-Gurion. The agreement was based on the IZL and the LeHI accepting the authority of the resistance's headquarters, to be made up of personnel from the Haganah and the two other organizations. The IZL and the LeHI undertook to refrain from actions not approved by the joint headquarters under Sneh. Sneh, contrary to Galili's opinion, agreed to the demand of the dissenter organizations to reserve freedom of action in arms procurement. This was the weak point of the agreement, and the dissenters were quick to take advantage of it to carry out actions unacceptable to the Haganah.

The Resistance Movement agreement granted legitimacy to the IZL's and the LeHI's actions and, in some respects, was a recognition of their separate status. This made it worth their while to accept the constraints imposed on them. Ben-Gurion hoped that the dissenters would agree to defer to the authority of the Jewish Agency (JA). This did not happen. But the agreement did ensure joint operational planning, and coordination prevented potential clashes between the various fighters. It also gave the resistance's headquarters (Sneh, in fact) the right of veto over actions exceeding the policy approved by the JA and the right to fix the date of operations.

The agreement was concluded with much ambivalence and a good deal of mutual suspicion. No one was really ready to unite, no side was willing to relinquish its autonomy, no organization was prepared to expose its men to the others. The operations were planned in such a way that each body acted separately with no contact between the three ranks. Each organization received its orders and carried them out. Nonetheless, when they required concealment, members of the IZL and the LeHI received shelter and assistance from Labor settlements.

Allon, of course, was in favor of armed struggle against the British. But he opposed the agreement with the dissenter organizations: he considered the agreement unnecessary because it was possible to take steps against the British without the dissenters. He thought the agreement was a mistake because it granted the dissenters the status of "equal partners," legitimating dissent and neutralizing the positive impact of the *saison* on the Yishuv's public opinion. The more resolve the Haganah showed in its war against the British, the more the status of the dissenters would drop. Operationally and politically, he thus saw no reason to make them partners.[37] Galili and Sneh, in contrast, were sharply aware of the dangers involved in separate action and pressed for the agreement.[38]

The Resistance Movement's explicit policy was to avoid, as much as possible, injury to life and limb: the struggle was not against British soldiers but against the policies of the British government. But the dissenters found good reasons, before and after the fact, to justify killings that deviated from this position. The Palmah, in contrast, made it a principle to avoid bloodshed, at real risk to its members. For example, ten minutes before blowing up the Givat Olga police station, which monitored illegal immigration, with the explosives already activated and the men lying near the station fence, one of the men hooked up to the station telephone, notified those inside about the charge, and hung up. This enabled the policemen to leave the building, but it endangered the fighters. The retreating unit immediately came under fire from all directions. The same caution was responsible for the first failed attempt to blow up Haifa's radar station: after receiving a warning, an intrepid British soldier approached and dismantled the explosives. Allon justified taking the risk. He contended that the policy had moral value and political wisdom: when a small, weak people took on a world power, it had to choose its mode of war carefully so as not to arouse the sleeping lion. It was better to sting the British lion, to hint at the Yishuv's military capability, but on no account to cause it come at the Yishuv full force. This thin line, the moral and political boundaries between permissible and impermissible, divided the dissenters from the Palmah.[39]

Despite ideological and moral restraints, the Palmah was eager for battle. After years of training, it was only natural for this body of daring, young people to long for adventure, for an opportunity to prove their mettle and demonstrate their readiness to put their lives on the line. As the Palmah poet Hayyim Gouri had written, "just let the old man give the order"—and now he (Yitzhak Sadeh) did. Very large numbers took part in the undercover operations. Young people walked about tent camps with a spark in their eyes and a secret smile on their lips. It was exciting, a shot of adrenalin—a real-time exercise of everything they had been taught and trained to do. It was not life threatening at first. However, four men, two from the Palmah, two from the field units, fell in the attack on the bases of the notorious British Special Police in Sarona. These were apparently the first of the Palmah's fatalities. Soon Brakha Fuld joined the list and then fourteen others perished when blowing up the a-Ziv Bridge. It was a terrible shock: two of the Palmah's most promising young commanders, Yehiam Weitz and Nehemiah Shein, had been killed. The Haganah had not taken such a bad blow since the disappearance of its twenty-three seamen. And this time, too, an element of mystery surrounded their deaths. Weitz was known to have been hit before the explosives carried by one of the "porters" blew up, apparently killing the others. But speculation remained: Had they been taken captive? Were they roaming the hills stunned? All investigation proved fruitless, and only then was the loss accepted. This was the Palmah's baptism of fire. It grieved with reserve and a stiff upper lip, heralding a culture of bereavement that was to prevail throughout the War of Independence.

The campaign against the British furnished Allon with his first opportunity for relatively broad-scale military action from the perspective of a senior officer. Yitzhak Sadeh was the acting CGS; Sneh was the head of the National Command, and Galili worked alongside him. Allon could not have hoped for a better-disposed constellation for himself and for the Palmah. There was trust and friendship between the various figures of command and operational plans were often the result of informal brainstorming.

The appetite for action on the part of Allon and the Palmah often outstripped the digestive ability of the political leadership or even the

High Command. In principle and praxis, Allon accepted the precept of "purity of arms," but he tended to interpret it flexibly. For example, the Palmah's headquarters conceived a plan to avenge innocent civilians injured by British soldiers during demonstrations or weapon searches. One of the instruments of the people's war used by the Yishuv was passive, mass resistance. It appears that in this period more Jews fell in clashes with the British army on kibbutzim and in towns than in the Palmah's actions. The Palmah proposed to ambush and strike at army units that had conducted the violent searches. The proposal was not totally removed from the LeHI's actions. According to Allon, the Haganah High Command approved of the plan, but the political institutions scrapped it.[40] On another occasion, he suggested blowing up military aircraft. Sneh gave the job to the two dissenter organizations. "I really couldn't forgive him for this," Allon noted.[41] Jealousy of the dissenters resurfaced when Sadeh informed him of the IZL's planned action at Jerusalem's King David Hotel, for him to warn the Palmah units at Ramat Rachel and other kibbutzim in the area of the danger of searches. "I confess I was eaten up by jealousy and I asked why we weren't given this target. But Yitzhak replied that it had been their idea."[42] One daring scheme was to blow up a British warship at the Port of Malta. Allon and David Nameri flew to Malta (Allon's first flight ever) and returned within twenty-four hours. While there, they took a rowboat and reconnoitered the port. The mission did not seem particularly difficult or dangerous. But the political leadership vetoed it, limiting the sabotage of British ships to the port of Haifa.

While the Palmah was careful to follow the High Command's instructions, Allon took some liberty if he thought an action was likely to be approved. Thus, without waiting, when the opportunity presented itself he allowed Yohai Bin-Nun (later the commander of the naval commando force and of the Israeli navy) to install an explosive device at the refueling pier in the port of Haifa to be activated when a ship was next in dock. But when he asked for final permission, he received a "resounding no." The British discovered and dismantled the device. Allon was interrogated by the High Command and tried for acting without authorization. But his "defense," that he would never have carried out the mission without authorization, was ultimately accepted; he got off with a reprimand.[43] It is hard to imagine a more smarting outcome in the highly sympathetic High Command constituted of Sadeh and Galili.

The most complicated and impressive operation of the Jewish Resistance Movement fell to the Palmah. This was the "Night of the Bridges," carried out on 17 June 1946, in which ten of the eleven bridges connecting Palestine with its neighbors were blown up. It was a miracle of coordination and cooperation. The units set out without any means of communication, neither receiving nor transmitting information. Everything hinged on the capability, resourcefulness and single-mindedness of the commanders. It involved hundreds of Palmahniks, from porters to patrol and diversionary forces to sappers. Following detonation, every unit was to retreat quickly so as not to implicate nearby settlements and to elude the British, who had gone on high alert right after the first explosion. Apart from the mishap at the a-Ziv Bridge, described earlier in this chapter, the missions were all successful, all the units got away. It worked like a well-oiled machine, arousing the admiration even of the British high commissioner, Alan Cunningham. His "sportsman-like" reaction somewhat reassured Chaim Weizmann, the president of the Zionist Organization and the architect of the Jewish-British cooperation, who had shrunk from armed struggle; he believed it could bring down disaster on the Yishuv. The high commissioner's reaction notwithstanding, the government of Palestine clearly could not ignore so blatant a challenge to its authority.

The reaction came on 29 June 1946. In what came to be known as "Operation Agatha" by the British and "Black Saturday" by the Jews, leaders of the Yishuv were picked up and arrested at Latrun. Searches were conducted to unearth material implicating the Jewish Agency in the Resistance Movement, and numerous documents of the JA Executive were confiscated. The British went after Sneh, Galili, Sadeh, and Allon, but they had managed to go underground. There were mass searches and arrests on kibbutzim suspected of being the Palmah's training grounds, though most of the Palmahniks managed to hide. The detainees were imprisoned in Rafiah. Mizra's Palmah headquarters was discovered and the members' card index seized; luckily, it was in code and the British failed to crack it. There was nervousness about the British finding the Palmah's archive if the hunt went on. Haganah personnel at Mizra thus decided to burn the archive—much to the misfortune of future historians. One of the most dramatic searches was at Kibbutz Yagur, where the British tracked down the Haganah's main arms cache. The Haganah's orders ruled out armed resistance to British actions; there could be passive resistance only.

The blow of Black Saturday was mainly psychological. Relations between the Yishuv and the government of Palestine rested on the latent assumption that the British were not Germans, and there was no great fear of brutal suppression. This now proved false. To be sure, the British did not behave like the Nazis (though such accusations were heard in the propaganda war), but they could, if they so desired, crush the Yishuv economically and militarily. The mass arrests, seizure of arms, neutralization of the political leadership—all signaled that the British had removed their gloves. After the dust settled, the blow turned out not to have been all that severe: the Haganah and the Palmah suffered minimally; the military leadership retained its autonomy. Ben-Gurion was in Paris and avoided arrest, continuing his political efforts with the help of other Zionist leaders from Palestine and the Diaspora. The Zionist movement and Jewish Yishuv in Palestine remained intact. Politically, however, the realization that the British authorities had the power to destroy the Zionist enterprise was of the greatest significance.

Right after Black Saturday, Weizmann demanded that Sneh put off all of the Resistance's actions until after the JA Executive convention in Paris. Plans raised before Black Saturday, though not yet approved, included an IZL and LeHI strike at two key government buildings as well as an arms "procurement" operation by the Palmah at Bat Galim to compensate the Haganah for the confiscation of its arms cache at Yagur. These plans were now approved by Sneh. When Weizmann heard of it, he took what was for him an extraordinary measure, bringing his weight to bear as president of the Zionist Organization and threatening to resign. Sneh put the matter to the X Committee, the civilian body that decided on all actions. When it backtracked and decided to stop all activity until the JA Executive session, Sneh resigned as head of the Haganah National Command. He meant to sail, undercover, to France and put his case for "continuous armed struggle" before the JA Executive. At the same time, he sent Begin a note asking him to delay the operation. While waiting at the port of Haifa to embark for France, he received word that the IZL had blown up the King David Hotel in Jerusalem. A hotel wing was destroyed and eighty people killed. The IZL claimed that it had phoned in a warning to the chief secretary of the government of Palestine, whose offices were on the premises, but that the latter had high-handedly refused to evacuate the building. Sadeh protested that the IZL had changed the original plan that he himself had approved before Black Saturday. The action, he said, was to have been undertaken when the building was empty; the IZL had carried it out at noon, when the hotel was filled with people.[44]

The action was the undoing of the Resistance Movement. As far as the Haganah was concerned, it was also the end of the "continuous struggle," that is, military operations unrelated to "illegal immigration." The Zionist Organization withdrew from the use of force; it concentrated on a worldwide public opinion campaign targeting both Jews and non-Jews and revolving around the epos of clandestine immigration and on diplomatic efforts.

Allon and his people accused the Haganah of defeatism: "A wave of resentment washed through Palmah camps. The fighters would not accept the lull," claimed Allon. Some said the Zionist leadership had no right to be in charge of the struggle, some suggested that the Palmah act on its own authority. But the Palmah's headquarters nipped these trends in the bud.⁴⁵

Ben-Gurion explained the need to stop the armed struggle to Galili and his colleagues at the Zionist Congress in Basle in December 1946. He said the orientation had to be changed from anti-British struggle to the showdown over Palestine's future, a matter that was fast approaching and would entail war with the Arabs. This war, he claimed, would not be only against Palestine's Arabs, but also against Arab states supported by the British. The new orientation meant stepping up illegal immigration, giving priority to arms procurement, and strengthening the Haganah and the Palmah. Allon did not conceal his distrust of Ben-Gurion.⁴⁶ Some in the KM suspected that Ben-Gurion was merely adopting an ideology that fitted the alliance he had struck with the president of the World Jewish Congress, Nahum Goldmann, to promote the political solution of Palestine's partition and to justify ending the struggle.

Advocates of the "continuous struggle" thought in tactical not strategic terms: Was the damage inflicted on the government of Palestine in the anti-British struggle worth wearing out the Yishuv's military force? But the youngsters clamored for action: again, the fighters, the doers, posed a front against the old political guard, the talkers. Allon found it hard to change over from the thrills of the struggle to the drab days that followed. This, as Galili saw it, was Allon's greatest test prior to the War of Independence.⁴⁷ He, like his friends, was downcast.⁴⁸ Galili, meanwhile, was going through one of his toughest periods: Ben-Gurion and Sneh were in Paris, Moshe Shertok (Sharett), the head of the JA-PD, was imprisoned at Latrun, and he found himself the acting head of the National Command after Ze'ev Sheffer (Feinstein) was made Sneh's acting replacement. A member of Kibbutz Ayelet Ha-Shahar, Sheffer was a good man, but he had no authority in defense matters.

The major arena seemed to have moved from Palestine to Europe: that is where the Berihah (Flight) Movement was, directing the flow of Holocaust survivors from eastern to western Europe; that is where "illegal immigration" was being organized; that is where the 22nd Zionist Congress was to take fateful political decisions. In addition, Ruth Allon was there—she had been sent as an emissary to an orphanage of survivor children at the displaced persons' camp in Landsberg, Germany. All roads led to Europe. Galili too was about to set out as a delegate to the Congress. He suggested that Allon join him, see his wife, and broaden his horizons. Allon was pleased. He obtained permission from Sadeh, the CGS. Shaul Meirov (Avigur), who was in charge of the Mossad's clandestine immigration activities, agreed to Allon's request to call on the Palmah marine companies scattered all over the Mediterranean coast, which were responsible for sailing the immigrant ships. The trip to

Europe lasted four months. Allon came face to face with the Jewish people on the move and the trials of Jewish existence. The journey began in Basle. From there, Allon and Galili traveled to Germany and stole their way into Austria, Czechoslovakia, and Poland. Allon returned to France and then set out to tour the embarkation ports of immigrant ships.

The Congress in Basle was highly charged: it was the first Congress since the parting of ways in Geneva in August 1939 when news arrived of the Molotov-Ribbentrop Pact and everyone had rushed home in advent of the war. Seven years had passed—and what years they were! The 22nd Congress brought together delegates from the free world and delegates of survivors, and tale after horrific tale was heard from the podium. It was also the scene of another drama: the weary, old president of the Zionist Organization, Chaim Weizmann, speaking in Yiddish, delivered his final major speech against the use of force, against armed struggle. It was the swan song of a great leader and so it was received, with lingering applause. Weizmann's ousting by an activist coalition led by Ben-Gurion and Abba Hillel Silver, the leader of U.S. Jewry, did not see the struggle resumed. The Executive decided to conduct further negotiations with Britain, to exhaust diplomatic channels, while stepping up the pressure of illegal immigration.

Allon seems to have remained untouched by these dramas. His impressions of the Congress's discussions, his meetings with delegates, the great Zionist drama—there are no reports on this. He strolled through Basle like a casual tourist visiting Europe for the first time: museums, scenery, architecture—all that was so very different from little Palestine. One assumes that his encounter with European culture must have been intoxicating. But there is no testimony of this either.

One meeting he described as "very important to [him]" was with Itzhak Ciukerman (Antek), one of the commanders of the Warsaw Ghetto uprising and a leader of Poland's Dror Zionist youth movement.[49] The two formed a close friendship and met up again in Paris. They would sit for hours over a chess board speaking little. Every now and then Antek would say something out of context. Allon understood; there was an intuitive rapport between them. The Kielce pogrom in the summer of 1946 furnished a main topic of their conversation. Local Poles had taken axes to Holocaust survivors, murdering dozens. Allon probed Antek on the motivation of the assailants, their socioeconomic status, the attitude of the regime, and so forth. Their friendship continued through the years. Allon had great respect for the ghetto fighters. When Antek's spouse and co-commander of the Warsaw Ghetto, Zivia Lubetkin, came to Palestine, Allon escorted her on visits to Palmah units. He did much to instill the legend of ghetto fighters in the collective memory of Palestine's young.[50]

But the encounter he considered most important, "certainly more so than the Congress itself," was the convening of Haganah members with Sneh, Avigur, Galili, Dori, and Shadmi. The mini-convention centered on Berihah work and illegal immigration, the Haganah in Europe, and arms procurement. One of the meetings was attended by the Haganah emissary Hayyim Slavin, who reported on arms purchases from American surplus.[51] This was the start of the psychological and practical transition from armed struggle to the illegal immigration campaign. Soon after Sneh became the head of immigration at the Jewish Agency.

From Basle, Allon and Galili journeyed via Austria to Germany, where Galili headed for Munich and Allon joined Ruth at Landsberg. From Innsbruck to Germany, Allon and Galili drove in Shimon Avidan's car. The window was broken, there was no heating, and the cold crept into Allon's bones. Avidan was greatly perturbed by the question of revenge and he spoke to his two guests about it. He had inherited the mission of vengeance from the poet and ghetto rebel Abba Kovner, who had been arrested in Egypt en route to Germany, carrying poison from Palestine on him; he had intended to poison the water system of a large city. Avidan set up a unit made up of Kovner's people, graduates of the Palmah's German Platoon, and ordinary Jews on hand.

The Kovner group viewed all Germans as responsible for the murder of Jews. They sought mass revenge, making no distinction between saints and sinners. Avidan found it hard to swallow the idea of total revenge. His approach was more selective, based on guilt: former SS members, concentration camp staff, and so forth. But this too presented problems: How was the German public to know that someone who had vanished had been executed in revenge? And if they were not to know, what was the point of the execution? Moreocver, any action drawing public attention could endanger the entire Berihah and illegal-immigration operation. The Allies might respond by sealing escape routes, blocking the way of the Jews to the ports. Was it legitimate or worthwhile to place at risk the larger issue of Jewish immigration out of petty revenge? What's more, since the war's end, hundreds of thousands of Jews had gathered in displaced persons' camps. There, they were in a protected environment, under the U.S. or British army, living among Jews. Yet at the same time, thousands of Jews had found places for themselves in German cities and towns. Their choice might be reprehensible—to live among people who had committed genocide against their own. But did this make it legitimate to expose them to possible German reprisal? On the other hand, it was hard to watch tight-lipped Germans back from the war going about their business as if nothing had happened. These are the questions and issues Avidan grappled with in the conversation with Allon, especially after Galili alighted in Munich. It was a moment of grace in the long, complex relationship between the two men. Avidan felt that he could talk to Allon openly, that his words fell on an attentive, sympathetic ear. He found an Allon more mature than in the past, inquisitive and receptive. Allon did not attempt to conciliate Avidan; he gave the matter careful consideration. Avidan surmised that Galili and Allon had been instructed by the Haganah High Command to curtail the revenge activity because of more immediate Jewish interests and the larger picture of Zionist policy. But Allon did not reject individual revenge. He encouraged Avidan to continue striking at the guilty without resorting to mass killings.[52]

At the mini-convention of the Haganah's leadership at the Congress, Berihah activists gave a report on their work. Galili and Allon were fired up by the idea of visiting Poland, paying their respects at the mass grave that it was, and viewing the Berihah network from up close. Looking back, it was a foolish, irresponsible act: the commander of the Palmah and the acting head of the Haganah National Command—the two top figures in the Yishuv's defense network—dressed up as displaced persons, obtained forged documents, and stole across borders in the reverse direction of Beriha operations; from Germany to Czechoslovakia and from there to Poland. They spoke no Polish, yet their documents stated that they were Poles. Zevi Netzer of the Mossad, who was active in Poland's Berihah, took charge of the trip and their security. Considering that Raoul Wallenberg ended his life in a Soviet prison without having stolen across any borders, the escapade cannot be said to have been all too sensible. But these were stormy times: thousands of refugees were on the march, the communists had not yet gained complete control of Poland and Czechoslovakia, and the borders were not hermetically sealed. The group crossed into Poland in early January 1947.

Poland was on the eve of a referendum about its future and the air was thick with tension. The poll was scheduled for 19 January 1947. A right-wing underground struck at Jews and communists and the communist authorities clamped down with an iron hand. It was hardly a time for tourists, particularly illegal ones, to visit the country. Allon and Galili spent ten days there escorted by Netzer, who both watched over them and acted as their interpreter. In the midst of this, Galili received word that he was to return to Basle for consultation by Ben-Gurion. That same night, the three boarded a train to the kibbutz-*hakhshara* training camp at Katowice, near Auschwitz. They spent the day chatting with local activists, and the next day they were driven to Auschwitz and Birkenau. Everything was still fresh, raw, exposed. Polish boys were digging up skulls in their treasure hunt for gold teeth. Words spilled out of the local hosts about the colossal German duplicity, about the medical experiments. Galili reached for a biblical phrase to describe the visit as "a burn by fire" (Leviticus 13:24). As for Allon—Galili said that he absorbed mammoth lessons in hate and could not stop saying that it was beyond the human grasp: he kept citing the incongruity between Germany's cultural breadth, even as it lay in ruins, and this savagery. In their meetings with the people of *hakhshara* and the Berihah, however, the two men were businesslike, asking pertinent questions about escape routes, the number of people streaming to the border, the modus operandi. The "locals" were stirred by the meeting. Said one of them: "When I saw Galili with his fair forelock and Yigal, a handsome young man, the words got stuck in my throat: here I was, a refugee who had survived, privileged to welcome the commanders of the Haganah from Eretz Israel."[53] In the evening, on the few minutes' walk to the train station, an army truck pulled up beside the men, and soldiers jumped out with weapons ready. There was no way of knowing at first if the soldiers belonged to the Right's underground or to the regime. Netzer, a master of improvisation, quickly drew the soldiers' attention to himself, brandishing his gun, for which he had a permit, and his forged papers. Had the soldiers tried to have the others speak, the War of Independence would have been written up differently.[54]

Allon never spoke of his trip to Poland. He kept a special place in his heart for Antek and Zivia, for Holocaust memory. In his letters to Ruth from that period he referred to Europe as the "cursed continent." Was he moved by a measure of pain and compassion at the tragedy of his people? Or merely by rage and vengeance at the shame and humiliation—a natural reaction for a native son of Eretz Israel raised on values of Jewish defense, freedom and honor? In his talks with Netzer, he showed no emotion. In his meetings with the *hakhshara* people, he was matter-of-fact. Perhaps this was because he did not know them, did not know Polish, and was not comfortable baring his feelings to them. Even years later, he and Galili both found it hard to speak of the experience. Was this a cultural reticence of silent stoicism, even as one longed to cry out? What impression did the events leave on Allon if still years later he would not speak of them? According to Avidan, Allon thought with his heart as well as his head, but he did not wear his heart on his sleeve.[55]

He may have clamped down from an aversion to what he saw in the displaced persons' camps. Conditions were intolerable; overcrowding, no privacy, minimal hygiene. The Jews lived out of suitcases, and many were prepared to do almost anything to eke out a penny: the figures entitled to UNRRA (United Nations Relief and Rehabilitation Administration) assistance were inflated with "dead souls"; black marketeering, smuggling, and dealing in foreign currency were not uncommon. There was virtually no meeting ground between the Palestinian emissaries and the displaced persons. The emissaries saw idleness and the playing of cards and games of chance and put these down to the negative experience of life in Exile, exacerbated by the Holocaust; the exigencies of camp life and its unending, unbearable state of limbo escaped them. Products of Palestine, the emissaries measured the survivors by the yardstick of Palestinian calm rather than European devastation. They failed to understand what the displaced persons had been through and that their current distress led many to "round corners" and pursue borderline activities. So shocked was Ruth by the refugee experience that after her first visit to a displaced persons' camp she wrote: "How are we to absorb this human material by the thousands; will we be able to make them forget this sort of life style and set them on utterly different lines, straight and productive? How are we to turn them into working people with a love of homeland?"[56] Not only did Allon not like what he saw, but most of his information was second-hand, via the emissaries. Instead of admiring the zest for life and astounding vitality displayed by the survivors, the emissaries came away with the impression that the survivors were not "aesthetic." In the camps, for the first time, the young man from Mes'ha came across anti-Zionist Jews who wished to make their homes in America. Tolerance was hardly the strong suit of Eretz Israel's young: he could not stand them.[57] (He forgot that his own father had also tried his luck in the United States, returning home only after not making it there.) Avidan, in a long talk, tried to explain to Allon what these people, for whom the war had not ended, were undergoing. He thought Allon understood. But Allon apparently did not delve into the matter. He asked about the Haganah's organization in the camps but made no attempt to come into direct contact with the survivors. On his visit to Ruth's place of work, an orphanage of the Coordination (a nonparty organization locating and retrieving Jewish children deposited with Polish gentile families or in monasteries), he grasped the enormity of the task, the enormity of her responsibilities. Yet he clung to a petty, partisan, party view: in the face of the nonaffiliated orphanage, he voiced to Avraham Givelber, the KM's senior figure in Munich, his doubts about the "movement" value of Ruth's work since the orphanage was not a project of Dror, a KM affiliate.[58]

Allon visited every European location where there were Palmah personnel, including radio transmitters and seamen. He listened patiently to their problems, offered an encouraging word, championed them before the Mossad. He was able to chat for hours with two female radio operators in Milan and elaborate to them the entire Zionist struggle, gravely and with concern. He skipped no one.[59] "These meetings with our members, wherever they were, were my most pleasant and important hours while I was in Europe, despite the depression often emanating from them," Allon wrote to his people upon returning home.[60] His intervention with the Mossad was due to the tension that had arisen between the organization and the Palmahniks who had been co-opted to it. The Palmahniks as usual thought they could do everything better, and the Mossad people, older and more experienced, hardly appreciated their arrogance.⁶¹ The Palmahniks were not given key organizational tasks in the clandestine immigration plans; rather, they were meant to serve as seamen, officers, and captains responsible for sailing the ships to Palestine. In Allon's negotiations with the institutions in Palestine, he jealously guarded the rights of Palmahniks in the Diaspora.⁶² But he did not manage to have the functions changed.

In the tradition of the Labor Movement, Allon believed that the road to salvation lay not in diplomacy but in "the constructive deed of deliverance."⁶³ This meant clandestine immigration, settlement, and, of course, armed struggle. The center weight of Zionist activity, however, had shifted to the diplomatic plane. The Palmah could not look forward to exploits in the near future.

From the start of the summer of 1946, the organized Yishuv no longer really operated against the British. The only active measure was the resistance of illegal immigrants to being transferred to deportation ships that would take them to Cyprus for detention in British-built camps. A British warship would approach an immigrant ship filled with men, women, and children and demand surrender. The immigrants would refuse, defying the British Empire by throwing tins of food, flourishing sticks, and wielding any other "domestic" weapons that came to hand. The British responded with tear gas and brute force, dragging the immigrants onto the evacuation ships. It was an unequal contest and the immigrants always lost, incurring casualties. The order to resist stemmed from the perception that the banishment of Jews who had made it to their homeland's shores was not to be countenanced. This is how Allon and other Haganah commanders saw it. In time, it was also considered necessary to signal to the British that they were not to contemplate either tougher measures or the deportation of immigrants back to their embarkation ports. Regarding worldwide public opinion, it was enormously important to show the resolve of immigrants to remain in Palestine.

But as it became clear that the Yishuv itself was not actually joining the immigrant struggle and that the city of Haifa was not even breaking curfew while dramas of exile and desperate resistance were unfolding at its port, it became increasingly harder for the Palmah men to maintain "unarmed resistance" in the scuffles. One of Allon's bold friends from the field company days, Joseph Harel (Hamburger), appreciated the human suffering with the very first refugee ship he captained, the *Knesset Yisrael*. Suddenly, the refugees were no longer a Zionist slogan but flesh and blood. He had a rough time and met with Allon at the end of the trip to describe the practical implications of the order to resist. There had been some four thousand people aboard, including about a dozen infants—the oldest being eighteen days old—and resistance had been left to the young and able-bodied. The chaos had been appalling. The British had sprayed the deck with tear gas, it had been hard to breathe, the roof caught fire, and people had jumped into the water from a height of nine meters without knowing how to swim. In the stampede to reach the open air of the deck, children had been in danger of being trampled. It was heart stopping: would the infants survive the tear gas? As he described the scene, Harel sensed Allon's complete identification, almost as if he himself had been there. And then Harel said that Allon had given the order to resist and they had resisted. Furthermore, if Allon gave the order again, they would do it again. But as long as Allon did not order the children's house at Kibbutz Ein Harod to endure tear gas, he did not have the moral right to command these refugees whose infants *were* being exposed to the gas.[64] His words angered Allon, but they also jolted him. All at once, he understood the human import of the order he had given. Yet he did not waver. At the end of May 1947, he wrote to the personnel of the Palmah Marine Company: "My order, for unarmed resistance to the capture of ships and the transfer to deportation ships, stands. Organize accordingly. Alert the immigrants. Buck up the escorts prior to every sailing."[65] A month later, he had to send another sharp letter to the escorts in Europe, warning against "the negative turn in the attitude of several escorts to the principle of 'resistance,' so much so that in recent ships, resistance has waned almost totally." He summed up: "Fully conscious of the responsibility I am assuming, I say: resistance must go on despite the victims."[66]

It was neither callousness nor incomprehension that caused him to fan the embers of the Zionist struggle on the backs of survivors. "Nothing distresses me more than the casualties at the homeland door of these survivors who escaped the seven gates of hell," he wrote to Ruth after the episode of the *Exodus*, whose resistance and final deportation back to Germany made front-page news in the summer of 1947. He simply was convinced that, at this stage, there were no other weapons available and that, ultimately, the struggle was as much for the illegal immigrants as for the Yishuv as a whole. "I regard them as soldiers who fell in battle. The blood of justice fighters is not in vain and in the end will help save many lives," he elaborated to Ruth.[67] But it was also the obduracy of a young man whose empathy and compassion reached only as far as his narrow cultural sphere. The refugees were "others." In time, he referred to the subject delicately in *Sefer Ha-Palmah*: "On the whole, for no few years, many of Eretz Israel's native sons were impaired by a lack of understanding of the problems of the Diaspora and even by some sense of superiority toward its Jews. Even the Palmah did not all at once come to recognize the common [destiny and peoplehood]."[68]

Ruth and Yigal journeyed to Europe in the same month—December 1946. Ruth went for a year while Nurit was placed in care near Tel Aviv. Ruth seems to have needed the break from her daughter, who was now six. The Yishuv's emissaries to the Diaspora were not always chosen on the basis of qualifications. Often enough, the candidates were sent off to solve personal problems: a woman separated from her husband, a young man who could not find his feet on a kibbutz. Ruth's mission was aimed at granting her a breather from the unrelieved strain of caring for Nurit. To everyone's delight, she proved herself eminently capable in her work in Germany. Allon heard glowing reports of his wife's talents from all the emissaries returning from Germany. Even Tabenkin sang her praises.

Nurit's development was heartbreakingly slow. She was a lovely child, but there was a frustrating imbalance between her physical and mental development. Grandpa Paicovich refused to accept that his granddaughter was retarded. She is fine, he claimed, she just tends to be on the quiet side.[69] Allon assumed the responsibility for her care after his return from Europe in March 1947 and bore it with love and devotion, beyond what one might expect from someone so busy. He set aside weekends for visits and took her to Ginossar, to members of the large Paicovich family (one of whom was arrested by the British on suspicion of involvement in the IZL[70]), or to Ruth's sisters. He spent long hours playing with her, on outings, at shared meals. Right after his return, he took her to buy sandals at a well-known children's shoe store in Tel Aviv,[71] and he showed an interest in the cloth chosen to sew her clothes (at Ginossar). Their visits were warm and cheerful. "My visits to her always give me great pleasure and gratification though I won't conceal from you that my pleasure is tempered with a drop of pain at our beloved's fate," he wrote to Ruth. While out of the country, he had hoped for an improvement in her condition, "and sometimes, on long train journeys in Europe, I would fancifully visualize her greeting me like a completely ordinary little girl. My imagination of course played tricks on me and I did not find her so. But why depress you? Forgive me."[72] Allon did not often pour his heart out about Nurit in order not to grieve Ruth. Rarely did a note of pain creep into the cheerful demeanor he presented. If this is the face he showed his wife, one may suppose that he was far less open with friends and acquaintances.

There was little knowledge of child psychology at the time, and not only in Palestine. The very diagnosis was uncertain as was the distinction between mental illness and brain damage. Allon accepted Nurit's retardation as one accepts a natural disaster, yet there was always hope . . .

perhaps in America, perhaps in Switzerland.[73] When Dr. Hannah Sneh, Moshe's wife and a pediatrician, suggested that Nurit be examined by Dr. Brock, a specialist in childhood retardation on a visit from Paris, Allon jumped at the chance, exposing a raw nerve.[74] Dr. Brock was unable to see her in Palestine and Allon began to weave plans to take Nurit to him in Paris.

From May to November 1947, these plans—to take Nurit to Paris and meet Ruth there—were the secret axis of his life. The times were tense, reminiscent of the eve of the Arab Disturbances and he was hardly avid to leave. But his daughter came first. He began to prepare the Palmah and HGS for the possibility that he might have to be away for a couple of months.[75] He obtained detailed medical reports on Nurit, saw to visas for France, and outfitted the child for the European climate. He also began to scrounge around for funds: the first sacrifice he made was the radio; Allon was fond of listening to classical music on Friday evenings (a habit he apparently picked up from Ruth). That precious radio was now sold on the altar of the trip.[76] Soon to follow was the dining room set.

Amid his preparations, Ruth wrote to him that she did not see herself leaving her post before her year of duty was up, which meant postponing the trip until the winter. Allon was not happy about it. The European winter appeared sinister, while the postponement itself was not a good sign; the doctors might advise a visit to their American colleagues, in which case it was a pity to lose time. Additionally, the security situation in Palestine was heating up in anticipation of the UN session on Palestine, which was scheduled for the autumn. "It will obviously be hard for me to leave the country in times of unusual emergency,." he wrote.[77] But he accepted Ruth's decision not to cut short her mission.[78]

The countdown had begun to the UN deliberations of 29 November 1947. At the port of Haifa, one of the great dramas in the epos of illegal immigration was unfolding before the eyes of the United Nations Special Committee on Palestine (UNSCOP). Immigrants of the *Exodus* were being forcibly removed to deportation ships and sent back to Europe. Meanwhile, the IZL executed two British sergeants by hanging in reprisal for the hanging of their members in a British prison. At a cafe on the bank of the Yarkon, an Arab gang caused mayhem, robbing and killing Jewish clients. The field force retaliated and Allon welcomed the move: "Were it not for the disaster that an entire Arab family was killed, this action of theirs could be regarded as a successful operation," he wrote.[79] Because of swelling Arab-Jewish tension, Allon intimated in his letters to Ruth that it would be better to advance the trip to Paris. She yielded but gave him cause to feel guilty about cutting short her work. "I'm sorry if my letters put any pressure on you and caused you to speed up the trip to Paris," he apologized. "Of course if you receive the rest of my letters meanwhile and change your mind and decide to put off the trip for a couple of months, I will not complain but wait patiently."[80] He made sure to add Nurit's name to his passport and arranged with Galili that Sadeh would replace him ("meanwhile, for the duration of the trip").[81]

In his correspondence with Hannah Sneh, Dr. Brock recommended certain tests and electric therapy for Nurit before she was brought to him. During this period, Allon installed Nurit in his room in Tel Aviv, where Ruth's younger sister looked after her. He left no stone unturned; he asked acquaintances traveling to the United States to check out what was happening in the field there. The sale of the radio had apparently impressed Ginossar's secretariat and it demanded that Allon allow the kibbutz to help defray the expenses of Nurit's care. He deferred the offer "until [he would] have no choice."[82] He kept putting funds together from the sale of possessions and planned to take a loan of £200 from the Haganah, against his severance and pension funds.[83]

Throughout, Jewish-Arab tensions rose with the level of uncertainty. No one knew what was going to happen: Would the British really leave Palestine? Allon did not believe it. Would the Arab states embark on war if the UN voted in favor of partition? Allon doubted it. Would a Jewish state rise? He thought this an illusion born of mistaken policy. The winds of war were blowing in the country's north. Allon's reaction was: "The Arab states are waging a war of nerves against us. For several days now, Syria's mechanized force has been poised on the country's northern border *pretending that it is planning to invade. . . . Upon the make-believe evacuation of the English,* they—that is, the Arabs—will try to establish the fact that they are the rulers of this country" (emphasis mine).[84] Allon traveled up to the Galilee with Galili and Sneh to inspect preparations to stop the Syrians. "I will write you tomorrow when I return, if I'm not too exhausted," he advised Ruth.[85]

As he continued his arrangements for the trip, his colleagues in the Haganah looked for ways to help him out financially. One suggestion was that he again go on an inspection of Palmah units in Europe or perform some other duty. He dismissed it outright: "I'm not looking for a cover to spend public funds on private affairs," he said. But then Galili surprised him, suggesting a short mission that, if he, Allon did not take on, someone else would have to. Allon knew that this was Galili's way of coming to his aid. But it was presented to him in a manner that left no room for refusal.[86]

In early November, Ruth sent a telegram asking Allon to postpone the trip. She had left her post and had met with Dr. Brock in Paris. He planned to be in Palestine in April 1948, at which time he would be able to examine Nurit at leisure, in her natural surroundings. Allon had travel fever and his "friends were already divided into those for or against the trip (at this time)."[87] Yet he carefully turned the matter over: "Though from my youth I have been able to make decisions, even on extremely serious questions, this time I find it immeasurably hard to reach a decision." In the end, he postponed the trip and applied himself to assuaging Ruth's guilty feelings over having cut short her tour of duty for nothing. He asked her to come home at once, to the family that so eagerly awaited her. "If we are together, we will find solace in one other and do better than any other way."[88] Less than two weeks later the country was at war: the War of Independence had erupted.

During those long months when Allon's thoughts were with his child and wife, great changes had been taking place in the country. True to his word at the 22nd Zionist Congress, Ben-Gurion became deeply involved in the Haganah. He invited the Haganah's commanders, members of the National Command, and anyone connected with the High Command to a "seminar" to enlighten himself about the state and capability of the defense forces. He asked questions, probed, and tried to form his own opinion regarding the professional level of both the commanders and the lower ranks, all leading up to the question: Would they be able to withstand the Arabs on the day that the British evacuated the country? The younger the respondents, the more confident was their reply. The older ones (Joseph Avidar, Yohanan Ratner) believed it doable but showed caution and qualified it with conditions. Ratner pressed for reorganization and predicted heavy losses.[89] A major question concerned the High Command: Who was to be the chief of general staff and who the head of the National Command? As mentioned earlier, Yitzhak Sadeh had taken over for Dori as the CGS in the autumn of 1945. Ze'ev Sheffer, with Galili's assistance, had acted as the head of the National Command since Sneh's resignation in July 1946. Both appointments were not up to scratch: Sheffer was clearly not the man to lead the defense forces at this critical time, while Sadeh—as even his closest friends agreed—was not CGS material. Yigael Yadin, in charge of the planning bureau, had left the job in exasperation with Sadeh's haphazard working methods.[90] Sneh had already written Dori in August 1946, announcing, "I see your return to your former post as a must,"[91] even though the two men had often clashed in the past. At a meeting with Eliezer Shoshani and Yigal Allon, the two representatives of the Palmah, Ben-Gurion asked how they would "fill" the positions of the CGS and the head of the National Command; in other words, who would they place at the top of the pyramid? They were hard put to supply a satisfactory answer. There were three candidates: Dori, Avidar, and Sadeh. Avidar, it was agreed, did not have the necessary abilities to be the CGS. They categorized Yitzhak Sadeh as having "intelligence, courage, ability to command, initiative, knowledge. He had no organizational sense." To characterize Ya'akov Dori, they referred back to Sadeh: "Ya'akov has what Yitzhak lacks and lacks what Yitzhak has." As for the head of the National Command, they thought that Galili could fill the job but expected snags because he belonged to the LAHA opposition party.[92] In early June 1947, Ben-Gurion finalized both appointments: Dori returned as the CGS and Galili was made the head of the National Command. Ben-Gurion had offered him the post on his summons to Paris from Poland, where he had been with Allon.[93] Militarily, Galili was the natural choice: he knew the defense forces from up close and had the trust of the National Command. Politically, it was far from natural: Galili's party was in opposition to Mapai and Ben-Gurion. But the two men went back a long way, to the pre-split period when they had been in the same activist camp of the same party, and their relationship was based on trust, intimacy, and mutual respect. In the absence of a more suitable candidate, Ben-Gurion could thus turn somewhat of a blind eye to political affiliations, at least temporarily. Galili's colleagues could not really plumb the ambivalent relationship between the two. Galili hesitated, waiting for the "movement's judgment" to force him to accept the position. Allon and his friends in the Palmah and the Haganah rose to the occasion, and he agreed.[94]

Dori's return as the CGS was a blow to Sadeh. "I only feel sorry for the old darling who will be offended by the demotion," Allon wrote to Ruth. He acknowledged that Sadeh "had not properly displayed the extent of his abilities in his term in office," but he thought that the conservative Dori was even less fit to meet the needs of the hour. He explained Dori's appointment on the force of political circumstances: if the head of the National Command belonged to the opposition, the CGS had to be a Mapainik. Allon assumed that Sadeh would return to head the Palmah.[95] But Sadeh shied away from ousting Allon. Nor is it at all sure that the High Command would have agreed.

In 1950, Galili noted: "A while back I reminded Yigal Allon that when we came back from Europe together after calling on our men in illegal immigration, he tried to convince me that there was no longer anything for the Palmah to do."[96] Allon asked for leave to resign from Palmah's headquarters, return to Ginossar for a while, and then devote himself to movement affairs on the KM secretariat. In the vernacular of those days, his reason was that "there's no job to do."[97] Galili argued with him the entire way and almost, but not quite, broke him. It took David Nameri (whom Allon was fond of) and Shaul Avigur (whom he respected) to apply further pressure before Allon agreed to shelve the idea of quitting the defense force. But he was restless: the fact that Ruth was in Germany and he had sole charge of holding the family together and seeing to Nurit's care did not add to his peace of mind.[98]

In this period, Allon was apparently bitten by the political fly. His desire to leave the Palmah fell in with his ambition to try his hand at politics. A thwarted enthusiasm for action may have combined with a weariness of the Palmah's everyday affairs to make him think about forming a new party to challenge Mapai's rule. "After I returned from Europe, I began to think out loud and before friends that it was time to look into uniting the party with Ha-Shomer Ha-Tza'ir (HSHT) and creating a Left party."[99] He was well aware of the differences on foreign policy and the anti-British struggle between the KM, himself included, and the HSHT Party. He did not hold with the HSHT's conception of a binational state in Palestine or with its censure of armed struggle. But he did find a common language and shared outlook: "Class consciousness, loyalty to the workers party and the trade-union war, eagerness for ties with the forces of tomorrow [that is, the Soviet Union], political realism, and pioneering—constructivism."[100] The Palmah's HSHT youth served as the bridgehead for the talks.[101]

These views were presumably current among the KM's leadership. In 1946, the LAHA-Poalei Zion Party was created. But this union with veterans of the Poalei Zion left did not restore to the KM's members the feeling they had lost since quitting Mapai—the sense of playing an important role in steering the Zionist ship. The Zionist Congress in Basle marked an additional stage in their alienation from the central arena—Ben-Gurion set up a coalition without the two parties of the left (LAHA and HSHT), and for the first time in its history the KM found itself in the opposition. The dissonance between the KM's capabilities and its political weakness apparently led Allon to the conclusion that the root of the problem was the Left's split; the corollary was that a united Left party could pose an alternative to Mapai.

One unifying motif, according to Allon, was the attitude of the two parties to the "world of tomorrow," that is, to the Soviet Union. Probably, like other Palmahniks, he too had been profoundly affected by the brave war the Russians had fought in World War II and thought it incontestable proof of the Soviet regime's endurance and vitality. His admiration was no doubt bolstered by his intimacy with Yitzhak Sadeh, a great admirer of the Soviet Union and the Red Army. In addition, his fierce animosity toward the British, the fruit of education compounded by Britain's hostile policy, featured in the perceived division between the forces of light, that is, "the world of tomorrow," and the forces of darkness, namely the imperialistic West in cahoots with fascism. This shallow worldview, however, was restricted to the conscious level. Beneath the surface, other insights came into play. He had thoroughly revolted against a call from the HSHT leader Meir Yaari in Poland for the Jews to halt their flight until the chances of *aliyah* became clearer: Allon agreed that the situation of Germany's displaced persons' camps was deplorable (which was the reason for Yaari's call), but the borders of Poland could close at any moment. "One must not forget that one of these days Poland might become fully Soviet and the fate of its Jews the same as the fate of the Jews in Russia itself."[102] His affiliation with "the world of tomorrow" did not blind him to the nature of the Soviet regime and its attitude toward Jews. At the same time, he was party to the popular KM perception that the United States was Britain's reprehensible ally. Little knowledge and limited understanding of the United States were significant components of the local, distorted leftist worldview. The United States was conceived as a capitalist power doomed to exit the stage of history in the clash with the forces of light. Yet, when Allon explored treatment possibilities for Nurit, he chose the United States over Europe. The United States, he believed, had the most advanced medical science. There was a dichotomy between the world of ideas, which ascribed to the Soviet Union every virtue and saw it as the society triumphing in the battle for world control, and the actual world, which made it necessary to relate to real factors: the attitude toward Jews, scientific power, economic capability. This dichotomy was part of Eretz Israel's leftist mentality, especially of its young, for whom Russia was not a mother land and Russian was not a mother tongue. Their attachment to Russia was based on Soviet war literature translated into Hebrew, the Russian songs they sang around the campfire, and the image of an ideal society projected by the communist regime.

From July 1947 onward, Allon had repeatedly told Galili that he wished to leave the Palmah. He made it clear, as he wrote to Ruth, "that upon our return from Europe, I am coming home [to Ginossar] (except in the case of total 'disturbances' of course, please don't smile at this addition in parentheses)."[103] Allon hoped to use the trip with Nurit as a break that would enable him to part from the Palmah on good terms. "When the trip becomes concrete, I will bring it also before the [Ginossar] secretariat and it is my hope that we will receive its approval."[104] Allon's desire to leave the Palmah and change his pursuits was, as described earlier, related to his political awakening. He had grown aware that a strong, well-organized political party was a prerequisite for maintaining the KM's influence in all walks of life.[105] Allon presented himself to the party's strong man, Israel Idelson (Bar-Yehudah), declaring his desire to help recruit for party activity all members who were on missions in youth movements, the defense force, and abroad.[106] "It is time for the younger generation to begin to express itself in political life, injecting political content within the framework of our positions wherever they may be," he wrote to Ruth, adding with pathos, "and if I must fall as the [first] victim in this endeavor, so be it."[107] The norms of Eretz Israel's Left at the time called for modesty and self-restraint when it came to political ambition, which was disparaged as "careerism." Allon was not free of these cultural conventions: his volunteering for party activism, he explained, was not driven by political ambition but by the party's pathetic state. The party was disintegrating and fast losing its conceptual clarity. Internally, social relations left much to be desired, and financially, it was at an ebb. The cause of it all was that its top people had volunteered for national tasks and did not look out for the party's own interests.

Galili was adamantly opposed to Allon resigning. Most likely in order to take the edge off of his insistence, he agreed to consider a leave of a few months to allow Allon to devote himself to party affairs—until he set out for Europe with Nurit. As for resignation, that discussion would wait until he returned.[108] In the end, no replacement was found for Allon and the idea died a quiet death. Ben-Aharon was appointed the party secretary and the unification with HSHT was accelerated. Allon remained the commander of the Palmah.[109]

Allon's sterile attempt to quit the Palmah in 1947 and turn to politics raises questions about the connection between military and political work in his thinking. He viewed his military position in political terms. In his estimation, his party comrades denied his request to leave the Palmah because they could not come up with a replacement from their own cadres (not because they thought he was the right man in the right place at the right time). This indicates that he regarded his job as a position of power, important to retain in the LAHA's hands. The split from Mapai in 1944 had exacerbated the politicization of every aspect of the Yishuv and the Zionist movement: everyone maneuvered to seize positions of power—in youth movements, in He-Halutz, on missions abroad, in the refugee ships, in the defense forces. The survivors termed it the "Eretz Israel plague." Allon exhibited the political fanaticism of one who had formulated his worldview rather late and had to prove his loyalty. Tabenkin and Galili were allowed to show tolerance—their loyalty was not in any doubt: Tabenkin, because he had founded the movement and because a rabbi may do what his *hasidim* may not; Galili, because he had acquitted himself with distinction in tests of loyalty set by Berl Katznelson and Ben-Gurion. He was above all suspicion as far as the KM's old-timers were concerned. This was not so regarding Allon. He was the outsider who had come to the movement as an adult. He never got over his need to prove his loyalty. What's more, he had never belonged to the large Mapai before the split. He was not intimate with its codes and customs, he had not suffered from its shortcomings, he was not bound by friendship ties with its members. The LAHA conception of national responsibility was a legacy from its days in Mapai. The "common good" espoused by Galili and his comrades belonged to the lost paradise of the Greater Mapai, predating the Fall (that is, the split). Allon's commitment to the "common good" withered before it ever ripened.

Allon, in this period, toed the party line unreflectingly, unhesitatingly. The idea of an international trusteeship in Palestine, the LAHA's proposed solution for the woes of the Jewish people, was aimed at deferring independence until such time as the Jews constituted a majority in the country. Premature independence meant partitioning the land between Jews and Arabs, which the LAHA spurned, connecting it with an end to pioneering, settlement, and socialism. Whether or not there was a necessary connection between partition and the enervation of pioneering and Labor settlements, or even between the integrity of the land and a socialist regime, remains in doubt. But this was how the LAHA's adherents explained things to themselves when they brushed aside Ben-Gurion's idea of "a state now." Their rejection stemmed from the psychological difficulty of relinquishing part of the land, from their suspiciousness of diplomacy (among other things, because it was alien to them since they had no inroads in the corridors of power), and from their hostility toward Western capitalist powers. Labor's other opponents to the idea of "a state now" were the Marxist HSHT Party, based on the Kibbutz Artzi movement. This party held onto the idea of the brotherhood of man, hoping that a binational state would rise in Palestine wherein Jews and Arabs would live peacefully and happily; rather than a divided territory, there would be shared rule. Unfortunately, the HSHT's matchmakers never consulted the bride: it never dawned on Palestine's Arabs to agree to any sort of regime that would leave Jews the right to immigration and settlement. The LAHA suffered from the same ailment: the question of the trusteeship's composition, and why it would agree to grant Jews what the British had not, never came up for serious discussion. Government by an international trusteeship was a stillborn idea, never seeing the light of day. But in the summer of 1947, in advent of the UN deliberations, Allon still believed in it. He thought the program of a binational state unrealistic because of Arab opposition to immigration and settlement, whereas the trusteeship plan "could be realistic if a Zionist majority supported it."[110] It was wishful thinking, skirting realities: Was there even a chance that most of the Zionist movement would back it? Moreover, why would the powers assume responsibility for a country on the verge of exploding merely because the Jews did not yet feel ready to take responsibility for their own fate? It was the sort of thinking that suited pre–World War II days. As 1947 drew to a close, it seemed out of touch.

With the benefit of hindsight, one wonders how seasoned, intelligent people like those of the LAHA could cling to a slew of assumptions that now appear totally misguided. But the crystal ball was opaque, withholding its secrets. Had anyone told contemporaries that the Jewish state was about to rise, within a matter of months, the bearer of the tidings would no doubt have been taken for a madman. Sini Azaryahu reckoned that he would not see a Jewish state in his lifetime.[111] Moshe Sneh, in setting up Jewish self-defense in Europe in 1947, assumed that statehood was far off and that meanwhile the Jews needed protection.[112] Several times in the course of 1947, Ben-Gurion said that a Jewish state would arise within a year or two. But the start of the countdown was postponed time and again, indicating that this was a slogan rather than a targeted date. At the end of May 1947, upon conclusion of the security "seminar" he held after returning from abroad, Ben-Gurion noted in his diary a plan to build up a military force, which was to take two years—not even he anticipated the imminent breakthrough of statehood.[113]

On the eve of 29 November 1947 Yigal was the Palmah's acknowledged commander and well-loved leader. He saw himself as the representative of the younger generation opposite the veteran political leadership, as the man who would have the Palmah's young take their proper place among the movement's leaders. He felt ready to take the leap to leadership.

Chapter 8
Countdown to Statehood and the Onset of War

On 29 November 1947, as the Sabbath made way for Sunday, the Yishuv was glued to the radio. The UN General Assembly was voting on the recommendations of the United Nations Special Committee on Palestine (UNSCOP), and the vote was being broadcast live. The UNSCOP had proposed partitioning Palestine into two new states, one Jewish, one Arab, allotting the Jews a more generous area than previous commissions. The UNSCOP allocated the Jewish state the Eastern Galilee and most of the valleys, the coastal plain from Haifa Bay to north of Ashdod, and most of the Negev. It included the city of Haifa and left Jaffa as an Arab enclave. Jerusalem was to come under international aegis with the road to it passing through Arab territory. Also in Arab territory were some thirty Jewish communities: Nahariyyah and Hanitah in the north, the Etzyon Bloc in the center, the Jerusalem Corridor, the area north of the Dead Sea, and others in the south. In population terms, it translated as follows: out of some 1.2 million Palestinian Arabs, about 400,000 were to be left inside the boundaries of the Jewish state; out of some 500,000 Palestinian Jews, about 100,000 were to be left outside the Jewish state. The recommendations earmarked some 55 percent of western Palestine for the Jewish state, but that territory had two drawbacks: first, it was mostly the Negev, a desert (12 million of its 16 million dunams, or 1.2 million of its 1.6 million ha). Second, apart from the Galilee, the entire area was in the plains and thus defensively at a disadvantage, while the hilltops remained in Arab hands. Nonetheless, the plan's shortcomings and latent dangers could not veil the extraordinary opportunity it presented: an independent Jewish state in a large portion of Palestine. As the votes were counted, the Yishuv held its breath. The announcement soon came: based on a two-thirds majority, the United Nations had resolved on the end of the British Mandate in Palestine and the establishment of two states—a Jewish state alongside an Arab state.

Contemporaries tended to believe that the World War II Jewish catastrophe had caused most European states from both blocs to vote in favor of a Jewish state. As they saw it, after all that had happened to the Jewish people, the enlightened world realized that Jews had a right to national liberty in their own country. New studies, however, cast doubt on the importance of the Holocaust in the considerations of the large powers. Each was impelled by its own interests, not necessarily by considerations of meta-historic justice.

The fact that both great powers voted for the UN resolution seemed to defy all logic, contradicting the predictions of all of the Yishuv's wise men: the Soviet Union had been hostile to the Zionist movement since the rise of the communist regime. The dramatic turn in its position, heralded by Ambassador Andrei Gromyko's famous speech at the special UN session of April 1947, was so unexpected, so astounding that the Yishuv could hardly digest it. Furthermore, since the end of World War II, the Soviet Union's relations with the West had deteriorated. And yet the United States and the Soviet Union had banded together to vote for the establishment of a Jewish state! Their accord in the historic resolution seemed almost a mirage.

The Yishuv may have been unsophisticated and untrained in the ways of world policy, but it was not alone in disbelieving such accord possible. Britain's government, which in the winter of 1947 decided to hand over the question of Palestine to the United Nations in acknowledgment of its failed policies, also gave the resolution little chance since it warranted the agreement of the two superpowers, a totally unrealistic scenario. This opinion was shared by Palestine's Arabs. Yet the vote went as it did, and what was a miracle for the Jews was a scandalous, unpardonable injustice for the Arabs. The Arabs utterly rejected the idea of partition, spurning any solution that meant recognizing Jewish national rights in Palestine and demanding the establishment of an Arab state in all of western Palestine. Arab-Jewish confrontation was inevitable: for the Jews, the issue of free Jewish immigration was axiomatic; for the Arabs, it was a *casus belli*. In the final analysis, the Jewish state arose because no solution was found to the problem of Jewish immigration.

The British were the one party that might have forced a solution on Palestine. But they had no wish to promote a pro-Zionist solution, such as partition, since the government in London considered it strategically vital to retain the goodwill of Arab states. Nor could the British promote an anti-Zionist solution, such as the establishment of an Arab state in all of western Palestine since, economically and politically, they were increasingly dependent on the United States. Their every attempt to force an anti-Zionist solution was sabotaged by President Harry Truman of the United States. They decided to transfer the question of Palestine to the United Nations out of an awareness that there was no peaceful solution. What's more, they were frustrated and tired of being the punching bag for both sides. The British were determined to evacuate Palestine at any price, though they took pains not to spoil their relations with Arab states. Neither the Jews nor the Arabs believed that the British really meant it. When the British colonial secretary, Creech-Jones, declared in the UN General Assembly at the end of September 1947 that, if an Arab-Jewish agreement were not reached, the British would leave the country, reactions in the region and across the world were downright skeptical. On 2 October 1947, High Commissioner Sir Alan Cunningham met with David Ben-Gurion, the chairman of the Jewish Agency (JA), and Dr. Hussein Khalidi of the Palestine Arab Higher Committee. In both meetings, he made it clear that Britain was resolved to exit Palestine even if the two sides had not reached an accommodation. Khalidi, incredulous, dismissed the notion.[1] Ben-Gurion had his doubts.[2] Nevertheless, he grasped the historic opportunity by the horns and issued a challenge: if the British government would not undertake the implementation of the UN resolution, then "[the Jews] are willing, ready and able to act as a government immediately, from the start of the transition period, in place of the British government leaving the country."[3] His words rang of a historic moment, a one-time opportunity not to be missed, even if it was fraught with danger.[4]

His opinion was not shared by the entire Yishuv. Some feared that the premature birth of the Jewish state would end in disaster. Hesitation was voiced at the Mapai secretariat: "It seems to me that in the Yishuv there is no [emotional] conviction that we will be able to hold out," said Jonah Kosoy (Kesseh). "Why should we be ashamed to ask for help—a small nation, surrounded by Arab states, being abandoned by the British?" asked Avraham Katznelson.[5]

In Tabenkin's camp of activists, distrust of Britain was complete. These activists certainly did not believe in a British departure. Allon concurred: in 1950, when summing up the war, he said: "None of us believed then nor do I believe today that they really intended to evacuate the country and leave it forever." Allon had no doubt that the British had expected a Jewish downfall, and thus, after suffering resounding defeats, "[the Jews] would ask for their intervention to save at least the women and children." Allon even claimed that the British had prepared camps in Greece to receive refugees from Palestine after the Jews lost the war.[6] Distrust and demonization of Britain had several breeding grounds: Palestine's Labor movement—especially under the historic triad of Yitzhak Tabenkin, Berl Katznelson, and David Ben-Gurion—had always been extremely suspicious of British rule. This stemmed from a skepticism born of the bitter experience of Eastern European Jewry who had received their political education under the czar's anti-Semitic regime. In addition, there was the political factor: a built-in contradiction between the desire of the British government to protect the interests of the Arab population, which sought to maintain the status quo, and the British commitment to help establish a Jewish National Home in Palestine. As the Jews grew stronger, the Arabs showed increasing opposition to the idea of a Jewish National Home, and the British found themselves curbing Jewish aspirations. Matters came to a head during the war when the British sealed the escape route from Europe for Jews seeking a safe haven in Palestine. At this point, the dissenters began to demonize the British, and the image seeped into activist circles during the anti-British struggle. The common explanation for British conduct rested on the dualism between socialism and imperialism: the British were hostile to the Jews because they wished to remain in Palestine forever with the help of Arab feudal forces. Ben-Gurion and members of the JA-PD did not share these assessments. Ben-Gurion's political outlook was underpinned by a recognition of the importance of British rule in Palestine for the establishment of a Jewish National Home. Before the resolution of 29 November 1947, he had hinted to the British that they would be able to maintain bases in a future Jewish state. It was not the antithesis between imperialism and socialism that was responsible for his suspicion in this period, but the fickle policy of the British government.

Still, partition was not agreeable to everyone. The aspirations for a "Greater Israel"—the integrity of Eretz Israel—did not evaporate. Before the resolution of 29 November 1947, the Le-Ahdut Ha-Avodah (LAHA) had consistently called for an international mandate and Ha-Shomer Ha-Tza'ir (HSHT) continued to demand a binational state. Neither explained how its aspirations were to be realized. While Soviet support for the UNSCOP's recommendations did lend the plan a certain legitimacy, it did not soften the pain of Partition. Members of the KM, including Allon, thought that partition chipped away at the hopes of the Jewish people.

But the people "voted with their feet": the circles of dancers bursting onto the street at the vote's outcome represented the entire gamut of the Yishuv, including those who dreamed of a Greater Israel and even those who dreamed of both banks of the Jordan River.[7] Synagogues opened at night to offer up prayers of praise, the dancing stretched into the new day. And, for one brief moment, the animus toward the British was forgotten; the sinister armored cars in Jerusalem's streets welcomed children who draped them with flowers.[8] But the spontaneous outburst of joy did not include Ben-Gurion. Always the realist, he knew that the country was on the brink of war and the toll would be high.[9]

The next day, on 30 November, before the merrymaking had subsided, Arabs attacked Jewish cars and killed seven people. The Arab Higher Committee (AHC) called a general strike. On 1 December 1947 a mob poured out of Jerusalem's Jaffa Gate into the business district outside the Old City, where both Jews and Arabs had shops. The mob headed for Jewish shops and set to pillaging. The Haganah sought to stop the violence, but it encountered opposition from British forces positioned between Arabs and Jews that blocked its advance toward the commercial district. Although there was no loss of life, the district was burned down. Thus began the war between Palestine's two national communities.

Like a creature of habit extrapolating from past experience, the Yishuv prepared for a campaign that had already been fought: it measured the new incidents by the yardstick of the Disturbances of 1936–39. Initially, the Arab outburst was considered a passing incident, the letting off of steam. Allon, too, thought so in the first week of December.[10] Large parts of the country were peaceful; in others there was violence. There were clashes in cities of mixed population, on border zones between Arab and Jewish areas, on the roads, and in the Negev. Tel Aviv's outlying neighborhoods came under sniper fire and there were Arab attempts to attack isolated quarters. Transportation to Tel Aviv was dangerous: the village of Abu Kabir, at the entrance to the city, was known for its truculence. The village of Salameh was a center for hostile forces. Villagers from Yazur had hit Tel Aviv's traffic on more than one occasion. Yet, it was citrus-marketing season and both sides had a clear interest in keeping the road to the port of Jaffa trouble free. For a while, with British mediation, there was a kind of truce between Jaffa and Tel Aviv, even if tensions continued elsewhere. Jewish neighborhoods in Jerusalem were cut off. The Jewish Quarter of the Old City was under siege. Certain neighborhoods that had come under fire were being abandoned.[11] In the month of December 1947, close to 250 Jews were killed countrywide. In comparison, in the three years of the Arab Rebellion, some 500 Jews had been killed all told.[12]

In early January 1948, a broad forum met to try to assess the situation. It consisted of members of the JA-PD, intelligence personnel in Arab affairs, and the Haganah's top brass—Yadin, Allon, Sadeh, Galili—and was headed by Ben-Gurion. The question was, were these Disturbances or not? This was to lead into the question of retaliation, yes or no. And if yes, then how? The "Arabists" still believed in "appropriate conduct" as warranted by an understanding of the Arab "mentality"—that is, a blend of a show of force and caution in human relations. This would make it possible to curb the Disturbances. A show of force was to be directed at attackers only, the aim being not to broaden the clash or hurt innocents.

The first person to express doubt about the feasibility of distinguishing between the guilty and the innocent in conditions of war was Moshe

Sharett. He also put the political dilemma on the table: on no account were the Jews to show weakness. The partition plan rested on the assumption that the Jews were able to control the situation. To undermine this assumption would cause the United Nations to abandon the plan. At this discussion, Sharett joined the chorus demanding a hard-hitting reaction; he considered this extremely important in the campaign for world opinion.

The main discussion was between the Arabists and security people. The former sought to minimize confrontation, limiting it to areas "on fire." Yadin, in contrast, called for the implementation of the May Plan—a countrywide contingency plan put together by the Haganah in case of unrest; it called for targeting anti-Arab objectives, including economic interests. Widening the front and taking the initiative meant accepting the fact that there was no way not to harm innocents: Shalom Aleichem's well-known method of killing the flea would not work here, Yadin argued: "You can't first catch the flea, tickle it, and then put poison in its mouth."

When Allon's turn came to speak, he chose a position midway between the Arabists and Yadin. On the one hand, he agreed with the Arabists that there was no need for countrywide action, that it was better to confine the fire to areas already burning. On the other hand, he declared in no uncertain terms that gone were the days when it was possible to strike at a solitary object in an Arab village or town. Every Arab house now harbored weapons, and any entry into a village or town spelled casualties. He was thus in favor of striking at the assailants' bases "even though in consequence of such action the innocent, too, will fall. ... We cannot afford the luxury of entering a house, even if it is a single story, and begin separating the guilty from the innocent. The innocent, too, will fall." The Arabs, who practiced blood vengeance, would understand collective punishment. "They sometimes avenge themselves even against a child if it is impossible to get to the father of the family himself."

Galili brought a fresh perspective to the meeting. In contrast to the arguments of whether these were or weren't Disturbances, he suggested by "way of compromise" the acceptance of his opinion that "this is war." His opinion was not based on intelligence reports but "on political analysis and facts." It was an instructive example of the limits of assessments by intelligence personnel who at times do not see the forest for the trees. In time, Galili took pride in his foresight, and with justice. Nevertheless, the action plan adopted the next day was a compromise between the conclusions implicit in the realization that the country was embarking on war and the operational constraints owing to the presence of the British army; the Jews were to defend themselves actively when attacked and carry out crushing counterattacks as the Haganah demanded. At the same time, the Arabist line was also accepted: the war was not to be extended to quiet areas.[13]

The roads passing through Arab areas were the Yishuv's Achilles heel. With the exception of the main road between Tel Aviv and Haifa (and it, too, around Tira), all the roads were dangerous. Transportation to isolated settlements had to be undertaken in convoys. The Haganah published a "Ten Commandments of Bus Travel"—a guide to the anxious traveler. Among other things, it said, "Don't look for 'safe' spots in cars—no one knows what these are. . . . While traveling, don't think about the dangers. Keep yourself occupied, reading or talking about something that interests you. . . . Don't interfere in convoy arrangements. There is someone in charge."[14] British policy was to avoid intervening as much as possible so as not to be seen as furthering the implementation of the UN partition plan. In some cases, the British army came to the aid of convoys attacked on the road to Jerusalem. In others, the British confiscated the weapons of Haganah personnel. On occasion, they in effect delivered Haganah personnel into the hands of an Arab mob. The high commissioner had announced that the Jewish defense force was no longer to be hampered, but British soldiers were careless about complying with the directive. In early December 1947, British officers advised the JA that it would do well to evacuate the Negev south of Beersheba since in current circumstances, militarily, the Jews would be unable to hold it. A report in "Pinkas ha-Maarakha"—a summary of the fighting published in the *Davar* almanac for 1948–49— attributed to a reliable source that "the advice was rejected without any discussion. The decision is not to abandon a single Jewish settlement, to fight, to defend, to hold out and to possess the Negev."[15]

The decision not to evacuate settlements was both ideological and military. The myth of Tel Hai held that "the built-up is not to be abandoned." A new slogan now came into being: "The entire land [is] a front," meaning that no place was safe. In the first months of fighting this was more or less true, although some places were safer than others. Tabenkin was adamant about not abandoning settlements. He even objected to evacuating women and children until the very last minute. He believed that people were prepared to make greater sacrifices when defending their homes and families than a deserted outpost. The importance he attached to frontier settlements stemmed from the Tel Hai ideology and the weight ascribed to the settlement endeavor in determining the country's borders. If, in fact, the Zionist plow did draw the boundary line, it was inconceivable that settlements be evacuated in wartime and fail to fulfill their historic mission. As was true of many issues, the 1948 war was a quasi-transition period between the spatial-settlement defense conception, which rested on citizen fighters defending their homes, and the IDF conception, which charged the army with the role of defense.[16]

This early in the war, the leadership did not seriously consider straying beyond the borders set by the resolution of 29 November 1947. At heart, some people may have hoped to do so, but several factors combined to banish the thought. Firstly, the UN resolution of 29 November 1947 was the basis of the legitimacy for the Jewish state. Second, the British were still in the country and any departure from the partition's borders might invite a strong reaction. Third, the Jews had not yet managed to take full advantage of the right to all of the areas earmarked by partition. Ben-Gurion, outlining his program in an address at the Mapai Central Committee after 29 November—an address published in the press—spoke out against irredentist ideas and for adherence to the borders of the UN resolution. He seemed to take it for granted that Jews would continue to live in an Arab state and an international zone (that is, Jerusalem), and Arabs in a Jewish state.[17] But as the war wore on, this idea appeared less and less feasible. There was no actual discussion of evacuating the Etzyon Bloc, among other reasons because it was regarded as Jerusalem's front line of defense, but statesmen of the stature of Moshe Sharret did reflect on the possibility, especially as the Arabs had meanwhile evacuated Tiberias, Haifa, and Jaffa; a new ethnic equilibrium seemed to be settling into place. It was the nascent thinking about ethnic uniformity in the two states-in-the-making, Jewish and Arab.[18] On the eve of 15 May 1948, representatives of the Western Galilee came to Ben-Gurion to discuss the future of the area, which was slated for the Arab state, and left heavy-hearted: they sensed that he did not mean to fight for the Western Galilee. He permitted the evacuation of women and children, recommending that "the combatants hold out as long as they could, though [there was to be] no 'Masada.' It is better to surrender." Moshe Carmel attested that the High Command did not wish to dispense forces for the conquest of the Western Galilee since it was not included in the partition plan; it would thus be a pity to waste resources on an area that might have to be evacuated.[19] Yigal Allon linked suggestions of evacuation to a readiness to compromise over borders, darkly warning against the leadership's lack of resolve: "Those who sought partition and agreed to the proposed borders might easily agree also to 'border amendments',"[20] the allusion being to the UN resolution. Before 15 May 1948, the leadership did not initiate any acts of conquest outside the partition's borders except around Jerusalem (which was to be internationalized) and on the road leading to it.[21]

The Negev's defense posed a serious problem all in itself. The road to the Negev, like that to Jerusalem, passed through Arab areas. Unlike

Jerusalem, however, few Jews lived there, a mere thousand versus one hundred thousand Arabs, many of them armed Beduin. The UN resolution, which included the Negev in the Jewish state, was not backed up on the ground by a Jewish hold on it. Eleven settlement points had been thrown together in 1946; they were small, isolated, and dependent on a pipeline laid by the Mekorot Water Company. In the first month of fighting two Palmah patrols were wiped out there, a loss that reflected Jewish weakness.

One Palmah battalion, commanded by Nahum Sarig and scattered among the settlement points, was also responsible for protecting the pipeline and roads. Clearly, if the Negev were to remain in the Jewish state, the points had to be fortified, the defense forces strengthened and enlarged, and means of defense and transportation improved. In short, there had to be some combination of "civilian" and military preparations. To this end, in mid-December, the Negev Committee was created with Ben-Gurion's full backing.[22] It busied itself with building shacks to quarter Palmah battalions, fortifying settlements, patrolling and repairing the pipeline, and bringing in supplies: equipment, food, and, of course, the means of war to enable the settlements to withstand sporadic attack and plan for the expected invasion. The committee, chaired by Joseph Weitz and including Allon, worked efficiently and in a spirit of cooperation. Reporting on one of its meetings, Weitz remarked about Allon that "he is pleasant to be with. He has an open, lively face."[23]

Meanwhile, behind the scenes, the Palmah and Ben-Gurion sparred over authority. Nahum Sarig had commanded the Palmah units in the Negev from which the Negev Brigade was formed in March 1948. Weitz was impressed by Sarig's personality and leadership.[24] Not so Ben-Gurion: Sarig left him cold. He referred to him as a "partisan," meaning not the commander of a regular army; he sought to subordinate the military command to a civil "governor" loyal to him. This was one of the first signs of the ensuing battle over the Palmah's continued autonomy.[25] By early March 1948, the arguments between Ben-Gurion on the one hand and Galili and Allon on the other became overt. Ben-Gurion wanted to remove the new Negev Brigade from the Palmah's command and, in fact, oust Sarig, who had been appointed by Galili. The situation was also an opportunity to hint to Galili that it was no longer within his authority to appoint commanders.[26] Ben-Gurion met with Allon on 5 March 1948. Allon objected to removing the Negev Brigade from the Palmah's headquarters: the Palmah was the best body to defend the area. It had esprit de corps, inner cohesion, and valuable assets that might be lost if the brigade were severed from the Palmah. Ben-Gurion probed; he was leading up to the conclusion that there was no difference between the servicement of the Palmah and the Haganah and, therefore, it made no sense to maintain an intermediary body, that is, the Palmah's headquarters, between the brigades and the general staff.[27] Meanwhile, Avigur, whom Ben-Gurion had designated as the governor of Negev, decided not to accept the appointment, setting out instead for a mission abroad. In the traumatic chaos of the end of March (the crisis of the convoys, the retreat of the United States from the partition plan—see below), Sarig's appointment as commander of the Negev Brigade looked like a fait accompli.[28] But Ben-Gurion neither forgot nor forgave. Whenever Sarig's name was mentioned, he acted as if he had only just heard it.

Exacerbating the tensions between the Palmah and Ben-Gurion was the founding of Mapam on 23 January 1948 in Tel Aviv. Comprising two parties, HSHT and LAHA-Poalei Zion, it sought to constitute a real political "alternative" or at the very least a "corrective," to Mapai. The two parties were different in character, in political and cultural tradition, and ultimately, also in goals. The KM (LAHA's driving force) was the flesh of Mapai's flesh. It had split off in 1944 because its members thought that the mother party was pushing them into a corner and denying them their proper place. Furthermore, the Zionist Left regarded itself as revolutionary, whereas Mapai, despite its continuing use of revolutionary terminology, had in fact drawn nearer social democratic parties, that is, abandoning the road of revolution in favor of welfare-state ideology. Yet another main bone of contention concerned the Soviet Union. Mapai's majority regarded the Soviet regime as tyrannical and oppressive; the Left tended to ignore its faults and see only its lights: Soviet resistance during the Nazi invasion and the Soviet Union's victory in World War II were evidence of the communist regime's superiority over crumbling Western democracies (the stress was on the fall of France; British and U.S. roles were ignored). The majority in both kibbutz movements—the KM and the Kibbutz Artzi, the movement behind HSHT—supported these opinions. On Zionist policy, in contrast, the two were miles apart: As part of the activist current, the KM rejected the idea of "statehood now" because it meant partitioning Eretz Israel; it wanted an international trusteeship or mandate. The HSHT, however, opposed "statehood now" because it meant imminent confrontation with the Arabs; instead, it advocated a binational state and shared Jewish-Arab rule. Both opposed partition, but there was a yawning gulf between the aspirations of an Arab-Jewish brotherhood and the aspirations of a Greater Israel. And yet the young people of both movements formed a brotherhood-in-arms. The same was true of the ghetto fighters of both movements, who had walked a common path and chosen a common destiny. After the Soviet about-face on the question of partition, the ideas of binationalism and international rule were no longer either options or impediments. The political agenda was partition and it had been anointed with the blessing of the Soviet Union. Yesterday's differences appeared irrelevant. Moreover, the two bodies shared a sense of power and a great hope that in unity they would manage to displace Mapai as the dominant Zionist-socialist party.

Mapam was born under false assumptions: that the drift of the times was toward the Left and that the Soviets would continue to support the Zionist enterprise; that the Left was strong enough to force Mapai to accept its terms; that the basic conditions of a voluntary society would be retained also in statehood; that the immigrants who would be flocking to the country would choose to place the government in the hands of the Left.[29] None of this happened.

At the founding meeting it was Allon who delivered the word of the young of both parties, especially that of the combatants. He spoke the local idiom, using clichés acceptable to his kibbutz crucible. He elaborated the idea of retaining a Haganah "out of uniform" even after the establishment of a Jewish state: "Let's not forget"—he said—"a very large Arab population remains within the borders of Jewish territory . . . every Jew and every Jewish settlement must therefore be able to defend themselves . . . until the arrival of reinforcements." Additionally, Jewish settlement points would remain in Arab state territory and Jews would be living in an internationalized Jerusalem. All of this made necessary the continuation of an army "out of uniform." At this stage, he apparently surmised that the partition plan would be implemented in spirit and in letter, with the borders as stipulated, and that an Arab population would remain inside the Jewish state.[30]

His address was not militant. On the contrary, it bore the official stamp of consensus. He made sure to mention that the younger generation, a "fighting, self-realizing cohort," was not restricted to members of Mapam and that the spirit of cooperation and comradeship would prevail. He said nothing contrary to Ben-Gurion's positions. Still, the mere fact that the Palmah's commander appeared at the founding convention of a new party challenging the leadership of Mapai and Ben-Gurion could not help but arouse Ben-Gurion's chagrin and wariness. In this stormy interval between Yishuv and state, it was not yet considered inappropriate for an army man to take part in a political event.[31] Beyond the proprieties, however, Allon's and Galili's place in the new oppositionist party could hardly enhance their standing in Ben-Gurion's eyes.

In the first months of war, Allon was stationed at the Palmah's headquarters at the Ritz Hotel on the Tel Aviv beachfront. From there, he supervised the conscription of Palmah reserves for active service and the operations of Palmah brigades in the Galilee, on the road to Jerusalem, and in the Negev. In early February 1948, the number of Palmah members doubled to some four thousand recruits.³² Though buried in work, Allon was presumably frustrated by his desk job. As the war developed, the Palmah's headquarters increasingly lost its operative significance: battalion and company commanders managed campaigns, each in their own areas. They did report back to the Palmah's headquarters, but they received their orders directly from the Haganah's general staff (HGS). As the army moved toward general conscription, the Palmah lost its uniqueness as the only standing army, along with the initial justification for maintaining a separate headquarters.

The fighting at this stage was influenced by the fact that the British were still in the country and there was no way of knowing when or if they would react. The Haganah's actions thus targeted spot problems rather than attempting to change the situation radically. Reprisals were allowed, such as harassing Arab traffic (with instructions to remove passengers before setting vehicles alight)³³ or blowing up a house in an Arab village. Outposts could be occupied and held until a convoy passed. But territory was not to be seized and held. By March 1948, these limited measures seemed to have exhausted themselves or at least had not led to the desired results.

At the end of March, three convoys met with disaster. One was to the Etzyon Bloc, which ran into Arab forces on the way back to Jerusalem and went down in history as the "Nabi Daniyal Convoy" after the site of the confrontation. British help was needed to evacuate the dead and wounded, and, as part of the "rescue deal," the British handed over the weapons and armored cars to the Arabs. Another convoy, to Jerusalem, set out from Kibbutz Huldah and came under heavy fire. The wounded were numerous and the convoy had to retrace its route, never making it to the city. The third and worst case was the attempt of a supply convoy to break through to besieged Kibbutz Yehiam in the Western Galilee. Dozens fell and the convoy never reached its destination. Gloom set in and only spread when it was learned that the United States had backed off from partition, proposing instead a trusteeship, a new version of the British Mandate at worse conditions. Contemporaries had no doubt that the American position was prompted by the display of Jewish weakness. As a result, a decision was taken to launch a major operation on a novel scale: Operation Nahshon.

Everyone involved applauded Ben-Gurion's boldness in deciding to act on such a scale. To gain control of the road to Jerusalem, fifteen hundred men were marshaled in what was the largest Jewish force ever; it was the first time that battalions the measure of a brigade were put into the field. Gone was the conception of capturing outposts to permit convoys safe passage. The idea was to gain control of the area and destroy the villages from which the Arab combatants set out to block the road. This would prevent their returning to outposts that previously had to be taken and retaken. In scope, organizational capability, and audacity, it was a turning point—an unprecedented step with the British still present. Historians writing on the War of Independence from the British perspective did not receive the impression that the British were aware of any turning point.[34] But from the point of view of the Haganah and political leadership, it marked a new stage in the war, even if in purely military terms it may not have been a real breakthrough.

After the Nabi Daniyal fiasco of 28 March 1948, Allon flew to the Etzyon Bloc to organize the defense force. The decision on Operation Nahshon was made while he was there. He was meant to take charge of it, but force majeure intervened: his aircraft got stuck in the mud and could not take off. The operation fell instead to the Givati Brigade's Shimon Avidan, the oldest, most experienced brigade commander.[35]

Allon's feelings as he sat in the Etzyon Bloc missing out on the most challenging military maneuver of the period were concealed from contemporaries. Allon was good at hiding his feelings, he had remarkable self-control. No one had ever seen him flare up.[36] Now, too, he did not share his frustration with anyone. Very soon, however, within weeks, he was presented with the military challenge he had been looking for.

On 25 April 1948, Allon sent a telegram from the Palmah's headquarters to Yitzhak Rabin at the Harel Brigade's headquarters in the Jerusalem Corridor: "I'm leaving to manage an operation named 'Yiftah' in the Eastern Galilee. Atzmon [Shalom Havlin] will be taking my place. Continue to maintain contact information with the council [HQ]." An "urgent" telegram promptly arrived the next day from Harel to "Sasha" (Allon): "We were astounded by the news that you received command of the Galilee instead of the entire Palmah. A circumstance fraught with danger for the campaign and the entire matter, explain what happened." The telegram was signed by Rabin and other leading figures of the Palmah.[37] The anxiety of the Palmah's commanders about a hidden agenda behind Allon's dispatch to the Eastern Galilee reflects the covert tension in relations with the political leadership in the War of Independence, that is, with Ben-Gurion. Allon's comrades and subordinates feared that his removal from the Palmah's headquarters would herald its liquidation. It was not a groundless fear. But what Rabin and his friends had missed was that Allon was craving to get to the front: his stint at the Palmah's headquarters in the Ritz Hotel was cutting him off from the war's key experience.[38] The decision to send him to the Eastern Upper Galilee as the commander of Operation Yiftah was based on his own initiative.

The pace and timing of developments in the Eastern Galilee were determined by the British army's evacuation. The Jews viewed the British in the Galilee as favoring the Arab side, whereas the Arabs believed they favored the Jewish side.[39] The British were worried about security along their departure line, the road between Rosh Pinnah and Tiberias, and they had no interest in clashing with the Arabs, whom they saw as more menacing. They refused to secure the conveyance of supplies to Ein Zeitim, a small community virtually surrounded by Arabs, or to permit the evacuation of the wounded. As for guarding borders against infiltration by irregulars—they claimed that this would require enormous forces and was thus infeasible. In their opinion, the Jews would not be able to withstand the anticipated Arab invasion and the entire Huleh Valley and the Upper Galilee would fall to the Arabs.[40] In mid-April, the British began their exit from the Upper Galilee. The Nabi Yusha police station, which dominated Malkiah, Ramot Naftali, and Misgav Am and controlled the only road connecting these settlements to other Jewish locales, was delivered into Arab hands. The same thing happened with the Mount Canaan police station, which dominated Safed and the Mount Canaan hotel district, as well as the Safed police station, known as the "Fort" (the highest point). On the "seam" between Jewish and Arab neighborhoods, the Jewish school seized by the British to separate the two populations was also handed over to the Arabs. Safed itself had some ten to twelve thousand Arabs and about fifteen hundred Jews. Safed's Arabs were reputed to be brave and bellicose whereas its Jews were mostly pious, carrying no arms. Topographically, the Jewish Quarter was below the Arab one and frequent sniping was the pattern of life. The British did nothing. Given that the Eastern Galilee, Safed included, was earmarked for the Jewish state, the British seem to have grasped every opportunity to show that they were not promoting the implementation of partition.

The Palmah's Third Battalion, stationed in the Eastern Galilee under Mula (Shmuel) Cohen, was scattered over Safed, Mount Canaan, and Kibbutz Ayelet Ha-Shahar. Now and then, it carried out raids, reprisals, and sabotage against Arabs in the region and irregulars endeavoring to penetrate from Syria. It was trounced in its attempts to capture Nabi Yusha. The second traumatic attempt tallied twenty-two dead. Made up of *hakhshara* members, the troops of the Third Battalion cut their teeth in this battle. Depression descended on the Upper Galilee.[41]

To bolster the troops, Allon set out on a tour of the dispirited Palmah units in the Eastern Galilee. He traveled by light aircraft since the roads were unsafe. He returned with a plan for a potential line of Jewish defense against the expected invasion. His report, termed "pessimistic-optimistic," noted that if the current tactics in the Galilee continued, the region had little chance of standing up to the invasion; but the situation could be reversed by resorting to offense. He submitted the report to Galili and Yadin and was summoned, along with them, to Ben-Gurion. Allon's evident enthusiasm must have been infectious for the next day Ben-Gurion offered him the command of the proposed operation.[42] Operation Yiftah was part of the Haganah's Plan D to be implemented upon the departure of the British. Its aim was to occupy the areas slated for the Jewish state prior to the anticipated Arab invasion.

It was not the largest operation commanded by Allon, although it was undoubtedly one of his favorites.[43] The collaboration of military and civilian forces, the combination of battle and psychology, subterfuge and fateful decisions—all lent it a special flavor.

Allon accepted the command of Operation Yifah on 25 April 1948. The first thing he did was set up a battle headquarters: from Palmah's headquarters, he co-opted only Yeruham Cohen, to serve as intelligence officer, as well as a secretary. As the operations officer and the acting second he appointed Mula (Shmuel) Cohen, whom Moshe Kelman replaced as battalion commander. The rest of his headquarter's staff was recruited from Palmah reservists in the area and from kibbutzim.[44]

"The Galilee and its boundaries and villages were well familiar to Yiftah HQ," Allon wrote in *Sefer ha-Palmah*.[45] His presence there as he planned the operation felt like "the return of the native." Allon was a son of the Galilee. He knew not only the geography and topography inside out, but also the people, the moods, the local culture, the colors and scents, the Jews and Arabs. His plans were drafted from this intimate knowledge. Before embarking on any military action at all, he called together settlement representatives at Kibbutz Ayelet Ha-Shahar. Everyone came to the meeting called by Paicovich's son of Mes'ha—all of the old-timers and walking legends, the veterans of Rosh Pinnah and Metullah, the *mukhtars* of the old colonies. One by one, they rose to explain that they needed more weapons and more people and, perhaps, additional ammunition; nor would it hurt if they were issued another Palmah squad to help out, or at least a guard unit. Allon responded with a plain and unadorned description of the situation. He did not minimize the dangers or exaggerate the strength of their forces. But his conclusion was the opposite of theirs. He announced that not only was he unable to place the few available forces at their disposal, but—on the contrary—he was asking them for some of their weapons and some of their manpower. He explained that in order to take the offensive, he needed to muster all the strength he could get for a knockout blow. To split that strength was to endanger the settlements, one by one. To concentrate it held out a chance of qualitatively changing the situation. "It must be said that they were surprised, but also captivated," he recounted in time.[46] The meeting forged an alliance between the settlements and Yiftah's headquarters, and an improbable scenario unfolded: the farmers gave Allon their weapons from the crates and caches they had been keeping, weapons that they had paid good money for, and they formed their people into special units to come to the aid of settlements in distress.

The first few days of Operation Yiftah passed in nervous anticipation of the British evacuation from the Rosh Pinnah police station and the nearby base of the Transjordan Frontier Force (the base was later renamed Filon after one of the casualties in the battle for Nabi Yusha). Rosh Pinnah's Jewish police guards were on their toes and succeeded in taking the station as soon as it was empty. The base, too, was secured without incident. Yiftah's headquarters moved from Ayelet Ha-Shahar to the Rosh Pinnah police station. Meanwhile, Allon was engaged in a war of nerves with the HGS over the transfer of the Palmah's First Battalion under Dan Laner to Yiftah. Allon won. To recruit vehicles for the battalion's transportation to the Galilee, Allon advised Laner to install a roadblock on the Yokne'am Road and requisition trucks along with their drivers. This was done. For the battalion's safe passage, Palmah units captured outposts on the road between Tiberias and Rosh Pinnah, and the soldiers moved north in broad daylight, fully armed—a long convoy stretching for kilometers. This was calculated: "I wanted to open by psychologically breaking the local Arabs, who are among the boldest and most arrogant," said Allon.[47] In tandem, actions around Safed attempted to break the siege of the Jewish Quarter and create territorial contiguity between the forces stationed in town and on Mount Canaan. Ein Zeitun and Biriyyah were seized, the capture of the former—a large, strong village—involving real battle. All day long, the troops blew up village houses as Safed's Arabs looked on, unable to do a thing; this was yet another stage in the psychological warfare.

Meanwhile, Jewish settlements were beleaguered on the slopes of the Bashan and north of the Huleh. Most of the fire was absorbed by the small *moshav* of Ramot Naftali. Though contemporaries believed that the Lebanese army took part in the assault, the assailants were apparently units of the Qawuqji Arab Liberation Army under Adib Shishaqli (later the ruler of Syria). In any case, the attack impressed locals as highly professional. It looked as though the *moshav* would not withstand the barrage of artillery and repeated charges by infantry and armored forces. It kept sending out cries for help. One telegram informed Allon in no uncertain terms that if he did not send reinforcements soon, the defenders would evacuate Ramot Naftali at nightfall. Allon was on the horns of a dilemma: should he split his forces—sending Third Battalion units to Ramot Naftali and postpone the attack in the Safed area—or stick to his original plan? He chose the latter course, believing that relentless offense would ultimately undo the enemy's plans and push it onto the defensive.⁴⁸ Moreover, he thought that the battle for Safed could ultimately change the face of the entire Galileean campaign, while the battle for Ramot Naftali was not likely to do so. Apart from strategic considerations, there was also a practical problem: there was only a slim chance of getting through to Ramot Naftali since the Arabs controlled the road northward. Allon telegrammed Ramot Naftali with the message that a machine gun had been placed at the bottom of the track the evacuees would be taking; anyone coming down against orders would be shot on the spot.⁴⁹ His tough stance aside, he sent out a Primus light aircraft to drop home-made bombs on enemy forces. These must have done their work because the attack on Ramot Naftali stopped. At the same time, he also organized reinforcements from nearby agricultural settlements, which arrived at nightfall. Ramot Naftali did not fall.⁵⁰

Allon's cool resolve bore fruit. After Ramot Naftali's panic of 1 May 1948, local defense and reinforcement became routine in bearing up against shelling. On 7 May 1948, Ramot Naftali was again rattled by artillery fire. In the interim, the first aborted attack on Safed took place (6 May 1948): after initial progress, the Third Battalion failed to take the "Fort" and was forced to retreat from positions it had won (8 May 1948). Their near success, however, sowed alarm in the Arab Quarter. "They began dispatching the kind of telegrams that I received from Ramot Naftali," said Allon. In light of the attack's failure, Allon took a Palmah squad and went by foot at night from Rosh Pinnah to Safed to check out the situation and revise the battle plan. On the way back to Mount Canaan and Rosh Pinnah, he made out a new sound, unlike the whistle of mortars that had been shelling Safed's Jewish Quarter: it was the muted whirr of artillery (9 May 1948). It clearly came from the same battery that had bombarded Ramot Naftali: his course of action had compelled the enemy to change its plans. This, for him, was the most important lesson of the whole episode: "On that day when, as a result of the cries of Safed's Arabs, Qawuqji or Shishaqli moved their artillery batteries from Malkiyyah to Meron—I thought to myself: this is the beginning of the end, at least for the local forces, if we continue to act as we should."⁵¹

The show of force exhibited by the First Battalion's northward march had an immediate consequence: the Bedouin tribe of Arab-el-Heb applied to the Haganah to join its ranks. The small tribe, whose past was studded with robbery and smuggling, had maintained good relations with its Jewish neighbors. Allon decided to look into the application. "There are things I have a weakness for. To this day, I have a weakness for a good Arab cauldron and I decided to go see for myself what the Sheikh [Abu Yusuf] was up to." Well versed in local custom, he took

Figure 11. A Jewish-Arab alliance: Allon and Abu Yusuf of the Arab el-Heb Bedouin, 1948. Photographer unknown. Courtesy of the Allon family.

along respected Jewish *mukhtars* and pretended to be representing his commander lest his young years detract from the occasion's formality. The visit appears to have been his first display of diplomatic acumen: "It was important to show the world that there are Arabs rooted in this country who side with the Jews."[52] The Pal-Heb unit was duly formed and served under Yitzhak Henkin, who was fondly remembered by Allon from the British invasion of Syria in 1941. Its exotic aura aside, the unit also played an important part in raids across the Syrian-Lebanese border. Allon knew how to utilize Bedouin talents, whether in harassing the enemy or fetching cattle booty. These skills were not to be belittled in an army not yet fully organized that left the procurement of provisions and vehicles to local officers. At a later stage in the war, the Arab-el-Heb were ousted by a local commander who knew not Abu Yusuf, at which point Allon applied to the defense minister and secured their prompt reinstatement.[53]

Operation Yiftah concentrated on two chief tacks. One was the opening of roads: from Tiberias to Rosh Pinnah and from Rosh Pinnah to Dafna and Kfar Szold. The other was the capture of Safed. Both sides of the road along the Ginossar, Jordan, and Huleh rift were inhabited by thousands of Bedouin. Allon resorted to psychological warfare once more. Using his connections with regional Jewish *mukhtars*, he had them whisper into the ears of Arab notables: look, awesome forces have arrived, the Jews will crush the Arabs in the Huleh, you would do well to leave. The ruse worked: in a matter of days, the Huleh area was virtually empty, and with hardly a shot having been fired. Seizure of the area south of the Huleh was left to the First Battalion under Laner. The operation took less than a day; "the tents were systematically torched, the houses demolished, the flocks sent to the rear, the population sent eastwards." All day and all night a sea of flames rose skyward. Only the tents of the Arab-el-Heb remained. For all of his love for an Arab cauldron, Yigal had no qualms about clearing the area: the road to the northern Eastern Galilee stayed open and safe until the end of the war. Moreover, by evacuating the population, the forces "created an empty expanse impeding infiltration between Syria and Safed."[54] Operation Broom (*Matateh*), as it was called, created a contiguous, Jewish-controlled territory in the Eastern Galilee. It was the prelude to the capture of Safed.

The battle for Safed entered the folklore of the War of Independence via a saying attributed to Moshe Podhortzer regarding Safed's Jewish community: "Safed was saved by deed and miracle: the deed was that yeshiva boys recited Psalms day and night. The miracle was that the Palmah arrived."[55] The sense of miracle stemmed from the town's Jewish-Arab balance of forces. In addition, there was the traumatic memory of the Arab massacre of local Jews in the 1929 Disturbances and the profound fear of a recurrence. According to rumor, the mufti intended to come from Lebanon to settle in Safed and establish a Palestinian government there. Allon, unlike most of his peers and social milieu, retained a warm spot for Safed's pious Jews. Their enlistment to help the Palmah build fortifications and their sharing of their food with the Palmah had not passed unnoticed. The fact that Safed's rabbis permitted work to proceed on the Sabbath and Passover for the sake of the town's defense reflected mutual trust. After the first aborted attack on Safed, General Hunt Stockwell the British commander of the northern part of Palestine, had suggested to Allon via Moshe Carmel that he evacuate the Jewish population. Allon rejected the idea. He also rejected an appeal from the town's population to evacuate women and children. In his assessment, matters hung by a hair, and evacuation could tip the scales toward defeat. Besides, evacuation was not easy to carry out, entailing exposure to fire.

Allon's decision not to evacuate was accepted by Safed's community leaders without complaint, which he never forgot.[56] When he entered the town with the Palmah squad early in the morning after the climb from Rosh Pinnah, they were greeted by Jews just coming out of synagogue from morning prayers. They knew Allon, but they noticed the new forces and stopped to pray for their welfare. "They had the feeling that the children were coming—'*die kinder kumen*,'" Yigal recounted.[57] "Anyone visiting their diggings—I did so that day and saw the ruins, the number of graves, and I must say: they deserve respect." This is how Allon summed up the relationship with Safed's townspeople.[58]

The Safed campaign highlighted Allon's ability to recoup. Right after the first attack failed, he went up to Safed to plan the next move with Moshe Kelman, the commander of the Third Battalion. This time, the force stormed the police station repeatedly. The toll was heavy, but Safed was conquered. In parallel, the First Battalion took the village of Akbara. During the battle for the town's main buildings, key sites were shelled in the Arab Quarter while Arab bombardment continued of the Jewish Quarter. The shelling, loss of control of important positions, and the capture of Akbara threw the Arabs into chaos. A mass exodus began from the Arab Quarter. The stream of refugees headed for the Wadi Ammud road toward Meron-Sasa, which was open; Allon had made sure to leave the Arabs an escape route. The next day, when the Palmah entered the Arab Quarter, they found a ghost town.[59]

Yigal later learned from the Haganah's intelligence that Yiftah's thrust had forestalled an Arab attack on Safed's Jewish Quarter by one day.[60] Years afterward, during the Peace of Galilee War in 1982, one of Safed's Jewish elders met up with an Arab refugee from Safed who was living in Lebanon. The latter recounted [for what it's worth] that on the flight northward, the refugees had come upon the mufti and his provisional Arab government in the village of Safsufa; they were making their way to Safed, which, as far as they knew, was about to fall into Arab hands. The news that the Jews had taken Safed came as a complete shock.[61]

The sandglass was running down to 15 May 1948. All over the country, tensions rose in expectation of the proclamation of statehood and the invasion. To pre-empt invasion from the north and a possible link-up of hostile forces in the Arab-controlled central Galilee, Allon brought up Dan Laner's First Battalion to occupy Malkiyyah and Kadesh, the gateway to the central Galilee. It was a hard ascent, with the troops on foot and weighed down by equipment, yet they managed to win the two sites in battle that night. The next morning, however, the Arabs launched a counteroffensive. They had the advantage of both firepower and armored cars, and the battle was etched in the memory of the soldiers as the bloodiest they had known. Laner communicated the gravity of the situation, the toll of dead and wounded. Allon demanded that they hold out at least until dark: to retreat in daylight could incur heavier losses. Laner obeyed. Meanwhile, Allon demanded that the HGS fly in a plane to drop provisions for the fighters and bomb the enemy. Just before noon, he asked that water containers be added to the provisions: it was

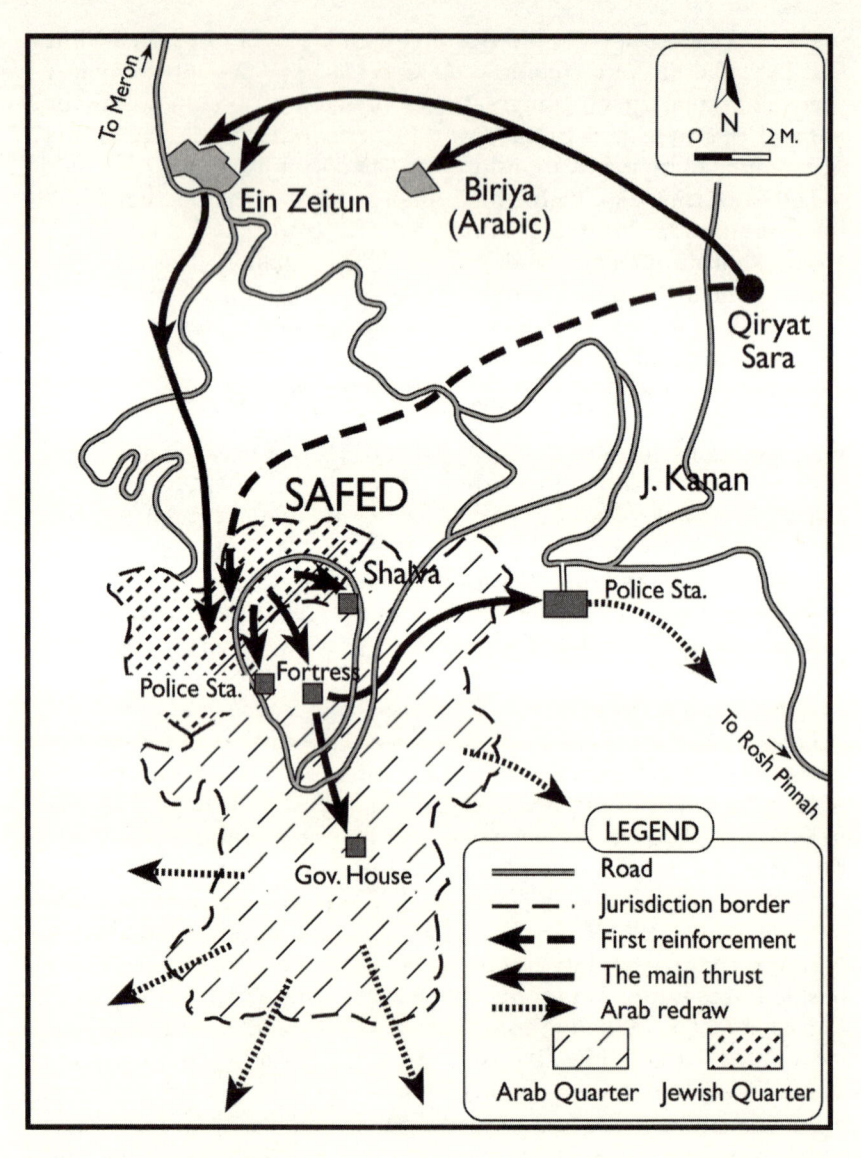

Map 1. The Battle of Safed

a hot dry day and the thirst was draining, some of the men had been left without canteens. But that day, day one of the State of Israel, the campaign faltered on all fronts. The general staff was forced to stint on its scant resources, and the defenders of the Malkiyyah Ridge, as well as those of the Jordan Valley settlements, the Negev, and even Tel Aviv under bombardment, could not expect any help. The situation deteriorated. There was no choice but to order retreat without waiting for nightfall. Allon tried to keep up the men's spirits, among other things with the news that the State of Israel had been born. Laner, in the thick of battle up to his neck, did not bother to pass on the news to company commanders.[62]

Despite the beating at Malkiyyah, Allon again showed initiative: as he saw it, his forces were too weak to leave the offensive to the Arabs. The First Battalion had been defeated, but it held the Kadesh outpost, straddling the road from Malkiyyah southward. It was now time to release the Third Battalion, which he had kept in reserve and out of Malkiyyah, for the conquest of Nabi Yusha, the foreboding fort at which they had already spilled their blood. The operation faltered at first but ended with the opening of the road to Manarah and Ramot Naftali. The Arab route from Lebanon to the Galilee was blocked.[63]

In the two weeks of Operation Yiftah, a continuous Jewish strip was created from Tiberias to Metullah. Safed and Mount Meron were captured, the siege from Ramot Naftali and Manarah was lifted. The preliminary preparations for the test of invasion had been successful.

The first days of statehood were grueling. The Etzyon Bloc fell. The Negev and Jordan Valley settlements evacuated women and children. Enemy equipment and ammunition were superior. Every day that the enemy advance was delayed allowed the IDF to organize and incorporate the weapons and equipment that had begun to arrive from Europe. The Syrian invasion came via the Golan Heights toward the Jordan Valley. On the morning of 18 May 1948, after heavy bombardment, Syrian tanks and armored vehicles burst through and conquered Tzemah on the southern edge of the Sea of Galilee. Tanks suddenly appeared near Deganyah. The Golani Brigade commander Moshe Mann sent notice of this momentous development by telegram—not bothering with encryption because of the haste and urgency.[62] It was the war's most dangerous breakthrough into a densely-populated Jewish area.

At the same time, an Iraqi force crossed Hussein Bridge and attacked Kibbutz Gesher to advance toward Wadi el-Bira. The Arabs aimed to cut the Jewish state in half and reach Haifa, winning a land strip between Samaria and the central Galilee in the hope of conquering all of the Galilee. New research reveals that the invading army was limited in size and riven by disagreement and lack of coordination, but this does not lessen the anxiety that gripped the northern settlements. In a spate of urgent telegrams, Yadin informed Allon and Carmel of events, demanding that each instantly dispatch a company to assist the Golani Brigade, which was stationed in the Jordan Valley. One indication of the critical state of affairs can be seen in Yadin's order to the Golani commander to immediately organize a second line of defense, on the Poriyyah and Yavne'el Ridge, to block the Lajjun-Afulah and Jenin-Afulah routes against the eventuality of the Jordan Valley falling to the enemy. Mishael Shaham (Schechter), a senior Haganah officer, was sent to help Mann organize the defense.[65]

Allon sent a company under Mula Cohen to assist Golani as Yadin ordered. As Mula Cohen's family lived at Kibbutz Deganyah there was an element of coming to the rescue of an esteemed commander's home. The overriding recognition, however, was that the regional commanders had to cooperate to block the breach in the defense line. The company attempted to recapture Tzemah but was repelled under heavy fire.[66] These efforts aside, there were apparently budding thoughts about evacuating the Jordan Valley. "No [settlement] point should be evacuated. Every place must be fought for," Yadin directed in an urgent telegram to Golani.[67] But in the night between 19–20 May, the people of the kibbutzim of Massadah and Shaar Ha-Golan abandoned their homes. When they reached Kibbutz Afikim, "they were forced to return." They tried to do so but came under fire and backtracked. The next day, they watched the Syrians torch their homes. On the morning of 20 May, the attack began on the settlements of the Jordan Valley. Meanwhile, an artillery battery had been brought in to the Poriyyah Ridge and the next day the Syrian offensive was halted.[68] The benefit of artillery in stopping the Syrians remains a subject of debate. It may not have hit a single Syrian, but it undoubtedly affected morale and the resolve of the people of the Jordan Valley; this, too, was valuable ammunition.

In this blazing mesh of front and rear, Allon showed admirable sangfroid. His family was at Ginossar, in the heart of the battle zone. His companies carried out raids across the Syrian and Lebanese borders, confounding the enemy. Light Primus planes took to the air and dropped bombs on Kafr Hareb and on Kuneitra. The idea was to keep up the initiative and sap the enemy's confidence and operational plans. The Arab invasion of the Galilee petered out. Within days, Allon grew aware that the Arab force had lost its momentum. It was time for an offensive, but he lacked the wherewithal. Never had the instruments of war been in such short supply: "I am in the same position as the Syrians at the Bnot Yaakov [Bridge] segment—today, neither of us has an advance quartermaster base," he telegrammed Yadin ironically after the attack on a Syrian base near Mishmar Ha-Yarden; "the solution is in your hands," he added.[69] He was in the throes of drafting a plan to recapture Malkiyyah and Kadesh more effectively than the previous bitter attempt.

He charged the operation to the troops that had spilled their blood on Malkiyyah's rocks a few days before—the First Battalion. The second attempt left him with warm memories, "one of my favorite operations in my military career."[70] It began with the building of an "armored column" based on two vehicles captured in Safed and on the handiwork of Galileean metalsmiths, who fitted armor onto transport trucks and buses. The column's crowning glory was a canon originally meant to stand on the ground, which was now mounted on one of the two armored vehicles thanks to the ingenuity of local artisans.[71]

Allon's sentiments for the operation seem to be related to the finesse and chicanery he employed—the finesse of a local farm boy at home with the geography of the area and the psychology of the inhabitants. Over several nights, "column" cars climbed up to Manarah in the guise of supply vehicles and nonarmored vehicles came back down, clattering noisily and in full light so that there could be no mistaking their descent. The armored cars were left hidden at Manarah. Arab fortifications had planned against an attack from Nabi Yusha. On the night of the operation, diversionary maneuvers confirmed the enemy's misapprehension that Malkiyyah and Kadesh were indeed under a frontal attack. While the Arabs turned their attention in this direction, the "armored column" proceeded from Manarah—with lights doused through a plowed field until it hit the Lebanese road parallel to the border. It then continued through Arab villages to Malkiyyah from behind. Taking these for Lebanese forces, the villagers cheered them and wished them well. The force arrived at Malkiyyah's rear, which was exposed. By morning, the First Battalion had captured Malkiyyah, including the Lebanese part of the village, the police station, and the army base. The battalion also took Kadesh. This time there were no casualties. In his report to the general staff, Yigal called the battle "saucy," hardly concealing his youthful relish at the subterfuge.[72]

The "month of battles," between the proclamation of statehood and the subsequent Arab invasion and the First ceasefire (15 May 1948–11 June 1948), is considered the hardest part of the War of Independence. Some sixteen hundred Jews were killed in this month, more than a quarter of the war's total losses. At this stage, there were the evident difficulties of a fledgling army meeting regular armies, even if the latter were not particularly advanced. That the Arab attack was halted was due primarily to the self-sacrifice of people who bravely and staunchly defended their homes against Syrians, Iraqis, and Egyptians. It was also due to the fact that the Arab states did not fully exploit their military potential, dis-

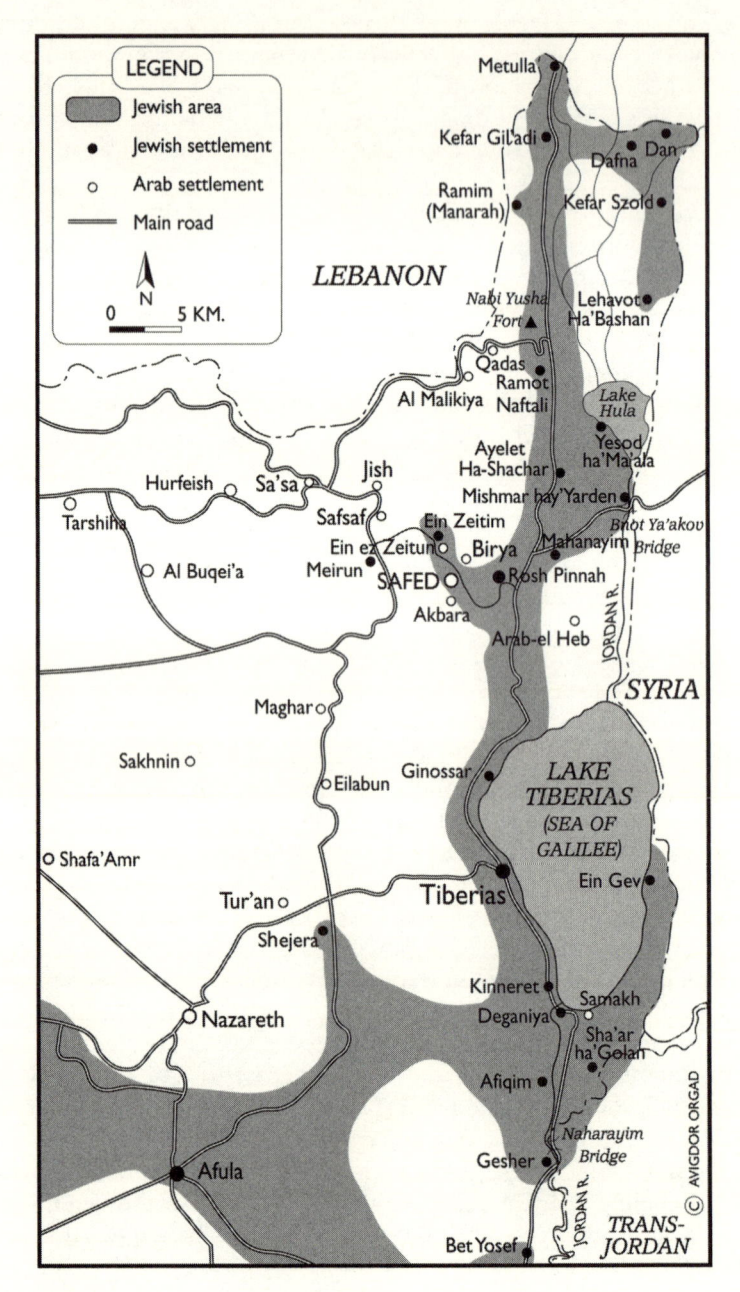

Map 2. The Eastern Upper Galilee at the Beginning of the War of Independence.

patching a limited number of troops. Their equipment, which the Jews regarded as ominous, was outdated and in disrepair. Their command was neither uniform nor coordinated. For all of these reasons, the Arab offensive soon faltered and the Arabs found themselves on the defensive. Until the end of the "month of battles," the balance of forces was quite even: Jewish settlements earmarked for the Jewish state, such as Mishmar ha-Yarden and all of the Negev settlements, either fell into enemy hands or were under siege, severed from Jewish population centers. Thirteen settlements outside of the allotted partition borders fell to the Arabs and were destroyed.[73] Jerusalem was under siege and heavy bombardment. Most of the fighting took place around the partition's boundaries. The conquest of the Western Galilee on the day that the State of Israel was proclaimed, and then, of the Gilboa area (in an attempt to take Jenin), did breach the partition's borders. But it was far from clear who was extending borders and who was maintaining the status quo. The Arabs were determined to reject any partition plan. Meanwhile, however, they endeavored to take as large a bite as they could out of the new Jewish state. The Jews were still fighting to ensure sovereignty in the areas allocated to them. The borders of 29 November 1947 thus did not vanish all at once.

The major front in the "month of battles" was Jerusalem. For both sides, Jerusalem was the most symbolically charged: for Jews all over the world, it was the Zion to which they lifted their eyes; for Arabs, it was el-Kuds, Islam's third-holiest city after Mecca and Medina. If the Arabs were to conquer the city, they could have dealt a mortal blow to Jewish national morale and greatly boosted Arab prestige. Some 20 percent of the country's Jewish population lived in Jerusalem, so its fall could have had serious demographic implications as well. Geographically, Jerusalem is situated at the crossroads between north and south, and between east and west, which makes it the most important strategic point in Western Palestine. Politically, its future was veiled in mist: according to the partition plan, it was meant to be under international rule, though it did not look as if this would be implemented. The policy of both sides regarding Jerusalem was to "grab what you can," each striving to ensure territorial contiguity and safeguard its population. The United Nations procrastinated on implementing internationalization, its remissness leaving the decision to the forces on the ground.

The entry of the Arab Legion into Jerusalem (18 May 1948) marked a new stage in the struggle for control of the city. For the first time Israeli forces faced off with a regular army on this sensitive front. The legion was considered the best of the Arab armies. On the eve of the war, Colonel David Daniel Marcus (Mickey Stone), an American-Jewish volunteer who had seen active duty in World War II and was recruited to help the young Israeli army, had appraised the legion's options. Stone believed the legion had two avenues to choose from: either a speedy campaign for the Sharon Plain, bisecting the Jewish state near Netanya; or a battle for Jerusalem. If they chose the first case, the situation was grave, he said; if they chose the second, the Jews were saved. Warfare in populated, built-up areas would exhaust the legion, dampening its advantage as a regular army against the IDF's quasi-regular forces. The battle of Stalingrad was clearly etched in the minds of contemporaries as a model of house-to-house fighting.[74] Stone's opinion was consistent with Yadin's, Yadin was worried about the bisection of the Jewish state and did not think it likely that Jerusalem would fall. Ben-Gurion, in contrast, regarded Jerusalem as making or breaking the course of the entire war, and he had nightmares about it falling. Yitzhak Rabin, then the commander of the Harel Brigade, which encountered some of the bitterest combat on the road to Jerusalem, shared Ben-Gurion's view.[75]

The road to Jerusalem had been blocked since the legion's entry into the fortified police station at Latrun on the night of 17–18 May 1948. One hundred thousand Jews lived under siege. The city's store of supplies, including food, fuel, weapons, and arms, was running out. Heavy bombardment had caused numerous civilian casualties. Attempts to break through to the Old City's Jewish Quarter and reinforce its defenders had failed. The quarter surrendered to the legion toward the end of May and its residents were taken captive. In the southern outskirts of Jerusalem, Kibbutz Ramat Rachel was overrun and razed by Egypt's Muslim Brotherhood irregulars and then retaken by the Palmah. Repeated battles for Latrun (Operations Bin-Nun A and B) in the latter half of May to open the road to Jerusalem failed. All of these opposing pressures were exacerbated by the time factor: at the end of May, the United Nations was clearly aiming at a ceasefire. In those days, with independence only two weeks old, Israel never even contemplated defying the United Nations. The picture on the ground was therefore worrying, especially as regarded Jerusalem. Would the Jews gain control of the road to Jerusalem by the time the ceasefire went into effect? If so, supplies would no longer pose a problem. If not, they would have to rely on arrangements determined by UN supervisors.

The military command suffered from a multiple chain of command: the Etzyoni Brigade, which was responsible for defending the city, was under the command of David Shaltiel, a controversial figure. The heavy responsibility for the road to the city, from Shaar Ha-Gai upward, fell within the purview of the Harel Brigade under the young Yitzhak Rabin. The section of Latrun was under the Seventh Brigade, commanded by the Haganah's Shlomo Shamir, a World War II veteran of the British army. Every field commander behaved as his own boss, with little cooperation between the three brigades. To complicate matters further, there were sporadic operations by the dissenters (IZL, LeHI), their recognition of state authority remaining ambiguous.

After the failure of Operation Bin-Nun A, Ben-Gurion made Colonel Mickey Stone the chief commander of the Jerusalem front, subordinating the three brigades to his authority.[76] In the heat of the Latrun campaign, the HGS feared an Arab thrust from the Ramleh-Lydda area toward the coast, whether against Tel Aviv or Rehovot. The Arab Legion and the Iraqi army were poised against the Sharon Plain, which was sparse in Jewish population. It was a highly dangerous line. These fears spawned the LuDaR (acronym for Lydda-Ramleh) Operation. Yadin ordered Allon to the Jerusalem Corridor region with the Yiftah Brigade in order to prepare for Operation LuDaR.[77] The brigade's dispatch to the plains was a "first": never before had the IDF organized so quickly to deploy so large a force.

Meanwhile, Operation Bin-Nun B took place on the night of 30–31 May while the brigade was redeploying. Despite a promising start, it too ended in failure.[78]

By the time the Yiftah Brigade arrived and began to organize, Operation LuDaR was no longer relevant. Latrun began to take on mythic dimensions: it was no longer a fortress to be captured on the road to Jerusalem, but a symbol of failure of the young Israeli army in its encounter with a regular army. On 1 June, a day or two after the second defeat at Latrun, there were reports from the Seventh Brigade and the Harel Brigade that a convoy of jeeps could possibly make it to Jerusalem by a route south of the main road, in between two conquered Arab villages, Bet Jiz and Bet Susin. That night, 150 novices wended their way on foot up to the Jerusalem Corridor as reserves for the Harel Brigade, which had seriously dwindled. Equipment and arms were brought in the same way.[79] But the general staff was still concentrating on breaching the main road to Jerusalem and, at this point, Allon too did not think it worthwhile to focus on an alternative route.[80] Time was breathing down the necks of the decision makers: from Lake Success, there were reports that the Arabs had consented to a ceasefire. Had it been implemented, the situation would have been frozen with Jerusalem cut off and the road to it blocked.[81] The need to get through to Jerusalem grew increasingly urgent.

Mickey Stone and Allon enjoyed a warm relationship. Stone, a graduate of West Point and a professional soldier, was noted for his informality, as well as his readiness to listen to the opinions of others and to adapt to local conditions. He had captured the heart of the Palmahniks on a visit to the country during the convoy period, before Operation Nahshon. To remedy the lack of armored cars, he had suggested fitting trucks with double panels filled with gravel. The improvisation matched the Palmah's thinking.[82] On his tour of Galilee, during Operation Yiftah, he had shown empathy for the Palmah's "barefoot army." Now, two Palmah brigades, Harel and Yiftah, were under his command on the road to Jerusalem, in addition to Etzyoni, which was in the city. Stone needed a headquarters: Harel's was on-site, and Yiftah's was co-opted to it. On 5 June, the united headquarters of the two brigades was officially designated Yoram, under Allon's command.[83] Stone served as an intermediary between Ben-Gurion and the Palmah command or rather as an umbrella for it against Ben-Gurion's rain.[84]

Just as Operation Yiftah had been Allon's first large campaign—in which he commanded a unit larger than a battalion—now, for the first time, he took charge of two brigades. It was one of the first campaigns to muster more troops than the size of a brigade. At Allon's request, Yitzhak Rabin was appointed operations officer of Yoram's headquarters. Mula Cohen, the commander of the Yiftah Brigade, was put in charge of the operational forces.[85] The Yiftah Brigade had come from the Galilee after long weeks of incessant battle with no rest and no time to regroup, yet it was in better shape than the Harel Brigade, which had suffered heavy casualties and was low in morale. Yiftah was deemed more fit for the coming battle.

The operation was marked by the times: everything was done in haste and under pressure. On 6 June, Yitzhak Ben-Zvi, a leading member of Mapai and a central figure in Jerusalem's civil society, telegrammed Ben-Gurion and Yadin warning of the city's possible collapse: the bombardment did not let up, there was no food and no fuel: "With all due respect for the valiant spirits of besieged Jerusalem's citizens, there is a limit."[86] Operation Yoram came to fill the breach.

At Yoram's headquarters in Abu Ghosh, a two-pronged plan was worked out: from the east, one arm was to attack Ramallah, the Arab Legion's main base in the country. The other arm was to attack and capture Latrun and, from there, continue on to Ramallah from the west. The assumption was that the success of both missions would result in winning also the hilly region in between because, once the roads were taken over, the Arab Legion would retreat for fear of being cut off from its rear. It was a typical Allon approach—and would serve well in the future. Now, however, it died a premature death because the Fifty-second Battalion of the Givati Brigade, which was to reinforce Harel on the eastern arm, was removed from the arena and sent south owing to pressure by the Egyptian army on the Negev. The plan was therefore trimmed down to the Latrun arm. The aim was to seize the village of Latrun along with the police station, after overrunning the two dominant outposts known as 13 and 14.

Luck was not on Yoram's side. A navigation error threw the whole plan out of kilter and Latrun again took a heavy toll: fourteen dead and more than forty wounded.[87] Were it not for the navigation error, the campaign might have ended differently. As it was, after the attack on the outposts failed, the whole operation ground to a stop. There was no assault on Latrun.

The Arab Legion's forces, as it later turned out, were on the verge of collapse. Intelligence had reported that "the Arab forces are tired to death and without ammunition";[88] another moment, and Latrun would have been taken. But these were hectic times with defeat and triumph coming fast on the heels of one another. There was no breathing space, which might have made all the difference.

The next day, a truce was about to begin. Both sides, totally worn out, rallied for a final effort to establish facts on the ground before it went into effect. On 10 June 1948, all the fronts were ablaze: Gezer was taken by Arab forces and retaken by the First Battalion under Dan Laner.[89] Mishmar ha-Yarden fell to the Syrians. On the Jerusalem front, the Arab Legion's chief thrust aimed at thwarting activity on the alternative route to the city, known as the "Burma Road," particularly around Bet-Susin.[90] The wise thing to do was to drop Latrun as a major target and secure the Burma Road instead. Stone and Allon were not overly eager to present the option to Ben-Gurion: it was an admission of the failure of Operation Yoram. Both men had believed in it, both had declared it feasible. Moreover, it meant openly relinquishing Latrun, which, apart from being a geostrategic target and a military challenge, was now a myth. For Ben-Gurion, Latrun was more than a national, political interest: it was the symbol of the struggle for the road to Jerusalem and an expression of a policy that he personally had molded, of priorities that he himself had set, in opposition to military experts, who, in his opinion, did not understand the importance of Jerusalem. The more it became the rock on which Israeli offensives were broken, the more it became his obsession. The messenger bringing Ben-Gurion news that Latrun had been dropped could expect to be on the receiving end of Ben-Gurion's wrath. Stone and Allon chose the young, inexperienced Yitzhak Rabin to lay the decision before Ben-Gurion and explain its reasoning.

Ben-Gurion did not spare Rabin. He blasted him with questions about what had gone wrong, why the plan had not been fully executed, what had happened in the course of battle, and so forth. Rabin attempted to convince Ben-Gurion that there was no chance of taking Latrun that same night: the forces were exhausted, there were no replacements and no time to bring any in before the ceasefire. However, there was an alternative route and it was best to use the night to capture the outposts and secure the new road. Jerusalem could be reached without Latrun. Ben-

Gurion's rage erupted: Yigal should be shot, he shouted. Rabin was shocked into silence. The rage was at both Stone and Allon, although mostly at Allon; perhaps because Ben-Gurion realized that Allon was the de facto the commander of the forces.⁹² Or, perhaps, his rage reflected the increasing tension between Ben-Gurion and the Palmah. The Seventh Brigade had twice failed in its efforts to take Latrun without drawing Ben-Gurion's fire. On the contrary: it was the brigade closest to his heart. This was not so for the Palmah and its commander: Ben-Gurion's feelings were a mixture of respect and suspicion, affection and hostility. After several hours of deliberation, Ben-Gurion acknowledged that there was no choice but to accept the recommendations of the field command. Time was short and no other decision was possible.⁹³ But he was soon to show his frustration with Allon, in the ensuing controversy over appointments.

Chapter 9
The Ten-Day Campaigns

The lull in the fighting on 11 June went down in history as "the First Truce." The lull, it was decided in advance, would last only four weeks, and it got off to a bad start. On the first night, Colonel Mickey Stone, who was wrapped in a blanket, stepped outside the fence of the camp in Abu Ghosh and was shot by a sentry by mistake. Stone was accepted by Ben-Gurion as a military authority; at the same time, Stone's heart and head were open to the desires and creative thinking of Israel's young.[1] With his demise, the man who might have shielded the Palmah from Ben-Gurion was gone.

About a week into the truce, on 18 June 1948, the Israel Defense Forces High General Staff (HGS)[2] met with senior officers. A sigh of relief rose from all units: the month of fighting had been grueling. "The truce descended on us like rain from heaven," said Moshe Carmel. The Negev and Yiftah brigades had been in combat without leave for more than seven months. Some units had suffered overwhelming losses: 220 in Harel, 250 in Yiftah, and these figures excluded the wounded and the shell-shocked. All the gripes that had been held back during the fighting now surfaced: the sense of alienation between front and rear; the charges of discrimination between older and newer units in terms of equipment and provisions. The tough battles and transition from elite units to general conscription had raised issues not encountered before in the Haganah and the Palmah. For example, how was desertion to be dealt with? Imprisonment for desertion was less frightening to soldiers than the danger of death. Even in the Harel Brigade, some soldiers had had to be threatened at gunpoint to go into battle. No one took care of the recruits' families, and many deserted out of concern for their loved ones: "In some cases, commanders refused to eat their meals when remembering that their families went hungry." There were numerous complaints about shortages in fighting units: the greatest demand was for hats and canteens. One commander claimed that his people went to war in pajamas because they had nothing else to wear. It was not enough to preach a firm stance in the name of morale, the Givati commander Shimon Avidan protested: "no shoes—morale, no clothes—morale, no aid for the families—morale." Commanders gave vent to the anger and frustration that had been building up in the month of battle: weapons arrived packed in grease half an hour before the troops were to set out on an operation; provisions were badly organized, detrimentally affecting the fighting ability of the soldiers. The burden was not equally shared by front and rear or between the fighting units themselves. Much was said about the lack of discipline, its main flag-bearers being Ben-Gurion, Shamir, and Dan Even, the commander of the Alexandroni Brigade. Allon, a restless colt, stressed the opportunities he believed had been missed in the Galilee, the center of the country, and Jerusalem. He proposed striking at Arab capitals. He pressed for taking the initiative and using the advantage of surprise. He urged that forces be mustered, that a supreme effort be made to recruit manpower. With the thoughtlessness of youth, he demanded the cancellation of the special exemption that kept only sons out of active duty: "Wingate would have called some of our considerations 'Jewish considerations,'" he noted with irony. Most of his words revolved around the need to establish divisions larger than brigades, compact "fists" to change the balance of forces after the truce. Though he did not spell it out, there is no doubt that he saw himself as one of the commanding officers of these large formations.[3]

The discussion reflected the long road traveled by the young army in the previous month: despite all of the weak points under review, the month of battles had ended with the halting of the regular armies of the Arab states and with initial counteroffensives. The fighting force had crystallized with remarkable speed and, in the heat of battle, had learned about organization, supplies, and the deployment of forces and auxiliary weaponry. It had even made a start on field intelligence. The fighting unit was no longer the company; it was the battalion, the brigade, and even larger units. There was general agreement among Ben-Gurion, the general staff, and the field commanders that it was time to move beyond the deployment of brigades and to organize fronts. It was equally clear that the main front was to be the center of the country, between Tel Aviv and Jerusalem.

A few days after the meeting, the *Altalena* affair took place. An arms ship, named after Jabotinsky's pseudonym, was brought by the IZL from France to the country's shores, an action that was both forbidden according to the terms of the truce and a challenge to the authority of the young state. The *Altalena* affair has been documented in detail by the IZL's supporters and admirers as well as by bitter opponents.[4] It raised the specter of civil war amid the Jewish state's fight for its existence and was certainly one of the most dramatic moments in state history. Ben-Gurion and his adherents regarded its outcome as a miraculous deliverance for the Jewish state. Begin and his supporters viewed it as a reprehensible abuse of state power. The *Altalena* affair, according to Ben-Gurion and the Left in those years, was understood as an attempt by the IZL to defy the provisional government in wartime. It was seen as a sign of the IZL's aspirations to continue to maintain an independent military force, which, in the best-case scenario, would claim the status of equal partner in its dealings with the government, and, in the worst case, would intend to hold onto its forces for an armed coup d'etat. According to the Right, in the best-case scenario, the *Altalena* affair was a tragic misunderstanding between the IZL and the government; in the worst case, it was a treacherous trap providing Ben-Gurion with an opportunity to liquidate his IZL rivals once and for all. Both versions flourished over the years, each side embracing the less generous interpretation. In the Left's version of the 1950–60s, Ben-Gurion was depicted as having acted on the principle of state, forcing state authority on all organizations that would challenge it. He thereby secured Israel's lasting democracy. Ben-Gurion applauded the artillery barrage that was fired at the ship and set it alight; the press quoted him as having dubbed it the "holy canon," and he offered no denial. In the twilight period between the Yishuv's volunteerism and a structured state authority, the fact had to be driven home that one era had ended and another had dawned. The price had indeed been terrible—Jews at war with Jews—but without it the fledgling state would have toppled before it ever got on its feet. The gunfire put an end to any independent import of arms, as well as to any idea that the IZL and LeHI might still have harbored about maintaining military frameworks separate from the state's. That is how Ben-Gurion saw it.

In the rightist camp, the story of the *Altalena* served as an extreme example of Ben-Gurion's arbitrariness and authoritarian tendencies: he was prepared to spill Jewish blood so long as he could deny the IZL the right to decide what was to be done with the arms it had brought to Israel; nor was he prepared to accord the IZL units conscripted into the IDF priority in receiving those arms. Instead of conducting negotiations or agreeing to the good services of mediators, Ben-Gurion chose to sanctify war. It was a resort to extreme and unacceptable measures, no matter the case or circumstance, against valiant combatants who had mobilized for the good of the people to furnish arms of deliverance without any ulterior motives. The protagonist of the *Altalena* episode, for better or for worse, was Ben-Gurion.

The *Altalena* was grounded off Tel Aviv opposite the Ritz Hotel, the location of the Palmah's headquarters. On the orders of the HGS, the Palmah's headquarters company enlisted to defend the coast and its own headquarters, and to prevent the offloading of the arms. Yitzhak

Rabin was there by chance and took charge of the headquarters' personnel, who were under fire by the IZL. The IZL continued to offload the cargo with the help of dozens, perhaps hundreds, of supporters on the shore, and, in the skirmishes with the Palmah, both sides scored casualties. The HGS instructed Allon to prevail over the IZL forces and the operation, called "Purge," relied on the Kiryati Brigade and the Palmah's forces placed under his command. The decision of the HGS stemmed from the failure the previous day to get the Alexandroni Brigade to act against the IZL when the ship (on the IDF's instructions) had reached Kfar Vitkin to deposit the arms there. The *Altalena* affair began when it transpired that the arms were not being handed over to the IDF, as had been agreed. Dan Even, the commanding officer of the Alexandroni Brigade, was ordered to arrest the IZL commanders at the site and block the ship's movement. He did not carry out the order. When the ship arrived at Tel Aviv, Michael Ben-Gal, the commanding officer of the Kiryati Brigade, voiced doubts about his ability to rouse his men to the action. The High Command thus called on the Palmah, certain that it would undertake the mission both because it was "ever ready for duty" and because of its emotional and ideological animus toward the dissenters. Both the Left and the Right had resorted to demonization as a vital element in constructing their own self-identities. When Allon rose to "purge" Tel Aviv on the orders of the High Command, he was convinced that he was fighting against the forces of fascism threatening to take over the state. Nor was he alone in this view; an entire echelon of fighters and commanders felt the same way. Nevertheless, the "holy canon" was not placed at the disposal of the Palmah but of the Kiryati Brigade at the Jonah camp to the north of the Palmah's headquarters. The order to fire it did not come from the Palmah's headquarters even though Allon had no qualms about doing so if it would quash the incident. For a few days, Tel Aviv was like a war zone with curfews and army patrols in the streets. Then the crisis drew to a close and the Palmah units dispersed, whether for leave, for rest, or for return to their lines. The Palmah's share in the *Altalena* affair received no prominence in contemporary reports. Like the *saison*, it was not a tale to boast of, nor, however, was it a tale to be ashamed of. It was a marginal episode in the history of Allon and the Palmah. In the history of Ben-Gurion's leadership, in contrast, *Altalena* Day remained an important milestone; another sign of his determination and iron will.[5]

The period of the First Truce brought to the surface tensions that had been seething unseen for months if not years. The key figures were Ben-Gurion, Galili, and the HGS generals. Allon was more or less a passive player, even though he himself was the subject of one of the conflicts.

But there is no doubt that in this conflict the fate of the Palmah too was sealed.

The tensions between Ben-Gurion and the Palmah went back to the Palmah's very beginnings. Ben-Gurion had always been guarded in his attitude toward the Palmah, which was half youth movement, half army, and which over the years had become increasingly associated with the activist left in Palestine's Labor movement. He liked to refer to the Palmah as "Tabenkin's private army," a label borrowed from another of his rivals, Yaakov Hazan (the leader of Ha-Shomer Ha-Tza'ir).[6] The Palmah's unique blend of idealism, which combined Zionism and socialism, universalist aspirations, and fierce patriotism, struck no chord with Ben-Gurion. Ever since the Second Aliyah period (1904–18), he had preferred hierarchical institutions to the anarchic creativity that characterized the youth organizations of Labor Palestine.

This was compounded by the differences during World War II concerning whether or not to recruit the Palmah into the British army; the conflict had left a residue of mutual suspicion and acrimony. One widespread story tells about Ben-Gurion's review at Kibbutz Ashdot Yaakov in April 1943 of the Palmah's Company A, which had outdone itself in spit and polish for the visit by the chairman of the Jewish Agency (JA). According to Allon, Ben-Gurion reviewed the formation with the Palmah commander Yitzhak Sadeh, and then he gave a talk on the affairs of the day, summing up with: "I hope that it will not be long before I see you as a recognized, celebrated unit in the framework of the British army's Jewish units, as is appropriate for you for the sake of the war against Hitler, [who is] the enemy of humanity and the enemy of the Jewish people."[7] The facts remain in dispute: did Ben-Gurion really say what was attributed to him? And, if so, was his intention to minimize the independent Jewish force vis-à-vis the recruits to the British army? But there is no arguing with legends. This version of the story made the rounds of all of the Palmah's tents and was received as definitive evidence of the political leadership's obtuseness regarding the defense force "out of uniform," and of Ben-Gurion's ill will toward the Palmah. In the Palmah's discourse, the incident took on mythological proportions; it was a defining moment in its relations with Ben-Gurion.

The 1940s saw a growing rift within Mapai, ending in a split and the establishment of the Le-Ahdut Ha-Avodah (LAHA) Party. The schism had all the hallmarks of a family spat: mutual recrimination, loss of trust, extremist positions, each side's demand for utter loyalty. The Palmah, to its detriment, was drawn into the whirlpool; its commanders and patrons were associated with the LAHA. The mood of the youth at the time favored the LAHA: it was considered anti-establishment and a challenge to Mapai's rule. Like every ruling party, Mapai was suspect in the eyes of the young idealists; they perceived it as hypocritical, corrupt, and far removed from its original values. Youth is the springtime of absolute ideals not yet compromised by life's imperfections. Ben-Gurion and Tabenkin may have belonged to the same age group and Yitzhak Sadeh may have been the "old man," but the latter two had the kind of naïveté that bestowed eternal youth, freeing them of the need to look at reality open-eyed. The mature figure among them was Galili. He, however, was unable to shed his loyalty to Tabenkin. Thus, even if he semi-recognized the justice of Ben-Gurion's way and was not party to the Palmah's rampant demonization of him, he was unable to reverse the rising tide of anti-Mapai hostility.

Ever since Ben-Gurion took over (or rather created) the security portfolio at the Basle Congress in December 1946, he had been trying to prepare for what he saw as an inevitable clash with Arab states. He assessed that when the Jewish state arose it would have to fight for its existence against regular armies.[8] It was thus necessary to conscript a regular Jewish fighting force. He considered the veterans of the British army a large fount of real military experience—as opposed to the Palmah's guerrilla games—as well as a command echelon true to the JA Executive; they did not look to any other source of inspiration, such as the KM leadership. First, he tried to reconscript the entire units of the Jewish Brigade, officers, soldiers, everyone. But a number of years had passed, everyone had scattered, and it proved unfeasible. He then tried to replace the HGS with a staff consisting entirely of Jewish Brigade veterans. Before he could do so, the War of Independence erupted and disrupted his plans, which, many believe, was a bit of good luck for the Jewish people. Nevertheless, he kept on trying to man key positions with people he believed had the necessary military knowledge as a result of service in a regular army, be it British, Austrian, or American. Whenever his intentions were stymied, for whatever reason, he suspected that there was something behind it. At best, it was the short-sightedness of his challengers, the people of the Haganah, who failed to grasp the enormity of the task at hand. At worst, there were political motives afoot.[9]

Every now and then, Ben-Gurion's stifled fury at obstruction or at insubordination would rear its head. Thus, for example, he refused to recognize the appointment of Nahum Sarig as the commander of the Palmah's Negev companies, which later became the Negev Brigade. The appointment touched on his relations with Galili: Ben-Gurion sought to ensure his unquestioned authority over the security forces and remove all trace of the old Yishuv order: the system of involving political and social bodies in setting security policy and, especially, the intermediary institution between the army and the political authority, that is, the head of the National Command. Ben-Gurion had appointed Galili to this position in 1947, but from 1948 onward he was determined to clip his wings, particularly as concerned appointments. Sarig was appointed by Galili and Dori without Ben-Gurion's approval. Ben-Gurion consequently treated him as if he did not exist and tried to oust him and replace him with his own man, Shlomo Shamir, a veteran of the Jewish Brigade.[10]

Another issue that got Ben-Gurion's goat was the navy. The Palmah's headquarters had regarded the seafaring Palmahniks, who captained and escorted the ships of clandestine immigration, as the core of a future navy, combining sea duties and commando warfare—much like the U.S. marines. This was not true of Ben-Gurion: he wanted to build a navy umbilically severed from the Palmah. He created the Sea Service and put Gershon Zack in charge of it; Zack was a Mapai hack who—by broad consensus—lacked the qualifications for the job. The Palmah marine companies were ordered to join the Sea Service. The seamen, who were under the command of Yosef Tabenkin (Yitzhak Tabenkin's son), refused to follow orders and deserted back to the Palmah, to Harel's Fourth Battalion under Tabenkin junior.[11] Ben-Gurion never forgot the insubordination.

The war's progress made the Palmah's headquarters obsolete. The brigades received field orders directly from the Haganah's Operations Branch without the mediation of the Palmah's headquarters. The old Palmah, whose reserves had been conscripted at the outbreak of fighting and which bore the brunt of the battle in the war's early stages, had lost most of its men (some were killed, some were wounded). General conscription directed thousands of novices to the Palmah to fill the dwindled ranks, but, unlike their predecessors, the new recruits had not been through the youth-movement crucible and had no long-term ideological and social education under their belts. The Palmah's spirit was diluted by its changed composition and the lack of time for bonding. There still was team spirit and the strength of the camaraderie and fellowship of comrades-in-arms. But the Palmah's headquarters, as an intermediary body between the brigades and the HGS, became less and less relevant. The fact that Allon was not a member of the headquarters, but a commander of active operations, did not enhance its prestige any. The acting commander of the Palmah's headquarters, Shalom Havlin, was a relatively older figure unremarkable either militarily or personally. In response to a HGS circular listing the various Palmah brigades separately from the Palmah's headquarters (code-named "Bulgarians"), Havlin issued a circular of his own. ". . . We hereby advise you that the Palmah designated 'Bulgarians' has not dismantled nor will it dismantle either de facto or de jure and that the brigades of the Palmah—Yiftah, Harel, and Negev—as well as the mechanized raiding unit will take no order or any other material from any institution, branch, corps, or service that [does not come] directly from the Palmah's headquarters and is not authorized by it."[12] Havlin never consulted anyone before projecting this bombshell into an air already filled with dynamite. The belligerent tone, the insistence on the independence of the Palmah's headquarters independence against the whole world may have suited the youth-movement mentality, but it was inconsistent with army conduct, even if that army was only ten days old. He was ordered to cancel his advisory immediately and recall the circular. If before the episode the status of the Palmah's headquarters had been obscure, Havlin's reprimand now exposed its vulnerability.

The comportment of Palmahniks and the light view they took of law and order did not make Allon's relations with Ben-Gurion any easier. When, to equip themselves for Operation Yoram, Harel's soldiers pilfered weapons from an officer of the Etzyoni Brigade, Ben-Gurion saw red: he demanded that the perpetrators be court-martialed.

There was no equality between Ben-Gurion and Allon, but there was a balance of forces in which one side (Ben-Gurion) called all the shots as to the arena and rules of the game while the other side (Allon) deluded itself that it was an autonomous player in the field. On one side of the scales there was the prime minister of Israel and the chief commander of the war; on the other side was the commander of the Palmah and then of one campaign arena. But the differences were not merely a matter of official positions; they stemmed from age, experience, and personal prestige. Ben-Gurion in 1948 was a seasoned leader who had met internal and external political tests and had known both success and failure over a forty-year public career. One of his unique qualities was the ability to learn and to change, to grasp reality and to recognize the limitations it imposed on anyone attempting to steer the tiny ship of Zionism. He understood the international power game, including the scant ability of the state of the Jews to influence it. Unlike other Israeli leaders of the period, he was conversant with the ways of the big wide world, knew the advantages and limitations of power, and with great caution navigated a course through the daunting rocks of reality.

Allon in 1948 was a young man sprung from the narrow world of Mes'ha, Kadoorie, and Ginossar, and then from the broader, though still restricted, local framework of the KM and the Palmah. His knowledge of the larger world amounted to one trip to Europe in the winter of 1946–47, and even then it is doubtful that he strayed beyond the turf occupied by his friends. He was a product of the local life-culture with all of its advantages and shortcomings, and it dictated his thinking and attitudes. He was used to relying on personal charm in confrontations with rivals or superiors. Failure was a stranger to him. In his local arena, he enjoyed a good deal of prestige among subordinates and superiors but it was a prestige confined to certain circles and certain spheres. It is not likely that his life experience prepared him for a personal contest with Ben-Gurion.

Ben-Gurion did not trust Allon; he associated him with the KM and Mapam. He had good reason to suspect that Allon reported to Galili (and through him to Tabenkin) about matters that he did not divulge to Ben-Gurion, and that he promoted Palmah commanders on the basis of political loyalties. Most of the Palmah commanders actually were associated with Mapam. This was explained away by the fact that promotions were made from the ranks of the old Palmah members and these were chiefly connected with the KM; after all, it had fostered and favored the Palmah over conscription into the British army. Allon, Galili, and their colleagues contended that promotion was based on professional considerations alone, that is, personal qualifications. But a degree of favoritism probably entered the equation. Ben-Gurion did not believe that the process was innocent. He had grown up in political frameworks and he found it hard to credit that the dominant principle in the military was merit. Allon and his friends, meanwhile, considered their involvement in Mapam and Mapam's involvement in the Palmah's affairs as legitimate and consistent with the Yishuv's norms of the time. The separation between the political and military spheres was not yet self-evident.

Ben-Gurion's suspicions went beyond politics, however. There was a cunning about Allon that came to the fore in his military planning as well as in his relations with those above and below him. His planning was bold and he was prepared to take calculated risks. But he did not always bother to fully share his plans with the High Command, whether because he was forever shielding his friends or because he was self-confident, which some people interpreted as insubordination, including Ben-Gurion. He radiated the chutzpah of a sabra that both attracted and disturbed Ben-Gurion. On the one hand, he too was charmed by the handsome, young Allon who emitted a boundless optimism and a belief that there was nothing his forces could not do; on the other hand, Allon's overdose of independence struck him as defiance.

Several factors at the start of the truce exacerbated the tension between Ben-Gurion and Allon. Allon and his peers sought a way to retain the organizational, operative framework of the Palmah's headquarters. The de facto situation created by the union of Harel and Yiftah in Operation Yoram placed Palmah brigades under a single command with the Palmah's headquarters actually functioning as Yoram's headquarters. The Palmah's headquarters issued the brigades their equipment and manpower. Ben-Gurion suspected Allon's motives and conducted a searching interview with him. Among his objections to the continuation of the Palmah's headquarters, he cited the Palmah's political identity, "Tabenkin's private army." Against this, he posed his ideology about a uniform army in which everyone is equal and answers to one authority, that is, the minister of defense. His long monologue contained an elaboration on a uniform army, drawing its inspiration from a single source and being centralized under a single command; a diatribe against the Palmah as a "proletarian" army demanding, ostensibly in the name of the proletariat, a separate staff and its own command; a reprimand to Allon for not having punished the guilty in the pilfering of weapons from the Etzyoni Brigade, which could have ended in a gun battle; and so forth. With seeming innocence, he made sure to intersperse in the monologue words of praise and bait for Allon. Relating to Allon's status among his underlings, he said: "You are more than a commander. You are in fact the leader of this thing. It is both a drawback and an advantage for a commander to be a leader. It is good for a commander to be admired by his soldiers." Allon's charisma aroused Ben-Gurion's reservations because it lent him a special status among his subordinates, a status that obstructed the High Command's freedom of action. After the praise, the bait was dangled: Allon did not have to be confined to the Palmah—Ben-Gurion could offer him a more senior position.[13] The compliments and hints of a senior appointment aimed at preparing the ground for Allon's detachment from the Palmah's headquarters, thereby opening the door to its dismantling. It was an attempt to drive in a wedge between Allon's personal career and the future of the Palmah's headquarters.

Following Ben-Gurion's harangue and Allon's predictable, defensively arrogant response, the two sides reached an amiable agreement. Neither bared their hearts. Allon concealed his intention of keeping the Palmah's headquarters under the mantle of Operation Yoram's headquarters with the camouflage of combining provisions for the two brigades. Ben-Gurion hastened to agree to unifying the two brigades under one headquarters, even announcing that meanwhile the Palmah's headquarters would remain.[14] But a few days later, at the Mapai Council, he sealed the Palmah's fate: "An attempt . . . has been made to make the Palmah the monopoly of one party, a party's military brigade, so to speak," adding that "factional rule in part of the army undermines the army's efficiency." He was effusive about the Palmah's spirit, then immediately summed up: "this spirit should not be the preserve of one brigade, but the preserve of our entire army! And all as one are capable of it."[15] It was an anti-elitist barb directed at the Palmah's avant-garde status and its pretensions to spearheading the camp: there was no longer any need for avant-gardism since the era of volunteerism was over.

The merging of the Palmah's headquarters and Operation Yoram's headquarters received official authorization, the former now being addressed as "Palmah HQ (Operation Yoram)."[16] The hidden tensions between Ben-Gurion and Allon did not abate. On 20 June 1948, Allon asked Yadin for "instructions for the future": "It is important that I know as soon as possible what commission you have in mind for me at the end of the truce."[17] Two days later the *Altalena* affair erupted and for a week Allon was busy with Operation Purge. There was also another issue in those frenzied days, this time far from the public eye and known only to a select few. As part of the army's reorganization in anticipation of the end of the truce, two decisions had to be taken: campaign priorities and new appointments. The first was a question of where to put the most weight—either on the central front, for which Operation LRLR (Lydda-Ramleh, Latrun-Ramallah) had been drafted, or against the Egyptian army in the south, breaking open the road to the Negev. Because of the threat to Jerusalem, Tel Aviv, and the large Jewish population on the coast, LRLR was given priority. This decision enjoyed the consensus of the High Command. The other decision, however, that of a new round of appointments, was a bone of contention from the first moment, reflecting the tensions of the previous months between Ben-Gurion and the rest of the High Command. Allon, though not actively involved in this dramatic dispute, was one of its key topics.

On 24 June 1948, with the smoke of the *Altalena* still rising and Tel Aviv still reeling from shock, Ben-Gurion jotted down in his diary a list of IDF appointments recommended by Yadin. There were to be four fronts under four commanders: Moshe Carmel—the Northern Front; Dan Even—the Middle Front (the Sharon area); Shimon Avidan—the Southern Front; Yigal Allon—the Central Front. After consulting with Chief of Staff Dori, who was ailing at home in Haifa, Ben-Gurion reached a decision. He wanted three fronts and three generals: Carmel in the north, Mordechai Makleff in the center, and Yigal Allon in the south. Allon appeared on his list with a question mark relating to his reliability, for Dori (according to Ben-Gurion's diary) had told him that "despite reservations, he does accept Yigal P. [Allon] for the Southern Front. He may be crafty and a politician, but capable." The allegation of "crafty and a politician" reflects Ben-Gurion's own thoughts. Dori did not counter Ben-Gurion's opinion, which was shared by the echelon of command; he merely added the comment, "but capable." Those two words best explain why the members of the HGS headed by Yigael Yadin were prepared to fight for Allon against Ben-Gurion. For the main front, Ben-Gurion earmarked his blue-eyed boy, Mordechai Makleff, a young, able, former major in the British army who had just been appointed brigade commander under Moshe Carmel. Apart from his suspicion of Allon, Ben-Gurion was locked into the conception that Palmah commanders, with Allon in the lead, were suited for guerilla warfare rather than the "traditional" warfare of a regular army. Since in the Negev there would be guerilla fighting against the Egyptians, Allon was to be sent to the Negev.[18] On 19 June 1948, Ben-Gurion announced his decision to the HGS members Yigael Yadin and Zvi Ayalon. There were a number of strange appointments on his list, but the one to arouse the most anger was Makleff's appointment as commander of the Central Front. Yadin was adamant in his demand that Allon be given the job. He argued that Allon was already engaged on that front, that he had been so since Operation Yoram, that he already had a headquarters as well as experience in commanding a division larger than a brigade. Makleff, in contrast, had no experience in commanding even a brigade, nor did he know the front.

Makleff's appointment encased all of the reservations felt about Ben-Gurion since he had become actively involved in the HGS. There may have been tensions between members of the HGS, but basically they were a cohesive group, bound by sharing a common endeavor and a defining experience. They admired Ben-Gurion but felt no intimacy with him as they did with Galili. They were a "non-party" party, what Yadin called the "Haganah Party." Ben-Gurion saw them as a bunch of amateurs who had taken on a job too big for them and did not allow others—worthier, more talented, and more experienced than them, veterans of the British army—to take the helm. On top of this, some of the command personnel were identified with the rival party, Mapam. His suspicions, while not groundless, were exaggerated. His remonstrance before Yadin that the HGS was "judenrein," meaning clean of British army veterans,[19] totally ignored the fact that one-third of the brigade commanders at that time were British army veterans and their numbers were augmented by officers in the professional corps and in the HGS who filled important positions.[20] The salient commanders, however, Yigal Allon and Shimon Avidan, had not served in the British army. What is more, they were identified with Mapam—a fatal combination.

On 1 July 1948, Ben-Gurion received letters of resignation from the HGS members Yigael Yadin, Zvi Ayalon, and Eliahu Ben-Hur, in protest of the appointments. Joseph Avidar, a member of Mapai, did not resign, although he too expressed his reservations about the appointments. Concurrently, Galili sent a letter to all members of the government to apprise them of the gravity of the situation. After a long government discussion of what Ben-Gurion termed "a political revolt in the army," the Committee of Five was set up, consisting of ministers from different parties.[21]

Ben-Gurion proclaimed that he could not continue to work with Galili since the latter had gone over his head to approach the government directly. It did not help any that the committee rejected Ben-Gurion's claims about a political revolt in the army and, in fact, agreed with Galili's reservations. Nor did it help that the committee's conclusions obliged Ben-Gurion to accept an oversight apparatus at the Ministry of Defense, including the establishment of a war cabinet. At the critical moment, Ben-Gurion drew out his threat to resign not only as minister of defense, but as prime minister. Clearly, no government or member of the HGS could contemplate his decamping at this decisive stage in the war, on the eve of renewed battle. No sooner did he threaten to resign than all of the committee's recommendations were shelved. Galili had to pay the price for his challenge. Though he did not resign immediately, he did not return to work at the Ministry of Defense. Allon met a different fate: a few days before the end of the truce, Yadin found a way to mollify Ben-Gurion and terminate the crisis. Ben-Gurion was sick in bed at his home in Tel Aviv, and his wife, Paula, blocked Yadin's way to her husband, taking him and his colleagues to task for having dared to upset him and make him ill. After this exchange, the head of the Operations Branch was allowed to come before the minister of defense. Ben-Gurion, when he caught sight of Yadin, turned his back on him and would not speak. Yadin appealed to his sense of responsibility, saying that they would not be able to forgive themselves if they did not find a way to cooperate at this trying hour. Yadin had come up with a semantic solution, which he now presented: Yigal Allon would not be appointed commander of the Central Front but of Operation LRLR. Ben-Gurion grasped at the straw; he agreed to the suggestion, thereby bringing the appointments crisis to a close.[22] This was on 7 July 1948. On 9 July, the Ten-Day Campaigns began.

From Allon's point of view, the appointments crisis ended with his receiving his greatest opportunity yet: the command of the most important operation, on the war's central front. All through the crisis, Allon and his soldiers had known that Ben-Gurion had disqualified him from command and that there was another candidate slated to replace him. It is no small thing for the leader of war to express lack of trust in a field commander. If Allon felt tension and frustration, he did not show it. He donned his mask and remained businesslike, conducting meetings at headquarters and holding discussions with the HGS and the auxiliary brigades as if there were nothing out of the ordinary. The headquarters' members continued to plan Operation LRLR even though it appeared that neither they nor Allon was to have a hand in it. The fact that not only Palmah brigade commanders took part in these operational discussions, but also members of the High Command, was a tribute to Allon's unquestioned leadership in the army as a whole. His abounding charisma affected everyone who came into contact with him. Even those

222   Chapter 9

Figure 12. The swearing-in ceremony of IDF's high command. In the middle row are Allon (first from right); Galili (third from right); Ben-Gurion and his wife, Paula (next to Galili). Yadin, sitting on the grass, is second from right. Photographer unknown. Courtesy of Yoram Sadeh (son of Yitzhak Sadeh) and the Yitzhak Rabin Center Archives, Tel Aviv.

who did not trust him, such as Ben-Gurion, were not immune to his charm. This was all the more so for his soldiers, who knew his loyalty to them, his concern, and his caring. Thus, for all his reservations about Allon's cunning, for all his concern about Allon's tendency to act irresponsibly, break discipline, and "stretch" orders, Ben-Gurion could not dismiss Yadin's demand that the most important front be placed in Allon's hands. But his ambivalence about Allon remained throughout the war.

An early order for Operation LRLR from 26 June 1948 outlined its plans, forces, aims, and so forth. The commander's name was left blank.[23] On 7 July the order was finally given for Allon's appointment,[24] and the next day, Allon issued a new operational order. First, he changed the name of the operation to Dani, after Dani Mass, the commander of "the thirty-five" who had lost their lives while coming to the aid of the Etzyon Bloc. Second, Allon dreamed of being the liberator of Jerusalem; though Jerusalem had been taken from his command and remained under the Etzyoni Brigade, he included it in the operational aims: "to totally liberate the city of Jerusalem and the road to it from enemy pressure."[25] The headquarters remained unchanged, that is, Yoram's headquarters, while administrative support was supplied by the Palmah's headquarters. Rabin continued as Allon's second and Zerubavel Arbel was the intelligence officer.[26] Unlike Operation Yiftah, this operation was initiated by the HGS. Allon was handed a preliminary plan.[27]

The plan was based on two assumptions: first, that IDF troops would be facing large Arab Legion forces in the war zone; second, that these forces were poised to attack in the direction of the coastal plain, the approach to Tel Aviv. Afterward, too, Allon remained convinced that the legion had been on the point of attack and was preempted by the IDF's offensive a mere six hours earlier.[28] An added fear was that the legion's forces would join up with Egyptian forces stationed at Bet Jibrin. All of the assumptions proved false. The aims and nature of the operation were apparently dictated by a case of anxiety based on lack of information and poor Israeli intelligence. In the Ramleh-Lydda sector, according to intelligence, there were some twenty armored cars, mortars, some two thousand legion soldiers, and another fifteen hundred irregulars;[29] the assessment was totally exaggerated. Furthermore, it was anticipated that the legion, concealed somewhere in the area of Latrun on the approach to Ramallah, would come out with a hard punch. It is thus hardly surprising that against such a force five brigades and auxiliary units were assembled, all told some nine thousand soldiers.[30] Numerically, the Israelis had the advantage by far; according to Glubb Pasha, the commander of the Arab Legion, the ratio was five to one. The legion had the advantage in armored strength because of the quality and quantity of its vehicles and the experience of the soldiers operating the equipment.

Operation LRLR was aimed at conquering first Lydda and Ramleh, including the Ono Valley and the airport, thereby removing the legion's threat to Rehovot, Tel Aviv, and the Jewish population center on the coast. The second LR in Operation LRLR signified the attempt to take the road to Jerusalem by occupying Latrun and Ramallah, two sites where the legion's forces were concentrated. An armored force was to come from the north to outflank Lydda and cause Ramleh to fall. Yiftah Brigade forces from the south were to secure the southern flank and permit speedy progress. The simultaneous offensive by both arms would ensure a speedy advance and a better chance of completing the operation before the UN Security Council could intervene with a cease-fire. The sooner the first stage was finished, the better the chance of carrying out the second stage. The aims were defined in terms of capturing territory, not destroying enemy forces.

As was customary on the eve of an operation, brigade commanders and headquarters' officers were invited to a briefing with the commanding officer and a dinner party. Allon, for the first time, now met up with Yitzhak Sadeh, the commander of the Eighth Armored Brigade, as his superior. Their roles had reversed: the teacher and architect of the Jewish defense forces found himself under the command of his senior pupil. Both were gallant: Sadeh gave a toast, saying he considered himself privileged to serve under his senior pupil and ending with the words, "long live the commander." Allon responded in kind, with words of affection, esteem and loyalty for his erstwhile teacher and mentor. Sadeh took care to follow etiquette and salute Allon. Allon responded by shielding Sadeh, which at times was detrimental to the campaign.

The northern arm, consisting of the Eighth Armored Brigade under Sadeh, was to reach Ben Shemen within a day and join up with Yiftah Brigade forces from the south. But the plan was upset. The Eighty-second Battalion, the more heavily armored of the two battalions comprising the Eighth Brigade, failed to advance according to plan and traverse its twelve-kilometer quota for the day. As a result, the two arms did not meet up. At the same time, the Eighty-ninth Light Battalion (also of the Eighth Armored Brigade) unexpectedly arrived at Ben Shemen. Meanwhile, the southern arm of Yiftah progressed, captured Innaba, Jimzu, and Daniyal, and reached Ben Shemen. Allon and Rabin set out for Ben Shemen to meet the forces and check out the situation. Indulging Allon's weakness for fancy cars, especially convertibles, they drove in an open Ford from Yazur, the site of the operation's headquarters, to the battlefield. The main road was not held by the IDF, so they had to travel along a bypass road and the trip took longer than envisioned. They grew impatient. Allon was driving and Rabin navigating and taking short cuts. East of Kibbutz Gezer, he suddenly noticed that they were driving through an Israeli minefield and managed to shout out to Allon to stop. Allon braked, but it was too late: the car hit a mine. The explosion was on Rabin's side and he was thrown from the car, badly injuring his foot. "Are you okay?" Rabin shouted in concern for the commander, and he was answered by a calm "yes." At the sound of the explosion, soldiers from a nearby post came running and warned the two not to move until sappers could lead them out since the field had both antivehicle and anti-personnel mines. They stood frozen in the minefield for half an hour before rescue came. Rabin was unable to walk on his own and Allon asked for a jeep. This is how the two drove into Daniyal, a freshly captured Arab village.[31] According to Allon, when he reached Daniyal, he found the Eighty-ninth Battalion of raiders there, in jeeps, under Moshe Dayan, instead of the Eighty-second Armored Battalion, which was still busy fighting around Bet-Naballah. Meanwhile, Dayan and Mula Cohen, Yiftah's commander, had planned an alternative option: the Eighty-ninth Battalion would storm Lydda, take the residents by surprise, and thus pave the way for the town's capture by Yiftah's Third Battalion under Moshe Kelman. Kelman was already on the march on the outskirts of Lydda.[32]

The romantic tale of Operation Dani belongs to Dayan and his battalion of raiders: the dauntless, charismatic, and unruly commander had mustered a plucky group of LeHI veterans and village lads, organized a column of jeeps headed by the "terrible tiger," an armored vehicle complete with a cannon looted in battle, and gone on a sortie against Lydda. Dayan had just returned from escorting Mickey Stone's coffin to the United States. There, he had met an American Jewish officer who, "on one foot," had taught him the doctrine of "movement" war, that is, mobile forces attacking with speed and surprise. He now decided to apply the idea, and the jeep battalion charged through Lydda shooting up the main street. The residents were stunned; they had not expected an invasion. It was several long moments before the Arab defenders rebounded to return fire. The battalion crossed Lydda and reached the police station between it and Ramleh. Shots were fired at it from the police building and it incurred casualties. Cars were damaged and had to be abandoned. Understanding that he could not hold out, Dayan retreated. The tactical effect of storming through the city was not lost on Allon.[33]

Dayan's daring captured the imagination and the headlines. It was a different sort of battle: in broad daylight, fully exposed, and using far more firepower than usual. True, the town was taken by Yiftah's soldiers, advancing cautiously, step by step, without any of the glory of Dayan's trail-blazing action, but who remembered that? Legend seemed to follow Dayan like a train: in Syria he had stolen the show from Allon and made the black eye-patch the symbol of an audacious warrior. Even in failure, when caught by the Transjordan Frontier Force and sent off to jail with the forty-three prisoners from the Haganah, he somehow managed to enter the annals of the intrepid. Now there was the story of Lydda: his appearance in Ben Shemen had not been coordinated with his commander, Sadeh, who was in a tight spot and could have used the battalion's help. Nor was Yadin bowled over by the indomitable but unpredictable soldier. But nothing succeeds like success: Dayan was summoned to Ben-Gurion to report on his trip to the United States, and meanwhile he recounted the "legend of Lydda." Things for which Ben-Gurion never forgave Allon—irresponsibility, lack of discipline, doing as he liked—skimmed over Dayan without touching a hair. Dayan was no less crafty than Allon and was far more ruthless in the pursuit of his aims.[34] Yet what aroused Ben-Gurion's suspicion of Allon aroused his admiration for Dayan. During the Ten-Day Campaigns, Dayan was a battalion commander and Allon was the front commander. Allon had risen far higher than Dayan since the photograph taken of the two of them at Hanita. The battle of Lydda, however, signaled Dayan's renewed penetration of Allon's military turf.

Meanwhile, soldiers of the Yiftah Brigade had managed to advance to the edge of Lydda and had begun to make their way into built-up areas. By dark, they had taken over the town center, yet Allon was now more worried than he had been at the start of the day of fighting: Yiftah's three hundred men had gained control of the mosque and both the southern and center parts of town, but the situation was extremely volatile. Lydda had a large population, which was not yet fully captured. Though the Arab Legion was still ensconced only at the police station and with a limited force at that, there were numerous armed irregulars in town. Throughout the day, the legion had received desperate radio transmissions from Lydda and Ramleh. A counterattack was expected. The fear was that the conquerors would find themselves overwhelmed by the residents.[35] Toward evening, thousands of people came to the mosque according to instructions they had received from the IDF forces. A civilian authority was ostensibly appointed, headed by Shemariah Gutman, the *mukhtar* of Kibbutz Na'an, who knew Arabic and had warm relations with members of the Arab community. He was to take care of the thousands of people whose entire world had been destroyed overnight.[36]

That night, 12 July 1948, people crowded into the mosque, dazed, frightened, thirsty, and hungry. Because of the overcrowding, it was decided to send the noncombatants home, leaving only the young men. Meanwhile, the fighting in town continued. An attempt by the city's notables to call on the legion at the police station to surrender ended with shots fired at the delegation. In the morning, after a night of curfew, some of the tension let up. But at 11:00 A.M. a legion force burst into town with several armored vehicles, performing much as Dayan's battalion had the day before: it sped through the city spraying bullets in all directions and then disappeared. The residents took heart. They thought that it was a rescue force to be followed up by more legionnaires. Operation Dani commanders thought the same thing. Irregulars and plain citizens began to shoot at soldiers walking about the town. Local commanders took this as an ominous sign—the legion's appearance followed by a local uprising. There were rumors of bombs being thrown from the mosque. An order was given to shoot at any source of fire and anyone on the streets. "I had no choice but to order a hard clamp-down and the assault was crushed," Allon related.[37] According to the Yiftah Brigade's report, 250 Arabs were killed, a very high number of fatalities compared to previous battles. Yiftah's troops, in contrast, suffered little loss of life.[38] More than anything else, the unbridled gunfire of Yiftah's forces was a sign of panic, of a lack of confidence in the troops' ability to hold the town, of their inexperience in governing civilians. Neither the troops nor Allon ever took pride in the measure, even if they thought it was a necessary evil.

Even after the uprising was crushed, there was a feeling that the town had not surrendered. Shemariah Gutman reported that inhabitants had not handed over their weapons despite repeated demands transmitted by loudspeakers all over town. The inhabitants grew dispirited only when it became clear that the police station had been abandoned in the night and had fallen to the IDF.[39] Meanwhile, elsewhere, a decision was made to evacuate the inhabitants.

The Haganah's Plan D empowered brigade commanders to expel civilian populations in the case of resistance or because they occupied strategic areas. In practice, the policy of expulsion of Arabs from areas conquered by the IDF was set at the local level and depended on a number of factors: the inclinations of the on-site commanders, the guidelines of the High Command, and the circumstances of the incident. The expulsion or evacuation of the residents of Lydda and Ramleh was exceptional in scope and in the fact that it was an IDF initiative; the IDF did not depict it either as flight in the heat of battle or flight due to fear of war, as was true of other instances. The uprising in Lydda seems to have tipped the scales against the residents of both towns. From the distance of years, the uprising may appear insignificant and negligible. At the time, however, it took on sinister proportions. Operation Dani's forces were meant to proceed to the next stage of the operation, not to be bogged down by having to deal with a civilian population that, though shocked, still hoped for a counterattack by the Arab Legion. "All the signs show that [we] are on the eve of an Arab offensive that is to rest on Lydda," Allon informed the Operations Branch on 13 July.[40] The removal of local residents would prevent their collusion with the legion, reducing the chances of an Arab offensive. Beyond the immediate arguments that hung on developments on the battlefield, a strategic threat emerged: that of leaving so large an Arab population mass in the center of the country, where it would be all too near the main airport, in Tel Aviv's backyard, and on the main road to Jerusalem.

The policy was not initiated from above. On the eve of Operation Dani, the HGS issued clear instructions forbidding the evacuation of Arabs except in special circumstances and with the authorization of the defense minister.[41] When the HGS learned that Yosef Tabenkin, the commanding officer of the Harel Brigade, had evacuated Abu Ghosh, Allon received a severe reprimand from the chief of staff and was asked to pass on the HGS directive to all units. When Mordechai Makleff considered expelling the Arabs of Nazareth (Operation Dekel, to occupy the central Galilee, took place simultaneously with Operation Dani), he received an urgent order in the name of the prime minister prohibiting him from carrying it through.[42] At the start of the campaign, Operation Dani's headquarters spread fliers calling on the residents of Ramleh and Lydda to surrender with the promise that the lives would be spared of those who did so.[43] Ramleh surrendered without a fight. Those with weapons left town prior to the surrender. The Kiryati Brigade took control of Ramleh. On 12 July 1948, Minorities Minister Behor Shitrit toured Ramleh. James Ben-Gal, the commanding officer of the brigade, reported to him that Allon had ordered that all men of conscription age be detained and "the rest of the residents be led across the border lines today and left there." As for the residents of Lydda, "the army is considering doing the same with them. . . ." Shitrit was shocked. He rushed to report to Foreign Minister Moshe Sharett, Sharett appealed to the prime minister, and the following policy was agreed upon:

a. It must be publicly announced in both towns that anyone wishing to leave may do so.
b. A warning must be issued that anyone who stays does so on his own responsibility from the point of view of food, and Israel's authorities are not duty bound to supply food.
c. On no account are women, children, the elderly, and the ill to be forced to leave.
d. Mosques and churches are not to be harmed unless there is overriding military cause.
e. Strict care must be taken [on threat of] full legal recourse that searches are not accompanied by acts of sabotage and destruction.
f. All steps must be taken to prevent acts of looting.[44]

That evening, 12 July, apparently before Sharett spoke with Ben-Gurion, there was a meeting also at Operation Dani's headquarters in Yazur. It was attended by Dani's commanders as well as by senior members of the HGS headed by Ben-Gurion. Allon presented the problem posed by a hostile population remaining behind the lines of an advancing army. This was the crucial issue. He raised also a tactical consideration: directing the refugees toward Bet Naballah and the Bet Horon axis would force the Arab Legion to look after the refugees, thus impeding it and tying it down there. He asked for authorization to evict the residents. Some fifty thousand residents were involved. In Ramleh, James Ben-Gal had reached an evacuation agreement with the town's notables, and the IDF had undertaken to supply buses to convey residents to the legion's lines.[45] In Lydda, there was resistance and the sense that there was no civilian authority in the town with whom to reach an agreement. At the meeting in Yazur, Allon pressed for instructions on the matter. Ben-Gurion was silent, not reacting. After the meeting, Allon and Rabin escorted Ben-Gurion to his car. According to Rabin, he saw Ben-Gurion gesture with his hand and say, "Remove them."[46] Allon was always careful in public to deny that Ben-Gurion had given his authorization for the expulsion. Very likely, he did so out of national considerations. "Ben-Gurion, as head of state, could not give the order. I do what a commander has to do in the heat of battle," Mula Cohen quoted Allon.[47] Ben-Gurion seems to have been both undecided and undesirous of being involved in giving the order. But the guidelines on which he and Sharett agreed and which were sent to Allon that same evening in an amended version by the Operations Branch said, "to warn that we are not responsible for protecting those who remain."[48] This is consistent with the account given by Shemariah Gutman in almost real time. Gutman reported that the residents were scared to death and feared a massacre among the detainees in the mosques if and when battle broke out again in town. The police station was captured only the next day, on the morning of 13 July; the situation was most uncertain and a column of the Arab Legion's armored cars and infantry was reported to be advancing on Bet Iqsa in the east.[49] When Gutman told the notables that they were all free to leave town, including the detainees, he heard relief.[50] Allon's account also stressed the significance of releasing the detainees: "The old men came to me and said: let the young men leave and we'll leave . . . when I saw that the arrest of the young was holding up the evacuation, I let the young go so long as they left."[51] The expellees were allowed to take all their portable goods but not motor cars. Households quickly organized for departure and column by column set their steps northward. Several hundred residents, mostly Christian, chose to remain in the town. The exodus was conducted in haste, in relative quiet, in the direction of Barfiliya, where the Arab Legion was still positioned.[52] Also that same day, Ramleh's exiles were bused on the Jerusalem road up to al-Qubab.[53]

Operation Dani soldiers and commanders never forgot the sight of an entire town going into exile. Lydda's exiles walked on foot to the legion's lines. In absolute terms, the distance was not great, some fifteen kilometers. But it was summer and hot. People collapsed under the travail. They littered the route with items cast off to ease their way. Here and there, a child or old man lay by the wayside, their strength having given out, or a woman crouched to give birth. It was a heart-breaking scene. Soldiers of the Third Battalion, members of youth-movement *hakhsharot*, could not reconcile themselves to the events, and commanders had to conduct elucidating talks to try to assuage their pangs of conscience.[54]

Some two years later, in a long, enlightening lecture on the War of Independence at a KM forum, Allon evidently unburdened himself

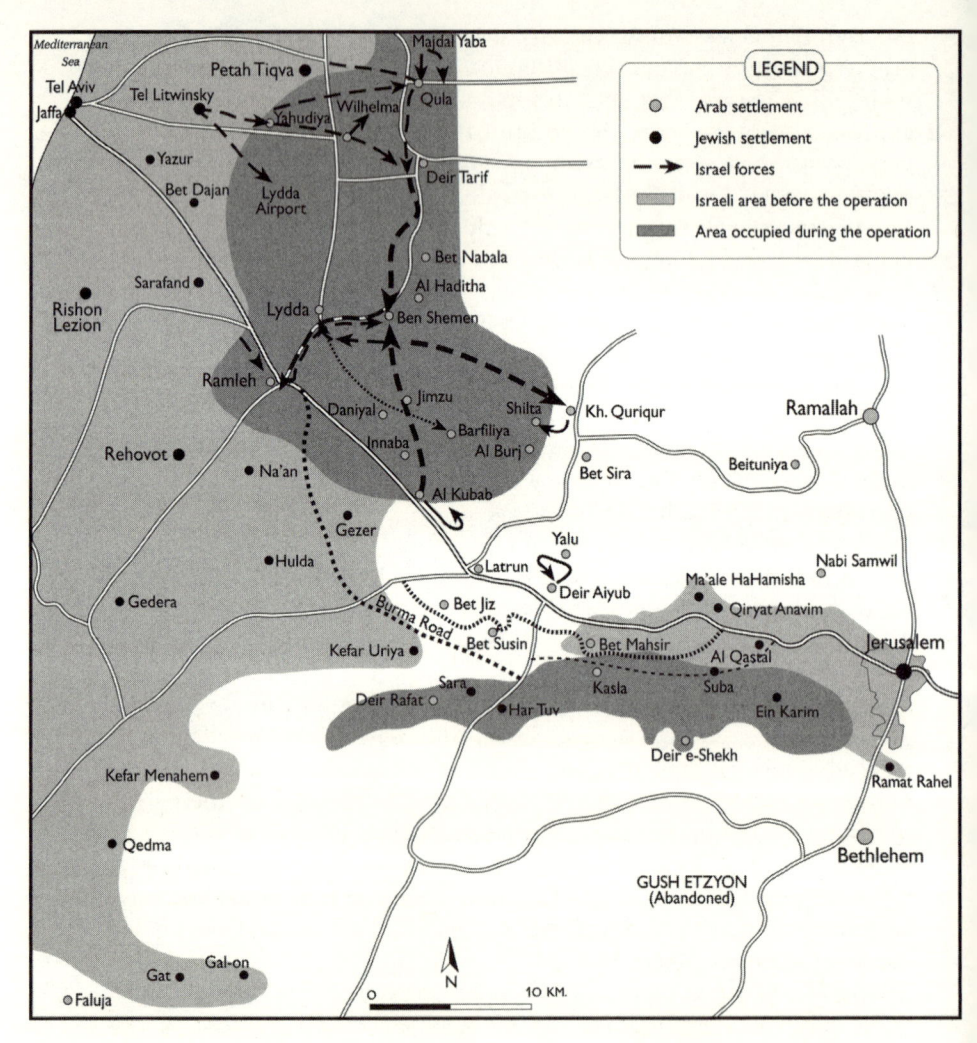

Map 3. Operation Dani, 7–19 July 1948

about the displacement of Palestinian Arabs. Relating to the phenomenon of mass Arab migration during the war, he noted three causes. The first was fright of the Jews: "Above all, I surmise that there was something here that stemmed from their own inner thinking; they thought of what they—not the invading Arab army, but the Arabs of Palestine—might do if they conquered a settlement of ours." Second, in places where they were on the losing side, both their leaders and the British encouraged them to leave so as not to serve as hostages for the Jews and on the assumption that they would return upon the victory of the Arab armies; the evacuations of Tiberias and Haifa fit this pattern. Third, "There were quite a few large cases of expulsion." Allon had no hesitation about this policy and he set out to defend it loud and clear. Militarily, he regarded the expulsion as the chief factor in halting the legion's assault: "So long as the Arabs were in Lydda and Ramleh, the legion did not cease their counterattacks on our outposts, with the intention of reconnecting with the Arabs in Lydda and Ramleh.... But from the moment that the expulsion began ... the legion's attacks grew weaker and, to the extent that there were any, these aimed at stalling our forward advance toward the hills." In so tiny a country as Palestine, with the Jewish zone so narrow and the distances so small, it is impossible in wartime to leave concentrations of hostile populations, "even if temporarily they pretend to be surrendering." They could be used as "an instrument of sabotage, espionage and also coordinated actions with the invading armies." He did not limit this view to the case of Lydda and Ramleh: "I think that the process of Arab flight was a positive process. Furthermore, I think that our activity to empty large, militarily valuable areas of a hostile Arab population, this too was a justified case of no-choice, not only momentarily, in the heat of battle, but justified over time." Allon would have welcomed the opportunity to conquer the country up to the Jordan River: "Had it happened that by completing the country's liberation up to the boundary of the west [bank] of the Jordan, there would have been an exodus of additional Arab population and their relocation to neighboring Arab countries; this would not, as such, have been historical injustice; it would have been a historic opportunity that fell into our laps—not thanks to us, but used by us to solve this problem, which would have remained a tough problem for a long time, both politically and militarily." Asked if it was true that it had been decided not to conquer the Gaza region because of the thousands of refugees there, he declared: "At the time, there was no factor known as refugees resulting in a decision not to take Gaza, especially as I am sure that had we been in Gaza, there would have been fewer refugees." "I stated my position on this question clearly and completely openly in my lecture"—Allon added—"I am not representing any public body here; I am presenting what I think about the war, and everything I said, I said openly, straightforwardly."[55]

The last sentence apparently provides the clue to Allon's uncharacteristic frankness. The things he said were unacceptable to the left wing of Mapam, which found it hard to come to terms with the expulsion from Lydda and Ramleh and summoned the operation's Mapam commanders to an inquiry. There are no minutes of this inquiry. It stands to reason that Mapam could not censure its most illustrious members. However, what Allon said at his lecture was probably unacceptable to the KM members as well. At the time of the lecture, Allon was in a "twilight period"—discharged from the army but not yet in politics—which may explain the freedom of reflection and particularly the outspokenness he permitted himself. For the moment, he felt no political or ideological restraints and he could speak his mind. Later, when he would shed his military outlook and adopt a statesmanlike approach, he was to take a totally different tack.

Allon was not insensitive to the Arab tragedy—forced into exile from a land they had inhabited for centuries. But he had no regrets: "I don't suggest that we beat our breasts over this outcome. War is war. In war things must be measured according to the criteria of war, the criteria of revolution. This was one of our revolutions. It was a national revolution. In every war and every revolution there are those who suffer; what's more, it is not we who voluntarily chose this route." The Arabs chose war and they lost. They paid the price for their policy. This reasoning was consistent with opinions voiced in the KM's circles at the time, regardless of Mapai or Mapam affiliation.[56] Transposing the tragedy from the personal to the national plane and from the private to the historical lent the events a more remote dimension released from the strictures of ordinary morality. Allon's more mature colleagues would most likely have referred back to the population movements of only three years earlier, which, following World War II, had encompassed millions of people; or they may have cited the bloody war of partition being waged in India concomitant with events in Palestine, which also involved a population exchange of millions. Allon did not cite worldwide precedents, either because his interests were purely local or because he saw no need to look for justifications.

There was no romantic sentimentalism about his attitude toward Palestine's Arabs. It was the attitude of a native son who knew the Arabs well and liked them on the personal level but was aware, from his boyhood, of the realities of the national clash. The very thought of abusing Arabs or resorting to brutality or looting was completely alien to him; to the extent that such things occurred, he considered them disgusting perversions. But as far as relations between the two peoples were concerned, he saw the War of Independence as a one-time, historic opportunity to change the Jewish-Arab balance of demography and settlement; it was an opportunity neither initiated nor, to his mind, properly exploited by the Jews. To the degree that matters depended on him, he had done his best not only to conquer the territory of Eretz Israel but also to clear it of Arabs. This was Yigal Allon at thirty; his political conception at this time was molded by his experience as a military commander who believed that destiny is to be decided by the sword.

While the exiles from Lydda wended their way to the legion's lines, the next stage of the operation was being worked out. At the UN Security Council, there was talk of a cease-fire and the clock was ticking. The estimate was that a truce would be called within days—three, four. The ambitious plans of reaching Jerusalem via Ramallah were obviously no longer feasible. Allon decided to concentrate on the Latrun segment, the stumbling block on the road to Jerusalem, which three times had already defied the IDF's commanders. Apart from straddling the road to Jerusalem, the area harbored the city's water pumps for the pipeline from Rosh Ha-Ayin (now in the IDF's hands) and had to be secured. The idea was to cut off Latrun from its hinterland by capturing the Bet Sira Junction and cause it to fall by an indirect maneuver.[57] Allon had a theory that Transjordan's Hashemite government survived because of the Arab Legion. If the legion were destroyed, King Abdullah's rule would topple. Therefore, Allon calculated, if the king had to decide between yielding territory or endangering the legion, he would choose the first option.[58] Allon figured that if the legion found itself in danger of being encircled at Latrun, Glubb Pasha would decide to evacuate the troops. The plan was fine, but removed from reality. Glubb, who had let Lydda and Ramleh fall because he saw no real chance of saving them, was determined to defend the road to Ramallah. He saw the Bet Sira Junction as the key to defending the legion's rear at Latrun and also its major force in Ramallah. He sent his troops out on vigorous counterattacks that surprised the soldiers at Qula (north of Bet Naballah). The legion took Qula back and, for a brief moment, the entire northern arm looked exposed. The tough fighting preoccupied the main armored force and prevented it from acting at Latrun.

The clearer it became that time was running out, the more Allon strove to establish facts on the ground even if it meant taking certain risks. The attempt to surround and cut off Latrun failed: the Harel and Yiftah brigades came near the road to Latrun and Bet Sira, and they won positions from which to open fire at it, and they even managed to harass passing traffic. But they did not succeed in gaining control of the road itself. Allon's assumption about the legion's retreat in the face of encirclement proved false. So he mustered forces for one final, hard strike at Latrun before the truce went into effect (the night of 17–18 July). The attack took place on 18 July 1948, the eve of the ccase-fire, and failed then too: by a piece of bad luck, a shell got stuck in the tank barrel and the tank was forced to withdraw. The second tank quickly followed suit, and the charge, which had begun with an effective barrage of artillery, ended in fiasco. "Circular motion" took on a new meaning: in the lexicon of the period, it came to denote a prebattle retreat. Operation Dani's headquarters, in the presence of Ben-Gurion and the High Command, watched the scene from al-Qubab. There seemed to be a curse on whoever attempted to take Latrun.

While all eyes and most of the troops concentrated on Latrun, one of the hardest—if not *the* hardest—battle of Operation Dani unfolded. A company of the Yiftah Brigade's First Battalion, under Pinhas Sussman (Siko), was ordered to capture an outpost dominating the Bet Sira Junction from the north, to disrupt traffic, and to prevent armored reinforcements from getting through to Latrun from Bet Naballah. The site was known as Khirbet Quriqur. Though intelligence was greatly improved in Operation Dani, in this instance it was wanting: there was another outpost next to the captured one, with a legion force the size of a boosted company—and there was no prior information about it. Its commanders watched the troops of the Yiftah Brigade settle into the taken outpost and called for reinforcements, including armored vehicles. The legion went on a dogged counterattack. Yiftah's troops were in a tight spot: caught in cross-fire, it was in danger of being surrounded by infantry and armored corps. There were no reinforcements to come to its aid and the company had to beat a retreat in broad daylight, in the burning heat. Forty-five soldiers were killed, many of them sixteen- and seventeen-year-olds. In terms of casualties, it was one of the worst battles fought. Most of the fallen lost their lives in the laborious retreat. The wounded left in the field were all killed.[59]

As the saying goes, success has many fathers but failure is an orphan. The same applied in this case. Quriqur's dead never made it into the pantheon of Israel's national memory. The foiled conquest of Latrun marked another fiasco in Israel's annals. To top it off, there was also an element of the ridiculous: as it transpired, the failure stemmed from a misunderstanding between the tank drivers, both of whom were deserters from the British army; it seemed to be the intervention of a higher power as it were, unrelated to the actions or errors of the commanding officers. The loss of forty-five soldiers, however, should have raised questions. But they died in a side arena that turned out to be unimportant since it did not decide the outcome of the campaign—the Bet Sira Junction was not blocked, Latrun was not cut off. Silence surrounded their deaths. It was a sign of hardening: the flower of Israeli youth perished in this long war. There was no time to mourn. To survive, a defense mechanism had to be developed against sensitivity to loss, a cover that might have appeared unfeeling. But it was more apparent than real. It made it possible to go on. An age-old fatalism surrounded Quriqur's dead: "For the sword devoureth in one manner or another."[60]

With Allon still trying to wring out a speedy reversal in the Latrun segment, the Harel Brigade's forces, assisted by the Etzyoni Brigade, were quietly expanding the Jerusalem Corridor southward to take over the railway lines to Jerusalem. An Egyptian force that was not large had failed to gain control of the area and the Harel Brigade encountered little opposition. Expanding the corridor southward made it possible to pave a new road, the so-called Road of Heroism, on the Eshtaol Ridge to Jerusalem. It was a great improvement on the Burma Road, which was made of dirt. As a result, the roadblock at Latrun could now be circumvented. In parallel, engineers from the Mekorot Water Company had been busy since the First Truce laying an alternative pipeline to Jerusalem. While the IDF had won control of the Rosh Ha-Ayin springs in Operation Dani, the pumps at Latrun had remained in the hands of the Arab Legion and were blown up during the Second Truce. Along with paving the Road of Heroism, a voluminous pipe was laid, supplying all of Jerusalem's water needs. Thus, even though Operation Dani succeeded only in the Lydda-Ramleh part, with the Latrun-Ramallah part being scrapped, it did achieve many of its strategic aims: the entire Ono Valley was taken, and the threat to the coastal plain and to the Jerusalem road averted. The Jerusalem Corridor was significantly widened, a paved road was opened to the city, and the water supply was assured. Latrun remained an enclave in contiguous Israeli territory, more threatened than threatening.[61] As one writer noted with irony, "Of all Operation Dani's accomplishments, the most important for the ongoing war turned out to be in areas not originally planned for capture," that is, in the southern part of the Jerusalem Corridor.[62]

Operation Dani showed up Allon's gift for commanding large forces, as well as his faults. It was rather a marvel that a young man whose most advanced military training had been the Haganah's course for platoon commanders could adapt so swiftly to the complexities of leading four brigades plus auxiliary troops. Allon did not gain his knowledge from military literature; unlike Yadin, he was no reader. He learned from exposure to the growing needs and an intuitive grasp of how to meet them. He was a natural commander. It was the ground he "read" and responded to. In the thick of the campaign, he learned about the need to coordinate the various military arms—infantry, air force, artillery, and armor. The air force and artillery did not have much of a role in Operation Dani. The Eighth Armored Brigade, in contrast, which was in action for the first time, bore the brunt of the battle on the northern arm. The brigade had been put together in haste and was far from consolidated: battalion commanders did not know either the arena or the soldiers; the soldiers spoke a babel of languages, barely understanding orders; armored vehicles suffered from poor maintenance and soon became inoperable; Yitzhak Sadeh did not prove himself as a commander of armored troops. And this is where one of Allon's weaknesses came to the fore: he could not bring himself to reprimand his former teacher and commander or pull rank on him. Sadeh may have saluted Allon, but salutes are not obedience. Allon was in charge of the whole operation, but, in fact, apart from drafting the plans, he really did not have control of the armored troops. It was otherwise with the Yiftah Brigade, which shouldered most of the fighting in the Ten-Day Campaigns. But in general, he was dependent on his brigade commanders and, in Sadeh's case, this was detrimental to the course of battle. Communication between Operation Dani's headquarters and the field was still defective, making for very loose control. The problems were mostly technical, but they stemmed also from a lack of tradition. Both the problems and the remedies were learned in the heat of battle.

Allon's strength lay in the preliminary planning. He and Rabin were an ideal combination: Allon supplied the leadership, an infinite optimism, an abounding self-confidence, and a bold blueprint. Rabin translated the ideas into spot-on, precise operational plans, weighing the odds and the dangers. Together, they were a winning team. Allon was the admired commander for whom soldiers were prepared to make that extra effort, which—often enough—made all the difference between defeat and victory. Rabin was an excellent second. Allon was also a master of improvisation and elastic adaptability. The very setbacks of the second stage point to his ability to draw lessons from failure, not to succumb to despair, and to quickly prepare for the next round: first, to drop the idea of taking Ramallah and downsize the operation to Latrun and the Bet Sira Junction; then, to give up on surrounding Latrun, which had failed, and change over to a frontal attack in broad daylight on the Latrun police station, which, though it also failed, demonstrated his quick reaction time and ability to bounce back.

In Operation Dani, there were no glorious victories on the battlefield, but rather conquests achieved amid minimal friction with the enemy. This campaign was more about capturing territory than destroying opposing forces. The battles were not aimed at pounding the enemy. Allon demonstrated a talent for identifying weak points in the enemy line, whisking troops to these spots and scoring facts on the ground. Their arrival at dominant outposts enabled the soldiers of the Yiftah and Harel brigades to fight a defensive battle in which they had the advantage, and to avoid a frontal attack, which required armor and artillery that they did not possess. Wherever the legion massed its forces, as in the battles at Canon Ridge, at Qula, at Quriqur, Operation Dani's forces got into trouble. The Arab Legion, a regular army led by seasoned officers, had the clear advantage over the army "just out of diapers." Allon managed partially to cancel out the legion's advantages by maneuvering, outflanking, surprise, and cunning. Dani's troops felt triumphant, but the legion's soldiers had no reason to feel gloom: the IDF certainly did not trounce them.

The losers were Palestine's Arabs. The conquest of the Ono Valley, the expulsion of the inhabitants from Lydda and Ramleh, dispossessed the Palestinians of a key chunk of land in the center of the country and set in motion the disconnection of northern Arabs from southern Arabs. Arab hopes of returning to the coastal plain were dashed. When the Second Truce went into effect, Allon issued the troops a clear order not to permit the return of villagers who had fled: "They are to be chased off with fire."[63] The instruction reflected policy that was taking shape in the government and was already being implemented in the field; it sought to make the Arab exodus permanent.

Operation Dani's partial success braced not only the fighters and commanders as to their ability to face off with a regular army, but also the leadership. A few days into the Second Truce, Ben-Gurion was already lecturing on future plans. He gave his view of the factors that would serve as cause for the resumption of war (impingement on "sovereignty, on *aliyah*, on the minimal territory we deserve"). But he related to peace as well: "a peace effort not necessarily based on our force's capabilities (which in my opinion encompass all of Eretz Israel)."[64] To some extent, this assertion divulges his thinking at that time: he already trusted in the IDF's superiority vis-à-vis Arab armies. This trust seems to have stemmed mainly from the gains of Operation Dani and Operation Dekel in the Galilee. At the same time, along with recognizing the IDF's military power, he set it limits: peace cannot be reconciled with full exhaustion of the military capabilities. After creating the power and demonstrating its ability, he had to rein in the knightly colts, such as Allon, who were itching to conquer the entire area west of the Jordan. One thing was sure: the partition borders stipulated on 29 November 1947 by the United Nations vanished irretrievably in the Ten-Day Campaigns.

Chapter 10
Commanding Officer of the Southern Front

After the Second Truce went into effect, the country succumbed to weariness. Partially, this was due to the summer heat, partially to war fatigue after more than six months of battles. Ben-Gurion tried to maintain the public sense of emergency and failed: most people believed that the war was over.[1] The High Command thought the military manpower inadequate but was hard put to find reserves. The idea of conscripting civilians to construct fortifications was shelved for fear of incurring public wrath. Even the government's alertness dropped. Yet the sigh of relief uttered at the cease-fire was, in fact, premature: the Arab Legion and an Iraqi spearhead were positioned in Samaria, Qawuqji's army was in the Galilee, and the Egyptian army controlled the south. Palestine's invasion by Arab states, which had begun on 15 May 1948, may have been halted with the invaders now on the defensive, but they were still in western Palestine and threatening to resume the war at will. In purely military terms, Samaria seemed to be the most dangerous area—the state's narrow midriff, easily bisected by a daring army. Politically, however, the most worrisome situation was in the Negev, which the Egyptian army had managed to sever from state control. In the month of battles, the Egyptian column had come to a stop between Ashdod and Yavneh, sending out two arms: one crossed the northern Negev from west to east, from Majdal to Faluja, cutting off the main western road along the coastal plain to the Negev; the other extended from Bir-Asluj via Beersheba and Bet Jibrin to Hebron. The Egyptian lines were bolstered by a thin though continuous strip of positions and posts. The two arms joined up near Bet Jibrin, where the Egyptian line was thinner. Egyptian irregulars had come as far as the outskirts of Kibbutz Ramat Rachel in southern Jerusalem.

Since the Egyptian invasion, Givati, the largest IDF brigade at the time, had fought doggedly to stop the enemy and stymie its northward progress. In time, historians claimed that the Egyptian column had stopped of itself, whether because it had no ambition to conquer Tel Aviv (as the HGS feared) or because it ran out of steam. It, in any case, suffered from very long lines of supply. But this is hindsight: in the summer of 1948 the Egyptian army was seen as the strongest of all the invading troops. Columns of supplies and war equipment were sighted arriving at bases along the Majdal-Faluja line across the northern Negev, apparently auguring imminent attack. In the appraisal of the HGS, the Egyptians were hatching an offensive: at the very least to conquer the southern part of the country; at the most to advance on Tel Aviv.[2]

In the whole of the Negev, there were only a few isolated Jewish settlements and two battalions of the Negev Brigade, while the road to the south was under Egyptian control—a situation that lent itself to political pressure. The UN partition plan of 29 November 1947 had earmarked most of the Negev for the Jewish state. Parts of the northern Negev, including Beersheba, were earmarked for an Arab state. The partition borders, however, had been swept away after 15 May 1948. Count Bernadotte, the UN mediator dispatched after the cease-fire to instate peace in the Holy Land, recommended Jewish-Arab territorial exchange. Alert to British sensibilities about controlling the Negev—a vital land bridge protecting British interests from the Suez Canal to Iraq—Bernadotte proposed that Israel relinquish the Negev in exchange for the Western Galilee (which had been slated for an Arab state, but had been won by the IDF). For Ben-Gurion and his colleagues, the proposal aroused all their anti-British demons, although, at the same time, it spotlighted the sorry situation of the Negev, which until then had hardly grabbed the High Command's attention.

In August 1948 the IDF was restructured according to region. Four "fronts" were created, each under its own commander, a major general.[3] The new structure reflected the High Command's thinking on the need to concentrate and coordinate forces under a joint command. Yigal Allon was appointed the commanding officer of the Southern Front (Front D). Shimon Avidan, the senior officer there who had successfully commanded the Givati Brigade during the long hard period since May 15, understandably felt frustrated and resentful at being passed over.[4] His own military leadership was almost the reverse of Allon's. Stern and strict, he smiled little and was certainly not in the habit of slapping people on the back. He projected worry, gravity, and concern. He cared so much about troop safety that it was a job to get him to attack. Before the battle at the Ad-Halom Bridge, where the Givati Brigade was defeated though it halted the Egyptian column, Yadin had to force him to go into battle. Allon, in contrast, was eager for bold though considered action. He was not irresponsible, but he was prepared to take calculated risks. In the view of the Operations Branch, he was the ideal commander.[5] His appointment as the commanding officer of the Southern Front meant that the south was to become the main thrust.

If in Operation Dani, Allon's posting could be seen as a temporary leave from the Palmah's headquarters for the campaign's duration, this was no longer true. The position of commanding officer of the Southern Front was a permanent commission demanding a permanent headquarters for the front and the cutting of the umbilical cord to the Palmah's headquarters. Allon made his "acceptance of responsibility for the Southern Front" conditional on solving the problem of the Palmah's headquarters and defining its powers. However, it is not likely that he really regarded this as a condition.[6] The Southern Front, for its headquarters, appropriated the top talents of the Palmah's headquarters: Allon, Rabin, Sini Azaryahu, Zerubavel Arbel, Yeruham Cohen, and Ithiel Amihai.[7] It also took two of the Palmah's three brigades under its wing. Allon did not succeed in uniting the three brigades in a single division under the Southern Front, as he had hoped, although as the Palmah's headquarters became less and less important, the Southern Front's headquarters increasingly replaced it as the chief focus for the Palmah echelon of command.

After the Ten-Day Campaigns (end of July 1948), the Givati Brigade managed to gain control of the Hatta and Karatiya outposts dominating the east-west axis, cutting off the Majdal-Faluja road and opening the way to the Negev. But after the Second Truce went into effect, the Egyptians captured outposts south of the road and blocked the way again. Observers from the United Nations, in an attempt to mediate, tried to get the fighting parties to lead their convoys through at specific times, but failed. The Egyptians contrived to bypass the Israeli blockade at the junction by what was called "Egypt's Burma Road" south of Majdal-Faluja, thereby dispensing with the need for Israel's good graces and the United Nations' exertions. In order to hold out and prepare the fighting force, the besieged Negev settlements and the Negev Brigade required supplies and soldiers. Most of the troops breached the enemy lines east of Iraq al-Manshiya or west of Karatiya, near the north-south and east-west crossroads mentioned above. A large part of the equipment was brought in by cargo planes that landed at an airstrip in Ruhama (Operation Dust). When the Egyptians espied the goings-on at the Ruhama landing pad, they regarded it as a violation of the cease-fire agreement, which honored the status quo. Mostly, they saw it as a threat to their ongoing siege of the Negev and to their east-west positions, which were now open to attack from both the north and the south. They thus decided to capture the hillocks around Ruhama and, taking the Israelis by surprise, they came very close to seizing Kibbutz Be'eri. Allon consequently ordered the Yiftah Brigade, in the Negev since September, to secure the airstrip from ground attack. Yiftah nabbed a few hillocks, including Khirbet Maqhuz near the dirt road between Faluja and Kibbutz Shoval. Thus began the epos immortalized in Hebrew literature by the monumental work of S. Yizhar, *Days of Ziklag*. The drama of Khirbet Maqhuz unfolded as the HGS was planning the upcoming offensive, with the Egyptians using planes, armored vehicles, and mortars to dislodge the Israelis from the bare hillock that nobody had probably even heard of until then. At the end of September and the start of October, the Egyptians charged seven times. Khirbet Maqhuz changed hands five times. Among the Egyptian officers leading the attack were Gamal Abdul Nasser and Zakarya Muhi a-Din, both of whom were to play key roles in Egypt's history. Demonstrating the competency of the Egyptian troops, the contest for Khirbet Maqhuz allowed Yiftah's soldiers (as yet unfamiliar with the Egyptian front and not worn down by it like the Givati and Negev brigades) a tiny taste of what it was like to fight a regular army primed for war.[8] Only on 8 October 1948, a day after Allon received orders for Operation Yoav from Yadin (see below), did the battle for the hillock die down. Observers from the United Nations who were visiting the site recognized the right of the Jews to Khirbet Maqhuz.

Ben-Gurion had to obtain his government's permission for the planned offensive in the Negev, which involved violating the truce, that is, defying UN authority. He wrote in his diary: "Today in the government, we adopted the gravest decision since the decision to proclaim statehood."[9]

The campaign plan was elegant in its simplicity: to split the Egyptian forces by driving in two "wedges," one in the east at Khirbet a-Ra'i on the road between Faluja Bet and Jibrin; the other in the west near the Arab village of Bet Hanun north of Gaza. The first wedge was to sever the strong Egyptian brigade along the east-west axis, especially at Faluja and Iraq al-Manshiya, from the Hebron hills. The second wedge was to pose a threat to the main Egyptian force around Majdal, cutting it off from the Gaza and el-Arish hinterland. In the second stage, there was to be also a third wedge, at the junction between the Iraq Suweidan police fortress and Majdal (Outpost 113), as a preliminary to conquering Majdal. The wedges were aimed at destroying each Egyptian brigade separately. The first stage was to undermine the enemy campaign in what was a new and rather revolutionary approach: the goal was not to win territory but to confound enemy forces, to strip them of initiative and to dictate the next steps. Allon stressed this at the decisive meeting at the Southern Front's headquarters: "We stay true to the plan to break the Egyptian forces, not to win territory."[10] The eastern wedge, it was hoped, would draw Egyptian troops from Majdal. Once the enemy had emerged from its fortified position, it would be quite easy to crush it. Commonly, the Israeli tactic was to conquer dominant outposts in night attacks, to dig in there and to force the enemy to come out on counterattack. This approach made allowances for the IDF's weakness in firepower and inexperience in storming fortified targets, basically changing offensive assaults into quasi-defensive battles. Majdal was to be taken in the second stage; Gaza in the third.

The question of how to optimize the Eighth Brigade's armored strength was left open. Headquarters was inclined to have the armor break through after the wedges were in place and the Egyptian force had begun to fold. The Eighth Brigade was to make good on the coup of the first stage to strike the Egyptian force at Iraq Suweidan, Faluja, and Iraq al-Manshiya.[11] But Yitzhak Sadeh, the commander of the Eighth Brigade, upset the applecart: he demanded that the Eighth Brigade enter the fray immediately, without waiting for the wedges to throw Egyptian positions in disarray. Headquarters, to a man, strenuously opposed a change in plan. The angriest exchange took place between Sadeh and Rabin, the Southern Front's operations officer. Rabin argued for the armor to hold back until the Egyptians could feel the effect of their being cut off in the hope that this would dent their morale to the advantage of the Israeli side. Sadeh pressed for a frontal armored attack on Faluja, in daylight. Rabin did not believe that Faluja could be stormed by armor attack coming from the direction anticipated by the enemy. "Moving on Faluja with tanks doesn't have a chance," he warned. "Faluja is primed for a tank attack."[12] He insisted on the old, tried, and tested approach—taking outposts under cover of night, and only after tanks were introduced. According to Rabin, Allon, at this moment, displayed weakness: he believed in the original campaign plan, but in the confrontation between Sadeh and the other brigade commanders and the headquarters' officers he could not bring himself to go against "the old man." Perhaps, he also had faith that if Sadeh promised success he would deliver. Sadeh, the former expert in guerrilla warfare, the master of night fighting and contained skirmishes, became in the War of Independence the greatest advocate of tanks, believing in their firepower and astounding effect on enemy soldiers. Allon yielded, changing the original plan.[13]

Operation Yoav began by creating a pretext for assault: the truce could not simply be broken as this would amount to a slap in the United Nations' face. Instead, the High Command chose to pull the wool over the eyes of the United Nations' observers. A convoy was organized and started out from Karatiya under Shlomo Lahat (in time, the mayor of Tel Aviv), ostensibly in order to bring in supplies to the Negev. Two fuel trucks were marked to blow up following Egyptian gunfire. The Egyptians rose to the role assigned to them and opened fire. The trucks burst into flame visible from afar. It was a dramatic sight. As was plain for all to see, the Egyptians were to blame for breaking the truce. That night,

Israeli forces set out to drive in the wedges at Khirbet a-Ra'i and Bet Hanun. The Egyptians responded vigorously but failed to dislodge the wedges. The next morning, the Eighth Brigade set out to attack Iraq al-Manshiya. Sadeh, Rabin, and Uzi Narkiss watched the maneuver from the headquarters' post near Kibbutz Gat. It was a fiasco, and would have been a veritable farce were it not for the large number of casualties involved. The heavy tanks (of Latrun's "circular movement" fame) got stuck in the wadi: one tank fired but failed to drive, another drove but failed to fire. Out of a dozen light tanks (Hotchkins), four were lost. The infantry soldiers on the tanks took mortal wounds; dozens were killed, wounded, or went missing; and the Seventh Battalion was ripped apart. Iraq al-Manshiya's conquest was dropped from the agenda. Rescuing the forces now became the main question.[14] The remainder of the Seventh Battalion was painstakingly reassembled. At night in Qastina, Uzi Narkiss rallied the soldiers, who were Holocaust survivors and recruits from displaced persons camps in Europe (Gahal), for most of whom this was their baptism by fire. He was to remember the occasion as an exercise in boosting morale: they spent the whole night singing Palmah songs around the campfire and in the morning the battalion commander put them through formation drills to try to shake them out of despondency. Miraculously, the battalion recovered. To replace their shrunken numbers, the company of Avraham Adan (Bren) was attached to them and they went back into battle.[15] Haim Gouri described the night in his book, *Ad Alot ha-Shahar*, noting that on the wall of one of the houses in Qastina an anonymous hand had scribbled, "The Seventh Battalion shall rise again."[16]

In the postmortem following the action, Allon said that the armored attack had ostensibly lacked three vital components: artillery support, coordination with infantry, and, most of all, a real armored force. In retrospect, he accepted Rabin's view that Iraq al-Manshiya would have been taken had they opted for stealthy penetration. His verdict was, "We tried to carry out an operation according to accepted technique without [the] means [to do so]."[17] Even years later, he voiced not a word of criticism against Sadeh. If he blamed himself for the defeat, seeing as the absence of the three components was hardly a secret in advance, he shared these feelings with no one.

The attack had lost its momentum: the main mobile force, which was meant to have used the wedges to sweep away the Egyptian forces in between, was broken and put out of action. Allon had to rethink the whole plan. He had no ready and eager units waiting in the wings, but rather a beaten army.[18] The Egyptian army had been thrown out of kilter, especially by the Bet Hanun wedge, and was apprehensive about the severance of its Majdal and Gaza brigades, and about supply lines. But it was not beaten and could even boast of its performance against Israel's armored force. Yet there was one bit of good news on the morning of 17 October: squads from the Givati Brigade had managed to take Outpost 113 above the junction. Allon assembled his brigade commanders to consult on the next move. Most had despaired of breaching the Egyptian force. Rather than trying for decisive skirmishes, they suggested leaving the road in the west and finding a bypass route to the eastern Negev: a new "Burma Road," as it were, in the Judean foothills southeast from Gat to Ruhama. The idea was a dirt road, far from the main traffic axes.[19] Allon stuck to his guns and the overall drift of the original campaign plan: to rout the Egyptian army while opening up the main road to the Negev. This meant a frontal attack on the junction outposts, a form of warfare contrary to Allon's general conception of indirect ploys. He thought that there was no other choice. Years later, he recounted, "I remember that day, it was one of the most fateful of my life, certainly the most fateful of the operation."[20] After failing to convince his commanders, he resorted to what was for him an extraordinary step: he ordered them to comply. Those opposed included his intimates Mula Cohen and even Israel Galili.[21] Most of the opposition was voiced by Shimon Avidan the commander of the Givati Brigade. Avidan was cautious, experienced in warfare against the Egyptian army, and concerned about a high casualty toll. But there was no chance of carrying out the operation without the Givati Brigade, which was the largest of all. Allon had to call on all of his persuasive powers to get Avidan to agree. To make it easier for him, he ordered the Yiftah Brigade to attack the outposts of Huleiqat from the south, while soldiers from the Givati attacked the outposts of Kaukaba and Bet Tima. The operation order issued by Allon after this discussion set the date for the night of 17–18 October and added a rider: "In view of the importance of the above campaigns, they are to be carried out at any cost."[22]

On the night of the action, the Givati Brigade attacked from the north and the Yiftah Brigade from the south. Givati's Fifty-fourth Battalion managed to capture Kaukaba and Bet Tima while Yiftah's First Battalion failed to take Huleiqat. The road to the Negev remained closed. Political time was running out as the UN Security Council's deliberations progressed toward a cease-fire, and the operation had yet to show any visible gains. The soldiers of the Eighth Brigade and the Yiftah Brigade were in a dark mood. Only the soldiers of the Givati Brigade had known a gratifying moment.[23] Somewhat to the north, the Harel Brigade managed to take Bet Jimal and nearby villages.[24] But in the south, the Oded Brigade, which had been brought to the front as reinforcement, also failed to overrun the junction outposts. Nor was the attack on Iraq Suweidan, planned for that same night, carried through. Ben-Gurion jotted down in his diary: "Something's wrong. I'm afraid that Yigal Allon is incapable of commanding a front as broad as this."[25] At this very moment, as Ben-Gurion doubted his capability and his soldiers and officers lost faith in victory, Allon exhibited his leadership qualities. He retained his optimism, his ability to act, and his resolve to open the road to the Negev. Of all the forces, the only one still fit for action was Givati's Fifty-second Battalion. It had been slated for Iraq al-Manshiya on the night of 19 October. But in view of the Yiftah Brigade's vain attempt to take Huleiqat and the countdown to a cease-fire, Allon decided to redeploy the battalion for Huleiqat and Iraq Suweidan. Once the main road was opened, Iraq al-Manshiya would in any case be unimportant. He now came up against opposition from Yadin, who considered the change of plan a sign of Allon's wavering. To avoid direct confrontations with Yadin in the past, Allon used to have Rabin lay forth his positions, acting as a sort of mediator. Rabin assumed that job now as well, though to no avail: Yadin insisted that the Fifty-second Battalion attack Iraq al-Manshiya. After lengthy discussion, Allon declared that he was convinced that the new plan was a good one, but that he would do whatever Yadin ordered. Silence fell. Finally, Yadin said he would leave the decision up to the commander of the front. Allon chose the attack on Huleiqat.[26] On the night of 19–20 October, the Givati Brigade's Fifty-second Battalion (joined by soldiers from the Fifty-fourth) charged and captured the Huleiqat outposts, gallantly acquitting themselves in face-to-face combat and the use of bayonets.[27] The road to the Negev was opened. The forces to the north and the south of the east-west axis joined up, and, overnight, the Egyptian forces at Iraq Suweidan, Faluja, and Iraq al-Manshiya found themselves under siege. The result was the "Faluja Pocket": Israel held the road to the Negev east and west of the pocket. But only the first stage of the operation's plan seemed to have been realized; Majdal had not been taken and Gaza was not even under threat. At this instance, Allon improvised a new plan—the capture of Beersheba.

A few days before the campaign was launched, Allon had rejected Nahum Sarig's idea to divert a force to capture Beersheba.[28] Now, with the cease-fire about to go into effect even before the Huleiqat battles had died down, Allon suggested to the High Command that troops be expedited to conquer Beersheba. Yadin and Ben-Gurion were hardly overenthusiastic at first: Ben-Gurion was still disappointed by the failed attempts at Iraq Suweidan, the quasi-Latrun fortress of the Negev, and suspected that Allon had exaggerated when he said he could win Beersheba and then Gaza.[29] Yadin claimed that the situation in the northern Negev was still unstable: the Egyptian army at Majdal on one side, and in Faluja on the other, had still not shown any signs of knuckling under. Splintering the troops to conquer Beersheba might jeopardize the gains of the breakthrough and the opening of the road. He did not approve the campaign when he spoke with Allon at the headquarters of the Southern Front in Gedera. But that same day, military intelligence intercepted a telegram from Egyptian officers to Cairo, requesting consent to retreat from both the east-west axis and the coastal area north of Gaza, in view of the IDF's breakthrough at the junction and the link-up of its forces. The Egyptian army wished to redeploy along a new line, Beersheba-Gaza.[30] Yadin and Ben-Gurion quickly authorized Allon to take Beersheba. To allow the operation to proceed, Ben-Gurion withheld his agreement to the cease-fire for another night. But, as indicated by the time that the forces set out, Allon had apparently not waited for official authorization: he had put his men in the field in the hope that events would justify his decision. The troops earmarked for Beersheba made their way to the regrouping point even before Huleiqat fell. They crossed the Egyptian lines via a dirt road while the battle at Huleiqat provided background and lighting for their southward trek.[31]

The conquest of Beersheba was meant to repair the status of Sarig, who had known setbacks,[32] restore the Seventh Battalion as a fighting force, and reinstate Yitzhak Sadeh's prestige, which had been tarnished by the defeat at Iraq al-Manshiya. It succeeded beyond all expectations.

The battle for Beersheba was not one of the hardest of the war. The Egyptian army did not expect an offensive and was not prepared for one. The world press reported that the IDF was about to attack Gaza. The image of Avraham Adan's (Bren's) company charging with drawn bayonets that twinkled in the sun of that October morning remained etched in the mind of participants. The Egyptians fled for their lives. On 21 October 1948 Beersheba was in the hands of the IDF. Ben-Gurion telegrammed congratulations to Allon: "Pass on the congratulations of the Jewish people and the government of Israel to our soldiers who liberated the Negev and conquered Beersheba. With your blood, you renewed the connection to our Patriarch, Abraham.[33] Beersheba's conquest was important not only because it accorded control of a vital intersection—north to Mount Hebron, east to Sodom and Ein Gedi, south to Aqaba Bay, west to Gaza, and southeast to Auja al Hafir (Nitzana). Following the previous bitter battles against the Egyptian army, it marked a turning point in the morale of the corps. The defeats of the Yiftah and Negev brigades had eroded the common Israeli conception that the Egyptian army was a backward feudal Arab army unprepared for war. The Egyptians, as it transpired, knew how to fight and were in no hurry to run away. The battle for Beersheba restored the self-confidence of Israeli commanders and soldiers. It helped them forget their prior whippings. Beersheba may have been a sleepy backwater in the heart of the Negev, but it conjured up biblical scenes. "The Bible awarded it world public-

Figure 13. Ben-Gurion and Allon in Beersheba during Operation Yoav, October 1948. Photographer unknown. Courtesy of the IDF Archives.

ity," Ben-Gurion rightly noted.[34] Names such as Faluja, Iraq al-Manshiya, Outpost 113, and Huleiqat said nothing to either the Israeli public or the world press. They were merely points on a map. This was not so of Beersheba. It fired the imagination because of its connection to the Patriarchs and the ancient myth. Thus, a last-minute improvisation, implemented after the foundering of the original plan, earned Operation Yoav and its commanders world fame. Ben-Gurion came to visit and partook of a festive lunch with the commanders. It was a moment of grace.

By the time the new truce began, on 22 October 1948, only Beersheba's conquest was complete. Territorially, the operation had not chalked up impressive gains. As for trouncing the Egyptian army, there was still much to do. This, however, was apparently not the Egyptian assessment after the battles died down and the dust settled. The Egyptians lost hope of holding onto their positions north of Gaza and decided to pull back their forces, which were positioned north of the Bet Hanun wedge. Consequently, the capture of Majdal, Isdud, and the rest of the coastal plain up to Kibbutz Yad Mordekhai was achieved without battle.[35] On the front's eastern sector, in the foothills of Mount Hebron, fighting continued past the truce.[36] Two days after the truce began, on 24 October 1948, Allon proposed at a headquarters meeting to capture Bet Jibrin, one of the country's most important strategic junctions—despite the truce. Mundek Pasternak, who represented the HGS Operations Branch at the Southern Front's headquarters and was meant to supervise Allon's actions, responded: "It is clear to me that the truce has to be violated wherever necessary."[37]

On 27 October 1948 the village of Bet Jibrin was taken along with its police station and a series of villages on the road between Bet Jibrin and Hartuv. As part of the "creeping annexation," Qubeiba (Lachish) and Tel Maresha were also captured. Their conquests once again posed the question of how the Arab population under the IDF's rule was to be treated. Allon issued directives on the subject on 27 October 1948. The first clause instructed that there was to be "no harm done the population." The second and seemingly chief clause noted that "a most severe warning is hereby issued against looting." The threat of speedy court-martial was meant to deter delinquents. In addition, there was another warning: "Officers are personally responsible for abiding by this directive."[38] The instructions were based on past experience. Until then, there had been no reports of brutality, but there had been reports of reprehensible plunder and looting. These priorities were about to change.

On 29 October 1948, the village of Dawayima was captured by the Eighth Brigade's Eighty-ninth Battalion under Dov Chesis (who had played an active role in the period of the *saison*). Many of the soldiers involved had belonged to LeHI. Sadeh had managed to gain their trust and shape them into a combat battalion. The episode was not the battalion's finest hour. Reports soon trickled out of a massacre against the inhabitants, including the abuse of women, children, and the elderly. While the Arab numbers may have been exaggerated, the horror of the deed cannot be diminished.[39] As in previous cases when it was imperative for Allon to confront the "old man" (Sadeh), now too he lacked the necessary firmness: there is no doubt that he was revolted by the conduct and the very fact that such conduct was even possible in the IDF. "An abhorrent act of murder," he termed the events.[40] His revulsion was expressed in his order to the perpetrators to bury the victims with their own hands.[41] But he did not throw the book at them, not at the men, not at the officers. He wrote to Sadeh about the rumors of the massacre in the village. "Since I know your negative attitude to such manifestations, I am sure that you will find a way to sharply react should the rumor prove to be true."[42] Sadeh did not reply. Allon did not persist. Allon's silence looks like acquiescence in Sadeh's whitewashing of the affair. Sadeh made do with a reprimand, charging no one. When the CGS appointed Isser Be'eri of intelligence to look into the matter, Sadeh disrupted the investigation by refusing to appear before him.[43] Rabin testified that the massacre shocked and enraged Allon. But Allon could not bring himself to force his will on Sadeh. In time, at his first open mention of the Dawayima incident, which till then had been kept from the Israeli public, Allon did not moralize. "I do not come to preach ethics about the war," he said, but he held the massacre responsible for the halt to the creeping annexation. "It might well be that, were it not for the justified worldwide commotion raised by this murder, we would have managed to steal another two or three villages, yielding us greater control."[44] The criticism, in veiled language, was readily intelligible to both speaker and audience: even though everyone believed that the massacre of civilians was to be thoroughly condemned, the fact that it was also to blame for halting Israel's takeover of the Mount Hebron foothills added military invalidity to the moral lapse: the episode was both morally inexcusable and detrimental to national interests. There was a tendency to view purely moral objections as "lily-livered" and insufficiently cogent; to lend them added weight, they thus had to be couched in expediency as well.

In summing up Operation Yoav, Allon stated: "Operation Yoav did not make fame as the greatest of the Negev campaigns. Others were far more imaginative. I nevertheless consider it the most important."[45] It seems to have been an accurate assessment. Despite setbacks, it was the first show of the IDF's capability of wining battles against a regular army. It was not an all-out victory, but it dealt a severe blow to the Egyptian army, the strongest of the Arab armies, which did not recover from it. It dispelled the danger of an Egyptian counteroffensive. As a result of Israeli actions during the truce (the conquest of Iraq Suweidan, Bet 'Affa), the besieged Egyptian brigade at Faluja found itself in a shrinking enclave. It was still able to hold out, though no longer to pose a threat to the road to the Negev. The second Egyptian brigade, in Gaza, retained its strength and was even reinforced by the retreating troops from Majdal, but it was a defeated army that had lost its momentum and dug in to defend its own territory. On the operational level, the most important conclusion Allon drew from the experience of Operation Yoav was that for a decisive outcome either more time or more manpower was needed. Outflanking and encirclement—the basics of the "indirect approach"—made it possible to avoid frontal offensives that relied on large forces. But they demanded forbearance. The factors of time and manpower were to decide the next campaign too.

The significance of Operation Yoav went beyond the military. As said, it was the first time that Israel violated a UN resolution, embarking on battle despite the truce set by the Security Council. Ben-Gurion was apprehensive about international repercussions. But the operation brought no sanctions; it was received as predictable, given the Egyptian

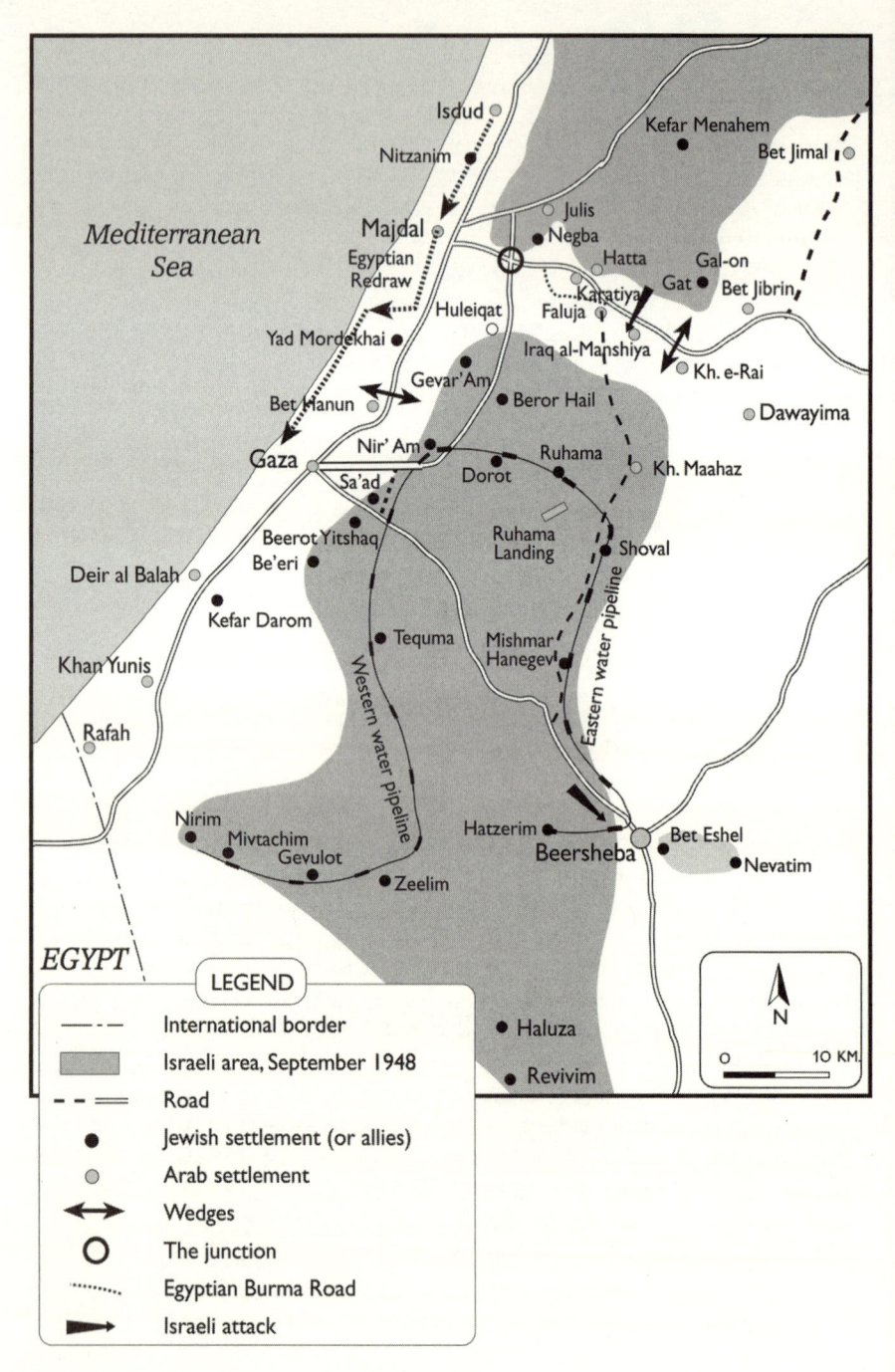

Map 4. Operation Yoav, 15–22 October 1948

blockade of Israeli convoys to the Negev. Moshe Sharett reported from the UN Assembly in Paris that there was wide enthusiasm for Israel's victory.[46] Fear of a concerted Arab reprisal also evaporated: no Arab army rushed to the rescue of the Egyptians. These two lessons were of the greatest importance for the leaders planning Israel's next moves. Operation Hiram, aimed at liberating the Upper Galilee from the Qawuqji army, was the first fruit of Israel's broadening policy: Israel no longer acted with the caution of previous months, but with a sense of confidence that the IDF had the initiative, that the Arab side had lost its self-assurance and the residual cooperation of its diverse components, and that the international community accepted the gains as a fait accompli, as it would have done had the opposite side been triumphant. For sure, nothing succeeds like success.

Allon's star was shining brightly: if formerly he had been known in the circles of the Haganah and the Palmah, he now became the "darling" of the local and world media. The young, handsome, and winning commander was perceived as the symbol of the sabra, the new Israeli. But even as Allon's stock skyrocketed, Ben-Gurion waged a high-handed campaign to liquidate the Palmah.

The continued existence of the Palmah's headquarters had been constantly debated since the establishment of the Southern Front. In August 1948, Allon agreed to limit the headquarters' functions to training, culture, and adjutancy.[47] Week by week, more and more of the headquarters' functions and duties were transferred to the HGS or the fronts. The establishment of the Southern Front's headquarters sharply curtailed its maneuverability. Allon manned the Southern Front's headquarters with "refugees" from the Palmah's headquarters.

On 14 September 1948 Ben-Gurion invited himself to a meeting of some sixty Palmah commanders and headquarters members at Kibbutz Na'an. He said it was an opportunity to advise them of his thoughts on the headquarters and to hear from them why they thought the Palmah was still unique now that it was no longer the IDF's sole permanent force. When he asked how new Palmah conscripts differed from new conscripts to other units, he touched a nerve. Most of the Palmah brigades were now filled by Gahal recruits or novices channeled to them by the induction center: while the command level was still peopled by the hard core of the Palmah, this was not so of the rank and file. The Palmah framework managed to absorb new immigrants who quickly imbibed the esprit de corps and became fiercely loyal to their units. But this Palmah characteristic left Ben-Gurion indifferent. As far as he was concerned, the Palmah's special components could and should have been instilled in the entire IDF. He would not be persuaded that the unique Palmah spirit would dissolve if its people were scattered or that there was a difference between an elite unit and a mass army. The arguments of the commanders fell on deaf ears. As a great (and simplistic) believer in the power of education to instill values and knowledge in every Israeli boy and girl, Ben-Gurion repudiated the uniqueness of elites and preached egalitarian democracy.

Allon was the last to reply to Ben-Gurion. Speaking for the headquarters, he attempted to counter with arguments that were chiefly professional and military: the Palmah trained its fighters better than did other bodies, its headquarters took care of its units while the quartermaster's branch was found wanting, its conscription was much speedier, and so on and so forth. The problem was that the arguments were true of the past, not the present. As for the future, Allon again tried to suggest that the Palmah form a single division of the IDF; just as a division had its own headquarters, so the Palmah should have its own headquarters. This was not unusual. There were separate headquarters for the artillery corps, the signal corps, and so forth. Aware that these were specialized corps, Allon sought to lend the Palmah a professional quality: the Palmah should be the IDF's elite division with marines, paratroopers, and other special units. "I am sure," he predicted, "that if disaster strikes and the Palmah is dismantled by the liquidation of its headquarters, soon afterward it will be necessary to establish a Palmah. A different Palmah may well rise then."[48]

In his opening remarks Ben-Gurion referred at length and unfavorably to the arguments of the Left about a political need for the Palmah to exist as a quasi-praetorian guard to protect the democratic, socialist character of the State of Israel against threatening, subversive forces of the fascist Right. The conception of a military unit subordinate to one part of the government (for example, the Histadrut), he said, went against state sovereignty and was destructive to the army. Allon, like others present, did not notice Ben-Gurion's carefully laid minefield and got caught up in political argument. The Right was dangerous to state welfare, he said, and the Palmah was necessary to prevent civil war. The political argument played into Ben-Gurion's hands. He was only too happy to don the robes of state protector and decry a sectoral army that had outlived its time.

At the end of the long discussion, Ben-Gurion went over the same old points: the whole army should have Palmah-type training; the Palmah was not a professional body, not unique. As for political reasons—yes, he had used the Palmah in the *Altalena* affair. But that had been a necessity, he said; it should not be made permanent policy.[49] As for pragmatic considerations—that there was no reason to dismantle a framework that had proved itself; or the assertion by Pinhas Rosen, the minister of justice, that it was better to leave the headquarters alone while war raged because, although the Palmah's sectoralism did pose a danger, the Egyptians were more dangerous still—all of these Ben-Gurion chose to ignore.[50]

Two weeks later, Ben-Gurion summed up his conclusions and instructed CGS Yaakov Dori to dismantle the Palmah's headquarters. On 7 October 1948, about half a year after congratulating Allon "and all the other comrades" on the occasion of the Palmah's seventh anniversary, Dori oversaw the transfer of the three remaining duties (induction, training, and culture) of the Palmah's headquarters to the pertinent branches of the HGS and the fronts.[51] The next week, the storm erupted: Allon dashed off a letter to the CGS: "I was astonished to learn that you have ordered the dismantling of the Palmah headquarters by the fifteenth of this month." It was the eve of Operation Yoav and Allon warned against impairing the war effort: "There is much bitterness and I fear a drop in morale" among the Palmah's soldiers. Of the CGS, he demanded that "an official order be circulated among the Palmah's soldiers about postponing the dismantling until further review in order to calm things down."[52] The protest encompassed large circles; the HGS was inundated with hundreds of protest letters from all ranks, from brigade commanders to privates and new recruits. The reasons listed read like a song of Palmah's praises: its moral weight, state loyalty, fighting spirit, defense capability, and border settlement; its comradeship-in-arms, esprit de corps, and numerous casualties. If the order were not to be rescinded, the writers stated, then at least its implementation should be deferred: to liquidate the Palmah's headquarters on the eve of battle was a blow to morale. Many letters poured in from Gahal people who had been absorbed into the Palmah and who now rushed to its defense. One of their frequent phrases was that "even overseas we had heard of the Palmah." Some of the letters were in fluent Hebrew, others in broken Hebrew. Many were in French (apparently by members of the "French Commando," recruits from North Africa), Yiddish, Polish, and Romanian. Some of the non-Hebrew letters had been written at the induction center, raising questions about their spontaneity.[53]

Outside the military orbit, Mapam rose to the protection of its "pet" unit. The Histadrut Executive's discussion of the matter on 14 October 1948 was surrealistic: the prime minister and minister of defense, army commanders, and representatives of Mapai and Mapam met at a forum of Histadrut workers to talk about the dismantling of a military unit. The strange mixture of a social-economic framework, political representation, and military figures who had come to appeal the verdict of the minister of defense and the CGS was typical of the twilight period between the Yishuv and the state. The state may have been several months old, but the principles of statehood that make the separation of army and politics imperative had not yet been internalized. The fact that Ben-Gurion himself did not invalidate a discussion of a clearly military issue in the framework of the Histadrut, but actually attended, indicates how blurry the boundaries still were.

This discussion of the fate of the Palmah's headquarters highlights the spirit of the times. From the point of view of the headquarters, it was insignificant. A two-thirds majority of the Histadrut Executive backed Ben-Gurion, determining that it was not the business of the Histadrut to interfere in military considerations. Meanwhile, Operation Yoav was in swing (beginning on the same day as the Executive discussion) and in the heat of battle a last moment appeal by Palmah's headquarters was rejected.[56] On 29 October 1948, Dori advised the Palmah's headquarters that the minister of defense had rejected the appeal and it was to carry out the dismantling order by 7 November 1948.[55] In early November, guidelines were issued on the disposition of the Palmah's assets—training bases, a convalescent home, a vacation camp, and so forth—and their transfer to the various units. The soldiers and officers involved were also scattered over relevant units. A question remained only about personnel at headquarters itself.[56] On 6 November 1948 Shlomo Shamir, an old friend and a rival of Allon and the Palmah and now the head of the Department for HGS Duties, issued an "order on unit liquidation—Palmah headquarters," which took effect on 8 November 1948.[57] That same day, the Palmah's headquarters issued its last order of the day to its brigades. It mentioned seven years of action by the Palmah and the functions of the headquarters as "a headquarters of command, education, image molding and strengthening of the force." It closed with two statements: first, that the dismantling of the headquarters was a decisive step in the dismantling of the Palmah (which Ben-Gurion strenuously denied at the time but soon implemented), and second, that despite everything, "we have been taught to maintain discipline—and have accepted the order."[58] The last was meant to silence the denouncers who drew parallels between the IZL, the LeHI, and the Palmah, as if all three were "private armies" disarmed by Ben-Gurion.

On the day that the Histadrut Executive discussed the fate of the Palmah's headquarters and Ben-Gurion let his barbs fly at the attending KM members, he also sent off a personal letter to Yitzhak Tabenkin, his old friend from the days of the Second Aliyah. Since their dispute over the Ben-Gurion–Jabotinsky agreement (1934), Ben-Gurion and Tabenkin had found themselves on opposite sides at every key juncture: in the controversy over partition in 1937, Ben-Gurion had led the supporters and Tabenkin the opponents. The establishment of Faction B and the split in Mapai in 1944 had revolved, among other things, around the Biltmore Program, which was Ben-Gurion's idea and was rejected by

Tabenkin. The man they both loved and admired was Berl Katznelson, but he had passed away in the summer of 1944, his death severing yet another link between them. In January 1948, the founding of Mapam sealed any residual hope of regaining the lost golden age of a united Mapai. In addition, Ben-Gurion's war on the Palmah had targeted "Tabenkin's private army." All of these things only makes one wonder at the letter he now wrote Tabenkin:

Yitzhak,
 The distances, alienation, strangeness, lack of contact between the closest of people perhaps—the last close people, perhaps, of that generation, who are already preparing or being summoned to walk toward their friends who have departed never to return—is an odd and bitter fate, especially in these times, *this* year. And yet not everything is totally or only in the hands of bitter fate. . . .
 I chanced upon a partisan pamphlet today, "La-Megguyas" [To the inductee] from the Liaison Committee of the Kibbutz Secretariat (No. 5), and I read your delivery at the Givat Brenner Assembly—and I had a strange feeling, a feeling mixed with wonder, sorrow, joy: here were echoes of my own inner feelings, as if the words had come from my heart, and the person who uttered them—it is a whole year (and what a year!) since I have seen him, heard him, since he saw or heard me, and yet we live on—amid the artificial, bitter distances we have erected around ourselves—with a single emotion and a single consciousness; and I could not tell which was more amazing and which more real—whether the alienation or the identification? . . .
 But I could not rest without writing you these few words.
Be strong and of good courage
As wished by your brother-friend
D. B. G.[59]

Beyond their political and ideological differences, veterans of the Second Aliyah retained a springtime warmth for one another. Ben-Gurion wrote Tabenkin with an intimacy harking back to the memorable threesome of Berl–Ben-Gurion–Tabenkin. No outsider could gain entry into it. At the height of the campaign to dismantle the Palmah, he sought out Tabenkin's friendship, tried to re-spark the old solidarity. He invoked a common heart and asked him to forget the alienation and strangeness that were not part of the true fabric of their relations. At the pinnacle of his success as the nation's unquestioned leader, Ben-Gurion felt cold, lonely winds blowing at the top and a need for the old friendship. "Your brother-friend"—it is not likely that he used this adjective toward party comrades. His feelings for Tabenkin—the sense of closeness and of spurned love—did not apply to the younger generation, to Allon, Allon's peers, or even Galili, who psychologically belonged to a more mature generation. Allon and his generation had not shared the romance of the Second Aliyah's pioneering "barefoot order." Ben-Gurion had a shorter fuse for them. In this respect, his anti-Palmah stance was another battle in his long-standing campaign against elitist groups that challenged the hegemony of the Second Aliyah. It was a generational struggle as much as an ideological, political, and cultural gap.

The dissolution of the Palmah's headquarters reinforced Allon's inclination to gather around him in the Southern Front's headquarters a "Palmah B" staff, so to speak, to maintain the close group that had worked together, that would ensure headquarters loyalty to himself, and probably could retain the Mapam character of the command echelon. In 1944, when Mapai split and the Le-Ahdut Ha-Avodah (LAHA) movement was formed, Aharon Zisling, one of Kibbutz Ein Harod's more zealous members, declared: "They won't be able to do without us." It was a proud statement, and it was received as unforgivably arrogant; it egged Mapai on to prove to its former party comrades just how wrong they were. But its spirit persisted and was widely shared by the Palmah's commanders. It radiated from Allon. He did not properly appreciate the vulnerability of his position or the suspicion that his behavior aroused in Ben-Gurion or even the CGS. The fact that Ben-Gurion was rankled by the close contact between the Southern Front's headquarters and Mapam leaders was a direct result of Allon's conduct and indiscretion. When he visited Beersheba a week after the conquest, Ben-Gurion noted in his diary, "I found all of Mapam's leaders [there]."[60] This was exacerbated by Allon's smart-alecky behavior in deceiving the military system so that he would have the freedom to build his own headquarters. This only raised the defense minister's antennae—was Allon preparing a Mapam hotbed in the Southern Front?

The appointment of a cultural officer for the Southern Front was a case in point. In October 1948, Joseph Kariv, the head of the Cultural Service at the HGS, notified the commander of the Southern Front that he intended to make Ahuvya Malkhin the cultural officer of the Southern Front. The choice was above board; no one doubted Malkhin's abilities. It was equally clear that the fact that he belonged to Mapai had stood him in good stead. The appointment was an attempt to deal with the Southern Front's smear campaign against Ben-Gurion and to dent the ideological uniformity of its headquarters by introducing a figure from outside the Palmah's inner circle.

Allon, however, wanted Zerubavel Gilad, a member of Ein Harod and a poet-writer, as his cultural officer: Gilad had been the Palmah's cultural officer for seven years, was part of both the Palmah and the KM inner circle, and edited the Palmah newsletter. Allon thus took steps to cancel Malkhin's appointment. Sini Azaryahu met with Ahuvya Malkhin and without mincing his words explained to him that should he get the post, he could expect no cooperation from the Southern Front but rather the reverse. Following this frankness, Malkhin withdrew his candi-

Figure 14. The Palmah's headquarters in the summer of 1948 before the Palmah was dismantled. Yigal Allon is in the center of the photo; Rabin is the second from the left; Azaryahu is the second from the right. Photographer unknown. Courtesy of the Haganah Archives, Tel Aviv.

dacy. Allon hastened to ensconce Gilad in the position in the hope of establishing "facts on the ground." He did not take into account that his lobbying and manipulations were hardly a secret, arousing suspicion and anger. About two weeks after Gilad assumed the post, he was informed by Kariv that his appointment had been reviewed and annulled. The CGS was determined to give the position to someone the High Command could trust.[61] Ultimately, Allon and his colleagues accepted Malkhin's appointment and straightened out matters with him. Malkhin served as the Southern Front's cultural officer in 1949.[62]

The episode would hardly be worth mentioning were it not for its illumination of Allon's misjudgment. Allon's prestige and standing were at a peak at the time, between Operation Yoav and Operation Horev. Everyone had high praise for him. At the same time, Ben-Gurion's dismantling of the Palmah's headquarters was a clear signal of what was politically permissible and what was not. Allon should have understood that his sly, naïve maneuvers to construct the Southern Front's headquarters as a B version of the Palmah's headquarters would not escape the leadership's notice. Yet he jumped in up to his neck in an issue of no military consequence, although it did have a political one. His assessment, that he was strong enough to force his will on the CGS, showed that he did not understand the limits of his position. This was one instance of his misreading of the signals in his relationship with Ben-Gurion.

Operation Yoav ended with two interlocked armies on the ground, each threatening and fearing the other. The Egyptians refused to enter into negotiations on a cease-fire, demanding that Israel first withdraw to positions prior to the operation. General Riley, head of the UN's team of observers, fruitlessly shuttled back and forth between the two sides. Meanwhile, the economic burden, especially widespread conscription, put the government under pressure to bring the war to a close. In mid-December after the UN Assembly in Paris adopted several resolutions that were difficult for Israel, Ben-Gurion decided to launch another campaign to rout the Egyptian army in Palestine and try to conclude the fighting. The force mustered was the largest till then: the Eighth, Harel, Negev, Golani, and Alexandroni brigades as well as additional, second-line forces. The command level kept its eye on the sandglass: every campaign was harder than its predecessor for the United Nations and Western powers to digest. Whatever remained undone in this operation would not likely have an opportunity to be rectified. The hope for a breakthrough explains the HGS's relative generosity in allocating forces.

Egyptian deployment was now based on the well-fortified Gaza Strip and the line from Abu-Ageila via Auja al Hafir (Nizannah) to Bir-Aslui (near Kibbutz Revivim). The line was secured by a series of shored-up stretches viewed by the High Command as a threat to Beersheba. The two arms were joined by the Auja al Hafir Road to Rafah, which followed an arc on both sides of the international border. Operation Horev's operational blueprint was much more inventive and canny than earlier campaigns. It reflected all of the accumulated experience, self-confidence and readiness to take risks. Vital roles were played by intelligence, the air force, and the artillery, though it was the jeep-mounted raiders that captured the imagination, swallowing up the white, dust-covered southern expanses and opening up infantry routes by storm. The operation started with a diversionary tactic. There was widespread expectation that the major thrust was to be against the Gaza Strip and, to buttress this impression, units of the Golani Brigade were sent to conquer Post 86 between Gaza and Rafah (23 December 1948). The measure, it was hoped, would act as a wedge much like the Bet Hanun wedge in Operation Yoav, causing the Egyptian army to fold north of Post 86. The Golani Brigade managed to take the post but was thwarted by force majeure: incessant rain wreaked havoc on the road to the post and the supply convoy delivering ammunition and cannon got stuck in the mud. Golani's brave stand was not up to holding the post. The Egyptians, under General Mohamed Nagib, who was wounded in battle and later became the leader of Egypt's young officers' revolution, directed a counteroffensive forcing Golani's retreat.[63] Despite the defeat, Allon attributed great importance to the maneuver: it prevented the Egyptians from rushing forces to Auja, which made it easier for the main troops acting against the southern arm.[64]

With the Egyptians and the Israelis still clenching their teeth over Post 86, a unit set out, amid a communication blackout, from Beersheba via Kurnub to Mount HaMisrafa to outflank the enemy and strike deeply. The Eighth Brigade was dispatched from Halutza to Auja (26 December 1948) in a maneuver that Allon was later to recount fondly and frequently. He wanted to take Auja by surprise so that there would be no need to fight for every post, thereby saving both men and time. There was an old Nabatean road from Halutza via Er-Ruheibe (apparently the biblical Rehovot) via Wadi Abiad (Nahal Lavan) that came upon Auja from the northwest, that is, the direction from which the Egyptians did not foresee danger. Though Allon was wont to credit the road's discovery to the exploration of Palmah scouts in the area, Yadin claimed that it appeared on a map of Roman roads hanging in his office; the map related to the doctoral dissertation he meant to write on warfare in the ancient East. Whatever the case, the road was impassable, buried in dunes. The engineering corps checked it out thirty-six hours before departure and announced that it would not take responsibility for the troops' safe passage along it.[65] The scouts, in contrast, pronounced it manageable. This was what Allon wanted to hear. He and his men weighed the option at the advance command headquarters in Halutza. There was to be another reconnaissance tour by both engineers and scouts with the participation of Allon and Rabin. Rabin had insisted on Allon's presence because of the deadly stakes. At the last minute, however, Allon was summoned to the HGS and Rabin went on his own. After a long, hard trek by night, the men returned to Beersheba at dawn with no consensus: engineers—against; Southern Front personnel—for. Allon turned to Rabin. Rabin replied that it was very difficult, but doable. Allon had the assessment he wanted—and from the person he most relied on. Ten years later, he revealed that when he had driven along the arduous route on the heels of the Eighth Brigade, he could hardly believe his eyes. His generosity toward Rabin was unstinting: "Had I had gone earlier instead of Yitzhak Rabin, I might have been deterred."[66]

It was in fact doable. For two days, while battle raged in the Gaza Strip over Post 86, engineers covertly prepared the route for vehicles and armored cars. Nets were spread over the dunes and overlaid with steel tracks from dismantled railways and old Bailey bridges left behind from the days of the British army. On the third night, the convoy began its procession. It was a December desert night. The cold crept into the bones. The troops removed their jackets and laid them on the route before the tanks.[67] Progress was slower than expected. Workers and tractors from nearby kibbutzim enlisted to help. In parts of the road, soldiers had to push the vehicles until they reached Wadi Abiad and, from there, to the Auja-Rafah Road. The entire venture was a calculated risk. Because of the topography, traffic was only one way, southward—with no return, no retreat. Based on the balance of forces between the Egyptians at Auja and the Eighth Brigade, the command was confident that the brigade could capture the site.[68] The surprise was that it did not. The Egyptian commander, realizing that the movement of troops before his eyes was not a diversion as he had initially thought, regrouped for a counterattack and drubbed the Eighth Brigade. The battalion that had penetrated the post was forced back and incurred casualties. A company commander, "Blonde Dov" (formerly a celebrated member of LeHI), was killed and the company fell apart.[69] Allon arrived after the retreat had begun. He did not criticize Sadeh. A decade later when he told the tale, he said about Sadeh what he had declared about Dayan in the Lydda episode: "I always knew that if Yitzhak Sadeh was forced to retreat—apparently nothing could be done."[70] But in practice, he acted otherwise. Though he found the Eighth Brigade "psychologically battered," he decided to launch another attack. He bucked up Sadeh and Dov Chesis, reinforced the brigade with troops from the Harel Brigade that had been kept in reserve, and organized the force for an assault at dawn. At the same time, he notified the officers that the Negev Brigade was advancing on the main road toward Auja—turning its conquest into a competition. The contest was won by the Eighth Brigade in the morning offensive (27 December 1948). Bir-Asluj, which had been cut off, fell to the Southern Front without a battle.

This was the end of the first stage of Operation Horev. The southern arm of the Egyptian army was destroyed. Allon did not waste much thought before ordering the Negev Brigade and the rest of the Eighth Brigade to regroup for another measure. In his report to Yadin, he noted that more than half of the Eighth Brigade's battle vehicles were inoperable and advised of preparations for the next move. He did not spell out the target,[71] but Rabin went to explain it to the HGS. The next afternoon, Allon announced that his forces were moving toward Abu-Ageila and soon afterward he reported that they had crossed the international border. Israeli airplanes were not expecting IDF forces on the road to Abu-Ageila and assumed these were enemy units. They opened fire, killing one soldier and wounding two.[72] Nor did Yadin know that the column was on the road. He was sick that week, and at home, and only in the afternoon did he prepare to respond to Allon's telegram.

"Advance on Abu-Ageila is to be avoided until you see me. If there has already been movement, there should be no more than a raid and withdrawal to base," Yadin informed Allon.[71] Allon replied that the forces en route to Abu-Ageila could no longer be stopped. Once the site was taken, a decision could be made to abandon it, if that was what the High Command wanted. As for presenting himself to the HGS (or Yadin's home)—that too would have to wait, since Rabin was currently with the HGS and Allon could thus not leave the front.[74] It is clear from the exchange that Allon acted at his own discretion, "broadening" the mandate he had been given by the High Command. He himself said as much. At a summation with commanders of the Southern Front, he explained his manner of dealing with the HGS. He said he always "stretched" and expanded operational approvals, then presented the HGS with facts and obtained retroactive authorization. "We logged Abu-Ageila as a raid. The HGS did not authorize the advance to Abu-Ageila, I replied that we were going on a raid and if we managed to take it, the HGS would then decide what was to be done. After the conquest, the HGS gave its consent."[75] Also in his lecture ten years later, Allon acknowledged that he had acted on his own authority amid "broad" interpretation: he knew that he could not hope for authorization to enter Sinai, so he defined the action as a raid aimed at neutralizing Egyptian air power by overrunning the airports on the Sinai front. They were in fact raids, although with proper reinforcement they could have been the basis of a more serious operation.[76]

The raids in eastern Sinai entered national memory as one of the high points of the War of Independence. On 28 December 1948, Rabin ordered the Negev Brigade and Eighty-second Battalion to capture Abu-Ageila and dig in.[77] Abu-Ageila fell on 29 December 1948. That same day, the UN Security Council adopted the cease-fire resolution. The Egyptians played into Israeli hands, refusing to accept the cease-fire unconditionally. Also that day, Rabin issued an operational order for 30 December 1948, charging the Negev Brigade and the Eighty-second Battalion to raid el-Arish "in order to conquer and destroy it."[78] On 29 December 1948 at 16:20, Yadin sent the following telegram: "1. I have been informed by the intelligence service and air force surveillance that our units have moved toward el-Arish. 2. You are hereby ordered to stop all movement of your units without prior authorization. 3. Confirm urgent."[79] Adopting a conciliatory tone, Allon replied that these were mere raids. He reported on the fighting of the forces at airports near el-Arish.[80] Yadin again forbade any action north of Abu-Ageila without prior authorization and demanded that Allon report to his (Yadin's) office the next morning.[81] Allon must have reassured Yadin for a document of the Operations Branch on the next stage of the operation,

Figure 15. At the el-Arish Junction during Operation Horev, December 1948. Photographer unknown. Courtesy of the Israeli Government Press Agency.

issued 30 December 1948, approved Allon's plan, allowing him to proceed against el-Arish and Quseima while digging in at Abu-Ageila.[82] Yigal was allotted another three hundred soldiers for the campaign.[83]

By advancing his troops to el-Arish, Allon hoped to achieve one of two results: either to seal off the whole Egyptian army in the Gaza Strip within a huge enclave, like the Faluja Pocket, or to make it move its forces from Rafah and Gaza in order to defend el-Arish, the only road that joined Gaza and Egypt. The latter case would have raised the possibility of capturing Gaza. Yadin, in contrast, believed that this sort of maneuver could take too long and opted for concerted action against Rafah. Because of the urgency, Yadin's approach had the advantage but lacked the thrust and daring of the el-Arish plan. Allon planned to repeat the Abu-Ageila exercise: to capture el-Arish and obtain retroactive approval; Yadin wanted Allon merely to create the impression of targeting el-Arish, thereby diverting Egyptian forces there from Rafah.[84]

The breach into Sinai lifted spirits and brought a sense of triumph, not only for the Southern Front but most likely for the High Command as well. From the clutches of existential fear they had gone on to become a blazing, victorious army: the swift transformation was intoxicating. Moreover, the glory had been won at a relatively low cost. Compared to Operation Yoav, the Sinai battles were easy, scoring high with few losses.

Figure 16. Allon (on the right) and Rabin during Operation Horev. Photographer unknown. Courtesy of the IDF Archives.

They looked like Palmah treks into new areas and landscapes and even retained some of the same amateurism: the Negev Brigade crossed the international boundary without maps but much enthusiasm. Bren (Adan) had no idea of the location of the Umm-Katef stretch on the way to Abu-Ageila, yet he managed to find it at night.[85]

Crossing the border was not regarded as such an unusual occurrence that it warranted prior discussion. Neither the Israeli government nor the IDF considered the international border between Palestine and Egypt a red line against trespassing. There was no thought of conquering Sinai permanently, not even by Allon. However, the notion that Israel should honor the international border while Egyptian forces sat in Palestine was unacceptable. Even the most cautious and sober of Israel's leaders, such as Ben-Gurion and Sharett, did not think that crossing the border would rouse sleeping dogs. Yet it did: the IDF's raids on Egyptian airports in eastern Sinai forced Egyptian airplanes into the air. For this, they had to ask permission of the British, who controlled the airways above the Suez Canal, to land at their airfields. From that moment on, the British sat up and took notice of Israeli actions, threatening to activate the 1936 Anglo-Egyptian Treaty, which Egypt sought to invalidate in an attempt to shake off British patronage. The British applied pressure on the United States to intervene. The Americans were not eager for international embroilment and bore down on Israel to cease its actions in Sinai. President Truman, who had just been re-elected, to Ben-Gurion's relief, issued an ultimatum making continued U.S. friendship contingent on immediate withdrawal. This piece of news caught up with Ben-Gurion in Tiberias, where he was spending the weekend. After consulting with Yadin, he ordered the army to pull back from Sinai but to continue the actions against Rafah and Gaza more forcefully. James McDonald, the U.S. ambassador and a long-standing friend of the Israeli cause, was not satisfied that Sharett had relayed the gist of Truman's message to Ben-Gurion nor with the notification he received that the army had indeed been ordered back eastward to the international border. He demanded an audience with Ben-Gurion in Tiberias so that he could tell him directly what Truman had to say and hear his reaction. In practical terms, the meeting changed nothing. But the drama of the ambassador traveling to Tiberias on the weekend signaled U.S. pressure on the Israeli prime minister. It did the trick.[86]

On 30 December 1948, Allon and Yadin finalized the next steps. The next day, a telegram came from Yadin, stating: "By tomorrow, 1 January 1949, 12:00, all our forces must leave Egyptian territory and return to Tarnegol [Israel]." To remove all doubt, he added, "You must ensure that Clause 1 is implemented at any price by the appointed time."[87] The order arrived while the commanders assembled to review the details of the next morning's charge on el-Arish. They were stunned. Dumbfounded and angry, Allon dashed off a telegram to Yadin and the minister of defense—a telegram not found in the list of those sent from the fronts to the Operations Branch ("Ha-Nes Ha-Nikhnas"). It cited a number of military reasons against withdrawal, the main one being the hurdles it would pose to the completion of Gaza's capture.[88] It began thus: "I have given instruction to prepare for carrying out your order to withdraw from the vicinity of el-Arish and Abu-Ageila to Auja." He did not yet despair. He still hoped that he would be able to stave off the order, and that night he flew to Tel Aviv. He met with Ben-Gurion and tried to convince him if not to rescind the withdrawal order then at least to delay it until the Egyptian forces were pressed to pull out of the Gaza Strip and the conditions for its capture were easier. But Ben-Gurion regarded the possibility of British intervention and the loss of U.S. support as real threats, and he ordered Allon to withdraw his forces. He did, however, throw Allon a bone: he gave him an additional day to complete the retreat, until noon of 2 January 1949.[89] Meanwhile, the commanders waited at the villa of Abu-Ageila's military governor for the results of Allon's lobbying. Rabin suddenly materialized in the clawing cold night, in an evident rage. All Allon's efforts, he announced angrily, had failed to budge Ben-Gurion. There was no choice but to retreat.[90]

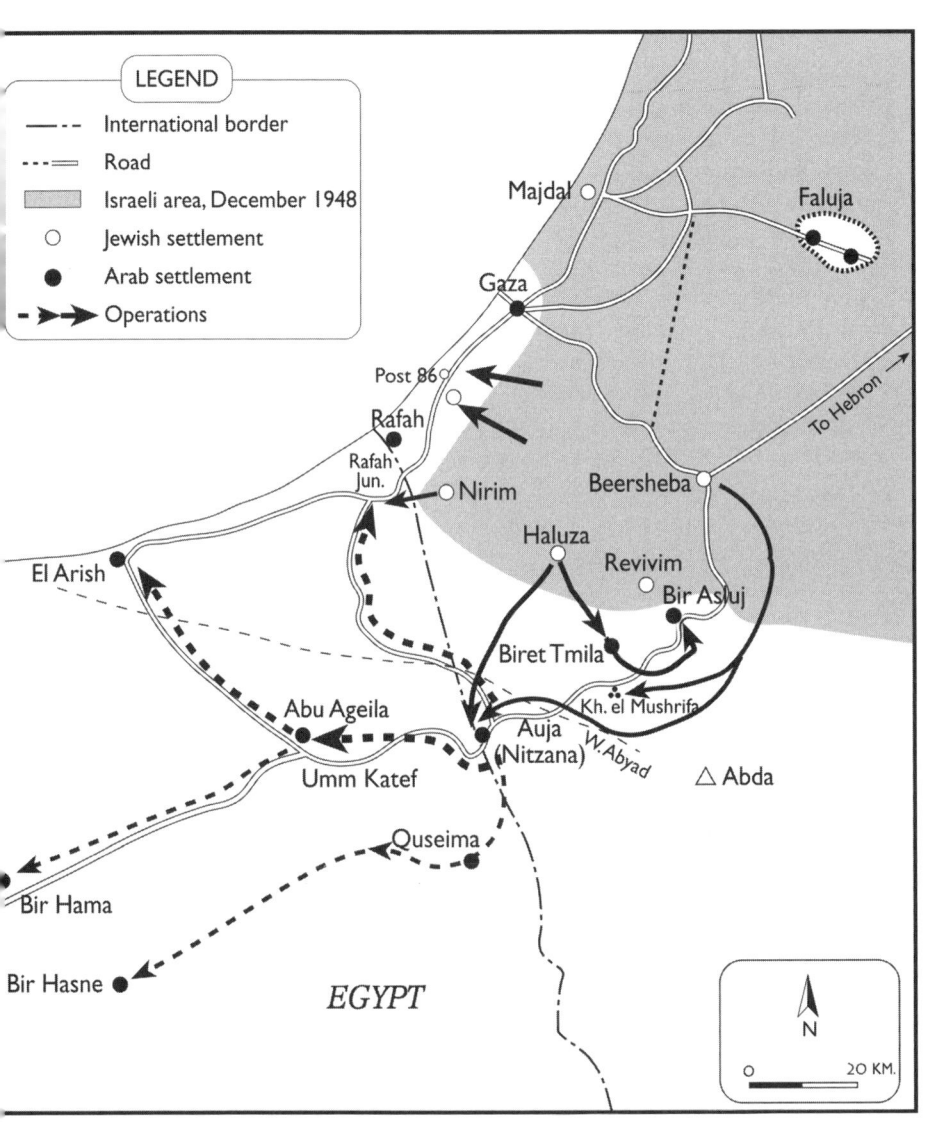

Map 5. Operation Horev, 22 December 1948–8 January 1949

The operation had been in swing for more than a week. The UN Security Council had still not imposed a cease-fire since the two sides had not agreed to it; there was some time left in the political clock. Allon improvised the next stage: an attack on Rafah. He wanted to use the Auja-Rafah Road and Ben-Gurion saw no obstacle even though the road arched through Egyptian territory.[91] The coming days were devoted to regrouping, planning, and redeployment at new departure points. On 4 January 1949 the fighting resumed. But the Israeli thrust had lost its punch. The troops were tired, the equipment worn. The joy of triumph and sense of intoxication at Sinai's primeval expanses had dissolved with the retreat. The adrenalin dropped; all at once everyone was aware of every pain, every blister. For the next four days, the Golani, Harel, and Eighth Brigades tried to take Rafah and failed. Golani's assault on the key Post 102 ended in a pullback. On the last night, a bad sandstorm clogged firearms and blocked visibility. Allon had to trim his aims to fit the capabilities of his troops. He decided on one final effort to capture the posts south of the junction, which straddled the road between Rafah and el-Arish. The action, by forces from the Harel Brigade, was successful.[92] As Harel wedged itself in, aircraft appeared overhead: they were British planes, as it later transpired, come to have a look at the battlefield. Incredibly, Israel's young, inexperienced air force managed to down four battle planes of the extolled Royal Air Force and a fifth was dropped by anti-aircraft fire (the British claimed the planes were unarmed and on reconnaissance). Allon reported the incident, including the capture of a number of British pilots who had parachuted into Israeli territory, coolly and straightforwardly, as if taking British pilots captive was an everyday event.[93] But when Ben-Gurion heard of it from Yadin, his face turned as white as snow: his fear of British intervention was real.[94] Determined not to provoke the British into intervening in the Palestine campaign, he quickly announced that Israel was ready to negotiate; it had agreed to a cease-fire earlier. Fortunately, Egypt announced at the same time that it was prepared to begin armistice talks. But, as a preliminary to the talks, it demanded that Israel evacuate the posts it had conquered across the international border. Ben-Gurion accepted and Yadin ordered Allon to vacate the "wedge" near Rafah.[95] Allon obeyed, but under strong protest now as well: "This is the second time in this operation that, with our own hands, we are destroying the sure chances of defeating the Egyptian army once and for all," he wrote Yadin. This telegram is also omitted from those that the Southern Front sent to the Operations Branch.[96] Allon's reaction sparked a prompt reprimand from the CGS for his interference in political considerations.[97]

Allon, in the postmortem of the operation, was convinced that if he had been given a few more days, he would have reaped the campaign's fruit and smashed the hold of the Egyptian army on the Gaza Strip. The two withdrawals—from el-Arish and from the wedge southwest of the Rafah Junction—really bothered him.[98] To him, they symbolized both the lack of determination and the weak will of the political leadership (that is, Ben-Gurion), which folded before political pressure. His attitude was marked by the self-confidence of an unvanquished commander who believed that nothing could stand in his way. This may be a necessary attribute for a military commander—to initiate, spur on, and aim for more than what "civilian" leaders are prepared to allow him. Nevertheless, it also had more than a grain of youthful hubris—the arrogance of a young man unequipped, inexperienced, and insufficiently knowledgeable to grasp the intricacies of international diplomacy, impelled by a rebellious instinct against the government and by a desire to make his own mark. Allon was positive that the British had no intention of acting against Israel. But, even if they did, Israel would manage to finish the job before the British reached its shores.[99] He was not alone in viewing Ben-Gurion's withdrawal order and fear of British intervention as a sign of weakness. The entire command echelon of the Southern Front felt the same way. It was an attitude that regarded international relations as a function of military force alone. It disregarded the importance of public opinion, of good will, of give and take in the world arena.

Rabin certainly did not remember weighing political considerations in the War of Independence: "Maybe we simply knew less." What he emphasized was the "experience of transition from a weak force to a relatively strong force against the opposite side."[100] Given how closed Israeli Jewish society in Palestine was at the time, and the self-confidence of its home-grown youth, one need not wonder at the intellectual limitations of the younger generation's leaders. Ben-Gurion, Sharett, and their colleagues were light-years ahead of them in statesmanship. Balancing the tactical convenience of holding el-Arish or the road near Rafah against Israel's international standing, they chose to concede military gain for political benefit. The opportunity to detach Britain from Egypt and to embark on negotiations with Egypt struck Ben-Gurion as a major step, one, moreover, that might predispose the United States toward the young State of Israel.[101] Israel made yet another gain when Britain, owing to domestic criticism of its involvement on the Palestinian front, announced on 29 January 1949 that it de facto recognized the State of Israel. For the political echelon, these were the desirable fruits of military accomplishments. Though the IDF did not manage to beat the Egyptian army in the Gaza Strip or the Faluja Pocket, the campaign ended with impressive achievements by Israel: control of the whole range of Mount Negev and Egyptian recognition of the need to talk with Israel in order to extricate its trapped brigade from Faluja and prevent encirclement at Rafah. The Egyptians came to the negotiation table only after they realized that they had no hope of forcing a military victory.

One arena of Operation Horev faded into a forgotten abyss: the battle for Iraq al-Manshiya. The campaign plan had assigned the Alexandroni Brigade a modest role: to stop the Egyptian army at the Faluja Pocket and prevent it from breaking out to join up with Egyptian forces in the Negev. Israeli forces had been hacking away at the pocket since Operation Yoav, but they failed to liquidate it. On 24 December 1948, at the start of military actions, Ben-Gurion came south to meet with Yadin and the headquarters' staff, and to see firsthand what was going on. From the launching of the IDF's large-scale offensives, he had not interfered in operational details. But at that meeting with Yadin in Gedera, he instructed the HGS to destroy the Faluja Pocket using heavy artillery. Its conquest would free up troops and make the IDF's work easier in the Negev, he contended.[102] Despite the surprise, no one voiced protest or opposition. After an adventurous drive southward, Yadin and Ben-Gurion reached Beersheba with their entourages and met with Allon (who reported on the problems at Post 86). Yadin relayed Ben-Gurion's instructions about Faluja to Allon, and Allon expressed no reservations. Ben-Gurion observed a Negev battalion setting out for battle and, even though the battalion's members sang Palmah songs, he was favorably impressed by their good spirits and high morale, as well as the welcome they had given him in his balaclava.[103] On 25 December 1948, the Southern Front's headquarters issued a "liquidation" order for the Faluja Pocket. It was a simple plan: the pocket was to be "softened up" by several days of massive artillery fire and then taken. The mission fell to the Alexandroni Brigade and auxiliary forces[104] and they broke through at Iraq al-Manshiya, the scene of battle in Operation Yoav. One battalion managed to consolidate a foothold in the village. Soon, however, Egyptian reinforcements arrived from the south, from Faluja, with armored cars and artillery and waged a smart counteroffensive. It was led by Major Abd-al-Hakim Amar, who later became a field marshal.[105] An IDF company found itself under heavy fire with no way of retreat. Trapped in the village, it was totally wiped out. Everything that could have gone wrong in battle did. It had the largest casualty toll of any single battle of the War of Independence—ninety dead, dozens wounded.[106]

Yet it scarcely left a mark on the national memory. Latrun was commemorated in songs, stories, and countless reports. Iraq al-Manshiya—where the IDF had been twice burned, the second time very badly—was forgotten. Allon's lectures on Operation Horev did not mention it. The memoirs of other contemporaries focus instead on the impressive breakthrough to Sinai. The Alexandroni Brigade's marginal campaign earned no publicity. The brigade soldiers themselves preferred not to dwell on it. Allon could hardly reproach the Alexandroni Brigade since it had operated on the Southern Front and under his command. But his attention had been elsewhere. He was forging ahead with the Eighth Brigade and the Negev Brigade. The mistake was that the HGS and Southern Front's headquarters had so casually agreed to Ben-Gurion's instruction to add the pocket's liquidation to Operation Horev. In the case of Latrun, Ben-Gurion could be blamed for having ordered the ill-fated battle contrary to the opinion of the HGS and the commanders of the Palmah. Latrun thus became the subject of myth, adopted in turn by one group after another according to the spirit of the times. In the case of Iraq al-Manshiya, in contrast, Ben-Gurion, the Southern Front, and the Alexandroni Brigade all had a hand in the debacle—and a common interest in avoiding publicity.

On the eve of Operation Horev, Allon, as directed by the CGS,[107] issued a "special addendum to the Order for Operation Horev." The document reflected the lessons learned by the IDF's command from "several shameful incidents that took place in the past on our and other fronts." The moral breakdown at Dawayima stung and a reaction from the senior level was imperative. The question of booty was secondary this time. The two main topics were prisoners and civilian populations. "The civilian population in enemy territory is not to be harmed except in clear cases of self-defense." To drive home the severity, the document warned: "Unjustified killing of civilians will be treated as murder during legal process. Torment or abuse of peaceful civilians will be met with a sharp response." Also prominent now were HGS orders against expelling Arab populations: "Arab populations must not be expelled from their habitations without special permission from the front's battle HQ." This was the first time that the question of prisoners was officially institutionalized: "The aim is to maximize the number of prisoners from the enemy army and, wherever the security of our units permits, to avoid killing them at the time of capture. From the moment that they are taken captive, they must receive kind and humane treatment."[108] Operation Horev took place in the desert. While there was almost no contact with civilian populations, it seems to have been the first operation involving hundreds of prisoners. As the war developed into an Israeli campaign against a regular army, the treatment of prisoners became more and more significant.

There were two known cases of prisoners being killed during Operation Horev: one, at Iraq al-Manshiya; the other, at Bir et-Tmila. Right after the battle at Iraq al-Manshiya, there was much talk among civilians in nearby settlements of the Alexandroni Brigade's terrible losses. The defeat was pinned on carelessness and inept command. But there were also rumors that after the Egyptians had raised their hands in surrender at Iraq al-Manshiya, soldiers of the Alexandroni Brigade had opened fire at them. The Egyptians defended themselves desperately, inflicting heavy losses on Alexandroni's forces.[109] In the campaign log of the Southern Front, the defeat at Iraq al-Manshiya was mentioned laconically. The number of dead was not given. The report was followed by a comment that reinforced the rumors: "It has come to our attention that in a number of cases, enemy soldiers who came to surrender were shot. In one case, the enemy soldiers went on fighting and tipped the scales after refusing to lay down their arms." The log continued: "We again warn our people against repeating such incidents. The enemy will lay down his arms sooner if he knows that he will not be harmed. Hurting prisoners will cost us unnecessary casualties."[110] Again, the attempt to institute humane conduct cited expediency.

The other case, at Bir et-Tmila, took place when one of the posts passed from hand to hand in battle. Four wounded soldiers from the "French Commando" were left there during the retreat. When the post was retaken, their disfigured bodies were found. In retaliation, soldiers of the "French Commando" burst into the infirmary, overpowered the medics, and killed two wounded prisoners.[111] This was the only official report on the killing of prisoners. After the operation, an intelligence officer could report with satisfaction: "In general, the order of the front commander on the humane treatment and non-killing of prisoners had been upheld," except in the above case. At the same time, there were reports of plundering goods and money from prisoners, eliciting a speedy reaction from the front's commander.[112] The more the war came to resemble a battle between two regular armies, the more attention was paid to accepted, civilized norms of conduct in war.

The Faluja Pocket remained surrounded until an armistice agreement was reached with Egypt at the end of February 1949 in Rhodes. Despite a lengthy siege and having been under shelling and bombardment by day and by night, the Egyptians refused to surrender. The Sudanese commander, Colonel a-Sayed Taha Bey, waged a wise campaign, protecting his men. Attempts by Allon and his fellow commanders to seduce him into an honorable surrender failed: he was resolved not to budge.[113] The Faluja Pocket was the school for a number of officers who were to cause a revolution in Egypt, among them, Gamal Abdel Nasser and Amar. The men were consumed by hunger. One of them accompanied Sadat to Israel in 1977 and recalled that the Israelis would throw them oranges out of pity, and they would eat the peels as well.[114] Following the campaigns in the Negev, Allon regarded the Egyptian army with respect. He had learned the hard way that they were a professional army who chose to fight tenaciously rather than flee. Their greatest strength lay in defense. They were unremarkable in surprise maneuvers or actions. But if their equilibrium was not upset by surprise or diversion, they fought well.[115] To a large extent, Egypt's consent to talks in Rhodes stemmed from the recognition that in the absence of an agreement with Israel, it would fail to extricate the brigade. For the same reason, Israel refused to allow the brigade to emerge until an agreement was signed. Nevertheless, Israel was unable to overpower the brigade. In time, during the siege of the Egyptian Third Army in Sinai in 1973, one of the veterans of Faluja told his fellow soldiers to have no fear: from his experience in 1948, he had learned that the United Nations would ultimately rescue them. There was a certain similarity between the two situations. In neither case was there a clear winner or loser, facilitating the move toward negotiations.

The battles ended. It was now up to the diplomats to negotiate the armistice's conditions. Yadin was sent to the talks as Israel's senior military figure. Rabin was sent to protect the achievements of the Southern Front. It was anticipated that the talks would take a few days. They stretched beyond a month. Egypt's opening position was a demand for an Egyptian governor in Beersheba and the withdrawal of Israeli troops from the conquests of the last two operations. Israel countered by asking that the Egyptians evacuate the Gaza Strip. These were clearly unrealistic positions and the two sides soon came close to common ground. The main controversy touched on Auja al Hafir (Nizannah). Egypt, with the support of the UN mediator Ralph Bunch, who had succeeded Count Bernadotte, demanded that a large chunk of the area be demilitarized and handed over to the United Nations for international supervision. Rabin, young and bashful, roamed the chambers of diplomacy, embarrassed and ineffectual. He did not see any reason to yield to the Egyptians since Israel could afford to be patient on key issues while the Egyptians were under pressure because of their besieged brigade at Faluja. He needed Allon's support and advice, fearing that a decision would be adopted contrary to his judgment and that, against his will, he would be compelled to add his signature to an agreement he found unacceptable. Allon was worried about the Auja sector; to his mind, if it were relinquished to the United Nations it would one day come under English or Egyptian rule. He considered this a "serious danger to our chances to control the southern Negev up to the (Red Sea) gulf, which is most of the Negev and our chief wish." But his long-term concern was about Egyptian rule in Gaza, on the one hand, and Jordanian rule on Mount Hebron, on the other: should the day come that the two joined forces against Israel, they could resort to a large pincer movement against the Israelis. He believed that the two arms, or at least one of them, had to be crushed. He added a pregnant comment: "I prefer to rout the mountain [Mount Hebron]."¹¹⁶ Though his letter to Rabin contained both implicit and explicit assumptions that revealed his diplomatic limitations, it showed, for the first time, mature and comprehensive thinking about Israel's military problems.

On 24 February 1949 Israel and Egypt signed the Armistice Agreement. That day, Ben-Gurion wrote in his diary: "After the establishment of the state and our victories on the battlefield, this is the greatest event in a year of wonders."¹¹⁷ Allon's fears that Israel's government would cave in to Egyptian demands were exaggerated. According to the agreement, Auja remained in Israeli territory but was demilitarized: a large zone on both sides of the international border was the seat of the Israeli-Egyptian Armistice Commission and of the United Nations' Supervisors.

One of the clauses of the agreement related to some three thousand villagers from Faluja and Iraq al-Manshiya. Caught up in the intensive battles, they had somehow survived the fighting, bombardment, and hunger along with the Egyptian army. The Egyptians introduced a clause that they be allowed to remain unharmed.¹¹⁸ But Allon had other plans. He regarded the villages adjoining the Bet Jibrin, Majdal and Beersheba junction as a security threat. "I consider it necessary to evacuate the residents of the above villages," he informed the CGS and Yadin. "I am confident that with proper information and real assistance in conveying their property across the border, we will be able to persuade them to evacuate the villages voluntarily (relatively speaking of course)."¹¹⁹ The "persuasion" was accomplished by spreading rumors that their safety could not be ensured; they were known to have killed many of the Alexandroni Brigade's soldiers who had been trapped at Iraq al-Manshiya, and the friends of the dead sought revenge and might perpetrate a massacre.¹²⁰ Yadin rejected Allon's suggestion. He said it was contrary to the obligations Israel had committed to in the Armistice Agreement. "We accepted the conditions and signed, and we must honor it in full."¹²¹ Allon did not relent. In the coming days, he waged a mini-war with Yadin, who reiterated that "no harm is to be done to the persons or property of the Arab inhabitants remaining in the [Faluja] Pocket."¹²² But the psychological pressure on the inhabitants did not relax. Night after night, shots and intimidating cries were heard in the villages. On one occasion, some of Faluja's villagers were beaten. The conduct of the command of the Southern Front was hardly a secret: observers for the United Nations reported the beatings. Nor did the "rumor factory" escape notice. The agreement's violation roused Foreign Minister Moshe Sharett to write the CGS a very sharp letter. He noted that this was the first agreement between Israel and an Arab government. "Our intentions as a party to an international contract and our real ability as a government to abide by its conditions are at stake here," Sharett rebuked the CGS. Furthermore, the State of Israel was in the throes of difficult discussions with the United Nations on the problem of the Arab refugees. Israel claimed that it was not responsible for the problem, that the plight of the refugees was the result of the Arabs' offensive war against Israel. In the case of the two villages, which had fallen to Israel without a battle, the sincerity of the state's declarations was being tested. "Should we fail in this instance, the failure will harm our entire position on the question of the Arab refugees," Sharett stipulated. In addition, Sharett harshly condemned what he termed an "unacceptable initiative by the local command on a matter relating to the policy of the State of Israel." "It is inconceivable that someone in the army will act on his own authority in these matters," he objected.[123] Dori relayed the letter to Allon with a clear directive to stop the scare campaign. Allon was undeterred. The Arabs of Faluja and Iraq al-Manshiya despaired in the end and asked to be evacuated to Dhahiriya.[124] The case of Faluja received publicity because it ran counter to Israel's obligations. But Allon and the Southern Front adopted the same policy of nonviolent expulsion or "unfriendly persuasion" throughout the southern coastal plain and the northern Negev on the approaches to Bet Jibrin. Ben-Gurion was not a party to it, nor, however, did he come out against it. Yadin did not oppose it for he viewed it as a positive development. This may explain why Allon was not punished even though he ostensibly defied HGS directives.[125]

While Sharett was indirectly exchanging unpleasantries with the commander of the Southern Front, the major thrust began to Eilat and was named Operation Uvdah (Fact). The United Nations map of 29 November 1947 had earmarked the entire Negev, including Eilat, for the Jewish state. Since then Palestine's borders had changed in Israel's favor and it was legitimate to question whether that map was still valid. The Jordanians had their own plans for the southern Negev, with Jordanian forces controlling the eastern section with no Israeli presence up to Aqaba. And the British too showed an interest in the southern Negev as an overland bridge between Egypt, the Suez Canal, and the Arab expanses in the Middle East. Following the downing of the British aircraft, the British navy had dispatched a marine force to Aqaba, either as a show of strength to deter Israeli aggression against Transjordan or in preparation to gain control of the region.[126]

The Negev had held a fascination for the Yishuv's leaders since the 1930s. In April 1935, Ben-Gurion, Berl Kaztnelson and members of the JA-PD had set out to explore the Negev, not out of strategic considerations, but to scour the area for a place to settle millions of Jews. While the landscapes captivated them, they were disappointed by the scant water resources, which put an end to their hopes of intensive Jewish settlement. Yet the romance of Etzyon Gaber and the merchant fleet in the Red Sea; the connection to the queen of Sheba; and the dreams of copper and iron in the Negev's soil caused both youth and leaders to pine for the distant south. In time, their pining diverged. The leaders came to appreciate the importance of a wedge between the strongest Arab state and the Arabs in the east. The youth enthused over the desert, the desolation, the landscapes, the legends. Youth movements and the Palmah traced routes to Masada, Ein Gedi, Bet Ha-Aravah, Sodom—Jewish landmarks. They did not venture further south.[127] Only a handful made it to Eilat (Umm-Rashrash, as it was then known).

Between Operation Yoav and Operation Horev, a force from the Southern Front was sent out to take control of the Dead Sea shore up to Sodom. As part of this action, the force took over Kurnub and Ayn Husub (Hazevah). Allon feared that the capture of Ayn Husub on the Arava Road halfway to Eilat would alert the Arab Legion to advance patrols to capture posts on the road to Eilat. He therefore pressed his officers to take Eilat quickly at the same time. But only after Operation Yoav, during the Rhodes negotiations, did Allon receive authorization "for the conquest of the Israeli Gulf of Eilat by means of a 'quiet thrust'."[128]

Operation Uvdah (Fact), as the name implies, was meant to ensure sovereignty over areas that Israel claimed on the strength of the UN resolution. Two brigades were to set out southward, one along the Arava Road to Eilat; the other, over rough terrain to the Ramon Crater. Flat ground was located near the crater to serve as an airfield for supplies and airlifted reinforcements. The two brigades were to join up north of the Israeli Umm-Rashrash, that is, Eilat. The Golani Brigade was to take the Arava Road in the east; the Negev Brigade, the western route. In parallel, the Alexandroni Brigade, freed from guarding the Faluja Pocket after the evacuation agreement, was to capture points south of Mount Hebron as well as Masada and Ein Gedi, which were a seeming no man's land in no one's control.[129]

Israeli-British tensions had not subsided nor had Ben-Gurion's fear of British intervention. It seemed as if any Israeli provocation were liable to cause a conflagration. Ben-Gurion therefore approved the expedition on the condition that Allon pledge to avoid all clashes with the Arab Legion. In Rhodes, it was agreed that Israel would thin out its forces west of the Negev's midline, which followed a straight line from Beersheba to Eilat. In the south of the Negev triangle, however, the distance between the Egyptian and Jordanian sides was tiny and the topography made it difficult to observe a midline.[130] The thrust to Eilat was thus a source of thorny political problems. On the eve of the brigades' departure (5 March 1949), a messenger from the HGS brought the Southern

Front command an urgent dispatch: on no account were the forces to enter into face-to-face combat with the legion; if their advance involved any such clash, it was to be halted. Allon was asked to put his signature to the assurance. Because the High Command was aware of Allon's tendency to take liberties and "stretch" authorizations, the document was to be co-signed by the brigade commanders Nahum Sarig and Nahum Golan. It was a slap in Allon's face, although not entirely undeserved.[131] The order came straight from Ben-Gurion. After recovering from the insult, Allon wondered what would happen if they were attacked? After all, forces can't be sent to a sure death! Yadin added a proviso to the order: "except in self-defense." This tiny loophole in the order of the HGS allowed Allon to slip two brigades inside. He had no problem with Nahum Sarig, the commander of the Negev Brigade. There was an intuitive understanding between them, the fruit of years of working together. But he was unsure of Nahum Golan, a veteran of the British army, the disciple of a different school. It was his brigade that was to take the Arava route, which was dotted with the legion's positions. He found himself having to explain to Golan the nature of the loophole. Golan had a quick grasp. "I'll 'defend myself,'" he winked.[132]

The forces advanced according to plan. Apart from reporting an encounter between the Golani Brigade and an enemy patrol, which opened fire and fled, Allon had nothing to say about skirmishes with enemy forces. A tactic evolved whereby forces approached and outflanked a manned post. If soldiers of the legion opened fire, the men were allowed to shoot back. But in most cases, when a unit the size of a platoon saw a column brigade coming to outflank it, it chose to abandon the site rather than engage the enemy. Allon requested a change in the instructions to permit attack on the legion's forces that had captured posts in Israeli territory. The request was rejected: "There is to be no deviation, not even by even a hair's breadth, from the orders you were given." Allon stepped up the pressure. Yadin informed him, "After receiving your letter I again consulted with the old man. Prior instructions remain unchanged." He did, however, add, "From the latest news, on the other hand, I feel that the problem may have solved itself."[133] The allusion was to intelligence reports that the Legion was evacuating Umm-Rashrash and Ras en-Naqb (two outposts in territory slated for Israel) and pulling back to Aqaba.[134] The Golani Brigade captured Ayn-Ghadyan. Meanwhile, the Negev Brigade column reached the cliffs above the Gulf of Eilat without incident, a distance of some 14 kilometers from the bay as the crow flies.[135] The two brigades were meant to reach the bay simultaneously and share the honors. But now the Negev Brigade took the initiative. Instead of waiting on the cliffs, members of the brigade struck up a conversation with the Egyptian sergeant man-

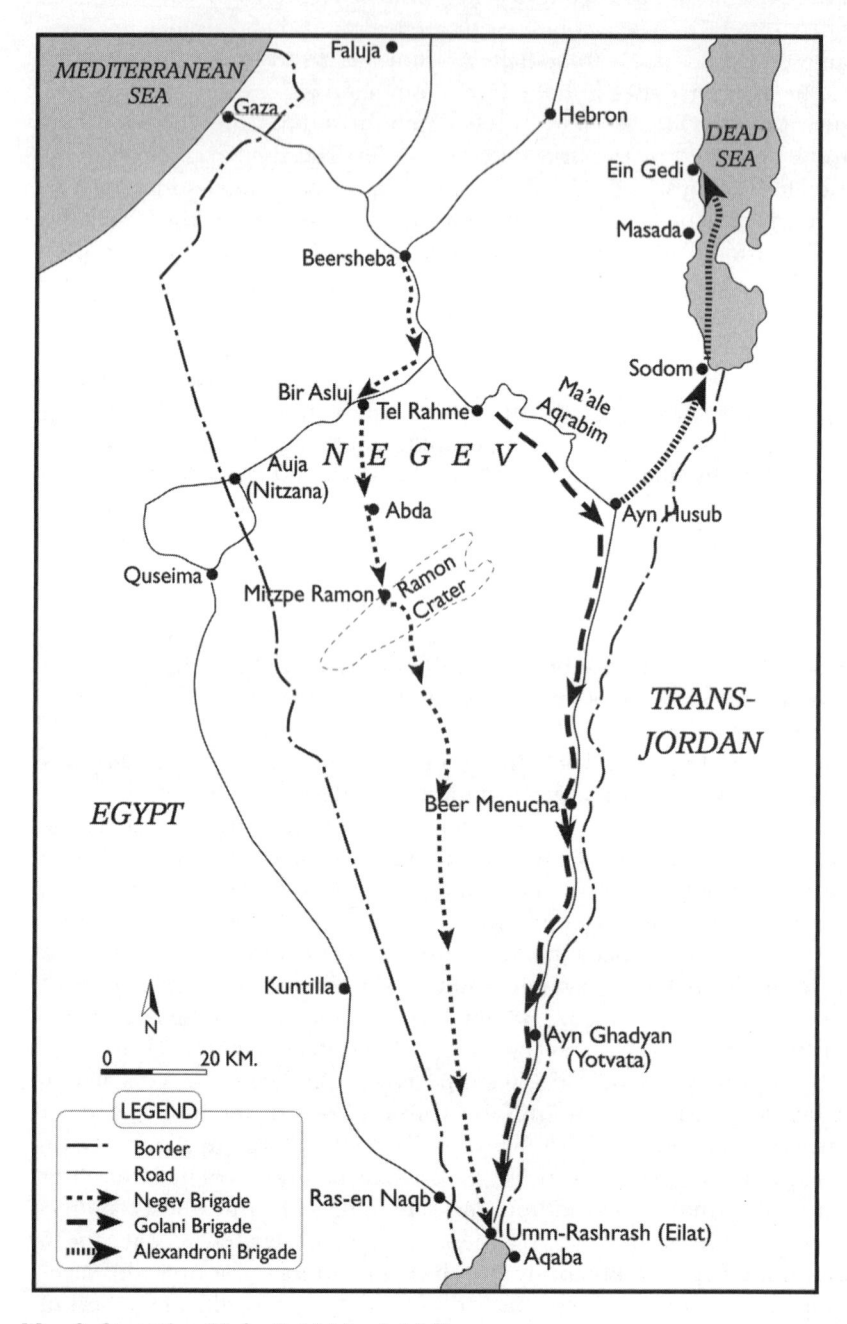

Map 6. Operation Uvda, 6–10 March 1949

ning the border station at Biqat Ha-Yare'ah (Moon Valley). An Arabic-speaking officer was sent to the border station with a white flag to make the peaceful intentions clear. He was welcomed. After a friendly exchange as befits the representatives of two states that had signed an armistice, the Israeli officer asked him to allow the brigade passage through Egyptian territory. The sergeant agreed though he wanted to get the permission of his superiors. The officer made it plain that it was not a good idea: What would happen if the request were denied opposite so large an Israeli force? The Egyptian understood. He agreed on two conditions: that the Israelis return the courtesy and allow him to convey vehicles to the border station at Taba through Israeli territory, and that he would not have to raise the barrier, meaning the Israelis would circumvent it. And so it was. The Negev Brigade took the high road and was the first brigade to reach Eilat, much to the chagrin of the Golani Brigade. The Golani Brigade followed orders and was too late.[136]

On 11 March 1949 Uvdah became a fact on the ground as well. Yadin telegrammed Allon, "Heartfelt congratulations. A great day for us all."[137] Ben-Gurion wrote in his diary, "We have reached Eilat. This is perhaps the greatest event of the past months, if not of the entire war of liberation and conquest. And not a single drop of blood was spilled!"[138] The tidings joined other good news: the Alexandroni Brigade, as the additional arm of Operation Uvdah, had captured the foothills of Mount Hebron, Ein Gedi, and Masada. These were the last exploits of the War of Independence in the south.

The operation had a few "epilogues." First, the Egyptians complained about the infringement on their sovereignty. Allon denied any trespassing prior to the descent from the cliffs and touched up the account somewhat: the initiative to convey the vehicles had been the sergeant's and the Israelis had agreed to it as a one-time gesture,[139] an act of friendly cooperation between neighbors. Second, following the complaint by the Golani Brigade's troops that the Negev Brigade had grabbed the Eilat crown from their heads, the brigade commanders were summoned to the front commander "for a preliminary clarification of the accusations voiced here and there about the entry of the Twelfth Brigade to Umm-Rashrash before the First Brigade not according to plan."[140] No doubt Allon used his charm to straighten things out. He owed it to Golan for his conduct during the operation.[141] Third, a crime always leaves traces. When the Southern Front's headquarters summed up the ammunition issued to the Golani Brigade for its outflanking maneuvers along the Arava border, the quantity could not be explained away as purely defensive. So, to avoid embarrassing questions, the headquarters did not report the full amount. Instead, for the next half year it inflated the quantities issued for training.[142] Rabin testified that there had been a number of clashes with the Arab Legion. He believed that if Allon had obeyed orders to the letter, the brigades would not have reached Eilat. In the reports of the Operations Branch and the headquarters of the Southern Front there is no mention of this, but merely Allon's repeated attempts to obtain authorization for attack. Yadin seems to have known what was happening and did not reprove Allon. He did regard Allon's behavior as a breach of discipline, but also as the desirable, necessary initiative of a field commander who always strove to perform over and beyond the mission. If Ben-Gurion suspected that his orders had not been honored in spirit, he showed no disapproval. On his visit to Eilat a few months later, he was content, cheerful, indulgent: the war was over, Eilat was in Israeli hands. It was the last moment of grace in the relations between Ben-Gurion and Allon.

Figure 17. The golden hero: Allon, the commander of the Southern Front, 28 March 1949. Photographer: Hugo Mendelsohn. Courtesy of the Israeli Government Press Agency.

Figure 18. Reviewing an honor guard with President Chaim Weizmann in Beersheba, 30 March 1949. Photographer unknown. Courtesy of the Israeli Government Press Agency.

Figure 19. Watching the parade of the Givati Brigade in Rehovot, spring 1949. From left to right: Yigal Allon, Shimon Avidan, Yigael Yadin, David Ben-Gurion, and Ya'acov Dori. Photographer: Fred Chesnik. Courtesy of the Allon House Archives, Ginossar.

Figure 20. Yigal Allon addressing the 12th Brigade in Tel Nof, at the end of the war, 5 May 1949. Standing behind him are Yitzhak Sadeh and Uzi Narkiss. Photographer Unknown. Courtesy of the IDF Archives.

Chapter 11
Triumph and Tragedy

After learning that Operation Uvdah had succeeded, Ben-Gurion wrote in his diary: "Has the time come for the Northern Triangle [the populated Arab area of Samaria]? Much will be decided by the Rhodes talks."[1] Negotiations were in progress with Jordan's King Abdullah. Since the end of November the two sides had agreed to a "a sincere and full cease-fire" and were discussing an armistice agreement. Ben-Gurion believed that Israel had achieved as much as possible in the given political conditions. At times, he feared that it had overstretched itself, that it might evoke the anger of the Western powers, which he regarded as the country's long-term political mainstay even though the Soviet Union had supported Israel's establishment and helped arm its military. He looked ahead to building the country and absorbing mass immigration. This meant shifting the center of gravity from military to economic endeavors. Prepared to risk far more than what military personnel considered acceptable, he sought to disperse the hugely expensive large army and set Israel on the road to peace. He was therefore pleased by the progress in the negotiations with King Abdullah.

But when negotiations veered from the Israeli scenario, an order went out on 11 March 1949 to prepare for a "tooth for a tooth" campaign to take over the small triangle (Tira-Taibeh-Qalansawa), namely the range of hills overlooking the coastal plain. About two weeks later, Israel and Transjordan reached an armistice agreement: Jordan was to gain the West Bank; the Iraqis, positioned in Samaria, were to fold up quietly, and Israel was to gain Wadi Ara, including the over-hanging hills from the south, and the first ridge of Samarian Hills dominating the coastal plain.

Allon did not question the armistice agreement with Egypt. Jordan was another matter. He would have liked to conquer the land of Israel up to the Jordan River. There were several reasons for this. First was the topography: western Palestine was dominated by the Judean and Samarian Hills, which sat above the lowlands and the coastal plain. It did not require a military genius to grasp Israel's vulnerability if this territory, soon to be called the "West Bank" by the reconstituted Kingdom of Jordan, were ceded. Second, there was the Anglo-Jordanian Treaty: Allon's experience in operations Horev and Uvdah only confirmed his suspicions about the British and added to his hostility; he appeared more anti-British than ever. There seemed to him to be a real danger that the British would use any pretext connected with Transjordan to punish Israel or to win control of the southern Negev.²

He was not alone in regarding the Jordan River as Israel's natural eastern border. Speaking to officers, Moshe Dayan, the commander of Jerusalem at the time, announced, "We must take the triangle; otherwise the State of Israel will not be able to survive." His words nonplussed his Mapai listeners, who wished to know: "What is really our party's political platform on borders and territorial arrangements?"³ The incident corroborates Allon's assertion that "to the best of [his] knowledge, this is more or less the opinion of most of the top officers in the army regardless of political or party outlook."⁴

The opinion strayed from the strictly military purview, which made Allon uneasy about putting it to the political leadership. Nevertheless, he plucked up courage and approached Ben-Gurion directly "on a matter I consider fateful." After outlining the main principles, he suggested that all of western Palestine be taken quickly, for the time was ripe: at that moment, the military balance with Transjordan was in Israel's favor. This advantage, however, would increasingly be lost as the IDF downsized and the Arab armies grew stronger. Consequently, Allon stated, "Let's utilize the tremendous effort we have made to reap its fruit to the maximum. In this respect, time is not on our side." He got to the heart of the matter: One question rarely voiced explicitly but couched in hints and innuendos was the question of the Arab population in conquered territories. Allon took the bull by the horns. He assumed that in war a large part of the Arab population would withdraw eastward. Based on prior experience, he suggested that the planned attack leave an escape route for the retreating army and the accompanying population. For Arabs who would choose to stay, he claimed, "We will likely find a way to allow them to live in dignity without posing a military danger to us."⁵ In an analysis a year later, after he had shed his uniform and stood before a civilian forum, he made his position clearer, as will be recalled: "Had it happened that by completing the country's liberation up to the boundary of the west [bank] of the Jordan, there would have been an exodus of additional Arab population and their relocation to neighboring Arab countries, this would not, as such, have been historical injustice; it would have been a historic opportunity that fell into our laps—not thanks to us, but used by us to solve this problem, which would have remained a tough problem for a long time, both politically and militarily." While the agreements signed with Abdullah did give Israel a dominant ridge, they were not good enough: "The topographical improvement of our borders in the Sharon was the bait we fell for, but thirty thousand Arabs living on the borders are the hook." Allon regarded the armistice agreement with Abdullah as a historical mistake, a missed opportunity that would not come again.[6] After his discharge from the military, he would frequently say, "We won the war but lost the peace."

The conquest of the area west of the Jordan was a bone of contention between Allon and Ben-Gurion. On one side of this contest was Ben-Gurion, the veteran, the seasoned statesman, a confirmed prophet of doom, a product of Jewish weakness and the protean effort to shake it off. In the new realities of 1949, he was left marveling at the year of wonders that had achieved more than he had ever imagined in his rosiest dreams—and he was not given to rosy dreams. It seemed to him that to conquer the area west of the Jordan was to temp fate, to gamble arrogantly with Israel's future. Ben-Gurion was prepared to "peer into the abyss" and take existential risks at fateful moments, but he was not prepared to play Russian roulette. If he could obtain by agreement what he considered the necessary minimum, he preferred that alternative to war. On the other side of this contest was Allon, a young general who did not know the meaning of failure. He saw no reason to limit expansion other than military capability or political aims. Politically, Ben-Gurion rightly understood the limits of power and the importance of restraint: what is forgiven the weak is not forgiven the strong. Militarily, Allon rightly claimed that the War of Independence had furnished Israel with a one-time opportunity to take the area west of the Jordan. In the public climate of 1949, war-related population movements, expulsions, and evacuations were part of the political order in the aftermath of World War II and the world might have accepted the mass flight or expulsion of the Arab population. From the point of view of "raisons d'état," the young Allon, pragmatic and morally uninhibited, may have analyzed the situation accurately. It remains a moot point, for this course of action was not taken.

Ben-Gurion did not speak of expelling Arabs, either as a policy or as a possibility. He was surrounded by numerous people during the War of Independence; none of them ever testified to his active involvement in the displacement of Arabs to solve a demographic problem rather than as a consequence of war.[7] Rabin recalled a discussion of the HGS in 1955 in which he and Uzi Narkiss had contended that Israel's greatest long-term security problem was the eastern sector, although Egypt posed a more severe political and military threat. Ben-Gurion had lashed out at them: they did not understand, he said, that the real danger was from Nasser and Egypt. He referred to the War of Independence as though he were continuing his argument with Allon in Allon's absence. There was a limit, he said, to what Israel could have achieved in the war. The world would not have consented to so small a community, as Israel was, ruling over so many Arabs. Even then, he did not mention the option of expulsion.[8] Allon, in contrast, considered Ben-Gurion's policy a surrender to political pressure from Western powers, forfeiting the fruit of victory.

The claim of collusion between Israel and Abdullah in the War of Independence has over the years become an entrenched myth voiced by spokesmen of the Far Left and slowly permeating the historiography. This claim originates in the dispute between Allon and Ben-Gurion. Allon and his young peers in Israel's Left of the 1950s interpreted Ben-Gurion's relative caution and reluctance to attack on the eastern front as emanating from an agreement concluded between Israel and Jordan.[9] Of all the Arab leaders, Abdullah was the only one with whom Israel's leaders had reached an understanding before the War of Independence. It included Israel's tacit compliance with his takeover of the area earmarked for an Arab state west of the Jordan River. The entire understanding, however, was washed away in canon roar when the Arab Legion bombarded Jerusalem in the war, and in the din of battle for Latrun, where the legion blocked the road to Jerusalem. From then on, it was a different ball game, one based on military capability rather than prior understandings. Each side fought to the hilt to defeat the other. In the last stages of the war, Israel did not fully utilize its military options. But this restraint was not a function of any secret agreements; it stemmed from Ben-Gurion's assessment of the situation. Obviously, his assessment took into account the history of prewar relations with Abdullah. For Allon and his adherents, this was another of Ben-Gurion's surrenders to imperialist forces. In history, ideas have a life of their own: thus, an idea born of the frustration of a patriotic military commander, who was not allowed to seize all of the land up to the Jordan River, in time became the cornerstone of a post-Zionist doctrine to prove Israel's "sin" in 1948, in thwarting the establishment of a Palestinian state.[10]

After the agreement with Jordan was signed, on 3 April 1949, the Southern Front's headquarters became irrelevant. The army was in the process of demobilization. Orders from HGS arrived daily on cutting down battalions, manpower, and headquarters. The regular Palmah brigades became reserve brigades; the soldiers were discharged. Gone were the days of glory between one operation and another, the excitement of opening new frontiers and changing the map of Israel. It was a time of small deeds. Allon busied himself seeing to the needs of the men formerly under his command: he helped one obtain a flat, another a new position, a third a position on the roster for settlement.

At the end of January 1949, Israel held its first elections. Out of a total of 120 Knesset seats, Mapai won 46; Mapam 19. It was not a bad showing for Mapam, the second-largest party. But it had apparently hoped for more: the party's leaders, true to their wishful thinking, had sought to challenge Ben-Gurion's rule. The party nevertheless emerged strong enough for Ben-Gurion to regard it as a real threat. The election campaign left a residue of suspicion and grievances. At the HGS meeting of 17 January 1949, Ben-Gurion condemned the fact that a military commander at an election rally had criticized orders he had received. The allusion was to Allon, and the order was the retreat from Sinai. That same day, an advertisement appeared in *Davar* accusing Allon of revealing military secrets at an election rally. Allon rejected the charges outright. He referred his accusers to members of Mapai who had heard him and found his words fitting and fair.[11] There was no denying Allon's electoral assets: a young and handsome commander, he projected authority and spoke a native Hebrew unlike other members of Mapam. These assets were exploited in the election campaign. But the very qualities that pleased his party comrades awakened Ben-Gurion's suspicions and animus. The attitude filtered down to lower ranks identified with Ben-Gurion who were eager to ingratiate themselves with the High Command.

In the autumn of 1948, amid the Palmah's dismantling, Ruth and Yigal Allon produced a son, Yiftah. They had been nervous about having another child since Nurit's birth, in case the source of her problem was genetic. Apparently, following fruitless attempts to have her seen by an expert in the summer and fall of 1947, the couple decided to take their chances. Yiftah developed normally and was a joy to his parents. But Nurit became more difficult to handle. She was nine by now and it was harder to control her conduct. Her presence in the home together with the baby became impossible and even dangerous. Yigal and Ruth made the painful decision to place her in an institution, and a search began for a suitable facility. After checking out centers in Israel and in Switzerland, an institution was located in Abderdeen, Scotland; it was reputed to be responsible and pedagogic, and it might even improve her condition somewhat. Moreover, the cost was relatively reasonable. Galili enlisted to get the KM to finance the child's keep, and Tabenkin too was involved. This privileged treatment no doubt raised eyebrows in the kibbutz: it was not every special-needs child who got to live in Scotland at the kibbutz's expense. To lend the arrangement the seal of approval, the intercession of the two men was vital.[12] Allon had struggled so hard the previous summer not to turn to the movement for support. Now he realized that he had no choice. He received assistance from the army as well. Though his trip to Scotland was presented as private, he was asked to use the opportunity for an introduction to British officers and, if possible, a military tour. The IDF was thus able to defray travel expenses.[13] To flesh out the military aspect, Allon asked that tours be arranged of other European armies as well. Since Yadin had been on a study tour in Switzerland, Dori suggested that a tour of the French army be arranged for Allon.[14]

On 15 August 1949 the IDF announced that Major General Yigal Allon was taking two months' personal leave and that his deputy, Lieutenant Colonel Yitzhak Rabin, would be filling in for him as commander of the Southern Front.[15] In early September, the Allons (Yigal, Ruth, and Nurit) traveled to London and from there to Aberdeen. They were impressed by the institution but the parting was a wrench. "I do not believe that there was another way open to us and yet we hope," Allon tried to describe his feelings.[16] After leaving the child in Aberdeen, Ruth returned home, and Allon embarked on his meetings with figures in the British Foreign Office and the War Office. British curiosity was whetted by the Israeli general crowned in military laurels, and the encounter had its piquant moments: Allon, who had only recently considered the British to be evil personified, now sat in the British War Office pleasantly and politely conversing with the devil's deputies and even relishing a meal with them. It was an important lesson in statesmanship. There was no chance of Allon visiting military installations or conducting a study tour of the British army. The reason was Israel's neutrality in the Cold War. Ben-Gurion, addressing the Knesset on the conscription law, had announced that Israel was prepared to send its officers for higher training in both the East and in the West. Moreover, the British made it plain that they had learned that Mapam, a party with pro-Soviet and even communist leanings, wielded considerable influence in the army. Allon could hardly believe that they thought Mapam and Israel would share sensitive information with the Soviets. "In their view, Mapam is a communist party or at least a satellite receiving orders from the Comintern," Allon wrote with surprise and irony.[17] The necessary conclusion was that Israel's policy of neutrality posed an impediment to its admittance to the club of Western states. The second subject that likely surprised him was the openness with which the British spelled out Britain's Middle East policy. Though there were people in the British military who accepted Israel's existence as a fait accompli and believed it had the strongest army in the Middle East, the fact remained that the balance of forces was in favor of the Arabs: "The reasons for your victory over Arab states derive more from their weakness than your strength. The causes of the victory are not permanent and can change. Time is in favor of the Arabs and there is no doubt that after training the military and educating the nations, they will be able to resume the war with better odds since it must not be supposed that they will repeat past mistakes and, in any case, fifty million are more than one or even five [million]."[18] Allon spared no effort trying to persuade his interlocutors that they were wrong about Mapam, Israel's neutrality, and the Israel-Arab balance of forces. He pulled out the old socialist-Zionist argument that Arab hostility was due to the Arabs' fear of Israel's social progress: "There is no doubt that Arab progress would be a factor of peace between us," he declared with the assurance of a neophyte in international relations.[19] On this trip, Allon learned to appreciate the beauty of London and the cultural treasures it offered visitors, and he even grew fond of the English. The climax of the trip was a lengthy stay at the home of the military expert Basil Liddel-Hart. The journalist Jon Kimche escorted him and acted as interpreter. Liddel-Hart was well-versed in the War of Independence and generous in his praise for Allon and his advice for the IDF. "In many areas, his military thinking is just like ours," Allon marveled, "as if reared in the school of Yitzhak Sadeh."[20] Liddel-Hart recommended that Allon and his colleagues acquire academic military training while retaining the unorthodox, original components of their military thinking.[21]

The evaluations Allon wrote after the trip were more lucid and reasoned than might have been expected considering his difficulties with English, his limited education, and the fact that this was his first exposure to the world of statesmanship. He did not succumb to animosity toward the British nor was he bowled over by their pleasant manners. In his judgment, the British were reconciling themselves to the war's outcome and their policy remained pro-Arab, but within several months it would be possible to promote mutual relations. Allon left his hosts with a good impression. They invited him to stay in touch when he visited his daughter, though no more than this because of Israel's pro-Soviet cloud. As a consolation prize for turning down his military tour, it was suggested that he watch the changing of the guard at Buckingham Palace. His escort, an Israeli diplomat, replied that Allon was not an Indian maharaja but a professional soldier and it was doubtful that he would find it interesting.

The whole while that he was in London, Allon had no certainty that his tour of the French army would materialize. He landed in Paris on 30 September 1949 and was met by an Israeli envoy who deposited him at a rather expensive hotel. When Allon protested, the diplomat informed him that "there was to be no lowering of standards lest this damage Israel and its army in the eyes of the nations."[22] The French Foreign Ministry advised him that the French army was prepared to host him and show him whatever it could. His pleasure at the news was tempered by a telegram from Yitzhak Sadeh announcing that the Palmah rally had been set for 15 October and demanding that he attend. It was clear to

Allon that he could not return on time. His military tour was to begin only on 10 October. After having imposed on Dori to arrange the tour and after the French hosts had tailored a program to his request, it was inconceivable that he "get up and run away before carrying out the plans." But he was no stranger to the Palmah's pressure and KM public opinion, and he added: "I'm in a great quandary in case my friends at home fail to understand my situation here."[23] He wrote to Sadeh, Galili, and other close associates, and he was apprehensive about their reactions. Sadeh dispatched another telegram insisting on his attendance. Allon was determined to see the visit through to the end. He wished his friends well and continued the trip. As far as he was concerned, this was his one opportunity to tour France and Algeria, and he was unwilling to forego the pleasure even if it meant incurring their wrath.

On 10 October Allon celebrated his birthday in Paris. He was thirty-one years old. Palmah veterans who were in Paris at the time as well as Israeli diplomats gathered for a festive meal. "If I am not mistaken, this is the first time in my life that my birthday is being marked by a celebration," he told Ruth. Aware of her puritan disdain for embellishment or self-aggrandizement, he noted: "I am sure that you know I am not at fault this time."[24] It was a benevolent interlude. Allon was enveloped in the admiration of his peers, enjoyed the respect of generals, and basked in a pinch of luxury. Only thirty-one, he was regarded the senior field commander of the War of Independence, the architect of the borders of the State of Israel.

In Israel itself that day, the IDF's reorganization was announced. The fronts were done away with and replaced by geographic commands responsible for border security and regional administration. All other functions—molding the army's image; organizing a career army, a conscripted army, and a reserve force—were taken away from the commands and charged to an operational team.[25] The biggest blow, however, awaited Allon personally: the Southern Command went to Moshe Dayan. Allon learned of the appointment from his hosts, French officers, who congratulated him on his promotion; they assumed that if Dayan had taken his place, he would move up in the hierarchy.[26] Allon was not informed of the imminent change by his superiors. Following a telegram from a shocked Ruth, who queried him on it, he replied, "I knew nothing, I was surprised but am smiling. Show to friends."[27] It was one of Ben-Gurion's more brutal, merciless moves. The shock was complete. Allon's friends in Israel were beside themselves. Most, especially Rabin and Ruth, urged him to come home quickly.[28] But now, too, his typical lifelong reticence was evident. He made sure to appear indifferent. "Happily, I have long schooled myself not to take umbrage from the affronts of rivals and the small-minded." Rather than respond with sadness or insult, he continued to smile. He did not react to the dismissal and gave a number of reasons for this. First, he would not humiliate himself by entering into a duel with Ben-Gurion: "I will not combat knaves as if they were knights." Second, "I am not in the habit of making a 'noise' over personal matters nor am I pleased by the noise that others might be making over it." Third, his tour of France fascinated him: the French treated him wonderfully, accorded him the military respect of a general, took him on enriching military tours, and so forth. "I am not prepared to act like a child and throw all of this away because of distress, insults, and so on."[29] The first reason smacked of weakness even if it was dressed up in moral superiority. The second smacked of the KM; the need to conceal wounded pride and ambition as well as leadership aspirations in favor of personal modesty and self-negation for the collective good—all of this was the product of a kibbutz education, conditioning ambitious members to treat their strivings for power as a moral ill. The third reason smacked of the forsaken Mes'ha: the child that had been ashamed of his miserable home suddenly found himself the object of admiration and pampering by officers with aristocratic traditions who were well versed in the good life and well able to overwhelm a young visitor. For Allon, to throw all of this away in a dramatic show of anger was to act like "a spoiled child, beating himself up when insulted."[30] The French withheld no temptations: a tour of an Alpine division in beautiful, snow-capped Grenoble, tours of the infantry, and so forth. The high point was a journey to French units in Algeria on the border of the Sahara. It all looked like a picture book: the temperate climate so reminiscent of Israel, the landscape so like the Negev's, date palms, the desert. He even found himself rethinking colonialism. "It is interesting to see how a handful of French have managed to leave their mark on this huge continent; how on the one hand, they tyrannize and exploit, and, on the other, they bring benefit and civilization."[31] It was an unforgettable experience. But meanwhile, in Israel, matters were being decided, appointments made. In one letter, Ruth apparently did not spare him criticism of his lingering abroad. "Your last letter, which greatly gladdened me, disturbed me in one paragraph that is almost mocking," he wrote her. "But I know it is merely a slip of the tongue," he rushed to defend them both.[32] Rabin expressed his gladness that Allon was enjoying his visit but wondered at his "lack of reaction to the basic issue." He was inclined to attribute it to his "difficulties in written expression," hinting at Allon's fear that his letters were being read by a censor.[33]

Allon did not seem to be in any hurry to return home. Only at the end of November, some six weeks after his dismissal, did he board an Israeli ship. The sea journey, which lengthened his absence by a few days, was due to a promise he had made to employee of the security establishment, to bring back his car in return for which he would enjoy its use in Paris. Allon, it will be recalled, had a passion for cars, yet another weakness that raised eyebrows in the kibbutz. His delay appears to have signaled confusion, hesitation, and anxiety over the future. He needed a breather to collect himself and make fateful decisions. Ostensibly, everything was plain. Since the spring of 1949 it had been clear to him that he would have to consider his course, plan his next steps. The position of commander of the Southern Front, which was no longer a front, was frustrating, even deflating. It was time to move on. Even before setting out for Europe, he seems to have tentatively weighed the possibility of resigning from the Southern Front.[34] In one of his letters to Ruth before the dismissal, he spoke openly of an expected change in his life, warranting his early return. "I know that at home I face a serious, perhaps fateful, decision about what comes next; nor will delays and evasiveness make it any easier for me, but the contrary."[35] Ruth had been aware of Allon's doubts. Still, he had gone out of his way to make sure that Brigade Commander Rabin would fill in for him on the Southern Front.[36] In other words, he had acted as if he feared for his position and wished to ensure a way back.

Some of Allon's behavior after Operation Uvdah remains a partial mystery. At the end of March 1949, he had attended a dramatic meeting with prominent figures of the KM at Yitzhak Tabenkin's home in Kibbutz Ein Harod. The source of information for the meeting is a strongly worded letter from Yitzhak Ben-Aharon to Allon the day following. Since the military thrust to Eilat, Allon had dropped the usual ritual of "reporting" on military measures to the KM's institutions. He had also avoided talking to Ben-Aharon face to face. At this meeting, the cat was let out of the bag. "In the moral, public sense, you threw us a divorce writ," Ben-Aharon defined the essence of the meeting. Allon's criticism of his comrades and the movement's political path was lethal. "Your words in Tabenkin's room were a mortal blow to us all," Ben-Aharon wrote. Allon had declared that he could not change the face of the movement, which was in the grip of a pro-communist ideology, and he had therefore decided to quit. His words seemed to show greater understanding for Ben-Gurion's policy than for Mapam's.[37] A large portion of his bitterness was directed at Galili, whom he blamed for his lack of promotion in the army. His listeners were stunned. The plans of the KM leadership had earmarked an important position for him. The leaders had expected him to leave the army and devote himself to politics: "Surely, it could not have escaped you that in the long run we are not prepared to see you as a gifted commander or career soldier." For the first time, the country's youth had produced a young man fit to take his place in the movement's leadership. "You are no longer a private person—you are an asset of the movement and it is calling you to take your place." Resigning from the movement would be disastrous to him, Ben-Aharon wrote: "You are not without political instincts." Ben-Aharon did not take Allon's "divorce writ" as final. He attributed Allon's swerve to "passing confusion and misgivings about plunging into the abyss of political life." He concluded the letter with a call to Allon to accept the "verdict of the movement" and return to its path: "Yigal, take careful consideration and do not break with your friends. These old men who call on you and the dear, confused young men who are holding you back are one camp and they pass judgment on you." "Please, let us regard yesterday as if it never happened and go on from the day before," Ben-Aharon entreated.[38] Allon's plans—his "lone, solitary path," as described by Ben-Aharon—were not made explicit in the letter. Likely, he had expressed a desire either to study abroad on behalf of the army or maybe he intended to organize a movement of the young, the combatants of the War of Independence, with a platform that would be relevant to the state's current problems.

Ultimately, Allon listened to Ben-Aharon, although his friends were not sure that he had really and truly returned to the movement's bosom. Now, in October, when he refused to come home for the Palmah rally, Galili was worried that this might be "a deliberately symbolic act of parting."[39] Looking back, it was apparently Allon's only attempt to distance himself from the KM and try to redefine his identity, his place in the state, his path and position. The attempt failed. The movement's smothering embrace, including his home at Ginossar, was stronger than his ability to break away. He had already broken once with hearth and home, with a way of life, a tradition. Was he to do it a second time? The ethos of chivalry to which he was committed dictated loyalty: to cross the lines was more than a reflection of changing attitudes, reassessment, or a change of heart; it was a betrayal of one's principles and, above all, of one's friends. Allon's attempt to spread his wings and leave the KM sanctuary for the open spaces was nipped in the bud.

His outburst was not incidental. He had come to feel that his active membership in the KM was disqualifying him from positions he coveted. It seems that more than anything, Allon wished to continue in the military. That is where he had achieved glory, that is where he had proved his ability and talents, succeeding more than any other commander in the war. He was attracted by the position of CGS and he understood that in order to win it, he had to do two things: first, to study, to expand his horizons, to learn English; second, to cut the umbilical cord to Mapam. But he could not bring himself to undergo the necessary surgery. The stumbling block was not ideology, but his loyalty to his friends.

Ben-Gurion knew nothing of all this. Relations between the two men were fraught with tension, suspicion, and distrust. The dismantling of the Palmah was a clear signal to Allon that Ben-Gurion meant to diminish Mapam's influence in the army. The Cold War was at its height, the communists had scored a victory in China, and the Soviet Union was experimenting with the atom bomb. In this climate, the war of Gog and Magog looked near. Zionism's "romance" with the Soviet Union had reached its zenith in 1948 and was now on the wane. For political and economic reasons, and even because of the relationship with American Jewry, Israel patently needed the friendship of the United States. The Soviet Union could not be a substitute, nor did it wish to be. Ben-Gurion's gradual progression from neutrality to a pro-Western stance was not yet discernible, although the helm had already turned. In this delicate situation, he did not want his hands tied by Mapam. More and more, Mapam seemed to be careening leftward. It appeared to have lost its Zionist anchor, drifting toward foreign shores, and where it would stop was anybody's guess. As far as Ben-Gurion was concerned, once the military campaigns ended there was no longer any reason to suffer Mapam's power in the army.

The Palmah rally was held amid the upheavals of reorganization and Allon's dismissal. It was a gathering of former Palmahniks, their commanders, and their supporters. Some twenty-five to thirty thousand people turned up for the ceremony, among them about six thousand Palmahniks. It was a strong endorsement across political divides. For veterans of the Palmah, it was an instructive, elevating moment. Ben-Gurion himself had inadvertently added to its limelight: on his demand, the CGS ordered soldiers and officers in active service not to attend. The Palmah's Mapai members were torn by dual loyalties. Ultimately, apart from certain commanders, they too participated in the assembly. That evening, Rabin, as he was to recount, was summoned by Ben-Gurion, who did everything he could to waylay him. As a result, Rabin was late to take his place on the assembly stage and earned suspicious glances from his friends. After the assembly, Ben-Gurion wanted to punish the high-ranking offenders who had disobeyed CGS orders by demoting and imprisoning them. But he was dissuaded by wise men around him. Most of the officers who participated in the Palmah assembly received no more than a reprimand and a warning, except for those who showed impudence at the disciplinary hearing with the CGS and were dismissed from the army.[40]

During his conversation with Ben-Gurion that evening, Rabin brought up Allon's dismissal as an instance of improper conduct. The defense minister responded that Allon had made his continued service conditional on his being sent for further studies. Rabin remarked that, at that moment, nobody seemed prepared to accept Israeli officers for training, and "even if the intent is to send [someone] to study, the [person] replaced should be informed of the replacement before the order is issued." Ben-Gurion answered that before studying abroad Allon had much to study on his own; as for the dismissal, "He [Ben-Gurion] really thinks it was a mistake from the point of view of human relations."[41] With this statement Ben-Gurion played down the whole matter, ostensibly removing the political barb and placing it on the interpersonal plane. It is no secret that Ben-Gurion was not overly sensitive in human relations. But the manner of Allon's dismissal exceeded even his own standards. It was indigestible. His attitude towards Allon had known ups and downs. According to contemporaries, he too was charmed by Allon. He had a soft spot for the young; Teddy Kollek was one, Allon was another—he matched his ideal image of the sabra. He was aware of Allon's attempts to be clever and steal a march on him. He also knew Allon's attitudes regarding the West Bank. But Allon was no different from Dayan in this respect, and Ben-Gurion was not bothered in Dayan's case. All Allon's failings seem to have paled in comparison with the political issue: Allon drew his inspiration from a different source. Ben-Gurion had chosen to dismiss Allon so humiliatingly because he wished to put him in his place: if Allon wanted to stay in the army, he would have to decide where his primary loyalties lay.

Allon, at this stage, had not yet decided to leave the army. When he returned to Paris from Algeria, he met with Foreign Minister Moshe Sharett, who was on his way to Lake Success. Sharett suggested that Allon choose a position that would enable him to prepare for future functions and, meanwhile, not cut his ties to the IDF. He offered him the post of military attaché in London. Allon took the offer as an insult and an attempt by Ben-Gurion to get rid of him temporarily. He wrote to Ruth: "I myself am sure that the offer is the fruit of BG's highly conniving mind. It is inconceivable that Moshe would dare make me this miserable offer without the defense minister's explicit agreement. They are certainly evil geniuses. Nevertheless, I continue to smile and with greater self-confidence."[42]

It is not clear what his confidence was based on; it may have been a sham. Rabin reported to him that Dayan was ensconced as the commander of the Southern Front. According to Rabin, "The fellow does not have a real handle on the business; in my opinion, beyond a company or a battalion, he does not have a minimal military grasp; he is totally without tact in his approach to people."[43] Dayan wasted no time informing Rabin that he did not require Rabin's services. Along with Rabin, Sini Azaryahu and others were dismissed.[44] By the time Allon returned at the end of November, only a shadow remained of the Southern Front's headquarters that he had put together. He was invited to lecture on his trip to the officers of the Southern Front and to a farewell party organized in his honor and attended by Yadin, who had meanwhile been appointed CGS. The activities were arranged by Zvi Zur, the head of the new headquarters on Dayan's behalf.[45]

It was one of the most chaotic periods in the IDF's history, with intrigue and double-dealing rife among army commanders.[46] The purge of army officers identified with Mapam was in full swing. In Ben-Gurion's circles, word was circulated that Mapam personnel had been instructed by their leaders to quit the army. With respect to the KM, the claim was unfounded. Tabenkin, Ben-Aharon, Galili, and their colleagues regarded military service as a national mission to be upheld fiercely. Tabenkin did all he could to convince the young to stay in the army, but they did not believe in Ben-Gurion's army or that they could expect opportunities for promotion. That being the case, members of kibbutzim chose to go home. For others, especially the urbanites and the politically unaligned, the army was now an occupation, a career. It satisfied their need to feel that they were carrying out a national mission while seeing to their own interests.[47]

Before Yadin took over as CGS, he talked to Ben-Gurion about the round of senior appointments. He wanted Ben-Gurion to finalize the new appointments before he assumed office. One of these personnel decisions obviously related to Allon. Yadin respected and admired Allon, but he did not come to his defense. He asked Ben-Gurion to wrap up the affair without involving him. He too had been utterly stunned by the handling of Allon dismissal, although he did not find the fact itself—of Allon's replacement by Dayan—unacceptable. Anyone with eyes in his head could see that Allon had no future in the army.[48]

During the month of December 1949, Allon still wavered about leaving the army. The CGS was prepared to discuss a new position, but Allon's dismissal grated him and he demanded an explanation and clarification: did the defense minister trust him and believe in him, or was the manner of his dismissal a sign of Ben-Gurion's basic attitude? In the two talks Allon held with Ben-Gurion, all doubt was removed: "It was made clear to me that my movement and comrades were under heavy suspicion of disloyalty regarding state security and independence (this was told to me explicitly). It was further made clear to me that this was not simply a hostile theoretical definition, but that the theory had practical implications for the place of my movement's members in the army's development and the echelons of command." Allon believed that Ben-Gurion threw him a rope: if he were to reply that he did not share Mapam's leftist views, his place in the army would be assured. But if he identified with the "tainted," he would have no future in the army. At that moment, his loyalty to the movement and his rage at the suspicions took precedence over all other considerations.[49] In the letter of resignation he sent to Yadin after the talks, he declared: "I told the defense minister everything openly, and obviously in the present circumstances my work can bring no good. Not out of irresponsibility, but out of responsibility, I must resign from active service."[50] Ben-Gurion's casting of Allon and members of the KM as untrustworthy in terms of state loyalty, along with Allon's proud stance, donned the aura of a myth among Allon's KM admirers in the KM: Allon had been given a choice and he had chosen loyalty to his friends over his own military career. This myth, which affirms both the KM's loyalty to the state and Allon's loyalty to his friends, presupposes that Ben-Gurion had expected, wanted, and even hoped for a different answer from Allon. This is by no means certain. There was no real reason for Ben-Gurion to make politics the condition of Allon's continuation in the army. Other members of Mapam who stayed in the army were not asked to denounce their friends. Ben-Gurion did not suspect Allon himself, but he demanded that Allon declare his loyalty to him and renounce his loyalty to Galili and Tabenkin. Ben-Gurion seems to have deliberately put matters in such a way that Allon would have to resign, thus dispensing with the need to dismiss him. At best, Ben-Gurion was indifferent to whether or not Allon remained in the army. Had Allon responded differently and unexpectedly to Ben-Gurion's gambit, Ben-Gurion would still have had the upper hand: an Allon who detached himself, perhaps even betrayed, his friends would no longer be the same Allon. He would be a shorn Samson; his leadership wings would be clipped. There is no evidence that this is what Ben-Gurion expected or that Allon would have been receptive.

Dayan's appointment to the Southern Command revealed Ben-Gurion's tendencies to man senior military positions with people who were either loyal to Mapai or unaligned. Dayan, who had not made his mark in the War of Independence, now became Ben-Gurion's protégé and candidate for leadership from among the sabras. Allon, against his will, was shoved out of the military circle. One cannot help wondering what would have happened had Ben-Gurion been patient with him and not forced him to leave. Would Allon have exchanged Mapam for Mapai in the coming years? It is not unreasonable. But like all unrealized historical options, it remains pure speculation.

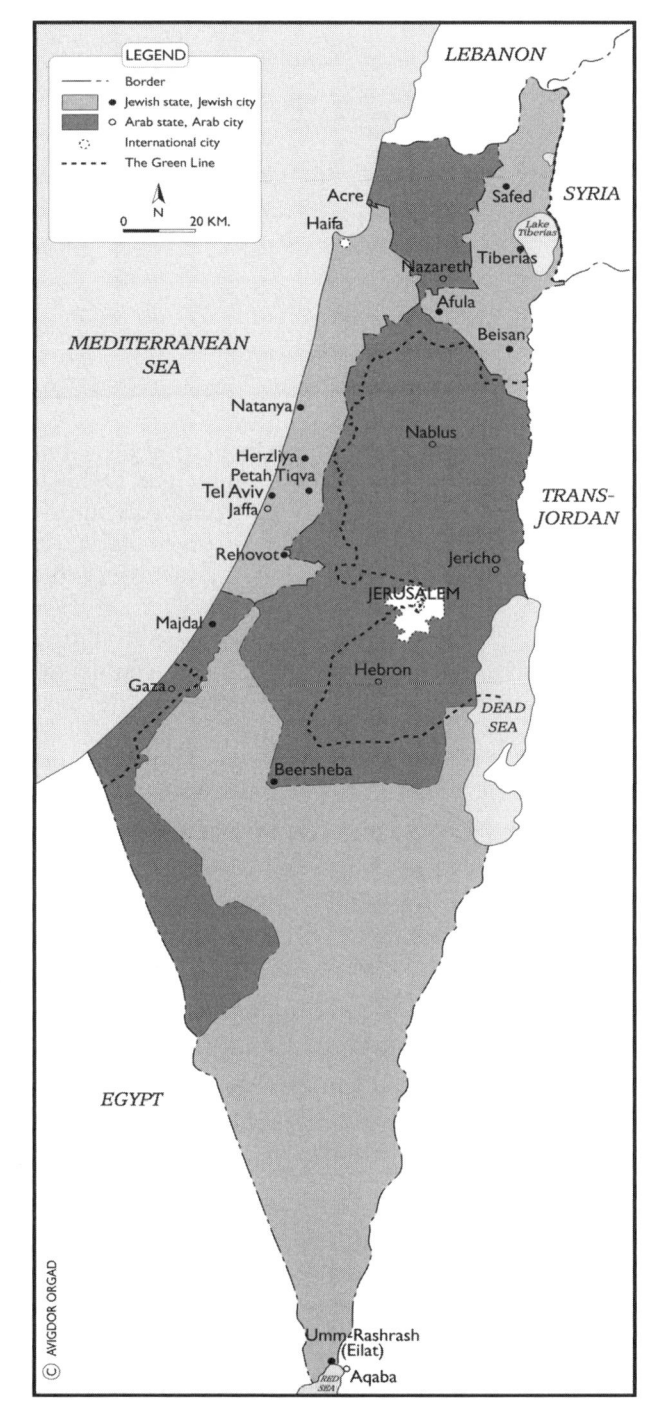

Map 7. The Borders of the UN Resolution of 29 November 1947 and the Borders of the Armistice Lines (Green Line) of 1949

Epilogue
The End of Things

On 22 August 1952, Yitzhak Sadeh passed away. Yigal Allon was in England, completing two years of study in London and Oxford. On the "old man's" last day, Israel Galili phoned Allon with the news that Sadeh's end was near.[1] Allon did not make it to the funeral. About two weeks later, the front page of *Maariv* featured a picture of him disembarking at the port of Haifa with Ruth and their son, Yiftah. The caption read: "Major General Allon returns from Oxford."[2] About two weeks after that, Palmahniks and Palmah supporters were to gather at Kibbutz Givat Brenner to mark the thirtieth day of Sadeh's passing. Some of the invitations sent out were signed by Allon, and the event received modest publicity in the press. It had been a few years since the Palmah's famous rally in 1949 (which Allon had not attended). He had now been away from Israel for almost two years and had vanished from the news. The organizers of the gathering at Kibbutz Givat Brenner feared a poor turnout. Their most optimistic forecast envisioned some five thousand people. The actual numbers were twice that. The estimates of *Haaretz* put the figure at eight to ten thousand; of *Ha-Olam Ha-Zeh*, at twelve thousand. People came to commemorate Yitzhak Sadeh, but mostly to hear Yigal Allon. Israel's young people voted for Allon with their feet: "Yigal Allon apparently greatly influenced the number of participants," *Haaretz* reported.[3] *Ha-Olam Ha-Zeh* capped a long, detailed write-up with the words: "The great show of strength in memory of Yitzhak Sadeh and in honor of Yigal Allon." At this dramatic moment, time seemed to stand still. "For seven hours, there were a sublime innocence and purity that many had believed gone forever," *Ha-Olam Ha-Zeh* wrote.[4] The reunion, the stories, the improvisations to accommodate the crowds all reawakened both the sense of togetherness and the amazing feats of bygone days. After paying their respects at Sadeh's grave, thousands of people filled Givat Brenner's amphitheater to listen to the main speaker, Yigal Allon. Allon had prepared a written address, toiling over it the previous night. "There are not many people who can read a speech before twelve thousand people—mouths closed, eyes open and gleaming, drawn to the speaker by an almost magical force," *Ha-Olam Ha-Zeh*'s reporter waxed lyrical.[5] The talk lasted a whole hour. Allon listed Sadeh's historic accomplishments in building the defense force and designing the field companies and the Palmah, and then he expanded on the Palmah's importance and principles. His words were polished in rich, rhetorical, elaborate Hebrew, abounding in oaths of loyalty to the Palmah's course and comrades.[6] Politically, the two years Allon had spent in England appeared not to have changed him at all: he portrayed Britain as the imperialist power fought by the Palmah in the War of Independence, the Arab armies its minions.[7] He identified Palmah loyalty with patriotism and the war to "liberate the entire country," and he defined the Palmah's opponents as the supporters of "passive defense, accepting the country's dissection."

Together, Hayim Gouri and Hayim Hefer composed a "yizkor" memorial to the "old man." It, too, was filled with pathos and looked to the past.[8] The *Haaretz* reporter noted somewhat cattily that the "yizkor" sounded much like the song "Hayu Zmanim"—"those were the days." Regarding "The address of the Palmah commander was not very different from the 'yizkor.' Mostly, it was devoted to past glories, not pointing to the future."[9] The impression was that Allon had gone out of his way not to say anything about his future plans. The *Ha-Olam Ha-Zeh* writer, who described the event as the founding moment of Allon's leadership of Israel's young, had to admit that his address did not divulge his plans. Moreover, despite the rapt attention paid Allon's address, the person who most excited the audience, according to the reporter, was Israel Galili: with a few off-the-cuff words he reached straight into the heart of his listeners. When he finished, they responded with a spontaneous outburst of the Palmah's anthem.

In the attempt to understand why the enormous charisma Allon had for his generation dissolved over the years, the Palmah gathering may provide a clue. His word was awaited with an air of expectancy. He still had his charm. But the Allon that returned from England was no longer the same person nor was the state the same country. He was the "tamed" native. He had learned the importance of a polished speech, the art of oratory. He amazed his admirers by speaking English to the president's wife, Vera Weizmann, who lent her patronage to the gathering. He had broadened his horizons; he had read, studied, and acquired new insights and new manners. He liked to dress well and took care with his appearance. In direct contacts, he still sparked instant liking. But this ability to spark empathy, so overwhelming in individual, face-to-face situations, did not have the same effect on crowds. His long, flowery speech at Givat Brenner was a sign of things to come: even his most loyal friends felt that he was not the same Yigal. Some of the spontaneity, the Palmah directness, the Eretz Israel originality had been eroded in his encounter with European culture. He returned better versed in worldly etiquette, capable of conversing with aristocrats such as Vera Weizmann, but less able to inspire his friends from the Palmah. In time Amos Horev noted, "I saw how much the British period had affected him—dulled his intuitive, healthy reactions. He had become more sophisticated, considering, balanced, less apt to show anger. A refined Yigal so to speak. Suddenly he was very cultured and this did not enhance his standing."[10] After the gathering at Givat Brenner, his peers watched him with concern: What had happened to the native returned from the cold?

Of course, Allon could not be expected to retain his youthful charm forever. His trip to England and the serious tone of his address reflected a deep-set desire to study, to learn, to train for research work or at least obtain an academic degree. In this, he was no different from the rest of his generation: after the war, many turned to education, something they had had to put aside during the traumatic decade in the history of the Jewish people. Many hoped to study abroad and some realized the dream—if not to gain a degree, then at least for the exposure to European culture, for spiritual fare, to see the world, to learn a foreign language. The fact that the KM sent Allon to study in England was a sign of the leadership's recognition that he was meant for greatness; it would therefore be good for him to step out of the narrow confines of Israeli culture and become acquainted with the world. The heads of the Labor movement regarded education as a vital key to leadership. People such as Yitzhak Tabenkin, Ben-Gurion, and Berl Katznelson—autodidacts who had never completed higher studies, yet moved worlds—nevertheless put great store by education and revered the educated. Allon had internalized this approach; just how much can be seen from his advice to CGS Yitzhak Rabin after the Six Day War that he study overseas. Rabin thought he was being underestimated: he felt no need to prepare himself for future functions. He felt ripe and ready. Nor did he feel a lack of intellectual baggage.[11]

Allon did not complete his studies. Every now and then they were interrupted by the "call of the movement." He did, however, acquire etiquette, comportment, manners. He learned to mingle with dignitaries. These skills, which both he and the leadership considered vital to the attainment of senior positions, his own generation regarded as alien, as a barrier between them. The tendency to expound at length in lacquered Hebrew and the overdose of flowery phrases hindered his encounters with his friends and in time also with the wider Israeli public.

The press reports on Sadeh's death and funeral showed his coffin borne on the shoulders of senior IDF officers. The front row of pallbearers included Moshe Dayan. The caption described him as closely associated with the Sadeh family, as a friend and a helper. Also featured was the famous picture from Hanitah of Sadeh standing between his two loved protégés, Moshe Dayan and Yigal Allon. It was even reported that Dayan had given the picture to Sadeh and that he had been very fond of it.[12] Dayan was not asked to speak at the Palmah gathering. This was Allon's home turf and that of the KM. But against Allon's flawless form of address, contemporaries cited Dayan's directness and simplicity, which had not changed with time. Dayan's articulation, originality, and sparkle were juxtaposed with Allon's starched solemnity and ponderous verbosity.[13] The most common charge heard was that Dayan had retained the authenticity of a sabra while Allon had lost his.

The hawk-eyed *Haaretz* reporter spied an interesting fact about the Palmah gathering: the thousands of attendees included numerous young Palmah veterans and bereaved families of the Palmah's fallen from all of Israel's tribes and ethnic communities. But "conspicuous by their almost utter absence were members of the immigration waves [who had arrived] after the establishment of the State [of Israel]." This marked the gathering: "For moments it seemed as if the hands of time had turned back four years."[14] The absence of the new immigrants signaled a phenomenon that was to erode the essentials of Allon's charisma: for them, the War of Independence was a thing of the past. Ben-Gurion was considered the founding father of the state. Preoccupied with absorption worries and making a living, they did not bother about who should wear the crown of glory. As they saw it, the prime minister and minister of defense was a source of inspiration and power. Nor were they captivated by the charm of a sabra. In any case, new concerns soon pushed aside old victories. The growing tension on the borders, the infiltration of *fedayeen*, the reprisals, and then the Sinai Campaign—all of these fixed new names in the public consciousness, especially Dayan's. For the broad public, Allon was virtually anonymous.

The absence of these immigrants, however, symbolized also a wider phenomenon involving the ability of the Israeli Left to beat a path to their hearts. Mapai, the ruling party, created dependency groups among the new immigrants, a policy that generated a good deal of bitterness among them. Ostensibly, the natural candidate to cash in on this bitterness was the Left, Mapam. As the second largest party in the First Knesset, its position seemed promising. The Left was certainly not unattractive; even after the LAHA split off from Mapam in 1954 and stood for elections on its own, the LAHA still garnered ten mandates. But there was something about the Israeli Left in the 1950s that made it anachronistic, marginal to the new Israeli realities. Against Ben-Gurion's dignified slogans, which spoke in the name of the state, Mapam evoked partisanship and organizational frameworks only vaguely relevant to the new reality. The burning question on the Left's agenda was Israel's political orientation. In the early 1950s, the attitude to the Soviet Union was the rock that split the KM, divided families, and sowed hatred between parents and children. But this question hardly interested the newcomers.

Allon, unlike Mapam's fervent young, was not captive to the Soviet aura. He may have brandished the same hackneyed ideological slogans as most of his generation, held up the glory of the Red Army, and expressed a clear preference for the sun rising in the East as opposed to the decadent, capitalist West. And in his address, he did vigorously demand that Israel guard its independence from Western powers, thinly criticizing Ben-Gurion's desire to integrate Israel in the region's pro-Western alliance. Yet ideology was not his chief interest. He was not involved in the KM split and he even succeeded in preventing a split in Ginossar. He did not take part in the emphatically ideological debate of ideas. His interest lay in political, international, and security issues. These he understood. To these he felt he could contribute. But the agenda of Israel's Left was dominated by Soviet-related ideological issues. Few of the new immigrants had Soviet leanings. Here and there, one could find leftist pockets among immigrant youth from Iraq and Egypt, or even among immigrants from the Balkans and Eastern Europe. They were, however, small and unrepresentative. Members of the leftist Kibbutz Harel enlisted to educate the residents of the adjacent immigrant camp in the lore of Marxism, endeavoring to instill in them the "three L's": Lenin, Luxembourg, and Liebknecht. It is hard to imagine that this doctrine, strange and foreign and dressed in outdated formulas, could capture the hearts of new immigrants from the lands of Islam. As for European immigrants, they hardly had good memories of their encounter with Soviet rule. The Left's orbit of influence was not enlarged by Israel's increased population nor did it make inroads among them.

In January 1962, Allon and Ben-Gurion had a long conversation attended by Galili. Mapai had just won a resounding election victory, and at Ben-Gurion's behest Levi Eshkol put together the new government, including the LAHA and excluding Mapam. The talk centered on the eternal topic of uniting the Labor movement, which is what Ben-Gurion pushed for. Among the reasons he gave was his apprehension at the rise of the Right: the evolving differentiation in Israel's employee sector; and the emergence of the engineers union and of the high-school teachers union, pointed to a widening gap between the white collar intelligentsia and the working class. At the same time, the Right was highly influential in disadvantaged neighborhoods. Ben-Gurion regarded as lethal the connection between an intelligentsia and public sectors that had not been raised on the values of manual labor: within

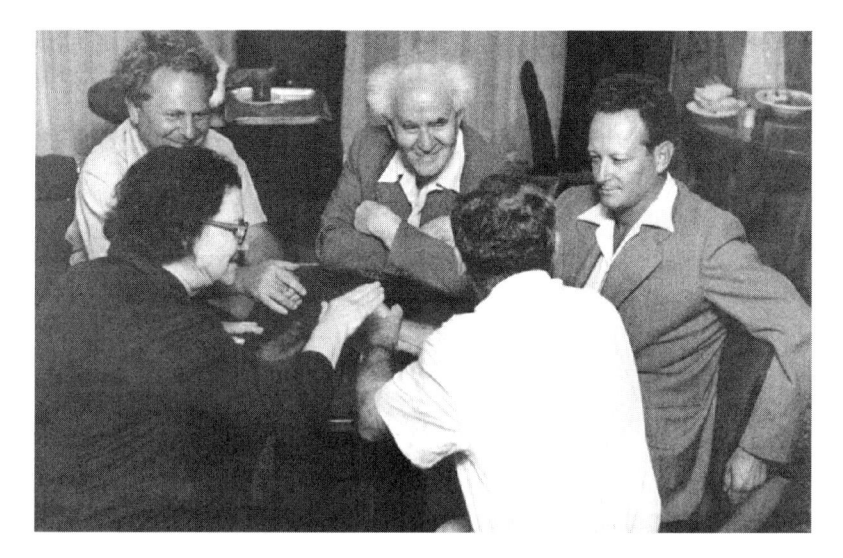

Figure 21. Beyond love, beyond hatred: Yigal Allon in the company of David Ben-Gurion, Paula Ben-Gurion, and Israel Galili, late 1950s. Photographer unknown. Courtesy of the Allon family.

several years, he predicted, Menachem Begin would come to power. The change of power would be destructive to the character of the state. It would mark a turning point from a pioneering society to a bourgeois one, a devaluation of labor and a switchover to nonproductive professions. The army's top brass would be entirely replaced. Ben-Gurion did not need to explain what this meant to Allon. Allon agreed with him about the dangers. He had noticed a similar development during his stay in England in the early 1950s among Labor supporters: "There is a huge gulf between the leadership class and the working masses, a conceptual gulf and [a gulf in the] standard of living." Numerous workers voted for the Conservatives, Allon reported.[15] Yet in his response to Ben-Gurion he resorted to slogans: doing away with social and cultural disparities, inculcating a respect for manual labor, energizing development towns, and so forth. These were truisms. On the practical level, he had two suggestions: restoring the youth movements to the schools (Ben-Gurion had removed them for fear of politicization) and renewing Labor's education stream (instead of state education). Ben-Gurion's reaction was keen: "You all live too much in the past, and you are much younger than me."[16]

In make-up, the psychological depths and understanding of the three men were not very different. They shared a worldview that gave clear preference to labor and workers over other classes in society; that regarded affluence with suspicion and consumer society with hostility; that feared a rise in the standard of living lest it lead to a depreciation of values. Modesty, making do with little, a quasi-communism of poverty—these were the appealing qualities. They conceived of a frontier society, mobilizing its members for national missions, whether voluntary or by state coercion.[17] The daring, and perhaps the audacity, to mold the image of the nation and of the new Jew struck them as desirable and self-evident. Ben-Gurion, however, seems to have been well able to distinguish between the ideal and the real, between desire and ability. He acknowledged the power of spontaneous processes to which a state lent itself (stychic processes in his terminology) and treated them with appropriate humility. He recognized the difficulty of maintaining a state-guided democracy in the long term, for the world's cultural climate had changed since the 1950s; the willingness to subordinate personal desire to the general good had dissolved as World War II's era of emergency became a distant memory. In contrast, Allon believed that the rug could be rolled back. If socialist youth movements were reintroduced into the schools, if the Labor stream were revived in the education system, the basic development trends of Israeli society could be transformed. It was the idealization of a non-ideal past. Even in their heyday, the pioneering youth movements had managed to attract only small groups of youngsters. Moreover, the Labor education stream suited only a small part of the Israeli public, no doubt falling far short of Allon's expectations. Submitting the Labor stream and the youth movements as a wonder remedy for the ills of Israeli society reflected the tendency of the Left to rest on the splendid laurels of the period of the Yishuv. It ignored the fact that the tools that had served the Yishuv's small, closed society no longer suited Israeli society, which, more and more, was opening up to the Western world. Misgivings about the invasive influences of Western democratic society were not limited to the radical Left. Ben-Gurion too watched the penetration of materialistic currents with concern. But he knew that the old means of battling these currents were no longer appropriate. In his heart of hearts he also seems to have known that it was a quixotic battle for it was about processes that could not be controlled by the instruments of an open, democratic society. Allon, Galili, and their colleagues, in contrast, still believed that the campaign against Western influence on Israeli society was not lost. Though weaned from their pro-Soviet romance, they continued to believe in the existence of an ideological, political alternative to Western capitalism. Their conversion from their faith in the triumph of "the world of tomorrow" had been a long, hard process. In 1960, Galili made his first visit to the United States. When he returned, he reported to Tabenkin: capitalism is alive and well and is not about to collapse.[18] In the KM's circles, this was considered momentous news. In the first half of the 1950s, Israel's Left guarded its innocence and sat in the opposition. This allowed the Left to appear as an oppositionist party, unsullied by the charges of "melting pot" distortions. The Left felt neutralized of influence though freed of the need to adapt ideology to reality. It had the image of the righteous, but also of evading responsibility, while Mapai took the necessary, harsh steps for the good of the state, arousing animosity and rage.

Allon was without question the most popular figure in the LAHA with the broader public. He was nevertheless a limited success. He increasingly lost his charm before large audiences, not only because he had matured and lost the allure of youth—though this no doubt played a part—but also because his messages spoke to a small public that did not increase with the state's demographic growth. The messages of the Yishuv period— equality and poverty, making do with little, individual commitment to the collective, subordination of private interests to the general good, a sense of "mission" as opposed to a career (in the army or government service)—all seemed out of place in a society that had recently emerged from a period of rations and had begun to enjoy a measure of well-being. Even in circles culturally and mentally close to Allon, the collective doctrine sounded worn and torn.

These social changes help explain Dayan's rising star; he was a detached, individualistic hero acting on whim without any ties or commitments except to himself. Yadin, defining the difference between Allon and Dayan, gave the following analogy: Allon was a plant raised in a flowerbed, healthy and strong and tall, above all the other plants there, but still a part of the flowerbed. Dayan was a solitary tree, sprouting without any connection to the surrounding vegetation; some people described him as a lone wolf. Allon belonged to the opposition party but was a conformist by birth and outlook, umbilically tied to his social milieu and constitutionally unable to sever those bonds. Dayan, a member of Mapai and the establishment, carried the image of a nonconformist his whole life. He always took liberties that others did not dare to take. He was able to surprise, astound, infuriate or excite. He was unpredictable, uninhibited, and, according to many, unscrupulous. Allon, meanwhile, carried with him some of Mes'ha's image—shrewd and manipulative. "If he pats you on the shoulder, watch out—he's out to get you," Galili voiced the feelings of many about being unable to resist Allon's lavish love. Yadin imagined him as an eel moving about in a pond and believing itself unobserved. His were small-scale manipulations, mostly innocent. Dayan's cunning was far more brutal, reckless, and concerted.[19]

Dayan was withdrawn and inaccessible. He was not in the habit of patting anyone on the shoulder. He neither gave nor received love. He could turn his personal charm on people when it suited him, as a calculated, instrumental ploy. Allon turned his charm equally on his secretaries, on his drivers, and on the generation's greats. Dayan felt no allegiance to anyone; people were a means to an end. Rabin cited him as saying that a commander was allowed to decide to abandon a mission only after half of his men had incurred casualties. A member of the Mossad to whom he gave an order told him that while the mission was possible, Dayan had to understand that a whole unit would be wiped out. Dayan's reply was: "People are like alfalfa—you reap it and it grows back." These are things that Allon could not have said even though in war he led whole armies into battles that took many lives. Dayan suited the growing individualism of Israel's early years. If Allon reflected the values of the Yishuv, Dayan heralded the culture of the statehood generation: a loathing of togetherness, a contempt for the self-adorning innocence of youth and for anything that smacked of the Palmah spirit; a culture of proud individualists that fostered amoral heroes or heroes who had despaired of innocence. Against Allon's infinite optimism, Dayan was a confirmed pessimist who was glum and moody. His egoism was shameless, unapologetic, unconcealed, as befit a Nietzschean hero dismissing the right of society to judge him. Dayan identified with the Mapai establishment, with Ben-Gurion, and he enjoyed the privileges that this identification brought. The protégé of the ruling system, he nonetheless knew how to nurture the nonconformist image. In their life paths, Allon and Dayan were very similar: both were village boys who made their way to security work and the rest has been told in the annals of the State of Israel. But Allon was more of a "convert" to the Labor movement, a product of Mes'ha who had moved to Ginossar and in time taken on the socialist faith, whereas Dayan was born into the Labor movement; he was flesh of its flesh. Allon did not permit himself to stray from his adopted faith and loyalties. Dayan always felt that he belonged to the Labor movement ("I am Labor," he said toward the end of his life), but he was never committed to any of its specific paths. He had no qualms about following Ben-Gurion to the Rafi Party or back to the Labor alliance of Maarakh, or about "sitting on the fence" and threatening to leave Golda Meir's government if she did not accept his policy, or even about "crossing the lines" to serve as a minister in Menachem Begin's government. If he ever hesitated, it was for tactical reasons, not because of principles. This sort of changeability was out of the question for Allon. He constantly saw himself as answering to the judgment of his friends. If he had passing thoughts about going against them, he would not make any moves that could be construed as abandonment, betrayal, or offensive. Friendship was the source of his charisma: a hand on the shoulder, a warm smile, genuine concern, a caring that asked for nothing. But it tied his hands.

His primary loyalty was to the KM. The relationship was fraught with tensions and questions and can probably not be fully fathomed. Allon was an unusual plant in the kibbutz flowerbed. The kibbutz movement rested on the recognition that the individual was to be modest, without political instincts, submissively accepting the "movement's judgment." The heart of any action, decision, understanding was the collective. One had to submit to its will at any time. The tendency to stick out or aspire to power was treated by the KM as a deviation. It was to be stamped out or at least concealed. Allon's friends, among themselves, marveled at his overt ambition; it ran counter to kibbutz modesty. After returning from England, Allon wanted to separate the KM from Mapam and gradually reunite his party with Mapai. His encounter with British Labor had taught him the doctrine of a broad class party embracing various currents and forces. If truth be told, Mapai before the split of 1944 had been just such a party. The split had been a tragic mistake for the KM. Its sway in Mapai had far exceeded its numbers: its members filled positions of influence and power and had the status of moral superiority. The break from Mapai had sidelined the KM; it lost the advantages it had enjoyed within. Allon endeavored to revert the situation. In addition, he was impelled by the feeling that his party was too small for him. If it reunited with Mapai, he might be able to pave his way to the top of the state pyramid, what Galili termed "his goal." He thus looked for a way back, to reunite the Labor movement, to regain the lost paradise of party unity. He played a key role in the break from Mapam, backed the LAHA's co-option to the government, and supported the creation of a new alignment (the Maarakh) and then of the Labor Party. Finally, he pushed with all his might for the establishment of the United Kibbutz Movement. The coalescence of his personal ambitions and political positions did not escape his friends: Ben-Aharon, Carmel, and even Galili thought that he was driven by too much careerism and too few of the movement's principles. Carmel believed Allon's conduct was egocentric and narcissistic, bending general interests of the movement to his own personal interests, especially as the transaction turned out to be futile. Allon believed that there was a "good" Mapai as embodied by Levi Eshkol and then by Golda Meir and Pinhas Sapir, and that it would place the leadership crown on his head, if not for love of himself then for hatred of his rival: following Mapai's antipathy for members of Rafi after the succession struggle between Eshkol and Ben-Gurion. The struggle ended in Ben-Gurion's breakaway from Mapai with Mapai's young (Moshe Dayan and Shimon Peres) and the establishment of Rafi. For Allon to achieve the position of favored successor, he had to blot out his factional past. His colleagues in the KM did not think he had a chance, although it is unlikely that anyone ever said so to his face. Among themselves, they wondered at his naïveté in his dealings with Mapai's veterans. As party men burned in the schismatic fire, they did not believe that Mapai would ever agree to have a member of a Kibbutz at its head, and one from the LAHA at that. Allon's past political involvement carried no wounds. He believed that by virtue of his personality, talents, and integrative approach to the problems of the State of Israel he would be able to win over the leaders of Mapai.[20] His comrades in the movement may have disapproved of his blatant ambitiousness, but they agreed that he was suitable for the position. This was not so of Mapai's veterans, however. On more than one occasion, Ben-Gurion, Eshkol, Golda Meir, Zalman Aranne, Mordekhai Namir, and Pinhas Sapir had discounted Allon, convinced that his ambition outstripped his personality. They questioned his reliability, his leadership qualities, his loyalty to government colleagues. They doubted that he had the necessary force of personality, decisiveness, and resolve. He was turned down not merely for party reasons, but also because of personal shortcomings.[21]

The crisis point was reached during the three-week waiting period leading up to the Six Day War. Allon, the minister of labor at the time, was frustrated by the recession and unemployment in 1966–67. He looked for nonroutine avenues of action. In early May 1967, the ministry received an invitation to the conference of the International Social Security Association in Leningrad and he jumped at the chance to attend.[22] The Soviet Union had been closed to most Israelis and he was keen to travel there, to promote relations between the two states, and to meet with Soviet Jewry. It was an unofficial visit, and, on the spur of the moment, he used his friendship from the early 1950s, "when [they] were both young and fair,"[23] with Harold Wilson, the British prime minister, to try to arrange a meeting with Alexei Kosygin, the Soviet premier. Wilson wrote to Kosygin, requesting an audience for Israel's Minister of labor.[24] On 9 May 1967, Yigal and Ruth Allon arrived in Moscow. The Israeli delegation attended Sabbath services at the Leningrad synagogue followed by a festive concert, which turned into a pro-Israel mass rally of the young. Also his visits to Tiplis and Riga aroused solidarity rallies. The Israeli body for Soviet Jewry, the Liaison Bureau, attached great importance to the visit and its head, Shaul Avigur, insisted that Allon exploit it fully.[25]

At the time of Allon's departure for the Soviet Union, Israeli intelligence assessments predicted that things would be quiet for two to three years, with no danger of a flare-up on the Egyptian border. But during the IDF's parade on Independence Day (15 May 1967), CGS Rabin was slipped a note and passed it on to the prime minister: Egyptian armored forces had moved into Sinai. The situation in the Middle East promptly changed. In the early days, which went down in history as "the waiting period," things remained unclear. Allon continued the trip in Russia. Within days, Galili grew worried. On 21 May, he telegrammed the embassy to ascertain if Allon was scheduled to meet with a ranking Soviet figure. On 23 May Nasser seized Sharm al-Sheikh and closed the Straits of Tiran. War looked inevitable. Galili urgently insisted that Allon return at once, despite Avigur's opposition. But Allon wished to utilize the visit to the full: in those days, a visit by an Israeli minister to Moscow was an extraordinary event. Just as he had refused to cut short his tour of the French army after being dismissed as commander of the Southern Front, so now he was in no hurry to return. He managed to meet with senior labor figures in the Soviet Union, but not with political figures. On 24 May he returned home.[26]

In time Allon's supporters liked to blame Galili, the master planner, for the poor advice he had given the golden boy of Eretz Israel. As a result, Allon was late to return and missed the historic opportunity to be appointed minister of defense. Aside from the fact that Galili had pressed Allon to hasten his return, there were eleven days between Allon's arrival and the outbreak of war. It was not his absence that had seen the appointment go to Dayan.

The waiting period was marked by a steadily rising anxiety level fed by rumors that the IDF was unprepared, that tanks lacked engines, that gas masks and other equipment were unavailable, and so forth. Every passing day, it was said, spelled another five hundred casualties. Forecasts envisioned tens of thousands of dead in the coming campaign. At the government meeting on 27 May, participants were equally divided between going to war and sitting tight: diplomacy had not yet been exhausted; both Germany and the French were reluctant about war while the United States still contemplated driving a fleet of ships through the Straits of Tiran to break Nasser's sea blockade on Israel. The idea of going to war unallied to any of the powers was very worrying, especially as Ben-Gurion, long retired but still carrying weight, led the camp opposed to the measure. Eshkol was afraid to embark on a predictably hard campaign without broad political support and he did not want to be the tiebreaker at the government meeting.[27] The state leadership under him did not inspire the confidence needed to allay public anxiety. He was not seen as the man to lead the nation in time of war even though he was an activist and had worked to bolster the IDF. There was talk of reinstating Ben-Gurion as the prime minister and installing a national unity government. The public sentiments about the government's helplessness and the leaks about divided opinion between the government and the CGS were such that an esteemed professor of political science sounded out Yadin about leading a military putsch.[28] Most of the pressure was on Eshkol to relinquish the defense portfolio in order to avert the government's fall. There were a number of candidates for the job of minister of defense: Allon, a member of the government and an IDF general whose protégés now filled key positions in the army, including CGS Yitzhak Rabin; Yadin, a former CGS and "the great hope" of Israeli politics, who had not got his hands dirty in politics; Dayan, a member of Rafi and a former CGS glorified in reprisal actions and the Sinai Campaign. Eshkol, however, had no wish to relinquish the Defense portfolio. After having prepared the army so well, he believed he was being unjustly hounded. He semi-promised the job to Allon, who meanwhile brushed up on the CGS's plans and prepared for the post. The public was not enthusiastic about his possible appointment. Nineteen years had elapsed since 1948 and it was now a different public. Allon's name was no longer bound up with military laurels, nor did it convey victory. Yadin's candidacy suffered from the same drawback. But his advantage was that he was not aligned with any party, meaning that his appointment would not extract a long train of political concessions. However, even Yadin himself preferred Dayan. Dayan's appointment was to be part of a package deal to expand the government by admitting the Herut-Liberal bloc (Gahal) led by Begin. The deal was backed by the National Religious Party (NRP) under Moshe Haim Shapira. Shapira, a moderate, believed that appointing Allon, an activist, was a prelude to war, which he sought to forestall. He hoped that Dayan's appointment would tip the scales in favor of the moderate members of the government: after all, Rafi, led by Ben-Gurion, had called for restraint. Shapira also wanted a broad government as a confidence-building measure for the public's sense of security. He threatened that the National Religious Party would leave the government unless a national unity government were formed with Dayan as the minister of defense. This would have caused a government crisis. On 30 May Eshkol agreed to relinquish the defense portfolio to Allon. Allon was sure the job was his. He had already made arrangements for Galili to replace him at the Labor Ministry.[29] The climax came the following day, on 31 May. Mapai ministers who were meeting that day decided to appoint Allon defense minister, to give Dayan a senior position in the Southern Command as he asked, and to co-opt Gahal and Rafi to the government, each to receive three ministers without portfolios.[30] At that meeting, most of the ministers preferred Allon to Dayan. Rafi, especially its members Ben-Gurion and Shimon Peres, were accused of causing public hysteria. That night, however, and the next day, Mapai's secretariat met twice in expanded form. The air was filled with anxiety and the discussions were affected by the public mood. Most of those present agreed with Haim Zadok that if Esh-

Figure 22. Close and distant: Yigal Allon with Moshe Dayan as GCS, at the Knesset buffet in the mid-1950s. Photographer unknown. Courtesy of the Allon family.

kol relinquished the Defense portfolio it was to go to Dayan; he symbolized Israel's military determination, which was just as important internally as externally, and his appointment would enable the government to be broadened. At this moment, it transpired that the Gahal Party insisted on Dayan's appointment as a condition of its joining the government, and that the National Religious Party really meant to quit if a national unity government were not formed. Golda Meir and Zalman Aranne fought in vain to retain the decision of the Mapai ministers to appoint Allon. After two stormy meetings, the Mapai secretariat vanquished the party's government representatives. The majority of the party supported Dayan's appointment.[31]

Allon backed down. He withdrew his candidacy for defense minister. "My words were received with emotion by everyone and 'with appreciation' from the prime minister," Allon wrote. It may have been a chivalrous, noble act, but politically it was disastrous. He was a hair's breath away from the coveted post, he knew he was right for it, and he had to give it up. In the circumstances that had developed, he apparently judged that Dayan would in any case win the appointment. It was thus better to relinquish it and enjoy the martyr's status than be spurned in humiliation.[32] As was his way in moments of crisis, he clamped down on his anger and frustration, gave no vent to his feelings, and guarded his self-respect. The most important thing to him, as he said, was not to be humiliated.³³ Yet the slap in the face had been public: at the crucial moment, Dayan was chosen over him and even his friends accepted the verdict.

It was a defining moment in Israeli society: Dayan reaped the glory of a war for which he had not prepared the army. In the festival of victory that erupted after the tremendous tension of the waiting period, Dayan became the symbol of the IDF's splendid triumph. His portrait, with his black eye-patch, adorned victory albums, books, posters, and even films all over the world. His prestige and public status towered over those of the rest of his generation. In the semi-latent competition between Allon and Dayan since the days of Hanitah, Dayan now leaped forward. Allon was left to straggle behind.

Two weeks after hostilities ended, Allon formulated the basics of a political program, which earned the title of the Allon Plan (discussed below). It was never adopted as a government program, although the government in fact went by it in its settlement policies in the occupied territories. Allon did not go to battle over the program, neither in the KM, which was suffering from the ideological recidivism of a Greater Israel, nor in the government. His great rival, Dayan, also hardly excelled when it came to standing up for his opinions. When it suited him, Dayan could nevertheless threaten to resign and strip the Labor Party of his electoral assets to enforce his will. Allon never threatened, never laid down conditions. After the Yom Kippur War, he believed that the entire government should resign, but he did nothing to make this happen. He continued to sit in the government without explaining why he did not resign.³⁴ He behaved chivalrously toward CGS David Elazar, who had been discredited and dismissed by the Agranat Commission, and even lent him a supporting hand in his time of trouble. But, again, this was a gesture, not an act that changed anything. When the Rabin government, yielding to Gush Emunim, refrained from removing the Kadum settlement that had been erected in the West Bank despite a government decision, Allon deemed this a serious mistake. He was upset, he was deeply opposed, yet he continued to sit in the government.³⁵

Allon reached his nadir as the the Foreign minister and the deputy prime minister in Rabin's government. After Eshkol died, Pinhas Sapir initiated Golda Meir's election as prime minister, skipping over the two candidates of the Palmah generation—Allon and Dayan. Sapir sought to avoid a confrontation between the two "young men," staving off a possible crisis in the party. The contest between them was thus deferred as Meir's appointment could not have been perceived as a slight. However, when Mapai's veterans picked Rabin to head the government, it was a hard blow: when the time came for the old guard to move over, it was not Allon they put in the top position. The choice fell to his subordinate, whom he loved and respected, but whom he considered an excellent second. Now Rabin, too, moved ahead of him on the ladder of advancement, while he, Allon, served in Rabin's government.[36]

Since the Six Day War, Allon had served as the deputy prime minister, under Eshkol, Meir, and Rabin. He had become the eternal successor-designate, always passed over, always seeing someone else appointed the head of the government. Deputy prime minister was a figurehead position of no value, conveying weakness and exaggerated attention to one's personal status.

In the War of Independence, Allon had been the source of authority and power while Rabin had relied on his support, encouragement, and patronage. As a team, they worked in complete harmony, Allon's seniority never being in any doubt. Rabin was a shy young man lacking in charisma, who found it difficult to cope with the strong personalities trying to oust him from the Harel Brigade. Allon gave him his backing and saw to his promotion. Over the years, Allon was apt to take pride in his protégé. At some point, Rabin got fed up with his image as Allon's star pupil. As CGS, he was hard put to conceal his resentment at Allon's conduct. It soon evolved into disparagement, with Rabin unable to mask his attitude toward his erstwhile patron. The contempt he showed his former commander was spoken of by Amos Horev and other members of the Palmah who did not conceal their dissatisfaction with Rabin's behavior from Allon himself.[37] When Rabin was elected prime minister, Allon had to swallow the fact of being passed over yet again. Rabin's attitude had no hint of the respect that he, Allon, had shown Sadeh when they found themselves in a similar situation. Around the cabinet table, Rabin's disdain was open. According to press reports, he was impatient and intolerant while listening to Allon's reports as foreign minister. More than once, he cut him short, causing Allon to snap, "Let me finish what I have to say."[38] Friends protective of Allon's honor urged him to slam the door on the government table. He continued to sit there and suffer abuse. He reached rock bottom in his career. In this period, his friends, too, despaired of his ability ever to recoup and regain his former status.[39]

In the years following the Six Day War, his name became identified with the Allon Plan. He had sketched the chief lines of the program two weeks after the war. It rested on three pillars: demography, security, and morality. Its goals were to preserve the Jewish majority in the state, to ensure that the Jordan River would be Israel's strategic border, and to refrain from ruling another people. The idea of territorial compromise was a direct consequence of these principles. It was a very daring step—a sea change for a member of the KM who after the War of Independence had continued to say that the war was not over, that Israel had lost the peace because it had not conquered the West Bank.[40] The Allon Plan sought to annex to the State of Israel a ten to fifteen kilometer strip along the Jordan Valley, as well as the Judean Desert, the Etziyon Bloc, and Greater Jerusalem. At first, he assumed that it would be possible to thin out the population of the Gaza Strip by settling its Arab refugees east of the Jordan or in el-Arish, and to annex the Gaza Strip to the State of Israel. At a later stage, he understood that the problem of the refugees was more complicated. He then suggested that the Gaza Strip be given to Jordan in exchange for an outlet to the sea. As for the West Bank, initially he sought to disconnect it from Jordan; still wary of Hussein and driven by anti-imperialistic reservations, he regarded Jordan as a transitory state. Subsequently, he defined Jordan as the most stable regime in the Middle East. The first version of the plan thus visualized autonomy for the West Bank, to allow residents to govern themselves, apart from sparsely populated pockets that would serve as Israeli security strips and come under Israeli military law. There was no talk of an independent Palestinian state, merely of autonomy. Nevertheless, at a time that Israel's government denied the existence of a Palestinian people, Allon's stance was considered very bold. At a later stage still, he adopted the "Jordanian Option": Jordan would take back the territories of the West Bank and the Gaza Strip that would be evacuated by Israel within the framework of a peace treaty. In 1974, he floated the idea of a foothold for Hussein in the West Bank as part of an interim agreement, similar to the interim agreement signed with Egypt as a preamble to an overall settlement. The Jericho area was to be the Jordanian bridgehead in the West Bank. This arrangement dovetailed a later version of the Allon Plan that severed Israel's contiguous control in the Jordan Valley and suggested a corridor connecting Jordan and the West Bank. These ideas proved fruitless after the Rabat summit in the summer of 1974, which, contrary to expectations, did not empower Jordan to represent the Palestinians, but put the PLO forward instead.

The Allon Plan offered a compromise between two polarized camps in Israeli society: the advocates of Greater Israel for whom the conquests of the Six Day War had revived the bond to the biblical Promised Land, and the advocates of total concession and full unilateral withdrawal. From both the personal and movement perspectives, Allon's ostensibly moderate position was revolutionary: he had turned away from the views that had molded his world and forged an independent road. He rebelled against the KM tradition and shook off Tabenkin's yoke—Tabenkin called for a settlement drive in the occupied territories. In an atmosphere saturated with messianic fervor, Allon offered a pragmatic stance, which was no mean feat in those days.

Did the Allon Plan ever have a chance? When Allon first presented it in the government, in July 1967, it was a bold and independent move.[41] It was one of the few times that he acted independently, not coordinating with Galili in advance. He may have feared that Galili would attempt to modify, dilute, and ultimately dissolve the program. Galili represented the KM's position of Greater Israel.[42] But to present the plan without preliminary preparations or garnering support or coordinating it with Galili was to sentence it to failure. This was so obvious that Sini Azaryahu, a close friend of both Allon and Galili, was sure that Allon merely wished to float the idea, not really intending that the program be adopted. If his intentions were serious, he would have laid the program before the prime minister and suggested that he present it to the government as his own proposal.[43]

The Allon Plan lay on the government table for half a year, subjected to partial discussions but not put to a vote. It was a national unity government. The Right opposed the plan because it relinquished Greater Israel. The Left opposed it because it involved annexations. Dayan's policy was based on the premise that time was in Israel's favor—he waited for a phone call from Arab leaders. Taking its cue from him, the government decided not to decide. Allon, in contrast, contended that Israel had to come up with a peace plan of its own, and quickly, for a number of reasons: to influence the superpowers when they put their minds to the Middle East to force a solution on the region; to take advantage of Palestinian shock at the resounding Arab defeat; and to preempt a reawakening of Arab extremists.[44] Galili managed to get the government to approve settlements according to the map of the Allon Plan, that is, where there was little Arab population, not on the hilly ridge. This principle was observed for ten years. Thus, even though the Allon Plan was not adopted as a government decision, to no small extent it did determine policy in the territories—until the Likud came to power.[45] It was not officially accepted by anybody, but it trickled down as an unofficial proposal for Meir's talks with Nixon and other U.S. leaders. It was also raised in talks that Israeli statesmen conducted with Jordan's King Hussein, who dismissed it as inadequate. Allon, the confirmed optimist, did not cease to present it as a realistic option to which the two sides would ultimately accede.

Allon took credit for coining the term "defensible borders." The phrase gradually penetrated the international political discourse and in the end was adopted as the basic conception for any peace settlement in the Middle East. "Defensible borders" meant that there would be no retreat to the borders of 5 June 1967; at the same time, the slogan of "not [giving] an inch" would be invalidated. The central motif was territorial compromise. The fact that the Allon Plan was the only one to be named for its formulator lent Allon the aura of a political thinker. He probably did not deserve the title when he first drew up the plan. He diverged from it several times: he supported the settlement of Rabbi Levinger's coterie in Hebron and he established Maaleh Adumim east of Jerusalem. These "zigzags" reinforced the impression that the plan was meant as a tactic against Dayan rather than as a solution to the basic problem. This may have been true in 1967. But over the years Allon increasingly identified with the program, making it the chief tenet of his faith. His political conception deepened, and when he was appointed foreign minister in Rabin's government, he brought to the Foreign Office a clear acknowledgment of the existence of a Palestinian entity. This entity was to achieve self-determination in a Jordanian-Palestinian state, which was to take over most of the West Bank. His position at the time was more "dovish" than the prime minister's.[46] Nevertheless, when Uri Avneri sought to report to him unofficially on his contacts with the PLO's leaders, he refused to listen for fear that this spelled indirect recognition of the PLO. Rabin, in contrast, agreed to hear out Avneri, although he was opposed to the entire measure.[47]

Beginning in the early 1970s Allon struggled to head the camp of the doves in the Maarakh (Labor Alignment), perhaps because Dayan led the hawks. For the doves, the territorial compromise he suggested did not seem enough. He was not prepared to return to the Green Line and in this he was consistent. In other things, he was inconsistent. He favored extending Jerusalem's jurisdiction, but he sharply opposed the settlement at Kadum. He encouraged settlement in the Jordan Valley, yet he repeatedly attempted to convince King Hussein of the virtues of the Allon Plan. He was prepared to concede to Egypt a chunk of Sinai larger than that stipulated in the second Separation Agreement of 1974. He proposed a separation agreement with Jordan, including the transfer of the Jericho area to Hussein, but he abstained in the Knesset vote on the 1978 Camp David Accords. He believed that to concede all of Sinai to Egypt, up to the last inch, was to set a dangerous precedent for the eventual accommodation to be reached in western Palestine; he also believed that it would have been possible to reach an agreement for less. Allon was prepared to adapt his positions to changing political realities based on the principle that peace efforts were to be accompanied by territorial compromise, that the Jewish character of the State of Israel would be preserved, and that its borders would be defensible. It is the irony of history that toward the end of his life, his basic position was not essentially different from Ben-Gurion's in 1949.[48]

The years after 1967 were marked by the rivalry between Allon and Dayan. This rivalry, to a large extent, determined the twists of Israeli politics. Their positions often seemed to be based on what the other would say or do rather than on pertinence. The last drop of poison in their relations was Dayan's appointment as foreign minister in Begin's government. Not only did Allon have to give up a post he liked and move to the opposition, but his successor in the foreign ministry was none other than Dayan, the man who had replaced him in the Southern Command, the man who had been appointed defense minister instead of him.[49]

Allon and Dayan, the two princes of the Israeli Labor movement, were not entirely different: both believed they were meant for greatness but expected others to hand them the scepter on a silver platter. Both displayed feebleness in moments that demanded forcefulness and decisiveness. Unlike the leaders of the previous generation, both felt comfortable with Arabs, were happy to socialize with them, liked their way of life, and treated them with empathy and respect. This was both political acumen and the natural penchant of members of the native generation who spoke Arabic and had always had direct relations with Arabs. But both distinguished between Arab rights on the individual level and the rights of Arabs as a nation. On the individual level, Allon and Dayan were open and generous, but not so with respect to Arab national aspirations. The older Allon was much more cautious and moderate on the "Arab question" than the younger: it is not likely that he would have supported the idea of expelling Arabs, which he had voiced openly in the early 1950s. At the end of his life, his "dovishness" was his banner, his humanism mature and genuine. But when it came to the national interest, even in the 1970s he did not hesitate to choose what he considered the national good over humane considerations. As foreign minister, when he was asked to decide whether to sell weapons to dictators, he did not let moral scruples stand in his way.[50] In this respect, there was no difference between him and Dayan.

Allon appears to have respected Dayan more than Dayan did Allon. But, "Beyond the love, beyond the hate," there seemed to remain a spark of mutual empathy and esteem. In the summer of 1967, Zerubavel Arbel wrote to Allon, "My great joy [at the victory in the war] is still today mixed with rage and indignation at the despicable [way] our Mapai partners treated you." He judged that two parties would rise in the state: a Left, under Allon and Galili; a Right, under the "one-eyed [Dayan]." Allon rejected Arbel's political analysis and added a comment in the margins: "Incidentally, I am not happy by the characterization of Moshe Dayan as one-eyed. He did, after all, lose an eye in battle."[51] He would not permit his aides to speak badly of Dayan in his presence. When Dayan underwent surgery at the end of the 1970s, Allon visited him in the hospital and sat long hours near his bed. To his aides, he explained: "For all that has passed between Moshe and myself—we did fight together." When Allon passed away, Dayan attended the funeral and sat in a corner, looking glum and forlorn.[52]

The question of why Allon's race to leadership failed has preoccupied his friends and cohort. Was it personal failure? Was it an expression of the limitations of the Palmah generation, the first generation of sabras? Champions of the former theory would cite his graveside elegy, which was delivered by President Yitzhak Navon. Navon likened Allon to King Saul: according to the Sages, Saul lost the kingdom for he was unblemished. The image of King Saul, it will be recalled, had accompanied Allon from his days in Mes'ha. Tchernichowsky's address had fired his imagination and he had told his father of his admiration for the king who had galloped by night on a light-footed horse to Ein Dor, to hear the verdict of the wrathful Samuel and to set out the next day on a doomed campaign. The towering king chosen from behind the herd of sheep symbolized the pristine innocence of creation before the realm rose and became corrupt. Saul's failures stemmed from his virtues: he had pitied Agag king of Amalek. Must one be prepared to trample corpses in order to rule? To reach the top, must one shed morals, loyalty to a path and a way of life, loyalty to one's friends? Many thought that, indeed, just as in the case of King Saul, Allon's virtues were the reason for his failures. Benyamin Galai pinned Allon's failures on Allon's emotional need to be enveloped in love, to give and to receive it. "Allon was always a man of warm waters, loving and loved. If rulership meant the cold of snow—not merely its purity—he could not abide it."[53] Allon was unique in his lack of hypocrisy or pretense, qualities required in politics, Amos Elon wrote.[54] His virtues were his faults: "Intellectual openness without a trace of arrogance combined with an extraordinary personal charm that never had either the charismatic magnetism of the villain, said to be the only one to make history, or of the vanquisher quelling his surroundings via intellectual and moral subjugation."[55] Nathan Shaham wrote, "We demanded of Galilee's golden boy . . . that he be untrue to his warm nature, which thirsted for friendship and love, and place himself outside the law as befits a strong man who knows his will; that he disregard the binding framework of the movement, the kibbutz, party institutions, and all of the other shackles he chained to his legs."[56] "We loved him as a man, not as a politician," Elon said. Allon's charisma was based on human contact, warmth, and caring. He was not built for the loneliness at the top, the solitude of leadership. His friends cited Wilson as saying that Allon was unable to go for the jugular—he was unable to hurt people to get what he wanted. The magnetic villain, the person who placed himself outside the law, unfettered by personal or ideological loyalties in his race to the top, these images embodied the ideas of Machiavelli and Nietzsche, separating ethics and politics, and assuming that only "the great monsters of history" had leadership qualities. Behind these images, there was a veiled comparison to Ben-Gurion, on the one hand, and to Moshe Dayan, on the other. In the case of Ben-Gurion, the comparison does not seem to have been just: there can be only one founding father in a nation's history. The prime ministers of the founding generation (Moshe Sharett, Levi Eshkol, and Golda Meir) made it to the top, although they lacked Ben-Gurion's force of personality or his knack for recognizing and seizing a historic opportunity. Moshe Dayan, like Allon, failed to make it to the top, to become prime minister, despite his aptitude for solitude and emotional nondependency—the reverse of Allon.

Was the failure an expression of the limitations of the Palmah generation? That is how Amos Elon saw it: "With Allon's death, thoughts come to mind not only about him—and his failure—but about everyone we call 'the generation of the sons.' Sad heroes in a cruel land . . . Did they have too few thoughts? Or, maybe, unlike their fathers, they did not bother to think them through to the end? Allon was the hallmark of the generation of beautiful sun-children, doers who made an ideology out of not having an ideology." The fathers were steeped in the Jewish heritage of generations, while here in Israel everything sprouted fast, without roots, without spiritual baggage. The result was that the sons never grew up; they were eternally young with the charm of youth, but thus also lacking in the depths that come with maturity.[57] According to Amos Keinan, the Achilles heel of the first generation of sabras was elsewhere: It was a generation that could not rebel, could not free itself of the authority of the fathers. "Yigal Allon did not rise up against his father, Yigal Allon was a good boy." And for this reason, he lacked the spirit to demand his place in the sun: "He was shot because he did not know how to murder. Only revolutionaries and rebels, only they knew how to kill as well. Consequently, he roamed the land of Nod, the mark of Abel on his forehead."[58]

The expectation that the "sons" would rebel was part of the great hopes that the latter generation pinned on themselves. They had a utopian hope that when the guard passed to their generation, the realities would change beyond recognition. They thought they could change the world, Israeli circumstances, and leave their own mark. Their call to rebel was a mirror image of their disappointment with the Israel that took shape in the period of statehood. The call did not emanate from an alternative social view. It probably carried no ideological message, though it rebuked the generation of the "sons" for lacking ideology. It was based on the alleged uniqueness of the "native" virtues of sabras, harboring an arrogance vis-à-vis the newcomers from the Diaspora who had not grown up in the liberating air of Eretz Israel. It had a dual focus:

to change both the guard in power and the basic management of the Arab-Israeli conflict. As the native generation saw it, the leaders of the fathers' generation had been reared in an environment of Jewish weakness subject to the whims of their non-Jewish hosts. Jewish weakness molded their spiritual world and their attitude to Arabs. In contrast, Yigal Allon, a sabra, was to show spunk for bold solutions in Jewish-Arab relations, recognizing the great transformation in Jewish-Arab relations wrought by the state's establishment.

The purported weakness of the Palmah generation refers to the failure of Allon and Dayan to attain the post of prime minister. This overemphasis on the top of the political ladder seems to ignore the fact that for more than a decade the two men were at the center of Israeli politics. If success or failure are not measured solely by premiership, then one must remember that the two men played a key role in setting Israeli policy in the period following the Six Day War, for better or for worse. The anger at the Palmah generation originated in the dovish camp of the Left, which was annoyed that the two men did not contest Golda Meir or stick up for the Left's opinions against her. Did this weakness stem from a lack of cultural depth? Was it typical of "native" culture, the first generation in a land of immigration, divorced from an intellectual fount? The argument seems to have rhetorical force but no corroboration. Shimon Peres and Yitzhak Rabin, the next home-grown duo who were to mold Israeli policy in the coming fifteen years, developed from the same soil as their predecessors. Yet they did not have the same accusations flung at them: their political boldness indicates that the problem was not generational or even educational but primarily the compatibility of the figures and their characters with the times and the circumstances.

Allon's devotees saw him as the symbol of the perfect sabra: daring, doing, brave, honest, sincere, loyal, handsome, authentically "Israeli." But beneath the shell, he seems to have been also nonrepresentative of the sabra. In a secular country that spurned religion, Allon was always respectful of religion and the religious even though his way of life and political identity were far removed from theirs. No doubt this was due to the influence of Mes'ha and its traditional observances. He never forgot his mother's origins in ultra-Orthodox Safed. He considered himself integrally bound to the Jewish people down through the generations; he was not a "new Jew." At a time when his generation "negated Exile," he was uniquely conscious of his place as an immediate link in the chain of generations.[59] In a period when the "Canaanite" instincts of the native generation spawned condescension to Holocaust survivors, Allon was different. "Yigal Allon removed the veil of shame that enveloped us then. He spoke from a complete identification with the heroes of the Shoah. Before us stood a 'thoroughbred' sabra, an amazing integration of an oversoul, so to speak, in a healthy body," as Shevah Weiss, later a member of the Knesset, described his first encounter with Allon at an assembly in Kibbutz Lohamei Ha-Gettaot in the early 1950s.[60] Allon was acutely aware of his cultural shortcomings, thirsting for knowledge and questing after study. His quest was evocative of the fathers' generation. His dream of completing a dissertation in political science was reminiscent of the awe in which leaders of the founding generation held people with a formal education, who, in truth, were not fit to sit at their feet. He knew and loved the country's trails but expressed no longing for the ancient mythos, showed no interest in archeology, and did not look for Jewish precedence in the land of the Jews. Unlike others, he did not draw a straight line from the Bible to the Palmah, skipping over generations; his lineage passed through centuries of the Exile, without shame or apology.

The myth of the sabra cultivated a gruff manliness, a tough emotionless image. But Allon, despite his reticence in keeping pain and frustration to himself, hardly projected toughness or hardness. He emitted a spontaneous love that enfolded everyone in contact with him. His generation's distaste for displaying feelings only made his warm masculinity a refreshing change.

Allon passed away without having attained any of the three positions he desired: CGS, defense minister, prime minister. After his resignation from the army at the close of 1949, he had successfully filled a variety of positions (minister of labor, of absorption, of education, and foreign minister). But he left behind the image of a loser, repeatedly trying and failing to reach the top. His appearance at the Palmah gathering at Givat Brenner in 1952 seems to have been an omen of things to come: the great hopes pinned on him, the disappointments in him, the loss of his Palmah charm, his inability to replace it with an alternative charisma attractive to Israel's new publics. After he left the army, his charm gradually froze and melted. He reached the peak of his life before the age of thirty-one, fixing the borders of the state of the Jews. All that came after was like a continuing preamble to the next chapter that was never written.

His sudden death (29 February 1980) called forth a tide of love and sorrow. Walking beneath black umbrellas in heavy rain at the funeral in Ginossar were Jews and Arabs, young and old, those who had loved him and those who had not. The journalist Nahum Barnea wrote: "I see a great deal of longing for what is termed the beautiful, sabra Israel as opposed to [Menachem] Begin's mystical Israel or [then finance minister Simha] Ehrlich's shopkeeper Israel. The radio played the 'Kinneret' songs of Rachel and Naomi Shemer and the eyes of an entire generation welled with tears. . . . Not over the demise of an important person do they weep, but for themselves, for a land that was theirs and is no more."⁶¹ Barnea directed his words at the Left, the generation of statehood that, upon the political upheaval of 1977, felt that the state it had believed would always be theirs was slipping through their fingers. He lamented the decline of the Labor movement's culture, which was characterized by an immediate bond to the land, reticence, modest patriotism as expressed in the songs of Rachel and Naomi Shemer, a flight from pathos, and a respect for kibbutz life, work, and the soil. For a single moment, Allon's funeral stopped the clock; a generation that felt increasingly alien in its native land suddenly felt a sense of togetherness and belonging. If this is how Barnea, a member of the statehood generation, felt, it was harder still for Allon's generation. Wrote Amos Keinan: "Yigal Allon died without a homeland. The state he established robbed him of his homeland." In a powerful, lyrical piece, Keinan portrayed Allon as the prince of the Eretz Israel experience, which had vanished from the world in 1948, in his terms, "the revolution that never was." The story of Yigal Allon is the story of the "brilliant star, supernova, that exploded emitting intense heat and blinding light, imploding to become a black hole." Allon, to him, represented the "Canaanite" dream of the "new Jew" sprouting from the country's soil: "Eretz Israel was born, for the most part, by the plow and by the Hebrew language." Once the state was established the dream came to naught: "In 1948, when he ran forward, he was shot in the back." Between the lines of the elegy for Allon there is an elegy for the uniqueness of Eretz Israel as expressed by the "Canaanite" culture, which steadily dissolved in Israel's mass culture: a love of landscape, of the plow and the rock, the spring and the thorns; a pristine, premodern entity that came to life in the paintings of Nahum Gutman, in Yitzhak Danziger's sculpture *Nimrod*, in the poems of Yonatan Ratosh, in the bond to the Bible. Keinan concluded the lament for Allon with the following words: "Rest in peace, dear Yigal, exiled king in his own land, its dominion not yet come, its war not yet done."⁶²

The longing for the rootedness of Eretz Israel, for native authenticity, held onto the figure of Allon as a symbol of all the unrealized hopes of the generation born and bred in the land. It reflected the alienation of part of the Palmah generation from the state that had arisen, the disappointment of front-line soldiers at the realities they found when they returned home. It was a longing for the essence of the Yishuv, which had vanished upon statehood. In that unanticipated outburst of sorrow over Allon's death, an entire generation mourned the waning of their world.

Notes

Chapter 1

1. Yigal Allon, *Bet Avi* (Kibbutz Me'uhad, n.d.), p. 75. (In English: Yigal Allon, *My Father's House* [New York, 1976.])
2. Allon, *Bet Avi*, p. 75.
3. Ibid., p. 79.
4. On the history of Grodno and the Hibbat Zion movement there, see Dov Rabin, ed., "Grodno," *Entziklopedia shel Galuyot*, vol. 9 (Jerusalem, 1973).
5. The memoirs of Yosef Reuven Paicovich were recorded by Menachem Ben-Aryeh, Rosh Pina, KMA, Section 15—Allon (hereafter: Paicovich Memoirs); Eliav Paicovich (Allon), *Masekhet shel Bazelet* (pub. by the family); Allon, *Bet Avi*.
6. This account follows the Paicovich Memoirs. Eliav's description is less accurate.
7. Paicovich, *Masekhet shel Bazelet*, p. 1; Allon, *Bet Avi*, p. 82.
8. Paicovich Memoirs.
9. Ibid.
10. Paicovich, *Masekhet shel Bazelet*, the former; Allon, *Bet Avi*, the latter.
11. Paicovich Memoirs.
12. Paicovich, *Masekhet shel Bazelet*, p. 3.
13. Allon, *Bet Avi*, p. 86; Paicovich, *Masekhet shel Bazelet*, p. 3.
14. Amihud Schwartz, interview by the author.
15. Ibid.
16. On Mahanayim, see Shimshon Stein, *Mahanayim: Moshava Kitzrat Yamim* (Jerusalem, 1978); Ran Aaronsohn, "Shlavim be-Hakamat Moshvot ha-Aliyah ha-Rishona u-ve-Hitpat'hutan," in *Sefer ha-Aliyah ha-Rishona* (Jerusalem, 1982), pp. 64–65; Allon, *Bet Avi*, pp. 87–90; Paicovich, *Masekhet shel Bazelet*, p. 3; Amihud Schwartz, interview by the author, Paicovich Memoirs.
17. Paicovich Memoirs.
18. Ibid.; Paicovich, *Masekhet shel Bazelet*, pp. 4–5. The two accounts differ somewhat. I followed the first.
19. Paicovich Memoirs.
20. Arieh Bitan, *Tmurot Yishuviyot ba-Galil ha-Tahton ha-Mizrahi: 1800–1978* (Jerusalem, 1985–86), pp. 50–62.
21. Ibid., pp. 56–57, 62–67.
22. Ibid., pp. 67–70, 81–82.
23. Aaronsohn, "Shlavim," pp. 74–75; Bitan, *Tmurot Yishuriyot*, p. 82; A. Ever Hadani, *Ha-Hityashvut ba-Galil ha-Tahton*, Massada and Hitahdut ha-Ikarim ba-Galil ha-Tahton (Tel Aviv, 1955), p. 12.
24. Ever Hadani, *Ha-Hityashvut*, p. 141.
25. For an example of contracts between the ICA and settlers, see CZA J15/

6548; Bitan, *Tmurot Yishuviyot*, pp. 82–87. Curiously, one clause obliges the tenant farmer to use *European* plows.

26. Ever Hadani, *Ha-Hityashvut*, p. 71.
27. Allon, *Bet Avi*, pp. 20–30; Ever Hadani, *Ha-Hityashvut*, p. 203.
28. See, e.g., Ever Hadani, *Ha-Hityashvut*, pp. 113–14.

29. *Hashkafa*, 19 May 1904, quoted by Shulamit Laskov, *Kol Koreh* (Tel Aviv, 1986), p. 47.
30. Aaronsohn, "Shlavim," p. 17; Meir Hareuveini, ed., *Kefar Tavor (Mes'ha)*, (Kefar Tavor, 1976), p. 12.
31. Vitkin, Mikhtav le-Sum, 24 November 1904, cited by Laskov, *Kol Koreh*, p. 47. Cited here from the original.
32. Laskov, *Kol Koreh*, pp. 47–48.
33. Vitkin, *Mikhtav le-Sum* (1904?), cited by Laskov, *Kol Koreh*, p. 53.
34. Asher Ehrlich, "Sefer Hayai," in Yitzhak Ogen, ed., *Asher Haya* (Tel Aviv, 1949), pp. 25 ff.
35. Shalom Atiya, "Ha-Moshava le-Gvurot," p. 77.
36. Contracts between Mr. Jules Rosenheck and Mr. Reuven Paicovich, 1 November 1908; 1 November 1901, CZA J15/6548.
37. Paicovich's letter to Rosenheck, n.d., CZA J15/6548; contracts between Rosenheck and Paicovich of 1 November 1901 and 1 November 1908.
38. Ever Hadani, *Ha-Hityashvut*, pp. 199–202; Paicovich Memoirs; Paicovich, *Masekhet shel Bazelet*, p. 7.
39. Ever Hadani, *Ha-Hityashvut*, p. 202.
40. The positive quality is in Ever Hadani, *Ha-Hityashvut*, based on the memoirs of Mordekhai Paicovich, p. 202. The negative quality follows the accounts given by Mes'ha members Shimon Zefira, Shimon Mattveyov, and David Goldman in interviews with the author.
41. Paicovich Memoirs.
42. Shimon Zefira, Shimon Matveyov, and David Goldman, interviews by the author.
43. Ever Hadani, *Ha-Hityashvut*, pp. 205–6.
44. Ibid., 178.
45. Paicovich, *Masekhet shel Bazelet*, p. 14.
46. Allon, *Bet Avi*, pp. 114–17.
47. Ibid., pp. 49–51.
48. Ibid., p. 26.
49. Ever Hadani, *Ha-Hityashvut*, pp. 75–76, 122.
50. Allon, *Bet Avi*, p. 46.
51. Amihud Schwartz, interview by author.
52. See, e.g., the letter from A. Y. Azdin to the ICA's Rosenheck, 5 Elul 5673 (1913), CZA J15/6536.
53. CZA J15/6548.
54. A. Y. Azdin's letter to Rosenheck, 5 Elul 5673 (1913), CZA J15/6536.
55. There are a number of sources on Ehrlich. The main ones are Ogen, *Asher Haya*, which includes his autobiography; and Yehuda Salu, *Ha-Moreh ha-Arokh* (Merhavia, 1965), which is dedicated to him.
56. Ever Hadani, *Ha-Hityashvut*, pp. 210–12.
57. The affair, involving the doctor's employment, is mentioned in Ogen, *Asher Haya*, pp. 29–30.
58. Ever Hadani, *Ha-Hityashvut*, pp. 237–41.
59. Paicovich Memoirs.

60. Allon, *Bet Avi*, p. 84.
61. Paicovich Memoirs.
62. Allon, *Bet Avi*, p. 102.
63. A letter from a Mes'ha group to council members at Yavne'el and Melahamiya, 5th Tebeth 5669 (1909), CZA J15/6521.
64. See council correspondence, 5673 (1913), CZA J15/6536; Ever Hadani, *Ha-Hityashvut*, p. 240.
65. Mes'ha interviews with Goldman, Mattveyov, and Zefira.
66. See, e.g., Allon, *Bet Avi*, pp. 110 ff.
67. Paicovich, *Masekhet shel Bazelet*, p. 12–16; Paicovich Memoirs; Allon, *Bet Avi*, p. 18.
68. *Maariv*, 20 July 1973.
69. The tale of the robbers appears in various versions in Paicovich Memoirs; Zvi Allon, *Le-Zikhro*, family booklet; Allon, *Bet Avi*, pp. 14–15; Ever Hadani, *Ha-Hityashvut*, p. 442–44; *Ha-Poel Ha-Tza'ir*, 2 June 1920; 11 June 1920.
70. "Me-ha-Galil ha-Tahton," *Ha-Poel Ha-Tza'ir*, 11 June 1920.
71. "Me-ha-Galil ha-Tahton," *Ha-Poel Ha-Tza'ir*, 25 June 1920.
72. David Goldberg lost 12 head of cattle; Yona Bizler and Mendel Goldman lost 10 each. In total, 185 head were stolen. The list of the cattle taken from Kefar Tavor, 29 May 1920, CZA J15/6677.
73. Bitan, *Tmurot Yishuviyot*, pp. 192–93.
74. "Kefar Tavor," *Ha-Poel Ha-Tza'ir*, 20 January 1922.
75. "Me-ha-Galil ha-Tahton," *Ha-Poel Ha-Tza'ir*, 3 December 1920.
76. "Mes'ha," *Ha-Poel Ha-Tza'ir*, 4 February 1921.
77. "Kefar Tavor," *Ha-Poel Ha-Tza'ir*, 20 January 1922.
78. "Me-ha-Galil ha-Tahton," *Ha-Poel Ha-Tza'ir*, 11 November 1921.
79. Paicovich Memoirs.
80. Allon, *Bet Avi*, p. 85.
81. Ibid., p. 103.
82. See CZA J15/5566; J15/5557; J15/5558; J15/6677; J15/10183.
83. Paicovich to Mr. Gottlieb, the PICA director in Haifa, 3 September 1930, CZA J15/10183.
84. The letters are in the Paicovich file, CZA J15/10183.
85. The PICA to Paicovich, 30 December 1934, CZA J15/10183.
86. Paicovich letters to the PICA, 1931–32, and PICA's answers, 29 October 1931, 29 September 1932, CZA J15/10183.
87. CZA J15/5557; J15/5566.
88. Ever Hadani, *Ha-Hityashvut*, p. 514.
89. The PICA to the Kefar Tavor Council, 2 July 1931, CZA J15/5566. See also the PICA's letter to the Kefar Tavor Council, 14 August 1931, CZA J15/5566. See also M. Z. Ben Sasson, "Ha-Avoda ha-Ivrit be-Moshvot ha-Galil ha-Tahton," *Ha-Poel Ha-Tza'ir*, 17 November 1933; Aleph, "Mikhtavim me-ha-Galil," *Ha-Poel Ha-Tza'ir*, 31 March 1933.
90. Ever Hadani, *Ha-Hityashvut*, p. 518.
91. On the water supply problems and the attempt to build a well on their own, see CZA J15/5558. See also Aleph, "Mikhtavim min ha-Galil," *Ha-Poel Ha-Tza'ir*, 31 March 1933. On the opposition to the "progressives," see "Mikhtavim min ha-Galil," *Ha-Poel Ha-Tza'ir*, 16 February 1934.
92. Ever Hadani, *Ha-Hityashvut*, p. 543.
93. Paicovich to the PICA official Frank, 19 June 1935, CZA J15/10183.
94. Allon, *Bet Avi*, pp. 119–22, 138–39.

95. Ibid., p. 65.
96. Ibid., 110–12.
97. Ibid., p. 98.
98. Ibid., 114–16.
99. Yigal's letter to his teacher, KTA.
100. Yigal Paicovich, "Ha-Geshem," school newspaper vol. 1 (surmised), 1928, KTA.
101. Moshe Grinker to the PICA, 3 May 1934 (18 Iyar 5694); 12 June 1934 (29 Sivan 5694); 14 July 1934 (2 Av 5694); CZA J15/5557.
102. Allon, *Bet Avi*, pp. 113–14.
103. Ibid., p. 31. In his interview, Shimon Zefira mentioned the great influence exerted by Saul and "Be-Ein Dor" on Mes'ha's youth, and he even quoted the ballad.
104. Allon, *Bet Avi*, p. 33.
105. Ibid., p. 126.

Chapter 2

1. A section of Sir Ellis Kadoorie's will, CZA S25/2698.
2. On the establishment of the Kadoorie school, see Eliezer Dumka, "Hevlei Hakamoto shel Bet ha-Sefer 'Kadoorie,' *Cathedra* (April 1985). On the Zionist version of Kadoorie's intentions, see the article by Moshe Kleinman, *Ha-Olam*, 18 January 1924, cited at length by Dumka, "Hevlei Hakamoto," p. 91.
3. Memo of the councils and towns, 14 January 1925, CZA S15/294a. A photocopy of Mes'ha's letter appears in Dumka, *Kadoorie—Alei Giv'a* (Kefar Tavor, 1982–83), p. 20.
4. Arlosoroff to the chief secretary of the Mandate Government; 26 October 1932, CZA S25/2700.
5. See Dumka, "Hevlei Hakamoto," pp. 104–6; CZA S25/2700.
6. Reuven Paicovich to Zemach, undated, KA, 16/5/18.
7. Zemach to Paicovich, 23 August 1934, KA, 16/5/18.
8. Paicovich to Zemach, 29 October 1934, KA, 5/678.
9. Zemach to Paicovich, 13 November 1934, KA, 5/519.
10. Paicovich to Zemach, 10 December 1934, KA, 16/2/34.
11. Sini Azaryahu (Sini), interview by the author.
12. Transcript of Kadoorie's first graduating class, 1934–37, KA.
13. Joel Prozhinin, Amos Brandsteter, Ada Zemach, and Sini Azaryahu, interviews by the author.
14. Shlomo Zemach, *Sippur Hayai* (Jerusalem and Tel Aviv, 1983), p. 156.
15. The first story is according to Dumka, *Kadoorie*, p. 37, the second story is from Azaryahu, Brandsteter, Prozhinin, and Ada Zemach, interviews by the author.
16. Zemach, *Sippur Hayai*, p. 156.
17. Sini to his parents, 6 February 1935, private archive.
18. Amos Brandsteter and Sini Azaryahu, interviews by the author.
19. Sini Azaryahu, interview by the author.
20. See a slightly different version in Allon, *Bet Avi* (My father's house), p. 165–68.
21. The described romance with Ada is based chiefly on her own account during an interview with the author. Her parents' purported disapproval is based on the author's interviews of Prozhinin, Azaryahu, and Brandsteter.

22. Sini Azaryazhu to his parents, 21 October 1935, private archive.
23. Zemach, *Sippur Hayai* p. 157.
24. Zemach himself discusses the dilemma; Zemach, *Sippur Hayai*, p. 159. The part of his memoirs dealing with Kadoorie is fraught with ambiguity about his role and the British, Zemach, *Sippur Hayai*, pp. 153–59.
25. Brandsteter, Azaryahu, and Prozhinin, interviews by the author. There are inaccuracies in the testimonies, but on the whole they correspond.
26. Brandsteter, Azaryahu, and Prozhinin, interviews by the author.
27. Pupils of Kadoorie's first graduating class to the JA-PD, 19 February 1936, CZA S25/7028.
28. Ada Zemach, interview by the author.
29. Dumka, *Kadoorie—Alei givah*, p. 37; Sini Azaryahu, interview by the author.
30. Sini Azaryahu to his parents, 21 October 1935, personal archive.
31. Brandsteter, interview by author; Allon, *Bet Avi*, pp. 151–52; Zemach, *Sippur Hayai*, p. 158.
32. Allon, *Bet Avi*, p. 152; Zemach, *Sippur Hayai*, p. 158, Brandsteter, interview by the author.
33. Ibid., pp. 153–54.
34. Hoter-Yishai to Bernard Joseph, Jerusalem, 1 November 1936, CZA S25/7028.
35. Brandsteter, interview by the author.
36. Allon, *Bet Avi*, p. 153; Bransteter, interview by the author.
37. Sini Azaryahu to his parents, Kefar Javetz, 24 September 1936, private archive.
38. Sini Azaryahu to his parents, Kefar Javetz, 5 October 1936, private archive.
39. The only existing description of Allon's actions in this period is his own in Allon, *Bet Avi*, pp. 169–73.
40. A group of Kadoorie graduates to the director of the Agriculture and Fisheries Department, Jerusalem, 26 January 1937, CZA S25/7028.
41. Prozhinin, interview by the author.
42. See note 40.
43. Yehezkel Rubin to the JA-PD, 6.3.1937, CZA S25/7028.
44. Allon, *Bet Avi*, p. 178.
45. Ada Zemach, Prohinin, and Azaryahu, interviews by the author.
46. Allon, *Bet Avi*, p. 168.
47. Ibid., pp. 158–69.
48. Ada Zemach, Azaryahu, and Prozhinin, interviews by the author.
49. Allon, *Bet Avi*, p. 181.
50. Ibid., p. 186.
51. The story is given in detail in ibid., pp. 182–86.

Chapter 3

1. Ginossar Newsletter no. 909, 17 March 1981.
2. The *kevutzah* (literally, "group") was the smaller forerunner of the collective, agricultural, pioneering kibbutzim. The movements of *kevutzot* and kibbutzim belonged to the Histadrut—the General Federation of Jewish Labor in Palestine—and they were organized in the Histadrut's Agricultural Center. The Histadrut embraced the entire Zionist Left and engaged primarily in creating infrastructure for Zionist settlement, defense, construction, and so forth. It also ran trade unions, and the HNHO youth movement, for working youngsters,

operated under its wing. *Kevutzot* and kibbutzim drew their members from organized youth groups, who usually trained (*hakhshara* stage) and settled (*hityashvut* stage) together.

Until 1951, there were three kibbutz movements, which were based on political leanings (the Social-Democratic right and the pro-Soviet left) or organizational size: Hever Ha-Kevutzot, Ha-Kibbutz ha-Me'uhad (KM), and Ha-Shomer Ha-Tza'ir (HSHT). The former two were associated with the Right or Left streams of Mapai (the Eretz Israel Labor Party)—the ruling party in the Zionist movement, the Yishuv, and the State of Israel from 1933–77. In the period considered here, Mapai was headed by Berl Katznelson and David Ben-Gurion. The KM was the largest, most dynamic, and activist component in defense, settlement, and the like.

In 1944, Mapai split and its left, led by Yitzhak Tabenkin, set up the Le-Ahdut Ha-Avodah (LAHA) Party. The issue divided the KM along party lines, with one-third of its members remaining with Mapai and two-thirds going over to LAHA. The KM advocated a "greater Israel," took an activist stance in matters of security, and was pro-Soviet, as opposed to Hever Ha-Kevutzot, which remained Social-Democratic and did not lean toward activism.

3. Joel Prozhinin, interview by the author.
4. Contract between the PICA and the Migdal youth *kevutzah*, Haifa, 22.21937, CZA J15/5343.
5. Absalom Zoref, *Ginossar, Hamesh Esrei Shana le-Hivasda* (Tel Aviv, 1949), pp. 128–29. There is another version in the same book, pp. 24–26. The first version, also published in 1935 in *Ba-Maaleh*, the journal of HNHO, strikes me as more authentic.
6. A. Zoref, *Ginossar*, pp. 37–41; Absalom Zoref, *Israel Levy, Ish Ginossar* (Tel Aviv, 1964) pp. 57–59.
7. Contract between the PICA and the Migdal youth *kevutzah*, Haifa, 1 July 1934, 22.21937, CZA J15/5343.
8. A. Zoref, *Levy*, p. 61; A. Zoref, *Ginossar*, pp. 39–40.
9. Wolfson, PICA, Haifa, to Kevutzat Migdal youth, 14 April 1937, CZA 115/5343.
10. Yehoshua Rabinowitz of Ginossar's HNHO *kevutzah* to PICA administration, Haifa, 23 April 1937, CZA J15/5343.
11. Hartzfeld, Agricultural Center, to Gottlieb, PICA, Paris, 14 May 1937, CZA J15/5343.
12. Minutes of the Ginossar assembly, 29 November 1937, Ginossar Archives (hereafter GAR).
13. Minutes of the Ginossar assembly, 8 February 1938, GAR.
14. Absalom Zoref, interview by the author.
15. PICA executive to Ginossar, 19 August 1938, CZA J15/5343; A. Zoref, *Ginossar*, p. 43; A. Zoref, *Israel Levy*, pp. 76–77.
16. Ginossar to PICA executive, Haifa, 23 August 1938, CZA J15/5343.
17. PICA correspondence, September–October 1938, CZA J15/5343.
18. Meir Rotberg to PICA executive, Haifa, 11 October 1938, CZA J15/5453.
19. Nahum Shadmi to PICA executive, Haifa, 12 October 1938, CZA J15/5453.
20. Letter from Sini Azaryahu to his parents, Ginossar, 21 October 1938.
21. See, e.g., A. Zoref, *Ginossar*, p. 45.
22. A. Zoref, *Ginossar*, p. 45; A. Zoref, *Levy*, pp. 78–83.
23. PICA correspondence, October–December 1938, CZA J15/5342.

24. Letter from Sini Azaryahu to his parents, 1 December 1939.
25. Hartzfeld to PICA executive, Haifa, 17 January 1939, CZA J15/5343.
26. Kupat Holim head office to the Kevutzat Ginossar secretariat, 24 April 1939, GAR, Ginnosar file.
27. Ruth Allon, interview by the author.
28. Sini Azaryahu, interview by the author.
29. Minutes of the Ginossar assembly, 1 November 1941, GAR.
30. Minutes of the Ginossar assembly, 2 December 1939; 8 March 1941 GAR.
31. Minutes of the Ginossar assembly, 8 March 1941, GAR.
32. *Bitui* (Ginossar newsletter), 22 December 1941, GAR.
33. Minutes of the Ginossar assembly, 8 March 1941 GAR.
34. Ruth Allon, interview by the author.
35. Newsletter of Migdal's HNHO *kevutzah*, 28 October 1938, GAR.
36. *Bitui*, 27 March 191940, GAR.
37. See Sini Azaryahu, minutes of the Ginossar assembly, 18 January 1942, GAR.
38. Ginossar newsletter no. 909, 17 March 1981.
39. A. Zoref, *Israel Levy*, pp. 55–56.
40. Sini Azaryahu, interview by the author.
41. The entire description is based on Ruth Allon, interview by the author.
42. Yehudit Zoref, interview by the author.
43. Joel Prozhinin and Sini, Azaryahu, interviews by the author.
44. Yehudit Zoref and Ruth Allon, interviews by the author.
45. Ruth Allon and Yehudit Zoref, interviews by the author.
46. Ruth Allon, Absalom Zoref, and Yehudit Zoref, interviews by the author.
47. Ginossar to PICA executive, Haifa, 1 October 1939, 15 October 1939, CZA J15/5343.
48. A. Zoref, *Israel Levy*, p. 88; A. Zoref, *Ginossar*, p. 58.
49. The details of the battle are based on A. Zoref, *Israel Levy*, pp. 88–89; A. Zoref, *Ginossar*, p. 58; and Yigal's account of the "water war," which is from the taped film of Yehoshua Baharav's program, "Haim she-ka-Eleh," Ginossar, 14 September 1977, GAR.
50. See Yigal's account of the water war, Baharav, "Haim she-ka-Eleh."
51. A. Zoref, *Ginossar*, pp. 59–64; A. Zoref, *Israel Levy*, 90–92; Absalom Zoref, interview by the author.
52. Letter from Israel Levy, 15 July 1960, quoted in A. Zoref, *Ginossar*, pp. 74–75.
53. Katznelson's letter to Ginossar's prisoners, first intermediate day of Passover, 1940, A. Zoref, *Ginossar*, p. 82. Yehoshua Baharav's letter from Acre, 29 April 1940, A. Zoref, *Ginossar*, pp. 71–72.
54. Agricultural Center to PICA, 9 May 1940, CZA J15/5343. See also the correspondence with PICA in this file on the preceding months (and the legal suit).
55. Hartzfeld to PICA, 21 May 1940, CZA J15/5343.
56. Ginossar to PICA executive, Haifa, 30 June 1940 and PICA's response, 1 July 1940, CZA J15/5343.
57. Minutes of the Ginossar assembly, 3 June 1940, GAR.
58. A. Zoref, *Levy*, p. 107–8; Sini Azaryahu to his parents, 21 August 1940; PICA correspondence, October 1940, CZA J15/5343.
59. Agreement between the colony of Migdal and Kibbutz Ginossar, 1 December 1940, GAR, Ginossar file; A. Zoref, *Ginossar*, pp. 50–51.
60. Minutes of the Ginossar assembly, 3 November 1940, GAR.

61. Allon's summary of the situation at the Ginossar assembly, Minutes, 8 December 1940, GAR.
62. Katznelson seems to have helped the *kevutzah* out on a number of occasions. The papers left by Yaacov Efter include a letter (dated 4 August 1940) from Katznelson, thanking him for obtaining a ten-year, interest-free loan in the sum of P£100 from the Ha-Mashbir board for the Ginossar *kevutzah*.
63. On relations with Berl Katznelson and his part in the attempt to end the disagreement with the PICA, see Minutes of the Ginossar assembly, 3 November 1940, GAR, Allon's words.
64. Absalom Zoref, interview by the author.
65. Promissory note, Tel Aviv, 4 December 1940, signed by Y. Paicovich, guaranteed by Z. Aharonowitz, GAR.
66. At the kibbutz assembly, 8 December 1940, Allon said: "We managed to receive the donation to Solel Boneh and it will be earmarked for buying a tractor . . . the money was obtained with Berl's intervention and personal guarantee. . . ." Minutes of the Ginossar assembly, GAR.
67. Minutes of the Ginossar assembly, 1 January 1941.
68. Shemarya Gutman, KMC at Givat Ha-Sheloshah, 17–19 January 1941, KMA, Efal, section 5, container 6, file 1.
69. Allon, KMC at Givat Ha-Sheloshah, 17–19 January 1941, KMA, Efal, section 5.
70. A. Zoref, *Israel Levy*, pp. 40–42; 46–49.
71. Minutes of the Ginossar assembly, second day of the New Year, apparently 27 September 1938, GAR.
72. Allon, KMC at Givat Ha-Sheloshah, 17–19 January 1941, KMA, section 5, container 6, file 1.
73. Minutes of the Ginossar assembly, 31 November 1941, poll on joining KM, 2 December 1940, GAR, Ginossar file; Yigal's words, KMC at Givat Ha-Sheloshah, 17–19 January 1941, KMA, section 5, container 6, file 1.
74. Abraham Givelber, KMC at Givat Ha-Sheloshah, 17–19 January 1941, KMA, section 5, container 6, file 1. Israel Idelson's moderate criticism of the Soviet Union immediately raised a demand for a response by M. Majhibovsky, ibid.
75. Minutes of the Ginossar assembly, 22 January 1941, GAR.
76. Ibid.
77. Minutes of the Ginossar assembly, end March 1940, GAR.
78. Minutes of the Ginossar assembly, 22 January 1941, GAR.
79. KMC at Givat Ha-Sheloshah, 17–19 January 1941, KMA, section 5, container 6, file 1.
80. Ibid.
81. Ibid.
82. Ibid.
83. On the Rehovot seminar, see Anita Shapira, *Berl* (Tel Aviv, 1980), pp. 632–37. On the letters of refusal, see the account by the seminar secretariat (published in hectograph), LA-LI, p. 19ff.
84. Minutes of the Ginossar assembly, 15 February 1941, GAR.
85. Ibid.
86. Berl Repetur, *Le-Lo Heref* (Tel Aviv, 1973), 2: 86–87.
87. Leni Yahil and David Koren, interviews by the author.
88. *Bitui*, 8 March 1940.
89. Appeal to British commander, January 1941, KMA, section 15, Allon, container 4, file 1.

90. A. Zoref, *Ginossar*, p. 58.
91. Nurit's story is based on the author's interviews of Ruth Allon, Absalom Zoref, and Yehudit Zoref. The quote is from the latter.
92. Allon, *Bet Avi*, p. 195.
93. According to Ruth Allon, he was the first. According to Yehudit Zoref, there were others before him.
94. Allon, *Bet Avi*, p. 195.
95. Ruth Allon, interview by the author.
96. Absalom Zoref, interview by the author.
97. The description of Reuven Paicovich's life at Ginossar is based on the author's interviews of Ruth Allon, Absalom Zoref, and Yehudit Zoref, as well as Allon, *Bet Avi*, pp. 195–99.
98. A. Zoref, *Ginossar*, p. 52; newsletter no. 67, "Eser Shanim li-Isud ha-Kevutzah."
99. Report of Dr. P. Lander, 28 May 1941 and 4 November 1942, GAR, Ginossar file.
100. Correspondence between Ginossar and the health fund's head office, 3 December 1942; 10 December 1942, and 19 January 1943, GAR, Ginossar file.
101. Letter from parents to Ginossar secretariat, Tel Aviv, 5 May 1943, GAR, Ginossar file.
102. PICA correspondence, 1942–44, CZA J15/5342.
103. The correspondence on the question is quite hefty. See, for example, the letter from PICA to I. Marshak, the Agricultural Center, 27 December 1946, CZA J15/5342.
104. A. Zoref, *Ginossar*, pp. 55–56.
105. Ruth Allon, interview by the author.
106. A. Zoref, *Ginossar*, pp. 145–46.
107. Ginossar to Mr. Levhar, district officer, 9 February 1942, GAR, Ginossar file.
108. Ginossar newsletter, 15 May 1939; 19 May 1939, GAR.
109. See Ginossar's letter to the Central Appeals Committee, 16 June 1943, GAR, Ginossar file.

Chapter 4

1. Israel Galili to his father, 4 September 1938, KMA, Galili Section, container 5, file 3. On the growth of the offensive (as opposed to the defensive) ethos, see Anita Shapira, *Land and Power* (New York, 1992).
2. See the detailed discussion in Slutsky et al., *Sefer Toldot ha-Haganah* (Tel Aviv, 1964), vol. 2, part 2, pp. 631–722; 1014–32.
3. In ibid., vol. 2, part 2, pp. 798–850. For the debate on restraint, see Anita Shapira, "Bein Havlaga le-Terror—Ha-Kinus ha-Yishuvi be-Yuli 1938," *Ha-Zionut* 6 (1981): pp. 350–426; Shapira, *Land and Power*, pp. 234–57.
4. Allon's words at the seminar for KM envoys, Givat Ha-Shelosha, 29 May 1945, KMA, section 2, container 16, file 105; hereafter Envoys Seminar.
5. Yitzhak Sadeh, *Ma Hidesh ha-Palmah* (Merhavia, 1950), pp. 22–28. For a summary of the question, see Galili's talk at the 37th Histadrut Council, LA-LI.
6. Sadeh, *Ma Hidesh ha-Palmah*, p. 24.
7. Yohanan Ratner, *Hayai ve-Ani* (Tel Aviv, 1978), p. 269.
8. There are a considerable number of accounts about Sadeh's key role in

this. Especially conspicuous is that of Joseph Harel, interview by the author. See also Ratner, *Hayai ve-Ani*, p. 269.

9. According to the manpower report (21 September 1936) of police and prison authorities, he was conscripted on 1 August 1936, and his I.D. number was 1853. He belonged to the Nazareth Brigade and his salary was paid by the Haganah rather than by British sources.

10. On the Jewish Settlement Police (JSP), see Slutsky et al., *Sefer Toldot ha-Haganah*, vol. 2, part 2, pp. 881–910.

11. Allon, *Bet Avi*, p. 172.

12. Ibid., pp. 173–74.

13. Slutsky et al., *Sefer Toldot ha-Haganah*, vol. 2, part 2, pp. 942–43; Shosh Spector interview by the author.

14. Allon, *Bet Avi*, pp. 176–77.

15. Ibid., p. 177.

16. In an interview by the author, Shlomo Shamir attested to Allon's participation in the course. This also emerges from the situation report of the field company, 15 March 1938, LA 161V, file 21, which lists the Ayelet Ha-Shahar course as the first in a series, with the participation of field company members from the Upper Galilee, the Lower Galilee, and the Jordan Valley.

17. Shlomo Shamir, interview by the author.

18. Field company situation report, 15 March 1938, LA 161V, file 21.

19. Absalom Zoref and Joel Prozhinin, interviews by the author. The apprentice was Prozhinin.

20. Joseph Harel, interview by the author.

21. For biographical details on the Dayan family, see Shabtai Teveth, *Dayan* (Tel Aviv, 1971), pp. 9–26.

22. Joseph Harel, interview by the author.

23. Rare testimony of this in a contemporary document may be found in a letter by Israel Galili from early 1941: "You know that I am looking for people and you know how few there are." He attached a list of English-speaking youngsters from Afikim, Deganyah Bet, Kibbutz Anglo-Baltic, Tirat Zvi (a variety of movement affiliations), adding: "I would like to ask for your assistance, meet them and see what you think of them, we will still speak of this face to face." Galili's notebook, 23 January 1942, p. 23, KMA.

24. Israel Galili, interview by the author.

25. Nahum Shadmi, 1981, KMA, 15, Shadmi, personal archive.

26. List of vans of Nazareth and Galilee region (apparently March 1938), CZA S25/159.

27. Joseph Harel and Meir Davidson, interviews by the author.

28. Report on the attack on Hanita road workers, 25 March 1938, Hanita 26 March 1938, KMA, section 15, Ben-Hur series, container 11, file 3.

29. According to Shlomo Shamir, he took the picture, interview by the author.

30. Meir Davidson, interview by the author.

31. See Gershon Rivlin, ed., *La-Esh ve-la-Maggen* (Tel Aviv, 1964), pp. 375, 430.

32. Yehoshua Gordon to Abraham Ikar, 13 November 1938, mobile squad, CZA S25/159.

33. Circular to sergeants from Yehoshua Gordon, 13 November 1938, mobile squad, CZA S25/159.

34. On the restraint and its abandonment, see note 3.

35. Allon at the Envoys Seminar.

36. See, e.g., "Yoman ha-Nesiya le-Ju'ara, 9 April 1938–10 May 1938," KMA, section 15, Ben-Hur series, container 11, file 1.
37. "Mi-Yomani," Report of 12 February 1938 (it says 1937, which is certainly a mistake), signed no. 6 (Joseph Pressman?), KMA, section 15, Ben-Hur series, Container 11, file 3.
38. Yitzhak Henkin, interview by the author. These rumors are corroborated by a contemporary report, 19 November 1938, on the actions of one (of Wingate's) special night squads (SNS) at the village of Metzar under a commanding officer by the name of Bridan, CZA S/25-8768.
39. "Mi-Yomani," KMA, section 15, Ben-Hur series, container 11, file 3.
40. This is Allon's number in the list of vans of the Lower Galilee District, CZA S25/159. See the report by Sergeant Yigal Paicovich to the Auxiliary Police Guard in Afula, 26 October 1938, on the joint action with the SNS at Hittin on 20 October 1938, CZA S/25-8768.
41. See report by no. 4, "Hatzlakha o kishalon," 9 June 1938, HA, Field Company, file 26; the letter, *nun* (Nahum Kramer?), "Min ha-shmira bi-sdot ha-Galil ha-Tahton," 10 May 1938, KMA, section 15, Ben-Hur series, container 11, file 3; "Al ma she-hitrahesh be-Migdal be-yamim ha-ahronim," 16 May 1938, KMA, section 15, Ben-Hur series, container 11, file 3.
42. Allon's words at the Envoys Seminar.
43. Sini Azaryahu, interview by the author.
44. Report of no. 4, "Helkeinu be-Leyl Tveria," 2 October 1938, KMA, section 15, Ben-Hur series, container 11, file 3.
45. The description is based on Slutsky et al., *Sefer Toldot ha-Haganah*, vol. 2, part 2, pp. 818–24; Rivlin, *La-Esh ve-la-Maggen*, pp. 177–79; "Helkeinu be-Leyl Tveria," 2 October 1938, KMA, section 15, Ben-Hur series, container 11, file 3, Nahum Shadmi, 1981, KMA, 15, Shadmi, personal archive.
46. Sini Azaryahu, Meir Davidson, Yosef Tabenkin, and Nahum Shadmi, interviews by the author. Shadmi in his testimony (KMA, 15, Shadmi, personal archive) elaborates on the erroneous *Davar* report that upset Wingate because it was his forces that carried out the action that was attributed to the field companies.
47. "Helkeinu be-Leyl Tveria," 2 October 1938, KMA, section 15, Ben-Hur series, container 11, file 3.
48. Ibid.
49. "'Bikur' ba-Kefar Daburiyeh," HA, field companies, file 26.
50. In those days (June 1939) the field companies were dismantled and a new field force established. The commanders of the new districts, which had just risen (in place of the old blocs) vied with the command of the Field Force for leadership. This rivalry found expression in the Lubya action in the complex structure of the forces. See Ratner, *Hayai ve-Ani*, pp. 277–84; and the Shadmi, 1981, KMA, 15, Shadmi, personal archive.
51. Allon related the difference between this way of doing things and the Palmah's in an allusion to the Lubya operation: "Not according to the system that was in place, when in order to damage a home inside an Arab village all the district's top brass assembled to carry out the action." Allon's words at the Envoys Seminar.
52. The description is based on the author's interviews of Shlomo Shamir and Joseph Harel, as well as the account of David Yitzhaki, KMA, section 15, container 10, file 1. See also Slutsky et al., *Sefer Toldot ha-Haganah*, vol. 3, part 1, p. 72, which explicitly cites the operation as an example of local commanders shedding responsibility.

Notes to Pages 97–106

53. The first version is from Shlomo Shamir, interview by the author. The second versionis from David Yitzhaki, KMA, section 15, container 10, file 1. The third version is from Joseph Harel, interview by the author.
54. Allon at Envoys Seminar.
55. The quotation is according to Slutsky, *Sefer Toldot ha-Haganah*, vol. 3, part 1, p. 72.
56. Shlomo Shamir, interview by the author.
57. Ben-Gurion, Minutes of Mapai Center, 8 September 1939, Labor Party Archives, Bet Berl, 23/39.
58. The description is based on Allon, *Bet Avi*, pp. 188–94; Teveth, *Dayan*, 175–80; Slutsky et al., *Sefer Toldot ha-Haganah*, vol. 3, part 1, p. 122. The latter description contains inaccuracies.
59. Allon, *Bet Avi*, p. 190.
60. Ibid., pp. 192–93.
61. Teveth, *Dayan*, pp. 176–80.
62. Allon, *Bet Avi*, p. 191.
63. Israel Galili, interview by the author.
64. Joseph Harel, interview by the author.
65. Israel Galili's eulogy. I assume that it was around this period for it is hard to imagine that Galili's words related to the period when Allon was already a well-known commander on a clear road to advancement.
66. Shosh Spector, interview by the author.
67. The first version is according to Zerubavel Gilad, ed., *Maggen ba-Seter* (Jerusalem, 1949); the second version is based on the author's interview of Shosh Spector, which also helped reconstruct Zvi Spector's biography.
68. Shosh Spector, interview by the author.
68. Joseph Harel, interview by the author.
70. Anita Shapira, *Berl* (Tel Aviv, 1980), p. 643.
71. Galili touches on these matters in a letter to his wife, Zippora, 23 March 1942, KMA, Galili, container 5, file 3. From the discussion during the panic at Rommel's renewed approach to Alexandria in 1942, it is clear that the matter came up earlier. On collaboration with the Germans, see also Galili's words at the KMC at Ein Harod, second (evening) session, 5 July 1942, KMA, Galili, container 6, file 2.
72. Shosh Spector, interview by the author.
73. Ibid.
74. Elazar Galili, interview by the author.
75. Shosh Spector, interview by the author; Zerubavel Gilad and Matti Megged, eds., *Sefer ha-Palmah* (Tel Aviv, 1953), p. 80.
76. Yigal Allon, "Megamot u-Maas," in Gilad and Megged, *Sefer ha-Palmah*, p. 10. According to Galili's testimony (HA), the decision to establish the Palmah was made in the absence of the National Command's representatives on the Right, who firmly opposed the creation of a permanently conscripted force.
77. Yitzhak Sadeh, "Shlihut Ha-Khaf Gimmel," in Gilad, *Maggen ba-Seter*, pp. 89–90.
78. David Hacohen, *Et Le-Sapper* (Tel Aviv, 1974), pp. 171–74. In the discussion of 27 November 1944 at the JA on the lessons of cooperating with the British, Ze'ev Sherf, in mentioning the mistakes of the cooperation, referred to this operation as "insufficiently thought out perhaps," and David Hacohen too related to it, CZA S25/7902.
79. Israel Galili, interview by the author.

80. Haeohen, *Et Le-Sapper*, p. 170; testimony of Shosh Spector, interview by the author.
81. Gilad, *Maggen ba-Seter*, pp. 90–92; HA documents, taken from the CZA, on the Sea Lion, HA 3158. A separate question deserving attention is that of British compensation to the families.
82. Joseph Harel, interview by the author.
83. Meir Davidson, Shlomo Shamir, Joseph Harel, interviews by the author.
84. See the letter of 28 July 1941, addressed to P, HA 3158.

Chapter 5

1. There is an elaborate description of this in David Hacohen's book, *Et Le-Sapper* (Tel Aviv, 1974), p. 135ff. Also see the remarks of David Hacohen and Reuven Zaslany, the Zaslany Report on Cooperation Activities, Jerusalem, 27 November 1944, CZA S25/7902. The document is central to the present chapter and contains also Allon's report. Yigal Paicovich's report on undercover activities in Syria, Jerusalem, 17 November 1944, CZA S25/7902 (hereafter, the Paicovich Report). See also Yehuda Bauer, *Diplomatya u-Mahteret* (Merhavia, 1966), pp. 95–143.
2. Hacohen, *Et Le-Sapper*; remarks of Hacohen and Zaslany in Zaslany Report on cooperation activities; Bauer, *Diplomatya u-Mahteret*.
3. Zerubavel Gilad, ed., *Maggen ba-Seter* (Jerusalem, 1949), pp. 154–56; the Parcovich Report.
4. See, e.g., the remark by Yitzhak Sadeh, in Gilad, *Maggen ba-Seter* (Tel Aviv, 1953), p. 16.
5. Emergency Order No. 2, in Zerubavel Gilad and Matti Megged, eds., *Sefer ha-Palmah*, p. 77; initial recruits (as told by Yitzhak Rabin, Israel Liebertovsky, Amos Horev), ibid., p. 132; report by Moshe Dayan on the invasion of Syria, Gilad, *Maggen ba-Seter*, p. 127ff; and Dayan's original report, LA 161V, file 3. The quote is from the original report.
6. Dayan's report, LA 161V, file 3.
7. Gilad, *Maggen ba-Seter*, p. 146; Yigal's talk, KM Envoys Seminar, 29 May 1945, KMA, section 2, container 16, file 105.
8. Dayan in his report (LA 161V, file 3) speaks of inducting thirty men, but it is not clear if this was the overall figure or the total for his men. The latter appears to be the case.
9. Dayan's report, LA 161V, file 3; Yigal's talk, KM Envoys Seminar, 29 May 1945, KMA, section 2, container 16, file 3.
10. For details, see Shabtai Teveth, *Dayan* (Tel Aviv, 1971), pp. 203–16.
11. Yigal's report, in Gilad, *Maggen ba-Seter*, pp. 152–53; Yitzhak Henkin, interview by the author.
12. Yigal's talk, KM Envoys Seminar, 29 May 1945, KMA, section 2, container 16, file 3.
13. Any optimistic assessment by Allon of his men is to be taken with a grain of salt: three years later at the Givat Ha-Shelosha Envoys Seminar, when reviewing their performance, he stressed their inexperience. Dayan's pessimistic assessment was also exaggerated: one of the participants, after all, was Meir Davidson, a field company veteran not mentioned by Dayan for some reason.
14. Dayan's report, LA 161V, file 3. According to one description, apparently by Zalman Mart, Dayan's partner in the action, from the moment that the police station was taken, the Australian commander ceased to command and Dayan

ostensibly managed the whole affair. The report is typically disparaging of the British. *Palmah Newsletter* no. 2, February 1942, HA.

15. Gilad, *Maggen ba-Seter*, p. 147.

16. Operation No. 8, 7 June 1941, in Gilad, *Maggen ba-Seter*, pp. 151–53. Though not explicit, the reference seems to be to a mission in which Allon and Henkin participated, the reporter is Allon, and it is his suggestion to come at the Beaufort from behind. See also, his talk in the same vein at the KM Envoys Seminar, KMA, section 2, container 16, file 3. Another version attributes the idea to Yitzhak Sadeh, but this strikes me as less reasonable.

17. Allon's talk, KM Envoys Seminar, KMA, section 2, container 16, file 3.

18. Gilad, *Maggen ba-Seter*, p. 146.

19. See a detailed discussion of this in Bauer, *Diplomatya u-Mahteret*, pp. 144–88.

20. Said Reuven Zaslany: "In this respect, it is a pity that the danger did not last longer, for perhaps then various precedents could have been created that might have served us in the future." David Cohen said: "And we would have achieved far greater results if the country had been in a difficult position longer." Zaslany's report, 27 November 1944, CZA S25/7902.

21. See the document signed by D/H52, undated (apparently summer 1941), HA, Cooperation file 3158.

22. The Paicovich Report.

23. Letter of Y. P., Beirut, 14 August 1941, HA, Cooperation file 3158.

24. In a letter from Reuven Zaslany to Moshe Shertok of 10 September 1941, Zaslany, disappointed at the petering out of the cooperation, wrote that "the only serious operation that we are still involved in is the operation in Syria (the project of the 30)," CZA S25/359.

25. The Paicovich Report.

26. See reports on Beirut cafe conversations, 14 August 1941, HA, Cooperation file 3158; the Paicovich Report.

27. Yigal Paicovich, HA, Allon file; debriefing of undercover agents, Efal conference, KMA.

28. The Paicovich Report.

29. There are a good many personal accounts of this, notably by David Ha-Cohen, Yigal Allon, and the agents themselves (Efal debriefing, CZA, Efal). Also, CZA and HA Cooperation files furnish a number of indications. See, e.g., the request to Solel Boneh's comptroller in the minutes of the 14 November 1942 meeting about the Syrian scheme, HA, Cooperation file 3158.

30. Minutes of the 14 November 1942 meeting on the "Friends" Syria scheme, HA, Cooperation file 3158. Participating in the meeting was Group Captain P. Domville, Major J. M. Collard, Captain P. G. Francis. On the Jewish side, there was Shaul Meirov. They formulated the operational requirements of the planned Syrian platoon.

31. See, e.g., an unsigned letter from 3 February 1942 sent by one of the British partners to a member of the JA-PD, outlining the organization and training of the Palestine scheme, HA, Cooperation file 3158.

32. "Our organisation will have to function if ever, next spring," HA, Cooperation file 3158.

33. P. T. Wilson to Shaul (Meirov), 22 May 1942, HA, Cooperation file 3158.

34. Letter from P. T. Wilson to Shaul Meirov, undated and unsigned (identified by the attached response from M. Shertok of 19 June 1942), HA, Cooperation file 3158. See also Ratner, in Gilad and Megged, *Sefer ha-Palmah*, vol. 1, p. 141.

35. The source of his information seems to have been Major Ringross, who later replaced him.
36. Shertok to Wilson, 19 June 1942, HA, Cooperation file 3158.
37. See Ratner, in Gilad and Megged, *Sefer Ha-Palmah*, vol. 1, p. 142. And in Shertok's letter to Wilson (19 June 1942, HA, Cooperation file 3158), Shertok reminds Wilson that he is about to take up a new post, indicating the brevity of his current one.
38. A letter signed "Pat" to Reuven Zaslany, Cairo, 31 August 1942, HA, Cooperation file 3158.
39. The Paicovich Report.
40. Reports of Beirut, café conversations, 8–14 August 1941, HA, Cooperation file 3158.
41. The Paicovich Report.
42. Major Collard to David Hacohen, 19 October 1942, HA, Cooperation file 3158. See also a report in the same vein by David Hacohen, Zaslany Report, 27 November 1944, CZA S25/7902.
43. Teveth, *Dayan*, pp. 221–22.
44. Minutes of the 14 November 1942 meeting on the "Friends" Syria scheme, HA, Cooperation file 3158.
45. The Paicovich Report.
46. Major Collard to David (Hacohen), Beirut, 5 March 1943, HA, Cooperation file 3158.
47. Ibid.
48. Domville to Moshe Shertok, Cairo, 17 March 1943, HA, Cooperation file 3158.
49. See, e.g., the letter from Major G. S. I. (J) to Shaul (Meirov), 27 March 1943 (the letter is stamped "1942," which is an error), HA, Cooperation file 3158.
50. See the reference to this in the letter from Reuven Zaslany to Major Gardner, 31 August 1943, HA, Cooperation file 3158.
51. Major Gardner to Shaul (Meirov), 14 June 1943, HA, Cooperation file 3158.
52. Major Collard to David (Hacohen), Beirut, 5 March 1943, HA, Cooperation file 3158. Remarks by Zaslany and Hacohen, the Zaslany Report, 27 November 1944, CZA S25/7902.
53. See, e.g., Zaslany, Zaslany Report, 27 November 1944, CZA S25/7902.
54. Letter from Major Gardner to Shaul (Meirov): "The sum paid in Palestine, which is the man's actual salary and a family allowance," HA, Cooperation file 3158.
55. Major Gardner to Shaul (Meirov), 14 June 1943, HA, Cooperation file 3158.
56. "Im Hiluf Mishmarot," *Davar Le-Almonim*, no. 1, KMA, section 15, series 6, container 4, file 6.
57. Yeruham Cohen, interview by the author.
58. Debriefing Conference, KMA, Efal.
59. David Hacohen, Zaslany Report, 27 November 1944, CZA S25/7902.
60. Zaslany to Major Gardner, 31 August 1943, HA, Cooperation file 3158.
61. The Paicovich Report.
62. Major Gardner to Shaul (Meirov), 14 June 1943, HA, Cooperation file 3158.
63. Y. P., "Yesod ha-Hashutfut," *Davar Le-Almonim*, no. 1, KMA, section 15, series 6, container 4, file 6.

64. Ibid.
65. Draft of Galili's letter to Shertok (end 1942?), Galili Archive, KMA.
66. In the discussion of cooperation, 17 November 1944, Zaslany spoke of the reluctance of paratrooper recruits to wear British uniforms and of at least one case in which conscripts, after training, refused to take part in an action because they were asked to swear allegiance to the king. The intercession of political leaders (apparently Tabenkin or Yaari) only strengthened the objection of the young to accept British authority. According to Zaslany, these considerations were damaging and impaired cooperation. Relating to this at the discussion, Ze'ev Sherf said that a conscript's connection with the organization (the Haganah) was detrimental, as was party affiliation: "One must demand that people be requisitioned on a one-time basis for the disposal of the body carrying out the operation, and it cannot be daily dependent on the Haganah, whether it is supplying people or not, and so I say: the requisitioning of the people from the Haganah, the requisitioning of the people from the parties." The Zaslany Report, 27 November 1944.
67. The Paicovich Report. 27 November 1944.
68. Letter from P. Domville, M.O.4 to Moshe Dayan, 10 September 1943, HA 613715.
69. Ginossar secretariat to Central Appeals Committee, addressed to Nathan Friedl, the Histadrut (General Federation of Jewish Labor), 16 June 1943, LA 208IV, file 3412.

Chapter 6

1. Lecture by Eliyahu Golomb, LA 1041V, Golomb file 23.
2. KMC at Givat Brenner, 15–16 April 1942, KMA, section 4, container 6, file 6.
3. Ibid.
4. Minutes of interview with the high commissioner, 1 July 1942, CZA S25/23. There is also a report in the (unclear) minutes of the Emergency Council on Security Matters, apparently from July 1942 at the Kibbutz Artzi Movement, with Nathan Friedl reporting. Here the phrase "decent Arabs" is attributed to the commissioner, GHA, 24.90 (4 c).
5. Golomb, KMC at Naan, 22 August 1942, KMA, section 5, container 6, file 8. See the detailed report in the minutes of Mapai's head office, 15 July 1942, LPA-BB 23/42; as well as the minutes of the Histadrut Executive, 1 July 1942, LA-HE 1942.
6. See n. 4, the Emergency Council on Security Matters. The quotation is from Galili at the KMC at Ein-Harod, 5 July 1942, KMA, Galili, container 6, file 2.
7. See confirmation of this by Golomb at the KMC at Naan, 22 August 1942, KMA, section 5, container 6, file 8.
8. Galili mentions the matter at the KMC at Ein-Harod, 5 July 1942, KMA, Galili, container 6, file 2. and at the KM Movement's ideological brainstorming on state and security, 18 June 1950, KMA, Galili. For confirmation of the fact of the meeting, see Ben Zvi's diaries from 1942: "In the evening I spoke to Eliezer [Kaplan, A. S.]. The meeting took place with the government, Katznelson took part in it," BZI 8/1835.
9. On this, see Galili, KMC at Ein-Harod, 5 July 1942, KMA, Galili, container 6, file 2; as well as Yigal Paicovich, KM Envoys Seminar at Givat Ha-Shelosha, 29 May 1945, KMA 2, container 16, file 105.

10. Y. Eshed, KMC at Ein-Harod, 5 July 1942, KMA, section 5, container 6, file 7.
11. Tabenkin, Eshed, and Galili, KMC at Ein Harod, KMA, section 5, container, 6, file 7.
12. Yosef [Rokhel], quoted by Galili in a letter to his wife, Zippora (hereafter, Letters to Zippora), 23 March 1942, KMA, Galili, container 5, file 3.
13. Tabenkin argues the point at the KMC at Ein-Harod, 5 July 1942, KMA, Galili, container 6, file 2. The suggestion is attributed to Ben-Asher, as identified by Galili in his address on state and security, 18 June 1950, KMA, Galili.
14. Galili, KMC at Ein-Harod, 5 July 1942, KMA, Galili, container 6, file 2.
15. Galili, Letters to Zippora, 23 March 1942, KMA, Galili, container 5, file 3.
16. Ibid.
17. Yigal Paicovich, KM Envoys Seminar, 29 May 1945, KMA 2, container 16, file 105.
18. Ibid.
19. Galili, Letters to Zippora, 23 March 1942, KMA, Galili, container 5, file 3.
20. Galili, KMC at Ein-Harod, 5 July 1942, KMA, Galili, container 6, file 2.
21. Golomb, Histadrut Executive Secretariat, 7 May 1943, HA, Golomb file 52.
22. Galili and Tabenkin at KMC at Ein-Harod, 5 July 1942, KMA, Galili, container 6, file 2; see also the Histadrut Executive discussion, 1 July 142, LA-HE 1942.
23. Sini Azaryahu, interview by the author.
24. Sini Azaryahu, interview by the author; lecture by Yigal Paicovich, Envoys Seminar, 29 May 1945, KMA 2, container 16, file 105; Zerubavel Gilad and Matti Megged, eds., *Sefer ha-Palmah* (Tel Aviv, 1953), p. 21.
25. See what Allon says about this in ibid.
26. Galili, Letters to Zippora, 23 March 1942, KMA, Galili, container 5, file 3; Israel Galili, "Siha ba-Hug," 17 May 1942, KMA, Galili, container 6, file 2.
27. Idelson and Alexander, minutes of Youth Committee and Security Committee, 30 August 1942, KMA, section 1b, container 6, file 28.
28. Draft of Tabenkin's talk at the KMC at Naan, 21–23 August 1942, titled originally "Ha-Meshek—Basis la-Neshek," KMA, section 5, container 6, file 8. See also Idelson and Alexander, Youth Committee and Security Committee, 30 August 1942, KMA, section 1b, container 6, file 28; Kibbutz Artzi Executive Secretariat, letter no. 1, Merhavia, 8 September 1942, GHA (16)1.18F, which tells about the suggestion to conscript four hundred Palmahniks into the British army. Golomb, speaking before the Palmah's Company A in October 1942, said that he supported sending small groups from the Palmah to the British army to ensure the loyalty of Palestine's Jewish conscripts. *Alon Ha-Palmah* 32 (July 1945). Addressing KM members (1944?), Golomb said that when 200 Palmahniks had left for the British army, he had proposed organizing them into a 150-man company sent by the Palmah rather than quitting it. LA 104IV, Golomb 23.
29. Galili, "Siha ba-Hug," 17 May 1942, KMA, Galili, container 6, file 2.
30. "Sikkumim ve-Hahlatot," KMC at Ein-Harod, 5 July 1942, KMA, Galili, container 6, file 2.
31. Tabenkin, decisions of the KMC at Naan, 23 August 1942, KMA, section 5, container 6, file 8. The quote is from the unedited minutes.
32. Ibid.
33. Idelson, KMC at Naan, 21–23 August 1942, KMA, section 5, container 6, file 8.
34. The passage is based on the comments of Palmah members at the gathering of Company B on 19 October 1942, HA, 116 (Golomb), file 9.

35. Shneour Lipson, Company B gathering, 19 October 1942, HA, 116 (Golomb), file 9.

36. According to all of the evidence, this was said by Meir Davidson and so it appears in Galili's response, KMA, Galili, container 6, file 2. But Davidson is not quoted in the minutes of the discussion or in the summary in Galili's notebook, October 1942, KMA, Galili, container 6, file 4.

37. Shneour Lipson, Shurika, Shulia, Matityahu Sternboim, Company B gathering, 19 October 1942, HA, 116 (Golomb), file 9. On the bank robbery, see also Tabenkin at the assembly of 19 November 1942: "There are members who have a prescription: Barclay's Bank," KMA, Allon, section 15, container 6, file 1. Similar things were said by Eliyahu Golomb at the gathering of Company A, *Alon Ha-Palmah* 32 (July 1945).

38. Galili, Faction B on the continuation of the Palmah, KMA, Galili, container 5, File 2.

39. Based on Golomb's estimates, about two hundred left the Palmah for the British army, LA 104IV, Golomb 23.

40. Galili's notebook, October 1942, KMA, Galili, container 6, file 4, provides a summary of a lecture by Tabenkin, from 30 November 1942, in which Tabenkin says: "I see that in the Palmah there is a repeat of the Shomer [Second Aliyah organization] case. This is exactly my argument against the Shomrim. This is a valuable, unique professional group that sees only the professional value of what is achieved and [what it] wants to achieve."

41. Testimony of Israel Galili to Yehuda Bauer, 1957, HA, Galili file 18.

42. Letter no. 2 of the Kibbutz Artzi Executive, Merhavia, 9 October 1942, GHA (16)1.18F.

43. Ibid.

44. Meeting of HNHO secretariat with representatives of all the movement's settlements, 30 December 1942, LA 213IV, file 29.

45. Uri Brenner, *Ha-Hakhshara ha-Megguyesset ba-Palmah* (Tel Aviv, 1983), pp. 20–25. According to *Tzror Mikhtavim*, KMP, 4 June 1943, p. 306, it appears that five training groups of KM kibbutzim were in fact transferred to work and training bases. Two additional groups, at Geva and Maoz, "did not join because of their special conditions." The number of members who left for the Palmah, along with the two groups that did not go, tells us that HNHO had 120 graduate members in agricultural training, of whom more than 90 joined the Palmah.

46. Census of the camps, *Yalkut Ha-Mahanot Ha-Olim*, no. 4, 30 November 1942, KMA, section 9, Ha-Mahanot Ha-Olim, container 1, file 2.

47. Had, "Im ha-Giyus la-Palmah," *Yalkut Ha-Mahanot Ha-Olim*, no. 4, 30 November 1942, KMA, section 9, Ha-Mahanot Ha-Olim, container 1, file 2.

48. *Yalkut Ha-Mahanot Ha-Olim*, no. 8, 4 June 1943, KMA, section 9, Ha-Mahanot Ha-Olm, container 1, file 2.

49. Lecture by Tabenkin, 30 November 1942, according to Galili's notebook, October 1942, KMA, Galili, container 6, file 4. Regarding Allon's opinion, see his lecture at the Envoys Seminar, Givat Ha-Sheloshah, 29 May 1945, KMA 2, container 16, file 105. Regarding Galili, his views are implicit.

Chapter 7

1. Yigal Allon, "Meggamot u-Maas," in Zerubavel Gilad and Matti Megged, eds., *Sefer ha-Palmah*, vol. 1 (Tel Aviv, 1953), pp. 233–34; Shosh Spector, interview by the author, 18 January 1983.

2. Author's interviews of Uri Brenner, 22 January 1987; Shosh Spector, 18 January 1983; and Sini Azaryahu, 1 June 1982.
3. Uri Brenner and Shosh Spector, interviews by the author; Zvika Dror, *Matzbi le-lo Serara, Sippur Hayav shel Yitzhak Sadeh, "Ha-Zaken"* (Tel Aviv, 1996), pp. 232–33.
4. Dror, *Matzbi le-lo Serara*, p. 232.
5. Israel Galili, interview by the author, 8 June 1982.
6. Uri Brenner, interview by the author, 22 January 1987.
7. Shosh Spector, interview by the author, 18 January 1983.
8. Uri Brenner, interview by the author, 22 January 1987.
9. Sini Azaryahu, interview by the author, 1 March 1982.
10. Author's interviews of Galili, 8 June 1982 and Azaryahu Sini, 2 June 1982.
11. Shosh Spector, interview by the author, 18 January 1983.
12. Israel Galili, interview by the author, 8 June 1982.
13. Sini Azaryahu, interview by the author, 19 May 1982.
14. Hayyim Gouri, "Misvivenu Mastema Goeshet," Gilad and Megged, eds., *Sefer ha-Palmah*, 1:130.
15. Gilad and Megged, eds., *Sefer ha-Palmah*, 1:212–17; Yigal Allon, "Ha-Yehida ha-Megguyesset," lecture at Envoys Seminar, Givat Ha-Shelosha, 29 May 1945, KMA, section 2, container 16, file 105.
16. Gilad and Megged, eds., *Sefer ha-Palmah*, 1:226–31; Yigal Allon, "Ha-Yehida ha-Megguyesset," lecture at Envoys Seminar at Givat Ha-Shelosha, 29 May 1945, KMA, section 2, container 16, file 105.
17. Gilad and Megged, eds., *Sefer ha-Palmah*, 1:231–33; Yigal Allon, "Ha-Yehida ha-Megguyesset," lecture at Envoys Seminar at Givat Ha-Shelosha, 29 May 1945, KMA, section 2, container 16, file 105.
18. See the summary of the discussion in Yitzhak Kafkafi, ed., *Shnot ha-Mahanot Ha-Olim*, vol. 2, *Ha-Asor ha-Sheni* (Tel Aviv, 1984–85), p. 419.
19. Begin in conversation with Sneh, 8 October 1944, according to Sneh's report at HA, KMA, Koah Ha-Maggen, Porshim (dissenters) container (not organized), *saison* 1944–46.
20. Eliyahu Golomb, meeting of the Histadrut Executive and the council secretariats, November–December 1944, HA, Golomb, no. 116, file 52, LA 208IV, 207IV.
21. Ben-Gurion, Special Session of the Histadrut Convention, 20 November 1944, LA 206IV.
22. Part of the discussion on the war against the dissenters (Porshim) at the Fourth National Council of the Le-Ahdut Ha-Avodah (LAHA) Party, 27 October 1944, KMA, Koah Ha-Maggen, Porshim (dissenters) container (not organized), *saison* 1944–46.
23. Letter to Ram (Sneh), Galili's notebook, 24 August 1944, KMA.
24. The Fifth LAHA Council, 10 November 1944, KMA, Koah Ha-Maggen, Porshim (dissenters) container (not organized), *saison* 1944–46.
25. Faction meetings at the Histadrut and LAHA Council, 20 November 1944, 21 November 1944, KMA, Koah Ha-Maggen, Porshim (dissenters) container (not organized), *Saison* 1944–46.
26. Account of Yigal Allon to Uri Brenner, 26 March 1970, KMA, section 15, Allon, container 6, file 3. Account of Yigal Allon to Yehudah Bauer, 10 June 1958, the Institute for Contemporary Jewry, 12 (79).
27. Account of Israel Galili to Yehudah Bauer, 1957, KMA.
28. See Yigal Allon, "Ha-Prisha—Zera ha-Puranut," *Haaretz*, 30 July 1971; and Israel Galili, interview by the author, 17 February 1982.

29. Account of Yigal Allon to Yehudah Bauer, 1958, and to Uri Brenner, 26 March 1970, HA.
30. Account of Dov Chesis to Uri Brenner, 19 March 1970, KMA.
31. Account of Meir Pa'il, 1 December 1969, KMA.
32. Shimon Avidan, interview by the author, 9 August 1982; account of Shimon Avidan to Ya'akov Yunish, 1 November 1985, KMA.
33. In April 1966 *Maariv* published, in installments, in its Passover and subsequent Saturday editions, a symposium on the undergrounds conducted by Ge'ula Cohen, with the participation of Moshe Sneh, Ya'akov Riftin, Eliezer Livneh, Menachem Begin, Nathan Yellin Mor, and Shimon Peres. In retrospect, the symposium was attacked as unbalanced and unrepresentative. One of the reactions was from Ya'akov Dori, who said that even though participation in the *saison* was on a voluntary basis, "The Haganah Command and General Staff could not shake off responsibility for the 'hunts'"; "to diminish the image of the Haganah, there could be nothing better than to allow Sneh and Livneh to represent it in the symposium" (*Maariv*, 20 May 1966). Haim Ya'ari also responded ("Tahbulah Itona'it she-Kar'u la Symposion," *Davar*, 13 May 1966), saying: "Moshe Sneh is now trying to shake off his responsibility for the affair, but in 1944 he was not an anti-*saison*ist and as a member of the Jewish Agency Executive and head of the Haganah National Command, he bears full public responsibility for everything done in the '*saison*.'"
34. Shabtai Teveth, *Moshe Dayan* (Jerusalem, 1971), p. 236.
35. Azaryahu Sini, interview by the author, 19 May 1982.
36. David Ben-Gurion, "Ba-Derekh le-Tzava ve-li-Medinat Yisrael," *Davar*, 8 May 1964. On Zionist political questions, in the postwar period, see Yehudah Bauer, *Diplomatya u-Mahteret* (Merhavia, 1966); Slutsky et al., *Sefer Toldot ha-Haganah* (Tel Aviv, 1972), vol. 3, part 2, 801–53; Joseph Heller, *Ba-Maavak le-Medinah: Ha-Mediniyut ha-Tzionit, 1936–1948* (Jerusalem 1984); Dahlia Ofer, *Derekh ba-Yam, Aliyah Bet bi-Tekufat ha-Shoah* (Jerusalem, 1988); Arieh Kokhavi, *Akurim u-Politika Beinleumit* (Tel Aviv, 1992); Yehoshua Freundlich, *Mi-Hurban le-Tekuma* (Tel Aviv, 1994); and many more. For all matters concerning Moshe Sneh, see Eli Shaltiel, *Tamid be-Meri* (Tel Aviv, 2000).
37. Allon, "Meggamot u-Maas," in Gilad and Megged, eds., *Sefer ha-Palmah*, 1:545–47.
38. Israel Galili, interviews by the author, 18 May 1982, 29 June 1982; account of Sneh to Slutzky, 20 March 1968, HA.
39. Allon, "Meggamot u-Maas," in Gilad and Megged, eds., *Sefer ha-Palmah*, 1:547–50.
40. Ibid., 1:551.
41. It was a decision of the Resistance Movement's headquarters and approved by the X Committee. Three airports were attacked on 25 February 1946. See David Niv, *Maarkhot ha-Irgun ha-Tzva'i ha-Leumi* (Tel Aviv, 1973), 4:234–37.
42. Account of Yigal Allon to Uri Brenner, "Tekufat Tnuat ha-Meri," KMA, Galili papers, container 7(1), file 6.
43. Ibid.
44. Slutsky et al., *Sefer Toldot ha-Haganah*, vol. 3, part 2, pp. 896–901; Israel Galili, interview by the author, 18 May 1982; account of Sneh to Slutsky, 20 March 1968, HA; Yitzhak Sadeh, "Klapei Pnim," Mi-Saviv La-Medurah, Yediot Le-Ahdut Ha-Avodah, 8 August 1946.
45. Allon, "Meggamot u-Maas," in Gilad and Megged, eds., *Sefer ha-Palmah* 1:572–73.

46. Israel Galili, interview by the author, 5 May 1982.
47. Israel Galili, interview by the author, 8 June 1982.
48. Ibid.
49. Account of Yigal Allon to Uri Brenner, "Ha-Nessiya le-Europa be-1946," 5 June 1969, HA, Allon file.
50. Israel Galili, interviews by the author, 5 May 1982; 8 June 1982.
51. Account of Yigal Allon to Uri Brenner, "Ha-Nessiya le-Europa be-1946," 5 June 1969, HA, Allon file.
52. Shimon Avidan, interviews by the author, 9 August 1982; 4 November 1982.
53. Zvika Dror, *Bi-Netivei Hatzala* (Tel Aviv, 1988), p. 167.
54. The description is based on ibid., pp. 165–67; Israel Galili, interview by the author, 5 May 1982.
55. Shimon Avidan, interview by the author, 4 November 1982.
56. Letter from Ruth Allon to the members of Ginossar, 10 January 1947, Ginossar newsletter no. 98, 14 March 1947.
57. Interviews by the author of Shimon Avidan, 9 August 1982, 4 November 1982; and Israel Galili, 5 May 1982.
58. Letter from Yigal Allon to Ruth Allon , Paris, 4 February 1982. (Their correspondence is from Ruth Allon's personal archive.)
59. Joseph Harel, interview by the author, 2 August 1988.
60. Letter from Yiftah (Allon) to all the emissaries, 21 June 1947, in Gilad and Megged, eds., *Sefer ha-Palmah* 1:838.
61. Yigal Allon to Haim (Avraham Riklis, Ashdot Ya'akov), Rome, 9 March 1947, KMA, section 15, Allon, series II, container 4, file 1.
62. Letter from Yiftah (Allon) to all the emissaries, 21 June 1947, in Gilad and Megged, eds., *Sefer ha-Palmah* 1:838.
63. Letter from Yigal Allon to Ruth Allon, Rome, 7 March 1947.
64. Joseph Harel, interview by the author, 2 August 1988.
65. Letter from Yiftah (Allon) to Leonard, 27 May 1947, KMA, section 15, Allon, container 5, file 1.
66. Letter from Yiftah (Allon) to all the emissaries, 21 June 1947, in Gilad and Megged, eds., *Sefer ha-Palmah* 1:838–41.
67. Yigal Allon to Ruth Allon, 12 September 1947.
68. Allon, "Meggamot u-Maas," in Gilad and Megged, eds., *Sefer ha-Palmah* 1:596.
69. Yigal Allon to Ruth Allon, 19 September 1947.
70. Yigal Allon to Ruth Allon, 7 September 1947; 22 November 1947.
71. Yigal Allon to Ruth Allon, 30 March 1947.
72. Yigal Allon to Ruth Allon, Ashdot, 14 April 1947.
73. Yigal Allon to Ruth Allon, 18 May 1947.
74. Yigal Allon to Ruth Allon, Tel Aviv, 2 May 1947.
75. Yigal Allon to Ruth Allon, Ginnosar, Shabbat, 31 May 1947.
76. Yigal Allon to Ruth Allon, 6 July 1947.
77. Yigal Allon to Ruth Allon, 7 July 1947.
78. Yigal Allon to Ruth Allon, 26 July 1947.
79. Yigal Allon to Ruth Allon, Tel Aviv, 12 August 1947; 17 August 1947.
80. Yigal Allon to Ruth Allon, 7 September 1947.
81. Ibid.
82. Yigal Allon to Ruth Allon, Tel Aviv, 27 September 1947.
83. Yigal Allon to Ruth Allon, 4 October 1947.

84. Yigal Allon to Ruth Allon, 15 October 1947.
85. Yigal Allon to Ruth Allon, 17 October 1947.
86. Yigal Allon to Ruth Allon, Tel Aviv, 21 October 1947; 5 November 1947; 11 November 1947.
87. Yigal Allon to Ruth Allon, 15 November 1947.
88. Yigal Allon to Ruth Allon, 16 November 1947.
89. BGD, April–May 1947, BGA.
90. Letter from Yigael Yadin to Israel Ber, September 1950; Israel Ber, "Makor shel Mahshava Tzva'it," *Al Ha-Mishmar*, 11 August 1950.
91. Moshe Sneh to Ya'akov Dori, Paris, 27 August 1946, HA, Sneh file.
92. BGD, 17 April 1947, BGA.
93. Israel Galili, interview by the author, 29 June 1982.
94. Yigal Allon to Ruth Allon, 8 June 1947.
95. Ibid.
96. Israel Galili, KM ideological seminar, 18 June 1950, KMA, Galili archive, 3.
97. Israel Galili, interview by the author, 8 June 1982.
98. Yigal Allon to Ruth Allon, Tel Aviv, 30 May 1947.
99. Yigal Allon to Ruth Allon, 30 March 1947.
100. Ibid.
101. Ibid.
102. Yigal Allon to Ruth Allon, Ashdot, 14 April 1947.
103. Yigal Allon to Ruth Allon, 7 July 1947.
104. Yigal Allon to Ruth Allon, 26 July 1947.
105. Yigal Allon to Ruth Allon, 17 August 1947; 20 August 1947; 24 August 1947; 29 October 1947.
106. In Allon's letter to Ruth (20 August 1947), he writes of I. Id., calling him "party secretary." In the opinion of contemporaries, the reference is to Israel Idelson (Bar-Yehduah), who did not hold the minor position of secretary but was widely believed to be the key man.
107. Yigal Allon to Ruth Allon, 20 August 1947.
108. Ibid.
109. Yigal Allon to Ruth Allon, 29 October 1947.
110. Yigal Allon to Ruth Allon, 13 June 1947.
111. Azaryahu, Sini, interview by the author, 2 June 1982.
112. Conversation with Sneh on 3 March 1967, HA, Sneh file.
113. BGD, 27 May 1947, BGA, Galili's letter to Ben-Aharon, undated (eve of the *Saison* 1947), KMA, Defense Force, Dissenters Container (not filed), file: Dissenters, *saison* 1947.

Chapter 8

1. For a detailed discussion of this, see Gabriel Cohen, "Mediniut Britania Erev Milhemet-ha-Atzma'ut," in Yehuda Wallach, ed., *Hayinu ke-Holmim* (Ramat Gan, 1985), pp. 13–170; minutes of cited conversation are on pp. 134–35.
2. Ben-Gurion's words before the Yishuv's Constituent Assembly, 2 October 1947, in David Ben-Gurion, *Paamei Medina, Zikhronot min ha-Izavon*, ed. Meir Avizohar (Tel Aviv, 1993), p. 381.
3. Ibid., p. 382.
4. Ibid., p. 383.

5. Mapai Secretariat session, 11 October 1947, in Ben-Gurion, *Paamei Medina*, p. 383.
6. Lecture by Yigal Allon (apparently at the KM Seminar), 17 June 1950, KMA, section Allon, container 6, file 2. A possible source of the rumor about the refugee camps may perhaps be seen in the story by Moshe Shertok at the People's Council (13 May 1948), about a question directed by the Italian delegate in Greece to the Greek foreign minister: the delegate asked whether or not Greece would be prepared to grant asylum to several thousand Jewish refugees when their exile or flight from Palestine began. People's Council, Minutes, 18 April–13 May 1948, Jerusalem, May 1978, p. 128.
7. See, e.g., Ephrai'm Shmueli's reference to the attitude of the KM's members to the celebrations of 29 November, "Mikhtav le-Merkaz Miflegget Po'alei Eretz Israel," *Ha-Poel Ha-Tza'ir*, 16 December 1947, as well as Joseph Shapira, "Ihud shel Levavot," *Ha-Poel Ha-Tza'ir*, 30 December 1947.
8. David Ben-Gurion, BGWD, 1 December 1947, 1:14.
9. Ben-Gurion, *Paamei Medina*, pp. 502–3.
10. Minutes of the meeting on "Shem" affairs, 1–2 January 1948; HA, section 80, private archive Israel Galili 21/50.
11. Ibid.
12. The description is based on ibid.; Zalman Rubashov, ed., "Pinkas ha-Maarkha," in *Be-Mivhan ha-Kravot, Shnaton Davar, 1948–49* (Tel Aviv, n.d.), pp. 300–307; Yehudah Slutsky et al., *Sefer Toldot ha-Haganah* (Tel Aviv, 1954–72), vol. 3, part 2, pp. 1371–92.
13. Minutes of the meeting on "Sham" affairs, 1–2 January 1948, HA, section 80, private archive Israel Galili 20/50.
14. Ha-Homa, Inyanei Bitahon ve-Haganah (no date), LA-LI, section IV/16, Haganah files, file 31.
15. Rubashov, ed., "Pinkas ha-Maarkha," 7 January 1948, in *Be-Mivhan ha-Kravot, Shnaton Davar, 1948–49*, p. 306.
16. See the extensive discussion of this in Osnat Shiran, *Nekudot Oz* (Efal, 1998).
17. Ben-Gurion, "L'isud ha-Medina," *Ha-Poel Ha-Tza'ir*, 16 December 1947.
18. A note written by Moshe Sharret to Israel Galili, apparently in April 1948: "Have you ever thought seriously about evacuating the Etzyon Bloc, especially after Tiberias-Haifa-Jaffa and the villages? In New York I resisted thoughts of evacuation of some of my colleagues in Jerusalem (of the serious kind), but the bug has not left me." Galili Archive, KMA-TI.
19. Joseph Weitz, *Yomanai ve-Iggrotai la-Banim*, Tel Aviv, 2 May 1948, (Tel-Aviv, 1965), 3:278; Moshe Carmel, "Ha-Mivtza'im be-Hazit ha-Tzafon," lecture at a course for military history instructors, 15 June 1953, IDFA, 1046/70, file 327–333.
20. *Ve'idat ha-Ihud shel Mifleget Po'alim Ha-Shomer Ha-Tza'ir be-Eretz Israel ve-ha-Miflaga Le-Ahdut Ha-Avodah-Po'alei Zion*, 23–24 January 1948, Tel-Aviv, Mapam publication, p. 41.
21. The conquest of Jaffa was an exception, but it was the result of a chain of events, not planned beforehand.
22. See, e.g., Weitz, *Yomanai*, 3 March 1948, 3:247.
23. Ibid., 20 January 1948, 3:227.
24. Ibid., 10 February 1948, 3:235; 6 February 1948, 3:243.
25. When Ben-Gurion raised before Weitz the possibility of Avigur's appointment as governor of the Negev, Weitz had his reservations. But Ben-Gurion kept

up the pressure until Weitz understood that the matter was connected to Ben-Gurion's relations with the Palmah. Weitz, BGWD I, 2 March 1948, p. 283; Weitz, *Yomanai*, 2 March 1948, 3:278; 18 March 1948, 3:279.

26. BGWD, 2 March 1948, 1:273; 3 March 1948, 1:275; 5 March 1948, 1:278.
27. BGWD, 2 March 1948, 1:279.
28. Weitz, *Yomanai*, 2 April 1948, 3:261.
29. The most extensive work on the topic is Eli Tzur, *Nofei ha-Ashlaya, Mapam 1948–1954* (Beersheba, 1998).
30. Yigal Paicovich, *Ve'idat ha-Ihud*, 23–24 January 1948, Mapam publication, pp. 39–42.
31. Ibid., pp. 89–90.
32. IDF/Staff Operations Archive, History Branch, file no. 1214-922/1975. See also Slutsky et al., *Sefer Toldot ha-Haganah*, vol. 3, part 2, pp. 1487–90.
33. Minutes of the meeting on "Shem" affairs, 1–2 January 1948, HA, section 80, private archive Israel Galili 21/50; Moshe Carmel, "Ha-Mivtza'im be-Hazit ha-Tzafon," lecture in a course for military history instructors, 15 June 1953, IDFA, 1046/70, file 327–333.
34. Motti Golani, "Mifneh Haifa—Britania u-Milhemet ha-Ezrahim be-Eretz Israel: December 1947–May 1948," in Anita Shapira, ed., *Medina ba-Derekh* (Jerusalem, 2001), pp. 13–59.
35. There are many accounts of this: see the author's interviews of Yigael Yadin, Israel Galili, Yitzhak Rabin, Zerubavel Arbel, and Shimon Avidan; and Galili's words, "Kfitzat Nahshon," 9 April 1948, in Zerubavel Gilad and Matti Megged, eds., *Sefer ha-Palmah* (Tel Aviv, 1953), 2:50–51.
36. Yitzhak Rabin, interview by author, 30 September 1982.
37. IDFA, wireless log of Harel, 25.27 April 1948.
38. Israel Galili on Yigal Allon, interview by Yitzhak Livni, *Mi-Bifnim*, 43, 1–2 June 1981, p. 166.
39. Report of a conversation held on 16 February 1948 with the officer of an Irish army battalion stationed in Safed, IDFA, 922–1226/75.
40. Ibid.
41. A literary description of the sense of pain, loss, and drop in morale can be found in Netivah Ben-Yehudah, *Mi-Baad la-Avotot* (Tel Aviv, 1985). See also Mula Cohen, interview by the author, 29 April 1984.
42. Yigal Allon, "Mivtza Yiftah," in Gilad and Megged, eds., *Sefer ha-Palmah*, 2:276; Yigal Allon, "Mivtza Yiftah" (lecture), 14 April 1958, KMA, section 16, container 6, file 2.
43. Allon, "Mivtza Yiftah" (lecture), 14 April 1958, KMA, section 16, container 6, file 2.
44. Allon, "Mivtza Yiftah," in Gilad and Megged, eds., *Sefer ha-Palmah*, 2:277; Allon, "Mivtza Yiftah" (lecture), 14 April 1958, KMA, section 16, container 6, file 2; Mula Cohen, interviews by the author, 29 April 1984, 3 May 1984, 4 May 1984; Yeruham Cohen, interview by the author.
45. Allon, "Mivtza Yiftah," in Gilad and Megged, eds., *Sefer ha-Palmah*, 2:277.
46. Allon, "Mivtza Yiftah" (lecture), 14 April 1958, KMA, section 16, container 6, file 2.
47. Ibid.
48. Allon, "Mivtza Yiftah," in Gilad and Megged, eds., *Sefer ha-Palmah*, 2:280.
49. Allon, "Mivtza Yiftah" (lecture), 14 April 1958, KMA, section 16, container 6, file 2.
50. Ibid. For details of the attack on Ramot Naftali and the telegram from the

point of view of the local defenders, see Varda Schulman, *Ramot Naftali ba-Maarkha*, (Tel Aviv, 1984).

51. Allon, "Mivtza Yiftah" (lecture), 14 April 1958, KMA, section 16, container 6, file 2; the reconstruction of the dates is based on the log of Operation Yiftah, IDFA, 922–1226/75.

52. Allon, "Mivtza Yiftah" (lecture), 14 April 1958, KMA, section 16, container 6, file 2.

53. Ibid.

54. Ibid.

55. Mula Cohen, interview by the author, 5 April 1984.

56. Allon, "Mivtza Yiftah," in Gilad and Megged, eds., *Sefer ha-Palmah*, 2:284; Yigal Allon, KMA, section 16, container 6, file 2.

57. Allon, "Mivtza Yiftah" (lecture), 14 April 1958, KMA, section 16, container 6, file 2.

58. Ibid.

59. Operation Yiftah log, IDFA, 922–1226/75; Allon, "Mivtza Yiftah" (lecture), 14 April 1958, KMA, section 16, container 6, file 2; Allon, "Mivtza Yiftah," in Gilad and Megged, eds., *Sefer ha-Palmah*, 2:284–286; Mula Cohen, interview by the author, 5 April 1984.

60. Allon, "Mivtza Yiftah," in Gilad and Megged, eds., *Sefer ha-Palmah*, 2:285.

61. Mula Cohen, interview by the author, 5 April 1984.

62. Yiftah to Operations (Yadin), 15–16 May 1948, IDFA, 1175-922/75.

63. Allon, "Mivtza Yiftah," in Gilad and Megged, eds., *Sefer ha-Palmah*, 2:288–89; Yigal Allon, "Mivtza Yiftah" (lecture), 14 April 1958, KMA, section 16, container 6, file 2.

64. Golani's telegram to the general staff and Yadin, 18 May 1948, IDFA, 922–1175/75.

65. Yadin's telegrams 18 May 1948, IDFA, 922–1182/75. Moshe Carmel, "Ha-Mivtza'im be-Hazit ha-Tzafon," lecture at a course for military history instructors, 15 June 1953, IDFA, 1046/70, file 327–333. For an example of the approach of modern historians to the question of Arab forces and aims, see Yoav Gelber, *Palestine 1948, War, Escape, and the Emergence of the Palestinian Refugee Problem* (Sussex Academic Press, 2001), pp. 138–54.

66. Yiftah's telegram to Hillel (Galili) and Dan (Yadin?), 18 May 1948, IDFA, 1182-922/25, Mula Cohen, *La-Tet u-le-Kabel, Pirkei Zikhronot Ishiim* (Tel Aviv, 2000), pp. 121–22.

67. Yadin to Golani, 19 May 1948, IDFA, 1182-922/75.

68. Golani telegrams to Yiftah, Yadin, and others, 20 May 1948, 21 May 1948, IDFA, 1175-922/75. See too the telegram from Magi (Moshe Dayan) to Yadin, 21 May 1948, ibid., which questions the value of the artillery sent to defend the Jordan Valley.

69. Yiftah to General Staff Operations Branch, 20 May 1948, IDFA, 1175-922/75.

70. Allon, "Mivtza Yiftah" (lecture), 14 April 1958, KMA, section 16, container 6, file 2.

71. Ibid.

72. Ibid.; Allon, "Mivtza Yiftah," in Gilad and Megged, ed. *Sefer ha-Palmah*, 2:293–95; Sasha, daily report to the general staff (from the "Bulgarians," the code name for Palmah's headquarters), 29 May 1948, IDFA, 922–1222/75.

73. Gelber, *Palestine 1948*, pp. 148–49.

74. Ben-Gurion reported on a conversation with Agudat Israel leaders, who voiced anxiety about Jerusalem turning into Stalingrad, BGWD, 28 May 1948, 2:465.

75. Yigal Allon lecture, 17 June 1950, KMA, section 15, Allon, container 6, file 2; Yitzhak Rabin, interview by the author, 19 August 1982; see also Yadin's testimony before the Committee of Five, in Anita Shapira, *Mi-Piturei ha-Rama ad Peiruk ha-Palmah* (Tel Aviv, 1985), p. 111.

76. Ben-Gurion, BGWD, 28 May 1948, 2:465. Telegram from General Staff Operations Branch to the brigades, 28 May 1948, IDFA, 1045–41/70.

77. See Ben-Gurion, BGWD, 30–31 May 1948, 2:470–71.

78. *Stone report* IDFA, "Ha-Nes Ha-Nikhnas," 31 May 1948, nos. 41, 45.

79. Ibid., 1 June 1948, nos. 7, 9.

80. Sasha (Allon) to Operations Branch, 8 June 1948, telegram no. 16, IDF, "Ha-Nes Ha-Nikhnas."

81. Exchange of telegrams between Operations Branch and brigades, 2 June 1948, IDFA, 41–1045/70.

82. Yitzhak Rabin, interview by author, 24 August 1948.

83. Operations Branch telegrams to the council (Palmah staff), 5 May 1948, telegram exchange, nos. 87, 88, IDFA, 41–1045/70.

84. Yitzhak Rabin, interview by author, 24 August 1982.

85. A study by Yaakov Eshed on Operation Yoram at the Operations Branch Training Department, IDFA, 69–1046/70. The above exchange of telegrams was apparently collected for the above study, along with the testimonies. The study was conducted in 1957.

86. Ben-Zvi to the General Staff, 6 June 1948, telegram no. 16, IDFA, "Ha-Nes Ha-Nikhnas."

87. The description of the battle and preparations for it are based on the study by Yaakov Eshed, as described in n. 85; also testimonies of Zerubavel Arbel, Amos Horev, Yitzhak Rabin, Mula Cohen, and others taken down by Yaakov Eshed in 1957, IDFA, 73–1046/70.

88. Urgent telegram to Yadin and all the brigades, 10 June 1948, No. 162, exchange of telegrams, IDFA, 41–1045/70.

89. Telegrams from Givati to Operations Branch, 10 June 1948, no. 13; from Mundak (Pasternak) to Yadin, 10 June 1948, no. 14; from the Seventh Brigade to Yadin, no. 18, from Amiram (Rabin) to Yadin, no. 19; from Givati to Yadin, no. 22; from Yigal to Operations Branch, 11 June 1948, no. 28; all IDFA, "Ha-Nes Ha-Nikhnas."

90. Telegrams from Oded to Operations Branch, 10 June 1948, nos. 6, 15, 20; from northern front to Operations Branch, 10 June 1948, no. 16; from Oded to Operations Branch, 11 June 1948, no. 30; all IDFA, "Ha-Nes Ha-Nikhnas."

91. Telegrams from the Seventh Brigade to Yadin, 9 June 1948, no. 8; from Etzyoni to Operations Branch, 10 June 1948, no. 5; from Etzyoni to Operations Branch, 11 June 1948, no. 53; all IDFA, "Ha-Nes Ha-Nikhnas."

92. Testimony of Rabin, 8 May 1957, Operations Branch, History Training Department, IDFA, 73–1046-/70. Yitzhak Rabin, interview with author, 24 August 1982.

93. Telegram from Sasha, 10 June 1948, no. 21; from Conrad to Operations Branch, 11 June 1948, no. 38; all IDFA, "Ha-Nes Ha-Nikhnas." Yitzhak Rabin, interview with author, 24 August 1982.

Chapter 9

1. In 1953, Yigal Allon wrote a long, friendly eulogy on David Marcus at Moshe Perlman's request. (Perlman's letter was written on 11 June 1953, Allon's article has no date), KMA, section 15, Allon, container 4, file 1.
2. After 15 May 1948, the name of the general staff changed from "Haganah General Staff" to "Israel Defense Forces High General Staff," but the acronym "HGS" remained the same.
3. Minutes at HGS meeting after the start of the First Truce, apparently 18 June 1948, IDFA 121–172/50.
4. Shlomo Nakdimon, *Altalena* (Jerusalem 1978); Uri Brenner, *Altalena* (Tel Aviv, Israel), 1978.
5. Apart from the two books cited in n. 3, which were important sources for my description of the affair, I relied on documents from the IDFA 922–1241/75, which include Harel and HGS logs, reports by Palmah and Kiryati personnel and by others about the events, IZL radio transmissions, government press releases, and so forth. See also file 1950/121–178 of the Legal Service, containing documents on the arrest of IZL personnel following the affair. The orders of the Operations Branch about the conclusion of Allon's role in Operation Purge are from 27 June 1948. See too the Harel wireless log, IDFA 50–661/69.
6. See, e.g., Ben-Gurion's words in his talk with Allon, 16 June 1948, BGA, minutes of 1948 meetings.
7. Yigal Allon, "Meggamot u-Maas," in Zerubavel Gilad and Matti Megged, eds., *Sefer ha-Palmah* (Tel Aviv, 1953), 1:23.
8. See Slutsky et al., *Sefer Toldot ha-Haganah*, (Tel Aviv, 1971–72, vol. 3, part 2, p. 1324.
9. An extensive discussion of the whole issue can be found in Anita Shapira, *Mi-Piturei ha-Rama ad Peiruk ha-Palmah* (Tel Aviv, 1985), p. 111, both in the preface and in the minutes of the Committee of Five, held during the truce after Ben-Gurion accused the HGS of political revolt. See what Ben-Gurion himself had to say to the committee, pp. 124–30.
10. Minutes of the Committee of Five, in Shapira, *Mi-Piturei ha-Rama*, p. 77 (for Galili relating to Stone's words, see pp. 84, 87, and 115).
11. Ben-Gurion, BGWD, 1:294, 296, 299–300. Minutes of the Committee of Five, in Shapira, *Mi-Piturei ha-Rama*, pp. 190–93.
12. Atzmon (Havlin) on behalf of the headquarters brigade to Hillel (Galili), HGS, and the distribution list of all IDF units, 24 May 1948, BGA.
13. Meeting between Ben-Gurion and Yigal Allon, 16 June 1948, BGA, minutes of meetings of 1948.
14. Ibid.
15. Ben-Gurion, BGWD, 19 June 1948, 2:534–38.
16. See Allon's telegrams (brigade commander) 20 June 1948, IDFA 922–1018/1975.
17. Allon to Yadin, 20 June 1948, IDFA 922–1018/1975.
18. Testimony of Yadin, minutes of the Committee of Five, in Shapira, *Mi-Piturei ha-Rama*, pp. 154–55.
19. Ben-Gurion, BGWD, 29–30 June 1948, 2:567.
20. Testimony of Zvi Ayalon, minutes of the Committee of Five, in Shapira, *Mi-Piturei ha-Rama*, pp. 154–55.
21. For details, see the preface, in Shapira, *Mi-Piturei ha-Rama*, pp. 39–44.

22. Ibid., pp. 43–47; Yigael Yadin, interview by the author, 26 August 1982.
23. Operation LRLR, document, General Staff/Operations Branch, 26 June 1948, IDFA 922–1018/75.
24. Yadin to Allon, 7 July 1948, IDFA 1–666/1948.
25. Dani headquarters, Allon, 8 July 1948, Operation Dani (stage 1), operation order, IDFA 922–1237/1975.
26. Operation LRLR headquarters, 8 July 1948, 1975/922–1018.
27. Yigal Allon, "Operation Dani," lecture, 11 March 1958, KMA, section 15, Allon, container 6, file 2.
28. Yigal Allon, lecture on the War of Independence, 17 June 1950, KMA, section 15, Allon, container 6, file 2.
29. Summary of information on the enemy in advent of the end of the truce on the Ramleh-Lydda front and vicinity for 28 June 1948, IDFA 922-1237/1975.
30. The most comprehensive work on Operation Dani is the pioneering book by Elhanan Oren, *Ba-Derekh el ha-Ir* (Tel Aviv, 1976), p. 77.
31. Yitzhak Rabin, interview by the author, 28 October 1982. See also Avi Yiftah (Shemariah Gutman), "Lod Yotzet la-Golah," *Mi-Bifnim*, 13 March 1948–April 1949.
32. Allon, "Operation Dani," lecture.
33. Allon, lecture on the War of Independence, 17 June 1950, KMA, section 15, Allon, container 6, file 2. Allon drew an important lesson in warfare from Dayan's experience: the conquest of Lydda and Ramleh had been planned according to the principles of indirect approach of the renowned English military historian and tactician, Basil Liddell Hart. The strategic impact was to result from the two forces joining up in Ben Shemen after completing the pincer maneuver on both towns. But strategy and tactics are two separate things. The tactical effect was achieved by storming through the city. Had it not been for this maneuver, Lydda might have continued to hold out under siege for weeks, until the Arab Legion arrived to deliver it.
34. Yadin, interview by the author.
35. Allon, "Operation Dani," lecture.
36. Avi Yiftah (Shemariah Gutman), "Lod Yotzet la-Golah."
37. Allon, "Operation Dani," lecture.
38. Quite a few historians have dealt with the question of Lydda in light of the Arab charge of massacre in the small mosque. See versions by Benny Morris, *The Birth of the Palestinian Refugee Problem 1947–1949* (London and New York, 1987), PP. 203–12; and Benny Morris, "The New Historiography: Israel Confronts Its Past," *Tikkun* 3, no. 6 (November–December 1988): 19–23, 99–102. In contrast, see Alon Kadish, Avraham Sela, and Arnon Golan, *Kibush Lod, July 1948* (Tel Aviv, 2000), pp. 43–53. See too the overall report on the actions of the Third Battalion from Friday, 9 July to Sunday 18 July 1948; report including Yiftah's actions as part of Operation Dani, 9 July–18 July, IDFA 922–1237/1975.
39. Avi Yiftah (Shemariah Gutman), "Lod Yotzet la-Golah."
40. Allon to Operations Branch, 13 July 1948, telegram no. 4, IDFA 1–464/54.
41. In a letter from the chief of staff to LRLR headquarters of 13 July 1948, there is a reminder about the order from the chief of staff, No. A/4/8/50 of 6 July 1948 on the question; IDFA 922–1018/1975.
42. On Abu Ghosh, see Etzyoni Brigade's telegram to Harel Brigade, 10 July 1948 and the letter from the chief of staff to LRLR headquarters of 13 July 1948, IDFA 922–1018/1975. On Nazareth, see Operations Branch to Yirmiyahu, 9 July 1948, "Ha-Nes Ha-Yotzeh," IDFA 922–1182/1975.

43. Dani headquarters/Intelligence, "El Toshavei Lod ve-Ramleh ve-khol nosei ha-neshek," 11 July 1948, IDFA 922-1237/1975.
44. Shitrit report on trip to Ramleh and Lydda, 12 July 1948, State Archives, FM2564/10; Shitrit's letter to Sharett, 13 July 1948, FM2564/10.
45. See the telegram from Allon to Yiftah's battle headquarters on the surrender of Ramleh, IDFA 922-1237/1975.
46. Yitzhak Rabin, interview by the author, 28 October 1982.
47. Mula Cohen, *La-Tet u-le-Kabel, Pirkei Zikhronot Ishiim* (Tel Aviv, 2000), p. 144.
48. Operations Branch to Dani, urgent, 12 July 1948, time 23:30, "Ha-Nes Ha-Yotzeh," IDFA 922-1182/1975.
49. The report of Yiftah in Operation Dani, 9-18 July, reports the capture of the police station on 13 July at 10:00, IDFA 922-1237/1975. On the same matter, see the announcement by Dani 13 July 1948, IDFA 922-1018/1975.
50. Corroboration of Gutman's version is found in a telegram from Dani's headquarters to Yiftah, 13 July, saying: "Residents of Or (Ramleh) are to be expelled quickly regardless of age. They are to be directed to the (Bet-Naballah) road," IDFA 922-1237/1975. According to this, there seems to have been a prior instruction that the young men were to be arrested as prisoners. There is also an earlier telegram saying that women, the elderly, and children were to be allowed to flee Ramleh, and the men arrested.
51. Allon, "Operation Dani."
52. Avi Yiftah (Shemariah Gutman), "Lod Yotzet la-Golah."
53. To: Commanding Officer, Forty-third Battalion, from Kaman, Re: transferring refugees, 13 July 1948, IDFA 922-1237/1975.
54. Yitzhak Rabin, interview by the author, 28 October 1982.
55. Allon, lecture on the War of Independence, 17 June 1950, KMA, section 15, Allon, container 6, file 2.
56. See Anita Shapira, "Hirbet Hizah: Between Remembrance and Forgetting," *Jewish Social Studies*, 7, no. 1 (fall 2000): pp. 18-27.
57. Operation Dani's headquarters, "Te'uda," 14 July 1948 (signed on behalf of Commanding Officer Yitzhak Rabin), IDFA 922-1018/1975.
58. Allon, "Operation Dani," lecture.
59. Overall report on the activities of the First Battalion from 9 July to Sunday 18 July, 20 July 1948, IDFA 922-1237/1975. See memorial book issued by bereaved families, *Re'eh Otam Shotkim . . . 50th Anniversary of the Battle of Khirbet Quriqur, 18 July 1948* (Tel Aviv, 1998).
60. II Samuel 11:25.
61. The description is based on the reconstruction in Oren, *Ba-Derekh el ha-Ir*, pp. 186-90 and 208-24. The book helped both as a supplementary source and as a pointer for some of the topics mentioned above.
62. Ibid., pp. 225.
63. Operation Dani to Kiryati, Eighth Brigade, Harel and Yiftah, 19 July 1948, IDFA 922-1234/1975.
64. Ben-Gurion, BGWD, 20 July 1948, 2:605.

Chapter 10

1. Ben-Gurion, BGWD, 6 September 1948, 2:673.
2. HGS/Operations Branch, context of Operation 10, 16 August 1948, IDFA 922-1017/1975.

3. Order of Chief of Staff Yaakov Dori on the country's organization into fronts, 6 August 1948, IDFA 110–113.

4. On 2 August 1948 Avidan wrote a memo to the Operations Branch, "Hazit Ha-Darom—Haarkha, Maskanot ve-Hatzaot," IDFA 922–1017/75. It is clear from the memo that Avidan saw himself as the potential front commander.

5. Yigael Yadin, interview by the author, 7 September 1982.

6. See the mention of this in Ben-Gurion, BGWD, 20 August 1948, 2:659 and 29 August 1948, 2:665.

7. Yigal Allon, "Pekudot Hazit ha-Darom," 2 September 1948, IDFA 110/110.

8. Uri Elgom, "Kravot Khirbet Maqhuz," *Maarkhot* 294–95 (July 1984): pp. 99–106. See also the brigades' telegrams to the Operations Branch, "Ha-Nes ha-Nikhnas," IDFA, 922–1175/75.

9. Ben-Gurion, BGWD III, 6 October 1948, 3:736.

10. Meeting of Southern Front High Command, 11 October 1948, IDFA, 275-1046/70.

11. Southern Front headquarters/Operations (Rabin), Operation Yoav Order, 10 October 1948, IDFA, 12–401/52.

12. Rabin at the meeting of brigade commanders, Southern Front headquarters, 10 October 1948, IDFA 922–1227/75.

13. The reconstruction is based on the meeting of brigade commanders, Southern Front headquarters, 10 October 1948, IDFA 922–1227/75; Yitzhak Rabin, interview by the author, 28 October 1982; Meir Davaidson, interview by the author, 19 March 1984; Yitzhak Rabin and Dov Goldstein, *Pinkas Sherut* (Tel Aviv 1979), 1:65–66. For the change of plan, see the document "Shinuim ve-Tikunim bi-Fkudat Mivtza 'Yoav,'" 13 October 1948, IDFA 922–1017/75.

14. Rabin and Goldstein, *Pinkas Sherut*, 1:66; brigade telegrams to Operations Branch, "Ha-Nes ha-Nikhnas," 15–16 October 1948, IDFA; Yitzhak Rabin, interview by the author, 28 October 1948; Uzi Narkiss, interview by the author, 7 October 1982.

15. Uzi Narkiss, interview by the author, 7 October 1982.

16. Haim Gouri, *Ad Alot ha-Shahar* (Tel Aviv, 2000), p. 62.

17. Allon, lecture on the Southern Front, 11 March 1958.

18. Ibid.

19. Ibid.

20. Ibid.

21. Mula Cohen, *La-Tet u-le-Kabel, Pirkei Zikhronot Ishiim* (Tel Aviv, 2000), p. 159.

22. Front headquarters to brigades, Operation Order, 17 October 1948, IDFA 275–1046/70.

23. Ben-Gurion, BGWD, 18 October 1948, 3:753.

24. Brigade telegrams to Operation Branch, "Ha-Nes ha-Nikhnas," 19 October 1948, IDFA.

25. Ben-Gurion, BGWD, 19 October 1948, 3:754.

26. Yigal Allon, lecture on the Southern Front, 11 March 1958; Yitzhak Rabin, interview by the author, 28 October 1982; Rabin and Goldstein *Pinkas Sherut*, 1:68–69.

27. Brigade telegrams to Operations Branch, "Ha-Nes ha-Nikhnas," 19–20 October 1948, IDFA.

28. Meeting of brigade commanders, 10 October 1948, Front D headquarters, IDFA 922–1227/75.

29. Ben-Gurion, BGWD, 20 October 1948, 3:755.

30. Ibid., 3:756. Yigael Yadin, interview by the author, 3 October 1982.

31. See, e.g., Haim Gouri's description of the night trek in Gouri, *Ad Alot Ha-Shahar*, pp. 62–65.
32. Mula Cohen, interview by the author, 28 June 1984; Uzi Narkiss, interview by the author, 7 October 1982.
33. Ben-Gurion to Allon, 21 October 1948, IDFA 69–2539/50.
34. Ben-Gurion, BGWD, 22 October 1948, 3:760.
35. "Ha-Maarkha al ha-Negev," stenogram of lecture by Major General Yigal Allon to cultural officers, Southern Front (apparently January 1949), IDFA 434–1046/70; Yigal Allon, lecture on Southern Front, 11 March 1958; brigade telegrams to Operations Branch, 24–27 October 1948, IDFA.
36. Southern Front headquarters, Campaign Log, no. 9, 27 October 1948, IDFA 275–1046/70.
37. Front D Headquarters, meeting of brigade commanders, 24 October 1948, IDFA 922–1227/75.
38. OC Southern Front, "Conduct in Occupied Areas," 27 October 1948, IDFA 275-1046/70.
39. The Arabs claimed that five hundred people had been killed. In Ben-Gurion's diary, seventy to eighty are mentioned. BGWD, 10 November 1948, 3:807.
40. Allon, lecture on the Southern Front, 11 March 1958.
41. Zvika Dror, *Matzbi le-lo Serara, Sippur Hayav shel Yitzhak Sadeh, "Ha-Zaken,"* (Tel Aviv, 1996), pp. 406–9.
42. Allon to Yitzhak Sadeh, 31 October 1948, IDFA 69–2539/50.
43. On this, see the letter from Be'eri to Allon, 9 November 1948, Re: Dawayima—Investigation, IDFA 70–2539/50; letters from Rabin on 10/11/1948 on the summons to the investigation, IDFA 70–2539/50; letter from the front's general prosecuter to Allon, 21 December 1948, IDFA 70–2539/50; Dror, *Matzbi le-lo Serara*, pp. 409–10.
44. Allon, lecture on the Southern Front, 11 March 1958.
45. Ibid.
46. Ben-Gurion, BGWD, 25 October 1948, 3:773.
47. Ben-Gurion, BGWD, 20 August 1948, 2:659; 29 August 1948, 2:665. See also 7 September 1948, 2:673–74.
48. Na'an Assembly, 14 September 1948, IDFA 121-225/50.
49. The description is based on the full minutes of the meeting, IDFA 121–225/50. Various passages have been cited in various places. See Ben Gurion, BGWD, 14 September 1948, 2:686–69.
50. Na'an Assembly, 14 September 1948, IDFA 121–225/50.
51. Ben-Gurion, *Medinat Yisrael ha-Mehudeshet* (Tel Aviv, 1975), 1:276–77.
52. Allon to CGS, 10 October 1948, IDFA 69–2539/50.
53. File of letters protesting the dismantling of the Palmah's headquarters, IDFA 141–481/49.
54. Ben-Gurion to CGS, 28 October 1948, IDFA 121–225/50.
55. CGS to Uri Brenner, 29 October 1948, IDFA 121–225/50.
56. HGS/Adjutant General Branch to deputy branch commander, 4 November 1948, IDFA 121–225/50.
57. Shlomo Shamir (HGS, Department for HGS Duties) to branches and the Palmah's headquarters, unit liquidation order, 6 November 1948, IDFA 18–2433/50.
58. Orders of the Palmah's headquarters, 6 November 1948, order of the day, IDFA 5–2539/50.

59. Ben-Gurion to Yitzhak Tabenkin, 15 October 1948, KMA, section 15, Tabenkin, container 8, file 1, document 41.
60. Ben-Gurion, BGWD, 30 October 1948, 3:786.
61. Arnan (Sini) Azaryahu to CGS, 7 December 1948, IDFA, 69–2539/50; service head to CGS, 24 December 1948, IDFA, 70–2539/50.
62. Ahuvya Malkhin, interview with the author. Also, in IDFA 16–1011/1953, Malkin is mentioned several times as the cultural officer of Front D (e.g., in the circulars of 27 April 1949; 9 May 1949, 9 June 1949).
63. Yitzhak Rabin, interview by the author, 20 November 1982.
64. Meeting of Southern Front brigade commanders and operation officers (undated, immediately after the operation), IDFA 275–1046/70. "Ha-Nes Ha-Nikhnas," telegrams from 23 December 1948.
65. Yitzhak Rabin, interview by the author, 20 November 1982.
66. The description is based on interviews of Rabin and Yadin by the author, 20 November 1982. Allon's lecture on the Southern Front, 11 March 1958. meeting of Southern Front brigade commanders and operation officers, IDFA 275–1046/70; Yigal Allon, "Ha-Maarkha al ha-Negev" (apparently January 1949), IDFA 434–1046/70.
67. Yitzhak Rabin, interview by the author, 20 November 1982.
68. Meeting of Southern Front brigade commanders and operation officers, IDFA 275–1046/70; Allon, "Ha-Maarkha al ha-Negev" (apparently January 1949), IDFA 434–1046/70.
69. Yitzhak Rabin, interview by the author, 20 November 1982.
70. Allon's lecture on the Southern Front, 11 March 1958.
71. Front D to Operations Branch, 27 December 1948 (appears as telegram no. 1 on 28 December).
72. Commander of Front D to Operations Branch, 28 December 1948, telegram no. 9; Security Officer Sh. M. 3 Front D, first special overall report on Operation Horev, January 1949, IDFA 15–2539/50.
73. Yadin to Front D commander, 28 December 1948, 16:25, "Ha-Nes Ha-Yotzeh," IDFA 922–1182/75.
74. Front D commander to Operations Branch, 28 December 1948, 21:00, "Ha-Nes Ha-Nikhnaz."
75. Meeting of Southern Front brigade commanders and operation officers, IDFA 275–1046/70.
76. Allon, lecture on the Southern Front, 11 March 1958.
77. Front D battle operations headquarters, 28 December 1948, change in deployment order of 27 December 1948, IDFA 550–922/75.
78. Front D operations headquarters, 29 December 1948, Operation Order for 30 December 1948, IDFA 550–922/75.
79. Yadin to Front D commander, 29 December 1948, "Ha-Nes Ha-Yotzeh," IDFA 922–1182/75.
80. Front D to Operations Branch, 29 December 1948, 17:15 and 18:00, IDFA "Ha-Nes Ha-Nikhnas."
81. Yadin to Front D commander, 29 December 1948, 19:30 and 19:50, IDFA "Ha-Nes Ha-Yotzeh," 922–1182/75.
82. Yadin, HGS/Operations, "Document on Operation Ayin Second Stage," 30 December 1948,
IDFA 550–922/75.
83. HGS/Operations Branch to Adjutant General Branch and others, 30 December 1948, "Ha-Nes Ha-Yotzeh," IDFA 922–1182/75.

84. Meeting of Southern Front brigade commanders and operation officers, IDFA 275-1046/70; Allon, lecture on the Southern Front, 11 March 158.
85. Uzi Narkiss, interview by the author, 7 October 1982.
86. Ben-Gurion, BGWD, 31 December 1948, 3:914-18.
87. Yadin to Front D commander, 31 December 1948, "Ha-Nes Ha-Yotzeh," IDFA 922-1182/75.
88. Allon to Yadin, CGS and defense minister, 31 December 1948, telegram 311815. I have no source. It appears also in Allon's chapter headings for the lecture on Operation Horev, KMA, section 15, Allon, container 4, file 5.
89. Yadin to Southern Front Commander, 1 January 1949, 11:15; Yigal Allon to Yadin, 1 January 1949, 18:00, IDFA.
90. Uzi Narkiss, interview by the author, 7 October 1982.
91. Allon's lecture on the Southern Front, 11 March 1958.
92. See Southern Front telegrams to Operations Branch, 4-8 January 1949, IDFA "Ha-Nes Ha-Nikhnas."
93. Front D to Operations Branch, 7 January 1949, IDFA "Ha-Nes Ha-Nikhnas."
94. Yigael Yadin, interview by the author, 3 October 1982.
95. Yadin to Front D Commander, 9 January 1949, IDFA "Ha-Nes Ha-Yutzel," 922-1182/75.
96. Allon, chapter headings for lecture on Operation Horev, KMA, section 15, Allon, container 4, file 5.
97. I did not find the CGS's letter, but I did find Allon's reaction to it, 28 January 1949, IDFA 69-2539/50.
98. Meeting of Southern Front brigade commanders and operation officers, IDFA 275-1946/70.
99. Allon's lecture, 17 June 1950, KMA, section 15, Allon, container 6, file 2.
100. Yitzhak Rabin, interview by the author, 20 November 1982.
101. Ben-Gurion, BGWD, 9 January 1949, 3:939.
102. Diary of Nehemiah Argov, 24 December 1948, *Sefer Nehemiah Argov* (n.p., 1959), p. 195.
103. Ibid., pp. 196-97.
104. Front D operations headquarters, Liquidation Operation Order, 25 December 1948, IDFA 17-979/51.
105. Yitzhak Rabin, interview by the author, 20 November 1982.
106. The Third Brigade, Regrouping Order, 30 December 1949, IDFA 922-1017/75; HGS/Training Division, "Report on the Action to Conquer Iraq al-Manshiya," 15 January 1949, IDFA 922-1017/75.
107. CGS Dori to Front D commander, 14 December 1948, IDFA 70-2539/50.
108. Front D headquarters, special addendum to Operation Horev Order, 17 December 1948 (signed by Allon), IDFA 275-1046/70.
109. SHAY/3, Daily Reports for 31 December 1948, 1 January 1949; Daily Report for 3 January 1949, 4 January 1949, IDFA 15-2539/50.
110. Front D headquarters, Campaign Log, 29 December 1948, IDFA 38-1749/50. Ben-Gurion quotes Allon as reporting that one platoon gave an order to shoot prisoners and then those who were about to surrender began shooting from the houses, resulting in the losses. Ben-Gurion, BGWD, 17 January 1949, 3:954.
111. Section 12/SHAY/3, Special Report on the First Stage of Operation Horev, January 1949, IDFA 15-2539/50.

356 Notes to Pages 270–275

112. Front D/ShM./SHAY/3, Report on Operation Horev, 30 January 1949, IDFA 15-2539/50.
113. Yeruham Cohen, in his book *Le-Or ha-Yom u-va-Mahshakh* (Tel Aviv, 1969), pp. 195–222, tells of his meetings with Gamal Abdel Nasser and the commander of the Faluja Pocket, Colonel a-Sayed Taha Bey, including a meeting between Allon and Taha Bey at Kibbutz Gat, in an attempt to convince them to surrender.
114. Yigael Yadin, interview by the author, 3 October 1982.
115. Report of a conversation between Allon and Ben-Gurion, BGWD, 7 January 1949, 2:933.
116. Allon to Rabin, 15 February 1949, IDFA 69–2539/50.
117. Ben-Gurion, BGWD, 24 February 1949, 3:970.
118. Avner to Yadin, February 1949, IDFA 70–2539/50.
119. Allon to CGS, 28 February 1949, IDFA 69–2539/50. Yadin's telegram, 26 February 1949, IDFA "Ha-Nes Ha-Yotzeh," 922–1182/75.
120. Yigal Allon to CGS, 28 February 1949, IDFA 69–2539/50; Sharett's letter to CGS, 6 March 1949, attached to Yigal Allon's letter to the brigades, 22 March 1949, IDFA 69–2539/50.
121. Yadin to Front D commander, 1 March 1949, IDFA "Ha-Nes Ha-Yotzeh," 922–1182/75.
122. Yadin's telegrams to Allon, 3–4 March 1949, IDFA "Ha-Nes Ha-Yotzeh," 922–1182/75.
123. Sharett's letter to CGS, 6 March 1949, IDFA 69-2539/50, and attached letter from CGS to Allon, 15 March 1949, IDFA 70–2539/50.
124. Yitzhak Rabin, interview by the author, 28 October 1982.
125. The reconstruction is based on author's interviews of Yitzhak Rabin. It should be noted, however, that Moshe Carmel, the commander of the Northern Front, claimed in his interview with author, that he had never heard from Ben-Gurion either a word or a hint about any desire to remove Arabs for demographic reasons. Yadin, in contrast and, according to Carmel, knew if a location had been emptied of Arabs and viewed this positively, though in his case too there is no hint or sign of any instruction to expel Arabs, except as a consequence of the exigencies of war. Moshe Carmel, interview by the author, 22 November 1984.
126. See Ilan Assia, *Moked ha-Sikhsukh, ha-Maavak al ha-Negev 1947–1956* (Jerusalem, 1994).
127. Haim Gouri gives a number of reasons bordering on legend and romance in favor of the drive to Eilat: quarries, King Solomon's port, an outlet to the Indian Ocean. He includes not a word about strategic importance. Gouri, *Ad Alot ha-Shahar*, pp. 120–121.
128. Allon to Galili, 9.2.1949, KMA, Section 15, Allon, Container 4, File 1.
129. Allon's lecture on the Southern Front, 11 March 1958. See also the description of the expedition in Gouri's book, *Ad Alot ha-Shahar*, pp. 120–27.
130. Yigael Yadin, interview by the author, 3 October 1982.
131. Allon's lecture on the Southern Front, 11 March 1958; Yitzhak Rabin, interview by the author, 28 October 1982; Yigael Yadin, interview by the author, 31 October 1982.
132. Allon's lecture on the Southern Front, 11 March 1958; Rabin, interview by the author, 28 October 1982; Yadin, interview by the author, 31 October 1982.
133. Yigal Allon to Yadin, 8 March 1949, IDFA 69–2539/50; Yadin's telegrams to Allon, 9 March 1949, "Ha-Nes Ha-Yotzeh," IDFA 922–1182/75.
134. SHAY/2, 9 March 1949, "Ha-Nes Ha-Nikhnas," IDFA.

135. Telegrams of Southern Front headquarters to brigades 1 and 2, IDFA 67-401/52.
136. Yitzhak Rabin, interview by the author, 28.10.1982; Uzi Narkiss, interview by the author, 7 October 1082.
137. Yadin to Allon, 11 March 1949, IDFA "Ha-Nes ha-Yotzeh," 922-1182/75.
138. Ben-Gurion, BGWD, 11 March 1949, 3:974.
139. Allon to head of HGS Branch, 14 March 1949, IDFA 69-2539/50.
140. Allon to brigade commanders, 22 March 1949, IDFA 5-2539/50.
141. Allon's lecture on the Southern Front, 11 March 1958.
142. Yitzhak Rabin, interview by the author, 28 October 1982.

Chapter 11

1. Ben-Gurion, diary, 11 March 1949, IDFA.
2. The reconstruction is based on Allon's letter to Ben-Gurion, 24.3.2949, KMA, section 15, Allon, series B, container 4, file 1; Allon's letter to Yadin, 15 April 1949, IDFA 69-2539/50.
3. Letter (signatory unclear) to Moshe Shertok, 18 January 1949, Lavon Archive, Zalman Aranne file, 32-14-8.
4. Allon to Ben-Gurion, 24 March 1949, KMA, section 15, Allon, series B, container 4, file 1.
5. Ibid.
6. Allon's lecture on the War of Independence, 17 June 1950, KMA, section 15, Allon, container 6, file 2.
7. This is based on the author's interviews of Yigael Yadin, Israel Galili, and Moshe Carmel. See also Yitzhak Rabin, interview by the author, 28 October 1982.
8. Yitzhak Rabin, interview by the author, 28 October 1982.
9. Israel Galili reported on a conversation during the First Truce with Yosef Tabenkin, who suspected that Ben-Gurion did not wish to conquer all of Jerusalem. Galili rebuked him on this occasion, contending that there was no reason to think so. Israel Galili, interview by the author, 2 August 1982. Later, a similar charge appeared in Israel Baer, *Bit'hon Yisrael—Etmol, Hayom u-Mahar* (Tel Aviv, 1966).
10. On the dispute over the Israeli-Transjordan agreement in 1948, see Yoram Nimrod, "Hit'havut Dfusim shel Yahasei Yisrael-Arav 1947-1950," Ph.D. diss., Hebrew University, 1985; Dan Shiftan, *Ha-Optzia ha-Yardenit* (Tel Aviv 1986); Avi Shlaim, *Collusion Over the Jordan* (Oxford 1988); Uri Bar-Yoseph, *The Best of Enemies* (London, 1987).
11. Yaakov Dori to brigade commanders, and others, 18 January 1949, IDFA 18-2433/50; Allon to CGS, 20 January 1949, IDFA 69-2539/50.
12. Israel Galili, interview by the author, 11 May 1982.
13. Allon to Israel and Yitzhak (Galili and Sadeh), Paris, 5 October 1949, KMA, section 15, Galili, container 4, file 1.
14. Dori to Allon, 8 September 1949, KMA, section 15, Allon, series B, container 4, file 1.
15. Order of Twelfth Brigade's headquarters, 15 August 1949, IDFA 33-2539/50.
16. Allon to Israel and Yitzhak (Galili and Sadeh), Paris, 5 October 1949, KMA, section 15, Galili, container 4, file 1.
17. Ibid. The description is further based on Kidron's report to Michael Comay, 4 October 1949, KMA, section 15, Allon, series B, container 4, file 1; and

Yigal Allon's report on his trip to the minister of defense and others, 25 October 1949, KMA, section 15, Allon, series B, container 4, file 1.

18. Allon to Israel and Yitzhak (Galili and Sadeh), Paris, 5 October 1949, KMA, section 15, Galili, container 4, file 1.

19. Allon's report on his trip to the minister of defense and others, 25 October 1949, KMA, section 15, Allon, series B, container 4, file 1.

20. Allon to Israel and Yitzhak (Galili and Sadeh), Paris, 5 October 1949, KMA, section 15, Galili, container 4, file 1.

21. Allon to Ruth Allon, London, 26 September 1949.

22. Allon to Ruth Allon, 5 October 1949.

23. Ibid.

24. Allon to Ruth Allon, 7 October 1949.

25. Rabin to Allon, 10 October 1949, KMA, section 15, Allon, container 4, file 1.

26. This version was prevalent among Allon's associates. In a letter to Yigael Yadin of 26 December 1949, he partially confirmed it: "My hosts, officers of the French HGS, knew of the matter before I did," KMA, section 15, Allon, series B, container 4, file 1.

27. On Ruth, see Yeruham Cohen to Yigal Allon, 18 October 1949, KMA, section 15, Allon, series B, container 4, file 1; Allon's telegram to Ruth Allon, 14 October 1949.

28. Yitzhak Rabin to Yigal Allon, 10 October 1049, KMA, section 15, Allon, container 4, file 1.

29. Yigal Allon to Ruth Allon, Paris, 15 October 1949.

30. Yigal Allon to Ruth Allon, 25 October 1949.

31. Yigal Allon to Ruth Allon, 18 November 1949

32. Yigal Allon to Ruth Allon, Paris, 5 November 1949.

33. Yitzhak Rabin to Yigal Allon, 23 October 1949, KMA, section 15, Allon, container 4, file 1.

34. Yigal Allon to Ruth Allon, Paris, 15 October 1949.

35. Ibid.

36. Sini Azaryahu, interview by the author, 4 September 1988.

37. The reconstruction of Yigal Allon's eruption at the discussion is based on a telephone conversation with Yitzhak Ben-Aharon and also the letter. Ben-Aharon to Yigal Allon, 29 March 1949, KMA, section 15, Ben-Aharon, series B, container 4, file 6.

38. Yitzhak Ben-Aharon to Yigal Allon, 29 March 1949, KMA, section 15, Ben-Aharon, series B, container 4, file 6.

39. Israel Galili to Yitzhak Sadeh, early October 1949, KMA, Galili Notebook, Mapam 1949.

40. Yitzhak Rabin to Yigal Allon, 23 October 1949, KMA, section 15, Allon, container 4, file 1.

41. Ibid.

42. Yigal Allon to Ruth Allon, Paris, 18 November 1949.

43. Yigal Rabin to Yigal Allon, 23 October 1949, KMA, section 15, Allon, container 4, file 1.

44. Ibid.

45. Letters of Zvi Zur, 9–14 December 1949, IDFA 16–1011/53.

46. Yigael Yadin, interview by the author, 3 October 1982.

47. Israel Galili, interview by the author, 17 November 1982. A check of the commanders who stayed in the army bears this out.

48. Yigael Yadin, interview by the author, 3 October 1982.
49. Yigal Allon to Yigael Yadin, 26 December 1949, KMA, section 15, Allon, series B, container 4, file 1.
50. Ibid.

Epilogue

1. M. Gefen, "Be-Veito Sh-Nityatem," *Al Ha-Mishmar*, 29 August 1952.
2. *Maariv*, 3 September 1952.
3. "Reshamim mi-Kinus Ha-Palmah," *Haaretz*, 28 September 1952.
4. "Medurato lo Tikhbe," *Ha-Olam Ha-Zeh*, 2 October 1952.
5. Ibid.
6. Yigal Allon, "Moreshet u-Netivah," KMA, section 15, Allon, container 6, file 7.
7. Ibid.
8. *Al Ha-Mishmar*, 25 September 1952.
9. "Reshamim mi-Kinus ha-Palmah," *Haaretz*, 28 September 1952.
10. Amos Horev, interview by the author, 19 July 1991.
11. Leah Rabin, interview by the author.
12. "Yitzhak Sadeh: Sofa shel Tekufah," *Ha-Olam Ha-Zeh*, 28 August 1952. See also *Al Ha-Mishmar*, 25–26 September 1952.
13. Author's interviews of Moshe Carmel, Uri Avneri, and Amos Horev; account of Yaakov Hefetz to the Yitzhak Rabin Center. See also Yael Gewirtz, "Pnei ha-Dor ki-Fnei Allon," *Hadashot shel Shabbat*, 3 February 1989. She quotes Haim Gouri as saying that Yigal Allon returned from England a different man and how his bombastic, rhetorical address at Sadeh's memorial was not forgotten.
14. "Reshamim mi-Kinus Ha-Palmah," *Haaretz*, 28 September 1952.
15. Yigal Allon to members of Ginossar, London, 14 January 1951, GAR.
16. Meeting between Prime Minister and Defense Minister David Ben-Gurion and Israel Galili and Yigal Allon, prime minister's office, Jerusalem, 8 August 1962, file of limited collections, Levi Eshkol Institute, BGA.
17. See also Yitzhak Ben-Aharon interview by the author, 7 September 1983.
18. Israel Galili interview by the author, 10 January 1983.
19. Yigael Yadin, interview by author, 7 September 1982.
20. Moshe Carmel, interview by the author, 22 November 1984 and 9 December 1984; Yitzhak Ben-Aharon, interview by the author, 7 September 1983 and 9 October 1983.
21. Yitzhak Ben-Aharon, interview by the author, 9 October 1983.
22. Letters of Y. Kenav to Yigal Allon, 23 April 1967, KMA, section 15, Allon, container 16, file 4.
23. Yigal Allon to Marsha Williams, Jerusalem, 19 April 1967, KMA, section 15, Allon, container 16, file 4.
24. Abba Eban to Yigal Allon, Jerusalem 3 May 1967, Allon to Eban, Tel Aviv, 4 May 1967, collection of documents on the waiting period, Galili Archive.
25. Exchange of telegrams, 24 May 1967–4 June 1967, between Moscow's embassy personnel, the Liaison Bureau there, and Israel's Liaison Bureau about Yigal Allon's visit in the Soviet Union, Galili Archive.
26. Exchange of telegrams between the Liaison Bureau and the embassy in Moscow, 21–24 May 1967, Galili Archive.
27. Document no. 1, Galili documents on the waiting period, Galili Archive.

28. Yigael Yadin, interview by the author, 28 October 1982.
29. Note from Yigal Allon to Israel Galili, 30 May 1967, Galili documents on the waiting period, Galili Archive.
30. Documents 5–14, Galili documents on the waiting period, Galili Archive. Yigael Yadin (reading from his diary for May–June 1967), interview by the author, 28 October 1982.
31. Meeting of Mapai secretariat, 1 June 1967, Galili documents, Galili Archive.
32. Note from Yigal Allon to his friends, "I wanted to pre-empt the negative resolution following Gahal's insistence and the storm in Mapai." Galili documents on the waiting period, Galili Archive.
33. Amos Horev, interview by the author, 19 July 1991.
34. Amos Horev, interview by the author, 26 July 1991.
35. Ephraim Evron, interview by the author, 6 November 1986.
36. Amos Horev, interview by the author, 26 July 1991; Yitzhak Ben-Aharon, interview by the author, 9 October 1983.
37. Amos Horev, interview by the author, 26 July 1991.
38. Matti Golan, "Ha-Maspid," *Haaretz*, 23 October 1980.
39. Yitzhak Ben-Aharon, interview by the author, 1 November 1984.
40. He himself viewed the step this way; see Nahum Barnea, "Yoman," *Dvar Ha-Shavua*, 7 March 1980.
41. See Yaakov Hazan, "Hu Kavash et Libi mi-Pgishatenu ha-Rishona," *Al Ha-Mishmar*, 12 March 1980.
42. Yitzhak Ben-Aharon, interview by the author, 1 November 1984.
43. Sini Azaryahu, interview by the author, 14 September 1988.
44. Yigal Allon, "Second Working Draft on the Historical Background of the Allon Plan"; my thanks to Sheila Hattis-Rolef for making this lecture available to me.
45. Sini Azaryahu, interview by the author, 3 October 1988.
46. Ephraim Evron, interview by the author, 6 November 1986; 11 November 1986.
47. Uri Avneri, interview by the author, 22 June 2002.
48. The passages on the various versions of the Allon Plan and his political conception are based on his lectures from 1978 onward, which were made available to me by Sheila Hattis-Rolef, Yigal Allon's aide. I also drew on my interviews of Sini Azaryahu and Yitzhak Ben-Aharon. See also Moshe Zack, "'Yiftah' and His Generation," *Maariv*, 2 March 1980; Moshe Zack, "Ha-Optzia shel Hussein," *Maariv*, 10 September 1982; Moshe Zack, "Du Siah bli Tokhnit," *Maariv*, 15 April 1983; Yaakov Hazan, "Hu Kavash et Libi mi-Pgishatenu ha-Rishona," *Al Ha-Mishmar*, 12 March 1980; Eyal Kafkafi, "Ha-Maavak Rabin-Peres eino Ishi," *Maariv*, 11 April 1980; Banco Adar, "Shayara el-ana at Overet," *Al Ha-Mishmar*, 7 March 1980; H[aim] G[ouri], "Ha-im Yigal Allon haya Yona?," *Davar*, 25 February 1982.
49. Ephraim Evron, interview by the author, 6 November 1986.
50. Ephraim Evron, interview by the author, 6 November 1986 and 11 November 1986; Sini Azaryahut, interview by the author, 3 October 1988.
51. Zerubavel Arbel to Yigal Allon, undated; Allon to Arbel, 28 August 1967, KMA.
52. Sheila Hattis-Rolef, interview by the author, 6 February 1984.
53. G[alai] Binyamin, "Shahor al gabei Lavan," *Maariv*, 2 March 1980.
54. Amos Elon, "Gibor Atzuv be-Eretz Akhzarit," *Haaretz*, 2 March 1980.

55. Ibid.
56. Nathan Shaham, "Al Yigal Allon," *Monitin*, March 1983.
57. Amos Eilon, "Gibor Atzuv be-Eretz Akhzarit," *Haaretz*, 2 March 1980.
58. Amos Keinan, "1948 Zikhro li-Vrakha," *Yediot Aharorot*, 28 March 1980.
59. Yaakov Hazan, "Hu Kavash et Libi mi-Pgishatenu ha-Rishona," *Al Ha-Mishmar*, 12 March 1980.
60. Shevah Weiss, "Mifgash Rishon u-Mifgash Aharon," *Yediot Aharonot*, 28 March 1980.
61. Nahum Barnea, "Yoman," *Dvar ha-Shavua*, 7 March 1980.
62. Keinan, "1948 Zikhro li-Vrakha."

Selected Bibliography

Archives

Ben-Gurion Archive, Sde Boker
Central Zionist Archives, Jerusalem
Ginossar Archive, Ginossar
Haganah Archive, Bet Golomb, Tel Aviv
IDF Archive, Tel Ha-Shomer
Kibbutz Meuhad Archive, Tabenkin Institute, Efal
Labor Archive, Lavon Institute, Tel Aviv
Labor Party Archive, Bet Berl

Journals and Newspapers

Al Ha-Mishmar
Alon Ginossar
Alon Ha-Palmah
Davar
Devar Ha-Shavua
Shnaton Davar
Haaretz
Ha-Olam Ha-Zeh
Ha-Poel Ha-Tza'ir
Maariv
Maarakhot
Mi-Bifnim
Monitin
Tzror Mikhtavim
Yediot Aharonot
Yediot shel Shabat

Books, Articles, and Interviews

Aaronsohn, Ran. "Shlavim be-Hakamat Moshvot ha-Aliyah ha-Rishona u-ve-Hitpat'hutan." In *Sefer ha-Aliyah ha-Rishona*. Jerusalem, 1982.
Allon, Yigal. *Bet Avi*. Kibbutz Me'uhad, n.d. Translated under the title *My Father's House* (New York, 1976).
Allon, Zvi. *Le-Zikhro*. Family booklet.
Assia, Ilan. *Moked ha-Sikhsukh, ha-Maavak al ha-Negev 1947–1956*. Jerusalem, 1994.
Baer, Israel. *Bit'hon Yisrael—Etmol, Hayom u-Mahar*. Tel Aviv, 1966.

Bibliography

Bar-On, Mordechai. *Etgar ha-Ribonut: Yetzirah ve-Hagut ba-Assor ha-Rishon la-Medinah.* Jerusalem, 1999.
———. *Gvulot Ashanim: Iyunim be-Toldot Medinat Yisrael, 1948–1976.* Jerusalem, 2001.
———. *Zikaron be-Sefer: Reshita shel ha-Historiyographya ha-Yisraelit shel Milhemet ha-Atzma'ut, 1948–1958.* Tel Aviv, 2001.
Bar-Yoseph, Uri. *The Best of Enemies.* London, 1987.
Bauer, Yehuda. *Diplomatya u-Mahteret.* Merhavia, 1966.
Beck, Alexander. *Anshei Panfilov.* Tel Aviv, 1946.
Ben-Eliezer, Uri. "Kibbutz she-yesh lo Historion." *Zmanim* 24 (1987): 107–10.
Ben-Gurion, David. *Medinat Yisrael ha-Mehudeshet.* Vols. 1–2. Tel Aviv, 1975.
———. *Paamei Medina, Zikhronot min ha-Izavon.* Edited and annotated by Meir Avizohar. Tel Aviv, 1993.
———. *Yoman ha-Milhama.* Edited by Rivlin Gershon and Oren Elhanan. Vols. 1–3. Tel Aviv, 1984.
Ben-Yehuda, Netivah. *Bein ha-Sefirot.* Jerusalem, 1981.
———. *Mi-baad La-Avotot.* Tel Aviv, 1985.
Bitan, Arieh. *Tmurot Yishuviyot ba-Galil ha-Tahton ha-Mizrahi: 1800–1978.* Jerusalem, 1982.
Brenner, Uri. *Altalena.* Efal, 1978.
———. *Ha-Hakhshara ha-Megguyesset ba-Palmah.* Tel Aviv, 1983.
Cohen, Shmuel (Mula). *La-Tet u-le-Kabel, Pirkei Zikhronot Ishiim.* Tel Aviv, 2000.
Cohen, Yeruham. *Le-Or ha-Yom u-va-Mahshakh.* Tel Aviv, 1969.
Dror, Zvika. *Bi-Netivei Hatzala.* Tel Aviv, 1988.
———. *Matzbi le-lo Serara, Sippur Hayav shel Yitzhak Sadeh, "Ha-Zaken."* Tel Aviv, 1996.
Dumka, Eliezer. "Hevlei Hakamoto shel Bet ha-Sefer 'Kadoorie.'" *Cathedra* 35 (April 1985): 91–108.
———. *Kadoorie—Alei Givah.* Kefar Tavor, 1982–83.
Elgom, Uri. "Kravot Khirbet Maqhuz." *Maarakhot* 294–95 (July 1948): 99–106.
Eliav, Mordekhai, ed. *Sefer ha-Aliyah ha-Rishonah.* Jerusalem, 1982.
Ever Hadani, A. *Ha-Hityashvut ba-Galil ha-Tahton.* Tel Aviv, 1955.
Freundlich, Yehoshua. *Mi-Hurban le-Tekuma.* Tel Aviv, 1994.
Gelber, Yoav. *Palestine 1948: War, Escape, and the Emergence of the Palestinian Refugee Problem.* Brighton, 2001.
———. *Toldot ha-Hitnadvut.* Vols. 1–4. Jerusalem, 1979.
Gilad, Zerubavel, ed. *Maggen ba-Seter.* Jerusalem, 1949.
Gilad, Zerubavel, and Megged Matti, eds. *Sefer ha-Palmah.* Vols. 1–2. Tel Aviv, 1953.
Golan, Arnon. *Shinui Merhavi—Totzaat Milhama: Ha-Shtahim ha-Araviim Lesheavar bi-Medinat Yisrael, 1948–1950.* Beersheba, 2001.
Gouri, Haim. *Ad Alot ha-Shahar.* Tel Aviv, 2000.
Hacohen, David. *Et Le-Sapper.* Tel Aviv, 1974.
Hareuveini, Meir, ed. *Kefar Tavor (Mes'ha).* Kefar Tavor, 1976.
Heller, Joseph. *Ba-Maavak le-Medinah: Ha-Mediniyut ha-Tzionit, 1936–1948.* Jerusalem, 1984.
Joseph, Dov. *Kiriyah Ne'emana.* Tel Aviv and Jerusalem, 1960.
Kadish, Alon, Avraham Sela, and Arnon Golan. *Kibush Lod, July 1948.* Israel, 2000.
Kafkafi, Yitzhak, ed. *Be-Shnot ha-Mahanot ha-Olim.* Vol. 2, *Ha-Asor ha-Sheni.* Tel Aviv, 1984–85.

Kanuhel, Dov, ed. *Gush Etzyon be-Milhamto*. Jerusalem, 1954.
Karpin, Michael, and Ina Friedman. *Murder in the Name of God: The Plot to Kill Yitzhak Rabin*. New York, 1998.
Katznelson, Berl. *Iggrot 1930–1937*. Edited by Anita Shapira and Esther Reisen. Tel Aviv, 1984.
———. *Ktavim*. Vols. 1–12. Tel Aviv, 1945–50.
Kokhavi, Arieh. *Akurim u-Politika Beinleumit*. Tel Aviv, 1992.
Laskov, Shulamit. *Kol Koreh: Hayav u-Zmano shel Yosef Vitkin*. Tel Aviv, 1986.
Levy, Yitzhak (Levitza). *Tisha Kabin*. Israel, 1986.
Lorch, Netaniel. *Korot Milhemet Ha-Atsma'ut*. Givataim, 1989.
Milstein, Uri. *Toldot Milhemet ha-Atzma'ut*. Vols. 1–4. Tel Aviv, 1989–91.
Morris, Benny. *The Birth of the Palestinian Refugee Problem, 1947–1949*. London and New York, 1987.
———. *The Birth of the Palestinian Refugee Problem Revisited*. Cambridge, 2004.
———. *Israel's Border Wars, 1949–1956*. Oxford, 1993.
———. "The New Historiography: Israel Confronts Its Past." *Tikkun* 3, no. 6 (1988).
Nakdimon, Shlomo. *Altalena*. Jerusalem, 1978.
Naor, Mordechai. *Laskov*. Tel Aviv, 1988.
Nimrod, Yoram. "Hit'havut Dfusim shel Yahasei Yisrael-Arav, 1947–1950." Ph.D. diss., Hebrew University, 1985.
Niv, David. *Maarkhot ha-Irgun ha-Tzva'i ha-Leumi*. Vols. 1–6. Tel Aviv, 1973.
Ofer, Dahlia. *Derekh ba-Yam, Aliyah Bet bi-Tekufat ha-Shoah*. Jerusalem, 1988.
Ogen, Yitzhak, ed. *Asher Haya*. Tel Aviv, 1949.
Oren, Elhanan. *Ba-Derekh el ha-Ir*. Tel Aviv, 1976.
Ostfeld, Zahava. *Shlavim Ikariim bi-Vniyat ha-Tzava be-Hanhagato shel David Ben-Gurion*. Tel Aviv, 1994.
Paicovich (Allon), Eliav. *Masekhet shel Bazelet*. Published by the family.
Pa'il, Meir. *Kera be-Tashach*. Efal, 1991.
———. *Palmah: Ha-Koah ha-Megguyas shel "ha-Haganah."* Tel Aviv, 1995.
Rabin, Dov, ed. "Grodno." In *Entziklopedia shel Galuyot*, vol. 9. Jerusalem, 1973.
Rabin, Yitzhak, and Dov Goldstein. *Pinkas Sherut*. Vols. 1–2. Tel Aviv, 1979. Translated under the title *The Rabin Memoirs*. Boston, 1979.
Ratner, Yohanan. *Hayai ve-Ani*. Tel Aviv, 1978.
Re'eh Otam Shotkim . . . 50th Anniversary of the Battle of Khirbet Quriqur, 18 July 1948. Tel Aviv, 1998.
Repetur, Berl. *Le-Lo Heref*. Vols. 1–3. Tel Aviv, 1973–75.
Rivlin, Gershon, ed. *La-Esh ve-la-Maggen*. Tel Aviv, 1962.
Rubashov, Zalman, ed. "Pinkas ha-Maarakha." In *Be-Mivhan ha-Kravot, Shnaton Davar, 1948–49*. Tel Aviv, n.d.
Sadeh, Yitzhak. *Ma Hidesh ha-Palmah*. Marhavia, 1950.
Salu, Yehuda. *Ha-Moreh ha-Arokh*. Merhavia, 1965.
Schulman, Varda. *Ramot Naftali ba-Maarakha*. Tel Aviv, 1984.
Sefer Nehemiah Argov. (N.p., 1959).
Shaltiel, Eli. *Tamid be-Meri*. Tel Aviv, 2000.
Shapira, Anita. "Bein Havlaga le-Terror—ha-Kinus ha-Yishuvi be-Yuli 1938." *Ha-Zionut* 6 (1981): 267–359.
———. *Berl*. Tel Aviv, 1980. Translated under the title *Berl: The Biography of a Socialist Zionist, 1887–1944*. Cambridge, 1984.
———. "Hirbet Hizah: Between Remembrance and Forgetting." *Jewish Social Studies* 7, no. 1 (fall 2000): 18–27.

———. *Land and Power.* New York, 1992.
———. *Mi-Piturei ha-Rama ad Peiruk ha-Palmah.* Tel Aviv, 1985.
———, ed. *Medina ba-Derekh.* Jerusalem, 2001.
Sharett, Moshe. *Yoman Medini.* Vols. 1–5. Tel Aviv, 1968–79.
Shefi, Yigal. *Sikat Mem-Mem: Ha-Mahshava ha-Tzva'it be-Kursim le-Ktzinim ba-"Haganah."* Tel Aviv, 1991.
Shiftan, Dan. *Ha-Optzia ha-Yardenit.* Tel Aviv, 1986.
Shiran, Osnat. *Nekudot Oz.* Efal, 1998.
Shlaim, Avi. *Collusion over the Jordan.* Oxford, 1988.
Slutsky, Yehudah, Shaul Avigur, et al. *Sefer Toldot ha-Haganah.* Vols. 1–3. Tel Aviv, 1954–72.
Stein, Shimshon. *Mahanayim: Moshava Kitzrat Yamim.* Jerusalem, 1978.
Teveth, Shabtai. *Moshe Dayan.* Jerusalem, 1971.
Tzur, Eli. *Nofei ha-Ashlaya, Mapam 1948–1954.* Beersheba, 1998.
Veidat ha-Ihud shel Mifleget Po'alim Ha-Shomer Ha-Tzair be-Eretz Israel ve-ha-Miflaga Le-Ahdut Ha-Avoda-Poalei Zion. Mapam publication. Tel Aviv, 23–24 January 1948.
Wallach, Yehuda, ed. *Hayinu ke-Holmim.* Ramat Gan, 1985.
Weitz, Joseph. *Yomanai ve-Iggrotai la-Banim.* Vols. 1–6. Tel Aviv, 1965.
Zemach, Shlomo. *Sippur Hayai.* Jerusalem and Tel Aviv, 1983.
Zoref, Absalom, ed. *Ginossar, Hamesh Esre Shana le-Hivasda.* Tel Aviv, 1949.
———. *Israel Levy, Ish Ginossar.* Tel Aviv, 1964.

Interviews

Allon, Ruth
Arbel, Zerubavel
Avidan, Shimon
Avneri, Uri
Azaryahu, Arnan (Sini)
Ben-Aharon, Yitzhak
Brandsteter, Amos
Brenner, Uri
Carmel, Moshe
Cohen, Shmuel (Mula)
Cohen, Yeruham
Davidson, Meir
Evron, Ephraim
Galili, Israel
Geller, Israel
Goldman, David
Gouri, Haim
Hacohen, David
Harel, Isser
Harel, Joseph (Yossi Hamburger)
Hattis-Rolef, Sheila
Hazan, Yaakov
Henkin, Yitzhak
Horev, Amos
Koren, David
Liebertovsky, Israel

Malkin, Ahuvya
Mattveyov, Shimon
Narkiss, Uzi
Prozhinin, Joel
Rabin, Leah
Rabin, Yitzhak
Sarig, Nahum
Schwartz, Amihud
Shadmi, Nahum
Shaham, Nathan
Shamir, Shlomo
Shoshani, Eliezer
Spector, Shosh
Tabenkin, Yosef
Yadin, Yigael
Yahil, Leni
Yitzhaki, David
Zefira, Shimon
Zemach, Ada
Zoref, Absalom
Zoref, Yehudit

Index

Abdu. *See* Ben Yehuda, Israel
Abdullah, King of Jordan, 233, 282–85
Abdul Nasser, Gamal, 241, 270, 284, 309, 356 n.113
Abed al-Hamid, Sultan, 5
Aberdeen, 286, 287
Abu-Ageila, 258, 260–64
Abu Gosh, 206, 209, 227
Abu Kabir, 182
Abu-Shusha, 54, 63–65, 74
Abu Yusuf, Sheikh, 194–95
Abyssinia, 44, 80
Acre, 5, 65; prison at, 69, 101
Ad Alot ha-Shahar (Gouri), 243
Adan, Avraham (Bren), 243, 246, 263
Ad-Halom Bridge, 239
Afikim, 96, 105, 130
Afula, 13, 30, 41, 200
Agatha, Operation. *See* Black Saturday
Agranat Commission, 312
Aharonowitz (Aranne), Zalman, 67, 308, 311
Akbara, 197
Aleppo, 111, 116
Alexandria, 4, 127, 334 n.71
Alexandroni Brigade, 210, 212, 258, 268–70, 272, 277
Algeria, 289, 290, 294
Aliyah. *See* Jewish immigration
Aliyah Bet. *See* Illegal immigration; Mossad for Aliyah Bet
Aliyat Ha-Noar (Youth Aliya), 77
Allon, Nurit (Yigal's daughter), 74–75, 168–69, 170–71, 173, 174, 175, 286, 287
Allon (Episdorf), Ruth (Yigal's wife), 61–63, 71, 74–77, 160, 162, 164, 165, 167–72, 174, 175, 286, 287, 289, 291, 294, 298, 308
Allon, Yiftah (Yigal's son), 286, 298
Allon Plan, 312, 313–16, 369 n.48
Alonim, 142

Altalena affair, 210–12, 219
Alterman, Nathan, 143, 144; "Ha-Tur ha-Shvi'i," 145
Amar, Major Abd al-Hakim, 268, 270
Amihai, Ithiel, 240
Anglo-American Enquiry Commission, 153
Anglo-Egyptian Treaty (1936), 263
Anglo-Jordanian Treaty, 283
Anglo-Palestine Bank, 67
Aqaba, 273; Aqaba Bay, 246
Arab armies, 237, 249, 299. *See also specific armies*
Arab Disturbances, 94, 103; of 1929, 28, 84, 95, 196; of 1936–39, 46, 54, 79–82, 182. *See also* Arab Rebellion
Arab-el-Heb. *See* Bedouins
Arab gangs, 48, 57, 64, 91, 95, 169
Arab High Committee, 79, 180, 181
Arab labor, Arab laborers, 16, 28, 29, 54, 63, 85
Arab Legion, 203–7, 223, 226–29, 233, 235, 236, 238, 274, 275, 278, 285
Arab Liberation Army, 193, 238, 251
Arab Rebellion (1936–39), 46, 56, 57, 61, 64, 74, 79–81, 85, 90, 93, 95, 111, 128, 182. *See also* Arab Disturbances, of 1936–39
Arab refugees, 227–33, 273, 314
Arab state in Palestine, 79, 178, 179, 185, 188, 239, 285
Arab states, 79, 160, 170, 180, 214, 283; invasion of Palestine, 192, 199, 201, 203, 238
Arab terrorism, 46, 169, 181–82
Aranne, Zalman. *See* Aharonowitz (Aranne), Zalman
Arava Road, 274
Arazi, Tuvia, 111, 115
Arbel, Zerubavel, ix–x, 223, 240, 317
Arlosoroff, Chaim, 36
Armistice agreements: Israel-Egypt, 270, 272, 282; Israel-Jordan, 282, 284, 285. *See also* Armistice talks

370 Index

Armistice lines (Green Line), 297, 316
Armistice talks, 271–72, 274, 282. *See also* Armistice agreements
Arms, 83, 146, 199; exercises in the use of, 147; illegal arms, 85, 99; procurement of, 146, 159, 160, 162; searches of, 101, 149, 157, 158; smuggling in, 80. See also *Altalena* affair
"Army out of uniform," 109, 110, 123, 132, 188
Ashdod, 178, 238
Ashdot Yaakov (kibbutz), 213
Atlantic. See Immigrant ships
Attlee, Clement, 153
Auja al-Hafir, 246, 258, 259, 260, 266, 271, 272
Auschwitz, 163
Avidan, Shimon. *See* Koch (Avidan), Shimon
Avidar, Joseph, 171, 220
Avigur, Shaul. *See* Meirov (Avigur), Shaul
Avisar, Eitan. *See* Von Friedman (Avisar), Eitan
Avneri, Uri, 316
Ayalon, Zvi, 220
Ayelet Ha-Shahar (kibbutz), 86, 90, 160, 191, 192, 193, 332 n.16
Ayn Ghadyan, 275
Ayn Husub (Hazevah), 274
Azaryahu, Arnan (Sini), 38, 40–41, 44, 45, 48, 49, 61, 73, 125, 130, 177, 240, 256, 294, 315
A-Zbekh. *See* Bedouins
A-Ziv Bridge, 156, 158

Baharav, Yehoshua. *See* Rabinowitz (Baharav), Yehoshua
Balfour Declaration, 21
Barfiliya, 229
Bar-Kokhba, 108
Barnea, Nahum, 321–22
Bar-Tikva, Mundek. *See* Pasternak (Bar-Tikva), Mundek
Bar-Yehudah, Israel. *See* Idelson (Bar-Yehudah), Israel
Bashan, 193
Basle, 160–63
Bat Galim, 159
Beaufort Castle, 112, 113, 336 n.16
Bedouins, 5, 17, 22, 32, 147, 186; Arab-el-Heb (tribe), 194–95, 196; a-Zbekh (tribe), 11, 15, 18–19, 23, 36, 47, 84
Be'eri, 240
Be'eri, Isser, 248
Beersheba, 184, 238, 245, 246–47, 256, 259, 268, 271, 274
Begin, Menachem, 148, 149, 159, 211, 303, 306, 310, 317, 321, 342 n.33
Beirut, 5, 116
Beisan (Beit She'an), x; Beisan Valley, 49, 111, 142
Ben-Aharon, Yitzhak, 175, 291, 292, 307
Ben-Gal, Michael (James), 212, 228
Ben-Gurion, David, 45, 73, 80, 98, 109, 123, 142, 149, 151, 152–55, 159, 160, 161, 163, 171, 172, 173, 175, 177, 180, 181, 182, 185–88, 192, 204, 205, 206, 209–22, 225, 228–29, 234, 237, 238, 239, 241, 244–47, 249, 251–58, 263, 264, 266–69, 272, 273, 274, 275, 277, 278, 282–87, 289, 290, 291, 293–96, 300–304, 306, 308, 309, 310, 316, 319, 328 n.2, 345 n.25, 348 n.74, 353 n.39, 355 n.110, 356 n.125, 357 n.9
Ben-Gurion, Paula, 221
Ben-Gurion–Jabotinsky agreement (1934), 254
Ben-Hur, Elijah. *See* Cohen (Ben-Hur), Elijah
Ben Shemen, 224, 225, 350 n.32; Youth Village, 39, 54, 224
Bentwich, Norman, 77
Ben-Yaacov, Zvi, 91
Ben Yehuda, Israel (Abdu), 116, 121
Ben-Zvi, Yitzhak, 98, 127, 206
Berdyczewski, Mikha Joseph, 13
Beriha (Flight) Movement, 154, 160, 162, 163, 164
Bernadotte, Count Folke, 239, 271
Bet Affa, 249
Betar (youth movement), 42
Bet Avi (Allon's autobiography), 2, 50, 52, 100, 101
Bet Gan, 7
Bet Ha-Aravah (kibbutz), 137, 274
Bet Hanun, 241, 243, 247, 258
Bet Horon, 147, 228
Bet Jibrin, 223, 238, 241, 247–48, 272, 273
Bet Jimal, 244
Bet Jiz, 205
Bet Keshet (kibbutz), 11, 148

Index   371

Bet Naballah, 224, 228, 233, 234, 351 n.49
Bet Netofah Valley, 14
Bet Sira Junction, 233, 234, 236
Bet Susin, 205, 207
Bet Tima, 244
Bet Zekharyah, 147
Bevin, Ernest, 154
Biltmore Program, 127, 254
Binational state in Palestine, 173, 181, 187
Bin-Nun, Yohai, 157
Bin-Nun A, Operation, 204, 205
Bin-Nun B, Operation, 204, 205
Binyaminah, 26, 52
Biqat Ha-Yare'ah (Moon Valley), 277
Bir-Asluj, 238, 258, 260
Bir et-Tamila, 269, 270
Biriyyah, 193
Birkenau, 163
"Black Saturday" (Operation Agatha), 158–59
Blonde Dov. See Garnak, Yaakov
Blood vengeance (*gom*), 19, 22, 94, 95, 97
Bluvshtein, Rachel, 321, 322
Bnei Binyamin organization, 25, 26
Bnot Yaakov Bridge, 200
Borochov, David, 73
Brandsteter, Amos, 37, 38, 41, 48, 49
Britain, 39, 46, 70, 77, 106, 127, 129, 140, 161, 166, 173, 239, 263, 264, 267, 273, 298, 299, 300; British Criminal Investigation Department (CID), 142, 149, 150; British police, 46, 147, 149, 184; British government, 64, 79, 153, 155, 179, 180, 181; British intelligence, 105, 111, 115, 119, 142; British intelligence, Department D, 110, 114–15; British Parliament, 80; conquest of Palestine, 21, 79, 114; cooperation with the Jewish Yishuv, 109–25, 133, 150, 158; elections (1945), 153; end of the Mandate and evacuating Palestine, 114, 126, 127, 128, 171, 178–81; the Foreign office, 287; invasion of Syria and Lebanon, 111, 112–13, 115, 130, 146, 199, 201; Labor Party, 153; Mandate in Eretz Israel, 13, 22, 142, 189 (*see also* Government of Palestine); Ministry of Economy, 110; Royal Air Force, 266; rule/policy in Palestine, 35, 36, 37, 40, 44, 45, 46, 56, 64, 70, 71, 79–80, 82, 91, 92, 93, 98–99, 101, 127–28, 131, 142, 149, 153, 158–59, 160, 181, 184, 189, 190 (*see also* Peel Commission; Shaw Commission; White Paper); the War Office, 110, 287; in World War II, 110–11, 114, 119, 127, 143
British army, 81, 82, 95–96, 104, 119, 128, 162, 183, 184, 214, 217, 220, 234, 259, 275, 287; Australian soldiers, 112, 113; Jewish Brigade, 110, 148, 149, 214; Jewish enlistment and volunteering, 98, 109–10, 112, 123, 131–36, 138–39, 146, 204, 213, 339 n.28
Brock, Dr., 169, 170
Broom (*Matateh*), Operation, 196
Bunch, Ralph, 271
Burma Road, 207, 235

Cairo, 149, 246
Camp David Accords (1978), 316
Canaan, Mount, 3, 191, 193, 194
Carmel, Moshe. See Zalizky (Carmel), Moshe
Carmel, Mount, 105, 123, 129
Central Front, 219, 220, 221
Chesis, Dov, 151, 248, 260
Churchill, Winston, 149
Ciukerman, Yitzhak (Antek), 161, 164
Coastal plain, 178, 223, 238, 247, 282. See also Sharon Plain
Cohen (Ben-Hur), Elijah, 82, 220
Cohen, Ge'ula, 342 n.33
Cohen, Shmuel (Mula), 191, 192, 200, 206, 224, 229, 244
Cohen, Yeruham, 192, 240
Collard, Major J. M., 120–21, 336 n.30
Commissions of inquiry in Palestine. See Anglo-American Enquiry Commission; Peel Commission; Shaw Commission; United Nations, UNSCOP
Committee of Five, 220–21
Communists, 70, 143, 179, 187, 293
Concentration camps, 162, 163. See also specific camps
Coordination (organization), 165
Creech-Jones, Arthur, 180
Crete, 104, 111
Cunningham, Alan, 158, 180
Cyprus, 166
Czechoslovakia, 161, 163

Daburiyeh, 96
Dachau, 96
Dafna (kibbutz), 195

Damascus, 5, 23, 116
Dani, Operation, 219, 221–37, 240, 351 n.48
Daniyal, 224
Danziger, Yitzhak, 322
Davar (newspaper), 72, 95, 97, 184, 286, 333 n.46
Davidson, Meir, 87, 90, 91, 107, 135, 335 n.14, 340 n.36
Dawayima, 248–49, 269, 353 n.39
Dayan, Deborah, 88
Dayan, Moshe, 87–91, 99–102, 111–13, 115, 120, 123, 125, 143, 147, 152, 224–26, 260, 283, 289, 294, 295, 296, 300–301, 305–7, 309–12, 315–19, 335 nn. 8, 13, 350 n.32
Dayan (Schwartz), Ruth, 88
Days of Ziklag (S. Yizhar), 241
Dead Sea, 178, 274
Deganyah (kibbutz), 68, 88, 199, 200
Dekel Operation, 227–28, 237
Deportation ships, 166, 169
Dhahiriya, 273
Dinaburg (Dinur), Ben Zion, 73
Dinur, Ben Zion. *See* Dinaburg (Dinur), Ben Zion
Displaced persons, 153–54, 164–65. *See also* Jewish refugees
Displaced persons' camps, 153, 154, 160, 162, 164–65, 174, 243
Dissenters (Porshim), 148–52, 155, 157, 181, 212, 341 n.22. *See also* IZL; LeHI
Domville, Captain P., 336 n.30
Dori, Yaakov, 91, 142, 146, 150, 151, 162, 171, 172, 215, 219, 253, 254, 287, 289, 342 n.33
Dorot, 129
Dowe, Mr., 40
Dror, Zvika, 143
Dror Zionist youth movement, 161, 165
Druze, 15
Dust, Operation, 240

Education, 32, 41; Labor education stream, 304
Efter, Yaacov, 330 n.62
Egypt, 8, 45–46, 104, 124, 126, 129, 162, 201, 263, 268, 273, 274, 277, 284, 302, 308–9, 314, 316; armistice agreement with Israel, 270–72; Department of Agriculture, 46; young officers' revolution, 259
Egyptian army, 206, 223, 235, 238–49, 258, 262, 266, 267, 270, 272; Third Army, 271
"Egyptian Burma Road," 240, 244
Ehrlich, Asher, 9, 17–18, 35
Ehrlich, Dvora, 9
Ehrlich, Simha, 321
Eighth Armored Brigade, 224, 235, 242, 243, 244, 258, 259, 260, 266, 269; Eighty-second Battalion, 224, 261; Eighty-ninth Light Battalion, 224, 248
Eilat (Umm-Rashrash), 274, 275, 277, 278, 291, 356 n.127; Gulf of Eilat, 274, 275
Ein Dor, 318
Ein Gedi, 246, 274, 277
Ein Harod, 10, 54, 99, 100, 101, 133, 167, 256, 291
Ein Mahl, 31
Ein Zeitim, 191, 193
El-Alamein, 119, 120, 143
El-Arish, 241, 261–62, 264, 267, 314
Elazar, David, 312
Elon, Amos, 318, 319
Entebi, Jehuda, 13
Episdorf, Ruth. *See* Allon (Episdorf), Ruth
Eretz Israel, ix, 10, 16–17, 52, 53, 70, 80, 113, 164, 181, 232, 237, 319, 322; Arab invasion of, 192, 199, 201; British conquest of, 21, 79, 114; British Mandate in, 13, 22, 79, 119; end of the British Mandate in, 178–81; redemption of, 80; right to the land, 80. *See also* Palestine
Er-Ruheibe, 259
Eshbol, Ze'ev, 29
Eshkol, Levi, 302, 307–12, 319
Etzyon Block, 178, 185, 189, 190, 199, 206, 222, 314, 345 n.18
Etzyon Gaber, 274
Etzyoni Brigade, 204, 206, 216, 218, 222
Europe, 71, 110, 148, 160–61, 164, 168, 173, 174, 178, 199, 216; Central Europe, 70; Eastern Europe, 180; Jews, 7, 109, 110, 134, 153, 180
Even, Dan, 210, 219
Exodus. See Immigrant ships
Expulsion/evacuation of Arabs from occupied areas, 227–33, 269, 284, 351 n.49, 356 n.125

Faisal, Emir, 23
Faluja, 238, 239, 240, 241, 242, 245, 247, 272, 273

Faluja Pocket, 245, 249, 262, 267, 268, 270, 271, 272, 274, 356 n.113
Farmers, 4, 8, 9, 12, 15, 16, 19, 25, 37
Faza'a (Arab alarm), 47
Fedayeen, 301
Fein, Joseph, 111
Field companies, 85–88, 91–96, 99, 102, 111, 141, 332 nn. 16, 46, 50
Filon camp, 193
First Aliyah, 4
France, French, 23, 70, 77, 104, 111, 115, 116, 126, 161, 169, 210, 289, 290, 309; Vichy regime, 105, 107, 111, 112, 114
Francis, Captain P. G., 120, 336 n.30
"French Commando," 269
Front D. *See* Southern Front
Fuld, Brakha, 156

Gahal Party, 310, 311
Gahal recruits, 243, 251, 253
Galai, Benyamin, 318
Galilee, 2, 8, 11, 17, 18, 21, 23, 24, 26, 34, 80, 96, 142, 170, 178, 188, 206, 210, 237; Arab invasion of, 199–200; British exit from, 191, 193; Central Galilee, 197, 199, 228; Eastern Galilee, 178, 191–201 (*see also* Yiftah, Operation); evacuation of women and children from, 185; Lower Galilee, 3, 5, 7, 9, 11, 13, 14, 23, 24, 25, 29, 36, 37, 48, 90, 332 n.9; Upper Galilee, 23, 24, 90, 191, 251, 332 n.9; Western Galilee, 185, 203, 239
Galili, Israel, 80–81, 89–90, 101–2, 106, 111, 123, 125, 126, 127, 129, 134, 135, 136, 138, 142, 150–52, 154–58, 160–64, 170, 172, 174, 175, 176, 182, 183, 186, 188, 192, 212, 214–15, 217, 220, 244, 255, 286, 289, 296, 298, 299, 302, 304, 307, 309, 310, 315, 317, 332 n.23, 334 n.65, 338 n.8, 357 n.9
Gardner, Major, 121, 123
Garnak, Yaakov (Blonde Dov), 260
Gat, 243, 244, 356 n.113
Gaza, 231, 241, 242, 243, 245, 246, 247, 249, 258, 264
Gaza Strip, 258, 259, 262, 264, 267, 271, 314
Gedera, 245, 268
Gei Oni, 4. *See also* Rosh Pinnah
German-Jewish youth, 61, 62, 68, 71
Germany, 61, 70, 98, 104, 110, 111, 114, 115, 118, 120, 126–30, 133, 147, 148, 151, 161–64, 167, 172, 309; American-occupied zone in, 153; Communist Youth, 143
Gesher (kibbutz), 199
Geva (kibbutz), 340 n.45
Gezer (kibbutz), 207, 224
*Ghaffir*s, 48
Gideon, 10, 33
Gilad, Zerubavel, 256, 257
Gilboa, Mount, x, 10, 203
Ginossar (kibbutz), 43, 53–78, 86, 87, 99, 101, 125, 172, 174, 195, 200, 216, 292, 302, 306, 321, 330 n.62
Givat Brenner (kibbutz), 126, 145, 255, 298–300, 321
Givat Ha-Sheloshah (kibbutz), 70, 335 n.13
Givat Olga, 155
Givati Brigade, 190, 209, 238–41, 244; Fifty-second Battalion, 206, 245; Fifty-fourth Battalion, 244
Givelber, Avraham, 165
Glubb Pasha, 223, 233
Godfrey, Admiral John Henry, 110
"Going beyond the fence," 83, 147
Golan, Nahum, 275, 277
Golani Brigade, 199, 200, 258, 259, 266, 274, 275, 277
Goldman, Nahum, 160
Golomb, Eliyahu, 73, 98, 102, 109, 123, 126, 127, 129, 132, 142, 149, 339 n.28, 340 n.36
Gordon, Yehoshua, 83, 93
Gordonyia (youth movement), 138
Gouri, Haim, 156, 243, 299, 356 n.127
Government of Palestine, 35, 36, 46, 49, 79, 82, 110, 148, 149, 158, 159; Department of Agriculture, 36, 37, 40
Greater Israel, 181, 187, 312, 314, 315
Greece, 104, 110, 180, 345 n.6
Green Line. *See* Armistice lines
Grodno, 2, 3
Gromyko, Andrei, 179
Gush Emunim, 312
Gutman, Nahum, 322
Gutman, Shemariah, 226, 227, 229

Haaretz (newspaper), 298, 299, 301
Habonim (youth movement), 61
Hacohen, David, 106, 123, 334 n.78, 336 nn. 20, 29

374 Index

Haganah organization, 44–45, 47, 58, 61, 64, 65, 70, 73, 78, 80, 81, 83, 85, 92, 93, 96, 99, 101, 102, 103, 107, 110, 113, 115, 120, 121, 123, 126, 127, 129, 141, 142, 146, 155, 159, 160, 165, 170, 182, 183, 184, 186, 188, 189, 190, 192, 194, 197, 214, 235, 251, 332 n.9, 338 n.66; campaign against IZL (see *Saison*); command of, 90, 92, 93, 110, 111, 116, 123, 124, 129, 342 n.33; and enlistment in the British army, 132; the forty-three affair, 99–102, 225; General Staff (HGS) of, 142, 146, 169, 171, 172, 187, 189, 193, 197, 342 n.33; High Command of, 57, 58, 97, 111, 128, 130, 134, 135, 142, 144, 145, 152, 157, 162, 171, 185, 205, 217, 218, 219, 221, 227, 257; marine company, 105, 160; May Plan, 183; mini-convention at the 22nd Zionist Congress, 162, 163; National Command of, 81, 105, 142, 144, 146, 154, 156, 159, 160, 163, 171, 172, 214, 334 n.76; Operations Branch of, 215, 248; permanent staff of, 103; Plan D, 192, 227; SHAY (Secret Service), 150, 151, 152; smuggling in arms, 80; training courses, 86–88, 90, 99. *See also* Twenty-three seaman commando

Ha-Horesh organization, 18

Haifa, 39, 42, 51, 52, 55, 66, 96, 106, 142, 166, 178, 184, 185, 199, 219, 231, 345 n.18; Italy's bombing of, 129; port of, 105, 157, 159, 169, 298; radar station, 155–56

Ha-Kibbutz Ha-Artzi Ha-Shomer Ha-Tza'ir movement, 143, 151, 176, 187

Halutza, 259

Hamadyah (kibbutz), 137, 138

Ha-Mahanot Ha-Olim (youth movement), 137–38

Hamburger (Harel), Joseph (Yossi), 87, 88, 91, 96, 97, 102, 103, 106, 107, 166–67

Hamis, Sheikh Abu-Fais, 64, 65

HaMisrafa, Mount, 259

Hammond, Captain, 120

Hanita (kibbutz), 90–91, 103, 178, 226, 301, 312

Ha-Noar Ha-Oved (HNHO, youth movement), 41, 42, 50, 54, 68, 89, 101, 327 n.2; training groups, 137, 138. *See also* Kevutzat Ha-Noar Ha-Oved Migdal

Ha-Olam Ha-Zeh (newspaper), 298–99

Ha-Poel Ha-Tza'ir Party, 36

Harats, 14–20, 25, 28, 29, 30, 31

Hardalah Bridge, 112

Harel (kibbutz), 302

Harel, Yossi. *See* Hamburger (Harel), Joseph (Yossi)

Harel Brigade, 190, 204, 205, 206, 209, 215, 216, 227, 233, 235, 236, 258, 260, 266, 313

Harrison, Earl, 153

Hartzfeld, Abraham, 54, 55, 57, 58, 65–66, 67

Hashkafa (newspaper), 9

Ha-Shomer Ha-Tza'ir (HSHT, youth movement), 173–76, 181, 187, 213, 328 n.2

Ha-Shomer organization, 18, 340 n.40

Haskalah. *See* Hebrew Enlightenment

Hatta, 240

Havlin, Shalom, 215–16

Hazan, Yaakov, 213

Hazaz, Haim, 73

Hazevah. *See* Ayn Husub

Hebrew Enlightenment (Haskalah), 32

Hebrew language, 16, 18, 25, 36, 61, 70, 87, 174

Hebrew literature, 13

Hebrew press, 112

Hebrew University in Jerusalem, 51

Hebron, 95, 238, 316; Mount Hebron, 241, 246, 247, 249, 271, 272, 274, 277

Hefer, Hayim, 299

He-Halutz organization, 70, 71, 110, 175

Henkin, Yitzhak, 113 195, 336 n.16

Herodium, 147

Herut-Liberal bloc. *See* Gahal Party, 310

Herzliya High School, ix, 21

Hever Ha-Kevutzot, 68, 328 n.2; *hakhshara* farms of, 54

Hewer, Charles, 120, 121

Hiram Operation, 251

Hirsch, Baron Morris, 7

Hirsch, Siegfried, 44–45

Histadrut Labor Federation, 41, 69, 73, 89, 102, 109, 117, 139, 142, 149, 252, 254, 327 n.2; Agricultural Center of, 54, 55, 58, 71, 327 n.2; Central Appeals Committee of, 125; Executive of, 67–68, 253, 254; 47th Council, 135; Health Fund of, 59, 139; leadership of, 68; Sixth Convention, 149, 150

Hitler, Adolf, 61, 110, 132, 149, 213

Index

Holocaust, 164, 165, 178–79, 320
Holocaust survivors, 153, 160, 161, 165, 243, 320
Hope-Simpson, John, 28
Horev, Amos, 300
Horev, Operation, 257, 258–70, 274, 283
Hoter-Yishai, Aharon, 47–48
Huldah (kibbutz), 189
Huleh Valley, 130, 191, 193, 195, 196
Huleiqat, 244, 246, 247
Hussein, King of Jordan, 314, 315, 316
Hussein Bridge, 199

ICA. *See* Jewish Colonization Association
Idelson (Bar-Yehudah), Israel, 134, 174, 330 n.62, 344 n.106
Illegal immigration, 70, 131, 140, 147, 154, 155, 159, 160, 162, 166, 167, 169, 172, 215
Immigrant ships, 160, 161, 215; *Atlantic*, 70, 131; *Exodus*, 167, 169; *Knesset Israel*, 166; *Patriah*, 70, 131; *Struma*, 131
Innaba, 224
Innsbruck, 162
International border, 263
International Social Security Association (Leningrad, 1967), 308
Iraq, 35, 201, 205, 239, 282, 302
Iraq al-Manshiya, 240–47, 268–70, 272, 273
Iraq Petroleum Company, 100
Iraq Suweidan, 241, 242, 244, 245, 249
Isdud, 247
Iskandaron Bridge, 112
Islam, Muslims, 33, 116, 203; Muslim Brotherhood, 204
Israel Defense Forces (IDF), 146, 185, 199, 204, 205, 211, 212, 223, 224, 226, 227, 233, 235, 237, 239, 242, 246, 249, 251, 252, 260, 263, 267, 268, 283, 287, 294, 295, 309; the appointment crisis, 219–22 (*see also* Committee of Five); General Staff of, 209–12, 215, 220, 221, 223, 227, 228, 238, 239, 241, 253, 256, 258–61, 268, 269, 272–75, 284, 285, 286; High Command of, 238, 239, 242, 245, 261, 262; the navy, 215; Operations Branch, 227, 229, 239, 261, 264, 266, 278; parade (1967), 308; reorganizations in, 239, 289
Israeli-Egyptian Armistice Commission, 272
Israeli government, 238, 241, 263
Israeli intelligence, 308

Italo-Ethiopian War, 44, 80
Italy, 104, 129
IZL (Revisionist National Military Organization), 93, 97, 135, 142, 146, 148–52, 154–55, 159, 205, 254; and the *Altalena* affair, 210–12; blowing up the King David Hotel, 157, 159; campaign against IZL (*see Saison*); declaration of revolt against the British, 148; execution of British sergeants, 169

Ja'uni, 4
Jabesh-gilead, x
Jabotinsky, Ze'ev, 210, 254
Jaffa, 19, 53, 79, 89, 178, 182, 185, 345 nn. 18, 21; port of, 3, 44
Jenin, 203
Jericho, 314, 316
Jerusalem, 35, 51, 103, 105, 178, 186, 210, 222, 233, 235, 283, 285, 314, 316, 348 n.74, 357 n.9; Arab violence against Jews, 181–82; blowing up the King David Hotel, 157, 159; convoys to, 184, 189; entry of the Arab Legion into, 203; internationalization of, 178, 185, 188, 203; Jaffa Gate, 182; during the "month of battles," 203–4; the Old City's Jewish Quarter, 204; the road to, 185, 188–90, 204–7, 222, 223; under siege, 182, 189, 203, 206. *See also* Dani, Operation; Nahshon, Operation; Yoram, Operation
Jerusalem Corridor, 178, 190, 205, 235
Jewish Agency (JA), 36, 49, 55, 58, 81, 93, 107, 109, 118, 131, 142, 149, 150, 155, 158, 180, 184, 213, 334 n.78; Executive of, 45, 85, 131, 148, 158, 159, 214; Immigration Department, 162; leadership of, 110; Political Department (PD), 36, 44, 45, 47, 64, 106, 114, 115, 116, 119, 120, 121, 123, 127, 160, 181, 182, 273
Jewish-Arab national conflict, 82, 169, 170, 179, 320
Jewish-Arab relations, 16, 17, 18–19
Jewish-Arab territorial exchange, 239
Jewish Brigade. *See* British army
Jewish-British cooperation, 64, 105, 109–25, 133, 142, 158
Jewish colonies/villages, 3, 4, 7, 24, 39 (*see also specific colonies*); cereal-based colonies, 67; Galilean colonies, 13, 17, 21, 29, 36

376   Index

Jewish Colonization Association (ICA), 3, 4, 5, 7–8, 9, 11, 12, 16, 20, 24, 25; officials of, 5, 15, 18, 27. *See also* Palestine Jewish Colonization Association
Jewish guards, 17, 18
Jewish immigration (*aliyah*) to Eretz Israel, 4, 10, 51, 59, 79, 82, 153, 162, 166, 176, 179, 237; prevention of, 98, 131, 153–54; restriction on, 64. *See also* First Aliyah; Second Aliyah; Third Aliyah
Jewish labor, 16–19, 25, 29, 42
Jewish Legion, 98
Jewish National Home, 64, 90, 98, 119, 181
Jewish refugees, 70, 77, 131, 140, 142, 147, 153–54, 163, 165, 181, 345 n.6. *See also* Displaced persons
Jewish Resistance Movement, 152, 154–59, 342 n.41
Jewish settlement in Palestine, 3, 4, 5, 7, 24, 26, 46, 55, 66, 79, 83, 93, 141, 166, 176, 184, 186, 188, 193, 199, 239, 273–74; agricultural settlement, 7, 48, 148
Jewish Settlement Police (JSP), 64, 83, 85, 86, 91, 92, 93, 95, 98–99, 100, 111; Nazareth Brigade, 332 n.9
Jewish terrorism, 149, 150
Jewish Yishuv, x, 9, 24, 35, 36, 44, 46, 50, 61, 64, 66, 70, 71, 80, 86, 88, 91, 101, 103, 104, 105, 107, 108, 113, 118, 139, 142, 152, 159, 166, 175, 178–82, 188, 253, 304; anti-British education, 114; anti-British struggle, 98, 152, 154–60, 166, 173, 181; combat methods of, 82–83; cooperation with the British, 109–25, 150, 334 n.78, 338 n.66; demography, 25, 46, 79; institutions of, 67; leadership of, 82, 127, 128, 129, 132, 149, 157, 158, 273; new Yishuv, 4; policy of restraint, 46, 82, 93; public opinion, 77, 151; in World War II, 98, 104, 105, 109, 126–31, 135, 143; youth of, 102, 128, 141
Jezreel Valley, 8, 35, 80, 90, 111, 142
Jimzu, 224
Jonah camp, 212
Jordan, 271, 273, 274, 282–83, 285, 314
"Jordanian Option," 314
Jordan River, x, 22, 181, 231, 237, 282, 283, 285, 313, 314
Jordan Valley, x, 24, 60, 62, 65, 66, 96, 142, 199, 200, 314, 316, 332 n.9
Ju'ar, 55, 57, 63, 66, 74

Ju'ara, 99
Judah Maccabee, 147
Judea, 18; Judean Desert, 147, 314; Judean Hills, 244, 282

Kadesh, 197, 201
Kadoorie, Ellis, 35
Kadouri Agricultural School (Arab school), 35, 36, 40, 216
Kadouri Agricultural School (Jewish school), 30, 31, 35–50, 54, 60
Kadum settlement, 312, 316
Kafr Hareb, 200
Karatiya, 240, 242
Kariv, Joseph, 256, 257
Karnei Hittin, 95
Karniel, Nahman, 23
Kassam, Sheikh Iz a-Din al-, 80
Katowice, 163
Katznelson, Avraham, 127, 180
Katznelson, Berl, 65–68, 72, 73, 90, 102, 104, 109, 142, 145, 175, 180, 255, 273, 300, 328 n.2, 330 n.62
Kaukaba, 244
Kefar Giladi, 38, 53
Kefar Hasidim, 52
Kefar Javetz, 48
Kefar Tavor (Mes'ha), 1–2, 5, 7–34, 42, 44, 46–50, 62, 71, 72, 73, 75, 76, 84, 85, 86, 88, 90, 145, 192, 305; school of, 9, 32, 35, 36, 37, 50, 51, 52, 99, 100, 216, 318, 320
Kefar Vitkin, 90, 91
Kefar Yeladim, 90, 91
Keinan, Amos, 319, 322
Kelman, Moshe, 192, 197, 225
Kesseh, Jonah. *See* Kosoy (Kesseh), Jonah
Kevutzah, kevutzot, 54, 137, 327–28 n.2, 330 n.62
Kevutzat Ginossar, 55
Kevutzat Ha-Noar Ha-Oved Migdal, 54–71
Kfar Kama, 14, 15
Kfar Szold, 195
Kfar Vitkin, 212
Khalidi, Dr. Hussein, 180
Khirbet a-Ra'i, 241, 243
Khirbet Maqhuz, 240, 241
Khirbet Quriqur, 234, 236
Kibbutz, kibbutzim, 50, 53–54, 59, 137, 139, 142
Kibbutz Me'uhad (KM) movement, 54, 68–69, 71, 72, 75, 109, 143, 150, 160, 165,

172, 174, 187, 216, 217, 229, 232, 254, 286, 289, 291, 292, 296, 300, 302, 305, 307, 308, 313, 314, 328 n.2; and enlistment in the British army, 110, 131; Council at Ein Harod (July 1942), 133, 338 n.8; Council at Givat Ha-Sheloshah (January 1941), 69–72, 73; Council at Givat Brenner (April 1942), 126; Council at Naan (August 1942), 134; and the Palmah, 123, 133–34; and the *saison*, 150–51
Kibbutz movement/stream, 54, 67, 68–69, 136, 307, 328 n.2
Kielce pogrom, 161
Kimche, Jon, 288
Kinneret, Mount, 95
Kiryati Brigade, 212, 228
Kleyah, 113
Klimantovsky, Moshe, 23
Knesset, 286, 287, 301, 302
Knesset Israel. See Immigrant ships
Koch (Avidan), Shimon, 87, 143, 147, 150, 151, 162–63, 164, 165, 190, 209–10, 219, 220, 239, 244
Kofer Ha-Yishuv, 58
Kollek, Teddy, 294
Kosoy (Kesseh), Jonah, 180
Kosygin, Alexei, 308
Kovner, Abba, 162
Kramer (Shadmi), Nahum, 48, 57, 61, 85, 86, 90, 95, 96, 97, 162
Krasnianski, Israel, 41
Kuneitra, 200
Kurnub, 259, 274

Labor battalion, 25
Labor education stream. *See* Education
Labor movement, 34, 39, 41, 45, 65, 89–90, 103, 126, 134, 166, 180, 213, 300, 303, 306, 307, 317
Labor Party, 312. *See also* Maarakh Party
Labor settlement, 17, 32, 102, 103, 133, 139, 142, 151, 155, 176
Labor youth, 42, 102
Lachish, 248
Lahat, Shlomo, 242
Lajjun, 200
Lake Success, 205
"La-Megguyas," 255
Lander, Dr. P., 59

Land of Israel, x, 2, 4, 17, 61, 282. *See also* Eretz Israel; Palestine
Lands, 5, 63; acquiring of, 5, 7; PICA's lands, 54–58, 60, 65–67, 68, 71, 77–78; restriction on purchase of, 64, 98
Landsberg, 160, 162
Laner, Dan, 193, 196, 197, 198, 207
Latrun, 204–8, 233–36, 243, 269; prison at, 158, 160, 223. *See also* Bin-Nun A, Operation; Bin-Nun B, Operation; Dani, Operation; Yoram, Operation
Lavon affair, 124
Le-Ahdut Ha-Avodah Party (LAHA), 150, 172, 173, 175, 176, 177, 181, 213, 256, 301, 305, 307, 308, 328 n.2
Le-Ahdut Ha-Avodah–Poalei Zion Party, 173, 187
Lebanon, 111, 112, 113, 115; Lebanese army, 193
Lebanon Valley, 113
Left, 41, 42, 70, 81, 109, 173, 174, 175, 188, 211, 212, 285, 301, 302, 304, 305, 315, 317, 328 n.2
LeHI, 135, 142, 146, 151, 154–55, 157, 159, 205, 225, 248, 254, 260; Lord Moyne's murder, 149, 150, 151
Lehmann, Dr. Siegfried, 39
Lev, Raphael, 99
Levinger, Rabbi Moshe, 316
Levy, Israel, 56, 65, 68, 69
Liddel-Hart, Basil, 288, 350 n.32
Likud Party, 315
Lishavsky, Aharon, 116
Livneh, Eliezer, 342 n.33
Lohamei Ha-Gettaot (kibbutz), 321
London, 88, 287, 288, 298
London Conference (1945), 154
Lovers of Zion movement, 2, 4
LRLR, Operation. *See* Dani, Operation
Lubetkin, Zivia, 161, 164
Lubya, 95, 96–97, 333 nn.50–51
LuDaR Operation, 205
Lydda, 205, 223, 224–26, 235, 237, 260, 350 n.32; expulsion of Arab residents from, 227–33. *See also* Dani, Operation

Maaleh Adumim, 316
Maarakh Party, 306, 307, 316
Maariv (newspaper), 298, 342 n.33
Maccabi Ha-Tza'ir (youth movement), 41–42, 43, 45, 50

378　Index

Machiavelli, Niccolo, 318
Maghreb villages, 15, 86
Mahanayim (kibbutz), 4, 5, 75
Majdal, 238–43, 245, 247, 249, 272
Makleff, Mordechai, 219, 220, 227
Malkhin, Ahuvya, 256
Malkiyyah, 191, 194, 197, 198, 201
Manarah, 199, 201
Mann, Moshe, 199, 200
Maoz Haim, Kibbutz, ix, 340 n.45
Mapai Party, 68, 73, 103, 123, 138, 150, 172, 173, 176, 180, 187, 188, 206, 213–14, 232, 253, 296, 301, 305, 306, 308, 310, 312, 317; activists in, 109, 131, 127, 328 n.2; and the British army, 109–10, 131, 138–39; Central Committee of, 185; Council of June 1948, 218; Faction B of, 109, 110, 131, 139, 254; elections to the fifth Knesset, 302; elections to the first Knesset, 286; moderates in, 109; and the Palmah, 138; split in, 173, 175, 213, 254, 256, 307, 328 n.2
Mapam Party, 188, 217, 220, 231–32, 253, 256, 291, 292, 293, 295, 296, 301; elections to the first Knesset, 286; founding of, 187, 255, 287, 288; split in, 302, 307
Mapu, Abraham, 13
Marcus, Colonel David Daniel (Mickey Stone), 203–7, 209, 225, 349 n.1
Marjayoun, 112, 113
Marsa Matruh, 126
Marseilles, 5, 8
Mart, Zalman, 129, 335 n.14
Masada, 129, 147, 185, 274, 277
Mass, Dani, 222
Massadah (kibbutz), 200
Mattveyov, Shimon, 11
May Plan. See Haganah organization
McDonald, James, 264
McDonald, Malcolm, 64
McMichael, Harold, 127
Mediterranean, 1, 160; Mediterranean Basin, 104
Meir, Golda, 73, 306, 307, 308, 311, 312, 315, 319, 320
Meirov (Avigur), Shaul, 90, 102, 103, 106, 109, 121, 123, 142, 160, 161, 172, 187, 308, 309, 336 n.30
Mekorot Water Company, 186, 235
Menachemiya (Melahamiya), 7, 17, 48
Meron, Mount, 194, 197, 199

Mes'ha. See Kefar Tavor
Metullah, 8, 15, 16, 18, 130, 192, 199
Middle East, 80, 98, 114, 120, 152, 273, 287, 314, 315
Migdal, 54, 55, 57, 66–67, 68
Mikveh Israel Agricultural School, 28, 35
Ministry of Defense, 221
Misgav Am (kibbutz), 191
Mishmar Ha-Emek (kibbutz), 99, 118
Mishmar Ha-Yarden, 201, 203, 207
Mitzpe, 7, 96
Mizra (kibbutz), 142, 158
Mobile squad, 82–83
Moledet, 99
Molotov-Ribbentrop Pact, 70, 161
Montgomery, General Bernard, 131
Mossad for Aliyah Bet, 142, 160, 163, 165, 166
Mount Scopus, Hadassah Hospital, 125
Moyne, Lord, 149, 150
Muhi a-Din, Zakarya, 241
Munich, 162, 165
Musa Dag, 129
Mussolini, Benito, 44

Naan (kibbutz), 101, 134, 226, 251
Nabi Daniyal Convoy, 189, 190
Nabi Yusha police station, 191, 193, 199, 201
Nagib, General Mohamed, 258–59
Nahalal, 39, 88, 90
Nahal Lavan. See Wadi Abiad
Nahariyyah, 178
Nahash the Ammonite, x
Nahshon, Operation, 189–90, 205
Nameri, David, 135, 140, 143, 157
Namir, Mordekhai, 308
Narkiss, Uzi, 243, 284
National Committee (Vaad Leumi), 127, 131, 149
National Religious Party (NRP), 310, 311
Navon, Yitzhak, 318
Nazareth, 5, 13, 14, 31, 33, 227
Nazis, 61, 70, 98, 127, 128, 131, 136, 148, 151, 158, 187; medical experiments by, 163
Negba (kibbutz), 129
Negev, 130, 178, 182, 184–87, 189, 199, 203, 214, 220, 239–50, 268, 270, 273; eastern Negev, 244; Egyptian invasion of, 238; eleven settlement points in, 186;

Index 379

Negev Mount, 267; northern Negev, 238, 239, 273; settlements in, 239, 240, 273–74; southern Negev, 271, 283. *See also* Uvdah, Operation; Yoav, Operation
Negev Brigade, 186, 187, 209, 214, 215, 239, 240, 241, 260, 261, 263, 269, 274, 275, 277; Seventh Battalion of, 243, 246
Negev Committee, 186
Nehar-Tov, 17
Nes Ziona, 3
Netanya, 30, 52, 204
Netzer, Zevi, 163, 164
"New Jew," 320, 322
Nietzsche, Friedrich, 318
Night of the Bridges, 157–58
Nitzana, 246, 258, 271
Nixon, Richard, 315
Northern Front, 219

Occupied territories, 312
Oded Brigade, 244
Odessa, 3, 19
Ono Valley, 223, 235, 237
"Open season." See *Saison*
Ossowetzky, Yehoshua, 3, 5
Ottomans, 5, 21
Oxford, 298

Paicovich, Deborah (Yigal's sister), 20, 21, 26, 51, 75
Paicovich, Eliav (Yigal's brother), 20, 21, 30, 52
Paicovich, Mordekhai (Yigal's brother), 4, 6, 20, 21, 23, 26, 52
Paicovich, Moshe (Yigal's brother), 4, 6, 20, 21, 26, 52
Paicovich, Rachel (Yigal's grandmother), 2
Paicovich, Reuven ("al-Insari"; Yigal's father), 1–2, 3–5, 6, 8, 11, 13, 16, 18–24, 26–32, 34–37, 50–53, 75–76, 85, 89
Paicovich, Shmuel (Yigal's uncle), 2, 3
Paicovich, Zvi (Yigal's brother), 4, 6, 52
Paicovich, Zvi Yehoshua (Yigal's grandfather), 2–3, 20–23, 30
Paicovich (Schwartz), Chaya Ethel (Yigal's mother), 3–4, 5, 6, 12, 19, 23, 26
Pa'il, Meir, 151
Palestine, 2, 3, 5, 10, 16–17, 20–21, 35, 46, 53, 70, 104, 109, 119, 124, 128, 263; Arab majority in, 64; borders of, 273; international trusteeship in, 176, 187; invasion by Arab states, 192, 199, 201, 203, 238; legislative council in, 80; Palestine frontier, 2, 11, 24, 32, 49, 60, 184; partition of, 79, 160, 176, 178–81, 187, 188; question of, 124, 153, 154, 179; western Palestine, 283. *See also* Eretz Israel
Palestine Jewish Colonization Association (PICA), 27–29, 32, 66, 73, 76, 124; lands of, 54–58, 60, 65–66, 68, 71, 77–78; officials of, 28, 35, 55, 56, 58, 77. *See also* Jewish Colonization Association
Palestine Scheme, 115, 118–21
Palestinian Arabs, 13, 15, 16–17, 23, 31, 37, 60, 63, 64, 65, 71, 80, 86, 94–95, 98, 109, 112, 116, 117, 124, 127, 147, 152–53, 160, 176, 178, 179, 180, 181, 188, 191, 237; displacement of, 227–33; general strike, 79, 181; obstructing roads and traffic routes, 81, 182, 184. *See also* Arab Disturbances
Palestinian state, 285
Pal-Heb. *See* Palmah
Palmah, ix, 99, 103, 107, 108, 115, 121, 141–47, 150, 159, 160, 163, 165, 166, 168, 169, 170, 172–75, 177, 186, 204, 206, 208, 216, 218, 251, 269, 274, 285, 299, 300, 313; and the *Altalena* affair, 211–12, 252; Arab platoon, 124; archive, 158; attempts to create an air unit, 148; and Ben-Gurion, 212–21; blowing up the Givat Olga police station, 155; brigades (*see specific brigades*); casualties, 156, 209; companies of, 142, 214; Company A, 101, 116, 129, 130, 213, 339 n.28; Company B, 101, 135; cooperation with the British, 112–14, 123, 133, 151; dismantling of, 251–56, 257, 286, 293; enlargement of, 135–36 enlistment and volunteering, 111–40; establishment of, 105, 111, 126, 334 n.10; First Battalion, 193, 194, 196, 197, 199, 201, 207; German Platoon, 143, 147, 162; and the Haganah High Command, 130; *hakhsharot* (training groups), 136–38, 141, 144, 145, 148, 191; headquarters of, 125, 141, 142, 144, 157, 160, 186–90, 192, 215–18, 221, 223, 240, 251, 254; and the Kibbutz Me'uhad (KM) movement, 123, 133–34; Marine Platoon, 147–48, 167, 215; Pal-Heb unit, 195; participation in invasion of Syria and Lebanon, 111–13, 130, 146, 147; physical training, 146–47;

380 Index

Palmah (*continued*)
  rally of 1949, 288–89, 292, 293; rally of 1952, 298–301, 321; reserves of, 188, 192; and the *saison*, 150–52; scouting, 147; Syrian platoon (*see* Syrian Scheme); Third Battalion, 191, 193, 194, 197, 229; in the War of Independence, 184–278; work-and-training camps, 133–34, 136–38, 145, 148. *See also* Night of the Bridges; Twenty-three seaman commando
Palmer, Anthony, 111
Pardes Hannah, 52
Paris, 66, 159, 161, 169, 170, 172, 251, 258, 288, 289, 291, 294; Foreign Ministry, 288
Partition: partition borders, 203, 239, 297; partition plan, 169, 170, 178–81, 183–88, 191, 203, 237, 239, 273
Pasternak (Bar-Tikva), Mundek, 248
Patriah. *See* Immigrant ships
Peace of Galilee War (1982), 197
Peel Commission, 79
Penn, Alexander, 42
Peres, Shimon, 307, 310, 320, 342 n.33
Peretz, I. L., 13
Perlman, Moshe, 349 n.1
Philistines, x, 34
PICA. *See* Palestine Jewish Colonization Association
"Pinkas ha-Maarakha," 184
Plan D. *See* Haganah organization
PLO, 316
Poalei Zion left, 173
Podhortzer, Moshe, 196
Poland, 61, 70, 104, 161, 163, 172, 174; kibbutz-*hakhshara* training camps, 163, 164
Poriyyah, 200
Porshim. *See* Dissenters
Post 86, 258, 259, 268
Prozhinin, Joel, 38, 41, 45, 49
Purge Operation, 212. See also *Altalena* affair
Purity of arms, 95, 96, 97, 157

Qalansawa, 282
Qastina, 243
Qawuqji, Fawzi al-, 193, 238, 251
al-Qubab, 229, 234
Qubeiba, 248
Qula, 233, 236
Quseima, 262

Rabadiyeh spring, 63
Rabat summit (1974), 314
Rabin, Yitzhak, 190, 204, 206, 207, 208, 211–12, 223, 224, 228–29, 236, 240, 242, 243, 245, 259, 261, 264, 271, 277–78, 284, 287, 289, 291, 293–94, 300, 306, 308, 310, 312–13, 320
Rabinowitz (Baharav), Yehoshua, 54, 65, 97
Rabinowitz (Shamir), Shlomo, 87, 90, 96, 107, 204, 210, 215, 254, 332 n.16
Rachel (poetess). *See* Bluvshtein, Rachel
Rafah, 158, 258, 259, 262, 264, 266, 268
Rafah Junction, 267
Rafi Party, 306, 307, 310
Ramallah, 206, 223, 233, 235, 236. *See also* Dani, Operation
Ramat Ha-Kovesh (kibbutz), 135
Ramat Rachel (kibbutz), 157, 204, 238
Ramleh, 205, 223, 225, 226, 235, 237, 350 n.32, 351 n.49; expulsion of Arab residents from, 227–32. *See also* Dani, Operation
Ramon Crater, 274
Ramot Naftali, 191, 193–94, 199
Ras en-Naqb, 275
Ratner, Yohanan, 115, 118, 129, 171
Ratosh, Yonatan, 322
Re'ali School, 42, 50
Red Army, 83, 104, 134, 144, 173, 302
Red Cross, 127
Rehavia Gymnasia, 103
Rehovot, 3, 17, 205, 223; a month-long seminar, 72–73, 102
Reprisals, 97
Revenge group, 162–63
Revisionist Movement, 41, 151
Revisionist National Military Organization. *See* IZL
Revivim (kibbutz), 258
Rhodes, 270, 271, 274, 282
Riaq airport, 113
Riftin, Ya'akov, 342 n.33
Riga, 308
Right, 41, 68, 81, 142, 152, 212, 252, 302, 315, 328 n.2
Riley, General, 258
Rishon Lezion, 3
Road of Heroism, 235
Rokeach, Elazar, 4

Rommel, Erwin, 104, 109, 114, 115, 126, 129, 130, 131, 334 n.71
Rosen, Pinhas, 252
Rosenheck, Jules, 5, 27
Rosh Ha-Ayin, 233, 235
Rosh Pinnah, 3, 4, 8, 14, 16, 20, 191–96; police station, 193. *See also* Gei Oni
Rotberg, Meir, 57
Rothschild family, 55; Rothschild, Baron Edmond de, 3, 4, 5, 7, 10; Rothschild, Baron James de, 77
Rubashov (Shazar), Zalman, 73
Ruhama, 240, 244
Russia, 16, 89, 131, 139; Civil War in, 83, 104, 134, 144, 174; Germany's attack on, 114, 162; Russian Revolution, 80. *See also* Soviet Union
Russian army, 83, 87. *See also* Red Army

Sadeh, Aza, 143
Sadeh, Yitzhak, 82, 83, 85, 86, 87, 90, 91, 102–8, 115, 129, 135, 140, 142–47, 151, 156–60, 170–73, 182, 213, 214, 224, 225, 235–36, 242, 243, 246, 248, 260, 288, 289, 298–99, 300–301
Safed, 3, 4, 191, 201, 320; Arab Disturbances of 1929, 196; Arab Quarter, 191, 194, 197; battle for, 193–97; the "Fort," 191; Jewish Quarter, 191, 193, 194, 196, 197
Safsufa, 197
Saison, 150–52, 155, 212, 248
Salameh, 182
Samaria, 199, 238, 282; Samarian Hills, 282
Samuel, Herbert, 35, 36
Sapir, Pinhas, 307, 308, 312
Sarafand, 91
Sarig, Nahum, 130, 186, 187, 214–15, 245, 246, 275
Sarona, British Special Police, 156
Sasa, 197
Saul, King, x, 10, 33–34, 318
Scholem, Gershom, 73
Schutzbund, 108
Schwartz, Chaya Ethel. *See* Paicovich (Schwartz), Chaya Ethel
Schwartz, Rachel, 88
Schwartz, Reb Alter, 3, 4, 5
Schwartz, Zvi, 88
Schwiger, Beralah, 18

Sea Lion (motorboat), 105–8, 111, 131
Sea of Galilee (Kinneret), 54, 56, 57, 59, 63, 199
Second Aliyah, 7, 9, 17, 18, 72, 103, 213, 255, 256
Sefer Ha-Palmah, 167, 192
Sejera, 7, 36, 96
Separation Agreement (1974), 316
Seventh Brigade, 204, 205, 208
Shaar Ha-Gai, 204
Shaar Ha-Golan, 200
Shadmi, Nahum. *See* Kramer (Shadmi), Nahum
Shaham (Schechter), Michael, 200
Shaham, Nathan, 318
Shaltiel, David, 96, 204
Shamir, Shlomo. *See* Rabinowitz (Shamir), Shlomo
Shapira, Moshe Haim, 310
Sharett, Moshe. *See* Shertok (Sharett), Moshe
Sharm al-Sheikh, 309
Sharon Plain, 204, 205
Shaw Commission, 28
SHAY. *See* Haganah organization
Shazar, Zalman. *See* Rubashov (Shazar), Zalman
Sheffer, Ze'ev, 160, 171
Shein, Nehemiah, 156
Shemer, Naomi, 321, 322
Sherf, Ze'ev, 334 n.78, 338 n.66
Shertok (Sharett), Moshe, 119, 127, 160, 182–83, 185, 228, 229, 251, 263, 264, 267, 272–73, 294, 319, 336 n.24, 337 n.37, 345 n.6
Shfeya, 8
Shinan, Giora, 130, 143
Shishaqli, Adib, 193
Shitrit, Behor, 228
Shoshani, Eliezer, 171
Shoval, 241
Silver, Abba Hillel, 161
Simhoni, Assaf, 130
Sinai, 261–68, 271, 286, 309, 316; Sinai Campaign, 301, 310
Sini. *See* Azaryahu, Arnan
Six Day War, 300, 308, 312, 313, 314, 320
Smolenskin, Peretz, 13
Sneh, Dr. Hannah, 169, 170

382 Index

Sneh, Moshe, 142, 149, 150, 154, 155, 156, 158–61, 169, 170, 177, 342 n.33
SNS. *See* Special Night Squads
Sodom, 69, 246, 274
Solel Boneh (construction company), 117, 330 n.66, 336 n.29
Southern Front (Front D), 219, 239–78, 285, 289, 291, 294–95, 296
Soviet Union, 70, 71, 129, 143, 173–74, 179, 187, 188, 282, 293, 302, 308, 309; Jews, 174, 308. *See also* Russia
Spanish Civil War, 43, 103, 108
Special Night Squads (SNS), 95, 96
Spector, Aharonchik, 129–30
Spector, Shosh, 103, 105, 144
Spector, Yiftah, 104–5
Spector (Toledano), Zvi, 103, 105, 106
Stalingrad, 131, 143, 204, 348 n.74
State of Israel, 154, 199, 252, 267, 273, 289; absorbing mass immigrants, 282, 301; first elections (1949), 286; proclamation of, 201, 203, 301
Stern, Abraham (Yair), 135
Stockwell, General Hunt, 196
Stone, Mickey. *See* Marcus, Colonel David Daniel
Struma. See Immigrant ships
Suez Canal, 239, 263, 273
Susannah, Operation, 124
Sussman, Pinhas, 234
Syria, 7, 55, 111, 112, 114, 142, 143, 170, 193, 201, 207, 225; invasion of the Galilee by, 199–200; network of Palestinian Jews in, 115–17, 119, 121, 124
Syrian-Lebanese border, 195, 200
Syrian Scheme, 115–21, 124, 140
Szenes, Hannah, 78
Szold, Henrietta, 77

Taba, 277
Tabenkin, Yitzhak, 73, 90, 102, 109, 132, 133, 136, 138, 175, 180, 213, 214, 215, 217, 218, 254–55, 286, 291, 296, 300, 305, 314, 328 n.2, 338 n.66, 340 n.40
Tabenkin, Yosef, 215, 227, 357 n.9
Taha Bey, Colonel a-Sayed, 270, 356 n.113
Taibeh, 282
Tabor, Mount, 2, 8, 11, 17, 20, 32, 36, 40
Tchernichowsky, Saul, 33–34; "*Be-Ein Dor*," 33

Tel Aviv, 45, 67, 77, 89, 90, 106, 170, 182, 184, 187, 205, 210, 212, 219, 221, 223, 227, 238, 239, 264; bombardment of, 199; Exhbition Grounds in, 119; port of, 90; Ritz Hotel (Palmah's headquarters), 188, 211; school for workers' children in, 54
Tel Hai, 80, 108, 184
Tel Maresha, 248
Tel Yosef (kibbutz), 39, 61, 68
Ten-Day Campaigns. *See* War of Independence
Third Aliyah, 24
The thirty-five, 222
Tiberias, 13, 14, 24, 30, 47, 48, 57, 58, 62, 64, 78, 85, 95, 96, 99, 185, 191, 193, 195, 199, 231, 264, 345 n.18; British Government House in, 95; Kiryat Shmuel neighborhood, 95; massacre of Jews in, 95, 96
Tira, 184, 282
Tiran, Straits of, 309
Tower-and-stockade settlement, 55, 90
Transjordan, 1, 22, 23, 55, 273, 282, 283; Hashemite government of, 233
Transjordan Frontier Force, 100, 101, 193, 225
Tripoli (Lebanon), 116; oil refineries, 105, 106, 111
Truman, Harry, 153, 179, 264
Trumpeldor, Joseph, 108
Tubruk, 126, 129
Tul Karm, 35, 36
Turks, 22, 47
Twenty-three seaman commando, 105–8, 111, 156
Tzemah, 24, 199, 200
Tzofim (Scouts), 138

Uganda Plan, 4
Um-Ja'bal, 11, 35, 47
Umm-Katef, 263
Umm-Rashrash. *See* Eilat
Undergrounds. *See* IZL; LeHI
United Nations, 176, 179, 183, 203, 204, 242, 249, 271, 273, 274; General Assembly, 178, 180, 251, 258; observers from, 240, 241, 242; Partition Resolution of 29 November 1947 (*see* Partition, partition plan); Security Council, 223, 233, 244,

249, 261, 266; supervisors from, 272; UNRRA, 164; UNSCOP, 169, 178, 181
United States, 2, 5, 10, 146, 154, 165, 169, 170, 174, 179, 225, 263–64, 267, 304, 309; American-Jewish public opinion, 153; Jews, 161, 293; and the partition plan, 187, 189; U.S. Army, 162
UNSCOP. *See* United Nations
Ussishkin, Menachem, 9
Uvdah, Operation, 273, 274–78, 282, 283, 291

Vaad Leumi. *See* National Committee
Vilna, 2, 70
Vitkin, Joseph, 9, 10, 17
Von Friedman (Avisar), Eitan, 129

Wadi Abiad (Nahal Lavan), 259, 260
Wadi Amud, 54, 197
Wadi Ara, 282
Wadi Bira, 22, 199
Wallenberg, Raoul, 163
War cabinet, 221
War of Independence, x, 77, 141, 156, 160, 164, 171, 182–278, 284–85, 289, 292, 296, 299, 301, 313; casualties, 201, 209, 234, 243, 268, 269, 288; First Truce, 201, 209, 212, 235; killing of prisoners, 270, 355 n.110; massacre against Arab civilians, 248–49, 350 n.37; "month of battles," 197–204; plunder and looting during, 248, 269; Second Truce, 235, 237, 238, 240, 242, 247, 249; Ten-Day Campaigns, 221–37, 240. *See also specific operations*
Warsaw Ghetto uprising, 129, 161
Water, "water war," 13, 49, 63–65, 71, 101, 124, 273
Wauchope, Arthur, 36, 80; Wauchope Prize, 32, 38
Weiss, Shevah, 321
Weitz, Joseph, 186, 345 n.25
Weitz, Yehiam, 156
Weizmann, Chaim, 149, 153, 158, 159, 161
Weizmann, Vera, 299, 300
West Bank, 231, 282–85, 294, 312, 314, 316
White Paper, of McDonald (1939), 64, 98, 109, 114, 153
Wilson, Harold, 308, 318
Wilson, P. T., 118–19, 337 n.37

Wingate, Orde, 82, 94, 96, 210, 333 n.46. *See also* Special Night Squads (SNS)
World War I, 20, 24, 70, 83, 89, 98, 113, 114
World War II, 63, 98, 99, 102, 104, 105, 110–11, 115, 119, 126–31, 142, 143, 148, 152, 173, 176, 178, 179, 187, 203, 213, 232, 284, 304

X Committee, 159, 342 n.41

Yaari, Haim, 342 n.33
Yaari, Meir, 174, 338 n.66
Yadin, Yigael, 171, 182, 183, 192, 200–201, 204, 205, 206, 219–22, 225, 235, 239, 241, 245, 246, 259, 260–61, 262, 264, 268, 271, 272, 273, 275, 277, 278, 287, 295, 296, 305, 310, 356 n.125
Yad Mordekhai (kibbutz), 247
Yagur (kibbutz), 128, 158, 159
Yavne'el (Yemah), 7, 13, 28, 29, 30, 37, 49, 95, 97, 99, 200
Yavneh, 238
Yazur, 182, 224, 228
Yehiam (kibbutz) Convoy, 189
Yellin Mor, Nathan, 342 n.33
Yemah. *See* Yavne'el
Yiddish, 16, 161
Yiftah Brigade, 205, 206, 209, 215, 223–27, 233, 234, 236, 240, 241, 244, 245, 351 n.48; First Battalion, 234, 244; Third Battalion, 225
Yiftah, Operation, 190–99, 206, 223
Yishuv. *See* Jewish Yishuv
Yizhar, S., 241
Yoav, Operation, 241–51, 253, 254, 257, 258, 262, 268, 274
Yokne'am, 193
Yom Kippur War, 312
Yoram, Operation, 206–8, 216–20, 223
Youth movements, 103, 141, 145, 174, 175, 274, 304; and the Palmah, 136–38, 139. *See also specific movements*

Zack, Gershon, 215
Zadok, Haim, 310
Zakai, David, 72
Zalizky (Carmel), Moshe, 91, 99, 101–2, 185, 196, 200, 209, 219, 307, 356 n.125
Zaslany, Reuven, 115, 119, 123, 336 nn. 20, 24, 338 n.66
Zefira family, 11

Zemach, Ada, 42–43, 45, 49, 50–51, 62
Zemach, Shlomo, 36–41, 44–47, 327 n.24
Zikhron Ya'acov, 8, 16
Zionist Congress: of 1939 (Geneva), 154, 161; of 1946 (Basle), 160–63, 171, 173, 214
Zionist Executive, 81, 149, 161
Zionist institutions in Jerusalem, 88, 92
Zionist leadership, 110, 152
Zionist Left, 25, 187, 327 n.2
Zionist movement, 73, 98, 109, 110, 153, 159, 175, 179; youth of, 34
Zionist Organization, 149, 153, 158, 159, 161
Zionist press, 35, 66
Zisling, Aharon, 256
Zoref, Absalom, 65, 69, 73, 74, 76
Zur, Zvi, 295

Acknowledgments

This book was written over many years. Along the way, numerous people opened their hearts and their archives to me. Without their assistance this book would not have been written. Dozens of people were generous with their information and their time, allowing me an intimate look into their lives, their way of thinking, and their cultural codes. Of special importance were my lengthy interviews with Arnan (Sini) Azaryahu, Yitzhak Rabin, Shosh Spector, Israel Gallili, and Yigael Yadin.

I was blessed with gifted assistants. Batya Danziger, Osnat Shiran, Ofra Elad, Alon Gan, and Boaz Levtov did a meticulous job. Mordechai Bar-On read the chapters on the War of Independence and saved me from embarrassing mistakes. Professor Gideon Biger of Tel Aviv University helped locate old maps, and Avigdor Orgad sketched them anew. The photographs in this book are published by courtesy of the owners. The index was wisely and scrupulously compiled by Rachel Yurman.

The English translation of this work was done by Evelyn Abel, who did an excellent job, retaining the spirit of the original Hebrew manuscript while adapting it to the English reader. I cannot thank her enough.

The idea of having this book published in English was born during my stay at the Center for Advanced Judaic Studies, University of Pennsylvania. I am most grateful to Professor David Ruderman, the director of the center, without whose support this project would not have materialized. Jerome Singerman, humanities editor at the University of Pennsylvania Press, was very supportive throughout. Erica Ginsburg was a pleasure to work with. They, and no doubt also other people at the Press, were crucial to the successful publication of this book. I am indebted to them all.

The Ruben Merenfeld Chair on the Study of Zionism sponsored research expenses. My stay at the Institute for Advanced Studies at the Hebrew University in Jerusalem allowed me to complete the manuscript. Professor Itamar Rabinovich, the president of Tel Aviv University, helped provide the funds for the English translation. It is thanks to them that this book is published.